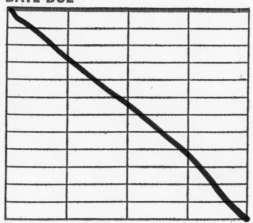

A SENATE JOURNAL
1943–1945

A Da Capo Press Reprint Series

FRANKLIN D. ROOSEVELT
AND THE ERA OF THE NEW DEAL
GENERAL EDITOR: FRANK FREIDEL
Harvard University

A SENATE JOURNAL
1943-1945

By Allen Drury

Illustrations by Joseph Papin

DA CAPO PRESS • NEW YORK • 1972

Library of Congress Cataloging in Publication Data

Drury, Allen.
  A Senate journal, 1943-1945.

  (Franklin D. Roosevelt and the era of the New Deal)
  1. U. S. Congress. Senate. 2. U. S. — Politics and
government — 1933-1945. I. Title. II. Series.
JK1161.D7 1972   328.73'073'1   76-38824
ISBN 0-306-70448-X

This Da Capo Press edition of *A Senate Journal, 1943-1945,* is an
unabridged republication of the first edition published in 1963.
It is reprinted by special arrangement with Drukill Company, Inc.

Published by Da Capo Press, Inc.
A Subsidiary of Plenum Publishing Corporation
227 West 17th Street, New York, N.Y. 10011

Manufactured in the United States of America

A SENATE JOURNAL

1943–1945

by Allen Drury

___

ADVISE AND CONSENT

A SHADE OF DIFFERENCE

A SENATE JOURNAL

ALLEN DRURY

A

SENATE

JOURNAL

1943 - 1945

WITH ILLUSTRATIONS BY JOSEPH PAPIN

McGraw-Hill Book Company, Inc.

NEW YORK   TORONTO   LONDON

Library of Congress Catalog Card Number: 63-18703

FIRST EDITION

17865

To the staffs
of the Press, Periodical, Radio-TV
and Photographers' Galleries
of the United States Capitol

*whose patient and skillful assistance is
an indispensable part of Washington reporting*

CONTENTS

FOREWORD

On October 1, 1943, I was discharged from the Army because of an old back injury and came East from my home in California to look for a job. On November 29 I found one with United Press in Washington and three days later was assigned to the Senate. I soon realized how little most Americans know about the very human institution which makes their laws and in large measure runs their country.

I began, at once and deliberately, to keep a diary of the Hill; partly to send to my family, partly because I had hopes that it might eventually be of some slight assistance in making my fellow countrymen better acquainted with their Congress and particularly with their Senate. There is a vast area of casual ignorance concerning this lively and appealing body. Its members in their deliberations do a great deal to decide your future and mine, and that of our country and of our world. Who are they? (Today, as twenty years ago, you have heard of a scattering, those who appear consistently on television or make the headlines regularly. The rest you couldn't name if you had to.) What are they like? How do they look, how do they act, what is their institutional slant on things? And over and beyond the special emphasis of the days here recorded, the days of the War Senate on its way to becoming the Peace Senate, how does the Senate function from day to day? What is this Congress?

I attempted to set down what I saw and heard in a time of testing. This is how we fought the war on Capitol Hill: not too nobly in some respects, not too meanly in others; no worse, on the whole, and no better, than everyone else who had some part to play in victory.

Here is the soldier-vote fight, the subsidy battle, OPA and FEPC, Barkley's resignation, the State Department debate, the Wallace nomination, the change in Presidents from Roosevelt to Truman, the manpower bill and reconversion, the Bretton Woods Agreement and the United Nations Charter.

Here are the people from Downtown who came to the Hill to

testify: Frank Knox, Donald Nelson, James Forrestal, Henry Stimson, General Brehon Somervell, Mayor Fiorello La Guardia, Philip Murray, Sidney Hillman, Francis Biddle, Fred Vinson, Chester Bowles. Here are Franklin Roosevelt and the Duke of Windsor, Clement Attlee and Colonel Robert McCormick. Here is Harry Truman—Senator, Vice-President, President of the United States.

Here are they all, all honorable men—or, at least, entertaining men. No one can deny them that.

Here also is the flavor of that special and fascinating amalgam that is life on the Hill. Here is the easy-going intimacy between politicians and press that makes of the latter virtually a formal branch of government; here is the pattern of the Press Gallery days, some slow, some hectic, the interviewing, the waiting outside committee rooms, the covering of debates and hearings, the exciting sense of being at the storm center of the government which, for good or ill, probably has the ultimate decisive impact upon these middle years of the twentieth century.

Here it is, caught in a time of tension when bitterness between President and Congress was rising to a point rare in American history; when the last of the eloquent isolationists were doing their best to turn the course of American involvement in the world; and when generations had not yet changed in the Senate, so that we still had delightful characters, one or two of them still in tail-coats and possessed of flowing hair, all filled with a lively awareness of their own egos, all imbued with a massive sense of the dignity and power of being a Senator of the United States.

The egos and the dignity remain, but this is a newer day: the suits are Brooks Brothers, the air is junior-executive, the average age is much younger now than then, and heavy sits the weight of time upon these earnest brows. Understandably so, of course: these are serious days, and a Senator now has even more demands upon his time and ability than a Senator then. The rush of history no longer allows much scope for characters. But it is permissible, perhaps, to say—too bad. For they contributed much, in their own cantankerous ways, and it is symptomatic of times grown grimmer and grayer that there is no longer much place for such individuality, even in the one body which above all others in our system gives free rein to individuality.

Many of those you will meet in these pages are no longer with us on the Hill. Bob Taft no longer bestrides the Capitol like Colossus. Arthur Vandenberg has smoked his last cigar and gone to rest. Ken Wherry, seemingly too alive ever to die, sleeps in his native Nebraska. Bob La Follette, dead by his own hand, trudges no more with dogged earnestness down the marbled corridors where his father walked before him. Barkley is gone, and Walter George.

Many are gone—but some are still here. More importantly, the Senate is still here. And here in these pages, unchanged, unchanging, indeed unchangeable, you will find it pickled in its own sometimes acerbic juices.

The editing I have done, with the perspective of two decades, has been slight—a word deleted here, a sentence or paragraph there, mostly because they have seemed too harsh or hurtful now, where once it seemed they must be said. On some things, particularly the soldier-vote bill, the manpower bill and the basic weaknesses of the United Nations Charter, the judgments were harsh and I have let them stand. Twenty years have not changed conclusions which seemed valid to me then, and to me seem valid still.

In a few places I have inserted a present-day comment to illuminate the flow of narrative. And here and there I have added an occasional historical clarification, such as the full name War Production Board for the casual WPB which in wartime was familiar to every informed American.

The record stands as it was written. In the interests of an honest account I have even decided to leave in something of the youthful wide-eyed approach that I find upon rereading characterized my first days on the Hill. Especially have I done so in my first impressions of Senators and Congressmen, even at the risk of arousing some antagonism among the gentlemen themselves. Henry Cabot Lodge, I imagine, will not be pleased to know that he first impressed me as somewhat supercilious, though I soon came to like and respect him. And it seems laughable now that my first impression of Kenneth McKellar was "a trifle slow on the uptake . . . shrewd but not in the way some people are shrewd." I swiftly learned that there were few people indeed as shrewd as Old Mack from Tennessee, in his day the most powerful and the most ruthless man in the United States Senate.

These things I have left in, however, for a very good reason: they were a lesson for me and will, I hope, be a lesson for the casual visitor who wanders into the gallery and wanders out and dismisses his Congress with a casual shrug. To him I would say: don't underestimate politicians; they didn't get where they are without abilities. With some exceptions, they are earnest, worried, overworked people who have a lot to recommend them. They wouldn't have gotten to Washington if they didn't.

One thing further I would say to this casual visitor:

This is your Senate I am writing about. These are the 100 men and women (96 then, before the admission of Alaska and Hawaii) whom you have elected to represent you in "the greatest deliberative body on earth." That is what they call it, and after twenty years' close acquaintance, that is what I call it too.

You will find them very human, and you can thank God they are. You will find that they consume a lot of time arguing, and you can thank God they do. You will find that the way they do things is occasionally brilliant but often slow and uncertain, and you can thank God that it is. Because all these things mean that they are just like the rest of us, and you can thank God for that, too.

That is their greatness and their strength; that is what makes your Congress what it is, the most powerful guarantor of human liberties free men have devised.

You put them there, and as long as they are there you're going to remain free, because they don't like to be pushed around any more than you do.

This is comforting to know.

One final word—because his partisans, I suspect, may be overly angered, his detractors overly happy. There has been no retouching, and no purpose other than honest reporting, in the portrait of Franklin Roosevelt that emerges from these pages. If he appears in a critical light, that is because this is how we saw him from the Hill. In his closing months in office there was an ugly hostility, a bitter jockeying for political advantage and power, a mutual mistrust and dislike that constantly clouded his relations with the Congress. It is not too much of an exaggeration to say that in those final days they despised each other, and not all the eulogies that flooded the April air in 1945 can obscure the underlying emotions that candid men voiced in the privacy of their offices or, often, in the public debate of both chambers.

They and the President appraised each other as politicians, and there were no illusions left in the glances they exchanged across a mile of Pennsylvania Avenue. Indeed, by that time there could not have been: he had simply been around too long, they knew each other too well. The time for pretense had long since passed.

He was still in such a commanding political position with the country that Congress, although its members understood his methods and could almost always see them coming, was powerless to do much about it. This made for a bitter resentment on their part, a spiteful arrogance on his. Toward the end there was precious little patience, and almost no charity whatsoever, left on either side—and this in a period when the close and friendly cooperation of White House and Hill was imperative to the making of peace and a smooth return to civilian economy. The hatred which existed threatened to become one of the major tragedies of American history. His death assuaged the immediate situation, though it did not solve many of the problems that had arisen, and would continue to plague the country long after, because of it.

And yet he was, of course, a fabulous and fantastic man—the most complex and unknowable human being that this observer, for one, has ever seen. Who was he, what was he? Who ever really knew—who, now, ever really can know? His mystery was great and that, too, fanned the resentment on the Hill. It gave him an advantage he unceasingly pressed. It presented them with a frustration they never resolved.

In a certain sense, for all Americans who lived through those years with him, the words *the President* will always mean just one man. Here in these pages is a view of him from one major vantage point—one portion of a portrait that neither his contemporaries nor history, in all probability, will ever see quite complete.

ALLEN DRURY

Washington, 1963

1

FIRST IMPRESSIONS

NOVEMBER 21, 1943. There was a soft warm haze over the city when I got into Union Station at 4 this afternoon. In it the Capitol loomed up massive and domineering across the Plaza. Behind me as I stood in the doorway looking out the great station echoed with the fretful rendezvous of trains, the murmurous clatter of many feet, the hectic excitements of arrival and departure, while down from on high magnified ten times over came the imperious voices of women calling the place-names of America. Around me in unceasing flood passed the travelers. Daily they come in their thousands and daily the city absorbs them, vomiting forth other thousands to make room. Night and day unceasing, humanity on the move, closing in on this focus of its hopes, desires, ambitions, fears and worries from all over America and all over the earth.

I for one am here to see what I can, and appraise it as best I can; disillusioned like all Americans about their ruling heart, not too certain that it is taking us in any very worthwhile or consistent direction, yet possessed still of some inner faith and certainty of its essential and ultimate purposes. We muddle, we blunder, we fall on our faces, and we survive; how, or by what peculiar grace, no man can say exactly. This is where it is done, however, and this is where I shall watch it, fascinated I know, encouraged perhaps—perhaps even, now and then, inspired.

NOVEMBER 22, 1943. This afternoon I visited the House, which had suspended regular business to eulogize two dead members. I was there for the opening benediction, a long, lugubrious affair during which Minority Leader Joe Martin of Massachusetts, a little, dark, shaggy man, nervously and audibly jingled the coins in his pocket. I left soon after to go over to the Senate and listen to a portion of the debate on the bill to make it easier for soldiers away from home to vote. This was distinguished chiefly by the wary way in which everyone circled around the issue of the poll tax, of which the Senate is apparently highly conscious.°

The House guards are informal, hasty, unconcerned; slap your pockets, slap your coat, and pass you. The Senate police are much more formal, making you get in line, spreading your coat out on a table, challenging servicemen to show their furlough papers or passes, and generally being more officious. It is much easier to get a good seat in the House gallery than it is in the Senate, which does not seem to be any too well constructed from an audience standpoint.

NOVEMBER 23, 1943. The Hill fascinates me, and I went back there again this afternoon to find that the House had given up its mourning to take up the anti-subsidy bill—more properly, the bill to continue the Commodity Credit Corporation and prohibit the use of its funds for farm subsidies. A large crowd was in the galleries, and nearly 300 members on the floor. A man in back of me asked the guard to point out Rep. Clare Boothe Luce of Connecticut and when he did, sucked in his breath in audible surprise. "Is *that* Representative Luce?" he said. "Isn't she an attractive thing! My, *my*, isn't she an attractive thing!"

It was a rather lively, acrimonious affair this afternoon. The Administration, which found death a godsend yesterday in delaying a showdown on the subsidies it desires, profited from it again today. Late in the afternoon Majority Leader John McCormack of Massachusetts, who gives the impression of being a rather slow but generally able man, arose to remark reasonably that a delegation was preparing to leave to attend the funeral of one of the deceased. Would the House, therefore, consent to limiting debate on all amendments to 10 minutes so that a vote might be taken at 5:15? This at once provoked a lot of argument in which John Rankin of Mississippi, a little man with bushy hair and a hallelujah voice, had his say at some length to demand an end to debate on the amendment then pending, and an immediate vote. A voice vote was taken. Administration men promptly demanded a standing vote, which was taken. After that Administration men demanded a teller vote, in which members walk up the aisle to be counted. Meanwhile time marched on. Finally that got settled, and late in the day, despite some neat parliamentary maneuvering, the final vote was taken and subsidies were snowed under. It was an interesting example of strategic politics.

° The Administration wanted to do away with this requirement for soldiers from the poll-tax states, at that time Alabama, Arkansas, Georgia, Maine, Mississippi, South Carolina, Texas and Virginia. The Southerners were violently opposed, because they felt removing the tax from their soldiers would be used to strengthen the drive to remove it from their Negroes.

NOVEMBER 26, 1943. This morning I visited the Senate Committee on Insular Affairs for a while. Senators Allen Ellender of Louisiana and Dennis Chavez of New Mexico were present; later Senator Robert A. Taft of Ohio came in. The issue is how far to go in giving Puerto Rico independence [ultimately extended, in 1952, to her present "commonwealth" status under the U.S. flag], and the committee shows a great reluctance to move too fast on the bill under consideration.

Taft is taller and larger than I had supposed him to be, with a bare, scrubbed-looking face, intelligent eyes, a pleasant smile, a thin-lipped mouth and the flat yet curiously attractive voice made familiar in the last campaign. He made frequent remarks to his colleagues which provoked their laughter, and seems to be well liked and respected. He is a very positive personality, despite the rather jocular and patronizing manner in which he was described by press and politicians alike in the pre-convention battles of 1940. Either he has gained considerable assurance since, or the jocularity was all part of the careful reduction of one Republican candidate, the Senator, and the building up of another, Wendell Willkie.

DECEMBER 2, 1943. Today I was assigned to the Senate staff of United Press and moved into the Senate Press Gallery, I hope to stay. Nothing could be a better break for a newspaperman and nothing could please me more. It is exactly what I wanted.

The afternoon I spent in the front row of the gallery directly above the Vice-President's desk. Henry Wallace, a weak but unmistakable voice from below adjuring the Senators to be in order or directing a roll call, was in the chair. Before me in their majesty sat the Senators of the United States. It very soon became apparent that, as I had expected, they are only human beings after all.

First impressions are not very good and I expect to revise them soon, but as of today this is how some of the members stack up from a front-row seat:

Taft continues to impress me as one of the strongest and ablest men here, one of the men who act consistently as though they think what is being done here really matters to the welfare of the country. He is quick in debate and quick in humor, as when Joe Guffey of Pennsylvania, a stocky, sarcastic gentleman, started to launch into a speech about all the soldiers who are going to vote Democratic. "Vote!" cried Taft hurriedly in an attempt to shut him off, "Vote! Vote!" The cry was taken up at once and echoed back and forth on the Republican side while Taft laughed heartily at Guffey's patient annoyance. It soon becomes apparent that Taft, perhaps more than any other, is the leader of the powerful coalition of Republicans and Southern Democrats which has things pretty much its own way right now. This makes him, in terms of actual strength on the floor, one of the three or four most powerful men in the United States Senate at the present time.

Henry Cabot Lodge of Massachusetts looks somewhat supercilious, and when he rises to speak it is with what seems a tacit assumption of superiority. He is a young man, forceful, apparently not too well liked.

Gone are the days of Pass the Biscuits for Pappy O'Daniel of Texas, apparently, for a sadder or more troubled-looking man I have yet to see in Washington. Something has him bothered, and he sits at his desk lonely and unloved as though he hasn't a friend in the world. Maybe he hasn't, although such an aura of hillbilly good nature has surrounded him in the press that one wonders what's wrong.

Allen Ellender of Louisiana is short, dark, swarthy, given to talking with his hands in quick, erratic gestures. He laughs a lot, sometimes without much provocation but always with a hearty awareness of the galleries.

Alben Barkley, the Majority Leader, acts like a man who is working awfully hard and awfully earnestly at a job he doesn't particularly like. Sweat almost visibly stands out at times on the man the President once addressed as "Dear Alben" in a famous letter. [A designation mockingly used by his enemies ever after.] Reasonably capable, though, I would say, and all in all a good man if not a great leader.

Guy Gillette of Iowa and Hugh Butler of Nebraska vie for the title of Most Senatorial. Both are model solons, white-haired, dignified, every inch the glamorous statesmen.

Chavez of New Mexico, looking like a smaller edition of Irvin S. Cobb, is able and earnest, a better-than-average Senator. Someone referred to him in print somewhere the other day as "suave." He is, but it seems to me that a good deal of the traditional dispassionate cynicism of the Hispanic peoples enters into it.

John Danaher of Connecticut already impresses me as one of the three or four ablest men in the Senate. Short, chubby, balding, with a round, earnest, serious face and an obvious lisp, he looks like some intent little teddy bear when he gets up to speak. But what he says makes sense and what he does makes more.

The topic under debate today was the soldier-vote bill. As interpreted for me by one keen reporter, the fight boils down to the fact that the Democrats think they can win the coming Presidential election if they have the soldier vote and the Republicans think they can win if they can manage to cut it off. Seen in that light—as Ed Moore of Oklahoma, a little old dried-up oilman, put it, "Of course it's a partisan bill, and we

all know it"—it becomes rather less of a patriotic contest than the public
has been led to believe.

I would say that on an average more backslapping and handshaking
are done in the United States Senate than in any other comparable area
or body of men in the world.

DECEMBER 3, 1943. Today I covered the Judiciary Committee hearing on
the bill to affirm the intent of Congress that the insurance business shall
not come under the Sherman or Clayton anti-trust acts, and got another
name to put near the top of my already-expanding mental table of ratings
for Senators—that of the sharp-eyed and sharp-minded, soft-spoken,
shrewd and hard-hitting Democrat from Wyoming, Mr. Joseph C.
O'Mahoney ("Oh-*Mah*-huh-nee"). So capable is the Senator, so logical
and so resourceful and so keen, that I came close to giving him straight
A on the basis of just one performance. He is conducting a brilliant one-
man *tour de force* in an attempt to show that the insurance business is
run as a monopoly from the top. By the simple device of asking gentle
questions and quoting from the constitutions and bylaws of the major
insurance firms, he pretty well tied up the witness in his own evasive
answers. The Senator appeared before the committee himself only as
a witness, is conducting his battle by himself, and does not have the
support of the committee, its chairman, Fred Van Nuys of Indiana, or
of any sizable number of his colleagues. He may be beaten on it, but it's
a good show and he is a good man.

This afternoon on a vote of 42–37, the Senate threw out the soldier-vote
bill offered by Scott Lucas of Illinois and Theodore Francis Green of
Rhode Island and substituted a milk-and-water version providing that
the states shall do what they can to extend absentee balloting to their
men overseas. In effect this simply cuts off the soldier vote. Few of the
men abroad are going to have time or interest to secure ballots from home.
The President's propitiary gestures on the measure are good but they
have come too late. The coalition of Republicans and Southern Democrats
is in the saddle now.

DECEMBER 4, 1943. Gradually the outlines of Congress' work are becoming
clear. What the Congress is, essentially, is a bill-machine: bills are introduced, they are considered, they are debated, and they are passed. A
secondary function which in recent years has assumed increasing importance is the investigating power: to establish by special resolution
committees which are empowered to subpoena witnesses, place them
under oath, and get the facts for the public record. The outstanding

example of this function is the Senate's Truman Committee to investigate the war effort. Sometimes investigative committees are empowered to originate legislation, but more often their duties are confined exclusively to fact-gathering. The regular standing committees of both houses, such as Agriculture, Foreign Relations, and so on, perform much the same function with regard to the bills that come before them. At the conclusion of their studies the committees issue reports disclosing, discussing, commending or condemning. Out of the reports legislation frequently comes, introduced by designated members of the committees or by other interested members.

The course of a bill is a basically simple process which can be complicated by a lot of side issues. The bill itself may be introduced by any member at any time about anything. Four things can happen to it:

If it is a Republican bill it will automatically be killed in committee and some Democrat will introduce a Democratic bill to do the same thing. [*A process, I eventually found out, which is exactly reversed when the Republicans come to power.*]

If it is utterly wild, or if the committee chairman or some other powerful influence such as the White House is against it, it can simply die in committee. The chairman never brings it up, it stays in the files, and at the end of the Congress in which it was introduced it automatically dies. This happens to the great majority.

If it manages to clear the committee hurdle and is "reported out" by the committee and placed on the "calendar," or printed list of bills awaiting action, and still arouses strong opposition, it can also die an automatic death. Somebody objects, or the motion to consider is voted down. It stays on the calendar and at the end of the Congress it goes into the wastebasket. Hundreds more are taken care of this way.

If a bill embodies a principle upon which there is general agreement (and no committee ever really bothers with a bill unless there is a good indication that it will pass in some form or other) then it goes through a standard process:

The first step is hearings. These may be open, in which case the press and the public are present and privileged to report what goes on; or they may be "executive," in which case the press and the public are barred and the press is privileged to report only what it can dig out of individual members. (This is usually sufficient.) Hearings may last a week or they may be scattered over a year or longer, depending upon the purpose for which they are being held. Usually the purpose is to get the best public advice on the bill, but sometimes it has to do with making headlines for both members and witnesses. Witnesses consist of people the committee has invited to testify and people who have asked that they be allowed to testify. Nearly all represent some organized group with special interest in the legislation.

At the conclusion of the hearings the committee goes into executive session to study the bill. If the committee accepts the bill as it stands, it may simply add a few "committee amendments." If the committee wants to take the basic principle and write its own bill, it will strike out everything after the "enacting clause" (carried at the head of all bills and consisting of the words "Be it enacted by the Senate and House of Representatives of the United States of America in Congress assembled ...") and insert an entire new measure as the committee amendment. Whichever is done, the next step is to "report it out"—send it to the floor with a formal report stating the aims of the bill and giving a digest of its provisions. The bill then goes on the "legislative calendar" of pending bills, where it may die the aforementioned natural death. If it is a major bill, however, answering a pressing and obvious need, agreement on the best time to debate it is reached between the majority and the minority at which time it is "called up for action."

After a bill has been called up, the committee amendments are considered first. If there is general agreement, they may be adopted or rejected by simple voice vote. If there is controversy a member may ask for "the Yeas and Nays"—a roll-call vote. The presiding officer asks for a show of hands. If there are enough (one-fourth of the members present), the presiding officer directs the clerk to call the roll. After the committee amendments have been disposed of, the bill is open to amendment from the floor. Any member may introduce any amendment; this is debated and disposed of, again either by voice vote or roll call, depending on the amount of controversy. After all floor amendments have been offered and disposed of, the presiding officer announces the "third reading of the bill" and the vote on final passage. Once again it may be voice vote or roll call. If a completed bill fails of passage—an extremely rare event— it is "recommitted" or sent back to committee, where it usually dies.

Bills may be introduced in one house, passed, and sent to the other, or similar bills may be introduced simultaneously in both houses. If the first procedure is followed, the house receiving the bill usually goes through the same procedure of hearings and rewriting and amending as the originating house. It then passes its amended version and the originating house asks for a conference. The bill then "goes to conference."

Conference consists of a certain number—usually 3 or 5—from each house. They are empowered to rewrite the bill once again on the basis of the best available compromise they can work out on the basis of their conflicting viewpoints. When they have finished, the "conference report" is sent to both houses. It cannot be amended and must be accepted *in toto*. If it is accepted by both houses, the bill goes to the President. If it is rejected, the conferees are discharged, new ones are appointed, and the bill goes back to conference until something acceptable is agreed upon. All major bills are written in conference by a handful of men after both houses have finished debate.

If similar bills are introduced in both houses at the same time, the house which concludes action first sends its bill to the other. The second house passes its own version, strikes out all after the enacting clause of the other bill, and substitutes its own version as an amendment. The first house then asks for conference, and the same procedure is followed.

When the bill reaches the White House the President may either sign it, permit it to become law without his signature if he doesn't like it but finds it politically inadvisable to block it, or veto it. The bill may be passed over the President's veto by a two-thirds vote of both houses, in which case it becomes law in spite of him.

DECEMBER 5, 1943. Joe Guffey and one or two other Administration supporters have come out with statements strongly critical of the "unholy alliance" of Democrats and Republicans who voted down the Green–Lucas soldier-vote bill. Apparently the split is getting to the point where really bad blood is going to develop.

At noon I went over to the Supreme Court for an hour or so to help our man there. It was a good chance to get a close-up view of the Honorable the Chief Justice and the Honorable Associate Justices of the Supreme Court, as their marshal (a gangling tow-headed kid on whose lips the stately words sound slightly incongruous) refers to them in the traditional prologue. They have quite a system, I found, particularly with someone they don't like. First Felix Frankfurter, pedantic and perky, pops a long, involved question. Before the lawyer has time to answer Robert Jackson, gracious and reasonable, leans forward and pops another. In the midst of the lawyer's confusion sandy-haired William O. Douglas contributes a bored and amused summation of what he really means to answer. Stanley Reed asks sharply if that is so, Frank Murphy stares at him with haloed disapproval, Wiley Rutledge looks disconcertingly thoughtful, Hugo Black leans over to murmur to Harlan Stone, while Owen Roberts gives the poor man an icy, appraising look. When he is sufficiently limp under all these flank attacks, Stone leans forward in a deceptively gentle, grandfatherly fashion and asks him kindly if he didn't really mean something entirely different, implying politely that he is obviously no lawyer at all, has no idea what the score is, and really ought to go back where he came from and raise hogs. It's a good show the nine gentlemen put on. In sum total they make a very good impression, and somehow one cannot help but feel that the law, whatever shots of adrenalin they may give it, is still quite safe in their hands.

Back in the Senate Office Building, the Banking and Currency Committee was conducting a hearing on the subsidy bill sent over by the House. As usual Taft was dominating the proceedings. Sober little Danaher was there, and George Radcliffe of Maryland, a kindly, fatherly old soul; Burnet Rhett Maybank of South Carolina, in his early forties, handsome, with sharp, intense eyes; John Bankhead of Alabama, old, bald, slowing with age and fanatic on cotton; Barkley, who really made a great deal of sense; and Arthur Capper of Kansas, a dried-up little old man who is going to blow away someday in a Washington high wind.

DECEMBER 7, 1943. We got our fireworks right off the bat today when Harry Byrd of Virginia, a red-faced, cherubic gentleman normally not concerned with much of anything except paring the Federal budget, rose to condemn Guffey's statement on the soldier vote in the most scathing terms. The Pennsylvanian's charge of an "unholy alliance"—of Republicans led by Joe Pew [of the Pennsylvania Sun Oil family] and Southern Democrats led by Byrd—was pretty well ripped to shreds by the Senator from Virginia. Josiah Bailey of North Carolina followed and made a colorful oration in which the Stars and Bars waved freely overhead and the threat of a new secession, at least from the Democratic Party, was freely voiced. There is a very real bitterness on this issue, and it began to come into the open today. Bailey looks like a professor or a deacon and is a good orator, rather than speaker, with a mild, dignified, schoolteacherly manner and a tendency to bite in the clinches. "Pennsylvania has produced some fine men," he remarked thoughtfully at the end of his speech, "Ben Franklin, William Penn. And then it has produced some others— Thad Stevens, Boies Penrose, Mr. Vare—and the junior Senator from Pennsylvania." The Republicans listen with attentive politeness and well-concealed delight these days while the Democrats fall apart across the aisle. All they have to do is sit tight and rake up the pieces.

There was apparent today the sometimes rather frightening fact of just how much democracy is founded upon good will—sheer human liking and ability to get along together. Out of the complex personalities of 96 men are rising prejudices and dislikes which could, under some circumstances, seriously handicap the country. In fact, they are handicapping it right now, and the tendency is increasing. So much depends, in a democracy, upon Joe liking John and John liking Bill; let the trio fall out and see how far we get. It was apparent this afternoon that mere dislike is turning, in some cases, into active hatred as the soldier-vote issue becomes embroiled in the growing general bitterness between the White House and the Hill.

Into this atmosphere Barkley tried to insert the House resolution extending the statute of limitations governing when the Pearl Harbor court-martials must be held to one calendar year after the end of hostilities and the ratification of the peace treaty by the Senate. He was at once chopped down by as neat and effective a piece of legislative axing as I have seen so far. Bennett Champ Clark of Missouri, a portly, tendentious and intelligent soul, swept aside Barkley's well-meaning but ineffectual arguments and rammed through a revision giving the War and Navy departments only six months to prefer charges and get the court-martials going. It went back to the House, was accepted, and presumably will determine the course of events in that affair from now on. Clark charged openly what everyone on the Hill claims to know for a fact, that the Administration is deliberately trying to string out the trials as long as possible for fear that evidence presented will lead into some very high places at the other end of the Avenue.

This morning the Interstate Commerce Committee held a hearing on the Wheeler–White bill to revise the powers of the Federal Communications Commission. Fourteen Senators were on hand at one point, including Cotton Ed Smith, Ernest McFarland of Arizona, Albert Hawkes of New Jersey, James Tunnell of Delaware, intense little Homer Bone of Washington, and Chairman Burton K. Wheeler. The last interested me most, and in his questioning of the witness confirmed an impression gained from several prewar radio addresses with which I did not agree: he is a very able man, and his views on foreign policy have little to do with his stature as a Senator, which is considerable. In fact, so amiable is he, with such a good sense of humor, that it is hard to reconcile the bitter partisan and the calculating politician who is undoubtedly biding his time in preparation for the reaction he believes to be inevitable.

Cotton Ed has a certain quality about him which is solid and rather impressive—the solidity and impressiveness of an old moss-covered ruin. His years are beginning to tell, and his colleagues evidently consider him quite a character, for they begin to laugh the moment he begins to speak. Usually what he says is funny, so it all works out all right in the end.

Lodge stacked up better today in debate. He gives the impression of a controlled and predatory bird, swooping down decisively upon his points and driving them into the other fellow with a crisp and rockbound air.

DECEMBER 8, 1943. The Senate took up the Deficiency Appropriations Bill today, some 300 millions; after a long involved quibble in which Lodge and Kenneth McKellar of Tennessee, with witty interpolations from Danaher, argued back and forth about whether or not to amend it to provide that 10 per cent of surplus funds held by the armed services be impounded as an emergency fund for them, it went like lightning through several hundred amendments and finally got itself passed around 5:30. Lodge went down to defeat 56 to 18, a vote which seemed to be to some extent personal.

McKellar is a slow, bumbling, absent-minded typical Senator, likable enough but a trifle slow on the uptake, well-meaning, reasonably honest, shrewd but not in the way some people are shrewd.

Late in the afternoon Richard Russell of Georgia, Happy Chandler of Kentucky and the handsome gentleman from West Virginia who bears the romantic name of Chapman Revercomb, got into a three-way fight on Russell's proposed amendment to grant the Surgeon General an emergency fund with which to subsidize doctors and send them into areas whose medical men have gone into service. Revercomb said it was the opening wedge for socialized medicine, Russell and Chandler said it wasn't. McKellar backed Revercomb, and the irrepressible Kenneth Wherry of Nebraska stuck his oar in at considerable length. Warren Austin of Vermont, a dignified, pink-faced, well-fed gentleman with a rather humorless manner and a rich, deliberate voice, also participated from time to time. The amendment was beaten.

Black-clad Senator Hattie Caraway of Arkansas, adhering to her standard ritual, came in with her big black handbag, fumbled in it for her glasses, put them on, sat for a while, read the paper, voted "No" on a few amendments and then walked out.

DECEMBER 9, 1943. Cotton Ed Smith arose today to uphold the honor of the South, white supremacy, the Constitution, Southern womanhood, Southern Democrats, and the poll tax. More or less incidentally he nominated Harry Byrd for President—after having said repeatedly, according to press-gallery gossip, that he wouldn't vote for Harry Byrd for dogcatcher, let alone President.

It was an old man's speech, the sort of speech that is beginning to mark the end, at last, of an era. There will not be many more such, filled with hell and damnation and a dirty story or two thrown in for good measure; presently, when Cotton Ed is gone, there will probably be no more. He is an old man and uncurbed any longer by the hesitancies of youth and middle age which once, in all probability, placed at least the minimum restraints upon his sentiments and tongue. That sort of thing is an echo of another day, an antique, as it were, brought forth at rare intervals and placed upon the counter; a rather obscene old book which somebody found somewhere and offers for a limited showing to a group of select customers. Byrd squirmed, Chandler played his usual stooge for the old man, and the Republicans listened attentively while a little more animosity was set afloat on the Democratic side. Taft seemed to take heart from it all and sounded quite like the future candidate when he rose to dispute Tydings of Maryland on a bill to establish a Filipino Rehabilitation Commission; coming, as he sometimes does, dangerously close to the line that separates the man of argument from the man of arrogance. Tydings, who is a thoroughly capable and logical man, got driven temporarily off base by Taft's attack, and got over into such flimsy defenses as "the Army and Navy want it," "it is necessary to the war effort," and all the other old turkeys which are trotted out when no real

Cotton Ed

justification exists for a thing. Taft demolished his arguments without any trouble and Tydings accepted with relief Taft's suggestion that it go over to Monday for further clarification.

After the session we went down onto the floor for our regular chat with Barkley, who is rapidly rising in my estimation. He is a good politician and a good-natured, easygoing man. I suspect he deserves his *E* for Effort. Certainly he has no simple job, and in fact frequently remarks these days that he does not rise "to make any comment because of any weight or influence I expect to carry with other Senators." He gains by admitting it, when all is said and done.

The Second Civil War seems to be three-tenths personalities, six-tenths bluff, and one-tenth real. Nonetheless, there are genuine animosities here, and the whole situation is not good from the standpoint of the peace legislation which will presently be tossed into it.

DECEMBER 10, 1943. Going downtown this evening after a rather relaxed day we got into a discussion of the "top men of the Senate." We finally concluded that the problem was highly complicated by the fact that, as one veteran reporter remarked, "What the hell, they're human." That's just about it. You start looking at somebody objectively and before you know it you're beginning to think about what a likable old cuss he is and that in spite of everything he's still a good egg. Even Cotton Ed gathers a little saving grace by this process.

Interstate Commerce Committee goes on and on with its hearings on the bill to revise the powers of the Federal Communications Commission. E. K. Jett, chief engineer of the FCC, testified this morning and made an excellent impression. Jim Tunnell of Delaware was acting chairman, assisted by Ed Moore of Oklahoma smoking his usual cigar and making his usual brief for the system of free enterprise which gave him, for one, all those oil wells in Oklahoma. There is something very typical about Mr. Moore, with his wrinkled, round, flat face, his unkempt hair and his wizened smile. No one from California needs to be told that he is from Oklahoma. The face is quite familiar.

McFarland contributed his customary slow, easy, humorous questioning. The Senator from Arizona is a pretty honest and pretty decent fellow. If an issue is good he will generally be found supporting it, and if it is bad he will generally be found opposing it. His instincts are right and he follows them with considerable diligence.

This afternoon most of us hung around the beautiful Caucus Room, with its massive oak tables, high ceilings, marble walls, tall windows and innumerable microphones and amplifiers, to listen in on the Van Nuys hearing on the liquor shortage, hard to explain to Senators whose states are producing grain surpluses. Homer Ferguson of Michigan, his silver hair rumpled above his earnest dark eyes, was industriously questioning the witness. The Senator is a good-hearted, idealistic soul with an outstanding talent for cross-examination. He made his great reputation in Michigan as a one-man grand jury, and on the strength of it came to the Senate last year. He has been investigating ever since. He is not so incisive or knifelike as O'Mahoney—his edges, so to speak, are rounded instead of square—but he does a capable job of it. Van Nuys, boiling with indignation because the head of Seagram's has refused to come down from Canada and testify, is apparently going to do dire things to the industry in retaliation. Or, more likely, it is all going to fizzle out into one of those gentle *pops* with which the gentlemen occasionally favor us.

DECEMBER 11, 1943. Guffey, apparently irrepressible, has issued another statement attacking opponents of the soldier-vote bill; and the ill and ancient Carter Glass of Virginia, absent from the Senate since his last election a year ago, has written to Lucas supporting it. The issue is not dead by any means, and it seems likely that we shall see more activity on it before long.

DECEMBER 12, 1943. There are minor isolated things about the Senate and the gallery, all of which contribute to their color, which I want to put down here before they become so much a part of everyday routine that I don't even notice them any more.

In the big oblong chamber with its emergency superstructure of frank ungainly steel put up a couple of years ago to support the cracking ceiling, a kind of sickly, sea-green light prevails, as though its occupants were debating at the bottom of a tank where little pageboys dart like minnows. Sometimes this becomes so overpowering on the eyes that the outlines of the desks begin to fade out and all you see before you for a second, before you shake your head and snap out of it, is row upon row of white papers, neatly circled against a murky and impenetrable background. It is a strange feeling. [*Changed now, following the postwar remodeling of the chamber which left it light beige, brightly lit, and handsome.*]

Sometimes late in the afternoon, looking down across the chamber to the farther door beneath the clock, you can see behind it a blazing streak of sunlight on the floor beyond, casting its bright reflection on the swinging glass panels as the Senators pass in and out. It is as though a glowing welcome were being prepared, a great burst of glory in which some hero, impossibly gallant and fine, might enter on a wave of light and the distant applaudings of a million hands. But no, sad luck: it's only little Raymond Willis of Indiana, wandering in like some fugitive gnome, or Bob Reynolds of North Carolina, with his plastered hair and puff-eyed face, or Arthur Vandenberg of Michigan, huge head wreathed in a pleased, complacent smile.

Visitors get herded into the galleries like sheep, sit a while hearing a debate whose origins and outcome they have no time to discover, and are herded out again bored and wondering. Their attention is diverted easily by the men they recognize, and to Mrs. Caraway they always pay the tribute of a lively interest. Servicemen sit more quietly and listen more attentively than others, seeming to strive to find here some portion of that glory for which they are told they fight.

Members of the House come in sometimes and sit on the couches that line the walls at the back of the chamber. Now and again former Senators come in and take their old accustomed places, listening with wistful interest to the proceedings on the floor.

When the Yeas and Nays are demanded, the Clerk goes down the list calling "Mr. Aiken! Mr. Austin!" and so following, in a loud challenging voice. Senators who come in after the call has begun wait patiently until it has finished and then rise to be recognized. The Chair then calls them out by title, "The junior Senator from Michigan!" whereupon the Clerk cries reprovingly, "Mr. Ferguson!" and the Senator votes. Then the Clerk reads those voting in the affirmative, followed by those voting in the negative. Then he adds them up and passes his tally up to the Vice-President's desk; the Chair announces the decision. Then we scramble up the steep gallery stairs and stream into the press room like something out of a movie, and the air is filled for half an hour with the loud excited clatter of typewriters and teletypes and the urgent ringing of telephones. Around the large table in the main press room, where the big mirrors stretch toward the ceiling and where in winter the fire is always lit, members of the fourth estate play poker in the best Hollywood tradition.

In the subway between the Senate and the Office Building, the operators must make close to a thousand trips a day, back and forth and back and forth along their block-long railway. The walls are painted a light, clean-looking gray; it is as though you were being whisked along the passageways of some sanitary modern hospital. Frequently Senators arrive at one end or the other to find the cars in transit, whereupon they apply themselves to the bell *For Senators Only* and the air resounds with three imperious clangings. In the same fashion, and with the same three rings, they are wont to summon recalcitrant elevators, which must take Senators where they want to go first, and only then attend to the needs of lesser breeds.

Whenever a message is sent to the Senate from the House or the President, the messenger stands just inside the doorway while the Chair asks the Senator speaking to "suspend for a moment while the Senate receives a message from the House of Representatives." The Chair stands, the messenger bows from the waist. "A message from the House of Representatives!" says a Senate clerk. The House messenger describes it ("Mr. President, the House has passed Senate Bill No. So-and-So, and has passed various and sundry enrolled bills to which the Speaker has affixed his signature"). The majority secretary takes the message and brings it to the Vice-President's desk. The interrupted Senator resumes speaking.

When you get off the elevator from the gallery onto the first floor it is as though you were entering a mosque; innumerable archways greet the eye, and an intricate brown design combining flowers and heros runs endlessly over the walls.

Whenever a quorum is demanded on the floor the Clerk goes down the list, calling each name. Meanwhile throughout the Senate side and in every committee room and office in the Senate Office Building, the two sharp rings of the quorum bell resound. Senators come in slowly from the hallways, are recognized and answer, "Here!" If the list is exhausted without a quorum of 49 being found, the Clerk goes through the roll of the absentees until it is.

There is frequently a lot of talking and visiting on the floor, and quite often the Chair is compelled to pound for order. It is always granted promptly, although the conversations are apt to continue *sotto voce* in little intimate huddles around someone's desk.

Legislation is followed by the press with more than professional interest: in a very real sense the press is an active part of the lawmaking process. Bills become living things, and arguments about them rage on the sofas and around the card table during slack periods in the Press Gallery. The press, by and large, combines a deep cynicism with some of the truest idealism to be found anywhere.

No one could do a really thorough job of reporting the Senate without the invaluable assistance of the gallery staff, who obtain copies of bills, distribute statements and speeches, keep tab on complicated parliamentary procedures, keep the list of committee hearings, furnish copy paper and reference books and in general keep the press supplied with whatever it needs.

DECEMBER 13, 1943. We spent the afternoon today over in the Office Building getting personal opinions on the McKellar–Butler squabble. Butler, dark eyes set in a dark face under the Senate's most Senatorial head of silver hair, has drawn a good many sparks with his assertions in *The Reader's Digest* that we are buying Latin American friendship to the tune of $6,000,000,000. McKellar has taken it upon himself to reply, and today asserted for an hour and a half that the figure is only $300,000,000. Butler is of course on his high horse now too, promised this afternoon that he will furnish a supplemental report in a few days, and the whole argument is resounding down the long corridors of the Office Building. It was against that background that we set out to get comments from various people. The first we talked to was the far-famed and ill-legended senior Senator from North Dakota, the Honorable Gerald P. Nye.

Mr. Nye is just about what one pictures him from his reputation and the things one has read about him: a shrewd, forceful, very political man, with an attractive, easygoing manner and obvious intelligence. Like Wheeler, he too is waiting; shrewdly, with what seems to be a deep personal conviction—perhaps more about his own future than about isolationism's—and with a friendly, down-to-earth manner that covers it up almost entirely.

Coming down the hall from Nye's office we ran into Lodge, who is a much bigger man than I had judged him to be, looking down from the Press Gallery—at least 6 feet 4 and heavy in proportion. On close contact he also makes a most favorable impression, friendly and matter-of-fact and intelligently humorous. When we began asking questions he grinned and remarked smoothly that in the days when he was here in the press— he is a newspaperman by profession and spent several years on the Hill before returning to Massachusetts to run for Senator—he used to know all the inside dope, but now that he is here as a member of the government he has to ask the press for everything he gets. [*Twenty years later, this child of the Roosevelt era can still remember the shock of Lodge's casual "member of the government." It was the first realization that "The Government" consisted of something more than just the inescapable, all-pervading personality that sat at 1600 Pennsylvania.*]

We saw then Ed Johnson of Colorado, a great bull moose of a man with a tolerant face, heavy eyebrows, and an aura of solid common sense. He is a member of the Military Affairs Committee, and we were trying to pump him about General Patton, who continues to be an issue because of the slapping incident. As Johnson said, "ugly stories are going around," but he would do no more than hint at them. He seems to be a thoroughly competent legislator, unruffled by the shifting currents of politics through which he seems to pass untroubled on a sure course of his own.

This morning I covered the Education and Labor Committee hearing on two bills, one sponsored by Chairman Elbert Thomas of Utah and the other by Claude Pepper of Florida, to give returning servicemen funds to continue their educations. Pepper is extremely liberal with the United States Treasury and extremely conscious of the fact that he came up by his bootstraps through Harvard and Phi Beta Kappa. He is one of the plainest men alive, but is intelligent and on the whole capable, I think. The witnesses included Major General Osborn of the Morale Division Special Services, a keen hawk-faced man whom Pepper heckled a good deal, and Colonel Francis Spaulding, also of the Morale Division and former Dean of the Graduate School of Education at Harvard—that perfect academic type, smooth as butter and sharp as a knife, ingratiating, reasonable, courteous, shrewd, ambitious. There is such a thing as a Typical Dean of the younger, more pragmatic type, and Spaulding represents it. It was an interesting fusion, this combination of the army and the academic. He gave Pepper as good as he got, with of course consistent suavity and courtesy and from time to time a gently acid irony, all in the best tradition of the little boy who didn't work his way through Harvard talking to the little boy who did.

DECEMBER 14, 1943. Education and Labor dragged on today, beginning to get out of the novelty class for all concerned and into the category of stout toil and earnest application. Thomas of Utah was again in the chair, a courteous, soft-spoken, precise old man who acts like what he is, a scholar in politics. It is with accommodating politeness that he accedes to the witnesses' desire to discuss his bill instead of Pepper's, but aside from that rather natural bias he seems to conduct the hearings on a fair and intelligent basis. He was flanked today by Raymond Willis of Indiana, a dumpy, sleepy-looking man with a face all folded in and wrinkled upon itself and a rather apathetic approach to life, and the press' fair-haired boy Joseph Ball of Minnesota, whose recent international-cooperation resolution has given him an aura of St. George versus the Dragon which may or may not be warranted. He is a huge young man, slow-spoken and slow-moving, with prematurely gray hair and a good-natured scowl occasionally alleviated by a skeptical and fleeting smile. Willis' questions were routine, Ball's more pointed. I should say offhand that Willis is not hard to catalogue but that Joe Ball will take some study before it becomes clear whether or not he lives up to his reputation or just profits from an appearance indubitably earnest and idealistic.

The afternoon went very slowly on the floor. Another Truman report, this time on transportation, has come out, and Jim Mead of New York and Ferguson both felt called upon to make speeches about it—both upholding it, of course, being committee members. Taft, Barkley and Bankhead have been named a special subcommittee of the Banking and Currency Committee to try to work out some compromise on the subsidy fight, and much of today's significant activity took place off the floor in the cloakrooms.

DECEMBER 15, 1943. This morning the hearings on the veterans education bills came to a close, distinguished chiefly by one of the witnesses' candid admission·that a good deal of the problem is the fight between the Veterans Administration and the U.S. Office of Education as to which one is going to administer the thing. Kenneth Wherry made his usual rather disruptive appearance, coming in late, chewing on his lip darkly for a couple of minutes and then proceeding to jump all over a perfectly inoffensive witness.

Debate got rather dramatic this afternoon when Moore read a long speech explaining why he voted against the Green–Lucas soldier-vote bill. He incidentally took occasion at some length to light into Roosevelt and the 1940 Democratic Convention, at which he was a Democratic delegate. He is now a Republican Senator, which perhaps explains something. Scott Lucas thought it did when he got up to reply with the most personal, below-the-belt, viciously specific speech I have yet heard in the Senate. He went so far, in fact, that Wallace White of Maine, who is acting minority leader in the absence of Charles McNary of Oregon, rose to make a point of order about one Senator impugning another's motives. He was upheld by John McClellan of Arkansas in the chair. Moore, who seemed rather baffled by the violence of the reaction he had provoked, attempted feebly to reply from time to time but Lucas refused to yield the floor and kept right on talking. Lucas became extremely bitter toward the end, telling Moore that "a one-armed veteran from Italy may run against you in the next campaign in Oklahoma, and he'll wave that one arm in your face and tell you about it" (Moore's vote for the substitute bill). It was an ugly display of dirty linen in public. There is a lot of bad feeling here, and no mistake. Under the surface amicability, a lot of things are festering.

The day ended with Bill Langer of North Dakota well launched upon a one-man filibuster to block a complicated piece of legislation to prevent private suits against frauds in government contracts. It was a humorous, disgraceful, saddening spectacle all rolled into one. The man ranted and raved and pounded and roared. He had abandoned his text and was well into the pages of the *Saturday Evening Post* when White finally rose and asked him to stop, with the promise of the floor tomorrow. During most of his speech three Senators were on the floor: White, minority; Mead, majority; and the gentleman with the handsome head and soothing voice, Harold Burton of Ohio, working away industriously at his desk, apparently oblivious of the racket in the room.

DECEMBER 16, 1943. Langer's filibuster collapsed this afternoon after a couple of hours. He eventually ran dry, moved to recommit the bill, lost the motion, the bill was passed by voice vote, and so ended the valiant stand of the Senator from North Dakota. He is an odd character, the maverick of the Senate, so proud of being turned out of the governorship of his state that he lists it in the *Congressional Directory* like an accolade. If his ideas have any value no one will ever know it, for he presents them at the top of his lungs like a roaring bull in the empty chamber, while such of his colleagues as remain watch him in half-amused, half-fearful silence, as though in the presence of an irresponsible force they can neither control nor understand. In some ways this Congress is a strange, strange thing, composed of the symbols of a people's erratic will.

DECEMBER 18, 1943. I interviewed Van Nuys this morning to get a week-end story on the liquor shortage, and found him a pleasant and friendly old man. I am beginning to think the chief requisite for United States Senator is personal amiability: it seems to be the one characteristic I find common to almost everyone. Van Nuys is no exception, and in addition seems to be honest and sincere in his approach to the problem before his committee. I think he is quite interested in developing some constructive legislation to solve it.

Going over to the Office Building to see him, it occurred to me what an institution a Senator is. They sit in their offices like a lot of independent little principalities, owing no subservience to anyone but their people, not possessed of too much loyalty to one another, only uniting from time to time on the issues that touch their particular boundaries. From them, stretching out into the depths of the country, run the long lines of power to the folks back home, the county committees, the state conventions, the friends, the acquaintances, the clubs, the people. It is a curious and rather moving thing, one of those features of our life in this land that sometimes amuse the mind and sometimes touch the heart.

This afternoon the Senate took four temporary recesses before the House would agree to a compromise on the subsidy fight and accept a proposal to continue the life of the Commodity Credit Corporation. Finally it did, and with that out of the way Barkley offered a concurrent resolution to adjourn *sine die* after next Tuesday's session, and a resolution to convene the second session of the 78th Congress at noon Monday, January 10. Both went through unanimously, although Pat McCarran of Nevada made some objection, wanting a recess to January 19 which he did not get. He too is an interesting character, with his huge square figure, his diamond ring, his perfectly tailored suits, his cynical face like one of Hans Holbein's, and his shock of white hair swirling upward like a cockatoo's.

It was an odd feeling to realize when the resolutions went through that in the normal course of things, with the single exception of the President calling a special session, no one on this earth could tell those men whether they could or could not take a vacation, or how long or how short it could be. Three sovereign branches: it comes out from time to time.

DECEMBER 19, 1943. Twenty-five members of the House have issued another statement on the hard-dying Green–Lucas soldier-vote bill. Obviously the Congress cannot let things ride as they are at present. Some attempt must be made to facilitate the soldier vote.

DECEMBER 20, 1943. Handsome, dynamic, suave, striking, forceful, dramatic, incisive—and all the other adjectives customarily fawned upon him by an idolatrous press-agentry—General Brehon B. Somervell got put on the griddle by the Truman Committee this morning and emerged from the ordeal still handsome, dynamic, suave, etc., albeit a trifle limp. The subject at issue was the ill-fated Canol Project, a wild dream that did not come true of oil in the depths of the Canadian Northwest begun, apparently, on a nod from Brehon B. and now become a great bone of contention between the Committee and the War Department. The committee damns it up and down while the War Department is as usual scrambling desperately to save face instead of having the guts to admit a mistake frankly and go on from there. All the desperate assertions of an embarrassed incompetence have been hurried forth to justify the thing, but the committee is unimpressed. In all this controversy Brehon B. occupies the central spot and today, his three stars glittering, was brought to book. Not much was gained by the whole business.

As a matter of fact, the committee got off base somewhat by concentrating on the project itself instead of on the way it was handled, which of course is the main issue in almost everything done by the Army. Few intelligent people can disagree with most of the objectives. The fault lies in the wasteful, sloppy, irresponsible methods.

The general was supported in his important mission by four brigadiers and a small covey of majors. At one point he asked for a glass of water and handed his glass to a brigadier. The brigadier promptly handed it to a major. The major looked around desperately for somebody lower down; finding no one, he filled it up and returned it to the brigadier, who returned it to the general. All very correct, right in line with regulations, and strictly conforming to the chain of command. I was glad to see that the finer things of life are still being treasured in the service.

Eight members of the committee were present, including Ferguson, Ball, Truman, Owen Brewster of Maine, Carl Hatch of New Mexico, Harley Kilgore of West Virginia and Tom Connally of Texas, who rose from a sickbed, so he told us, to attend. He and Hatch defended the general capably; others were more critical. Truman has very thick glasses, a conservative appearance, and a quick, humorous way of speaking. He seems to be a generally good man, probably deserving of his reputation. Brewster is bald and quiet, asking a few polite but loaded questions in a subdued voice from time to time. Kilgore, who handled most of the questioning and lit into the general rather thoroughly, seemed to be a capable man with a sense of humor, a sensible line of questioning and considerable common sense.

This afternoon I decided to do a piece on Senate Resolution 100, urging the State Department to negotiate with the British to permit passage of food to Occupied Europe, and S. Res. 203, urging the President to establish a commission to help save the Jews. Both were reported out today by the Foreign Relations Committee, and both are to be placed before the Senate tomorrow in an attempt to get unanimous consent to suspend the rules and pass them before the Christmas recess. I went

around to see Gillette and Taft, an interesting duo who were at swords'
points on the soldier-vote bill a couple of weeks ago but have managed to
get together on the humanitarian issues.

Gillette on close inspection is a nice fellow, friendly and voluble, im-
pressively handsome with a friendly twinkle in his eye. Interviewing
Gillette you say, "Senator, I wonder if you would care to comment——"
Then you say "Mmmhmm" for 45 minutes and you have your story.
Interviewing Taft, *you* talk for 45 minutes and *he* says "Mmmhmm."
Then you go back and work it out on your typewriter and you have your
story.

Taft is curiously quiet, at least on first acquaintance. Where is the
dynamic fighter of the floor, I wondered, where the indomitable tilter
at windmills and rattler of scabbards? Is all that fire banked in this quiet,
silent, uncommunicative man? I know it is, but it is still rather a surprise
at first to see the contrast between Taft the Man on the Floor and Taft
the Man behind the Desk. I came to the conclusion finally that the silence
which I took at first to be calculated politics is simply the shy nature
of a man who takes a while to warm up and a certain amount of knowing
before he will speak out. A bronze statuette of his father looks down
encouragingly upon an aspirant son.

DECEMBER 21, 1943. Today, in that atmosphere of lackadaisical inattention to everything but the business of getting through which apparently characterizes the tail-ends of sessions, the press became increasingly hard put to find anything to write about. Great stress was laid on personal interviews upon whatever subject could be thought up on the spur of the moment. This led me into my two most interesting so far. The first was with the determined and unyielding senior Senator from Montana, the Honorable Burton K. Wheeler. I found him pacing up and down his office like a nervous panther, and wrote most of my notes sitting at the desk while he ranged up and down behind me, editing and revising and furbishing his statements, taking out a word here and putting one

Truman Committee
From Left, Senator Mon. C. Wallgren, Harley M. Kilgore,
Joe Ball, Tom Connally, Harry S. Truman (chairman) James M. Mead,
and Ralph O. Brewster

in there with all the careful attention of a copy desk. From time to time an impatient smile would cross his face briefly as he told off some pet enemy with violent emphasis, but on the whole the impression I got was one of stormy moodiness, a rather grim humor, and not much tolerance.

The Senator is understandably bitter, and the vigor of his denunciations reveals that he has not modified in the slightest degree the opinions he held before the war and during its early stages. He swung out freely at "internationalist-minded crackpots—be sure and include that in your story" and "the same gang which wanted us to get into war and is now trying to smear everyone who wanted to stay out." He did praise the President's conferences with other Allied leaders, and he did favor the President's attempts to begin work now on a postwar peace plan, but for the rest his statements were angry, embittered, and gave no quarter. He has had a rough time of it in recent years, giving and receiving haymakers on all sides, and it has left its mark.

Later on I stopped in to see Joe Ball, who represents the other side of the picture, and found him slow-spoken, friendly but not too communicative, not much concerned with any over-all program but apparently content to go along until an issue arises that appeals to him. He then attempts to get behind it and put it over. He is no match for Wheeler in out-and-out legislative rough-and-tumble, I should say. The old man has been here a long time, knows all the tricks, and fights with a skillful partisanship I don't think Ball could ever muster. Nonetheless, I am inclined to think that the young Minnesota Senator is one of the hopes of the nation, providing he can eventually gain some positive strength of the only sort that counts when the chips are down—votes.

The Senate met at 12 and recessed at 12:46 after disposing of routine business. White and Barkley agreed to block anything more, and Gillette's Jewish and food resolutions were held over until January. A few committee hearings and now and again a prepared statement are probably all we shall get out of the Senate for the next three weeks.

This morning I continued in pursuit of a story on what Burt Wheeler terms "internationalist-minded crackpots," and talked to Harold Burton of Ohio, whom I liked a lot. There is something franker and more forthright about him than about many here, and his ideas, while not startling in originality, are sincere and honest. He's a nice fellow, compactly built on a small scale, with a handsome head, silvering hair, and bright eyes set deep in very dark circles of flesh. He laughs a lot as he talks and seems to look upon the world with an idealistic generosity concerning other peoples' motives. He seemed not at all displeased with the fact that the Connally peace resolution blanketed out the Ball–Burton–Hatch–

Hill effort. "After all," he said, "it includes the language of the Moscow Declaration [of 1943, expressing the Allies' hopes for a postwar world organization] so really it's even better than ours." Like Ball, however, he said there was no over-all strategy on the part of himself and other internationalist Senators, no program of continuing legislation.

Wayne Morse thinks he may resign from the War Labor Board and run against incumbent Rufus Holman for the Oregon seat. The report is causing considerable interest in the Press Gallery.

Tomorrow I am going to beard the fearsome Langer in his den and ask him to comment on Willkie. That ought to be good for at least 45 minutes of roaring denunciation and a good story to boot.

DECEMBER 23, 1943. Bill Langer, who is dumb like a fox, is not to be drawn out on Willkie, at least right now. "No, no comment. Nothing at all, no." Then a bright friendly expression and a little silence. Then, "What's the latest on this railroad strike? I *am* interested in that!" Inconsequential chitchat for a couple of minutes and another jovial silence. Then, suddenly, "Cigarette? Cigar?" I rose and left, politely; we parted the best of friends. He's an odd character—that's about the best anybody around here can do when trying to describe him, and it's about the best I can do too. There is a disturbing sense about him, somewhere underneath the very smooth heartiness and the firm, lingering handshake, that here is a man of great violence and great anger. I have seen how it comes out on the floor; it dissipates itself into howling nothingness, but it is only luck that it does so. If it did not, here might be a man as dangerous in his way as Huey Long in his, one of those wild, harsh men out of the wild, harsh places of America, uncontrollable and elemental. He lacks the essential quality of appeal to the masses, but aside from that he was built for power—too much power. It is the nation's good fortune that he will never achieve it.

Hugh Butler says he is going to submit his second report on Latin America right after the recess, ahead of the tax bill and everything else; and the rumor is going around with increasing persistence that the Republicans, faced with the problem of McNary's continuing illness, are going to move White into the minority leadership. In a number of respects it looks like a lively session coming up.

DECEMBER 24, 1943. A little perspective, perhaps, is a bad thing. I have been wondering about the Hill today, and the people who inhabit it and what they do, now that most of them have gone home and things have quieted down. Certain nagging thoughts keep coming back. The terrible slowness of the legislative process, for instance; the mountainous

labors that bring forth mice; and, repeatedly recurring, the inertia of
the men who should furnish leadership, who should enunciate principles
even though action may not immediately follow. They are curiously voice-
less, suffering from the subtle apathy which seems to creep upon them
after their first few months on the Hill. Reading such things as Ernie
Pyle's classically simple book on the GIs and finding in it confirmation
over and over again of my own personal observations while in the service
—the great disinterestedness of the men, their wanting to get home, their
lack of any definite purpose or goal beyond—a kind of desperation sometimes rests upon the heart. No one here is talking their language, no one
here is inspiring them or giving them purpose. Nothing is planned to help
bring forth tomorrow's world, or if it is it will be referred to committee
and hearings will be held and someday, if it is rarely lucky, it will appear
upon the floor and become the center of a bitterly partisan fight that will
presently rob it of all its heart and spirit; and ultimately, many months or
even years from now, it will be passed, maybe, and maybe be approved.
Perhaps that is why the young men here, those who are young in years
and those others who are young in spirit, do not speak out in the living
words of a living people to put into this war the heart and the hope so
ominously lacking.

There are many men easily beaten on the Hill—too many men too easily
beaten—not by any great conspiracy, not by any dark and devious opponents, just by the sheer ponderous weight of an institution moving too
slowly toward goals too petty and diffuse.

O'Mahoney says Congress and the states could pass a constitutional
amendment to facilitate soldier voting in ample time for the elections. So
they could, in 30 days or less, *if they would.* But never, never, will they
act so quickly; and never, never, will there be any real excuse why they
should not.

One of the nicest men in the Senate came into the beautiful green room
of the Office Building cafeteria while Helene Monberg of UP and I were
indulging such dark thoughts this noon, and I said, "There's a nice guy. I
like him." "He's swell," she said. "If we had 96 men like that in the United
States Senate, you and I wouldn't be sitting here saying the things we
have been."

Yet I have already seen in him too a certain indefinable inertia, the
subtle influence of the Hill, the scarcely noticeable dessication of ambition, force and will.

It is a strange place, the Hill, and it does things to the men who come
to it with high hopes and gallant plans.

2

OPA AND GOP

DECEMBER 27, 1943. If you take the reputation he has in some circles as a standard, Wheeler has no right to be such a likable man, or such a capable man, or such a keen man. Nonetheless he is all three and no honest observer can deny it. I am getting to like him personally as well as anybody I have met in the Senate.

This morning he wanted to unburden himself about Ed Johnson's statement that the invasion forces will be composed 73 per cent of Americans, 27 per cent of British. The Senator doesn't like it, and with his unfailing skill at turning the knife in the wound, has seized upon it as one more lever against the British. It also gives him a chance to hit Roosevelt, something he enjoys doing. His comments on the election are interesting and more than a little pessimistic of Democratic chances. "Why, hell, the people won't stand for this nonsense, that's all. They won't stand for it."

Subsequently I talked to White, not having anything much to take up his time about, but just to get acquainted. As I expected, he pinned various suggestions for comment right down to the specific. Friendly, colloquial, and as New England as they come, the little man from Maine is a nice fellow.

I also saw Senator Caraway, a brief but interesting visit. "All I do is answer letters," she told me with a deprecating, noncommittal smile. So far it seems to have paid off at the polls.

After lunch I dropped in on O'Mahoney and after yanking and hauling to get something out of him, and taking a good deal of abrupt but good-natured bullying before he would condescend to say anything, finally got something on the insurance bill. After I got it all down he made me dictate it to his secretary and had her give it to AP. They tell me this is characteristic.

I wound up the day with a brief, cordial, unproductive call on Henry Cabot Lodge, who refused like O'Mahoney to say anything on the invasion percentages and told me once more that he doesn't know anything now that he is here in the government. All very friendly and jolly, "drop in any time when you haven't anything better to do," but no news.

DECEMBER 28, 1943. Today I met Clyde Reed of Kansas, a white-haired old man with prominent eyes, a belligerent chin, and very positive opinions on practically everything. The occasion was a meeting called by the Kansas delegation to try to get the Office of Price Administration to declare a 10-day holiday on ration points for pork in order to relieve a temporary surplus. Ed Johnson was for it, and Reed, and Bill Langer, and Eugene Millikin of Colorado, a very bald, plain man with prominent dark eyes, a wide generous mouth, and a lot of intelligence; and mousy little old John Thomas of Idaho; and, although he had some trouble getting the drift, Arthur Capper of Kansas. O'Mahoney was against it and proceeded to put on his usual pyrotechnic display of cross-examination, eliciting a lot of answers in opposition to the plan from the OPA and War Food Administration men who were present.

Capper is a dried-up, frail old man, a living shadow, very deaf, who listens with the intense concentration of the aged, one hand cupped behind his ear and a strained expression on his face, breaking in from time to time with some hurrying, querulous question.

DECEMBER 29, 1943. The railroads have been taken over by the government and the threatened strike has been called off. A great apathy is apparent on the Hill. After all that talk against government management, nobody gives a damn. I am beginning to wonder a little, in fact, just what they really do give a damn about—aside from Roosevelt, that is.

Concerning that gentleman, wild rumors circulate these days about deep dark Southern plots to do various things; the most fantastic, from a reliable source, being a wild dream about sending electors to the Electoral College who would confound the nation by switching their votes at the last moment, reversing the popular will (if Roosevelt were the popular will) and emerging with somebody else—surprise, surprise. Just how this could be done without revolution is not quite clear; unless, as somebody else suggested, the whole thing could be gotten into a tangle and tossed into the House where it could be managed with a fair show of legality and—perhaps—popular acceptance. All of which sounds like a marijuana jag but is an indication of the sort of gossip which is going around.

I dropped in on the farm-staters again today to get some more comments on the pork holiday and found a general undercurrent of feeling against the OPA. Reed, just leaving for Mrs. Bennett Champ Clark's funeral, paused long enough to tell me that "We expect the OPA to cooperate. If it will not cooperate, we shall insist." And John Thomas of Idaho said he "hoped OPA will see the light. If not, legislative action will follow." Ed Johnson said he wanted to try the experiment of selling pork without ration points and didn't think it would result in a wild scramble to get them taken off everything else. Millikin said frankly he thought it might, and indicated tacitly that he didn't give a damn if it did. Ed Robertson of Wyoming, O'Mahoney's quiet-spoken, Scotch-born colleague, said he didn't have much hope of a ration holiday but didn't see what good legislation would do, since the pork surplus won't be a surplus in another three weeks anyway. Apparently he is really concerned only with the immediate issue: others are digging a grave for OPA. Over on the House side charges of OPA incompetency were being aired today, and the whole atmosphere promises trouble for the unhappy agency.

I also saw O'Mahoney again, to see if he had anything to say on the matter after his stout opposition to it yesterday, and with his usual contrariness he said no, he didn't, and where did I get the idea he was against it? All he was doing was asking questions, trying to establish facts, trying to get at the basis for the thing. However, when he won't talk he won't, so I didn't pester him about it but accepted instead another blast at the insurance industry.

DECEMBER 30, 1943. Treaties and executive agreements occupied me today. Wallace White made a tentative suggestion the other day that it might be a good idea to study the whole subject and clear up the vagueness which surrounds it, and taking that as a lead, I dropped in to see him in the hope of getting something more definite. He was willing to talk, as always, and wound up by proposing that either Judiciary, Foreign Relations or a special committee named for the specific purpose be given the task of defining the two types of international arrangement. When he concluded, however, he aroused in me once more that rather exasperated wondering about the Senate's constructive men, because he said, "Of course it would be simply advisory, just a suggestion expressing the sense of the Senate. It isn't as though it would bind anybody to anything."

Why *not* bind anybody? Why "just a suggestion"? Why not something more than "merely advisory"? Why is the Hill so reluctant to exercise its responsibility? Why are its worthy men so hesitant?

I doubt if I shall ever really find out.

From there I went on to see the round-faced, pink-cheeked, husky-voiced Abe Murdock of Utah, who said he was all for an investigation and the passage of a Federal statute to settle the argument of treaty vs. executive agreement once and for all. We then got onto the anti-poll-tax bill, which he seemed to think will be brought up on the floor almost as soon as the new session starts. "I guess if they want to filibuster they won't be able to filibuster all session," he remarked with a grin. Carl Hatch, whom I saw next, was vague on that subject and refused to commit himself at all one way or the other. He regarded the proposed treaty study as "interesting but largely academic," and repeatedly remarked that he sees "no possibility of a conflict between the Executive and Congress on the peace treaties." No one else I have talked to has been quite so sanguine.

DECEMBER 31, 1943. Admiral King says we are going to launch a big offensive against Japan in '44 and Ed Johnson, Elbert Thomas and Owen Brewster were all willing to comment upon it. All three were pleased, the two Westerners particularly so.

Brewster of Maine is bald and friendly, intelligent and perceptive, with a quick, dry, rather ironic humor and a pleasant manner. He had some interesting things to say about MacArthur and the Presidency, and then got off onto the whole management of the South Pacific campaign. He made some good points, too, but like so much of the stuff one hears around here it was off the record and not for publication.

I heard today from a source one always associates with moral uprightness, purity and all things holy, that Huey Long was a great man "and will be honored." He was not dangerous, my informant said with the gentle faith in the everlasting quality of American goodness which so noticeably distinguishes him, because "America would never stand for a dictator, or for anyone exceeding his authority." The armed guards, the suppression of free comment, the raucous shame of the Louisiana legislature—all these were nothing in the mind of my philosophic friend. He knew Huey and Huey was a great man. It is the one quality in the Senator which occasionally makes one wonder a little about his practicality and essential responsibility. All is for the best in this best of all possible worlds, and the evil men do, counter to the poet, is apparently interred with their bones.

JANUARY 2, 1944. OPA has added another 5-point ration bonus for pork to its list of propitiatory gestures toward the farm bloc, but whether it will do any good remains to be seen. Another meeting will be held Tuesday, and the pattern of future legislative policy toward the agency may become a little clearer then.

JANUARY 3, 1944. I had my first interview with Vandenberg this morning, very jolly, very cordial, very unproductive. One "no" right after another, with the big cigar poised in mid-air and the curiously little-boy smile on the big round face. I seemed to sense a terrific ego, but may have been mistaken.

I went over to the Court this noon and spent an interesting couple of hours. Last week I thought I could detect a fairly definite alignment of Douglas, Black, Jackson and Rutledge, but today everybody was going off in all directions, with concurring opinions, dissenting opinions and philosophic dissertations coming thick and fast. Douglas announced several of the majority opinions, speaking in a reasonable, rather dry tone. Frankfurter made his usual positive, didactic and coruscating statements, chiefly in dissent. Murphy, speaking in a gentle, low, reproachful voice like someone with the mental pouts, also found himself in frequent disagreement. Jackson, forceful, friendly, humorous, reasonable and logical, makes as effective and appealing a presentation as anyone on the Court.

JANUARY 4, 1944. O'Mahoney has smoked out the Court on the insurance matter. It seems Hatton Sumners, House Judiciary chairman, asked to be allowed to appear on behalf of the Southern Underwriters Association in the pending case, and the Senator, not to be outdone or miss a trick, promptly wrote asking to be allowed to appear for 30 minutes on the other side. The Court then went into a huddle, evidently decided the Wyoming wildcat would be too hot to handle, refused his application and told Judge Sumners today that they were sorry but he would have to withdraw his. The chances seem good that they will decide against the Association anyway, but apparently they didn't want to turn the Court into a sounding board for a very shrewd in-fighter.

Bob La Follette, chubby-faced and earnest, was concerned today about the desperate food situation in Europe and gave me a good statement on it. He's an idealistic and admirable soul, trying to hold with honest integrity to a position that is virtually untenable: the middle.

I dropped in on Clyde Reed this afternoon and talked about OPA and the price of wheat for a while. Another meeting of the farm group will be held Thursday, and I expect to attend. "We'll educate you on this farm business," he told me as I left, and I am glad of the chance to learn. Nothing I cover on the Hill bores me, for most of it is new and most of it is broadening. I regard this job, more than anything else, as an opportunity to learn. All the interests of America sooner or later center on this group of men. I am glad of the chance to find out what they are.

Reed is cantankerous, opinionated and able, and he certainly does work hard for his constituents. OPA, WFA and the Department of Agriculture all hear from him, I should judge, about 15 times a day. In that sense—in the sense of working for his people tirelessly and doggedly—he comes easily within the classification of a good Senator.

JANUARY 5, 1944. I should set down for the record some details of the great Battle of the Minority, now raging with intense undercover fury on the Republican side. Not since fraternity days at Stanford have I seen any-

thing to match the devious Machiavellianism of this struggle for the leadership of 37 men.

Since I first heard about it the conflict has grown and expanded, with
divisions and factions and groups and blocs springing up on every side.
The key to it all, McNary, is apparently not going to return to the Senate
for a long, long time, if ever. The chances of his full recovery from a recent
operation for brain tumor are considered slight. He sent White a telegram
yesterday telling him to carry on as he sees fit, thereby throwing the whole
thing wide open. The issue now seems to lie between the Young Republicans and the Old Republicans, the latter being willing to accept White if
he decides to continue as acting minority leader, or support him with their
votes if he wants to throw the matter into caucus and run for permanent
leader.

The young group, sparked by Kenneth Wherry, has been actively considering three men: Bridges, Taft and Danaher. Vandenberg has been a
sort of uncertain dark horse, much as he is at national conventions, and
much as he apparently is by nature. Styles Bridges of New Hampshire is
in poor health and not too sure he wants the job. Taft has not definitely
refused it and neither has Danaher. Taft has recently slipped from favor
somewhat because of his proposals for compromise on the subsidy and
soldier-vote issues. "Compromising Nelly," the young bloods call him.
What they want, Wherry says with that pugnacious look, chewing furiously on his lip, is somebody who will get in there and fight, show a little
opposition, organize the Republicans into a really strong unit capable of
Action. The nature of the action is apparently not specified, just so it's
action. The older group, and such parliamentarians as Danaher, conceive
of the minority leadership as simply a sort of glorified legislative counsel.
There is some talk of making Wherry minority whip if Bridges takes over.

All of this leads to a lot of secret meetings in various people's offices,
with Senators sidling surreptitiously down the halls of the Office Building
and gliding into sequestered rooms to indulge their ambitions. Only secret
panels and daggers dripping blood are absent from this picture. Wherry's
point is obvious, all right. The Republicans should do something constructive in the Senate and not continually oppose for opposition's sake; and
the coalition with the Southerners gives them overwhelming strength if
they can get organized. This will all reach a head next week when everybody is back and the session has begun.

JANUARY 6, 1944. I walked along to work with White this morning, as I
occasionally do when we both happen to take the same streetcar in, and
he remarked rather wistfully that "the atmosphere we're goin' to be workin'
in from now on is the worst possible atmosphere in which to legislate. It's

an election year, and people say a great many things which are off the subject." His own plans, and those of the minority, have not progressed much since yesterday, although it developed later on that Vandenberg, with Taft as whip, has suddenly spurted into the lead in off-the-record calculations. Way back in the beginning somewhere somebody had the idea that Taft would be leader with Wherry as whip.

I am coming to the conclusion that there is considerable to be said for Ken Wherry. All the things that people dislike about him—his blustering, his impatience, his didactic manner, his personality which at first rubs people the wrong way—still hold; but underneath them there is a certain dogged determination to keep slugging away at what he believes in, which is in its way quite admirable. He doesn't give up, and while he is by no means the most tactful man in the Senate, there is a certain basic durability about him which is a good thing to have around. The quality is there, and if he espouses a cause he gives it everything he's got. There's a lot to be said for that, particularly where the rough-and-tumble is as rugged as it is up here.

The farm-state boys had it out with OPA again this afternoon, a long and occasionally impassioned set-to which culminated when Reed told the agency spokesmen bluntly that if they didn't take action by the middle of the next week on the pork situation he would "introduce a resolution to take it out of your hands." It was the first time I have seen a Congressional committee really go to work on a witness, and it's quite a bloody business. Bit by bit they get him down until finally, although he may still be self-possessed and still keep his temper, he is quite definitely obliterated. It is a hard thing to spot the moment when this process begins—when the subtle change comes over a hearing and a man who has been standing up to them is suddenly on the run. But it is a very definite psychological transition, and nobody in the room is in any doubt that it has occurred.

JANUARY 7, 1944. White gave an embarrassed but friendly exposition of his position in the minority fight this morning. He says it puts him in a terrific spot, and so it does, of course. He also said they would probably hold a meeting early next week and decide what's to be done. Apparently he isn't going to force the issue if they want him out. Later on in the day I was up on the fourth floor of the Office Building talking to Harlan Bushfield of South Dakota about OPA when Vandenberg phoned and asked him if he intended to "come down for the meeting." He said he'd be right down. Later we found out the meeting had consisted of Vandenberg, Bushfield and Wherry. Some sort of major compromise was apparently in the wind at that time. About 5 P.M. Bridges got back in town and promised to survey the situation. He said he was lukewarm about the leadership at first but wants it now if it will prevent certain more conservative elements from taking over. He may have made this decision too late, however. It looks increasingly probable that White will stay right where he is, simply because the minority split into two factions and then reached a deadlock, leaving him the only choice acceptable to both.

Bushfield, a tall, spare fellow with a long face and a mop of white hair, who strongly resembles Andrew Jackson, reduced the OPA fight to its basic terms for me this afternoon when he came out with the flat statement that rationing ought to be taken off everything. Wherry, with whom I had an amiable talk (or for whom, rather, I furnished an amiable audience while he emphasized his points with his usual candid vigor) didn't go quite that far, but apparently wouldn't be too sorry if it happened. Reed flailed out at "pig-headed bureaucratic theorists" with considerable indignation. And late in the afternoon, startling everybody, meek old John Thomas of Idaho suddenly issued a statement to the press in which he announced that he will introduce a resolution Monday "to remove meat rationing until thousands of tons of surplus pork, lamb and beef have been consumed."

This whole squabble is one more example of the tactlessness and stubbornness of the administrative agencies. They would lose nothing by tacking with the wind occasionally, and might gain immensely in prestige and influence on the Hill. But no, absolutely not. Somebody in Congress challenges a pet theory, and just because it is a pet theory—and just because it's somebody in Congress—*bango!* Their backs stiffen, their hackles rise, and they prepare to fight it out on this line if it takes all winter. They happen to be outnumbered in the campaigns this year will see conducted.

I also talked with George Aiken of Vermont, who is an awfully nice fellow, quiet and friendly and humorous, with a slow, crisp New England drawl and a dry New England twinkle. As one might expect from his manner and his fine, thoughtful head, his words were words of moderation and the things he had to suggest were constructive. It's too bad he doesn't carry more weight than he does on the floor, but he's such a maverick that his fellow Republicans usually regard him with more concern than approval. This bothers him extremely little, for he is a New Englander secure in his convictions as only a New Englander can be. He's George Aiken, and this is how he feels about things, and if the rest of the world doesn't like it, they can lump it. It is no wonder the more conservative are annoyed.

I have now had two of the Senators who may be considered leaders of the internationalist group tell me that they are convinced a postwar reaction is inevitable and that "this foreign policy fight isn't settled by any means." They don't talk that way for publication, they say, because they feel they have some responsibility toward keeping up public hope. But that is what they think.

JANUARY 8, 1944. The latest minority plan is now this: the Republican Conference, abandoned in 1935 when GOP representation in the Senate sank to 16, is to be revived with Vandenberg as chairman, Taft as whip, White to remain as acting minority leader and conference secretary. This is apparently a proposal to have your cake and eat it too, since it saves White's face, gives him some power, and still eases Taft and Vandenberg into influential spots. It is this proposed combine more than anything else that will probably kill it off unless it can be forced on the younger group by sheer weight of votes. They could stomach Taft alone or Vandenberg alone, they say, but by God they can't stomach both of them together. Consequently they plan to hold a meeting tomorrow and again on Wednesday to try to work out an alternate slate.

White is not entirely inactive himself these days. He turns up in the Office Building cafeteria eating lunch with various Republican Senators, and yesterday he stood outside the door having a long, earnest confab with Joe Ball. It looked like nothing so much as an earnest little terrier talking to a great big scowling St. Bernard. Ball did not seem overly impressed with White's logic, although the discussion remained on an amiable plane.

The OPA row continues to rumble. Thomas of Idaho has released the text of his resolution, which if passed will remove meat rationing until such time as the War Food Administration and the Price Administrator certify that the surpluses have been used up. Bushfield and Millikin are apparently the only ones who favor an outright end to everything. Both Ed Johnson and Clyde Reed told me with considerable sincerity that they regretted that the issue had reached a deadlock in which legislation is apparently the only way out. Both expressed disappointment at having to meddle in an administrative matter. I used to have the impression from statements in the press that Congress didn't want to yield its powers to the Executive. I am beginning to perceive that on the contrary the Constitution is very strictly interpreted in the Senate. They set the policy and then it's up to the Executive. Until, that is, the Executive begins to step on their constituents' toes, when a new interpretation is promptly handed down.

Which after all is what they're here for, and there's nothing wrong in that.

JANUARY 9, 1944. Tomorrow the session begins, and there is some talk that Roosevelt may put his State of the Union address off until next week because of a case of grippe. Everybody hopes not, for the effect would inevitably be to slow things up all around.

This week Thomas will introduce his OPA resolution, Lucas and Green will put in another soldier-vote bill, the tax bill will probably reach the floor, and the Gillette–Taft resolution on feeding the Europeans will probably also be considered. Also various incidentals, such as Presidential prospects and what one party thinks of the other.

JANUARY 10, 1944. It took the Senate about 35 minutes to reconvene formally this afternoon. Walter George of Georgia made a short statement asking unanimous consent to suspend the rules and take up the tax bill immediately, and later on, riding over in the subway, I heard him tell Bob Reynolds, more red-faced than ever from his Florida holiday, that he expects to get it out of the way in about two weeks of debate.

Apparently the OPA resolution, the Green–Lucas bill, and the new soldier-vote compromise that Austin and Lodge have suddenly concocted together, will all be introduced tomorrow. The President is going to send up his State of the Union speech and then go on the air tomorrow night. What this peculiar strategy means nobody on the Hill can quite figure out —unless, as one reporter put it, "Maybe he's afraid to come up here this year." How valid that is no one knows, but it is possible that he would rather skip the obvious hostility which the Republicans—and a good many Democrats—would evince were he to appear in person. Anyway, it spoils what promised to be a good show.

This afternoon we sounded out the Eastland–McKellar–McClellan crowd on the soldier-vote bill. James Eastland of Mississippi, a youthful, round-faced, slow-talking gentleman with a deep devotion to the Constitution and States Rights, was cagy and obdurate but did tell me they are planning a meeting to organize strategy later in the week. McKellar isn't back in town, so I wasn't able to get his particular version. McClellan of Arkansas, a dark good-looking gentleman with restless yet candid eyes, was reasonable in his approach to the problem and also frank in his off-the-record remarks. Portly John Overton of Louisiana said he felt the Senate was through with the matter, and in any case anything that attempted to remove the poll tax was absolutely unconstitutional and he would fight it. Rufus Holman of Oregon, whom I had never met before in my life, greeted me with a wild cry of, "Come in, Brother!" and carried on from there in a fashion that brought me closer to laughing in his face than I have come with anyone here.

Late in the day White announced that he is calling a formal conference of the Republicans for Thursday morning. The meetings planned for Sunday and tonight by the young group have been called off. Apparently they are giving up their fight for Bridges, and apparently also there is some division in their own ranks. There seems to be some criticism of Bridges because he didn't stay around to help them but went off to New York to indulge in his favorite pastime of criticizing the Soviet Union.

Thoughts of a United States Senator on the soldier vote:

"I'm as much for soldiers voting as the next man. Roosevelt says we're letting the soldiers down. Why, God damn him. The rest of us have boys who go into the Army and Navy as privates and ordinary seamen and dig latrines and swab decks and his scamps go in as lieutenant colonels and majors and lieutenants and spend their off time getting medals in Hollywood. Letting the soldiers down! Why, that son of a bitch. I took my oath to defend the Constitution of the United States and that's what I'm going to do, and any son of a bitch who proposes a soldier-vote bill has got to take that into account. Who's proposing this thing, anyway? Why, it's Mr. Lucas of Illinois, product of the Kelly–Nash machine of Chicago, that sinkhole of the nation; and Mr. Guffey of Pennsylvania, that noble soul whose election wouldn't have happened at all if it hadn't been for that God-damned Roosevelt and his WPA relief rolls; and Dear Alben. These three great statesmen, these three fine gentlemen, are asking us to set aside the Constitution 'because of an emergency.' And then we're 'letting the soldiers down' when we refuse, are we? Why, those bastards! Just a bunch of political thimble-riggers, that's what they are, them and that—that—that—*man in the White House!*"

Thoughts of another United States Senator on the 1944 election:

"If Roosevelt runs I'm going to vote for him, but of course I'm against a fourth term."

Merrily, merrily, merrily, life is but a dream.

JANUARY 11, 1944. White has suddenly called off the Republican meeting slated for Thursday and now says it will "probably" be held next Monday. Corridor gossip hasn't any very good explanation for this, although it would seem to many to indicate a progressive strengthening of the Old Guard and the ultimate collapse of the young bloods. Taft and Wherry got together for quite a while on the floor this afternoon. Taft, in fact, was chatting with a number of his critics on the Republican side, obviously a little embarrassed and ill at ease but managing to carry it off pretty well even with people like Bushfield, who were not overly warm.

Lucas and Green put in their version of a soldier-vote bill this afternoon, as did Lodge and Austin. Thomas of Idaho, shaking and nervous, finally got the floor to introduce his OPA resolution, after bobbing up and sinking back a dozen times as more agile members caught the Chair's eye.

The President's message was read by the Clerk soon after the session opened: a mild, reasonably constructive statement which advocated "national service" legislation that would, in effect, draft everyone, civilian as well as military. A cooing paean of praise from the Democratic side was only shattered by Ed Johnson who remarked bluntly that national service looked like national conscription to him and he was against it. Whatever the validity of his stand, at least it sounded sincere. No one else's did. Apparently no one else's was, either, for three hours later, in the first Administration test of the new session, the Senate voted 48 to 17 to freeze social security taxes for another year. So much for the deep, sincere, overwhelming love for Roosevelt evinced in the after-speech comment.

Austin promptly put in a revised version of his national service bill, a package of potentially totalitarian dynamite which seems rather incongruous when taken in conjunction with his deliberate, earnest, goodhearted intelligence and faint but likable pomposity. They say he knows what he is doing, and I know he is sincerely behind his bill, but it seems like a lot of explosive to leave lying around loose. In any case, however, it seems unlikely that it will ever pass.

I had occasion to talk to Tydings and Chavez today. Tydings made the same good impression close up that he does on the floor. His ideas are generally sound, his approach is intelligent. Chavez is a type most Californians are familiar with: very cordial, very polite, very cooperative—and completely elusive, uncommunicative and inscrutable. Uncommunicative in his case has nothing to do with the amount of talking he does, either. It is a condition more subtle than that.

JANUARY 12, 1944. I spent the morning in the Military Affairs Committee room today, covering a meeting on the Austin national service bill which started out to be executive and then was switched to an open meeting by Chairman Bob Reynolds. Lodge, Revercomb, Sheridan Downey of California, George Wilson of Iowa, Holman, and Elbert Thomas of Utah were there. Prior to the meeting a lot of amiable chitchat went back and forth between Reynolds, who is a pretty likable character of a certain fulsome Southern school, and Lodge. "What's new, Bob?" Lodge asked him. "Nothin' much, Henreh," he replied, " 'cept they's a lot uh pressuh bein' brawt to beah to make me run agin." Everybody laughed and he added with a chuckle, "Of coahse, Ah'm the wuhn who'se puttin' on most of it, myse'f. Guess the on'y thing Ah can do 'bout it is bow to pressuh and run." No one will be entirely surprised if this should turn out to be the case.

Holman asked Downey about Governor Earl Warren of California, and Downey gave a fair answer, praising Warren's "excellent record" in public life and the "excellent job" he is doing as governor. Of course, he said, he didn't want to give the Republicans advice, but they couldn't get a stronger ticket than Dewey and Warren. Gossip here emphasizes that as the probable choice when the last tally is in.

Austin was on hand to defend his bill, and did a weak job of it before a skeptical and critical committee. The Senator is a nice fellow, capable and sound and usually very conservative, which makes his espousal of this strange proposition one of the major mysteries of the Hill. Nobody can quite understand it, unless he is really as sincerely convinced as he says he is that the bill would be administered in good faith and not become an instrument of official fascism. His colleagues back away from it like startled horses, however, none of them being quite so naïve about the uses to which emergency powers can be put. Their opposition was fully evident this morning, and later on in the day when we polled them on it the vote was overwhelming against the measure. Only Downey and Elbert Thomas took refuge in the President's own doubletalk in which he made national service dependent upon four other measures. If they were passed, Downey and Thomas said, they would vote for national service, not otherwise. So much for the Military Affairs Committee, which Bob Reynolds says will not even report the bill out, let alone give it do-pass recommendation.

On the floor this afternoon the Senate whipped through all the committee amendments to the tax bill up to Title VII, renegotiation, which by mutual agreement was left for more extended debate tomorrow. Walter George did a smooth and able job of steering the bill, and Vandenberg made several brief statements which resembled his speech yesterday in that they were dull but excellent. He's a thoroughly capable Senator.

JANUARY 13, 1944. The liquor hearing resumed this morning, playing to a small gallery of casual tourists and bored reporters in the Caucus Room. A man from the California wine industry was the witness and received a pretty thorough going-over by Van Nuys, Ferguson and Murdock. Ferguson plows ahead like some great big shaggy bear with his questions, keeping one eye on the press table and exhibiting a very good nose for headlines. "Sen. Homer Ferguson (R., Mich.) charged today . . ." is a standard lead where he is concerned. He gets hold of something and worries it like a dog with a rag until he has extracted a sensation from it, whereupon he gives us an innocently pleased smile and settles back in his chair content. Fred Van Nuys has a low boiling point and is quite apt to grow indignant in a hurry when somebody displeases him, shaking and quivering, his face growing redder, his voice rising, rolling his head back and glaring through the bottom of his glasses. The husky-voiced, round-faced Murdock, looking pink, earnest and well-fed, has a habit of asking the witness innocently, "Now, wouldn't it be a fair conclusion to say——" and then going on into something which is by no means a fair conclusion and usually leaves the witness stunned, annoyed and/or flabbergasted. The Senator is a good man in an investigation—innocent, bland, astute and deadly.

The Republicans got together in the Senate restaurant for breakfast this morning, but so far haven't reported any great progress from it. A story is going the rounds concerning the *faux pas* of one of the younger group. It seems he went down to Vandenberg's office the other day to persuade him to get behind Taft for minority leader. "Senator," he began, "we're thinking about putting in a new minority leader. . . ." The great Van held up his hand, and across his huge round face came the beaming little-boy smile. "Why, thank you, Senator," he said in his heavy, hearty voice. "I'll be delighted to serve." Whereupon the other, so the story goes, beat a strategic retreat in some confusion.

JANUARY 14, 1944. Fourteen members of the Privileges and Elections Committee were on hand this morning to hear Lodge and Lucas defend their particular compromise versions of the soldier-vote bill. The gentleman whose name, always used in full, has even more of a resounding ring than Lodge's—Theodore Francis Green of Rhode Island—was in the chair, looking like a pleasant leftover from the Nineties with his walrus mustache, his sharp-boned face with its sharp shaft of nose, his scholarly eyes and kindly expression, his dignified schoolteacherly way of speaking, his long coat, and his busy, shuffling walk. Austin was there to help Lodge when the going got rough. The quiet, pleasant lawyer, George Wilson of Iowa; Chapman Revercomb, stocky of body, handsome of face, liquid of voice; Murdock; Moore; tall, bright-smiling Jim Mead of New York; Tom Connally; fair, decent Tunnell of Delaware were also there. The handsome Mr. Lucas, with his powerful face which so easily becomes sarcastic, his light voice, and his unhesitating willingness to scrap rational argument at the drop of a hat and get down to personalities, tarried long enough to argue with Lodge for a while and then departed. On the whole, the session was productive of a good deal of intelligent study. Apparently the initial burst of suspicion against the Administration has dissipated somewhat and Senators are now ready to work out some practical compromise. Murdock told Lodge sharply, and with what seemed honest indignation, that he was "shocked" that Lodge's bill does away with the Green–Lucas provision cancelling the poll tax for overseas servicemen. "I thought you agreed with me on that," said Abe in a reproachful voice. Lodge hastened to assure him at some length that he did, but that the difficulty apparently lay with Southern Senators who were afraid of states' rights being violated. Abe did not seem satisfied. Connally furnished several laughs, one of them coming when someone said something about "swallowing our oath to defend the Constitution to permi᠄ certain wartime necessities." "Swallerin' our oath!" Connally exclaimed. "Some of us have done so much swallerin' of our oath our throats are slick from it."

During debate in the afternoon Tydings introduced still another compromise proposal on the difficult issue. The good intentions are there, anyway.

The afternoon was largely dominated by Republicans, who did not put it to very good use. Bushfield made a long attack on subsidies—"a message of great bipartisan appeal," as we remarked in the Press Gallery when the entire Democratic side got up pointedly and walked out. Then Bridges took over and attacked official secrecy on the Cairo and Teheran conferences. A few Democrats drifted back; Connally challenged Bridges' obvious suspicion of the President. "Don't you believe the President's statement that there weren't any commitments?" he demanded. Bridges hedged and the decision, technically, went to Connally.

JANUARY 15, 1944. I had a pleasant visit in the State Department this morning with a friend of mine who has the typical downtown attitude toward the Hill. "Don't you find most of them pretty decent, reasonable, capable men when you talk to them?" he asked. I said I did. "Then how do you explain the fact that when they get together they act like such damned fools?" He strongly criticized their lack of initiative, their buckpassing to the Administration, their refusal to enact obvious legislation to meet situations as they arrive—making out, in short, a good case for that particular point of view, which is very characteristic in the bureaus and departments. Some things, I was forced to admit, are indefensible, but the better I get to know them the more I am coming to see that there are very sound reasons, some practical, some just human, for most of the things they do. The number of times when they "act like such damned fools" is considerably smaller than their country thinks.

Aiken wanders lonely as a cloud these days, no more a Republican than he is a Democrat—an Agrarian Republican if anything, but not even definitely that. He is one of the Senate's completely independent men, not having much in common with anybody. His opposition in Vermont seems to be dwindling, so he will probably come back all right. Fred Van Nuys at first wasn't going to run but has now decided to, and is apparently heading into a stiff fight. Hattie Caraway may also run into competition, enough to snow her under, if J. William Fulbright from the House decides to go after her seat. Charles Tobey of New Hampshire is under fire from the Willkieites, which may or may not affect him adversely. Scott Lucas says that he thinks he is licked already and so is going to do as he damn well pleases. For one with so much avowed independence he is nonetheless sticking close to the White House. Bob Reynolds has taken himself out of

the North Carolina race. Cotton Ed will probably run again in South Carolina, although 80. Barkley's opposition has not developed as yet, but with
Kentucky as much a variable as it is this year, it undoubtedly will. Taft
started on New Year's Day organizing Taft-for-Senator Clubs, and is going
ahead developing a campaign that will probably be blessed with success.

JANUARY 17, 1944. Clyde Reed put on one of his one-man shows in committee this morning, complete with all the elements one associates with
such a performance—the heavy-handed sarcasm, the violent indignation
against "you boys downtown," the portentous manner, the constantly reiterated "In my humble opinion—" ("Yes, I've often seen how humble you
are," Judge Marvin Jones, the principal witness, remarked drily), the constant references to "my long experience in this field." The issue this morning was the War Food Administration's order taking 200 boxcars out of
domestic traffic and diverting them to the Canadian run to bring in an
estimated 40,000,000 bushels of wheat by April 1. Jones, War Food Administrator, made a very good presentation of his reasons for the order
and was repeatedly interrupted by Reed. Time and again the Senator shut
him up with scant courtesy. The judge kept his head and his temper and
emerged the victor, at least in the eyes of the press. There was more talk
of "putting in a resolution to take the power away from you," and the
stuffy, crowded old Interstate Commerce Committee room resounded with
dark Senatorial threats of retribution which no one took very seriously,
not even those who made them.

This afternoon on the floor the Senate devoted some four and a half
hours to a debate on olèomargerine versus butter. All the dairy boys went
to town on this one, with Aiken and Wiley carrying the ball for the butter
league, and even Bob La Follette helping out. Maybank and Eastland put
on a brave fight for the other side, but it did them no good. Their amendment to the tax bill, which would have removed the 10-cent tax on colored
oleo, was defeated 55 to 23. The handsome Maybank, his sharp-featured
face uneasy and his distinctive Charleston accent at its most excited, got
suppressed as he usually does. He gives an impression of being honest,
rather naïve, and desperately in earnest about everything he says. A scion
of the Carolina aristocracy, there is no one in the Senate more courtly and
pleasant than he.

O'Daniel blandly got up and put in an amendment to have the Federal
government pay the poll taxes for all overseas servicemen, explaining
frankly that the Texas attorney general has ruled that Texans in service
must pay theirs by February 1. Tobey pounced on this immediately and
asked bluntly why the Texas legislature shouldn't pay them. Superior logic
and violent New Hampshire indignation delivered in Tobey's machine-

gun diction resulted in Pappy's defeat. But it was a grand idea, all right, and his manner in presenting it was full of dignified tolerance and sweet, innocent reason.

Langer delivered himself of a 57-page diatribe on Willkie, Hopkins, the 1940 Republican Convention, and the shortcomings of the current President, starting shortly after 4 and running to 6:20 P.M. During the last 45 minutes only game little White remained in the empty chamber to hear the fearful North Dakotan rave and roar.

JANUARY 18, 1944. The hearings on the shortage of boxcars in the grain belt wound up today. Reed and the able Wheeler were on hand to bring them to a close. After it was all over the Senators called us in for a press conference. The gist of it was another threatened resolution, which will be introduced if the order diverting 200 cars to Canada is not rescinded. Reed emphasized again how much the Senate hates to legislate on administrative detail. The hearing this morning was tiresome in several respects, not the least of them being the violence with which all concerned damned the Administration. There is such a thing as overdoing it, and it certainly occurred today. "I don't always like to be jumping on these bureaus downtown—" Wheeler began. "The hell you don't," Reed chuckled amiably. After a while, however, it became neither instructive nor funny.

OPA has apparently decided to trim its sails to suit the prevailing wind, and has come forth with an announcement releasing ration points to help ease the pork situation. This should take the props out from under all but the most rabid of its critics.

This afternoon, having settled the oleomargerine question yesterday, the Senate got around to labor. This is a touchy subject still on Capitol Hill, and it was done for the most part in doubletalk, with the notable exception of Josiah Bailey, who whatever his principles at least had the guts to speak them honestly. The issue that brought it up was a provision requiring charitable organizations to file—but not pay—income-tax returns. Bennett Champ Clark of Missouri opened the debate, his portly body and contentious, critic's voice being thrown wholeheartedly into the fray. He made a flamboyant plea for the poor harassed labor unions and farm cooperatives, which never before filed a tax return and now were going to have to, at God knows what cost in mental anguish to themselves. The mention of farm cooperatives immediately elicited support that Bennett Champ evidently didn't expect, but as soon as Aiken and La Follette got behind it he gracefully forgot labor unions and concentrated his ammunition on the farm angle. Brewster and Francis Maloney of Connecticut, who is also a contentious and able critic, kept close to labor. Walter George felt so deeply about it that he put on quite a forensic exhibition, the first

time I have heard him raise his voice since the tax bill came to the floor.
Even Chavez got aroused, arguing for the filing of returns. When it was
put to a vote, Clark's motion to strike the filing requirement failed 43 to
34. As far as practical value is concerned, as Taft pointed out scornfully,
no information will be given the Treasury which it can't already get under
existing law, and as La Follette also stated, in any case the returns are
confidential and nobody will ever hear about them anyway. There may
be a psychological value, however.

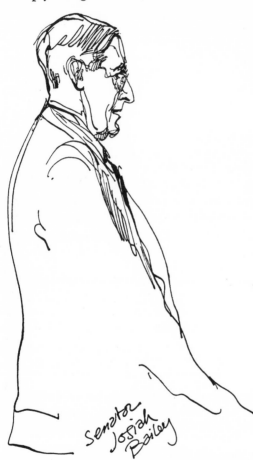

Senator
Josiah
Bailey

Josiah Bailey seems to
show no signs of the man-
ner in which some other
Southern spokesmen are
bowing low to the inevit-
able on the fourth term.
The President has had the
Southern governors up here
for the past couple of days
entertaining them royally.
In the papers this morning
it began to bear fruit.
Roosevelt, it seems, is the
only man for 1944, and the
South will go along. Gov-
ernor J. Melville Brough-
ton of North Carolina did
admit that there was "some
ferment" in his state, and
apparently the good Josiah
bespeaks it. He does it well.

It seems Scott Lucas and
Tom Connally were in the
Senator's barbershop the
other day. "Been home,
Scott?" Tom asked. "Yep,"
Lucas replied. "Everybody
mad out there?" Tom
asked. "They tell me there's
one man somewhere in the state who isn't," Lucas said, "but so far they
haven't been able to find him." When a nearby Republican laughed, Tom
demanded, "What you laughin' for? I guess you Republicans are goin' to
have quite a little difficulty naming your man for the Presidency. Now you
take us, our problem's already been decided for us."

And then there were the two Democratic Senators listening to the Clerk read the President's State of the Union speech last week. One of them turned to the other. "You know," he said, "if you or I made that speech people would say it was a damned demagogic address." "Well, hell," replied the other promptly, "that's just what it is."

JANUARY 19, 1944. There are few things, I am beginning to conclude, as monumental as the patience of a good United States Senator. Ferguson, Kilgore and Murdock were confronted with a representative of the OPA beverage branch during the liquor hearing today and managed, somehow, to keep their tempers and their patience. It was a notable triumph. The man squirmed and evaded and procrastinated and equivocated and qualified and and sidestepped and weaseled until it seemed that everyone would reach the breaking point and let him have it. You simply cannot get a straight answer out of some of these subordinate government witnesses—it almost seems that some fiendish personnel supervisor has deliberately picked them for their inability to be frank. They are all in deathly fear of their superiors, for one thing. Add to that a congenital inability to cooperate with the Hill (Clyde Reed has a certain point in his constant charges that the boys downtown just won't do anything the Hill wants them to) and you have a sad situation. It is rather pathetic, in a way, to see men so worried about what the men higher up will think. It provides a disturbing spotlight reaching down into the murky depths where the government politicians swim. There is one thing the Senate ought to investigate sometime—although of course it could never get any honest information on it—and that is the administrative fascism which makes the agency men so terrified that they will lose their jobs if they tell the truth.

As for the liquor hearing itself, it is turning into an endurance contest, a sort of glorified marathon in which all concerned are beginning to get groggy. The same evidence is being presented by successive witnesses, a general lack of purpose and plan is evident. Van Nuys' crusade against the industry is beginning to peter out. Even Ida B. Wise Smith of the Women's Christian Temperance Union has decided to pass it up.

Late in the morning I stopped in the Military Affairs Committee to hear Stimson and Under Secretary of War Robert P. Patterson testify in favor of the national service bill to create a civilian as well as military draft. Like everyone else they weakened their case immediately by urging the bill's passage and then promptly adding that of course it would be "just a psychological weapon and of no practical value" (in which case, why pass it?)—but the occasion was of interest because they were there. Stimson is an obviously old man, with a little mustache over a little mouth, pink cheeks, infinitely tired eyes, and a lifeless old man's voice, muffled and hard to hear. The impression he gives is of a man too old to carry the burdens of an exacting office. Patterson has close-cropped hair and a long face with deep, severe, monastic lines yet a somehow pleasant expression. He seems to be a very intelligent and efficient man; a trifle cold and impatient, perhaps, but able. Elbert Thomas, despite his earlier equivocations which seemed to indicate that he might support the bill, carried the ball against it. O'Mahoney was also critical.

JANUARY 20, 1944. Ida B. Wise Smith fooled us. Tiny, bright, perky, 72 years old and an expert in the expression of spontaneous emotion, she turned up before the liquor hearing this morning to furnish an hour's entertainment. The list of things Ida B. Wise Smith represents is rather long. Besides the WCTU it includes the American home, womanhood, motherhood, the armed forces, the future health of the nation, our future citizens, the sanctity of marriage, and the Forces of Good as contrasted with the Forces of Evil. Midway in a rather monotonous reading from various liquor-trade magazines she suddenly stopped and cried, "Oh! If you gentlemen could only know what the liquor industry is doing to our fine, brave boys in the armed forces! If you could only know—" Her voice trembled, the tears came into her eyes, she clutched wildly at the air for a handkerchief, which was swiftly placed in her hand by a secretary. For a moment, overcome, she stood choked and speechless before the startled committee. Finally with a valiant effort she recovered and went on.

At 12:15 this afternoon the President of Venezuela arrived on the floor amid polite applause from a standing Senate and galleries, was led to the rostrum by Barkley, Connally, White and Henrik Shipstead of Minnesota, and made a 10-minute speech in lightning Spanish. There was more applause and more standing and the President left. His speech, of which we were furnished the translation, was pious, platitudinous, and delivered in the same spirit in which all our Latin cousins address us. His skin was sufficiently white that Southern Senators remained in their seats while he spoke. They say in the Press Gallery that when Elie Lescot of Haiti addressed the Senate, they all got up pointedly and walked out.

Promptly after the Venezuelan had departed, Hugh Butler got the floor to make his own type of Good Neighborly gesture, giving a second report on Latin American expenditures which put the figure around $5,900,000,-000. McKellar sat a couple of desks away and listened intently, making a few challenges but not embarking upon any extended debate. So far there has been no indication that he will make another formal reply.

Following that, Barkley arose to tell his colleagues what a good job the New Deal has done for the past 11 years, and shortly after 3 o'clock the Senate recessed without having accomplished very much on the tax bill, although both the Banking and Currency Committee and the Privileges and Elections Committee laid the groundwork for the future by reporting the Bankhead farm-subsidy bill and the new Lucas–Green soldier-vote bill. In both cases the committees confessed frankly that they could not devise an acceptable substitute and so were deliberately throwing the issues onto the floor to be fought out there. The Bankhead bill would in effect do away with all subsidies save a very select few. Tydings, Lodge and Austin withdrew their soldier-vote bills in deference to Green and Lucas.

The Republicans settled their differences this morning, at least temporarily, by formally electing White as acting minority leader, and setting up a five-man committee to "study Republican needs in the Senate." White told the press that they were "getting ready to take over the Senate," and it may well be that he is not so far wrong. After all the hurrying and scurrying, the Battle of the Minority has petered out in a very minor engagement, and as many had expected, too much factionalism has resulted in the retention of the man who already held the job.

3

SOLDIER VOTE: Passage

JANUARY 21, 1944. On the floor today the Senate broke its usual pattern of meeting at 12 noon and met instead at 11 in order to get the tax bill finished. Even so it took them until 6:15 to do it and complete a process which Bob La Follette bluntly described as "laboring for months to bring forth a mouse." It was, in many respects, a La Follette afternoon. The senior Senator from Wisconsin successfully killed three amendments that would have given various corporations the right to duck out from under tax liabilities. He did it virtually single-handed, and with very little opposition from George—a rather significant thing considering the fact that George called down the wrath of God on Harry Truman when he tried to get acceptance of an amendment providing for court review of government war-contract renegotiation decisions. George is a powerful man: most amendments he didn't want were killed forthwith on his mere say-so. Apparently La Follette is one of the few men on the floor who can successfully overcome his influence. In the George-Truman set-to, Bennett Champ Clark jumped in and carried the ball against his colleague Truman with great gusto. It was quite a little Missouri family squabble, interspersed with the Biblical wrath of the Finance chairman himself, who combines a soft Georgia accent with a thunderous voice and an air of overpowering righteous indignation. The Administration beat him on the renegotiation issue, however, for he meekly offered a series of amendments that restored almost all the renegotiation features his committee amendments had previously taken out of the bill.

In the concluding 10 minutes of the session Lucas tried to get Barkley to promise that he would bring up the soldier-vote bill ahead of the subsidy measure on Monday, and Barkley sidestepped, refusing to give an answer. Later he told the press he was going to let the Senate decide it by resolution. Taft took exactly the same position that Overton did a couple of weeks ago and declared that the Senate had already acted and that it was "an extraordinary parliamentary procedure" to take time "from more pressing matters" for a bill "which has already been defeated once."

JANUARY 23, 1944. An aging man spoke on a newsreel screen I saw today and called the nation to worship a "new Bill of Rights," a "charter of economic freedom." Later on it was announced that the Democratic National Committee has addressed him once more as the all-high, the indispensable. Theodore Francis Green wrote the final concluding paragraph of eulogy in his own hand, the stories ran, and the only problem rose over the choice of a running mate. Henry Wallace, sitting aloof and other-worldly in his rooms in the Senate Office Building, or presiding amiably and not too adeptly in the chair, is apparently on his way out. Rather pathetically, he is trying to fight the tide, although it will probably not do him much good.

JANUARY 24, 1944. Today was an interesting day in a number of ways, and perhaps the most interesting of all was the way in which Taft handled the soldier-vote issue. It was the most partisan exhibition I have seen so far in the Senate, and on an issue which is sheer dynamite. This did not deter the gentleman from Ohio one little bit.

He was at his most vigorous, jumping up and challenging the opposition right and left, heckling Barkley, shouting at Lucas, using every possible parliamentary procedure to keep the soldier-vote bill from coming to the floor. It was an amazing performance. He even went so far as to shout that "Knox and Stimson are running for a fourth term!" The first test of strength came on his motion to bring up Bankhead's subsidy bill ahead of the Green–Lucas bill. The Republicans voted Yea right down the line; La Follette (the lone Progressive) left his seat on the minority side in some disgust after a vigorous "No!" and went to sit with the Democrats for the rest of the afternoon. Taft lost that one 33–38 and promptly notified Barkley he would move to bring the Bankhead bill up again at 2 P.M., a threat subsequently abandoned. He immediately thereafter engaged Lucas in a long, violent, partisan debate that went clear back to Colonel Knox's Bull Moose days at one point. His expression ranged from angry concern to open laughter and back again. It was a study in the Compleat Politician.

Concerning the bill itself, Green and Lucas came close to talking it to death themselves during the course of a long, long afternoon in which everyone, after the opening fireworks, grew more and more bored. Chances it will pass are about 60–40 against right now, but it may pick up strength during the week. The logical Mr. Danaher, who is quite as fast on his feet and quite as partisan as the next man when he wants to be, shot Green pretty full of holes when he brought forth a War Department release of

Robert Taft

Nov. 24, crowing about the way in which under present law they had been able to distribute ballots to Louisiana's soldiers in ample time for them to vote in the Jan. 18 primaries. Sometime between now and then the attitude of the department strangely changed. There is a lot of specious, suspicious stuff going on in the background of this bill, and although the Republicans and the Senate in general are going to receive endless criticism, they know what they are doing when they insist upon going over it with a fine-tooth comb. Too much is at stake on both sides for them to pass it through in two days, as Lucas maintained they could.

JANUARY 25, 1944. Nothing travels so fast over the Capitol grapevine as the news of death. When I stepped on the elevator to go up to the gallery this morning the elevator boy said, "You won't be doing anything in the Senate today. Van Nuys is dead." From then on until well into the morning each new arrival in the gallery announced, or had announced to him, the news of the kindly Indianan's passing, picked up from the elevator, or the dining room, or the Capitol police, or the post office. In an institution composed in the main of elderly men, death is a topic of vital interest and moves invisible but all-dominating through the halls.

The Senate met at 12, devoted itself to eulogies for 23 minutes and recessed. Most of the members were on the floor, sobered and saddened by the event. Everyone liked Fred Van Nuys; he was a kindly, decent, friendly old man, and the Senate side sincerely regretted his passing.

His successor, undoubtedly a Democrat, will serve out his term until January and then will yield to the Republican who will undoubtedly be elected. Indiana has moved far back toward Republicanism from the day it first sent Van Nuys to the Hill. In that way only his death was perhaps a blessing, for it saved him from the defeat his determination to run again had virtually guaranteed him.

JANUARY 26, 1944. The President, following the smoothly developing campaign by which he is moving gradually and imperceptibly from his position *vis-à-vis* the civilian population to a point where he can emerge as the Soldier's President, the protective Commander-in-Chief, took a hand in the soldier-vote fight today with a message to the Congress terming the Eastland–McClellan–McKellar bill a "fraud" on the soldiers and the people and urging the passage of the Green–Lucas substitute. More and more positively he is beginning to emphasize the soldiers' viewpoint, the soldiers' interest. All along the line this note is being sounded: Stimson and Patterson both expressed it in their testimony on the national service bill. The Presidential words which are so impotent when placed against the hard realism of Russia or the pragmatic politics of Britain still retain their old subtle strength at home, and by their use he is moving slowly but surely away from the civilians and toward the armed forces.

Following the reading of the message Taft at once arose and criticized it violently as an "insult." The subsequent debate went along without gloves on. The Republican case became a little better defined today, and certain of the more obvious jokers in the Green–Lucas bill were brought out. Unfortunately the Republican strategy, in essence a filibuster, is the sort that alienates the average citizen. And they are already smeared beyond redemption by the propaganda that in some way the soldiers have been "robbed" of their vote. They can still vote. They could vote if Congress never passed any legislation at all, if they cared to. It is entirely true, as Taft said, that Stimson and Knox have deliberately abandoned a hands-off position they maintained six months ago and are now deliberately using every possible influence to uphold the Federal ballot over the state ballot. The inferences Taft draws from this may or may not be true, but the fact is there, beyond denying. They are deliberately obstructing every proposal but the Green–Lucas bill, which would seem to indicate, in an issue where so much is at stake—the Presidency itself, in an election both sides feel may be very close—some interest over and above and beyond the mere mechanics of getting the ballots overseas.

Bridges, who is adept at give and take, did a little slugging with Scott Lucas and Barkley, provoking the galleries to laughter when he asked Barkley if he hadn't already been told who the Democratic nominee will be. "No, I have *not* been told!" Barkley shouted in an aggrieved tone that set everyone to laughing. Two minutes later he had crossed the aisle and was telling Bridges something that made them both laugh uproariously. In general the debate this afternoon was conducted on that plane—a lot of sound and fury, not meaning much or indicating any great personal animosity.

JANUARY 27, 1944. The ugly personal bitterness which cropped up last month when Lucas attacked Moore clouded the debate today. Abe Murdock, trying to make a reasonable speech but unable to resist the temptation to become partisan, told the Senate that "the American people want Franklin Delano Roosevelt for a fourth term!" Scattered applause broke from the galleries and Carl Hatch in the chair demanded order. Rufus Holman rose to remark: "If the Commander-in-Chief would remove himself as a candidate, this bill would pass in a day." This infuriated Hatch, who immediately turned the chair over to Hattie Caraway and came down on the floor to answer. Before he could do so Lucas had jumped up to make one of his characteristic personal attacks upon Holman, telling him his statements were "the most absurd, the most ridiculous, the most asinine

I have heard since I have been in the Senate. Shame on you!" he concluded. Holman, undaunted, shouted that he wanted to be quoted correctly if he was going to be quoted at all, and repeated what he had to say.
The galleries were inclined to be amused, but it was not amusing to the
white-faced men on the floor, and it was not amusing to anyone concerned
with the importance of Senatorial unity on the ultimate issues of peace and
war. To all who know the Senate day by day it was one more disturbing
indication of the ugly fissures which divide it on this issue.

There was no aisle-crossing and joke-passing today after the colloquies.
Most of the Senators concerned left the floor, and amicability was gone
from the atmosphere for the rest of the day.

Ten Senators left for Indiana tonight for the Van Nuys funeral, and
before they left Wherry got Barkley to promise that no amendments will
be voted on until Monday. More delay, and in the meantime the House
works feverishly to get its version of the Eastland soldier-vote bill passed.
Justice does not rest on either side of the aisle in this debate, but like so
many issues here, it is by no means so simple or so crystal-clear as out-
siders assume.

JANUARY 28, 1944. The Army and Navy released the story of the aftermath
of the Bataan surrender today, and overlooking the cruelly cynical fashion
in which the news was withheld for three years until it could be made to
coincide with a bond campaign, the Senate fell obediently into line.
Speech after speech, from Barkley's cry that he was "growing impatient
for the day of retribution," on through White's demand that it be visited
"not alone upon the Japanese army but upon the Japanese authorities and
the Japanese people," to Hill's somber plea that the Allies "bomb and
burn and gut with fire," the statements followed the same familiar pattern.

McKellar has chosen this moment, with impeccable shrewdness, to
bring up for the administration a $30,000,000 measure to provide funds for
the importation of migratory labor. The present grant expires on Monday,
and the soldier-vote begins again on Monday. No better time could possibly have been selected. The bill went through without opposition, and
La Follette for one paid tacit tribute to McKellar's political skill when he
remarked regretfully that he would have liked to spend more time discussing certain provisions but knew it was out of the question now. Old
Mack brought a lot of know-how out of the hills of Tennessee.

JANUARY 31, 1944. Dennis Chavez arose today to say the definitive word
on the timing of the Bataan release. Everything the country feels about it
he said, ably, bitterly, and with the righteous anger of a man whose state

contributed its entire National Guard to the ill-fated campaign. "Inopportune and inhuman," he called the timing of the release, and without saying so in quite so many words, he said it was done to sell bonds. The Senator of Mexican extraction who is always careful to use the words "so-called" before the words "Mexican people in my state," doesn't speak unless he has something to say, and when he speaks it is usually worth listening to. He has a way of going directly to the heart of a thing and stripping it down to essentials with the outwardly passionate yet at the same time curiously dispassionate candor of his race.

The silvery Gillette also spoke, criticizing the President's soldier-vote message on the ground that it was an unwarranted and unconstitutional attempt to interfere with the legislative branch; a reasonable, rather apologetic, sensible and sound address from a man who has repeatedly announced his own retirement. There are some here the country could do without, but it will be rather too bad if he has to bid the Senate farewell. He's a good public servant.

Vandenberg broke the ranks of the Republicans by coming out for the Federal ballot in a reasoned and cogent statement. Taft, Danaher and Ball have now put in extensive amendments, which should be good for at least another week's debate. Meanwhile the House is expected to vote Wednesday on its version of the Eastland bill, so that the move to block the Green–Lucas bill may succeed after all.

Representative Fulbright of Arkansas announced today that he will run for the Senate against Hattie Caraway. Arkansas needs positive, forceful leadership in these days of crisis, he said, thereby hitting Hattie where it hurts the most. It may well be—in fact the press and the Hill in general are sure it will be—that the days of the quiet little grandmother with the bright red fingernails who wanders in, reads a newspaper or sits solemnly in the presiding chair, and then wanders out again, having won nothing, lost nothing, and done nothing, are numbered.

FEBRUARY 1, 1944. Barkley made the astonishing statement today that the War and Navy departments shouldn't obey a law passed by Congress "because the Secretary of War and the Secretary of the Navy didn't tell them to." No utterance I have heard so far on the Hill matches that one in sheer voluntary abject abdication of the authority of Congress.

It can be said for Alben, of course, that he only made the statement in the heat of debate, and in fact was virtually tricked into it by Brewster, but even so it exhibited a startling frame of mind. Brewster jumped on it at once and made the most of it. Barkley retreated after a moment, although without retracting what he had said. It was one of the more surprising highlights of an afternoon that furnished a lot of them.

On the whole it was a Republican day, with Brewster, Bridges, Curley

Brooks of Illinois and Taft carrying the ball. Brewster made a good speech opposing the Green–Lucas bill and proved himself conclusively to be one of the fastest men on his feet in give-and-take debate when Green, Lucas and Barkley arose like some predatory trinity to go after him. The gentleman from Maine knocked them down, rhetorically, tied them securely, and tossed them out the window. Then, surveying the field with a smile which was more strained than he perhaps would have liked, he retired to rest on his laurels and let the others take over. Bridges made a reasonably good speech in connection with his amendment to have the names of the candidates printed on the Federal ballot. Brooks made an excellent speech —one of the very best I have heard so far. He has a light, earnest, reasonable voice which he uses with consummate skill and an actor's instinct for change of pace. In one more Republican attempt to puncture the myths across the aisle, he pointed out that some 2,000,000 boys under age will not be given the vote at all, so that the noisy breast-beating about giving *all* the soldiers the right to vote is so much political poppycock. He also stressed, as did Revercomb the other day, that he spoke as a former enlisted man when he warned that any voting conducted in the field was not apt, perhaps, to be entirely open and above-board. The Taft and Brewster charges that the men will be "herded up to the polls and voted by order" are a trifle flamboyant, but the subtle pressures of the chain of command exist nonetheless. Brewster said he didn't want a situation "in which regimental commanders will be put under pressure because only 10 per cent or 15 per cent of their troops voted." And Brooks reminded his colleagues on the Military Affairs Committee that they "know what promotions mean, where they come from, and how much they are desired." There may not be too much foundation in the charges that it will be done that way, but it certainly could be. It could be handled like war bonds or insurance: voluntarily—by request.

Midway in the afternoon the House overwhelmingly defeated a motion to require a roll-call vote on the Eastland soldier-vote substitute, and that was the tip-off that there are sufficient votes to pass it without a record tally over there. A decision is expected tomorrow, and after that anything can happen. The chances seem good that the Senate—or the Republicans and Southern Democrats in the Senate, rather—will recommit the Green–Lucas bill and the bitter debate will thereupon be over. It is a confused, a chaotic, and a rather tragic issue all the way around, and the only single certain thing about it—the thing which of course has made it tragic—is that the attitude of the Administration has been the farthest thing from objective, nonpartisan, statesmanly and fair.

FEBRUARY 2, 1944. There is a sentence which has engraved itself in the past 10 days upon the mind of everyone who has followed the soldier-vote debate. It is always delivered in the same earnest, ringing tone, with the same impassioned fervor and the same perfectly sincere emphasis. "Every man in this chamber wants the soldier to vote," it runs. "You want it, I want it, we all want it." If it has been said once since the debate began it has been said a thousand times, and each time it has been true.

Today in a brief burst of activity the Senate got the Overton amendments out of the way. In effect, they would have placed in the law one more guarantee—in addition to Section 14 of the bill, which as it now stands does everything the most reactionary could want—that the poll tax would be kept inviolate. One went down by voice vote and the other two on roll call; the vote was approximately 66–23.

Immediately thereafter the pace slowed down, and the eagerness with which the Senators had gathered for the opening of the session—Gillette, Shipstead, Bridges, Alexander Wiley of Wisconsin, Aiken and Elmer Thomas of Oklahoma put on a real sprint for the elevators in order to reach the floor in time to "stand up and be counted," as Aiken drily remarked, echoing the President's message—soon dissipated in a welter of endless talk. Danaher had the floor longer than anyone else today, with an amendment that would give the Federal ballot to soldiers overseas whose states had not taken action to give them the state ballot by June 1. Joe Ball, who nominated Harold Stassen for President last night in a radio talk, got up to remark angrily that "the Senate is being held up against the ax of time" on both the soldier-vote and the subsidy issue. Later Guffey took it upon himself to condemn Hugh Butler and *The Reader's Digest* for Butler's article on aid to Latin America, and later still Wherry put on an exhibition of uncontrolled partisanship—so uncontrolled, in fact, that he ignored the Chair and poured out a torrent of exclamatory talk at the top of his lungs. Noble Nebraska, Noble Hugh Butler and the Horrible Administration seemed to form the main burden of his remarks. He was completely sincere about it—so much so that he just had to talk himself out and unwind in his own way; nobody could shut him up until he was exhausted. Bob Reynolds followed immediately afterwards and was equally violent, although perhaps not quite so sincere. "The American people will be so sick and tired of international interventionists after this war," he shouted angrily, "that they will turn so quickly and so soon to nationalism that America will not recognize itself."

I talked to Happy Chandler today and found him to be an overwhelmingly friendly, impulsive soul. He says what he thinks with an excitable good humor, and from time to time takes a few nasty sideswipes at the British, all in a spirit of innocent, boyish fun.

Five Republicans and some 11 Democrats have drawn up a new soldier-vote compromise which will be put in tomorrow. There has been a terrific

Rush from the elevator

OUTSIDE ELEVATORS 3rd FLOOR MALL

amount of industrious politicking today. I was down on the floor for a
while, interviewing Chandler in the old President's Room where the Chief
Executive used to come to sign bills on the last day of a session, and the
number of Senators who hurried in and out and went into hasty conferences with each other was impressive. Taft carries a printed roll call with
him on such occasions and goes around buttonholing and checking names
with scientific ardor, leaving behind a wake of interested Republicans and
compliant Democrats. Meanwhile debate drones on in the chamber while
the real work gets done outside.

FEBRUARY 3, 1944. Taft remarked angrily today that "groups of people sent
down here by the C.I.O. Political Action Committee have been hanging
on my arm all day long telling me they want the soldiers to vote." And
Joe Ball added that they had been after him too, with the statement that
"unless the Green–Lucas bill is passed the soldiers will be denied the
right to vote." "Have you read the Green–Lucas bill?" Joe asked them.
Of course they hadn't.

Just for the record, the Green–Lucas bill:

1. Gives the states exclusive control of validation of ballots, which
means that poll-tax states will throw out the ballots of soldiers who have
not paid the poll tax, and other states which have other provisions will
judge their soldier ballots in the same fashion.

2. Provides for only four offices on the so-called "uniform Federal
ballot," President, Vice-President, Senator and Congressman.

3. Does not provide for the names of candidates to be printed on the
ballot, but simply says "write in your choice, or the party"—an obvious
invitation for the soldier, either wilfully or through ignorance, either to
write in a straight party label all the way down the line or write in the
names of candidates who aren't even running, the latter resulting only
in invalidation.

4. Deliberately attempts to make the Federal ballot dominant by giving
it priority over all other mail and specifically over state absentee ballots.

5. Deliberately attempts to make the Presidential office dominant over
the Congressional by refusing to name the candidates, urging use of the
party label, and thereby encouraging the tendency to make the choice
for lower offices dependent upon the choice for President.

In effect, these provisions:

1. Make it virtually certain that thousands of ballots will be thrown
out by the states if they do as the Green–Lucas bill wants them to do and
rely exclusively upon the Federal ballot without revising their own
statutes.

2. Remove the soldier vote entirely from local state elections.

3. Make it virtually certain that the choice of President will dominate the choices for all other offices on the short Federal ballot.

4. Make it virtually certain that the few state absentee ballots which the soldiers apply for will in all probability never reach them.

5. Make it virtually certain that a specific hour will be set for voting, that the men will be marched up to the polls—not because of any sinister design on the part of commanding officers, but simply because marching men in a body is the simplest way to handle them to get a specific job done—and that thousands who would never have voted at all will vote under orders, and consequently will either throw their ballots away by frivolously writing in the first thing that pops into their heads or will simply endorse with blind partisanship whichever party happens to appeal to them most at the moment.

All these things the opponents of the Green–Lucas bill are afraid of. Take them in conjunction with the Administration's grim insistence upon the bill as it now stands, plus the deliberate obstructionism of the Army and Navy, plus the propaganda with which the Administration and its partisans have been flooding the press in the past two weeks, and an excellent case can be made out for the policy of going slowly and with extreme care in the passage of a soldier-vote bill. The proponents of the Green–Lucas bill had hold of a good thing and they almost got away with it. Whatever else the Republicans have done, they at least have managed to block that.

Apparently the Administration is beginning to concede as much, because today, for the first time, Lucas accepted an amendment that makes some change in the essential structure of the bill. Danaher's proposal to restrict the Federal ballot to men overseas and to men in the country whose states have not given them the absentee ballot by August 1 passed 72–19. Taft immediately put in his substitute whose basic provision is that ballots will be sent only to those soldiers who apply for them. Barkley agreed to make it the first order of business tomorrow. It is impossible to predict on the basis of today's vote whether or not it will carry, because the motives of most of those who upheld what Green referred to jocosely as "the Connecticut Compromise" were not entirely clear. The whole tempo of the debate is beginning to speed up, at any rate, and that's something.

FEBRUARY 4, 1944. Lodge has resigned to return to the Army, for reasons which were candidly assessed on the Hill. No criticism was voiced of an action which many others would have been glad to take if they could.

Somehow, however, there was something more than a little noteworthy about the way it was done. Apparently the decision was reached without

DAVID WALSH

Henry Cabot Lodge Jr.

prior consultation with anyone, save possibly his colleague Dave Walsh. The old man made some reference to Lodge's indecision and doubt when he bade him a formal farewell from the floor. Secondly, the resignation was not submitted to Governor Saltonstall but was sent to Clark of Idaho as acting president pro tempore of the Senate. Thirdly, the Senator himself did not appear all day, nor was he available in his office; the resignation came in the form of a letter which was submitted to the Clerk and read by him a few minutes after the session began. In some subtle fashion the whole business seemed to suggest a rather unhappy, lonely, suspicious young man, not very content in his own mind and not very much at ease with his colleagues, finally forced to a decision after months of worry and not wanting to stay around and accept congratulations he was not sure he would receive. Henry Cabot Lodge is a brilliant, sardonic, reserved man, and it is probable that he can only be understood if one takes into account the self-conscious knowledge that people expect him to act superior—which tends to make him do so by way of self-defense —plus the shadow under which he feels himself to walk because of his grandfather's reputation. The influence of the legend of the first Lodge upon the career of the second will someday, perhaps, make an interesting psychological study. It may explain much in the life of a man who feels that, whatever else he must do, he must vindicate his grandfather. As Vandenberg remarked today, Lodge will probably come back to Washington. In this resignation, presented bluntly and unheralded to the Senate of the United States, there may possibly be discernible the future pattern of a man who, whatever heights he may rise to and whatever power he may achieve, will always walk alone, uneasy and essentially unbefriended.

The soldier-vote debate moved into its final stages today, with a number of very close votes. Taft's amendment was defeated 45–42, much to his chagrin. He had been quite certain it would pass, but some of his promised votes didn't pan out. Green himself even bowed to the inevitable and offered an amendment that would specifically ban any officer or non-com from suggesting in any manner whatsoever that a man vote for a specific candidate, or that he even vote at all. When Ed Johnson, whose separate amendments this one incorporated, asked Green if the War Department approved those safeguards, Green said that he would "not go so far as to say it approved, but I can say it did not disapprove." Which again casts doubt upon the integrity of the department in this matter. The amendment carried on a voice vote.

The debate today was very much under the shadow of the House action last night, in which the Rankin states'-rights soldier-vote bill was passed overwhelmingly at 10:55 P.M. Overton finally moved that the Senate take up the House bill, and on a vote of 42–42 the motion failed and the Green–Lucas bill remained the order of business. What will happen after the Senate passes it—if it does—remains to be seen. Today was a dramatic day, and for once the galleries got their money's worth, as roll-call vote after roll-call vote showed how close the division is on this embittered issue.

FEBRUARY 5, 1944. The Senate had hoped to complete work on the bill today, but Barkley fooled it by suddenly moving adjournment on the first quorum call of the day, some 20 minutes after the session began. Forty-four Senators had answered to their names and others were still arriving. To the Majority Leader's practiced eye, however, it became apparent that the antis far outnumbered the pros and consequently fast work was indicated if the Green–Lucas bill was to be saved at all. Accordingly he jumped up and on the pretext of no-quorum moved recess until Monday. It being Saturday and enthusiasm for a session not too high on either side, nobody tried to make an issue of it and the whole business went over. It was a close call for the Administration.

FEBRUARY 6, 1944. The War Department announced today with that bland innocence which seems to indicate a hope that everybody will keep right on talking and not notice, that it has begun making information available to the troops for the April primaries in Illinois, Nebraska and Pennsylvania and the general election in Louisiana. In line with Public Law 712 and the 1942 voting statute, post-card applications for absentee voters' ballots are being distributed to the men and they are being given every assistance if they wish to exercise their franchise. Even the men overseas are being encouraged, although the department does say reasonably that in some theaters the men should take the time element into account. They are not being discouraged if they wish to apply, however, and everything is being done to help them.

And then the department and the Administration, through Green and Lucas, try to tell the Senate that it is impossible for the soldiers to vote under the present law, and impossible for the Army to get state ballots to them—and in the face of all the facts it expects the Senate to believe it. Today, as in the November release on the Louisiana primaries, the true situation emerges. The Green–Lucas bill will not profit from this sudden, contradictory, and quite embarrassing candor.

FEBRUARY 7, 1944. Again the day was lively, with a series of votes that finally indicated a definite trend after days of jockeying. Overton again made his motion to take up the House bill and was beaten on it 44–42. An hour and a half later he made it again, and as one Green–Lucas man after another switched over, a happy smile of triumph spread across his round and amiable face. The vote was 50–38 in his favor when the final tally was concluded, and the Green–Lucas bill was laid aside for the time being. Barkley tried to get blanket rejection of the House amendments to the original Senate (Eastland–McKellar–McClellan) bill, but McKellar rose at his desk beside him and, fiddling with his watch chain and his Phi Beta Kappa key, proceeded to call down the wrath of God on his head. Barkley bowed to the inevitable and agreed to take them up one by one. The first two were accepted by voice vote. On the third amendment Barkley proposed concurrence with an amendment—the amendment being the Green–Lucas bill. Taft immediately jumped up to propose an amendment to Barkley's amendment—the amendment being his own original amendment defeated Friday. Things were then in an uproar as the Senate spent almost an hour trying to get the parliamentary situation clear in everybody's mind.

"Mr. President!" one Senator after another would say. "Parliamentary inquiry!" "The Senator will state it," Pepper, who had the chair, would say automatically. The query would be stated, and after some hurried whispered consultations with the official parliamentarian at his elbow,

Pepper would give the ruling. This went on for some time as the Senate went into every possible question of precedence of motions, the situation if Barkley's amendment should pass, the situation if the House amendments should be agreed to, the situation that would occur if a motion should be made to lay Barkley's amendment on the table and take it up tomorrow (the Green–Lucas bill would again be the order of business, and McClellan, who had the idea, withdrew the motion hastily), and the situation which would eventuate in any case when the matter went to conference. Finally McClellan asked unanimous consent to carry Barkley's amendment over until tomorrow as pending business—which did away with the possibility of its being displaced by the Green–Lucas bill—it was agreed to without objection, and the soldier-vote debate ground to a halt for another day. The House then reported back both the tax bill and McKellar's bill to import foreign labor, both went through on unanimous voice vote, and the Senate adjourned. Parliamentary law is a tricky and fascinating business in the hands of men who know every angle of it and use it to the utmost as a political weapon, and today was an interesting and entertaining example of it.

After the session when we went down on the floor to talk to Barkley, he opened up new vistas of conjecture by describing all the things the House could do to the bill when it gets back to it. The least is amend it some more and the most is kill it altogether. He said it has been a long time since a parliamentary tangle as complex as this developed between the two houses. He left us laughing with a good story and we went off the floor convinced all over again that he is a prince of a fellow. He has no trouble implanting this impression in the minds of newspapermen as they come to know him, because he is a prince of a fellow.

FEBRUARY 8, 1944. Shortly after 3 o'clock this afternoon the Senate completed the soldier-vote bill and all concerned were much relieved. In a series of votes the trend away from the Administration apparent in the vote on taking up the House amendments yesterday was reversed and sufficient strength was found to carry the day. Taft used every possible parliamentary maneuver. An amendment by Ferguson was accepted first, and then Taft's amendment was proposed; Ferguson objected, and Taft promptly moved to modify his amendment to include the language of Ferguson's amendment. Pepper, again in the chair, ruled that Taft had already proposed his amendment and modification could not be made. The amendment was accordingly defeated 41–45—the same four-vote margin which has turned up in all the close contests on this bill. A Barkley amendment was accepted, placing the language of the Green–Lucas bill in the body of the House bill. The remaining House amendments were considered, some being accepted and some being rejected deliberately to throw them into conference. On the last House amendment, which covered two sections of the original Senate bill, Taft asked innocently for a division of the amendment; Pepper granted it. The first section was accepted. The Clerk began to read the second section and Taft immediately jumped up to propose his entire amendment all over again as an amendment to the second section. More wrangling ensued, Lucas delivered himself of another masterful piece of flag-waving, eagle-screaming denunciation; the chamber waited in bored silence. Finally Brewster arose. "It seems to me, Mr. President," he said acidly, "that the question is not whether the soldiers will vote but whether the Senate will vote. Does the Senator want the Senate to vote?" "Of course I do," Lucas cried. "Of course I do. That's all I want." "You've been trying for three weeks and haven't convinced us of that yet," Brewster told him drily and sat down; a true observation, for Lucas strangely enough has done almost more to delay his own bill than anybody else. "Vote! Vote!" came from what the *Congressional Record* refers to as SEVERAL SENATORS. Once again the roll call came on the Taft amendment, now in its third trial before the Senate. Once again the same 45–41 vote knocked it down. Ferguson, Vandenberg, Wiley, Burton and Aiken consistently backed the Administration throughout; in those five Republicans Taft could number the men who beat his amendment. The House amendments were then considered, disposed of, and the Senate again took up, for the record, the Green–Lucas bill as perfected. On a vote of 48–37 it was passed and sent to the House. The parliamentary situation now stands:

The House bill has returned to the House with a Senate amendment inserting the language of the Green–Lucas bill. The House can now either accept it, reject it, or ask for a conference. In the meantime, the Green–Lucas bill in its original form has also gone to the House, where it will be referred to the Privileges and Elections Committee, which can either report it out or let it die in committee. Rankin and Martin over in the House have promised death to the House bill as amended with the Green–Lucas language, and the chances are good that if the Green–Lucas bill itself ever reaches the floor it will also be killed. The most the Administration can hope for now is a conference on the House bill.

So ends the great soldier-vote fight—at least, so ends, temporarily, the great soldier-vote fight. Underlying all the heat and the propaganda is one basic fact. Had the Administration been willing to accept amendments to the Green–Lucas bill at the very first it could have got substantially what it wanted, slashed debate to a week or less, provided a workable measure by which soldiers could vote, and done a generally creditable job. But somebody wanted to do it differently.

4

SOLDIER VOTE: Conference

FEBRUARY 9, 1944. The national service law is still being worried around in committee. Austin insists on prolonging the agony, and apparently Bob Reynolds doesn't want to cause any gratuitous bad feelings by refusing him. So the hearings drag on and on, bringing to the Hill one big name after another to deliver their insincere eulogies of a bill that lies dead at this moment on the committee table.

Today's performer was Ambassador Joseph P. Grew, a tall, dignified man with an intelligent face, gray hair and a clipped gray mustache, candid, perceptive eyes and a general air of sincerity. The sincerity is apparently genuine, for he stuck to what he knew best—the nature of the Japanese—and avoided, except in the most general terms, the national service law. Austin tried to draw him out into the flamboyant exaggerations that characterized the Stimson testimony, but he was not to be drawn. Very polite, very courteous, very gentlemanly, agreeable but reserved: he said he was for the bill and let it go at that. No dire predictions, no maledictions and ominous threats, just a discussion of the Japs and how tough they are and what it will take to beat them. The only thing he had in common with those who have come up here before was the candid and baffling statement, "Of course we shall win the war whether this bill becomes law or not." All this endless testimony we are hearing about why this bill is so all-fired imperative, and after it is all over, all that remains is the echo of a dozen different voices saying calmly, "Of course we shall win the war whether this bill becomes law or not."

The mind of Warren R. Austin continues to baffle the press utterly. "Would this not be the most noble kind of democratic action?" he queried Grew about the most openly fascistic measure ever broached to the Congress. "Would it not be a great, dynamic expression of the people's faith?" The amazing thing is that he means it. He is completely sincere. Whenever his colleagues back him into a corner he refers to "that higher law which is above the Constitution, that great, glorious expression of

73

the unity of a free people united in the prosecution of the war." All of
which is so much noble nonsense when brought right down to the specific
terms of a bill which would give the national government authority to
pick a man up out of one job, set him down in another, uproot his home,
break his union ties, force him, apparently at the point of a gun, to labor,
and in effect place the country squarely in the hands of a military
oligarchy. "There is no compulsion," Austin cries. "There is no military
law, there is no regimentation. No one will be forced to obey. It will be
a great, voluntary cooperation. No one will be under military duress."
Judge Patterson, who spoke acridly about "being able to get labor when
we want it and get things done without all this red tape and having to
ask people for their cooperation," had the grace to blush slightly when
Austin said that. The men who run the War Department are nowhere
near so innocent or so naïve as the Senator from Vermont. There are no
illusions there about "great, voluntary cooperation."

Bob Reynolds put in a few licks for the isolationist cause, asking Grew
a series of loaded questions about the military situation before Pearl
Harbor, the relative importance of Germany and Japan, and the wisdom
of concentrating everything in the Pacific now that Germany is (he says,
although the reports do not bear him out) on the run. Grew saw him
coming every time and with neat grace stepped suavely aside. The question on our preparations before Pearl Harbor was typical. "You say that
if we had been better prepared before Pearl Harbor we would probably
not have had to fight a war in the Pacific?" Bob asked. "Yes, that is true,"
Grew replied. "Now, who, in your opinion, was responsible for our not
being prepared?" Bob wanted to know. "I am really not qualified to
comment on that," replied Grew gently. "I was in Japan at the time."
When he left Bob thanked him, with the little lines of sardonic humor
around his prominent and encircled eyes which come and go when he
has met his match. Grew responded gravely. They understood one another
perfectly.

On the floor today Bankhead brought up his bill which will in effect
kill the emergency farm-subsidy program with only a few exceptions for
a handful of agricultural items. Debate was desultory until Maloney of
Connecticut, a small, solid gentleman with a sharp face and the general
appearance of a prosperous little businessman, offered an amendment
to give the Commodity Credit Corporation $1,500,000,000 for the subsidy
program. He put up a good defense of it, for he is forthright and very
able, and along toward 5 it became apparent that it might reach a vote
—something nobody had dared hope for so early in the debate. Walter
George then arose and with his magnificent voice, which rolls down into
the depths below the sea and then rises into majestic crescendo while

the lightning streaks and the thunder blares, proceeded to call down the wrath of God on the whole subsidy program. It was an impressive speech —the Senator is a generally impressive man—and when it was over the vote snowed Maloney under 49–26; a tribute, so he told us later, to the histrionic ability and Biblical fervor of the senior Senator from Georgia. He had a tally sheet in his pocket which showed him with enough votes to carry the amendment, Maloney said, but the boys turned tail when it came time to vote and left him in the lurch. The indefatigable Taft has an amendment he will offer tomorrow, which reduces the subsidy program to $950,000,000 but still preserves much more of it than the Bankhead bill. He said privately tonight that he hasn't got enough votes to carry it, either.

"Is this an Administration defeat?" somebody asked Barkley after the session.

"It sure isn't any victory," he replied with a chuckle.

All of which brought up once more the comment heard increasingly around the Press Gallery.

"How *can* he run again with this situation up here?"

No one can figure it.

FEBRUARY 10, 1944. Barkley and McKellar engaged in an amiable exchange today during an otherwise heated debate over the selection of conferees on the soldier-vote bill. Early in the debate Barkley made some reference to McKellar's general wisdom and sagacity. McKellar, he said, "came to the Congress when I was in short breeches." After the debate ended, McKellar got the floor, and the following colloquy, as reported by the official reporter, took place:

"Mr. McKellar: 'Some question was raised here about the ages of two Senators, I being one and the Senator from Kentucky being the other. The Senator from Kentucky made the astounding statement that when I was in the House of Representatives a good many years ago he was a boy in short breeches. I wish to read the biographical sketch of the Senator in the *Congressional Directory*. He was born in Graves County, Kentucky, Nov. 24, 1877. I went to the House in 1911. Therefore when my distinguished friend was wearing short breeches, he was just 34 years of age.

" 'I am utterly astounded that, though he came from Graves County, Kentucky, in the country, he should have been wearing short trousers there at that time. Thirty-four years old and wearing short breeches! The remarkable thing about it is that the very next year he was elected to the House of Representatives. I wonder whether he was in short breeches when he came to the House of Representatives in 1913?'

"Mr. Barkley: 'If the Senator will yield in that connection, I have never denied my age. It is in the *Directory*, where everyone can see it. I have searched in vain to find in the *Directory* the age of my very dear friend the Senator from Tennessee.'

"Mr. McKellar: 'Mr. President, I received hundreds of letters of congratulation and innumerable telegrams just a few days ago when I celebrated my birthday.'

"Mr. Barkley: 'How old was the Senator?'

"Mr. McKellar: '75 years old and the Senator is nine years younger than I am.'

"Mr. Barkley: 'Mr. President, I move to insert in the biographical section of the *Directory* the date of birth of the Senator from Tennessee.'

"The acting president pro tempore: 'Is there objection? The chair hears none.'

"Mr. Barkley: 'Getting back to short pants, I merely wish to say that when I came to the House of Representatives in 1913 at the age of 34, I was in long pants, but the Senator from Tennessee has been trying to pull them off me or shorten them ever since."

Amid laughter he sat down, poking Mack in the elbow and shaking with amiable merriment.

So much for Fun on Capitol Hill. It was typical of the two men involved, and typical of a good deal of the banter that goes on here between those who are good friends. There is also the Scott Lucas, or Curse You, Jack Dalton type of exchange, but it doesn't make for half as enjoyable reading—or listening.

The controversy over conferees came when Barkley moved acceptance of Green's suggestions, made as chairman of the Committee on Privileges and Elections. Stacked four to one for the Federal ballot, it included Green, Hatch, Kilgore, Austin, Bridges and Moore. Bridges being at present on his honeymoon, that left three Democrats and Austin opposing Moore, the lone states'-righter. Of course, as Bennett Champ Clark remarked with some acerbity during the debate that promptly followed, the conferees were theoretically supposed to represent the majority views of the Senate anyway, so what difference did it make how they felt personally? Nonetheless, White made the point that the various votes on the Green–Lucas bill had been so close that in all fairness the minority should have at least two men on the conference committee. After prolonged haggling and the citation of many precedents, McKellar managed to force Barkley into a compromise, and the ultimate choices turned out to be Green, Hatch, Connally, Austin and Butler.

Lucas cast some aspersions on Connally which Connally resented and rose to protest with some heat. He didn't want to put his integrity and good faith up to popular vote, Tom said, "but of course he couldn't expect the Senator from Illinois to understand the ethics of the case." Later Lucas went up to his desk and tried to laugh him out of it, but Tom wasn't having any. Along with a great many of the conservative Democrats, he is pretty well fed up with the sarcastic gentleman from Illinois.

On the subsidy issue, the Taft amendment was beaten severely by a combination of New Dealers and anti-subsidy Senators. The subsidy program, insofar as the Senate can kill it, is now dead as a doornail. There is some hope of disposing of the whole matter tomorrow.

FEBRUARY 11, 1944. The subsidy bill was passed today. Aiken and La Follette lost their fight for a food-stamp plan, Pepper lost his attempts to raise the Little Steel wage formula (tying wage increases to the rise in the cost of living since Jan. 1, 1941), and everybody but Bankhead, in fact, lost whatever it was he wanted. The bald little old gentleman from Alabama got what he wanted and was satisfied. The bill now goes to conference with the House.

After the session we went down on the floor and had our usual amiable chat with Barkley. "I see where Hannegan has set the Democratic Convention for a Wednesday, planning to wind up business by Saturday," somebody remarked innocently. "I wonder if you see any significance in that, Senator?" "Why," Alben began judiciously, "it means that we're all of us in a hurry in wartime. And then, too," he added slowly, "perhaps he thinks it will only take us a short time—" he paused and stared thoughtfully into space while the press stood around panting with its collective tongue hanging out—"to do a good job," he finished quickly, chucked the reporter under the chin and burst into laughter, in which we all joined. He doesn't know any more about the great Secret-Which-Isn't-A-Secret about Roosevelt's plans than we do, probably, but it helps make life amusing to go on the assumption that he does.

FEBRUARY 13, 1944. The impression seems to be growing over the week end that the House soldier-vote conferees may insist on a state-ballot measure, in which case things will probably be back just about where they started. If all the time, energy and exasperation which have been expended upon this annoying bill could be harnessed and converted to the production of electricity, it would run the nation's industries for 20 years.

FEBRUARY 15, 1944. The Senate conferees met in Green's office this morning, and after the session the press was called in. Theodore Francis, looking kindly and academic, addressed us in his precise, jocose and

Senator Richard Russell   Theodore Francis Green

scholarly fashion. There was no news, he said; they just met and talked. He had supplied them each with a mimeographed statement of "features of the Green–Lucas Bill not included in the House bill," and "Features of the Green–Lucas Bill as it passed the Senate." Of eight "features not in the House bill," seven were amendments bearing the names of Republican Senators. Of 11 "features of the Green–Lucas Bill," presented with pride by the bill's author, nine were amendments bearing the names of Republican Senators and Bob La Follette. In other words, the sum and substance upon which Theodore Francis Green based his proud statement—for the tone of his handout could only be termed that—was nothing more nor less than the amended material which he fought against bitterly for two months and only accepted at five minutes to midnight because the House passed the Eastland bill and his original bill was dead anyway.

FEBRUARY 16, 1944. "The fate of the Versailles Treaty in the United States Senate—'death by reservation'—may await the United Nations Relief and Rehabilitation agreement." With that doleful supposition I began my story this afternoon. After what happened on the floor it seemed not too flamboyant.

The magic formula devised by Theodore Francis Green and Francis Sayre of the State Department in an attempt to bypass the Senate's treaty-ratifying power is apparently not going to work. The method is classically simple—you simply take an Executive agreement made by the President, slap a preamble containing an authorization of money on one end and an epilogue expressing Congressional approval on the other, and put it through with a whoop and a holler. Except that somehow, in this first practical test, it doesn't seem to be working so well. The simplicity of the Senate, unfortunately for such lazy man's treaty-making, is not quite so great as the simplicity of the method.

It became apparent very early in the afternoon, despite a surprising one-man campaign by Vandenberg to pass the UNRRA measure single-handed, that opposition was going to develop. Tom Connally's optimistic forecast that the bill would go through in a day proved groundless, and by three o'clock when Guy Gillette had arisen to explain why he voted 1 against 16 in Foreign Relations Committee on reporting the bill favorably to the Senate, a definite trend was apparent. By the end of the day there was that feeling in the bones, which I am by now getting used to, which indicates that something you thought was going to be put through in a hurry is instead going to be dragged out and dragged out until it becomes a major issue. For, by some psychological process inherent in the Senate, the longer a thing drags on the more vocal and active becomes its opposition. If you can jam it through in 10 minutes, fine; but the moment the time element begins to enter you can be sure that the waverers and doubters are going to begin to waver and doubt, and with each expression by a waverer or doubter of his wavering or doubt other waverers and doubters are going to begin to succumb to the psychosis, until ultimately you have speeches and speeches and more speeches, and possibly some very close votes.

The end result today was the Taft–McKellar reservations, a series of five amendments, one by Taft and the other four by McKellar, specifically restricting UNRRA from making any expenditures or commitments beyond its authorized appropriations, specifically requiring that any future agreements for the United States in UNRRA must be approved by joint resolution, and specifically stating that "rehabilitation" means relief and nothing more. If these prohibitions indicate a trend, it is probable that UNRRA is going to emerge in a sorry and somewhat bedraggled condition as it goes about its stated purpose of giving aid to areas liberated from the Axis.

There are times when you sit in the gallery and watch the Senate as though you were observing some fearful force. You like them and you see why they do the things they do, and you know that nine-tenths of them are sincerely and honestly convinced that it is in the best interests of the country, but you can't help a certain amount of foreboding. In spite of all the ridicule that comes their way, and in spite of all the derogation they receive, they are still terribly important and terribly powerful people. If all this hullabaloo arises over poor old UNRRA, what chance would a full-fledged peace treaty have? It is something to think about.

Tom Connally left the floor in some disgust today when two of his most brilliant colleagues, one a Republican and one a Democrat, began to toss legalisms back and forth. It was a good thing the Ten Commandments were handed down when they were, Tom told the press, "otherwise those two would find some way to amend them."

This morning William Green, president of the American Federation of Labor, appeared before the Military Affairs Committee as the first witness in opposition to the national service bill—"this benevolent law," as Warren Austin calls it calmly. Green, a sober, earnest man with a worried, sorrowful set to his eyes and mouth, parried the Senator with some skill and consistent logic as Austin went back into Revolutionary history to find precedents for drafting labor. Green is agin it.

The usual ubiquitous colonels who hang around the Senate and advise and lobby the Military Affairs Committee were on hand at Austin's elbow, as were a few scattered naval officers. I have yet to see the services appear in behalf of a measure that would increase rather than complicate governmental efficiency, or extend rather than restrict civilian liberty.

FEBRUARY 17, 1944. UNRRA was approved today, and so were the Taft–McKellar reservations, and so was another by Raymond Willis. Vandenberg and Wheeler parted company on this measure, and today indulged in one of the sharpest colloquies of the entire debate. Van is for it and Burt is against it, and the crossfire with which they have mowed down isolationism's opponents heretofore was directed at each other. Bob Reynolds also made one of his rip-roaring, hell-for-leather denunciations, but it did him little good. The final vote was 47–14.

The soldier-vote conferees met twice today, and each time came forth to report no definite progress, but "amicable" relations. Both times the press, some eight of us this morning and five or six this afternoon, hung around outside the conference room and talked shop—always enjoyable. Colonel Robert Cutler, Stimson's legislative aide and one of the few officers around here who take some of the curse off military lobbying, hung around with us, relating with considerable wit and humor his work for the Army on the present law. He said he had "cooperated until I'm black and blue" with the state governments on the matter, and described at some length the difficulties he had encountered in trying to write the department's circulars to the troops concerning primary dates and voting restrictions. The press understood how the colonel does such a good job of winding the Military Affairs Committee around his little finger. His superiors didn't detail him to the Senate for nothing.

Theodore Francis Green told us today that he "couldn't understand this impression which seems to be in the public mind, that this is an issue between the Federal ballot and the state ballot, or an issue between whether the soldiers will vote or will not vote. Of course we have Public Law 712 right now which provides that they may vote. It is just a matter of extending it to permit more of them to vote. It isn't Federal ballots versus state ballots, but Federal ballots *and* state ballots. I don't see how the public has the contrary impression." We gulped a little, swallowed hard, and agreed that he was perfectly right. If he and Scott Lucas have said once on the floor that the soldiers couldn't vote at all unless the Green–Lucas bill was passed they have said it a thousand times, and the same ratio applies to the argument that the Federal ballot is absolutely the only solution. It is too bad his clarification wasn't developed earlier in the debate.

Democracy has its lighter side. It is generally understood now that the anti-poll-tax bill will not be brought to the floor before April. Jim Mead, who has been put in charge of it, has made an agreement with Theodore Bilbo of Mississippi that he won't call it up until Bilbo has finished getting a new set of teeth, after which he will be equipped to filibuster to his heart's content. [*The "new set of teeth" as it turned out with a fearful irony, was the official euphemism for the mouth cancer that would, in another year, silence Theodore "The Man" Bilbo forever.*]

FEBRUARY 18, 1944. The soldier-vote conferees began to consider the idea of compromise this morning, which is progress of a sort. Hunched-up, bushy-haired, rabble-rousing little old John Rankin remains obdurate, but others show signs of weakening. After the meeting broke up, Green informed us that three compromise proposals had been offered, one by Connally that would put state offices on the Federal ballot, one by Republican Harris Ellsworth of Oregon that would split the thing into two separate bills, one urging state action, the other providing a Federal ballot supplement. The third was offered by Green himself.

Theodore Francis is apparently fighting with his back to the wall and knows it, for with this proposal he backed water even farther than he did in his statement yesterday, has accepted the states'-rights doctrine altogether, and has accepted the principle of Taft's perennial amendment which would simply make the Federal ballot supplemental to the state. There is still no gauging whether or not this last-ditch offer to the House will be accepted, however. Rankin was terse and noncommittal when we swarmed around him as he came out of the committee room; not in a

82 A SENATE JOURNAL

very good humor because, he said, "the meeting recessed over my protest." Green said he had wanted to vote on the matter as it stood, without permitting new suggestions to be offered, but the others over-ruled him. It is possible he feels he is slipping and doesn't quite know—at the moment—how to stop the process. On the other hand it is quite likely that they will meet again next Monday, some personal quirk or animus will intrude itself into the conversation, and the whole thing will end in disagreement and go back to the houses.

I was struck today with the way in which this job brings history and legend right down to cases. Here was a historic moment, I thought, the Senate and House of Representatives of the United States of America trying to settle their differences—and yet what was it really? Why, aca-demically humorous Theodore Francis Green with his impeccable clothes and his habit of turning his whole body when he turns his head; and slow-spoken, shrewd and friendly Carl Hatch; and kindly Warren Austin; and Hugh Butler, and shrewd Tom Connally and ripsnorting Rankin and his confreres from the other side, meeting in the Senate District Committee room in executive session while outside the faithful minions of the press sat around and swapped stories of the trade through the long, dragged-out minutes. Just a little handful of familiar, thoroughly human men, sitting down around a table and slugging it out for what they believe in. This democracy, as commonplace and well-worn as an old shoe, is sometimes more moving than it knows.

FEBRUARY 19, 1944. Bernard Baruch has issued his postwar planning report, a long document placing its major emphasis upon action by the Executive in the process of reconversion. It is doubtful whether this will sit well with the Hill, and yet one sometimes wonders, even though much constructive thought is being given to the problem there, how much real good can be accomplished by the legislative branch in this particular matter. Reconversion, the redistribution of industry, the liquidation of war contracts—all of these touch upon interests which in turn touch upon the political and economic welfare of the states and their representatives. It may be that an objective approach is impossible to achieve. In the meantime, of course, the Army goes on canceling contracts right and left, throwing thousands abruptly out of work. Unless prompt action is forth-coming on the part of someone, we shall be converted into chaos long before either the Executive or Congress has had a chance to do anything about it.

FEBRUARY 20, 1944. As was apparently almost inevitable, the Senate has served notice, through Walter George and Vandenberg and Jim Murray of Montana, that it will not accept the basic premise of the Baruch report that reconversion must be handled by the Executive. It's a legislative matter, the gentlemen maintain, and they aren't acknowledging that anyone downtown should be allowed to handle it independently of the Congress. In other words, what it all boils down to is that they have been worrying for years because they let so much power slip out of their hands, but have been more or less stymied in getting it back by the war. Now they see a situation arising which is fresh and new and a virgin field for Congressional enterprise, and they're going to stake out their claim on it before anyone else can. George and Murray issued an exhaustive and competent survey of reconversion a couple of weeks ago, and others have been promised. There is the usual talk of "a comprehensive legislative program" this morning, and it is true that Murray has introduced an omnibus reconversion bill that would be of much constructive value if passed. If the Baruch report speeds action, it will have accomplished a great deal. Otherwise it will probably languish for months in committee while reconversion continues and the Executive, forced as usual into expediency, finds some way to dodge the law and take care of it.

FEBRUARY 21, 1944. Rep. Gene Worley of Texas, tall, young, dark-haired, clever, has perhaps found the way out of the soldier-vote controversy—when the conference broke up today the members seemed in a more optimistic mood than at any time heretofore. The Worley compromise, however, is not so much a compromise as a complete surrender—for him and for the Senate. It is rather surprising, particularly since he told us that he suggested it gratuitously and caught Rankin by surprise. He didn't even expect any such concession, Worley said—leading one to wonder a little whether such a concession was altogether necessary.

At any rate, under the terms of Worley's proposal, sections 1 and 2 of Public 712 (the sections that abolish payment of poll tax and registration as qualifications for absentee military voters) would be repealed, thereby restoring the poll tax and registration to states which love them dearly, those in the South. In addition, acceptance or rejection of the Federal ballot would be left entirely up to the states. Having been handed all that on a silver platter, with only the barest shreds of the Federal ballot remaining, Rankin emerged from the committee room in a reasonably good humor. Not showy good humor, for that would not become one who is finally, after great and sober struggles, winning the slow, uphill fight, but at least he seemed more pleased than usual. He said it "removes the constitutional issue altogether." He indicated judicious approval. Mississippi's statesman was beginning to perceive the dawn

breaking through the clouds. Virtue, conceivably, might be about to
triumph at last.

On the other hand—as we remarked when we sat down to write our
stories, "Now we've got to figure out some way to put ourselves 'way
out on a limb and still be able to get back if we have to"—it is still
perfectly conceivable that they may throw everything out the window
tomorrow and break up in complete disagreement.

5

"A CALCULATED AND DELIBERATE ASSAULT"

FEBRUARY 22, 1944. Somebody in the Press Gallery can always be counted on to sum it up in an apt, sarcastic, succinct wisecrack. Today was no exception. "Well," said someone while we were waiting around for the soldier-vote conferees to break up, "we heard two Farewell Addresses today."

The first, according to the rules of the Senate, was by General Washington, and it was given an earnest rendition by Elbert Thomas, obviously pleased with the honor.

The second was by Franklin Roosevelt, and it had to do generally with a veto of the tax bill. A nastier attack on Congress—"like a mad dog snarling at the postman," in the words of one reporter—has not been heard hereabouts for some time.

"It has been suggested by some," he said with that aloof other-worldliness that always precedes a dagger-thrust and invariably infuriates his targets, "that I should give my approval to this bill on the ground that having asked the Congress for a loaf of bread to take care of this war for the sake of this and succeeding generations, I should be content with a small piece of crust. I might have done so if I had not noted that the small piece of crust contained so many extraneous and inedible materials. . . .

"The nation will readily understand that it is not the fault of the Treasury Department that the income taxpayers are flooded with forms to fill out which are so complex that even certified public accountants cannot interpret them. No, it is squarely the fault of the Congress of the United States in using language in drafting the law which not even a dictionary or thesaurus can make clear. . . .

"I trust, therefore, that the Congress, after all these delays, will act

85

as quickly as possible for simplification of the tax laws which will make
possible the simplification of the forms and computations now demanded
of the individual taxpayers. These taxpayers, now engaged in an effort
to win the greatest war this nation has ever faced, are not in a mood
to study higher mathematics."

Crack! Crack! Crack!—laying open the backs of his opponents with
one blow after another.*

The effect has been to create, for the first time, perhaps, of all the
times in which he has differed from the Congress, a really grave crisis
in the relations between the Executive and the Legislature.

The House will meet tomorrow and the entire Ways and Means Committee has announced that it will make speeches in reply. The Senate
will do much the same, having already set the ball rolling today with
a resounding denunciation by Walter George. Not a man in the Congress
has dared to voice approval of the veto—in fact, there is some serious
doubt as to whether any man in the Congress does approve it. The rift
this time has gone too deep for any but the most temporary healing. The
words chosen were too deliberate, the basis for the action too flimsy
and illogical, the thing too obviously a deliberate blow at Capitol Hill,
for anyone to either forgive or forget.

In the Senate, after the session, Barkley told us in a cold fury such
as we have never seen him in before, that he had gone downtown twice
in the past week, the last time yesterday, and argued for more than an
hour and a half in an attempt to kill the veto. He said he intends to make
a speech tomorrow "without regard for the political consequences." It
remains to be seen whether he will or not, but at least the intention was
there today. For a man of infinite patience and the most persevering
loyalty, this is going far indeed for Alben. His anger is typical of that
of the rest of the Senate. This is the last time the Roosevelt Administration will get anything but the most essential war measures out of the
Congress of the United States. There is, in fact, serious doubt now that
it will get even those.

Several of the few remaining New Dealers among the press show signs
of wavering in consequence. One of them summed it up to me with honest
candor and a troubled heart. "This is the first time," he said, "when I
have really begun to think that maybe, if he runs again, I will have to
vote against him. I hate to vote against the Administration, because I
think it has done many fine things, and I think in a lot of things he has
a fine record. But after this, I don't know. It's going to be this story all

* The President had other objections, basically the assertion that the bill did not
provide adequate revenue, but these quoted words were typical of his tone which so
infuriated the Congress.

over again from now on whenever he wants something, and I honestly don't know whether or not the country can stand it."

If one were to pursue that thesis in the press, however, he would be accused of letting partisanship obscure his objective judgment. But it is absolutely true—desperately true. Those of us who are on the ground and know the Congress and know how these glib, arrogant, unkind and unwarranted attacks affect it, know that there is growing between the Hill and the White House a real, deep and ugly hatred that can have the most serious consequences for the country.

On the soldier-vote bill, all of us swung around at the ends of our limbs and dashed back to the trunk for cover after today's meeting. Without exception we had all played it yesterday along the line of compromise. Today Rankin did a complete about-face, refused to consider the Worley compromise, forced the House conferees to take an informal vote on where they stood, and in consequence managed to kill all attempts at a reasonable solution. As it now stands, the House has decided to insist upon its amendments to the Eastland–Rankin states'-rights bill and reject the Senate's amendment to Section 3—the Green–Lucas bill embodying the Federal war-ballot principle. Rankin would give no explanation for this sudden switch, nor could Worley or Green offer any reason. The press believes that he thought the Worley compromise over last night, came to the conclusion that it showed a weakness, and decided that if they would yield that much, they would probably yield altogether if he would stand pat. Consequently the abrupt overnight change. Consequently, also, the calculating politician's strategy by which the decision is rendered as if by fiat from on high, without deigning to give an explanation to anyone.

We meet for another deathwatch at 2 P.M. tomorrow outside the District Committee room. After a lot more instructive gossip and some jokes by Colonel Cutler, the door will open, the conferees will emerge carrying a flag-draped coffin, and we will go back to our typewriters and proceed to bury the Federal ballot. The few remaining possibilities —further votes by the two houses, the possibility of a Senate offer which might be accepted, etc.—seem very remote tonight. This thing has been bungled from first to last, and the Administration which wanted all or nothing at all stands an excellent chance of ending up with nothing at all.

On all counts it has been a disturbing day.

FEBRUARY 23, 1944. Barkley resigned as Majority Leader today, and the event will not soon be forgotten by those who were there.

Shortly before the session opened the rumor began to sweep through the Press Gallery and the Senate. By the time the Clerk had launched into the first quorum call, about five minutes past 12, the atmosphere—in the trite but inescapable phrase—was electric. Everyone who could possibly get away and get over to the Senate side was on hand; all the bureau chiefs rushed up from downtown; most of the special correspondents were there. As Barkley sat at his desk waiting for the quorum call to be completed, he glanced up from time to time with an almost questioning look at the Press Gallery. He saw it more crowded than he has seen it in many months.

On the floor the tension was also mounting in those opening minutes. As the Senators drifted in by twos and threes, the word spread rapidly among them. Several came over to shake his hand. Wherry was one, Scott Lucas another. Elbert Thomas walked past his desk, and noticing the manuscript rack on it, asked him if he was going to make a speech. We could see Barkley's reply—"I'm going to resign the leadership"—and Thomas' startled and disappointed protest, followed by Barkley's adamant reiteration: "I'm going to resign." McKellar entered, was informed of the situation by one of the Senate attendants, and went immediately to Barkley's desk, shaking his hand, urging him repeatedly to reconsider. Again the adamant refusal, and the reiterated statement—"I'm going to resign." In a moment Mack gave up and settled into his own seat beside him, a quizzical expression on his face. Once Barkley got up and crossed the aisle to Bob La Follette and Vandenberg, moved by some impulse to tell them of his decision. Both looked startled, started to protest, and then stopped in the face of an evident determination to go through with it. The quorum call droned on, came to an end; several Senators inserted material in the *Record*. Barkley rose and was recognized by Henry Wallace in the Chair. For a moment he looked straight ahead of him without expression, as almost the full membership of the Senate sat silently watching, and above in the gallery the press leaned forward expectantly. Then he began to speak.

For almost 45 minutes, point by point, he denounced the veto message and the man who sent it to the Hill. In a speech that very evidently came from the heart and at times rose to heights of moving passion and sincerity, he repudiated the President whose errand boy in the upper house he has been for seven years. The honor of a man who has been in the Congress for upwards of 32 years was at stake in the Executive's "calculated and deliberate assault." His own mind and his own conscience, he said, could not let him take it lying down. And finally, after specifically replying to every point raised in the veto message, he said that his happiness did not depend upon the office he then held, but upon the approval of his own mind and his own conscience. Accordingly he had

Bartley's resignation
as majority leader

called a meeting of the Democratic majority for 10 A.M. tomorrow, at which time he would submit his resignation as Majority Leader. He concluded with the statement that despite the President's veto message, he advised the Congress "if it has any self-respect yet left" to "pass the bill over his veto, his objections notwithstanding."

He then sat down, and immediately, against all precedent, while the press dashed wildly from the gallery and began to bang furiously on its typewriters and yell hurriedly into its telephones, his colleagues and the galleries stood and applauded for a good three minutes while he remained seated at his desk. Then from both sides of the aisle Senators hurried forward and stood in line to shake his hand while business suspended and Murdock, to whom Wallace had yielded the chair hastily at the end of Barkley's speech, banged futilely for order. Through the swinging doors across the way, Hattie Caraway could be seen from the Press Gallery, standing on the steps just outside the Senate wiping her eyes, apparently crying with emotion. Only a tiny handful of Senators remained in their seats, among them Theodore Bilbo, Joe Guffey, and kindly Jim Tunnell, whose partisanship for Roosevelt is apparently such that it traduced him into a glaringly obvious and ungenerous gesture. Aside from those, all other members were on their feet to honor a man who had finally, after many years and many humiliations, reasserted his own dignity and his own self-respect and gained thereby an increased stature among the men with whom he works.

Of the political repercussions of this day, and their effect upon the future course of the relations between the Congress and the Executive, much of a speculative nature will undoubtedly be written in the next few days. The resignation's bearing upon the fourth term will also be gone into exhaustively. The press gallery had its own interpretation today: the man who said "we heard two Farewell Addresses" yesterday was perhaps not far from right.

The Democrats are virtually unanimous tonight in their prediction that Barkley will either be refused permission to resign or will be overwhelmingly re-elected at the conference tomorrow. When that happens, as one remarked, "he will really be the Senate majority leader and not just the Administration's stooge." He has repudiated the President, almost single-handedly guaranteed an override of the veto, greatly strengthened his own prestige, and probably made unhealable the breach between Roosevelt and Congress. No, the day will not be soon forgotten by those who were there. Or by those who were not there, either.

On top of all this, the decision of the soldier-vote conferees to continue talking instead of disagreeing came as a decided anticlimax, particularly since we had all predicted collapse of the conference.

Coming down from the floor, a couple of us spotted a wandering lady tourist who had just come out of the gallery. "Did you find it interesting?" we asked her. "Yes, I liked it," she said rather uncertainly, "but I couldn't tell just what they were doing." "That was the Majority Leader of the Democratic Party denouncing the President and resigning in protest against the tax veto," we told her. "Oh, was it the Majority Leader?" she wanted to know. "Yes, Senator Barkley." The light of happy recognition broke across her face. "Senator Barkley!" she exclaimed. "I've heard about him. ... Can you tell me where I can find the statues of all the famous men?"

We all hope devoutly that there were at least one or two tourists who realized that they were seeing something more than just routine business today.

FEBRUARY 24, 1944. Today was the second day in the city of Washington in which there was just one story: Barkley. This morning and this afternoon it moved step by step in a logical progression toward an outcome no one can accurately predict, but about which many speculate. It was one of those rare times when issues transcend men, and beneath the petty battles of transitory politics the basic framework of the Republic can be fleetingly discerned.

A liberal Democrat summed it up for me when he said: "Those of us who would have voted to sustain the veto, because we agree in general with the President's objections to the bill, cannot do so now. The issue has gone beyond that. It has become an issue of the Executive versus the Congress, to determine once again which has the final say-so. Of course in the long run we do, and we shall vote in a way which will leave no doubt of it."

By 9:45 this morning, in the hallway outside Room 201 in the Office Building where the Democrats were due to meet and receive Barkley's resignation, upwards of 100 correspondents and cameramen were on hand, standing about in little groups, talking, joking, laughing, smoking hurriedly and nervously, with a mounting tension running through them. Presently, by ones and twos and threes, the Senators began to arrive: McKellar and Bilbo together; Scott Lucas by himself; Millard Tydings; Homer Bone of Washington on the crutches to which a bone infection has chained him; Connally and huge, portly, heavy-jowled old Dave Walsh of Massachusetts; Burt Wheeler, looking grimly pleased with the President's misfortune; Abe Murdock, spick and span and in a hurry, brushing reporters aside as though he were shaking off a pack of terriers; Cotton Ed and McClellan and Hattie Caraway; shrewd little Maloney of Connecticut, and the rest. As each appeared down the hall and started toward us, the line formed, until by the time he reached us the Senator found himself confronted with a solid mass of reporters, pencils raised.

Some talked, some didn't; around each we surged in the instinctive mass movement that characterizes the press on such occasions. Suddenly Barkley arrived at his office, right next door. Immediately the flashbulbs began to explode and the questions began to fly. He tried to open the door, dropped his keys, stooped to pick them up; somebody cried, "Senator Barkley!" He looked up, the flash went off, the picture was taken, he dropped his keys again. Eventually he got in. Meanwhile the press services were writing running stories—and the running was literal. One man would jot down a few words of comment or descriptive color and tear off at a dead run down the hall to the press room. A minute or so later another would detach himself from the crowd and hurry away to file additional matter on the news wire. Soon the first man would return, and a third would depart. Ten o'clock came and went, 10:30 arrived. Barkley appeared again in the doorway of his office, and again the flashbulbs went off and the pictures were taken. Shaking his head and refusing comment, he stepped down the hall to the door of the conference room, about thirty feet away, stepped inside, and closed the door. The press broke up again into little gossiping, nervous groups.

Half an hour later Barkley came out, and with a rush we surged around him. He told us with tears in his eyes that he had submitted his resignation and turned the chair over to McKellar. We followed him the short distance back to his office. He paused patiently for many more pictures and many questions, some of which he parried and some of which he answered. Then he disappeared inside and closed the door. We drifted back to the conference room. By this time dead flashbulbs and cigarette butts were scattered all over the floor.

Suddenly the conference door flew open. Again there was that swift, mass rush toward it. Tall Tom Connally, with his long black coat, bow tie and picturesque long hair, lacking only a stovepipe hat to make the picture perfect, pushed his way out crying, "Make way for liberty! Make way for liberty!" Dave Walsh followed him, and Walter George, Millard Tydings, Bennett Clark and Elbert Thomas. Single-file they pushed their way through us to Barkley's office and went in. Repeatedly reporters and cameramen pushed into the office and were pushed back by the Senator's secretaries. Presently that door, too, was closed, and we again took up our vigil.

Fifteen minutes later the door opened and the committee came out again. "Did you re-elect him, Senator?" somebody cried. "What did you do?" Dave Walsh smiled and murmured in his soft, hurried, plum-pudding voice, "You know what we did. You know what we did." Barkley appeared in the doorway and once more pictures were taken and questions were asked. He remained silent, walked swiftly to the conference room and went inside. The Senators rose and cheered, the door closed. Again we waited.

At 11:52 A.M. there was applause. We all wrote it down dutifully: "Appls, 11:52."

At 11:59 A.M. there was applause and cheers. We noted it.

At 12:03 P.M. there was prolonged applause and cheers.

At 12:05 the door opened, the Senators began to stream out and the press crowded in.

At approximately 12:10 McKellar began to tell us the story of the meeting at which the Democratic majority unanimously accepted the resignation of its Majority Leader and then with equal unanimity re-elected him.

"By his one-vote margin in the 1937 contest when he was first elected leader," Elbert Thomas told me later, "the impression was given, and it has been the impression ever since, that he spoke to us for the President. Now that he has been unanimously elected, he speaks for us to the President."

At 6 P.M. the press received the letter with which the Majority Leader replied to the President's politically desperate and cajoling "Dear Alben" telegram of last night.* Dignified, formally cordial, and firm, it reiterated Barkley's position that the Congress had been attacked and that more important than personal friendship or political loyalty was the mutual respect of the Executive and the Legislature. He hoped this incident would serve to clarify and emphasize that respect, Barkley said, and he closed with cordial regards.

"It has become an issue of the Executive versus the Congress, to determine once again which has the final say-so," my liberal friend told me. "Of course in the long run we do. . . ."

FEBRUARY 25, 1944. The Senate played to a full house today. The galleries were jammed, and along the walls at the side and back House members crowded in two-deep around the room. A constant hum of talk and laughter preceded the opening of the session, in the moments during which some of us went down on the floor to see Walter George, who remarked

* The President said he was sorry to learn from Barkley's speech that the Senator had thought he "had, in my message, attacked the integrity of yourself and other members of the Congress. Surely you know that was not my intention." They might disagree, he said, and still not question each other's good faith. He recalled that Barkley had objected on Monday to some aspects of the tax message, so he had "made certain changes." He said he did not realize then "how very strongly you felt." And finally, informed by his Senate supporters of the course events were taking, he said he hoped Barkley would not resign as Majority Leader, but that if he did, then he hoped his colleagues would immediately re-elect him.

that he hoped no one would make a speech before the vote, but that with the galleries full it was a mighty temptation; and Happy Chandler, just back from Kentucky, overflowing with friendliness but completely non-committal about his colleague's fight with the White House. Promptly at 12 Wallace convened the Senate, the chaplain said the prayer, and the session began.

During the inevitable quorum call immediately after, all eyes were on the first seat in the first row on the center aisle. For more than 15 minutes it remained empty, as more and more members drifted in to answer to their names. When the quorum call was completed a messenger from the House appeared to deliver the message on the defeat of the veto, which came there yesterday afternoon on a vote of 299–99. The Clerk of the Senate then began to read the veto message, striving, as he always does when reading a Roosevelt message, to give an approximation of the President's delivery. Sometime during the reading Barkley slipped in from the left, crossed to his seat, and sat down. No demonstration occurred, perhaps because he entered so swiftly that he was in his place before anyone really realized it. Wallace White stepped across the aisle from his desk opposite to shake his hand, and Nye came down from his desk two rows up to do the same. Midway in the veto message Holman surged to his feet to demand order in his querulous bleat. Wallace banged the gavel four or five times and the galleries quieted down. The Clerk read on. Barkley got up once and went up toward the back of the room to the desk where Pepper, just back from spreading the New Deal gospel in Florida, sat in morose silence. They shook hands and spoke for a moment or two. Then Barkley returned to his seat. The Clerk finished reading the message and Wallace said, "The question is on passing the bill over the President's veto. According to the Constitution, the vote will be by Yeas and Nays." Pepper jumped to his feet and was recognized.

There then briefly intruded upon the spectacle of a Senate about to complete the restoration of its self-respect the old, old war-cry of "Stand by the President." Pepper spoke quietly and sincerely, and with the excellent language that always characterizes his extemporaneous speeches. More than a tax bill was at stake, he told his Democratic colleagues, some of whom were trying to duck behind the pleasant fiction that the sole issue was revenue: the fate of the party and its leader was to be decided. In proof of his own sincerity he wanted to read a letter which he, as a newly elected member of the Florida legislature, had sent to the newly elected governor of New York on Dec. 22, 1928. As the Senate listened in close attention he launched into a statement of youthful and moving idealism. Somewhere toward the middle of it Chavez rose. "The Senator says this was written after the election of 1928?" he asked with innocent blandness. "It was," Pepper replied. "And what did Florida do in the election of 1928?" pursued Chavez gently. "In that election Florida went for Mr. Hoover," said Pepper soberly. It brought down the house, and Chavez sat down with an amiable grin, having completely destroyed the effect of a speech which before that had been mounting toward a peroration that might conceivably have swung a few votes.

When Pepper sat down, the Republicans and many Democrats at once began to shout, "Vote! Vote!" No one else desired to speak (Langer having been talked out of his intention to do so by his colleagues on the Republican side) and Wallace ordered the Clerk to call the roll. All sound ceased, and in dead silence the Senate began to vote.

Ten minutes later, 72–14, the 1944 tax bill was passed into law despite the President's objections.

Immediately the Senate broke up into milling groups of Senators and Congressmen, most of them crowding out the doors. In the galleries also the visitors began to leave. In the midst of the confusion Barkley rose and asked unanimous consent for the Clerk to read the President's telegram to him and his letter in reply. Scott Lucas had been handed the chair by that time, and repeatedly while the Clerk struggled to make himself heard, he banged futilely for order and said over and over in a voice without much conviction, "The Senate and galleries will *please* be in order." Barkley decided to give it up, and asked that the correspondence be printed in the *Record* instead. The Senate moved on to routine business, and an hour or so later recessed until Tuesday.

At 3 o'clock we received word in the gallery that the Minority Leader, Charles McNary of Oregon, had died in Florida, and for the next three hours were busy rounding up comment. Someone remarked that his death was "the worst thing which has happened to the Republican Party since it lost the Presidency in 1932." I got here too late to know him, which I regret, for never have I heard a Senator referred to with more affection and respect by everyone than "Charlie Mack."

FEBRUARY 26, 1944. Looking back in hasty retrospect, three days after the event and its aftermath, the Barkley resignation still looks like what it did on the day it happened: a basically sincere protest by a man who just got fed up. The professional cynicism of the Washington press corps, which sees an ulterior motive in everything, still has not managed to rationalize entirely the Senator's obvious anger, or the emotion that filled his voice during the delivery of his speech. Despite such museum pieces as *PM's* gala edition (CONGRESS IN REVOLT! 7 PAGES!) and the vicious sniping of some irresponsible commentators closer to home, the facts seem to remain. He took it and took it and took it and suddenly one day he decided he wouldn't take it any more. None of the wild rumors which have been going around—that it was a stage-piece framed by McKellar and the Southerners, that it was a carefully calculated maneuver to win re-election in Kentucky, that it was inspired by the Treasury, which didn't want the tax bill vetoed—has been in any way confirmed. As for the Kentucky situation, it is undoubtedly true that it crossed Barkley's mind, as it did everyone else's; but at best it was only a gamble, and to think he would risk his entire political future with the Democratic Party on that would seem a rather broad assumption to make. Probably, as happens so often at the other end of the Avenue, public good coincided happily with political advantage: the percentage of the former, in this instance, being about 80, and of the latter not more than 20. No one listening to that speech, or reading the letter to the President which followed it, or hearing Barkley tell in his own words at his press conference how he had been prompted to take the action he did, could honestly believe that it was much more than the faithful camel, finally back-broken with the one last straw. Probably no one summed it up more succinctly or more soundly than did the Washington *Daily News* in the title of its editorial: BARKLEY GOT A BELLY-FULL.

He has emerged from it immeasurably strengthened, and so has the Congress. From the professional mourner's bench in New York dire predictions of the fate of the country, distinguished as usual solely by their tortuous felicity in removing all blame from the President and placing it squarely somewhere else, are coming as a result. They are hardly valid. There comes a point in the consideration of the issues before it when the Congress feels instinctively in its bones that the time has come to call a halt. That time came on the tax bill when the Hill received a smart-aleck veto message. The only thing left for it to do was reassert its independence and rebuff the Executive. Had it not done so, then the hysterical headline in *PM* that first day might have come true. BATTLE BETWEEN FDR AND CONGRESS TO DECIDE POLITICAL FUTURE OF BOTH; PEOPLE WILL SETTLE ISSUE, it read. The writer of that headline, and the newspaper that printed it, apparently had no more idea of the full implication of those words than the man in the moon. Suppose for a moment that the President of the United States should ever win a "battle" with the Congress of the United States; suppose that it did "decide the political future" of Congress in the sense that headline meant. If that day ever came it would be the last for the Republic—as a republic. In the very nature of free government, the President *cannot* in the long run win over Congress. In the long run it *must* win over him. It should give him as much power and as much cooperation and help as it honestly can in meeting the country's problems, but when the time comes—as Congress instinctively felt this week that it had—when he attempts to turn that power back upon its creators and use it deliberately to weaken the Congress, then Congress has no higher duty than to crush the attempt. And this regardless of who, be he saint or sinner, sits at 1600 Pennsylvania.

FEBRUARY 27, 1944. The week-end round-ups in the Sunday papers are full of "the Congressional revolt" today. From them a fairly consistent picture emerges of a Legislature surfeited with insults, an Executive too willing to be clever and too apt to be personal. Judge Rosenman is selected by some to be the whipping boy, but I cannot forget that one Democratic Senator told me Thursday: "You talk to the other Senators around here and you'll find them blaming Jimmy Byrnes." Nor can I forget the way in which another, normally mild and gentle-spoken, banged his desk with the first show of temper I have ever seen him display and said flatly, "You can mark this down in great big black letters: Jimmy Byrnes will never be the vice-presidential candidate." Even those who blame Jimmy Byrnes, however, cannot totally ignore the fact that the ultimate responsibility lies above.

Economic
Stabilization
Director
James F. Byrnes

6

SOLDIER VOTE: Home Stretch

FEBRUARY 28, 1944. Things began to shake themselves back down to normal today; the first real sign that all was once more calm along the Potomac came when John Rankin emerged from the soldier-vote conference to announce that the meeting is again "going over until tomorrow to give us time to study the proposition." The stalwart symbol of Mississippi democracy, to whom *Time* has applied the adjective "poodle-haired," is blowing cold again in the blow-hot, blow-cold marathon by which he is deliberately trying to drag the issue out until the public has lost all interest in it. The Federal war ballot will be done to death by boredom if Rankin has his way; it is already a dead issue in the public press. The Congressman has been able to stall too long. Instead of forcing him into a showdown, the Senate conferees and Worley and Herb Bonner of North Carolina from the House have let him get away with his dilatory tactics, agreeing to one postponement after another. Each time, just as he has us all convinced that this, at last, is it, Silent John changes his mind with a great show of deep constitutional conviction and we go over for another day or two while the country has a chance to yawn just a little wider over the soldier vote. The issue is dead: Rankin has killed it with delay. We know it, he knows it, and sooner or later one of these long-drawn-out days Theodore Francis Green and his Senate colleagues will realize it too. He perhaps deserves the calumny which has been heaped upon him by his more perceptive critics, but there is no denying that on the soldier-vote bill John Elliot Rankin led the Congress of the United States around by the nose.

FEBRUARY 29, 1944. Compromise emerged at last from the soldier-vote conference today, and all was sweet, singing harmony. The obvious mortification of Our John put the finishing touch to it, adding immeasurably to everyone's delight and satisfaction.

The half a loaf the Senators finally accepted was offered by Bonner and Harold LeCompte of Iowa and to anyone who has stayed with them these past three weeks it was easy to see why they took it, even though it preserves the Federal ballot only in a thin and ghostly form. It is far more, perhaps, than they had any right to expect, particularly considering the House's original attitude. The Senate is probably lucky to get this much.

The Federal ballot remains, but it goes only to men who have applied for a state ballot, and only to those in that category who have not by Oct. 1 received their state ballot. And in all cases, validation of the Federal ballot is vested in the governors—a stipulation that causes some skepticism but which Green says will be taken care of by public pressure. He is probably right.

Rankin, of course, emerged from the conference room with the statement that "the fight has just begun," and promised to organize opposition to the conference report when it is presented to the House. He was the only man in the 10-man committee who voted against the compromise, and has apparently slipped badly. He still may be able to whip his cohorts into a frenzy on the floor, however, and when the bill gets over here the Eastland–McKellar crowd may filibuster. The soldier-vote bill isn't entirely over the bumps by any means, but at least a major advance has been made.

In a lot of ways it has been fun to cover, and although Green's little speech about "democracy in action" at the conclusion of the conferences was trite and obvious it was also true. Just a group of men sitting down around a table to battle out their differences, while the press hung around outside—the Senate and House of Representatives of the United States of America, taking care of the Republic.

MARCH 1, 1944. Once again the soldier-vote conference, just yesterday so amicably "concluded" with a "binding agreement," almost blew up in our faces. That it did not is due simply to the fact that the Senate has once more receded from its position and given in to another House demand. When they voted yesterday, the House conferees said, they never dreamed that the Senate meant to extend the Federal war ballot to men within the country as well as men overseas. When they found it out this morning they were shocked, outraged and well-nigh horrified. The resultant explosion threatened to rock the Capitol for a few moments, but by dint of fast talking and one more surrender the Senators managed to hold the conference together. One more restriction was clamped on the Federal ballot, and the final work on the bill could once more proceed. Theodore Francis Green says now that the conferees hope to be finished altogether by tomorrow; the conference report is on the Senate calendar for Tuesday. Barring a fight there, it should go through without much more than perfunctory approval. The House may well be a different matter.

The Federal war ballot that now remains is a shameful farce and a betrayal of the hopes of many soldiers. The Senate would have done better to stand by its guns or else disagree completely and rest its case on Public 712. One cannot help but feel that Rankin has done just about what he wanted to do. What the bill's reception at the other end of the Avenue will be, no one can quite imagine. If it includes the Federal ballot at all, the President would be taking a terrific political risk in vetoing it; a bigger risk, perhaps, than he did with the tax bill. And yet it may well be that he cannot conscientiously approve it as the measure stands now. Unfortunately, however, such an event could only be interpreted most unfavorably by the Congress, still acutely conscious that it has beaten him once and not averse to a chance to do it again.

Oddly enough, by a coincidence not altogether fortunate for the Administration, the same issue of Executive versus Legislature is developing along parallel lines this week in both houses. In the Senate, the Agriculture Committee's investigation of the Rural Electrification Administration has run headlong into the obstinacy of Jonathan Daniels, one of the President's executive assistants, who has refused to testify, apparently under orders. At the same time in the House, the committee investigating the Federal Communications Commission has run into stormy weather, with Republican members charging the chairman and other Democratic members with whitewashing the agency and attempting to suppress the facts about the purchase of a New York radio station. The issue is the recurring one of whether or not the Congress has a right to demand the testimony it needs from employees of the Executive branch. The committee is preparing a brief against Daniels, and is seriously contemplating taking the case to the full Senate for decision. In both instances, important government witnesses have been specifically ordered by the President not to give information to the Congress, the order in the FCC case having been given some time ago, but the Daniels incident occurring since the tax fight. Apparently the President's dander is up, a jolly and exciting situation for his partisans. Unfortunately the Congress is in no mood to take it sitting still either. The immovable object is evidently about to get involved with the irresistible force again.

Here again, the issue is basic; and here again, the Congress will win. So long as it holds the purse, it always has one last recourse: it can cut off the funds and in that manner cripple the office. If the present trend continues, and the President remains in office and his term runs beyond the conclusion of hostilities, it seems a reasonable prediction to say that when he finally leaves the White House the Presidency will have been reduced nearer impotency than it has been for many years. Should this mutual antagonism be unchanged, the moment the war ends the Congress will begin systematically stripping the Presidency of one power after another until only the irreducible minimum remains. [*But to this possibly flamboyant foreboding, death gave, as it did to so many Roosevelt might-have-beens, the final answer of no answer at all.*]

MARCH 2, 1944. The soldier-vote conferees voted on the conference report today, and the final tally found Green and Carl Hatch opposed. Both gave us the impression when we went in to talk to them afterward that they were tired out and disgusted. Green said the bill had been "whittled down and whittled down and whittled down, day by day, until what remained wasn't worthwhile." Hatch, speaking in the quiet, reasonable, rather courtly tones that distinguish him in argument, said that he had thought the purpose of the measure was to extend the Federal war ballot to more soldiers. "Instead of extending, it curtails," he said. "Its effect is not to simplify, but to complicate." Accordingly he could not honestly accept it. Green felt the same way, and for the first time in the whole long battle gave the impression today that he felt his 76 years—a rare thing for a man who goes to the Senate gym regularly, takes a stiff workout, and, generally chipper, looks and acts to be about 60. It was also the first time that he neglected to tell us that he is "always optimistic." Both he and Hatch seemed pretty thoroughly beaten down and worn out.

One more restriction was added prior to the final vote—state legislatures must now empower their governors specifically to accept the Federal war ballot. Of all the states, only California has already taken this step, which means that special sessions must be called for the purpose. Gene Worley, stretching his long and lanky form out in a tipped-back chair and employing his unhurried Texas voice at its most persuasive, could not agree with this interpretation: the new language—that the governors must certify the Federal war ballot to be "authorized by" their laws instead of "acceptable under" them—means only that if a governor wants to be absolutely sure he is complying with state law need he call a special session. Otherwise, Gene said, he can still certify on his own responsibility. Hatch and Green, while obviously liking the Congressman as everyone does, chose to take the opposite view. Worley was also tired and disgusted, but more disturbed than annoyed by the fact that the final vote had not been unanimous. Later he said there "still might be time" to work out something else before the conference report is finally issued on Monday. It seems a wan hope, even in this off-again, on-again marathon.

Both Green and Hatch indicated strongly that they will oppose the conference report when it reaches the floor of the Senate. That can mean any one of several things. If the original majority that passed the Green–Lucas bill still holds together, the report may be beaten in the Senate. If it has fallen apart, the report may go through and go to the White House. The reception it will receive there is already the topic of much speculation in the Press Gallery. If the word "fraud" could be applied to the Eastland–Rankin bill, an honest and forthright declaration of states' rights, certainly it could with far more justice be applied to this mongrel measure which holds out the promise of a Federal war ballot, only to snatch it back with a dozen restrictions.

Certain it is, however, that "fraud" is not the word with which to make a veto stick. The language had better be more moderate this time—or else. And *or else* with some justice, considering the endless patience and hard work that have gone into this thing.

Rankin still promises to fight the conference report in the House, although he voted for it in committee. He looked quite in his glory when he emerged from the conference room today waving his arm and crying "Eureka!"

Looked at from any angle, the possibilities on this ill-fated tangle are still infinite. As for the way everybody here feels about it now, Scott Lucas summed it up explicitly the other day when someone asked him. "Ah, the hell with it!" said the co-author of the Green–Lucas bill in frustrated disgust. The feeling is universal.

Frank Knox came up this morning to deliver one more eulogy over the dying body of the national service bill. A sincere man, pompous and a trifle bombastic but still basically sound, he impresses one as being quite capable, without much imagination or very much humor. Despite his effort, the patient is still not expected to live.

MARCH 3, 1944. The leading Republicans are in Oregon today, where 17 of them went for the McNary funeral. The minority situation is once more in the state of flux dear to the hearts of newspapermen—the Senator's death has thrown the leadership wide open again. Only two days before it occurred he had been re-elected leader, with White as acting leader, Vandenberg as conference chairman, Burton as conference secretary, and Wherry as minority whip. Wherry was the only one his selection seemed to really impress; other Republicans were not so cordial. Aiken for one is already complaining that he does not relish being bawled out for the way he votes. The Wherry approach is a trifle direct.

McNary's passing has now upset all these plans. Taft, White and Vandenberg are the leading contenders for the leadership. Taft, so the story goes, would like to have it because "he is very much interested in a place on the ticket this year." Vandenberg came out yesterday with the statement that White should retain it "as long as the present occupant remains in the White House," a rather startling suggestion in view of the possibilities. Vandenberg himself is playing coy as usual. The minority conference will have to meet again in a few days to elect its officers all over again. White, as someone remarked wittily if unkindly, will probably get it "if the law of inertia applies"—unless he defers to Taft's ambition.

Over in the House today, deliberately perverse as usual, Rankin came out with a ringing defense of the soldier-vote conference report. Simultaneously at the other end of the Avenue the President remarked at his press conference that the veto test of the bill would be whether or not it permits more men to vote than the present law. The words are an exact echo of Green's, and this may well be the tip-off.

MARCH 4, 1944. The Senate Agriculture subcommittee investigating REA decided today to recommend to the full committee that Jonathan Daniels be brought before the bar of the Senate to show cause why he should not be cited for contempt. Cotton Ed was in the chair as usual, perceiving at last a concrete means of forwarding his vendetta with the White House. The old man, with his slow, shuffling walk, his huge head with its heavy jowls, drooping moustache, tired old eyes and curly gray hair, faintly suggests, in some curious fashion, an appealing and willful little boy. There is something indefinably juvenile about his looks. Despite the allegations of his critics, it does not extend to his mentality. There is nothing childlike about a man who is one of the most amusing, and at the same time one of the grimmest, reactionaries on the Hill. Only a few days ago he sent a telegram of praise to the South Carolina legislature for its resolution condemning the "damned Northern agitators" who stir up the racial question. His endorsement of it was typical of a man who never misses a chance to say in his whispery, husky, petulant old voice that he has "one eternal platform—the Constitution, states' rights, and white supremacy." Thirty-five years in the Senate yesterday, and nothing has ever changed him.

The outcome of the Daniels case remains to be seen. There is a nice and delicate question involved: the confidential relationship between the President and his closest aides should be preserved, otherwise the independence of the Executive would be in as much jeopardy as the independence of the Legislature ever was. At the same time, the question does arise as to whether or not the Congress should have the power to compel testimony in order to prevent the Executive branch from corrupting its own agencies. The present mood of Congress, however, may obscure these finer considerations and tip the balance toward an active prosecution of every Executive assistant it can lay its hands on.

During the afternoon I went around and talked to a pretty fair cross-section of the Senate—a states'-rights Democrat, a liberal Republican, an all-out New Dealer, and a rock-ribbed Republican—on the soldier-vote conference report. With only one exception, and that very much qualified, they are against it. Apparently, to quote once more the words of Our John, "the fight has just begun."

The states'-rights Democrat, one of the soundest and ablest men here despite a few blind spots peculiar to the South, had some interesting observations to make on the whole subject of the soldier vote, the election, and the President.

"I've never been able to quite get away from the feeling," he said, "that the original soldier-vote bill as it was presented to us was pretty much of a phony. It looked entirely too much as though somebody was framing up a scheme to control the soldier vote by having them marched up en masse to the polls and put under pressure to vote for 'the Commander-in-Chief.' And don't think that 'Commander-in-Chief' stuff won't be played for all it's worth here, either. The whole idea is going to be 'indispensability.' Why,——. No man is indispensable.

"I can tell you one thing, though, and that is that no other man in the Democratic Party could ever hope to be a candidate. He's seen to that all the way through. He's cut down every possibility that's come along. As soon as they begin to get prominent, he gets rid of them. He uses you and then he throws you away. Why, hell, I could no more be one of these ass-kissing New Dealers! He'll be your friend as long as he can get what he wants out of you, and then it's good-by. That's not for me.

"I'm a Democrat, and I'll always remain a Democrat, but I'm not a New Dealer. And I think that's true of the majority of the Democratic Party.

"As for the Barkley affair, we may try to let that go, cover it up and forget about it as you might a family squabble, but do you think the Republicans will let us forget it, even if we want to? He's worked himself into a position where he's got to go on opposing Congress or back down and be discredited. How can he do anything else? He's put himself right out on a limb. I have an idea he'll veto this soldier-vote bill anyway, if it should be passed.

"I can tell you one thing, though—by God, it had better be a better-mannered veto than that last one, or he'll hear about it."

MARCH 5, 1944. Jonathan Daniels has written Cotton Ed an eat-crow letter in which he takes it all back and promises to be a good boy. After consulting with the President, he says, he has come to the conclusion that nothing he might say on REA could endanger his relationship with the President. The letter is sensational and the timing has made it even more so. Not until the subcommittee had definitely decided to proceed with its contempt action, not until Daniels'—and the President's—capitulation could be put in the most placating light, was the surrender forthcoming. Instead of placating, however, it has simply aroused contempt.

MARCH 7, 1944. What is apparently the most final of all the "final" agreements on the soldier-vote bill was reached today. It even got to the point of deciding who would and who wouldn't sign the conference report; and in fact Tom Connally, to whom Green turned over management of the bill, said he expected to bring it to the floor on Thursday. It will come heralded by omens of misfortune, with opposition guaranteed and a veto expected.

Green and Hatch on the final showdown refused to sign the report, and Green withdrew from all active connection with the bill, promising to fight it on the floor. Lucas has already started his campaign, both against the bill and for re-election. Once more, in today's session, we were treated to the sound of his savage voice attacking his enemies. It was the same old speech he has made before, with the same dark predictions and the same appeals to the servicemen's anger which, if they ever succeeded, would stir far more terrible consequences than Lucas ever dreams. Nonetheless, he bespeaks a very vocal and very bitter element in the Senate, and on the basis of his remarks today it is easy to see that his companions will demand their say in the matter too. We are in for more storms and tempests on the soldier vote.

So ends the conference after 14 meetings covering a period of 25 days. The bill as it stands now is very much restricted. Even so, if the states will cooperate ("90 per cent of the responsibility for the success of this law lies on the states," Gene Worley told us) the soldiers will be able to vote. For men overseas it will be some help, for men within the country it does not compare with Public Law 712. All in all, although Hatch frankly and honestly declared that it is "entirely impossible to judge whether more soldiers would vote under Public 712 than under the conference report," it seems probable that in the last analysis Public 712 is the broader and more effective law.

MARCH 7, 1944. Ferguson and Brewster made quite a spectacle for the press in the Truman Committee hearing on defective Liberty Ships this morning. Joe Curran of the Maritime Union testified, looking tough but amiable, and on the whole did a pretty good job of it, too. What he said made sense and he said it in a reasonable manner. However, he did make some reference—the stock reference, which some people who belong to a certain school of political thought (32nd degree Democrats, you might call them) are prone to make—about "some newspapers using this hearing for their own political ends." Ferguson and Brewster jumped him for that; he kept his temper but Truman got mad, a lot of hot words were exchanged and a statement that otherwise might have sunk into the silent depths of a committee record, there to gather dust and molder, was lifted into the class of news and spread across the country. Truman twice tried to shut his irrepressible colleagues up, each time growing angrier. Ferguson returned to the subject with the dogged persistence for which he is noted, and Brewster, his voice rising and a hot flush covering his face and forehead, became more and more personal. It was this more than anything else that seemed to annoy Truman. The chairman is a fine fellow, presiding like some trim, efficient, keen-minded businessman, which is just what he looks like, with his neat appearance, heavy-lensed glasses, and quick, good-humored smile. There are a number of times, in fact, sentimental though it may seem, when it is quite easy to find oneself thanking whatever powers there be that the country has Harry Truman in the Senate. He is an excellent man, a fine Senator and sound American. The debt the public owes to him is great indeed.

And Boss Pendergast put him in. Politics is funny business: or may be one should say politics is people, and people is funny business.

Later in the day I went around and talked to a few Senators on the soldier-vote bill. It is impossible to predict at the moment what reception it will receive when it comes to the floor. Taft said he would probably vote for it. States that have already had special sessions and have not validated the Federal ballot won't meet again, he predicted. "They just won't get the Federal war ballot. Anyway, they don't want it." This he said with the calm of a man entirely sure of his course. It is one of the things you have to hand Bob Taft. He never pulls his punches and he lets the chips fall where they may.

Jonathan Daniels came back to the REA hearing. "Are you the same Jonathan Daniels who appeared here on February 28?" the committee counsel asked him. "Approximately," Daniels replied with a grin. Today the committee decided to drop the contempt proceedings and forget the whole thing. The issue was there, basic enough, but everybody thought better of it and backed away before any damage was done.

MARCH 9, 1944. Tom Connally filed the soldier-vote conference report today and immediately got into a three-way argument with his fellow conferees Hatch and Austin. Ultimately it was agreed to postpone formal consideration until Monday. Lucas then delivered a 16-page speech attacking the Republicans, the conference report, "a Congressman from Mississippi who is still fighting the Civil War," and all who dare to criticize "the great man in the White House." He concluded by taking what is apparently to become the official line, that S. 1285, the conference report, is worse than Public Law 712, and accordingly 1285 should be killed and Public 712 be retained. The veto message, if any, will in all probability follow the same thesis.

MARCH 10, 1944. I went to my first White House press conference this morning and came away with rather mixed reactions. The physical routine of it was already familiar from the accounts of innumerable sources. Once my name had been checked off the list and I had passed through the north-west gate and entered the Presidential offices on the west side of the White House, it was more a matter of confirming things I had read about than of absorbing new impressions. There was the big front waiting room, just as described, with the red leather chairs and sofas along the walls and the huge oaken table in the center, piled high with hats and overcoats. There were the White House police, wearing uniforms, and the Secret Service men, not wearing uniforms. There were the correspondents drifting in by ones and twos, and a gradually mounting hum of talk and laughter as everyone stood around waiting. The whole atmosphere was one of con-trolled informality, with a slight but inescapable excitement in the air, increasing as 10:30 came and went and the President still delayed calling us in. Promptly at 11 the buzzer sounded three times and the regular White House correspondents streamed down the hall toward the executive office. After they had gone in the visitors were allowed to follow. As the last man came through the door into the oval room one of the policemen called out, "All in!" and the President began to speak. We were there per-haps 10 minutes.

I came away with two dominant impressions. The first was a curious sense of physical smallness, hard to understand in view of so many refer-ences to the man's size. Nonetheless, the impression remained, and even at the end, when the crowd began to thin out and I could get a better look at him, it still struck me forcibly. Perhaps it was because he was sitting low in his chair. Whatever it was, it made him seem relatively small with a rather small head and not a very great width to his shoulders. I had been prepared for someone of far more imposing proportions than this. It is the thing which struck me most forcibly.

The second impression was more subtle, something in his manner, in his tone, in the way in which he answered questions. "Subdued" is the word for Franklin Roosevelt at this particular juncture; whether subdued be-cause of his enormous responsibility, or because of political opposition, or because of age or of ill health, I have no way of knowing. But subdued he is, even though the standard gestures—the quick laugh, the upflung head, the open smile, even the intent, mouth-opened lack of expression when he is listening—are all there, just as they have been in a million newsreels and photographs. Underneath one detects a certain lifelessness, a certain preoccupation, a tired impatience, not lessened by an obvious mistrust of the press.

The press, in fact, came in for several thrusts during the course of the conversation. The Italian Navy was brought up, and the press was straightened out on that. He had said a third of it "or the equivalent" would be given the Russians. "Only, some people didn't use the key words"—this with a quick, unamused smile and a glance along the line of faces. He was asked if, in his opinion, the bombing of Berlin was preliminary to an invasion. "One of those iffy questions," he remarked, and added that, after all, why should he have an opinion. "Don't they always make up their own opinions?" "Who is they?" someone asked, for he has a habit of making elliptical remarks whose intent is not always immediately clear. "Why, the press," he told us with an edge in his voice. "They always make up their own opinions, don't they?" Dutifully we laughed.

The conversation slipped on and off the record for a moment or two. He told us a story by a member of the Swedish legation in Berlin whom he talked to recently; off the record. He commented that the bombing of Berlin, and whether or not there was anything left of Berlin, was something he didn't know much about, something which was worked out by the joint British and American staffs; on the record. He told us that Lewis Douglas was resigning from the Board of Economic Welfare; on the record. Because of his health; off the record. Sinus trouble, due to Washington weather—"and you all know my opinion of Washington weather," off the record. We laughed again. We shared the opinion.

President Roosevelt at news conference

A little silence fell; he examined something on his bric-a-brac-cluttered desk. Someone said, "Thank you, Mr. President." We all murmured it. He smiled, grinned, laughed; leaned back in his chair, one hand on the arm; seemed relieved. We left.

MARCH 11, 1944. From all the soundings taken so far on the soldier-vote, the formal debate which will begin on Monday looks like a free-for-all. Everyone you talk to has a little different shading of opinion. The basic argument of the strict constitutionalists versus the liberal interpreters remains unchanged.

Harold Burton, small, trim, intelligent and capable, seemed more amused than anything else when I asked him about his candidacy for the Republican nomination. So far it seems to exist mainly in Pearson's column; Drew has been running him furiously for the past two weeks. He didn't seem to be panting much this morning. He just emphasized that both he and Taft are pledged to Governor Bricker, and that he has no plans beyond that. "Who do you think will get it?" I asked. He laughed and reminded me that he could only stand on his official statement—"I am pledged to John W. Bricker." However, he added, Dewey seems the best bet now, with Willkie trailing badly. "He seems to have real opposition," he said thoughtfully, "not just people neutral, but people actively working against him. That's different."

Guy Gillette announced yesterday, in response to a petition signed by 24,000 Iowans (and a personal request from the White House, whose occupant tried to purge him in 1938 but now is worried about Iowa) that he has abandoned his plans to retire and will run again. He faces a very stiff fight, and the hopes of the Press Gallery go with him. "He's a good Senator," people say, and the way they say it, not with any exaggerated emphasis but just with firm conviction, is significant enough of the kind of good Senator he is.

Today John Overton announced that he will retire next January when his second term ends. Grateful Louisianans, however, may persuade him to change his mind too. The Huey Long machine, to which he has a habit of making curious, sentimental references in statements that mean nothing to the general reader but doubtless have a deep significance in the haunted bayous of the Pelican State, is probably still strong enough to send him back if he wants to come. One of the Senate's hardest-working members, with a round face and drooping eyes and a bland expression that says nothing and lots of it, he has a certain satiric humor that furnishes a good many laughs. They wanted to amend the Food and Drug Act the other day to call skim milk "dry milk solids." Very well, said Overton, let's be consistent: let's call spinach "health and strength greens," and let's call castor oil "the elixir of life and the nectar of the gods." He introduced two amendments to that effect, they went to the Government Printing Office at some expense to the taxpayer, reappeared formally in printed form, and were solemnly (more or less) considered by the Senate. The vote was somthing like 77–1, but at least it was a good try. Things like that, plus his very real industry, have kept Overton from being quite the typical figure he might otherwise be.

MARCH 12, 1944. Elbert Thomas and Warren Austin, earnest and idealistic both, have launched a drive which *The New Yorker* or some other satiric journal ought to note in Peace-Through-Glowing-Phrases Division. They will find "the lowest common denominator" for peace, the Senators say: they will compile the winged words of Henry Wallace, the statements of Wendell Willkie and Franklin Roosevelt and Herbert Hoover, and they will issue words of policy and principle. Out of all this, presumably, the just and lasting peace will finally emerge.

Someday (and someday far too late) someone is going to start out by enunciating some good sound wonderful principles, and then right after he has done so, he is going to say: now let's get down to cases. Let's see how this applies to Poland, and the Balkans, and Spain, and De Gaulle and Badoglio, and China, and India, and Yugoslavia, and Russia, and the rest. On the day that unlikely, mythical Somebody says that, we are going to begin to get somewhere with the peace. And not until.

In a way it is idle even to imagine that day, however, for already we have been left behind by our allies. The time has passed for generalizations while we still generalize. The time has come to be specific, and we refuse with all the vigor at our command to be specific. Meanwhile Britain and Russia have already become specific. We still talk on, in a vacuum and to ourselves. They go briskly ahead with their plans for Tomorrow. When it dawns we shall be sadly surprised, and when we are sadly surprised we shall be bitter, and we shall blame them. We shall not do so justly, however. They looked to us and we looked away, muttering the while a few more pious platitudes.

MARCH 13, 1944. Something known as the soldier vote was formally brought up in the Senate today. Somewhere we had all heard about it before.

Tom Connally opened the third debate on the issue with a short statement defending the conference report. More soldiers would vote under it than under Public Law 712, he said. It was the best possible compromise. If it should be rejected, in his opinion no satisfactory measure could be passed by the Congress. Gene Worley came in and sat beside Green, and presently Bonner followed, and shortly thereafter John E. Rankin. Much of the discussion was taken up with members of the conference committee explaining to each other what they had or hadn't done. Warren Austin made the longest speech of the afternoon, upholding the report. Green and Hatch denounced it. It was a long, windy day, in which not even one of our most rabid New Dealers could contribute much enlightenment, even though he tried very hard.

It provided a mild diversion from the more serious business of the chamber, from a man who has a flagrant reputation on the Hill. He gains a certain wry patronage from some of the President's more violent journalistic partisans, but it has none of the admiration in it which the sincerity of Pepper, for instance, brings him. The automatic devotion of this particular Senator to the White House, in fact, is such as to give rise to the stock story about him in the Press Gallery. In that hall of legend the tale runs that the Senator, when beset by the demands of insistent nature, gets on the telephone and the following conversation ensues: "Hello?" "Hello, Boss. This is Butch." "*What,* Butch? *Again?*" "Yes, Boss." "Well"— after a thoughtful pause—"O.K., Butch." "O.K., Boss."

Certainly that is how he votes—by a sort of inevitable, inexorable, legislative peristalsis.

Pat McCarran announced today that the Judiciary Committee has tabled "indefinitely" Gillette's amendment to permit ratification of treaties by a majority vote of both houses. This is no time to amend the Constitution, Pat says.

MARCH 14, 1944. The vote was 47 to 31 today when the conference report passed the Senate, three hours after the start of the second day of the third debate. The final minutes of discussion were taken up to good effect by Barkley, making his first speech since the resignation. He was against the report and he said frankly why, in an able and sincere address.

John Rankin came on the floor during his speech, looking self-satisfied and smug. Once Barkley praised the hard work of the Senate conferees— "I know they labored under very difficult circumstances"—and Rankin looked up at the Press Gallery, laughed openly and pointed to himself. Again Barkley referred to the fact that conferees from the upper house "were up against a stone wall"—and again Rankin grinned openly at us and pointed to himself.

So ends the soldier-vote fight in the Senate. The House gets the conference report tomorrow and is expected to vote overwhelming approval after a perfunctory debate. It then goes to the President, who will be on the spot. By rights he ought to veto it, but he may not have the guts.

MARCH 15, 1944. There is life in the old dog at the other end of the Avenue yet. Two hours after the House voted 273-111 today in favor of the conference report, he dispatched a bland telegram to the 48 governors. Tell me, he asked gently, tell me: will your state laws permit you to validate the Federal war ballot? And if they do not, will you call a special session of your legislature to amend them?

It was a clever move, and it puts a number of ambitious gentlemen squarely on the spot. Warren is in the clear in California, where the legislature has specifically provided that it will accept the Federal ballot, but all the rest (and that includes Tom Dewey and John Bricker) are going to have to do some fast talking—or doubletalking, as one reporter put it. It is a moot point at the moment whether doubletalking, however, will be enough. It looks very much as though the decision has been put squarely in their laps. Of all the President's political stratagems on the issue, this is the master stroke. Nothing could be more clever.

The responsibility for the bill now rests upon the governors. If they dare to say they will not amend their laws, the veto will be theirs, not the President's. If they say they will amend their laws, then they have given their formal promise before the nation and they will not be able to duck it. If a veto should be forthcoming, Congress could not override, for that would be a repudiation of the governors rather than the President. Mr. Roosevelt has tied his opponents' coattails together. They couldn't get away from one another if they tried.

Despite the hearts and flowers some sections of the press have tried to read into the relations between the Capitol and the White House since the Barkley affair, this is the act of a man still fighting bitterly against opponents for whom he has apparently only the most vindictive dislike. As such, while the first reaction is one of startled admiration for his supreme shrewdness, the second is far more sober.

The first real day of spring came to Washington today, and with it the soft haze so characteristic of the city's good weather. Through it, as a colleague and I rode downtown in the Pennsylvania Avenue car, we could look back and see the Capitol seeming to float above the town as if suspended in the still, warm air. My companion, not normally sentimental, looked at it for a long time. Then he said soberly, "You know, that's the most beautiful sight in the world." Contemplating the magnificent building, so strong, so powerful, so sure, I was moved to agree. It is a drab heart indeed that is not touched at least a little by the sight, for then, if no other time, is one inspired to feel that whatever the shortcomings of the men on the Hill, and whatever the shortcomings of the men downtown, the nation that has such a symbol and such a challenge and such a hope cannot ever really lose.

7

A FEUDIN' SON OF TENNESSEE

MARCH 16, 1944. OPA went into its second day before the Banking and Currency Committee today, having been introduced yesterday by the skilled, charming and capable Chester Bowles. A big earnest man with a big earnest face, who talks out of the right side of his mouth and has a brief but pleasant smile, the OPA Administrator has the Senators eating out of his hand nearly all the time. He is so reasonable about it, intelligent and sincere; plus the personality. He has not been a success in advertising for nothing. His appointment to head the nation's storm center was a stroke of genius of some sort. Even people like New Jersey's capable but extremely conservative Hawkes go out of their way to compliment him on his testimony. Only Taft, the eternally obdurate, sticks to his guns and continues to ask questions. They are asked with more tolerance than most witnesses receive, however.

The agency's life runs out in June, and legislation has been introduced to continue it for another year. It will undoubtedly pass, although it may be somewhat amended to satisfy Republican objections.

The subsidies issue was raised again, this time by Francis Maloney, who pointed out in his blunt, good-humored and able fashion that there is going to be another drive to do away with them by tacking on an amendment to the Price Control Act. This simply means, he said, that the bill will go to the President, be vetoed as was the Commodity Credit Corporation bill, and OPA will then be extended by simple joint resolution in the same manner as the Commodity Credit Corporation—subsidies will simply be continued by the transfer of other funds. What right the Executive has to do something which a majority of the Congress doesn't want is, of course, another question and beyond the purview of the gracious Mr. Bowles.

McKellar took up his recurrent feud with the TVA on the floor this afternoon. When the Appropriations Committee got ready to report out the Independent Offices Appropriations bill the other day, it included at his insistence several amendments designed to provide that TVA profits, instead of going back into the agency's revolving fund, should go into the Treasury and then be filtered back by Congressional appropriation. Also, Mack wants all executive appointees earning more than $4500 a year confirmed by the Senate. Cries of "Politics!" and "Patronage!" have been leveled at his head, and in reply he has once again concentrated his fire upon David Lilienthal. The battle was not completed today and will go over to Monday. Old Mack was in a pow'ful tempuh and made one of his hell-for-breakfast speeches, full of anti-Lilienthal quotations from Dr. A. E. Morgan, former TVA chairman, and George Norris of Nebraska. Morgan referred to Lilienthal's "smart strategies," and when bald Lister Hill of Alabama arose to read a telegram from Norris praising Lilienthal, McKellar's voice rose softly in pious triumph. "You see?" he cried. "You see? He will not defend himself, but gets othuhs to dew it. Smaht strategies! Smaht strategies!" And this is the man I used to think was "not shrewd." Over and over again I am learning not to judge politicians at first glance.

MARCH 17, 1944. Bennett Champ Clark got his omnibus veterans bill (the "GI Bill of Rights," the labelers call it) approved by the Finance Committee today, and next week will introduce it for himself and as many others as can get on board. The number to date is about 80. It includes everything but the kitchen sink, and its effect upon the portly B. C.'s chances for re-election is not overlooked on the Hill. He is apparently heading into a stiff fight, although Harry Truman, who is supporting him, thinks he will win. It will be close, though, Truman admits, and there is some chance that Forrest Donnell, the Republican governor, may get the seat. B. C., the story goes, hasn't been answering his mail—and that counts, heavily.

The Republicans had a meeting the other day and emerged with Vandenberg as conference chairman, White floor leader, and Taft chairman of a steering committee of nine members. Wherry remains as whip and Harold Burton as secretary. The great Van made a valiant reference to "taking over the Senate," a prospect that is coming more and more to fascinate the minority. Twelve seats will do it—just. That will give them control of committees, which of course is more than half the battle, but it certainly won't give them voting control. There are as many mavericks on the Republican side as there are across the aisle, and unless they change a lot it seems unlikely that they will stand still long enough to be counted.

MARCH 18, 1944. Jim Murray of Montana has issued another report from his subcommittee of the Military Affairs Committee, this time on war-contract terminations and the disruptive effects they may have on the economy unless carefully handled. It is a sound job, carrying the name of one of the busiest men in the Senate. We are always seeing him sprinting down the hall in the Office Building on his way to some committee meeting, a tall rangy man with his arms swinging widely as he strides along, a rather pinched, chipmunk-cheeked face, dark clothes like a preacher, an air of intense preoccupation. Although the Congress is not moving fast enough on contract termination, it is probably moving a lot faster because Jim Murray is pushing it than it would otherwise.

MARCH 19, 1944. Canny old Jack Garner has spoken up in Texas, urging upon his fellow citizens the necessity for returning all their incumbents to Congress. That way, he says, lies control of committees and speakerships and other pleasant emoluments of the righteous political faith. As one practical answer to the system of seniority, his program seems sound. Certainly it has given his state a powerful hold on the government.

"Theodore Gilmore Bilbo," remarked the Washington *Times-Herald* the other day with admirable candor, "is a pipsqueak." Whatever he is, it is certain that the wizened character from Mississippi has managed to make himself the most hated man in the District in the short month he has been chairman of the District Committee. Under an old law passed in 1934 Washington's "alley dwellers" were to be moved out within 10 years. Bilbo's first act as chairman was to announce to 20,000 Negroes who had never heard of the law that they would have to vacate by July 20. If they didn't have any place to go, Bilbo told them  blandly, they could go to the Virginias and Kentucky and find homes. If they didn't have anything to do, he was sure the farmers in those regions would help them out. Really, Bilbo said with unctuous self-righteousness and a characteristic sardonic cruelty, he was the Negro's best friend. "I'm getting him used to moving," he said, "so that after the war he will be ready to move to West Africa."

MARCH 20, 1944. Forty-two governors have responded so far to the President's query on the soldier vote. Four say definitely they can validate the Federal ballot; 10 expect their legislatures to take favorable action; 9 evade the issue; and 19 refuse flatly to cooperate. It is quite possible that Mr. Roosevelt's political cuteness has been the deciding factor to drive some waverers into the opposite camp. Anyway, the returns are sufficiently varied so that he can now do anything he wants to and still be able to make out a politically good, if morally specious, case for it.

The poll-tax issue has suddenly come alive again; an "informed source" has been sending up trial balloons in the press today. The story even includes some reference to Barkley's willingness to press for action on a bill "within a couple of weeks." If so, a filibuster is inevitable. John McClellan stated it succinctly the other day. "They've been given fair warning that we will filibuster if they bring it up," he told me frankly. "So they can't charge us with interfering with the war effort. They know what the result will be if they force the issue. They can't blame us for what happens." The principle may be questionable, perhaps, but the logic is unimpeachable.

After the session this afternoon we went down on the floor to talk to McKellar about his amendments to place tighter controls on TVA's use of funds, which will probably come up tomorrow. The Senator, fingering his Phi Beta Kappa Key and surveying us with drooping eyelids over his little uncommunicative eyes, was at his blandest. He didn't expect a bit of trouble, really; everything looked fine. Did he know that Boss Crump of Memphis, his bosom political buddy, had come out against him on this issue? Yes, he had seen that. Of course that wouldn't mean any permanent break, would it? "Oh, no! Oh, no! Oh, no!"—in the heartily scoffing tone which implies that the questioner is slightly touched—"At least Ah hope not. Mistuh Crump and Ah ah ve'y deah friends. Ve'y deah friends. Oh, no! At least"—thumping the questioner jovially in the chest—"Ah said Ah hope not." "He's a devil, that McKellar," one of his former constituents in the Press Gallery remarked the other day in grudging admiration. It was a true word. Seventy-five years old and the toughest in-fighter in the Senate, shrewd, tricky, unscrupulous and ruthless—a feudin' son of Tennessee.

MARCH 21, 1944. McKellar swung into his second day of battle today against David Lilienthal, the man who wasn't there. Although absent in Tennessee and necessarily silent, the TVA chairman managed to give the Senator quite a fight. Or at least McKellar acted that way. The air was empurpled with denunciations and derogations. From time to time some particularly apt phrase would occur to the Senator and he would repeat it with loving emphasis. "His eely, oily, ingratiating, insinuating ways," he cried once; and struck with it, paused for a moment and then went back over it with tender care: "His eely—oily—ingratiating—insinuating—ways!" It was a valiant contest, all right, only interfered with by Lister Hill, who took TVA's side of the discussion in a speech that managed to knock the props out from under Mack pretty well. This was particularly true when the bald, slender Alabaman challenged McKellar to produce evidence of the attacks which he claimed Lilienthal was "making against me night and day in my state." Mack attempted to duck this by quoting Dr. A. E. Morgan, but Hill kept returning to it with gentle persistence. Finally in desperation Mack left the floor, returning with a huge scrapbook full of newspaper clippings. Through it he hunted in vain for substantiation. Everything he read somehow failed to mention him by name, or even, in fact, by any very direct implication. He eventually sat down in frustrated anger and closed the book. Connally came to his defense at one point, asserting that "every Senator knows the sort of sly, insinuating, creeping" (this with the famous Connally gestures, the arms drawn in toward the sides, the shoulders hunched, the hands jabbing forward stealthily at appropriate intervals) "attacks which the Senator refers to." Hill hunched and gestured right back. "Of course," he said blandly, "if this is one of *those* attacks—where the knife goes into a man—" (his hand darted forward and the knife went into the man) "where he gives it a twist—" (he gave it a twist) "then I should certainly be against it, and so would every Senator." It was a perfect physical parody of the senior Senator from Texas, done with just the right amount of exaggeration. When all was said and done, although in all probability none of the votes McKellar claims he has were changed by it, Hill's speech had both defended the TVA and exposed Mack's opposition for what it is, simply a feud against Lilienthal who apparently hasn't yielded to pressure the way he was expected to.

McKellar cautioned his colleagues, of course, that he wanted them to vote "purely on the merits of the case and not because of any resentment they may feel concerning Lilienthal's attacks on me."

Midway in the afternoon I went over to the District Committee room, just off the floor, to cover a brief meeting of the Finance Committee. The bill under discussion was H.R. 4410, to extend for 90 days the duty-free importation of feed grains. After the government witnesses had unanimously testified against it on the ground that Canada was taking advantage of the tariff moratorium to boost the price of her grain to American purchasers, the committee asked them to leave and prepared to reach a decision. It was a rather instructive study in a certain type of legislation. Everyone agreed that it was a bad thing for Canada to gouge the United States, and everyone agreed that it probably wouldn't increase our grain supplies enough to make it worth while. But heavy-jowled old Dave Walsh of Massachusetts, speaking in his deep, soft, hurried voice, said that the governor of Massachusetts had written him that the farmers wanted it; and Bob Taft pointed out that the Quaker Oats people were very anxious to have it go through, with an amendment permitting importation of rolled oats for human consumption; and Walter George kept coming back in the midst of a logical statement against it to the fact, stated rather wistfully, that "the poultry people are certainly desirous of having it go through"; and thin, gray Peter Gerry of Rhode Island, encouraged by his closest crony, Harry Byrd, emphasized that the farmers certainly did want it, all right; and John Danaher, while admitting it wouldn't do much good, agreed; and then too, as Walter George pointed out once more, "the poultry people are *certainly* desirous . . ." "I move the chairman report the bill out favorably to the Senate," said Dave Walsh briskly. The motion was approved.

MARCH 22, 1944. Ed Johnson spoke in Chicago last night, formally breaking at last with the President after months of increasingly open criticism. It was an excellent speech of its kind, from the last Democratic officeholder left in Colorado. He has just gradually gotten fed up, and being like Barkley an honest man he has finally cut loose and said so. "That's one thing about Johnson," somebody remarked today. "He says what he thinks." It is an admirable trait. The big, slow-spoken Westerner may be a portent. If so, he is one of many.

The Democratic National Committee is apparently beginning to feel that it is fighting with its back to the wall. The Second District of Oklahoma has suddenly become a formal battleground. The Committee has decided to stop the Republican trend if it can, and all the rabbits are being pulled out of the hat. The most significant is Barkley, who has finally agreed after much beseeching to go into Oklahoma and speak for the Democratic candidate. Elmer Thomas, worried about his own chances for

re-election as Senator, is already in the district stumping it for the party, and from the House the very able Mike Monroney has also consented to participate. On the Republican side Senator Moore has left for home to throw his slight figure and dry, flat voice into the battle. Like Willkie in Wisconsin, the Democrats in the Second Oklahoma District have decided to make that district the Symbol. It will become clear next Tuesday whether they have made the right choice.

Debate this afternoon lasted for four hours and 54 minutes, and still we didn't reach a vote on the TVA amendments. Old Mack was at his most indignant, ranting and roaring one moment and sweet as a suckling dove the 'next. In the last few days, he remarked blandly, he had noted that the newspapers were "full of Lilienthal's feud with me." The matter has been exaggerated "out of all proportion to its true state," he added, intimating that the whole thing was rather surprising. Lister Hill was again diligently determined to spike McKellar's allegations, and was presently joined by John Bankhead, unhappily but doggedly opposing the man who once, untold years ago, was his roommate in college. Barkley also arose to condemn Mack's position. Even if Lilienthal had attacked McKellar and every other member of the Congress, Barkley roared in some wrath, he would not vote to punish the entire Tennessee Valley because of one

Kenneth McKellar

man. Bob La Follette and George Aiken also came to the agency's defense. Rankin came over from the House, "lobbying on the right side for once," in the dry words of one reporter. Homer Bone, the liberal Washington Stater with the crutches, the drawn, unwell-appearing face and the uproariously flamboyant line of chatter, finally got up and said he was going to make a point of order against every one of Mack's 16 amendments on the ground that they are legislation in an appropriations bill, something that is against the rules of the Senate. This was late in the day, and after some consultation back and forth between Barkley, White and McKellar, it was decided to go over until Friday—skipping Thursday for no good reason, apparently—except that, as Barkley said, "we just didn't feel like working." Either that, or both sides expect to do a lot of digging for votes all day tomorrow, which is more likely.

McKellar's opposition is picking up considerable strength, principally because his attack on TVA is so openly and blatantly dictated by his personal hatred for Lilienthal. As he does with everything, he is trying to put this on a personal basis—demanding that Senators vote his way out of personal friendship—and it is just possible that he may succeed with this tactic. But Barkley assured us after the session, "We're picking up quite a lot of territory—territory we didn't expect to get."

MARCH 23, 1944. The inside story of Secretary of State Cordell Hull's very hush-hush huddle with the Foreign Relations Committee yesterday is gradually coming out. Apparently it was simply one more attempt to pile words upon words to create a foreign policy. His pious and empty 17-point statement yesterday served, if anything, to make the fog which envelops the huge old pile of fantastic architecture housing the State Department even more dense and impenetrable. His chat with the Senators evidently did even less to dispel it. Questioned about it today at his press conference, he remarked blandly that he is "glad, at last, after two years of expounding foreign policy, that people are waking up to the fact that there is one." If they are waking up to the fact that there is one, which seems doubtful, they are also more than awake to the fact that whatever it is, it is being deliberately withheld from them.

Chairman William Davis of the War Labor Board came up today for the OPA hearings, a short, stocky man with a square stocky face topped by gray hair, a slow, drawling, unimpressed voice and a tendency to handle tendentious Senators as though they were unruly children. "Just a moment, please," he told Taft in unhurried reproof once. "Let me finish." The Ohioan, in fact, became quite heated over the Little Steel formula and the railway labor case. Dr. Davis backed out of that gracefully by pointing out that WLB was deliberately kept out of the picture, and then went on to expound his theory of how the Little Steel formula could be broken and still remain unbroken. It was all rather involved and put Taft in a stew from which he only barely managed to rescue himself and regain his good temper. Davis continued to talk on through the Senator's frequent interruptions, unmoved, unhurried, unimpressed. He makes an excellent impression, takes a middle-of-the-road view of things in general, has a good sense of humor, and handles himself with the instinctive but quietly unassuming arrogance of a man who knows exactly what he is talking about. One begins to see why he manages to hang onto his job the way he does in spite of storms and tempests.

McKellar tried strategy today. The Appropriations Committee was called into session this morning, and from its meeting Mack emerged with the news that it had decided to drop all of his TVA amendments with the single exception of the one requiring the agency to turn its funds back into the Treasury—everything but the one that would really deal it a body blow, in other words. This will probably pick up a few votes. Homer Bone is still going to raise his point of order though, he told me, explaining that TVA was by court decision virtually a private corporation and as such could not operate efficiently if it had to come running to the Hill every time it wanted to do something, and also emphasizing Jim Mead's point that in years of auditing by the General Accounting Office no irregularities have ever been discovered. And Lister Hill, while "delighted" at the amendments dropped, still doesn't like the one retained and will fight it on the floor. We shall see tomorrow whether McKellar still has his votes.

MARCH 24, 1944. Mack had his votes, as it turned out, 39 of them: not too many, but enough to overcome the 26 mustered on the other side. A dutiful group of his colleagues and a number of obliging Republicans fell obediently into line and delivered as promised. The McKellar method (which consists of two parts—first to wield that Appropriations Committee ax for all it's worth and second to make a feverishly personal, sentimental appeal for votes on the ground of friendship) proved itself again. He got his amendment through and also another which would necessitate Senate confirmation of all government employees earning $4500 or more. The House has killed both before in previous years and the hopes of TVA's supporters are now transferred there.

Homer Bone made his point of order, which under the rules is not debatable. Instead of ruling on it promptly as he should have done, Wallace delayed. McKellar immediately jumped up and asked that it be "considered." Millard Tydings, remarking innocently as he so often does that "in the interests of clarification" he wanted to make a point of order himself, thereupon raised the point that the Bone motion was not germane to the subject under discussion. Wallace, suddenly waking up to the situation, ruled that Tydings was out of order, and McKellar again jumped up and appealed Wallace's ruling to the Senate. There then ensued nearly an hour of parliamentary argument—simply an extended back-and-forth clatter about the rules of the Senate. Finally in exasperation the Vice-President remarked that he regarded the appeal of his ruling as "a parliamentary trick," and then the fat was in the fire. Old Mack surged to his feet roaring. The Chair had called his action a parliamentary trick. The Chair *knew* he was not the sort of man to trick people! The Chair *knew* he would never do such a thing. He regarded the Chair's statement as unfair and unwarranted. More than that, it was downright damnable! He demanded that the Chair retract that statement! Wallace, who had tried without success several times to interrupt this tirade, remarked in some disgust that he would withdraw his remark. After an hour of this sort of thing the Senate voted 47–16 to override his ruling. Comments on the V.P. in the halls and elevators afterwards were scathing. No matter what he does, he gets it in the neck—and this time quite unjustly, for he simply got caught in the path of the McKellar steamroller and wasn't nimble enough to jump aside.

Following that, Dick Russell's amendment to ban transfer of appropriated funds from established agencies to executive-order agencies which have been in existence for more than a year, without direct appropriation by Congress, was brought up. The Republicans then did some interesting flipflops. First C. Douglass Buck of Delaware, a tall innocuous man with a little black mustache, offered an amendment to the amendment which would specifically exempt the President's Fair Employment Practices Committee. This passed 37–31, nearly all the Republicans voting for it. Bennett Champ Clark arose in great indignation to denounce the pressure that had been put upon the Senate to retain FEPC. Lobbyist Edgar Brown, a tall ascetic Negro with a beard like Haile Selassie's who is always hanging around the Capitol, had buttonholed him, Clark cried, and told him that "the Senate is going to exempt FEPC." "Why are we?" Bennett wanted to know. "Because we want you to," replied Brown with serene arrogance. This is no way to handle Bennett Champ, or indeed any Senator, and the reaction on the floor to this little story was immediate. Dick Russell also took occasion to point out scathingly to the Republicans, and he was joined by Walter George, that for a party which condemned bureaucracy they were certainly inconsistent in wanting to leave FEPC unchecked. This was a nicely calculated line of attack by a Southerner who wants to get rid of FEPC for reasons of his own, and it successfully embarrassed the Republicans. When Ed Johnson moved to reconsider the vote, the motion was upheld 30–28, and presently by a vote of 32–35, after being amended to put FEPC back in and widened by Styles Bridges to include agencies set up as subsidiaries of government corporations, the Russell amendment carried. The Republicans in the space of an hour had made a voting record on both sides of the Negro question. Rather inadvertently, all things considered.

Before the session ended at 7:14 the Senate had also come within an inch of requiring a General Accounting Office audit of some 30 government corporations. It failed by a handful of votes on Aiken's motion to suspend the rules, the necessary two-thirds couldn't quite be mustered. All in all, however, the Senate had done pretty well for one day in its drive against the Executive. On few occasions has it ever passed so many restrictive measures in one legislative session—a significant enough indication as to just how far the spurious good fellowship of the post-Barkley era extends on the Hill. No farther, apparently, than it does downtown.

8

THE LOST CRUSADE

MARCH 25, 1944. Twenty-five Republicans from the House met with Cordell Hull yesterday for a vague, inconclusive, useless two-and-a-half hours of doubletalk. From it they emerged embittered a little more, feeling (and rightly so, considering they have supported the Administration consistently) that they should have been told much more. They commented again, and bitterly, upon Hull's "evident distrust of the people"—an attitude which in any other land would precede active fear of the people, followed by active suppression of the people, but here only means that the people, instead of being told the truth, will just be lied to with bland and paternal condescension.

More and more it becomes apparent that perhaps the major thing wrong with our war and our foreign policy is age. The men at the top are old, without imagination, without enthusiasm, without heart. It is an old man's war in which all the young men are permitted to do is the dying, and it will be an old man's peace in which all the young men will be permitted to do is prepare their sons for dying.

MARCH 26, 1944. The Truman Committee is beginning to succumb like everything else to the virus of politics, an unfortunate occurrence, and one which time and the passage of the election may heal. Certainly it is to be hoped, for it would be no small matter if the committee's fine work should be hampered permanently by partisanship.

Harry Truman has taken it upon himself to issue a statement urging support of "present leadership" until "the crisis" is over. In extremely careful phraseology he urges this thesis for about 250 words: so careful, in fact, that nearly everyone in the Press Gallery has concluded that this is the tip-off on the invasion. Few have interpreted the statement as another endorsement of the fourth term, even though the Senator is one of its most industrious backers. Perhaps the timing more than anything else, the fact that there is no good excuse for it right now—so far as we know officially—leads to this belief. At any rate the feeling is quite general.

Owen Brewster, however, one of the touchiest men in the Senate when it comes to anything implying Democratic favoritism, has decided that this is just one more declaration of war on the third front, and has persuaded Burton and Joe Ball to join him in a stern reminder to the chairman that he can back Roosevelt as a Senator if he wants to, but not as chairman of the committee. What effect this has had on Truman no one knows, for he has left for Seattle where the amiable Mon Wallgren is already on the ground getting ready to blow the Liberty Ships out of the water with another investigation. Perhaps when he returns oil will flow on the waters and all will be well. This is not too certain, however.

Aubrey Williams, one of the most double-dyed of New Dealers, had dinner with the President the other night and then returned to Atlanta to write a signed article about it for the Atlanta *Journal*. In it he says he was shocked at the President's poor appearance and very evident weariness, and came away with the "very strong impression" that he will not be a candidate. For the record it should be noted somewhere now that a good many people in Washington are beginning to have that hunch and have had it in varying degrees of intensity for months. For the record, though, let it be said that it is only a hunch. Only one man knows, and he isn't talking.

MARCH 27, 1944. Eric Johnston of the U.S. Chamber of Commerce came up today to testify in favor of continuing OPA; a neat, trim, efficient and forceful young man; "Candidate Johnston," as one Republican Senator remarked drily afterwards. In looks he suggests Robert Taylor of the movies, without the blacks and whites—done in halftone, as it were, on a somewhat smaller scale. There is something rather deliberate about the emphasis and the forcefulness, also; the word, I think, is "practiced." The charm goes on and off with brisk precision, lost, sad to say, on Taft and a line of stern-faced GOP cohorts, none of whom seemed overly impressed. All in all, despite characteristics which are vulnerable to a certain amount of attack, Johnston is a sound and capable fellow. Somehow I got the impression from watching the Senators look him over, however, that what they want this year is not someone young, not someone dynamic or forceful or imaginative. Just somebody safe. Somebody good and safe.

MARCH 28, 1944. Wendell Willkie, shadow-boxing in Wisconsin, has found his issue if he only has sense enough to stick with it. He hit upon it yesterday, and it is foreign policy—the only kind of foreign-policy issue the Republicans can pursue and still not seriously endanger the country. In a slashing speech he attacked the Darlan deal, the Vichy deal, the Badoglio deal, the Polish deal, lighting into the hypocrisy that has already come close to destroying the moral prestige and good name of the United States. The practice of fighting a war so that you can re-establish the very thing you were against when someone else wanted to do it has become Mr. Willkie's target. If he can stick to that, holding firm to the higher objectives of a truly international policy but flaying for all he is worth the tragic, deliberate stupidities which have characterized our policy to date in the war, then he may really have something.

A wistful letter from Bernard Baruch, released this morning, points out that although more than a month has passed since he filed his report on reconversion, and although the Congress had much to say at the time about the bypassing of the legislative branch, nothing at all has been done on the Hill. The point is well taken, especially since everybody is getting ready to go home on March 31 and not come back until April 17. Why, nobody knows—except that there is an "agreement." Barkley has agreed with White and Joe Martin has agreed with John McCormack and everyone else has agreed that that's just dandy. In actual cold fact it is inexcusable. Reconversion is hanging fire and a terrific rumpus has been raised because "Congress was being bypassed"—yet here goes Congress off home. There are many annoying things about the way the institution operates, but they are human mistakes, mostly, and they can

Wendell Willkie

be understood and suffered without too much protest. But there is one thing absolutely and truly inexcusable, and that is willful delay.

MARCH 29, 1944. The Democrats won in the Oklahoma Second District by around 4000 votes, despite the valiant efforts of Ed Moore and Pappy O'Daniel. Barkley returned today from his successful stump-tour in behalf of the Democratic candidate, exhilarated by the smell of the hustings. "You don't realize," he told us dreamily, "how much I enjoyed it, to get out there and talk to the people after sitting around here. You just don't realize...." If there has been any doubt in his mind about his own campaign—and there has perhaps been a little—this has probably settled it. Politics, besides being a great many other things, is also fun. If his decision to run again hadn't already been made, it is probably made now. They are after him to go into New York state and campaign for a candidate there, he said, but (with a sudden chuckle) "Maybe I'd better quit while my rep is still good." It is a rather interesting contrast with the old days, when the official endorsement came from 1600 Pennsylvania. Barkley seems to be the star performer now.

MARCH 30, 1944. A couple of the powers of Washington came up to testify on the OPA today. President Edward O'Neal of the Farm Bureau, a shaky, sly old man with an innocent expression and a Texas voice, and Albert Goss, master of the Grange, a pink-cheeked, small, grandfatherly old gentleman with an air of gentle reproof for all who consider his motives questionable, came up to see their boys and talk the situation over with them. O'Neal, whose quivering conversation is filled with "I was down at the White House the other day talking to Jimmy—," "I was down talking to Don the other day—," "I saw Fred Vinson about that, and he said—," conducts himself with the bland assurance years of cooperation from Capitol Hill have given him. "You do think price control will work all right for another year, then?" Bob Wagner of New York asked him. "If you will make the amendments we suggest and write in the changes we advocate, perhaps it will," O'Neal replied with serene self-confidence.

Goss, who took a much more reasonable view on the whole, said that the Grange was still against subsidies but that in order to be "realistic" about the situation it would probably be necessary to continue them, and consequently he urged a limitation of $1,500,000,000. Maloney said that he was delighted to hear that, because that was exactly what he had tried to get through the Senate a month ago. Goss then backed water abruptly, emphasizing that he was not in favor of subsidies—just embracing them out of necessity. "So am I," said Maloney promptly in his squawky, humorous voice. "I'm entirely against them, and I think it's too bad we have to have them, but—here we are." Maloney and Danaher, in fact, working with the cooperation which often distinguishes them, were rather inclined to take Mr. Goss apart and strew the pieces around the committee table. The firm of Danaher and Maloney is not one to tangle with unprepared. Both partners are shrewd, witty, keen-minded, sincerely patriotic and thoroughly capable. Nor is either one above a little blarney when the occasion calls for it. After he got through reducing the Goss logic, Maloney added, "Of course I want you to know that I am very proud indeed of my membership in the Grange." "And we're proud to have you, Senator," replied Goss with equal blandness. Maloney must have noted a certain amount of amusement at the press table, for he glanced over at us quickly with an impish grin and muttered, "Well, I have one apple tree."

The Senate met for an hour or so, principally so that it could recess again until Saturday. Technically the President has until midnight Friday to decide on the soldier-vote bill, and if Congress should be in recess by then and he had not signed it, there would be a pocket veto. Inasmuch as they want to give him ample opportunity to do whichever of the three things he is going to do—veto it, sign it, or let it become law without his signature—they decided to delay the start of their vacation for a day. The tall, heavy, broad-faced, white-haired Swede from Minnesota, Henrik Shipstead, finally got approval for his resolution to investigate the legal authority for Executive orders. Barkley supported it, but suggested that it be amended to restrict it to the legal basis for them and not to the occasion which gave rise to each one, something the Republicans rather wanted to go into. On second thought, however, they seem to have agreed that to do so would consume entirely too much time and get into political controversy in a field where they don't particularly care to go. After all, other Presidents will be issuing Executive orders after this one is gone, and you don't want to tie your own hands by being too particular—the same theory, in fact, which has prevented the Republicans, in this year in which they have virtual control of both branches, from doing anything about the amendment to limit the President to two terms.

MARCH 31, 1944. 'Way off in Wisconsin, so remote that only its faintest echoes reach the Hill, seeming to have nothing to do with the affairs of the country as they function here, a familiar husky voice is crying in the wilderness. The campaign to let Willkie talk himself to death in a vacuum is nearing the end of its second week. Next Tuesday will decide whether or not it has been successful. It was a shrewd move, a combination of circumstance, strategy and his own desire to join the issue and fight it out. The issue has been joined—with empty air. The battle is being fought out—with nothingness. If he can survive that, he will deserve to survive anything.

Ever since he entered public life four years ago, he has acted like a man who is not a politician but knows he ought to be and consequently is doing his damnedest. But politics is a good deal more than rules and formulas. It is an instinct, and Willkie apparently doesn't have it. If he does win the nomination and election he will still have to deal with a Congress dominated by leaders in whose faces barely a scant six months ago he threw the arrogant statement, "I can have the Republican nomination if I want it." On that day he came very close to guaranteeing that he would never be President of the United States. Politics is an instinct for handling people. You don't handle them that way.

As for the Republican Party, on the other hand, it will in all probability be muffing the best chance it has had for a long, long time if it turns him down and accepts a trimmer, a do-nothing, or a general. At least he is constructive, at least he is progressive, at least he represents an aggressive hope. At least he possesses the ability to grow to a stature somewhat commensurate with the office to which he aspires. The same cannot be said for most of his opponents within the party.

All over the country there is a great instinctive protest against the continuation of Roosevelt in power. It shows itself in a million places, and as noticeably as anywhere else in the liberal journals which are hopefully urging the Republicans to nominate *somebody* to whom progressive opinion can turn. Deep down under, America is restless under a domination which has continued too long: it just doesn't feel right about it. And yet unless the Republicans meet the challenge with a really good man, the country will turn once more to Roosevelt.

It is a curious thing, this vast psychological protest, unthinking, unvocal, truly instinctive, with which people are hoping so desperately that the Republicans will give them the answer. But people will know whether or not the Republicans *have* given them the answer, and they will vote accordingly. If the party comes forward with a trumped-up legend, an empty head and a platform of platitudes, it will have missed the great chance to return to power with a truly democratic and liberal administration.

APRIL 1, 1944. April Fool's Day couldn't really pass without a joke. Theodore Francis Green and Scott Lucas gave us one—another soldier-vote bill. It hasn't a prayer of passage, but it will annoy everybody intensely and keep the issue alive for a while longer, and maybe force the Republicans to extend their voting record on the matter a little more. All in all, it is probably worth it from one point of view.

That point of view was officially summed up by the President himself in a cogent and reasonable discussion of the conference bill. He didn't like it very well, he said; he regarded it as impossible to tell whether or not more soldiers would vote than under Public Law 712; accordingly he would let it become law without his signature. ("I wonder how that jibes with his demand that the Congress stand up and be counted?" Brewster asked tartly. "Where does the President stand and how shall he be counted?") And he urgently requested the Congress to at least— "at least," when it took four months and endless wrangling to get even the slim Federal ballot of the conference report—extend the Federal ballot to overseas servicemen. Theodore Francis popped up and put in the bill to do just this in today's brief session. All he wants to do is give the Federal ballot to all overseas servicemen who have not received a state ballot by October 1—the provision of the conference bill requiring application for a state ballot would be removed—the certification by state legislatures would be repealed. In other words, Green wants everybody to give up everything, write off five months of controversy, three debates, six separate bills, and more than three weeks of seesaw Senate–House conferences, and just go right back to the beginning and start all over again. But it will keep the issue alive, and it will furnish more campaign material, and perhaps that is reason enough for its introduction.

The President nominated Homer Bone to be a judge of the Ninth Circuit Court in San Francisco today, and the Senate confirmed it immediately without even the formality of referring it to Judiciary. The Senator had gone to the Naval Hospital at Bethesda, Md., for treatment of the bone injury and illness which have kept him on crutches for months. A quick, nervous man, his drawn, pale, sick-looking face conceals the infallible humor with which he manages by sheer will-power to keep 'em laughing. I remember offhand only one remark of his, but it is typical. A reporter approached him for a story one day, and—"What do you want to do, you scrivening jackal?" said Homer Bone. "Pillory me some more on the point of your unprincipled pen? Jesus Christ, my Samsonian locks have been cut so short already by the press that I'd hate to have anyone try to trim them with a blunt ax." All of this in a very rapid, quick, amusing way of speaking. It is the way he talks most of the time. At other times, also in a quick, somewhat more terse fashion, he will discuss some point of parliamentary order with great emphasis. His third mood is one in which the eagle screams and Homer becomes more and more flamboyant and indignant. He is a good man and a true liberal, and an excellent adornment for any court.

Every time a member of the Senate dies or moves on to some other office, the continuity of the Congress is re-emphasized. In the long run, aside from the great issues which confront it from time to time, the individual man matters little. Men come, stay for a while, and go, and others take their places. The institution lives on.

APRIL 3, 1944. Every once in a while in the press up here you get to work and dig out a good, sound, factual, dull story about the operations of Congress—one of those things you know perfectly well the office downtown will cut to pieces or withhold altogether because nobody has the space to run it, and anyway, who's interested? Nonetheless, from time to time in a sort of defiant desperation you say to yourself, "I don't care; damn it, people ought to know about this." So you go ahead and write it. It's purely a moral triumph.

In pursuit of such a worthy but foredoomed objective I went around today to see a few people about proposals to streamline Congress. The subject is in one of its periodic states of agitation at the moment, various articles are appearing here and there in some of the magazines, and Maloney is industriously filling up the *Record* with reprints of editorials. He has remarked frequently that if he doesn't do anything else while he is in the Senate he is going to start the ball rolling on that. His efforts are commendable, even though they haven't produced much so far but talk. Talk helps in the long run.

Maloney himself has gone off to Connecticut for the recess, but Taft was in, thoughtfully clipping his fingernails with a small pair of scissors as he slowly considered the legislative problem. "Obviously something should be done," he said in that flat, reasonable voice. "But I hardly hold with the theory that Congress ought to be turned into an executive agency. Congress *isn't* an executive agency. Congress is a jury, in a sense, expressing the will of the people and passing upon proposals put before it. I think you can overdo this streamlining business. . . . I do think, however, that much of the trouble lies in the fact that the agencies downtown and the Congress up here are working on different philosophies. I think perhaps if you get a Republican administration in" (this with a thoughtful examination of the right index nail, which received special attention by way of emphasis) "if you get a Republican administration in, then you won't have that disagreement. . . . They say 'Congress is just a debating society.' Well, it is, to a considerable extent, and to a considerable extent that's what it's supposed to be. No Congress can expect to become expert on all the many complex problems of administration. I do believe the number of committees should be reduced, and in the case of technical committees like Appropriations, a larger staff of expert assistants should be provided . . . but I don't hold with the idea that Congress ought to be an executive body."

White, looking kindly and benign as always, and as always swamped with work, said that one of the main things he wanted to see is a reduction in the number of committees. "The way it is now, why, my gosh, a man has so many things to keep up with that he can't possibly handle them all. Particularly in the minority, where there just aren't enough of us to go 'round. Unless you can keep up with the committees day by day, you've simply lost the thread of them and you never can catch up. But I'm workin' on it; I'm workin' on it. One thing I particularly want to do away with is this matter of proxy votin' in committees, and I want to enforce real committee quorums, and I'd like to see the number of committee membahships a man can hold cut down to three at the most. . . . The basic problem simply goes back to the fact that government has become so gigantic and complex, touching the life of the individual in a thousand ways never dreamed of a generation ago. But I'm a nut on this thing, and I'm goin' to have somethin' definite soon."

As for things now in the hopper, Guy Gillette on July 1, 1943, submitted a resolution providing for a study of the rules of the Senate. It was referred to Rules Committee and has been there ever since gathering dust. The same fate has befallen a concurrent resolution by Maloney, providing for a joint committee composed of six from the House and six from the Senate to study the whole problem of making Congress more workable; and a resolution by Bob La Follette which sets out in characteristic fashion to state exactly what objectives it hopes to achieve and then tells exactly how to achieve them. The last would boil the committees down to 13, have the majority of them composed of 12 members (24 for Appropriations, as befits the extent of its work), and authorize them to act jointly with corresponding committees of the House. It is entirely typical of the man who proposed it, an admirable character in a great many ways, not the least of them being the dogged persistence with which he has gone on fighting for 20 years for things he has only rarely succeeded in attaining. It would have broken a less determined man long ago, and even he sometimes shows a certain humorless tiredness. But he sticks with it regardless, and by that fact alone contributes much to his country.

APRIL 5, 1944. Wendell Willkie made his choice, and today can repent it in vain. With the same political ineptness that has distinguished him throughout, he chose to make isolationist Wisconsin the battleground for his internationalist ideas. Like the Republican Old Guard which went into the traditionally Democratic Oklahoma Second District and cried "We dare you to beat us!," Willkie in his turn walked blindly and deliberately into defeat under the strange impression that he could pick a fight and win it against people who wouldn't fight because their minds were made up long ago.

It was bad politics, stupid strategy, and inept planning. It was also a personal tragedy for a man who, whatever his faults, is honest and courageous and forward-looking. If it results in his losing the nomination, as everyone here is positive it will, then it will prove also to be a tragedy for a Republican Party which chose to play it safe in an age in which only the imaginative could succeed.

Old Guard jubilation on the Hill, of course, was resounding this morning. Butler and Wherry, in whose state Willkie makes his second primary bid next Tuesday, were smugly unsurprised. Joe Ball, whose lieutenant commander, Harold Stassen of Minnesota, came into port in second place, said he thought it showed Dewey's strength but also showed Stassen's, since he had made such a good record under the handicaps of absence and a relatively unorganized campaign. Wallace White remarked drily that one swallow doesn't make a summer, and Taft said much the same. "I might say that this kills Willkie deader than a doornail," he told me. And then with his sudden, sardonic chuckle, he added, "except that that might be premature." He ought to know.

APRIL 6, 1944. Willkie threw in the towel last night like a man who, scorning the use of the airplane, tried to fly by flapping his arms and when that didn't work gave up in disgust.

Comments on the Hill were judicious in some cases, disturbed in others, sincerely respectful in one or two. None were regretful. Only good-hearted Warren Austin, apparently seeing in the Wisconsin debacle the same reactionary triumph that Gerald Nye crowed into it, asked earnestly whether or not it meant that the Midwest has "sagged back" into isolationism. He regretted Willkie's withdrawal although he would not say so directly, preferring to maintain that "the cause is the thing." Who else will be found to carry it on in the Republican Party is something he did not venture to discuss. Taft remarked that it was "regrettable that Mr. Willkie in withdrawing should have expressed opposition to other elements in the Republican Party." The rest of his statement sounded a note of obvious relief. Wherry for one sounded respectful and quite sincere when he praised Willkie's courage—the Nebraskan's instincts are basically sound, whatever his personal enthusiasms. Others hailed "unity" with hysterical thankfulness. Tom Dewey, strong and silent, "attended to a stack of legislative matters" on his desk in Albany and refused to comment.

9

A RISING WIND

APRIL 7, 1944. Eastland, his round face beaming blandly and his figure drooped in its perpetual slouch, says happily that he and his buddies from the great Southland are all jest as busy as bees durin' recess, preparin' no less than a thousan' amendments to the anti-poll-tax bill. First off, Jim says, there are going to have to be 48 amendments to take care of some of the peculiar No'then state laws. After that, there's a good many other things have to be tended to. The whole thing is perfectly barefaced and candid. Since each of the amendments will have to be printed, to the extent of some 1000 copies each, it is also going to run into quite a little money before the fun is over.

Where there is so much smoke, however, there is bound to be fire. Apparently the recurring cautious hints we have been getting about the bill are correct: a definite date—the week of April 24—is even beginning to be bruited about. Despite the Democrats' own need for party harmony, which this issue will of course blow sky-high in a South already'profoundly upset, and despite the knowledge that to raise the issue this year will be to throw the Senate deliberately into a deadlock in the midst of the invasion months, the measure's sponsors are evidently going to bring it up. Their idealism cannot be criticized, although their sense of timing is appalling. The reputation of Congress is in for a new decline, this one self-imposed.

During the debate we shall hear two basic fallacies reiterated over and over again. The first will be offered by the anti-poll-tax forces, who will say that the bill is Constitutional; it is not, because it would set aside control of voting qualifications specifically vested in the states. The second will be offered by the Southerners, who will say that the poll tax is humanly and morally defensible; it is not. If everybody would just admit those two things on the first day, there might not be any filibuster at all. There would certainly be no debate. There would just be a vote.

Barkley is going to try to get cloture after a day or two of debate, and is apparently picking up a lot of support on the Republican side. If he can hold his New Dealers and middle-of-the-roaders together on the Democratic side, he may be able to get the limitation. It takes a two-thirds vote, and if he gets it, he indicates, the move then will be to drop the bill and immediately introduce and pass a constitutional amendment that would, if ratified by three-fourths of them, be binding upon the states.

APRIL 8, 1944. A certain Republican Senator, whose delight in intrigue can only be termed irresponsible when it is not downright vicious, has confided to the press that "a definite change" has occurred in the Truman Committee's reports of late. "Haven't you noticed it?" he asks innocently, and people who would never read into the committee's findings anything but the sober constructive criticisms they are begin to get upset and look at them cross-eyed. He's a smooth worker, this fellow, and I shall always remember one day in the Senate when he gave a most reasonable speech on a vital topic. "That would be a fine speech," one of the press remarked, "if that man only had a principle." Unfortunately he hasn't; on that we are all agreed.

His latest little campaign is complete with an inside story. It seems that Harry Truman got called down to the White House, he says, and from on high there were dangled before him two good jobs, the Vice-Presidency and the Secretaryship of War. Either would satisfy an honest man's ambitions, and in the case of one, at least, providing Roosevelt is re-elected and is overtaken by his frailties, the offer might far exceed the recipient's wildest dreams. But there was a price, our informant tells us, and the price was that the Truman Committee soft-pedal the criticisms and lay on with the trowel. This information, he says, has come to him from Republican sources on the committee and also from the Army, which of course has always gotten along beautifully with Truman and would certainly have no reason to smear him—much. Look into it, he urges the press; and being conscientious, and during recess hard up for a story, some of us undoubtedly will. In all likelihood the end result will be just what he wants it to be—a considerable shadow thrown upon the work of one of the finest and most constructive committees Congress has ever known.

If the facts alone could refute such a story, then it might be shown up for what it is. Unfortunately they will not be sufficient. This Senator, clever, cynical, and as far as anyone can see almost entirely unprincipled, knows perfectly well the intangible weapon with which he deals: suspicion. That's all he needs: implant it, and let nature take its course. The result is not hard to imagine or predict.

Most of us in the press prefer to consider Harry Truman an honest man who, whatever he may have been offered—and that part of the story is not too fantastic—would never permit his personal ambitions to hamper the work of his committee. Even if he weren't that sort of man, the committee's work would be its own protection. Honesty has just been too profitable where the Truman Committee is concerned. It has paid too-big dividends in fame and reputation and constructive results. Any man who would throw that away would be a fool indeed, and Harry Truman is not a fool. In addition to which, anyone who can read the latest committee reports objectively and without succumbing to the careful suspicions of the aforementioned Senator can see for himself that the story is without foundation. But it will grow, for all of that, in the frenetic atmosphere of the Hill, and someday not far off it will seriously hamper, if it does not altogether terminate, the fine activities of the Truman Committee.

APRIL 10, 1944. Hull, sounding a little less pious and a little more practical, made another of the State Department's stop-heckling-us-you-know-we're-noble speeches last night, touching at some length upon the situation in France and thereby confusing even more a picture which the President rendered reasonably obscure at his press conference Friday. At that time the Executive said no one could say what government France wanted, and that consequently the United States certainly wasn't going to get any too chummy with De Gaulle. Hull remarked calmly that the United States would certainly permit the Committee of Liberation and its leaders to supervise the restoration of civil government in the country.

Hull's invitation to Congress to name a committee to consult with him on foreign policy was received with some interest on the Hill. But looked at in the larger perspective, what does it matter how many committees you tell your secrets secretly to? It is not eight men in the Congress, or 96, or even 535 who will ratify or reject your foreign policy for you, in the last analysis. It is the 135,000,000 people out in the country.

APRIL 11, 1944. The names of the two overlords of Washington's most confused situation—manpower—are sufficient by themselves to provoke most people on the Hill to near apoplexy these days. "General Hershey *
made a speech the other day—" I began to one Senator. "He makes too God-damned many speeches," he replied promptly. "Maybe if he didn't make so many we might get somewhere." "Hershey and McNutt!" †

---

* General Lewis B. Hershey, Director of Selective Service.
† Paul V. McNutt, Director of the War Manpower Commission.

snorted another in great disgust. "Of all the mismanaged, stupid, inefficient, incompetent—— They couldn't have done any better job of tying it up in knots if they'd tried." Another Senator suggested that Hershey be given the boot and then commented philosophically on the way people get a little power and then try to run everything. It is only a matter of time before somebody threatens to put in a resolution authorizing an investigation.

Out of the day I put in on this story—it began as a story about the reaction to one of General Hershey's speeches suggesting that servicemen be retained in service until they have jobs waiting for them—I got several interesting comments, and one rather interesting dissertation, from a shrewd and dissident Democrat, on the political future. Elbert Thomas, as nice and fatherly as he could be and if anything more gently idealistic than ever, seemed a little disturbed by my ventured pessimism concerning the situation which will arise when 11,000,000 men decide they want to come home and their folks decide they want them to. He tried at some length to talk me out of it. The transition back, he said, will be gradual. Men will be subject to the needs of their units, just as they are now—some will be held for a while in armies of occupation, others will be released—it will be a gradual changeover. I was impressed again, as I have so often been before, with his innocent, simple and profound confidence in the country and the future. The Senator is a truly Christian gentleman, combining infinite idealism with a faith in America almost childlike in its simple acceptance. It is a collection of qualities enlightening to behold and conducive to considerable respect, if not always agreement.

My friend the dissident Democrat came forth with the following items:

1. David Niles, one of the President's administrative assistants (the Hill refers to him as "Devious Dave"), came up a little while ago and told Burt Wheeler flatly that Roosevelt won't run again.

2. The palace guard is "scared to death of Harry Byrd—of any potential third-party movements."

3. Dewey will win.

As for the first item, "I told Burt, 'Why, hell, Burt, you know why they did that, don't you? Because they want to head you off and block any third-party movement. All this talk about ill health and so on—that's just to quiet people like you down, so that they can come right up to convention and then put over a draft on us. Don't be a sucker for that stuff.'"

As for the second, "They're scared to death of Harry Byrd down there —oh, they're scared to death of him! This is going to get right down to cases. There aren't going to be any votes to spare in the Electoral College. If Byrd organizes a Southern Democratic Party it seems pretty likely that he'll carry Virginia and probably South and North Carolina. Even if he only took those three states—and it's quite possible with all the discontent in the South that he might take more—it would ruin Franklin right there. Harry'll do almost anything—*almost anything*—to stop a fourth term."

And as for the third, "I don't like Dewey. I don't like the way he treats bellhops and porters and waiters—the little people who wait on him. That's a good indication of the kind of damned snooty guy you've got on your hands. But he has an excellent radio presence, he makes an excellent speech, and he'd probably do a pretty good job of it as President. I think he can beat Roosevelt all right."

All of which may be election-year woolgathering—all but the message to Wheeler. That is apparently authentic.

APRIL 12, 1944. The V.P., as he is customarily referred to here, today did something only he would do—he welcomed seven South American baseball players to his office just off the Senate floor and posed with them amiably for the photographers, chatting with them in Spanish. It was my first oc-  casion to observe the V.P. at close hand, and after doing so my only comment is the same one everybody makes—the amused, rather frustrated laugh, the baffled shake of the head, the inability to put into exact words the combination of feelings he arouses. The man's integrity and his ideal- ism and his sainted other-worldliness are never in question: it's just the problem of translating them into everyday language and making them jibe with his shy, embar- rassed, uncomfortable good-fellowship that is so difficult. Henry Wallace is a man fore- doomed by fate. No matter what he does, it is always going to seem faintly ridiculous, and no matter how he acts, it is always going to seem faintly pathetic—at least to the cold-eyed judgments of the Hill. It is something indefinable but omnipresent.

He has a shy way of looking at you, ducking his head way down and peering out from under his eyebrows. "Ah, shucks, fellas," you expect him to say momentarily. With it there is a quick laugh—too quick, perhaps, and too frequent: "Whuh-whuh-whuh-whuh-whuh!" A certain tenseness never quite leaves his lips, and the lines around his eyes are uneasy and set from the strain of a public joviality he was never made for and would probably give anything to avoid. A shock of silver-graying hair sweeps over to the right of his head in a great shaggy arc. He looks like a hayseed, talks like a prophet, and acts like an embarrassed schoolboy.

For all that, he is in his way an excellent man, morally good and mentally idealistic, and no doubt worth much to his country. If it had been given to him to express it in some other context he would have been far happier, and so would the country. As it is, exposed to the pitiless glare of. the Washington spotlight, surrounded always by eyes which can never forget that he stands separated from power by the tenuous barrier of one human heart, it is perhaps inevitable that he should have become what he is, a butt of scorn and many cruel jokes.

The seven South American ballplayers, however, seemed too awed to be in the mood for such philosophizing. The V.P. spoke to them in excellent Spanish, quick and fluent, seemingly far more at ease in their tongue than his own. What did they call first base, he asked them, rapidly sketching a diamond on a piece of paper. Second base? Third base? What did they call shortstop? The press, on the whole less literate and numbering few bilinguals, stood around in amused silence while this went on. "Let's have the pictures, damn it," some photographer murmured; and after a moment, in the midst of a line of huge young Latin Americans dressed fit to kill and eyeing him with polite but thawing awe, the V.P. obliged.

Ten minutes later press and Latins had scattered and from his seat in the chamber Henry Wallace was opening the session of the United States Senate while the tourists ohed and ahed and pointed him out to one another.

The Senate met for 13 minutes. The only thing of note was the fact that Eastland, looking happy, was sitting next to Bushfield on the Republican side. Bushfield and Bridges have both announced that they will not vote to impose cloture on the poll-tax debate. It would be establishing a bad precedent, Bushfield says; it isn't a measure of sufficient importance, Bridges avers. Eastland looks awfully pleased.

APRIL 13, 1944. The Senate met again today—nine minutes this time— and Maybank seized the occasion to read a brief statement to the effect that the South, "regardless of what decisions the Supreme Court may make and regardless of what laws Congress may pass," will handle the Negro as it sees fit. The problem of translating this into practical action, or the ultimate implications of such action, is apparently something which never occurred to him, any more than it has occurred to his Southern colleagues or their people back home. A second Civil War is unthinkable, but there are times when the South comes awfully close to openly advocating one. From time to time there flits across the mind a certain disturbed curiosity as to just what *would* happen if the anti-poll-tax bill should actually pass. Of course it would be accepted in the South—or would it? Would all be sweetness and light below the Potomac or would there be local insurrections culminating in official state repudiation of the national government? Sometimes, for all our twentieth-century enlightenment, one cannot help but wonder.

APRIL 14, 1944. Aiken remarked today—knocking on wood—that so far he has no opposition for re-election from the Democrats; or—knocking on wood again—from the Republicans either. Reports drifting back to the Hill indicate that others are not so fortunate.

Betting so far on the Republicans' chances of taking the Senate this time is very cautious on the Hill. It is pretty generally conceded that they will take the Indiana seat, probably the Iowa, possibly the Illinois and Idaho, possibly the California, perhaps Missouri, possibly Washington. Given those, their total would be 44, still 5 short of the necessary 49.

APRIL 15, 1944. Congressman A. L. Miller of Nebraska has released correspondence with MacArthur which discloses the general to be more than a little interested in the Republican nomination and in all probability reduces even further the remote likelihood of his getting it. "That's about what you can expect from these first-term Congressmen," the old-timers remark sagely. Everybody has picked it up and given it a whirl and it has turned into rather more of a sensation that the Congressman probably expected. MacArthur has not been heard from yet.

Vandenberg, faced with the blow-up of his carefully nurtured candidate, has concealed his chagrin, if any, behind a cloak of silence. This has not been hard for him to do, because he rarely says anything anyway, but it has furnished the press with a little more exercise in devising ways to approach the sage of Michigan. This is a never-ending game in which we all indulge with relatively poor success. When I went in to see him on this particular matter—did he have any comment to make on the MacArthur–Miller correspondence? —he turned away rudely and barked out in his heavy, emphatic voice: "Not a word—*now* or *ever*." Others, I found, had had the same experience: we compared notes in some frustration. The episode was a vivid reminder of a recent conversation between a couple of my colleagues. "Shall we go and see Vandenberg?" one asked. "Let's," said the other agreeably. "I haven't given him a chance to sneer at me for three weeks." "He'll be glad to see you, then," said the first. "It'll give him the opportunity." Much as the great Arthur annoys us, however, we can't help liking him in a sort of exasperated way.

And as for his ability as a Senator, it is deserving of the respect it gets from all of us.

APRIL 17, 1944. The Senate met today for an hour or so while Tunnell talked about the poultry situation in Delaware, and then went over until tomorrow, when it will again go over to Friday. At that time minor legislative matters will be disposed of and the decks will be cleared. On Monday, unless some unforeseen circumstance arises, with OPA, the Navy appropriations bill, and reconversion all hanging fire, Jim Mead will call up H.R. 7 and the poll-tax fight will be on.

He said today that his forces head into battle somewhat stronger than they were a year and a half ago when the bill was killed by filibuster, but still not strong enough so that they can count with certainty upon success. A filibuster, he added, will have one of two results. Either it will force the Southerners, through an aroused public opinion—something they are quite impervious to—to abandon their stand and give in; or it will force the anti-poll-tax forces, through the same aroused opinion—which they are more amenable to—to abandon their stand and give in. He is not entirely certain, Mead said, which will occur, but as a matter of practical fact few people in the Senate are under any illusions. The anti-poll-tax forces are deliberately provoking a filibuster they know they cannot win. As time runs out and the event draws closer upon us, their reasons for doing so become increasingly obscure. The bad effect on the reputation of the Senate, the perhaps-disastrous effect upon the Democratic Party, the possible hindrance of the war and the memories of wasted time and ignominious argument that may someday come back to plague them at the polls—none of these apparently weighs in the balance against the reasons which to them seem sufficient. On the basis of hard, practical what-can-be-done-and-what-can't-be-done, however, it is a logic difficult to follow.

Of the effects upon the South, a Southerner told me today with reasoned emphasis and considerable concern. "When you hear Maybank get up and say, 'We shall do as we please regardless of any laws Congress may pass or any decisions the Supreme Court may hand down,' mark my words he is not joking; the South isn't joking any more. They mean these things. It isn't just this one issue here or that one issue there, but a whole accumulation of things, gradual pressures which are getting to the point where they may someday—someday not too far off—come to a boil. You see the lengths they are going to already in South Carolina, calling a special session of their legislature and abolishing all their primary laws, using every possible dodge to avoid registering Negroes. Back them into the corner a little further and see what they do. Or put all their discontent and unrest against the background of the postwar readjustment with all its stresses and strains and see the picture you get. No, don't make any mistake about it: you can take these things they say at face value, of that I am absolutely positive. The South isn't joking any more."

Thus succinctly a Southerner summed up a whole series of impressions, some of them small and insignificant, some of them larger and not so insignificant, which I have received since being here. We seem to be perched on a cliff, in Washington, above a vast and tumbled plain that stretches far away below us: the South, unhappy, restless, confused, embittered, torn by pressures steadily mounting. As far as the eye can see there is discontent and bitterness, faint intimations of a coming storm like a rising wind moving through tall grass; a storm which need not come, which indeed may never come, but a storm whose peaceful passage will be a miracle more of Providential grace than man's planning.

In such a mood I like to buy copies of certain New York journals and depart with them into their own particular Nirvana. There, all is rules and theories, and the human problems of human people struggling bravely and pathetically and confusedly with the terrible forces loose in their world are forgotten in the glib, easy, irresponsible convention of telling others how to live. It is so simple, up there—it is a cliff even above ours. Managing the South, after all, is very easy to do when you are far away and snug and safe, and feel yourself, however inaccurately, free from any compulsion to exercise the tolerance you preach so intolerantly, or act with the responsibility you clamor for so irresponsibly.

"Make no mistake: the South is not joking any more...."

I live on the edge of it now, and I am beginning to believe it.

10

BUTCH AND OTHERS

APRIL 18, 1944. Sooner or later they all come up here. Fiorello La Guardia came from New York yesterday to tell the Banking and Currency Committee about what a good idea OPA extension is, and today Phil Murray of the CIO stopped in to do the same. Tomorrow William Green returns. As we tell one another when the pace begins to get too pressing, "You meet such *interesting* people."

La Guardia is enjoyable to watch and listen to, an impish little monkey who occasionally overdoes the cuteness a trifle but on the whole is amusing and charming and good for a lot of laughs. There are a number of La Guardias, all passing in quick review before the beholder. There is the thoughtful La Guardia, his thick-rimmed glasses riding on top of his head, leaning forward intently with his flexible face screwed up into a living study of Concentration. In the flash of an eye this characterization can give way to the sly La Guardia, murmuring blandly to the committee and ending with a punch line that sets everybody roaring while he leans back in beatific innocence. From time to time the confidential La Guardia emphasizes his points by stretching forward over the committee table and forcing out his words slowly—and powerfully—and impressively. If the confidential La Guardia needs extra emphasis, he drops this manner instantaneously, his voice rises into its natural lisping shrillness, and he shouts it out. The reasonable La Guardia, his eyes suddenly blank and uncommunicative, his mouth puckered and earnest, sometimes intrudes a word or two. Sooner or later the sly La Guardia comes back to reclaim his audience with a quick sockeroo. Somewhere just offstage the managerial La Guardia stands by through all this, pleased and self-satisfied, peeking out from time to time to wink at the customers as much as to say: Isn't this a pip of a show, folks? Isn't this really damned good?

Phil Murray, on the other hand, is sober and indignant and intelligent and determined, not possessed of much humor. A tall man, small-faced and round-headed, with white hair, black eyebrows, dark eyes and a turned-up nose, he talks in a strong Scotch brogue that becomes more burry as he goes along. On the whole he seems reasonable, according to his lights, and constructive, according to his interests. He isn't in it for his health, but then few in this town are, and by now I have come to realize that there are other standards by which to judge a man in Washington. By those, Phil Murray measures up pretty well, as a moderately big man, active for the things in which he believes, and like so many here, more concerned for the welfare of the country than his popular reputation makes out. He and Taft don't get along too well: the fur flew frequently during the morning.

The Senator, who has consistently maintained that Congress never authorized the Little Steel formula, intimated to Murray that he sympathized with the CIO's opposition to it, at least on the ground of principle. "Senator," Murray said promptly, "I wish you'd get up on your hind legs on labor's side of the fence and tell people about that." "I have told them, told them repeatedly," Taft replied. Then, with his quick sardonic chuckle, "Anyway, I'm not altogether on your side—I'm half on your side and half on the other." "Stop straddling!" said Murray bluntly. "Stop straddling and tell people about it!"

There were also frequent occasions when both would start talking at once, or Taft would try to break in, or Murray would do likewise,

La Guardia

whereupon there would be much argument until one or the other by sheer will-power and lung-power drowned the other out. They shook hands and parted friends when the hearing ended, however, so at least the surface amenities were preserved.

APRIL 19, 1944. An interesting little story is going the rounds apropos the Southerners' dreams of a protest party. It seems that Josiah Bailey got into the elevator the other day with Colonel Edwin Halsey, the tall, dark, heavy-set old man who is Secretary of the Senate. The Colonel was in a joking mood, and turning to Josiah, he said, "Well, do you think your man [Harry Byrd] will win?" A moment of icy silence ensued. Then Bailey whirled—one of his slow, stately, freezing whirls—and with iron in his soft Southern voice he said coldly, "You say anything about my man and you'll hear from me!" The rest of the ride passed in silence, the ubiquitous Halsey for once at a loss for words.

APRIL 20, 1944. I went around to see Theodore Francis Green again today, hoping to smoke him out on his new amendment to the soldier-vote law. He was not to be smoked. "What's the hurry?" he asked. "The things that would be done under it won't be done until October, anyway. There's no rush. I've gathered some material, made a few inquiries—but there's no hurry. Plenty of time, plenty of time." Questioned about recesses—"What recess? All I've heard about is a week between the two conventions. Maybe along in September, October sometime, some of them may want to go home and do a little campaigning. Although I don't know" (with a chuckle) "but what it might do them more good if they just stayed here and didn't say anything. That usually crowns my efforts with success. No, there's plenty of time to take it up. I'm not worrying."

The OPA hearings drag on and on. The routine is unvarying. Each morning the committee is scheduled to meet at 10:30. About 10:20 the official stenographers and the audience turn up. By 10:30 the press has arrived. At 10:35 Bob Wagner comes in, looks around at the press table with an invariable chuckle and, "Well, the press is here anyway." By 10:40 he has requested the committee secretary to call the other members on the phone and find out if they will be there. By 10:45 the regulars, Taft, Hawkes, Maybank and Murdock, have come in. After a little more impatient looking around, nervous turnings in his chair, a wisecrack or two for the press, Wagner decides to go ahead and call the meeting to order. Usually by 10:50 the hearings are under way. Everybody then settles down for a session that usually lasts until about 1 P.M., when

Wagner breaks in apologetically on the witness and asks if he would mind coming back after lunch. A hurried conference with the other Senators follows—"How about you, Abe, will you be here?"—Wagner adjourns the hearing until 2:30. At 2:20 the official stenographers and the audience turn up. At 2:30 the press has arrived. At 2:35, with a wisecrack for the press, Wagner enters. By 2:40 the regulars are in their places. By 2:45——

At 5:30 the committee recesses until tomorrow at 10:30.

APRIL 21, 1944. The atmosphere is getting more and more tense here with invasion rumors. There is some possibility, perhaps better than we know, that the Senate will start its poll-tax fight more or less simultaneously with the drive on Fortress Europa. There is probably some sort of a moral there, but most on the Hill are too upset and annoyed to care.

Since the groups that are forcing the Senate into this hopeless and tragic struggle, incidentally, are the same groups that follow a consistent policy of derogating Congress, they stand to win no matter what the outcome. If they get H.R. 7, well and good, and if they don't—well, they've got some more ammunition with which to smear the Legislature. It all works out very neatly when you stop to think it through.

APRIL 22, 1944. Clyde Reed is seeking re-election by press conference this year, a method a trifle more subtle than Alexander Wiley's re-election by press release. Every five or six days, now, the crotchety Kansan calls us in for some long, involved attack on the government, full of hell and damnation and explanations about how "I don't want to annoy anybody any more than I have to." Even more often, averaging close to once a day, the junior Senator from Wisconsin peppers us with press releases. Release-A-Day Wiley, they call him in the Press Gallery, and the topics are many and wondrous. Quite occasionally, also, they contain the sound core of an excellent idea. The only thing wrong with them is that he never concentrates, he never pursues his ideas. Instead of real ammunition it's just birdshot. An amiable, bouncy soul with a pleasant, eager expression, he is always pumping somebody's hand, slapping somebody's back, poking somebody's ribs, or whooping wildly at his own jokes. Essentially good-hearted, he is one of the characters of the Senate.

Reed's latest blast came this morning, one of his semihumorous attacks on the OPA and Chester Bowles. The Reed sarcasm is acid and often uncalled for, considering that most of the people he uses it on are reasonably honest, hardworking folk whose chief crime, if any, is that they are caught in the meshes downtown. "I found your testimony very interesting," he wrote Bowles in a letter he released to us today. "Anyone who knew nothing about it would have been quite impressed." This really rocks 'em in Kansas.

Tom Connally has appointed his committee to consult with the State Department on foreign policy. It is perhaps the most important group of men in the whole Congress, or will be if Hull keeps faith with them. Besides himself, Tom picked Walter George, Barkley and Guy Gillette for the Democrats; Vandenberg, White and Austin for the Republicans; and Bob La Follette, the lone Progressive who for practical purposes is counted with the minority in committee assignments. It is an interesting selection, drawn from the subcommittee that handled the Connally peace resolution last year. And perhaps, if the sainted old gentleman who hangs his hat in the gingerbread castle at 17th and Pennsylvania does his part, they may be of some consequence to the future course of Senate–State relations. This move won't help much in educating the 135,000,000, but it is a gesture in the right direction, at least, and one much too long delayed.

APRIL 23, 1944. Knox, Stimson and Admiral Emory Land, busily whipping a dead horse, have come forth with another moving plea for national service. The reasoning is familiar, the hysterics also. It does little to bolster the case for the unlucky legislation. Andrew May, chairman of the House Military Affairs Committee, has reiterated his stand that the authority to handle manpower adequately already rests in the bureaus downtown—if they would only administer it efficiently. The Senate Military Affairs Committee has made no formal statement, but the sentiment of its members, as nearly as it can be judged from hasty soundings, remains unchanged. Bob Reynolds is not in town ("We-all don't know wheah the Senutuh is," his secretary told me the other day when I stopped by the office. "We-all haven't heard from the Senutuh in foh-five days. I 'spect he'll be turnin' up one of these days"), so the committee has not spoken officially. But there has been no shift. The bill is as dead as ever.

APRIL 24, 1944. Ken Wherry came up to the Press Gallery this afternoon to tell us about the War Production Board's cancellation of its order banning resumption of civilian production. The action was typical. Where most would have remained on the floor and later sent around a press release, the Nebraskan knew what he wanted and without hesitation went after it. Previously he had also gone after WPB, which is why WPB canceled the order.

He explained the significance of the agency's move to us in his usual didactic fashion, not much interested in his own position in the matter, not attempting to take credit for it, impatient with personal implications and interested only in results. His pet phrase, spoken with heavy emphasis—"If—you—get—the—idea"—was thrown in frequently; each time, we nodded. We got the idea. Somebody, just by raising hell and not stopping till he got action, had dislodged a highly important part of the logjam downtown. WPB is shot through with suave people loaned from industry, many of them busily taking care of the gang back home at the office. The resistance to reconversion among that tight little hierarchy is getting to be one of the scandals of Washington. When the inside history of this war comes to be written, a rather lurid chapter will be devoted to the way in which the automobile representatives, for instance, tried to block reconversion "until the big corporations have completed their war contracts and everyone can start together." That strange, blind fallacy—that little business should be throttled by government decree until the big boys have finished their war jobs and can "start even"—dominates the thinking of too many powerful men in WPB. It is an open invitation to government regimentation, and they are just too blind and selfish to see it. They would rather run the risk of destroying the free economic system altogether than yield in the slightest particular the preferred positions they held before the war. It is going to be a running fight all the way (it is already, in fact) to break their hold on the industrial machine and permit a fair, sound and honest reconversion. Some of them have learned nothing in the last 12 years.

In that running battle, Wherry's skirmish will probably rank among the more important engagements. The order had been issued and a complete ban had been placed on resumption of civilian production. Wherry and Tom Stewart of Tennessee both protested, and nothing happened. Then Wherry got mad. After that things did happen. Donald Nelson, chairman of the WPB, finding a very vocal and unexpected ally, apparently took heart and swung out at the men who continually try to run his agency out from under him. The order was withdrawn. Wherry, by sheer brass, lungpower, guts, impatience and stick-to-itiveness, had gotten results.

There is much to be said for the junior Senator from Nebraska—more for than against, I think. Blunt, direct, excitable, brash, he has a certain basic honesty nonetheless, and a dogged determination to get what he thinks is right. He probably never will be a parliamentarian, his manners will probably never be Senatorial, he will always seem like an excitable, naïve, unlicked cub, but when the time comes to look back over the next 20 years and pick the men who have made their mark on the nation, it will be surprising if Ken Wherry is not among them.

APRIL 25, 1944. Drew Pearson tangled with McKellar today. Like the fight Little Peterkin heard about in the poem, it was a famous battle. Pearson referred to the Senator's temper, retelling the old tale about the time he drew a knife on a fellow Senator and had to be virtually disarmed before he calmed down; he then went on into his patronage, his power as acting chairman of Appropriations, his feud with TVA. Old Mack put on a pow'ful good show in reply. He wanted to ask his fellow Senators—he wanted them to tell him—if any of the statements of this low-down, lying, contemptible scoundrel were true. If any Senator ever heard of him drawing a knife on anybody, he wanted him to get up and tell him about it. (At this Harry Byrd, sitting by Bennett Champ Clark, reached over and poked Bennett Champ's arm and they both grinned.) If any Senator ever heard of him using Appropriations to kill off anybody's pet project as a means of retaliation, he wanted him to get up and tell him about it. And as for patronage! Why! That was the most contemptible, sneaking, miserable, low-down lie of all the lies by this egregious ass. He wanted his fellow Senators to tell him—he challanged any Senator—he would let them pass the verdict on him as to whether he was any of the things this sneaking skunk had said. His voice roared one moment and sank to a grimly amused conversational tone the next. His right arm flailed the air and his forelock fell across his sleepy eye. He did not get a case of the weepy sniffles, as he is sometimes wont to do, but aside from that he put on quite a complete exhibition of the McKellar repertoire.

His fellow Senators, who regard him with a combination of affection, fear, and amusement, sat in amused or impassive silence and in effect assented to all his statements by so doing. Late in the day Pearson replied, apparently fed up, in a cold, blunt, factual statement. As for the feud with TVA, he ticked that off; as for the patronage, he ticked that off, with facts and figures; and as for the knifing incident, he took care of that too. Bennett Champ Clark told him that, he said, and the incident occurred when McKellar drew a knife on the late Royal S. Copeland of New York. This would seem to put the issue squarely in the lap of the lively B. C., who may confirm it tomorrow, or, thinking better of the whole thing, may find some graceful out.

APRIL 26, 1944. Bennett Champ says meekly that the McKellar knife story is a fabrication. McKellar did get mad at Copeland, he says, and he did calm him down, but as to whether or not he had a knife, B. C. couldn't say. So much for that. Clark will doubtless be next on Pearson's little list of those who won't be missed.

Fred Vinson, one of the six or eight most powerful men in the country, came to the Hill today to ring down the curtain on the OPA hearings. A reasonable man with a quick humor and an even temper, he wears the immense powers of the Office of Economic Stabilization as any other democratic citizen might—matter-of-factly, as though he were not very much impressed by them. Physically he is a fairly tall man, with a reddish face and a habit of blushing easily and frequently, a long nose at the top of which little bland, tired blue eyes are set close together beneath very bushy dark eyebrows which curl down around them at the sides; a small mouth easily provoked into a humorous smile, a small, receding chin, graying hair with many darks spots in it. He speaks with a rather flat Kentucky drawl and is a confirmed pencil-swinger. He and Taft, in fact, lectured one another with their pencils rising and falling at a great rate.

The testimony he had to offer was not new or unexpected. Naturally he was not there to damn his own program, and naturally he gave OPA, War Labor Board and War Food Administration a strong pat on the back. Nonetheless he was reasonable about it, candidily admitting errors and imperfections, but making a passably good defense of things accomplished in spite of them. On some points he was rather vague, as when Taft and Danaher pushed forth into the vast twilight zone in which things somehow just get done without anybody seeming to know just where the authority comes from. There is a lot of that downtown—these hearings have brought that out time and time again. Judge Vinson answered as best he could, and then gave up; never going quite so far as to shrug, but stopping right on the verge of it. Taft and Danaher did virtually the same. It is a characteristic frustration: everybody knows things like that go on, but they work, and they are necessary for the war effort, and so—well, they just happen. Criticism, even that of such cogent gentlemen as the two Senators, is never carried very far. There's a sort of tacit, mutual agreement that everybody understands and nobody violates. After all, as the saying goes, "You know what they're up against." And you may be faced with the same problems yourself tomorrow, and so—well, you just don't get too nosy, that's all. Live and let live.

Even so, some restrictive amendments are going to be proposed, for the latitude now is admittedly far greater than the Congress ever intended; far greater, perhaps, than the situation warrants. The twilight zone is going to be drastically reduced, there is no doubt of that. A certain section of it will always remain, particularly in wartime, but the understanding covers that. For the rest, powers and duties are going to be much more rigidly defined by the Congress this year than they ever have been before.

In these long, long hearings which have dragged on for over a month, many of the interests of America have come before the committee. The tale has been told over and over again of this group injured, or that group hurt. Labor has appeared, and the Chamber of Commerce, and a man who buys waste paper, and a man who raises cabbages, and a man who sells tires. The mighty and the small, they have taken the stand and had their say before the Senate of the United States. It has been a terrific bore to cover, but looked at in the broader perspective of a democratic land, it is good that it should be so.

APRIL 27, 1944. Fred Vinson came back today and, smiling, blushing, and parrying Senators skillfully, engaged in one colloquy that seemed to sum up pretty well the whole problem in Washington right now. It began when McClellan, speaking slowly, reasonably and, as he said later, "in order to make the record very straight," asked him if the rise in living costs would justify breaking the Little Steel formula.

Vinson (thinking for a very long time, blushing, starting to smile, looking up at the ceiling, looking down again. Finally, slowly): "So far as I am concerned, I have no purpose to break the Little Steel formula."

McClellan: "I take it on the record, then, that there would be no justification for breaking the Little Steel formula?"

Vinson: "I don't think the Little Steel formula should be discarded, no, sir."

Taft (hurling himself into this as is his custom, twisting his body from side to side and emphasizing his main points by leaning forward with quick, short, restrained half-lunges): "Wouldn't it be fairer to give a man a 25 per cent wage increase, say, justified by the increase in the cost of living, instead of establishing a flat wage ceiling and then trying to get around it in some way by dodging the wage formula?"

Vinson (with emphasis too): "I have not gone around the wage formula. The public shouldn't have the idea that Little Steel is the only formula for a raise in wages. There are other things, inequities, upgrading, relation with other jobs, and so on. I've done my dead-level best, Senator, to follow the formula."

Taft: "It seems to me that you are trying to follow two conflicting theories. First you have the principle established in the law, to do justice to the worker. Then you have the principle that you'll hold the line regardless of justice. First you'll hold the line, it seems to me, and if you can manage to do justice too, well, that's so much to the good."

Vinson: "No, sir. No, sir. The line must be held under the rules which say what the line is."

Taft (lunging again, bearing down hard on the emphasis in his flat, forceful voice): "What I'm maintaining is that you can't carry out the act as written without breaking the hold-the-line directive."

Vinson (more thought; very slowly): "Well, of course . . . there is one thing I might say to you. . . . If the Congress thinks this test is too severe, you can write language in the law to take care of it."

The law, in other words, states a principle. It does not, perhaps, say enough. Out of that omission the Administration has created a house of cards in which regulation piles on regulation in a shaky and precarious structure, sometimes too harsh, sometimes too easy, always seeking the will-o'-the-wisp of a perfectly controlled balance. The same thing applies to the subsidy program. As McClellan remarked, it's here—illegally, in the view of a majority of the Congress—and we're stuck with it. But the thing itself is threatening to turn into an endless juggling act in which the government, in the roll of performer, tosses up more and more colored balls in a rhythm faster and faster, until ultimately the foot slips and the balls go flying. The boys downtown have gotten what they wanted by deliberately evading the law and flouting Congress, but their plaything is turning into a mechanical monster which is showing alarming signs of independent and erratic movement.

Or such, at any rate, is the general view on the Hill. There is the other view, and Vinson, Davis, Bowles and Marvin Jones have all stated it most persuasively during the hearings now concluded.

Bob Wagner, shrewd and gentle and cynical and good-humored, told us a joke today, typical of the kind he does tell: more jest than joke. Something reminded him, he said, of the newspaperman who said he had a wonderful story. "He said he had a wonderful story," said Bob Wagner with a smile, "until something sperled it—there was an eyewitness. . . . That," he said with a thoughtful chuckle, "sperled it." It didn't sperl it for us, though; quite the contrary.

11

FUTILITY BY UNANIMOUS CONSENT

APRIL 28, 1944. All the groups who want to force the Senate into a filibuster are gradually achieving success. For almost two weeks now they have been swarming around the Office Building like ants, infesting first one office and then another. Senators like Barkley and Mead, faced with a flat ultimatum from the Southerners, and knowing perfectly well that the tide has been turning away from them day by day until now they know definitely they cannot get cloture, have ducked and dodged and procrastinated and put off a showdown in the desperate hope that they can somehow get out from under an ill-considered promise. But the lobbyists have been relentless in their pressure.

The strange, the peculiar, the tragic thing about it is that all this they demand in the name of democracy, and indeed and admittedly in the name of democracy it should be done. If they were at all interested in the practical mechanics of the thing, however, if they had taken time in all this shouting about democracy to study the Senate and find out how democracy actually operates in the hard, practical business of corralling votes, they would know that it cannot be done now. And they would disband their swarming, arrogant, self-interested hordes and go home to rest up for a later day when their efforts might be of some avail.

However noble the anti-poll-taxers may be, and however much their crusade should be blessed with victory, they are up against a cold, blunt fact:

They just haven't got the votes.

Nonetheless, they have finally forced Mead to call a meeting of the anti-poll-tax Senators. McCarran has returned to town after some weeks of campaigning in Nevada, and as chairman of Judiciary can now give the authority of his position to the strategy evolved. May 9 has been set as the date to call it up. There is no inside information yet as to the agreement which will be reached with the Southerners, but in all probability there will be a tacit understanding by which the bill will be called up, a filibuster will be begun, a sufficient number of speeches will be made for the record on both sides, a cloture vote will then be called for, it will fail, and the bill will be laid aside. It is not the best way out of the situation imposed on the Senate by the pressures it is under at the moment, but it is perhaps the only one feasible under the circumstances. It is too bad, and only the people who want to make themselves some ammunition with which to smear the Congress will be happy.

APRIL 29, 1944. The Montgomery Ward seizure * is agitating the Hill considerably today. The Republicans in the Senate decided at their regular weekly conference yesterday that they would try to get some ideas together preparatory to writing a bill to amend the Smith–Connally Act. Ferguson told me he would like to see provisions which would require: 1. That the President make a finding of fact in seizure cases, setting forth exactly why and on what grounds; 2. That he set forth the specific law under which he is doing it, and show how the facts conform to the law ("This business of saying he's doing a thing because he's Chief Executive or Commander-in-Chief or 'under the war powers of the Constitution' doesn't mean a thing; it's just generalities. In this country our laws are written"); 3. That court appeal be provided, and that such an appeal be given precedence over all other cases; 4. That appeal be permitted direct from the court below to the Supreme Court, and that it be given precedence in the Supreme Court.

"After all," he said, "unless we have martial law the normal channels of justice should be preserved. If martial law is necessary, then the people should be given all the facts so that they would know why it is necessary. We are supposed to have equal justice under law, that's the principle of this country. We don't want to take away from people the very thing they're fighting for."

Wherry, talking bang-bang-bang, is not so much interested in the legal aspects of it—which he considers virtually nil so far as the seizure is concerned—as in the political. "It seems to me the political effect is very bad," he said, "very bad. It's certainly caused a lot of bad reaction up here, on both sides of the aisle. Why, I wouldn't be surprised if all these acts—price control and Lend-Lease and all the rest of them—will emerge very restricted, more restricted than they would have been before. This looks too much like outright dictatorship. The reaction is very bad."

* The company's plant in Chicago was seized by the Army when the firm refused to comply with War Labor Board directives that it grant employees' demands for better working conditions, and thus avert a possible strike. Board Chairman Sewell Avery was carried out of his office by two soldiers, thereby giving the press one of the great photographs of World War II.

Pat McCarran explained in his light, husky voice that under the Shipstead resolution to investigate Executive orders he already has all the authority he needs to launch a study of the Montgomery Ward affair. In fact, he said, as chairman of Judiciary he had already dispatched an investigator to Chicago. Attorney General Francis Biddle's decision, he said in a formal statement issued after he talked to us, was "unlawyerlike"; and while he emphasized that he did not "want to comment on the issues involved," it was apparent that he did not approve. Harry Byrd put in a resolution specifically directed at the Montgomery Ward case Friday, expressing the sentiments of many on the Democratic side.

The President, this time, has a bull by the tail. Aside from living up to the Washington definition of an Attorney General—someone you appoint to tell you you can do what you want to do—Biddle has apparently done little in his decision to bolster the Executive's case. And the Republicans have been handed another good issue on a silver platter. From all standpoints, legal, political and moral, it is hard to see why it was done. "To get the CIO?" one reporter suggested. "He already has the CIO," another shot back. "That would be like asking Phil Murray to support the fourth term." The motive is obscure. Someone else broke in to wonder idly if it might not be that the President just got mad at Sewell Avery.

MAY 1, 1944. May Day has come and is going, and still no invasion. Signs are pointing, straws are blowing in the wind, the clever can wet a finger and calculate the breeze with it—but the event is not yet. Uneasily beneath the beautiful springtime weather lies the knowledge that carnage beyond description cannot be long delayed.

The Senate, still marking time today, was in recess, ostensibly out of respect to Frank Knox who died during the week end. A number of the members went to his funeral; the rest were busy catching up on correspondence and the myriad minor errands upon which constituents insist. A sense of lull rested on the Hill, extending to the House as well. Over there they met for seven minutes and adjourned, still muttering darkly about Montgomery Ward.

Tomorrow this picture will change. Some optimist—Barkley, I believe, abetted by White, two gentlemen who are always unfailingly confident of the vast amount of work the Senate can get out of the way in a short time—expects an agriculture bill, a war-contracts termination bill, and Lend-Lease, to go through before next Tuesday when the poll-tax bill comes up. This may occur, but if it does it will be sloppy legislating, done by guess and by golly and without much attention to detail. The bill establishing procedures for war-contracts termination, in particular, will probably be shoved through as though it were a routine claim for $50 to relieve Joe Doakes. Later on, of course, people will be very surprised and aggrieved at the way in which those bad boys downtown interpret it. They will be very positive then that it was never—not *ever*—the intent of Congress that any such thing should occur. There will be denunciations and condemnations, and maybe even an investigation. It will all be very upsetting, and of course the Administration's fault.

MAY 2, 1944. "Time after time," Taft shouted today in a heated exchange with Dick Russell, "we pass things up here only to have the agencies downtown find meanings in them which we never intended. I don't say this is the fault of the Executive, either. It is principally the fault of Congress for not taking time enough to legislate thoroughly, for not defining sufficiently the powers we intend to give." Not many on the Hill are honest enough to admit that, but the Ohioan makes no bones of it. It is perhaps the main reason why he will consume the time of the Senate, as he did today, in threshing out some point in a bill that everyone else wants to rush through.

The occasion today was the so-called Agriculture omnibus bill, a catch-all piece of legislation to give legal sanction to a lot of things that have been done through implicit powers derived from appropriations. Every so often the Congress has a habit of stopping to catch up with itself in this fashion. It will suddenly occur to somebody that maybe they had better have this all down in black and white instead of just making it a matter of administrative assumption based on the fact that money has been appropriated. Consequently, as in the present instance, a hodgepodge of items will be tossed together in an organic act and passed for the record.

Few of the authorizations in the Agriculture bill deserved challenge today, but Taft was upset about an apparently endless grant for school lunches. Being possessed of a brilliant but rigid mind, he applies its standards to each new problem that arises without much regard for the human element involved. The school-lunch principle, as humanitarian and worthy as any to come before the Congress in recent years, received the same treatment at his hands as an unlimited grant to buy fire hydrants might have. His constant cry to limit the powers, limit the powers, limit the powers, was turned full blast on school lunches. McFarland, slow, amiable and obviously frustrated by a vocal and parliamentary attack too swift and sure-footed for him to counter, defended the school-lunch provision heatedly for a little while and then suddenly asked Taft if he would accept it if it were limited to two years. Everybody laughed, Taft agreed, and it went through abruptly on a voice vote after a good half-hour's wrangle that had involved a number of people and frayed a number of tempers.

On the Montgomery Ward seizure the Senate was still in good voice today. Curley Brooks, his light voice soaring and sinking with consummate skill, made a violent attack upon the President's action. Wherry followed, starting in rather slowly and clearly, as is his custom, and then gradually winding himself up into an exploding tornado of emotion and emphasis. The Republicans very obviously do not intend to let their issue die.

MAY 3, 1944. Claude Pepper and Lister Hill both made fairly good showings in the primaries yesterday, and both are apparently out of danger. Out in South Dakota Chan Gurney, a short, stocky, impassive man with a smooth round face which gives him at 48 the look of one about 30, swept back in easily in a four-to-one victory over his opponent. By the same ratio Millard Tydings was renominated in Maryland Monday. All down the line, also, the Representatives are being returned. So far the apparently instinctive desire to stick with the known during wartime, plus the fact that none of the states contested to date has been doubtful, has resulted in victory for the incumbents.

Chester Bowles took off all meat rationing save that on beefsteak and beef roast today. Far from being happy, the farm-state boys were bitterly angry. In the first place, according to them, the move came three months too late; in the second place, it fitted into a picture that already included a War Food Administration order freezing corn, thereby cutting off feed in the Middle West; a War Food Administration order removing the support price on heavy hogs, thereby knocking the bottom out of the market; and a War Food Administration order clamping shipping embargos on Omaha, Kansas City and the other selling centers. With hogs already a glut on the market—the holdover today from yesterday alone was 100,000 —OPA's critics say that the farmer can't sell the hogs he has on the farm, because he can't get them into the market. Neither can he keep them on the farm, because he can't get the feed. And even if he could get the feed and could get them to market, he still couldn't sell because of the embargo. Into that chaotic situation Bowles blithely tossed his order taking off rationing, which immediately strains the market to the breaking point everywhere as consumer demand shoots up. There are times when it is easy to see why the farm bloc, so glibly condemned by its critics, fights the way it does against the dictates of the government.

On the floor today, after a number of speeches hailing Polish Independence Day, the Senate got around to the Murray–George war-contracts termination bill. Debate was desultory and interest slack. Thirteen Senators were on the floor at one point when it seemed the bill might pass. When it turned out it wouldn't, five of them left. Challenging one section, Langer asked Murray, "Then it isn't the intention that large staffs of

political employees will be set up around the country to run the thing?"
"No," replied Murray firmly, "that is not the intention." "It isn't the intention," remarked one veteran reporter drily, "but it will be done."

Around 5 o'clock the Senate recessed until noon tomorrow. In a day or
two, after more half-hearted discussion, it will rather absent-mindedly
pass one of the most important pieces of legislation to come before it in
this war, and one out of which there will subsequently grow many bitter
and indignant attacks upon the Administration as it reads into the loose
language of the law things which it was *never* the intent of Congress to
authorize. The answer to that one lies in 13 Senators, who subsequently
became 8.

MAY 4, 1944. In something like an hour and 15 minutes, the Senate passed
the war-contracts termination bill. Debate continued to be desultory, the
only active interest occurring when Harley Kilgore, chewing his invariable
wad of gum, tried to tack on his bill providing expanded unemployment
compensation as an amendment to the Murray–George bill. It was voted
down decisively on the assurance that it would be taken up immediately
following the end of the poll-tax debate. The main thing at the moment,
George and Murray maintained, was to get war contracts settled. And
settled it was, after a debate which ran approximately four hours.

Following that, Tom Connally put in a report from Foreign Relations
on Lend-Lease extension, and after him McKellar got the floor to make a
report from Appropriations. At the conclusion he began in routine fashion,
"Mr. President, I ask unanimous consent to put the committee's recommendations in the *Record*." "The committee's recommendations?" cried
Styles Bridges, jumping to his feet. "The committee hasn't even met yet!"
"Well," said McKellar with an ironic grin, "well, Mr. President, I withdraw the motion, and I ask that the members of the Appropriations Committee meet with me in the committee room immediately to approve this
report. Bridges! Russell!" And like an old hen trailed by her chicks, he
wandered off the floor followed by the members of his committee, amid
general laughter.

At 2 P.M. Military Affairs met to consider a new bill by Bailey and
Brewster that would draft into labor battalions all 4-Fs who do not take
essential war jobs. The committee room was as usual jammed to the doors,
with everybody falling all over everybody else trying to make room. A
star-studded cast was on hand. Bob Patterson was there to represent the
War Department, his tired patrician face impassive and intent. Undersecretary Ralph Bard of the Navy, a tall dark man with the air of controlled strain and impatience that characterizes the top men of the services,
represented his department. Hershey, bull-necked, with a big head of

bushy hair and an earnest, amiable face, talked in his light voice about how "I have so many men" in this classification and "I have so many men" in that. Bob Reynolds was in the chair, red-faced, flanked on the right by Warren Austin, silent and bitter at the apparent interest in a bill which is only a tentative gesture in the direction of his own national service law. Next to him sat Mrs. Luce, looking rather tired but turned out fit to kill. Andrew Jackson May, Chairman of the House committee, a graying man with deep-set dark eyes and a slow Kentucky manner, came next, and after him California's John Costello. Chapman Revercomb, only other member of the Senate committee present, came next, not very much impressed and given to asking questions in his liquid voice which became increasingly sharp-edged as he failed to get the answers he wanted. Bailey and Brewster completed the gathering. Sandwiched in between, all around, under the tables and over the mantelpiece, the press and a vast quantity of gold braid and stars and eagles rounded out the picture. It was quite impressive, even if it didn't accomplish much.

Bard, Patterson and Hershey were all for it, of course; Andy May said he approved, and so did Costello, and Clare Luce remarked in her rather prim and affected voice that "it seems to conform to the same principles as the bills which I introduced eight months ago." Asked to comment toward the end, Warren Austin tried desperately to be fair but couldn't resist the dig that "so far as I have been able to judge, the members of the Senate Military Affairs Committee are not any more disposed toward this bill than they are toward mine." Later Bob Reynolds told the press blandly "I have heard many expressions of general approval from Senators outside the committee." He repeated "outside the committee" with a thoughtful air and a brief, sardonic grin. Within 30 days, he said, he expects to bring it to a vote of the full committee and dispose of it one way or the other.

When the meeting broke up the photographers swarmed around Mrs. Luce. Watching Bob Reynolds, who is always in his element on the occasions when beautiful ladies are around, seeing him bow and scrape and play the gracious and fulsome squire, I could not help but be reminded of the remark made by a reporter friend of mine one day when we were sitting in the Press Gallery. Bob came on the floor, dapper and jaunty at age 60, and I said idly, "You know, you've got to hand it to the Honorable Bob. There's something about him." "There's something about him, all right," she agreed promptly, "but it isn't honorable."

MAY 5, 1944. I was over in the House today for a while, enjoying that lively, hectic atmosphere—voices booming out over the microphones, hordes of people coming and going, a constant babble of talk, a vigorous informality, an air of circus that makes you expect at any moment to see whitecoats suddenly burst down the aisles crying, "Popcorn! Candy! Soft drinks!"—always a good thing for someone from the sedate Senate side where all is (generally) dignity and decorum, and where (usually) a glossy veneer of heavy courtesy overlies everything. In the House the facts of life are considerably closer to the surface. If Joe Doakes thinks Bill Blow is a son of a gun he gets up and says so, and none of your "distinguished Senator from So-and-So" stuff. Members tell one another off in a roughhouse atmosphere through which, like figures surrounded by an unruly brawl to which they frequently contribute, the gracious Mrs. Luce, the dour-faced Ham Fish, the hulking Martin Dies, the pinch-beaked Clare Hoffman, the amiable Gene Worley, mop-haired John Rankin and the rest, move in and out.

In the Senate, debate began on Lend-Lease but ended in 40 minutes when Ellender asked that it go over to Monday so members might study the official figures in the administrator's report. Commenting on the imminence of the poll-tax fight, Barkley remarked yesterday that "every Senator knows that none of the speeches will change any votes," and virtually admitted that the supporters of the bill haven't got the votes to put it over. There is something passing strange in this charade by grown men in the United States Senate, too afraid of pressure to say outright what they know to be the fact, that the bill is dead at this moment and can never be revived in this Congress, and so moving forward step by step as though in some fantastic, mechanical minuet without purpose, without meaning, without result.

MAY 6, 1944. Nearly everyone went to the Derby today, so the Office Building was nearly deserted and pickings were rather slim. Clyde Reed stayed around, of course, for his Saturday get-together with the press. Wherry, Bushfield, Capper and Millikin dropped in too, and in no time at all another gripe session on hogs was under way. It produced a lot of indignation and another demand that the War Food Administration restore the support price on heavies. Round-faced Harry Reed, head of the livestock and meat branch, an easygoing gentleman with a mildly belligerent expression and a matter-of-fact voice, came up dutifully to go through one more of his performances for the farm bloc. The Senators are always very indignant and Harry is always very unimpressed. They tell him what they want and he tells them what he is going to do, and the thing always ends in a draw. It is sometimes rather amazing to stop and realize how consistently, deliberately and openly the men downtown defy Congress and do exactly the opposite of what it wants. The only thing is, it's such a standard practice that nobody really gives it much of a thought. The

Hill makes its protest, with varying degrees of emphasis depending upon
the amount of its real interest, and Downtown replies, and after that, with
the record made, everything continues as before. It's really quite a system
—the Washington system.

At 11 o'clock Walter George held a press conference on the tax-simpli-
fication bill, sent over yesterday by the House. Caressing his favorite
word—"mateeeriel"—with his organ-stop voice, the Senator said he antici-
pated little difficulty in getting the measure through the Senate with
speed, expedition and no mateeriel changes.

MAY 7, 1944. The latest rumor on the poll-tax fight now says two weeks.
That is considerably better than the original predictions, but still seems
unnecessarily long under the circumstances.

MAY 8, 1944. Lend-Lease went through today after a rather interesting
debate in which Connally, Vandenberg, Wheeler, McKellar, Ellender and
Curley Brooks all served notice on the Executive that the Congress is not
bound by his commitments. The fatal cleavage in government upon which
Wilson foundered by being too clever is inexorably, inevitably, bit by bit
developing again—and from exactly the same causes. Congress just doesn't
like to be hoodwinked, bypassed, patronized, lied to, or affronted in the
field of foreign policy. So long as this is a democracy, such practices will
succeed for a little while but they will not succeed forever.

On the whole, debate was slow. When the time came to vote, interest
was already shifting to the poll tax. As the Clerk droned on through the
names, the Senators began to crowd in from the cloakrooms and con-
gregate in little groups. Harry Byrd moved briskly about the Republican
side buttonholing; Bridges crossed over to talk to Connally. Through the
doors at the back, while the tally slowly piled up in favor of Lend-Lease,
the poll-taxers suddenly trooped in, Bankhead and Eastland and McClellan
and Lister Hill, Bilbo and Cotton Ed and the volatile Maybank, obviously
just done with a conference. Barkley hurried around from seat to seat
with a sheet of paper which we later learned was the petition to invoke
cloture. Vandenberg signed hastily and took it up to Brooks, seated at
his desk; he too signed and returned it to Barkley. Sheridan Downey
stopped by, took out his fountain pen, signed. Sixteen names, the necessary
number, were shortly inscribed upon it. The Lend-Lease vote droned
slowly on, concluded. Sixty-three had voted Aye; Bill Langer, moved by
some strange impulse no one ever did fathom, cast the lone No. The bill
was passed and Barkley moved the reading of the calendar. Several routine bills were passed while the tension mounted. Suddenly Barkley moved
the Senate adjourn until tomorrow. "Adjourn?" cried McKellar in startled

surprise. "Adjourn?" cried the press. The word went buzzing through the gallery. "The Senate will stand adjourned until noon tomorrow," said Jim Tunnell in the chair. Senators, rather puzzled, began to straggle off the floor. We descended upon Barkley from the gallery like a swarm of locusts. This was a strategy no one had foreseen.

Pressed for an explanation, he was innocent and reasonable. Been almost a month now, he said, since the Senate had a "morning hour." Seemed as though it ought to have one. It was only incidental, apparently, that the morning hour—the first hour of the session following an adjournment—is the only time when a motion to bring up a bill may be made without debate. Asked about this directly, he said either McCarran or Mead would move to bring up H.R. 7. He hoped the Southerners would "permit it to become the order of business without an argument." Argument might take many forms: reading the journal of the previous day's proceedings (customarily dispensed with by unanimous consent); quorum calls; amendments to the journal, each one necessitating a quorum call, each one subject to a Yea and Nay vote if so desired. "They can use up the two hours all right if they've a mind to," he said. However, he "hoped" they wouldn't. In any case, he had in his pocket the motion for cloture and would introduce it on Thursday. Not later than Monday it would come to a vote. Yesterday's two-week prediction has been reduced to one, a sensible procedure.

We wrote our stories from the angle of an agreement on the part of the Southerners to permit the bill to be called up without a filibuster in return for a cloture vote not later than Monday. Since they would never permit this if they didn't know they had the votes to beat cloture—Bankhead, in fact, has said as much—the move means that the bill will be formally buried on Monday.

MAY 9, 1944. The agreement held all right today. Pat McCarran moved at 12:30 to bring up H.R. 7. "All those in favor?" said Wallace promptly. "Aye!" shouted Barkley defiantly, and, "Aye," murmured many others. "All those opposed?" asked Wallace. "NO!" shouted Tom Connally defiantly, and "NO!" shouted a few others. "The vociferousness of those opposing does not conceal the fact that they are a minority in numbers," said Wallace jocularly. There was some rather grim amusement. Pat McCarran, dressed in a perfectly pressed blue suit, his huge square figure turning slowly from side to side, arms akimbo, fingers thrust deep into his coat pockets on both sides, began in his high, husky voice his introduction of the bill. He would not take long, he said, and he didn't. Everyone knew the issues, which "have been debated here at great length on previous occasions and will be debated here at great length on this one." The bill should pass, and he told why he thought so. At the end of five minutes he sat down and Wallace recognized Tall Tom, opening gun for the poll-tax states.

The rolling-haired Texan talked for upwards of three hours. It was a good speech, an able presentation of the constitutional side of the question, full of humor as well and including the famous gestures. The shoulders would hunch, the hands would shoot forward and pull back, the arms and body would sway first to this side to make this point, and then to that side to make that. Three seats away sat ex-Senator Gore of Oklahoma, white-haired, clean-cut, sightless. Toward him Connally would rush for emphasis. Frequently he would reach forth and poke Gore's shoulder for corroboration. The blind man, with his invariable kindly and interested expression, would nod agreeably each time. Then Connally would wheel and pace back along the row of seats toward someone else, gesturing, hunching, uttering his ironic and humorous statements in an indignant tone of voice. From time to time earnest Dick Russell would get up to ask dutiful leading questions: is the Senator aware that so-and-so, is it not true that such-and-such? "The Senator is entirely right," Connally would exclaim, "the Senator is entirely right." Toward the end dapper Abe Murdock, clearing his throat nervously and frequently and shifting the position of his shoulders and arms like a boxer seeking the right stance, attempted to tear down Connally's argument. "May I ask the Senator—" he began each time. After some eight or ten interrogations Tom suddenly remarked, "Now let me ask you something. You answer me for a change. I've been answering you all the time." They got off into hypothetical cases,

such as raising the voting age in Utah to 80 and its probable effect upon Section 2 of Article I of the Constitution. Ultimately Murdock found himself talked down and gave up. Connally finished triumphantly with an attack on cloture. Throughout his speech ran the constant refrain "certain individuals urged on by the necessity for gathering in each scurvy vote, each s-c-u-r-v-y vote," were in league with certain "fast-talking pressure groups" in bringing up the bill. "Sir Galahads leaping on their steeds to come down and reform us" might better be employed, he thought, than in this outrageous assault upon the Constitution. He sat down triumphant after an eagle-screaming, indignant peroration. Cotton Ed got up and heartily shook his hand. Josiah Bailey took the floor.

The good Josiah, pointing out that his own state abolished the poll tax 24 years ago, said he would not have entered the debate against the bill had it not been for two groups: the CIO Political Action Committee and the National Association for the Advancement of Colored People. Speaking in his customary slow, rather academic, but powerful and effective fashion, he threatened again to leave the party if certain things (specifically "Sidney Hillman coming in the window") were not stopped. At 4:43, with Bailey promised the floor again tomorrow, the Senate recessed. Sometime tomorrow the rebuttal is expected to begin.

This morning Tom Stewart and Wherry had Maury Maverick up before their Small Business Complaints Committee. The short, stocky, bull-necked, frog-faced Texan, who told Wherry that he has "tamed down a lot—you didn't know me in the old days"—is vice-chairman of the War Production Board and chairman of the Smaller War Plants Corporation. As such he is having an uphill fight. Most of the skeletons in the WPB closet were rattled during his blunt, honest testimony. "Throughout the fabric of Washington," he said, "runs the idea that the business a man did before Pearl Harbor must decide his reconversion to nonmilitary production. Throughout WPB's 700 industry advisory committees runs the theory that nobody can start reconversion until they can all start together." Unless the anti-trust acts can be enforced soon, he intimated, the already great centralization of American industry will proceed to a point where it cannot be stopped. Very few in WPB, he made clear, are interested in stopping it. Consequently little business, and little business' friends, stand in grave danger of "taking a hell of a beating."

MAY 10, 1944. "Time, time!" cried Danaher with a worried frown today, hurrying down in the elevator with us, riding over on the subway, sprinting for the Senate floor. "You never have time to do anything!" He looked like a little boy, disturbed and nervous and upset. The cares of a Senator, which are no joke, were weighing heavily on him. For all members the pressures of work mount higher and higher in a steady stream that seems to have no ending. Letters to answer, people to see, committees to go to, bills to prepare, documents to read, sessions to attend—the list expands almost without limit. The hired help earns its pay, in the United States Senate.

On the floor, Josiah Bailey finished his speech, threatening once again to bolt the party. Walter George took over, thundering against the bill. Jim Mead responded, neatly sidestepping several sallies by McKellar but otherwise making a rather weak defense of the measure along the only line its supporters can honestly follow—the humanitarian. A few attempt to maintain its constitutionality, but most do not stay long with that argument. The qualifications of voters are reserved to the states, and that's all there is to it. Furthermore, to establish the precedent that the Federal government can go into a state and dictate those qualifications is to establish a precedent that could be very dangerous in days to come. For the same reason cloture, in the last analysis, is probably unwise. It is being defeated in this instance in the name of a cause that is essentially reactionary, but it might be defeated later in a cause of far greater import to America. All these things have to be looked at in the perspective of what has been and what may be, and bearing in mind that in the continuity of the laws is the surest guarantee of the nation. Poll taxes will ultimately go altogether, but it had far better be by state action than by Federal intervention that might conceivably be used someday to tighten the chains on liberty. And cloture will be defeated this time, as it will in the future, and should the occasion arise when filibuster is used to maintain freedom instead of restrict it, we shall be thankful.

The Administration has relinquished Montgomery Ward abruptly. The CIO is annoyed and Sewell Avery still antagonistic. The Republicans are unanimous in placing the most uncomplimentary construction on the President's sudden termination of a rather embarrassing situation.

MAY 11, 1944. Lister Hill, his manner at its most reasonable and earnest, put the quietus today on the lingering hopes of anyone who still thinks cloture will be imposed next Monday. "I think it will be strongly defeated. I think when the vote is taken a large majority will be found to be against it." Wherry's private figures, which he has been diligently gathering for the past two days, show at least 77 expected in attendance. Thirty-three of these are expected to vote for, 44 against. The 1944 poll-tax fight will be over by 1:30 Monday afternoon.

There was a noticeable tendency on the part of the Southerners today to come down off the lofty plane of principle upon which they have heretofore discussed the bill. Leaving the realms of practical constitutionality where they had the company of such sound men as Warren Austin, Carl Hatch and Joseph O'Mahoney, all three opposed to the bill, they repaired instead to the ancient bloody ground upon which whites and "Nigras" contend. John Bankhead began the trend, warning direly of a reviving Ku Klux Klan "if you force this on us." Smacking his lips and managing to look dour, kindly and upset all at once, he remarked with the most exasperating yet the most innocently patronizing air that if you "treat the Nigras right, treat them good, give them justice, they'll stand by you." Why, he said, he has two Nigra servants who have worked for him for 40 years—his "pet Negroes," in the bitter phrase of one Negro writer—and he'd do almost anything to keep them from harm. But when you threaten white supremacy, then that's something else. "Our women, our children, our institutions" are in danger. The K.K.K., if need be, will ride again.

All of this John H., who personally wouldn't hurt a fly, said with nervous indignation. His own record was clear, he emphasized. He "took the stump, made use of the press and all other means, to fight the Ku Klux Klan." But he just wanted the warning to go out. As one who could not be responsible for the consequences, he was telling the North what would happen. Dotted here and there through the galleries Negroes, many in uniform, sat silent and impassively listening. Of the hopeless despair that must have been in some of their hearts they gave no sign. They were eloquent testimony to the human reasons why this bill *ought* to go through, even though there are the soundest possible reasons in law why it will not. It is increasingly hard to understand why the sponsors of H.R. 7 have never taken the course O'Mahoney consistently advocates and put in a constitutional amendment. If they had done so far back in the beginning when the Congress first became concerned, it might be passed and on the books by now. Certainly it would be much farther ahead than these repeated, futile attempts to make what Bailey called yesterday a "frontal assault" upon the Constitution.

Once during the afternoon McKellar had another sharp exchange with Mead, who kept his temper but grew increasingly acid. "All I am saying," Mead said sharply, "is that if you put this bill to a free vote of the American people, the Senator would be in the minority." Scattered applause, very light, unorganized, and white in origin, broke from the galleries. Tom Connally jumped to his feet immediately to demand that the Chair "order the attendants to throw these disturbers out." Kindly old Tunnell, who couldn't be so harsh with anyone if his life had depended on it, hemmed and hawed for a moment, long enough for Old Mack to interpose and say that well, now, he hoped the Senator from Texas would withdraw that request because he, McKellar, intended to read some names of the Communistic agitators who were behind this bill—and he hoped (with a sly grin), he hoped that they might be in the gallery to listen. Tom huffed and puffed a little for the record and finally sat down.

Noticeably during the day, and indeed during the whole debate, the Republicans have scrupulously refrained from taking part. Only Jim Davis of Pennsylvania, one of the 29 signers of the cloture petition which Barkley filed around 2 o'clock, made a brief speech supporting the bill. Millikin, bald, reasonable, with a heavy, grave voice and considerable matter-of-factness, has engaged in a few short colloquies from time to time opposing it. Aside from that, the GOP has kept hands off. Frequently during the debate White alone, or sometimes Burton subbing for him, has been present on the Republican side. Across the aisle Democrat fights Democrat tooth and nail. The minority sits tight, happy and well pleased.

MAY 12, 1944. Cotton Ed made his contribution to the poll-tax debate today, and so did Bilbo, hitherto suppressed by the Southern strategists. Neither's remarks were so very constructive. At one point Maybank jumped up and in a moment of real drama waved a framed picture of the South Carolina legislature of 1868—50 Negroes, 13 whites. This was the legislature which passed the poll tax, he cried: this was the government of South Carolina in her days of anguish. Bilbo is evil and ruthless, Cotton Ed is exclamatory and bombastic, Bailey denounces and Walter George thunders; only Maybank is really and truly bitter. He means what he says with all the sincerity—and it is great—at his volatile and excited command. Eastland was active again today, reiterating the Southerners' "policy argument"—that this whole incident is caused by "Communist agitators." John McClellan, sound, reasonable, intelligent, gave a brief but powerful speech. Even Hattie spoke yesterday. The record has been made, by all who cared to make it, and the Senate now goes over to Monday for the final vote. Wagner, alone of all those speaking, has demanded that the fight be continued even if the first cloture vote fails.

A very tall man with dark eyes beneath dark eyebrows, a wide, unhappy mouth, a straight sandy mustache, and an air of uneasy restlessness came up to the Press Gallery for a little while today: Col. Robert R. McCormick, the Emperor of Chicago, publisher of the *Tribune*. Around him clustered a number of reporters, anxious to see what he might choose to say on the historic occasion. He spoke in quick, rather nervous sentences, laughed little, and when he did forced it out abruptly and as abruptly cut it off. He left very soon, leaving the hasty but definite impression of a man not too happy in his power, uneasy, ridden by dark fears and hatreds, easily hurt and with his guard always up.

By contrast, Major Richard Bong the war ace, curly, pink and cherubic, 23 years old and one of the most destructive men alive, seemed strangely unsophisticated and innocent of the cares of the world when La Follette, speaking from the floor, introduced him in the family gallery and broke the rules of the Senate to lead the applause.

Barkley has finally come out for the fourth term, in an article in *Collier's* today. It is a very reasonable article, placing great stress upon respect for the opposite viewpoint, but it is one of the things which tends to lend increasing weight to the tax-veto comment by sardonic Paul Ward of the Baltimore *Sun*. The Senator's resignation, Paul remarked at the time, was an attempt to commit hari-kari with a rubber sword.

MAY 13, 1944. When I went in to see Aiken today he was thoughtfully scanning the headlines. "HOPE FOR POLL-TAX BILL HANGS ON SENATE CLOTURE VOTE," he read slowly, and added with a dry chuckle, "Seems like a slim hope."

Wherry's original figure of 33 for cloture, 44 against (which he has subsequently raised to 41 for, 44 against), was confirmed for me by Jim Eastland; exclusive, he said, of Gurney, Bob Reynolds, and Revercomb. Later Les Biffle, the slight, brisk, harrassed-looking and monumentally efficient Majority Secretary around whom the Senate revolves, came up with 34 for, 43 against. It is very probable that the final vote will not vary more than two or three at the most within the Eastland–Biffle range.

Wagner, fortified by Mead, is still thumping the drums for a continuation of the fight after the vote at one o'clock Monday. The parliamentary situation will be such as to make it virtually impossible. When cloture fails, H.R. 7 will still be the business before the Senate, but it may be displaced by a simple motion to take up another bill. (Someone suggested yesterday that it might suitably be the claims bill "For the relief of Winnie Left Her Behind," which has been on the calendar for some months.) Unless Wagner can muster enough votes to defeat this motion, H.R. 7 will be dead.

One of the South's most active younger spokesmen summed up the basic philosophy behind his own stand on this measure succinctly today. "Hell," he said calmly, "this wouldn't put niggers on the voting lists even if it did go through. Niggers don't vote in my state and niggers aren't going to vote in my state." And that, he intimated with a slow grin, was that.

MAY 15, 1944. Lobbyists infested the Office Building like vermin this morning, apparently trying to change a few votes. In their fashion they too were making a record. The votes they changed were not apparent in the final tally.

Pepper opened debate shortly after noon. While he spoke the galleries were filling up; before he finished his brief address most of the seats were

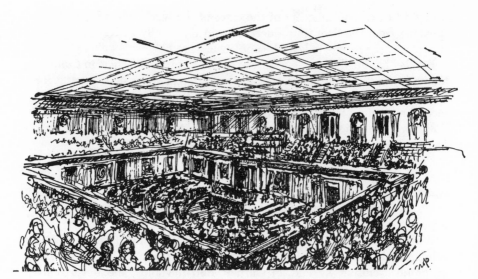

full. Along the back behind the rows of seats long lines of people stood against the wall. Negroes and servicemen dotted the audience. As on all the Senate's great occasions, an indefinable but all-pervading air of tension increased steadily throughout the minutes preceding the vote. Members gathered in small groups to talk, paying scant attention to debate. Pepper demanded cloture with violent indignation. Bilbo made the rebuttal, with equal violence. Chavez shouted that he would vote Aye on the bill "now, or a week or two weeks, or six months from now, but I will never vote for cloture!" Connally put in one last word for the South. Barkley obtained the floor and made the concluding argument as the clock moved toward 1 P.M. "If this motion for cloture fails," he said, "we all know the bill can never reach a vote." He begged his colleagues to permit a vote on the merits of the bill, begged them to support cloture. At 1 o'clock he sat down. Stumbling a little over his words and twisting his sentences slightly, as he does when under pressure, Henry Wallace put the question. With 78 Senators present the Clerk began the quorum call required by the rules. "Seventy-eight Senators being present," said Henry Wallace presently, "a quorum is present. The question is on limiting debate on the pending bill. The Clerk will call the roll." The slow tally began: "Mr. Aiken!" "No" ... "Mr. Austin!" ... "Mr. Andrews!" ... "Mr. Bailey!" ... "No" ... "Mr. Ball!" ... "Aye" ... "Mr. Bankhead!" ... "No" ... "Mr. Barkley!" ... "Aye" .... "Mr. Kilgore!" ... "Aye". .... "Mr. Pepper!" ... "Aye". .... "Mr. Russell!" ... "No" ... "Mr. Wheeler!" ... "Aye" ...

And presently Henry Wallace, matter-of-factly:

"On this vote the Yeas are 36, the Nays are 44, and the motion is not agreed to."

At once the tension snapped, Senators began to mill around the floor, and in the galleries the listening flocks arose obedient to some unseen compulsion and took their leave.

Aside from an hour-long harangue in which Pat McCarran tried to force continued discussion of the bill and Barkley and White both opposed him—ending when Bennett Champ Clark got an approving vote of 41–36 on his motion to take up a veterans' bill, automatically displacing H.R. 7— the poll-tax fight was at an end for one more Congress.

There are some who have written bitterly that this has been a "farce." Insofar as the end has been foreordained and known to everyone on the Hill for weeks, it may have been. Looked at from the standpoint of the Senate put deliberately on an embarrassing spot, however, and faced with the necessity for getting off that spot with as much neatness and dispatch as possible, the way the problem has been handled is commendable and reflects considerable credit upon Barkley, White, the poll-taxers and the anti-poll-taxers. The result should be a lesson—although it will probably not be—to all the proponents of this particular method of abolishing the poll tax. As Barkley frankly said at one point in the debate, "If any Senator thinks, or any outside organization thinks, that outside pressure can make the Senate change its votes, that belief is mistaken. I know the Senate of the United States, and it does not yield to that kind of pressure." Anyone familiar with the Senate can attest to the truthfulness of that. The last way on earth to handle the Senate is to try to beat it over the head with the club of high-pressure lobbying. Its back stiffens, its hackles rise, and that's the end of any hope for a reasonable discussion of the matter at hand. Members resent being bludgeoned. They will kill a measure rather than give in to the type of attack they have been under for the past three weeks.

As for the merits of the bill itself, and the tragic fact that it has been presented in this form in which it can never pass though it be introduced in a hundred Congresses, that is another matter. In all the freely thrown charges of "bad faith" that have been tossed at the Senate, there is perhaps a small section which might be reserved for some of the organizations backing H.R. 7. They are not really interested in getting the poll tax abolished, one suspects, otherwise they would have attempted to do so by the only honest method, a constitutional amendment. They are only interested in controversy, and should an amendment pass and the controversy be ended, they would be out of work in their peculiar employment of keeping dissension at fever heat. On the day a constitutional amendment is put in and they get behind it and give it the same highly organized support they have given H.R. 7, this doubt of their integrity will go. On that day also the Senate will truly stand before the bar of history, the Southerners' bluff will be called, the merits of the bill will be the only thing at issue, and a free vote on a fair challenge will at last be secured. Until that day, however, the black pall of the poll tax—and the black tragedy of the Negro with which it is so inextricably bound—will continue to furnish work for those who would rather profit from recurrent, futile assaults upon it than abandon their great investment in bitterness to seek the real, the only honest, solution.

12

THEY ALL COME UP

MAY 16, 1944. Humphrey Mitchell, Canada's Minister of Labor, stopped in to see Bob Wagner this afternoon, and Bob invited in the press. It was a typical amiable Wagner affair: the conversation hopped here and there in friendly fashion without getting much of anywhere. Mitchell, a huge, red-faced, clipped-speech man, spoke with candor on labor in the Dominion. Offhand, he listed for us his enormous powers: wage stabilization, civilian selective service, social insurance, war labor regulations, pensions —"What else is there, George? There're so many I can't remember them all." At some length he went into Canada's handling of labor and manpower, "all under one tent." "I don't intend to criticize another country's way of doing things; I'm just telling you how Canada does it." How Canada does it, we gathered, is pretty good.

Wagner, drawn out on OPA, became a trifle glum, as he does from time to time. "Each group who feels something is wrong wants to change the law. 'What did you do?' we ask them. 'Well, we appealed it.' 'And you had a hearing?' 'Yes.' 'Well, what was the decision?' 'It was against us. We want to change the law.'" He laughed rather morosely. Mitchell joined in with the knowing air of an old parliamentarian. Wagner skipped to his son: "Young Bob is in England now." "Bob La Follette?" asked Mitchell promptly. "No, my son Bob," Wagner said. He gave a thoughtful chuckle. "I'm a grandfather now." "Where's he stationed?" Mitchell asked. "Somewhere outside London." "I was in London," said Mitchell promptly. "Flew over just recently." Wagner looked pensive. He had been in London, too, once, when he introduced a slum-clearance bill and wanted some firsthand evidence from other lands as well as his own. "Those were the days when people said everything I did was unconstitutional. But they upheld it—they upheld it. There it is, on the wall." And there it was indeed, the front page of the New York *Daily News*, framed: WAGNER LABOR ACT UPHELD. He sighed. "This OPA, though. Gee, it's a fight. I hope there's still some progressives left in the Senate, but I don't know." Again he sighed.

"I don't know." Mitchell rose, hearty and huge, hands were shaken all around, the conference was over. We had spent a little while with a man who very obviously gets what he wants and no questions asked, and a man, once in the vanguard of an eager band, who now stands unhappily almost alone on his farther shore while the tide runs out and the waves recede and all the gallant company of other days falters and turns back.

MAY 17, 1944. The State, Justice and Commerce Appropriations bill went through in about 20 minutes this afternoon, followed by the Agriculture Appropriations bill. Both had been the subject of exhaustive hearings before the Appropriations Committee, and both were more or less cut-and-dried affairs. Little argument was expected and little arose, with the single exception of a no-politics amendment the House tacked on the Agriculture bill. This proviso, withholding salaries from any Department of Agriculture employees found to have engaged in any type of political activity whatsoever, stirred up quite a tempest. The committee threw it out and the Republicans tried to put it back in. A lot of names were called in the process. Not since the soldier-vote fight has politics come so close to the surface.

The committee stand, stated reasonably by fleshy-faced, soft-voiced Dick Russell, was that the Hatch Act covered all that anyway and therefore there was no reason for the amendment. McKellar strengthened this argument. Legislating in an appropriations bill! Why, Mr. President, that was too much. And to single out one department for special treatment, to attempt to set special restrictions on one department—that was compounding the felony. Old Mack, who a short time ago was singling out one department, TVA, and doing his damnedest to cut its throat, was as violently sincere about it as anybody could be.

MAY 18, 1944. James Forrestal, a slight, short-spoken, graying man with a hard-boiled face and a self-effacing manner, came up today to lend his weight as newly confirmed Secretary of the Navy to the drive to pass the Brewster–Bailey 4-F draft bill. Patterson also returned, looking tireder, more impassive than ever, obviously a man who drives himself relentlessly. Donald Nelson was there too, a big man with a long, oval face, a slick, thinning pompadour, little eyebrows that shoot up sharply, intelligent eyes, a small, severe mouth, a light voice and a great air of impatience with the Senate. He has been having rather rough going on the Hill lately, at the hands of both the Small Business Committee and McCarran's liquor committee, which has resumed hearings. All three of these busy men, who have nothing to contribute which can possibly persuade the Senate to approve any sort of labor draft, had been called away from their desks to endorse the bill all over again. Bob Reynolds, fulsome and sardonic, was no more impressed than he ever has been, and soundings in the Senate seem to indicate that the measure is as dead as Warren Austin's national service bill.

MAY 19, 1944. Today Wherry, for himself and 32 other Republicans, introduced a constitutional amendment to abolish the poll tax. The reaction has been interesting, and just about what one would expect. It is Republican politics; or it is an attempt to get the Negro vote; or it is a try at stealing the idealistic banner of a pure Administration. The Southerners, their talk about constitutionalism shown up for what it is, are against it. Mead and his cohorts, their issue stolen by the opposition, are showing strong signs of doubtfulness about it all, and people like Joe O'Mahoney, jealous of the fact that their pet thunder has been stolen, denounce it as a farce.

All these things may be true. The fact remains, however, that a constitutional amendment, backed by the largest organized group which has yet attempted to go after the poll tax with this method, has been introduced. The issue is squarely up to the Southerners and it is squarely up to Jim Mead and his friends. If everybody involved in this peculiar matter were sincere, it wouldn't make any difference who introduced it. They would all get behind it, taking advantage of the basic bloc of 37 Republican votes, and put it through. The amendment has been referred to Judiciary. "I don't think anybody's going to lose his head over it," says Pat McCarran drily. The Republicans, who have achieved their purpose whether it passes or not, would probably be the last to urge that anybody should.

MAY 20, 1944. Walter George's tax simplification bill went through today after Bill Langer had succeeded in holding it up by a three-and-a-half hour filibuster yesterday, forcing a Saturday session and thoroughly annoying his colleagues. His principle was sound, though his method as usual was rather flamboyant. Rather than accept a virtual *fait accompli* from the Finance Committee, Bill said, he wanted time to study the 50-odd page report on a 30-odd page bill. This business of rushing it through on George's say-so, he intimated, was hardly democratic. As one of the few men who never hesitate to hold up the Senate on some such point of order, he asked George to let it go over to Monday so that members might study the bill. George refused, so Langer filibustered. George said he was going to let him talk himself out if it took all night, but shortly after 5 P.M. capitulated and agreed to a Saturday session. Langer, satisfied, permitted the bill to pass about 1 P.M. this afternoon.

Out in Oregon, Rufus Holman, the Senate's first electoral casualty, has apparently lost the Republican primary to Wayne Morse. Quiet, self-effacing little Guy Cordon, McNary's successor, has won renomination to succeed himself for the remaining four years of the McNary term. It is a rather signal victory for a political unknown, a temporary appointee, who has only been in office four months.

The V.P., a Chinese grammar in his suitcase and good will in his heart, has gone off to Asia.

MAY 21, 1944. Jesse Jones was up the other day, a tall old man with white hair, rosy chipmunk cheeks, dark eyes, a Texas drawl, and an air of serene power. The air is not unwarranted, for Jesse does have the power, more power per square inch, perhaps, than anyone in town except the Boss himself. And Jesse, who plays this side of the street more carefully than anybody else in the government, takes good care to see that his power stays in good repair.

Jesse has this power for a lot of reasons: partly because he's a smooth old politician, partly because he's one of the Texas Gang, partly because he's a likable cuss, but more than anything else, maybe, because he just has his finger in so doggoned many pies. Sometimes it seems there's no limit to the things Jesse's head of, secretary of this and chairman of that and president of the other. When Jesse wants something done he consults with himself for a while, and then he tells himself he can do it, and then he does it. Sometimes the Hill objects, but Jesse comes up and talks to them a little bit, and then it's all right. Nobody really stays mad at Jesse for very long. Jesse holds the ends of too many strings.

Of course some people don't like Jesse very well. Clyde Reed doesn't like him. "I'm getting sick and tired," Clyde Reed says, "of the way Jesse tries to run this Congress." But Jesse doesn't care. He goes right on running it just the same.

Jesse, in a way, is the one real connecting link between the Hill and downtown. If any one man in himself represents the transmission belt of the Administration, Jesse's the man. This is because Jesse knows which side his bread is buttered on; Jesse knows the advantages of getting along with the boys. Jesse keeps them happy and they do the same for Jesse. Jesse's nobody's fool.

There are lots of places to go to get things done, of course, and if you want to, you can spend your time chasing around downtown going to them. But if you really want results, if you really want action—well, there's a lot of available advice but it all boils down to one thing.

You'd better see Jesse.

MAY 22, 1944. Donald Nelson was around again today, his fourth visit to the Hill in almost as many days. "I think Nelson does a remarkable job of running the war," one reporter remarked, "running it from these committees up here the way he does."

The occasion today was the Truman Committee's investigation of the paper shortage. Nelson, feeling himself among friends, was in a more amiable mood than he has been on other visits. Carl Hatch, his lined, weathered-looking face breaking into frequent friendly smiles, was an encouraging chairman. Mon Wallgren, just back from Washington, took care to look after his timber growers but was otherwise amiable. Homer Ferguson in his big shaggy-bear fashion was respectful though inquisitive, and Brewster, although pointed as he often is, with a sort of courteous New England intimation that the witness is trying to dodge the facts, gave his quick smile often and followed an earnest and reasonable line of questioning. Truman himself was speaking in Brooklyn and the rest of the committee was split up among other hearings.

The more Nelson comes around the deeper grows the conviction that he is a remarkable man, all things considered. Indubitably capable, there is also about him a firm conviction that he is in there to do a job—no less, and no more. Where some people downtown would welcome with eager delight the chance to allocate paper in such a way as to dictate editorial policies and news-play, Donald Nelson remarked with sincere emphasis that to do so, in his view, would be to impose censorship. "We cannot determine the less essential uses of the printed word," he said, adding with a sudden laugh and a humorous positiveness, "If the industry wants me to, I'll be more than glad to get together with them and draw up a bill to put this thing under an independent agency. I don't like the job, I don't want to do it, it gives me more headaches than any other thing I do." The newspaper business, he added rather thoughtfully, "is certainly the most com-

WPB chairman nelson

petitive I have ever been connected with." In the same way he testified before the liquor hearing that his job is not to tell the industry what to produce but simply to meet war necessities. Throughout his whole approach to his enormous job runs that philosophy: this is the job. I am here to do it. I shall do it the best I can. When it is over I shall give it up, thank God. He doesn't want to remodel the world or revise the social system, and while there is certainly a place in Washington for those who do, it is more likely, perhaps, that when the ultimate credit for winning this war is distributed, the major portion of it will go to America's Nelsons. They take care of the country while the others take care of the dreaming.

In the afternoon the interminable investigation of the Rural Electrification Administration dragged on to 5:15, Henrik Shipstead of the clipped accent and the dry, acid humor, in the chair, Aiken dutifully alongside, bored but sticking with it. The topic today, as often before, was the drive last year to oust REA Administrator Harry Slattery. This was carried on in several peculiar ways, some of them endorsed by the White House. A lot of suave people who appear on the stand, take the oath, and then play with the truth with the most matter-of-fact calmness, have told the committee about it. The facts have yet to emerge—the process is rather like using a bent pin on the end of a thread to raise an ounce of quicksilver from the bottom of a barrel of molasses. The committee flounders over its head in endless letters, memorandums, charges, countercharges, lies, assertions and denials. What the end result is going to be, nobody knows. The investigation of REA's practices and procedures has been running on for at least four months now, and the goal is not yet in sight. The only certainty is that something is certainly rotten. Sometimes when you lift one of the manhole covers downtown you find a cesspool underneath: this seems to be one of the times. When you grant that, though, you still haven't got much.

MAY 23, 1944. Three of the Senate's finest men, on what must certainly be the best committee in the history of the American Congress, went after an evasive, weaseling witness today with all the coordinated precision of a high-geared machine. Harry Truman, Carl Hatch and Homer Ferguson had themselves a field-day at the paper hearing, and the press had one too. It wasn't much to write about, the man was minor and the incident small, but as an exercise in technique it was a delight to watch. As always when the Truman Committee gets down to cases, it left us with a renewed appreciation for its work and the excellent men who compose it.

The party in question, a small sly man with a little mustache and a habit of looking candidly into his questioner's eyes while deliberately weaseling on the answer, represented a firm which had in some strange fashion been able to get four times the paper allotment in 1944 that it had received in 1943. This windfall had been granted on Aug. 7, 1943, three days after a Truman Committee hearing at which the gentleman and his employer had failed to show. The connection between these two circumstances—the failure to appear for Truman, the grant by WPB—intrigued the Senators. They wanted to know why. It took them almost an hour, but they found out. Truman led off with the opening questions, returning to them with the brisk good humor and blunt attention to detail that characterize him on such occasions. Ferguson, his dark eyes innocent and thoughtful, his lips pursed, staring off into space with an air of almost wistful patience while the witness ducked and dodged, softened him up. Carl Hatch, speaking in his slow, courtly, friendly fashion, and smiling his rather unique smile, warm, intimate, all-embracing, "this-is-just-between-you-and-me-and-forget-all-these-other-distracting-people," administered the *coup de grace.*

"Wasn't it really, then," he asked kindly, "that you refused to appear before us because you had reason to believe that it would prejudice your case with the War Production Board?" "That's right," said the witness promptly, misled as they always are by Carl's confidential manner. Inasmuch as this was an answer he had ducked, dodged and evaded for nearly an hour, it brought down the house. It had taken the committee a little time to get what it wanted, but as usual it had succeeded.

To a certain extent, also, it got what it wanted concerning WPB this morning. As always when the reassuring presence of Donald Nelson is off the scene, gnawing doubts about his organization return. Several of the small publishers present today, citing names and cases, made out a fairly sound argument for the theory that industry's on-lease boys are pushing things toward the big producers and deliberately squeezing out the little ones. Every so often—more and more frequently, these days—people lift the curtain of righteous integrity that envelops the agency and disclose strange areas of a self-interest far from Nelson's noble purposes. It is a disturbing situation, apparently verified from many sources, and it serves to indicate the dilemma of democracy in wartime. If you put in the pure of heart who have never had anything to do with business, you get a terrific mess. But if you put in the experts who know what it's all about, you get a lot of dirty work at the crossroads. You're damned if you do and damned if you don't. It's a situation for which there is apparently no real, permanent solution. As long as the Truman Committee is on the job, there will be some alleviations, perhaps enough fingers in the dike to keep the flood in check, but there will apparently never be any lasting correction while the war is on. Nelson does what he can, but he can't be everywhere. Behind his back the little foxes keep awfully busy.

On the floor today the Senate whipped through the Interior Department Appropriations bill while Carl Hayden of Arizona, a tall, bald, stringy old man with a sharp mind, presided over its destinies with efficient blandness. Around 3 the Senate recessed until Thursday. "How are things shaping up for the summer recess, Senator?" we asked Barkley. His lips set grimly and a little flush came into his usually good-natured face. "I don't think there's going to be any recess," he said shortly. "By God, I'm getting fed up with this. These Republicans come across the aisle here, wearing out my carpet all the time asking for a recess and then they issue a statement saying there shouldn't be one because we've got too much work to do. I imagine we'll go right on through the conventions. But—" Here, as always, he relented, "I wouldn't want to be quoted on that. Maybe we'll be able to work it out." And the chances are that good old Alben, who lets himself be imposed upon by Republicans as well as Democrats and, along with Biffle, carries nine-tenths of the detail of the Senate on his back, will probably "work it out" when the time comes, and the Republicans will get their recess.

MAY 24, 1944. Banking and Currency Committee has finally reported some progress on the OPA amendments. Bob Wagner, who sighs about the way he can't get any publicity, refused to tell us anything but others were not so reticent. "I can't tell you anything," Bob says with a smile and a wave of the hand. "I'm bound by this agreement, you know, and it's an executive session. No, I can't tell you anything. But the other boys will, I'm sure. They'll tell you. Good luck." Which of course places both the press and the other boys on a nice moral spot. The chairman won't talk because of a committee agreement but he urges you to ask other Senators and get them to break the agreement. Taft, pragmatic and blunt as always, obliged after he heard about this, in the rather scornful fashion which it deserved.

MAY 25, 1944. The Senate took up the calendar today, passing a number of private claims bills, among them Bushfield's bill to get government aid for his South Dakota Indian constituent, Winnie Left Her Behind. Wherry, irrepressible and inclined at times to use the Senate as an arena for horseplay, jumped up immediately and asked Bushfield to explain the bill, a request Senators often make of the sponsors of obscure minor bills. Barkley looked disapproving and Bushfield looked annoyed. With dignity he pointed out that he saw a number of other odd names on the claims list, and didn't see why Winnie had to be singled out for discussion. As a matter of fact, he said, he didn't know whether the name meant that "Winnie left someone else behind or someone else left Winnie behind." Everybody laughed, a jolly note in an otherwise boring session. The

Senate, which is beginning to crowd on the committees and get ready to jam through several pieces of important legislation as the convention deadline draws near, then went over to Monday, with an announcement by Barkley that inasmuch as Tuesday is Decoration Day, the plan is not to meet then; and that unless Walter George wants to bring up the debt-limit bill on Wednesday, it will be the purpose to go over to Thursday, at which time OPA will be taken up.

MAY 26, 1944. The most powerful man on earth was in a little better mood with the press today when I went to the White House for my second visit. The false joviality, the acrid edge to the voice that puts over the punch lines with the stinger in the tail, were not quite so pronounced this time. Even so it was not hard to remember that we were not all the best of friends. At best the amusement of these gatherings is never very profound, and underlying the dutiful sycophantic merriment is a mental reservation that is not flattering to the President of the United States.

Drawn out on the Great Enigma he remained enigmatic, though light-hearted. Someone enterprising pointed out that enough delegates are already pledged to assure nomination, the only barrier being the President's refusal to accept. "I'm not asking what your decision is," the questioner added, "only if you've reached a decision." This provoked quite a laugh, followed by the comment that that was a new approach to the question; the President said he would add it to his list. "Are you going to answer all of them at the same time?" someone else wanted to know. "Time will tell," he replied with a happy chuckle.

The Washington *Post*'s suggestion of the term "liberation" instead of the term "invasion" drew his approval. He read us a little lecture on postwar planning. He said the United States was doing a lot of it.

Somebody referred to Pat McCarran's critical report on the Montgomery Ward seizure, just out and severely castigating everyone from the President on down. What did he think of the Senator's suggestion for court review of War Labor Board decisions? He said he would ask a question himself in reply to that one. If a plant was closed down because an employer failed to comply, and people were out, maybe people starving, and the thing had to go to the circuit court of appeals and the Supreme Court and Congressional committees, who would pay for the poor devils' food and clothing?

Somebody asked if "Mr. Churchill's blueprint of the postwar world conforms with yours and Mr. Hull's?" This produced the usual hesitation, followed by the characteristic tone of voice which implies, "Oh, come now, let's be reasonable." "Oh, I can't say anything about that. We've been talking for over a year, now. We've been holding many discussions." Someone else wanted to know if there would be another meeting with Churchill. Perhaps in the late spring or summer or fall, he replied. "How about winter, Mr. President?" "Oh, I don't like winter, I don't like winter on the Atlantic." We laughed politely. "Thank you, Mr. President," said somebody crisply. It chorused from a hundred throats as we began to troop out.

Hanging back a little and looking him over as the crowd departed, I could see that he had a good coat of tan and looked thinner, the lines of his face pronounced, the same appearance of a man undeniably aging but still vigorous. He seemed today to be under a little less strain than before.

MAY 27, 1944. On December 3 last year, noting my first committee assignment, I remarked that I had covered Judiciary and watched Joe O'Mahoney go to town on the bill to exempt the insurance business from the anti-trust laws. Today, six months later, I have to note that I again covered Judiciary and again watched Joe O'Mahoney go to town on the bill to exempt the insurance business from the anti-trust laws. It gave me a curious feeling of this-is-where-I-came-in, something which I understand is characteristic in the recurring cycles of activity on the Hill.

MAY 28, 1944. The cancer of politics eats deeper into the Truman Committee as election nears and the partisan interests of the chairman take him more and more extensively onto public platforms. In a speech to the Connecticut Democratic Convention Friday Harry Truman charged that the Republicans were attempting to turn to advantage facts brought forth by "the Democrats themselves" through the committee. Joe Ball and Homer Ferguson both countered yesterday, Ball with the sharp comment that so far Truman seemed to be the only one interested in using the committee for partisan purposes, and Ferguson asserting that "in several cases" (which he did not further elaborate) the Administration had deliberately attempted to block the committee's investigations by withholding information and silencing witnesses. The whole situation is rather disturbing in view of the very great value of the committee's work and the sincerely nonpartisan spirit that has heretofore, despite occasional great provocation, dominated its activities. As nearly as any outside observer can see, the committee is going along just about as usual, fair, objective, not pulling its punches and neither unduly white-washing nor unnecessarily attacking. It seems rather too bad that a lot of charges and countercharges have to be hurled back and forth by men who should know better, men whose patriotic cooperation has made possible the finest of committee records.

MAY 29, 1944. After a long session in Judiciary this morning, the Republicans' poll-tax amendment was consigned to a subcommittee on a strict party vote of 10–7. O'Mahoney's amendment was also referred to the group, which includes himself, Hatch, and several other of the ablest members of the committee, and there is some reasonable chance that the two amendments may be molded into one that will eventually be reported out. At least they have not been killed off, and that is something. The proper method of handling this thing has been put in operation; the Senate is heading in the right direction at last, even though it may take some time to get there. [*It did. Not until August, 1962, did Congress finally pass the amendment. It is now before the states for ratification, with approval by 38, the necessary three-fourths, expected.*]

Late in the day Banking and Currency reported out the OPA extension act, carrying a number of amendments, the principal one being a package of dynamite concocted by Bankhead that would require the maximum price for cotton textiles to reflect the price of raw cotton, plus the cost of transporting cotton to the point of manufacture, plus the cost of processing, plus "a reasonable profit." OPA says this will cost the consumer "from $225,000,000 to $350,000,000 more per year for clothing." Taft says shortly that it will only cost $20,000,000 to $30,000,000. With the single exception of Danaher, who voted against it, the Republicans on the committee stood by the Southerners and put it through on a vote of 12–6. A subsequent Danaher motion to reconsider was lost 12–8. Wagner, Danaher, Radcliffe, Maloney, Murdock and possibly one or two others intend to file a "statement of minority views" and fight the amendment on the floor. It promises to cause a hot battle.

MAY 30, 1944. The whole issue of contract termination, the whole implication of postwar reconversion [*increasingly important now as the Axis appeared to be losing ground ever more rapidly*] was thrown suddenly into relief today when Jim Murray called before his Military Affairs subcommittee the leading participants in the Brewster Aeronautical Company case. The firm, holding a Navy contract for Corsair fighters, was notified on Friday, May 19, that its contract would be canceled. On Monday, May 22, the formal termination notice came. Over this past week end the CIO United Auto Workers, charging fantastic political plots in the Navy ("Is this an attempt to embarrass President Roosevelt and Senator Wagner?"), decided to remain on the job in an extraordinary protest against the Navy's action. The issue was dramatized, and Murray made the most of it.

Out of the day-long testimony, however, in which the president of Brewster, a small, trim, worried man; Richard Frankensteen of the UAW, a heavy, pragmatic young man; Rear Admiral DeWitt Ramsey, chief of the Bureau of Aeronautics; and Charles Wilson of the WPB, a big red-faced man with a belligerent jaw and heavy glasses, all gave their versions of the story. The only common denominator that emerged was confusion.

The Navy apparently consulted no one until the last minute. Once consulted, no one could do anything but offer temporary makeshifts and the constantly repeated idea that "other war work" should be given the corporation to keep it going. "Continuing production for production's sake," as Ramsey pointed out at one point with quiet desperation, is not the soundest policy imaginable, yet that is what the testimony of all concerned boiled down to. War work and more war work and more war work—and after that? No one dared to say.

In the afternoon the White House took a hand. The President said he had asked other government agencies and the Navy to give Brewster "other war contracts." This would solve everything, he intimated: the "test-tube case" had apparently been settled to his satisfaction. The union, mollified, agreed to withdraw its people and await the government's pleasure. Brewster's officials were pleased, and on the Hill Murray announced approval. All was well: the *status quo* had been restored. The thing about it, which none of the participants seemed to realize, was that the *status quo* was the *status quo* of war. In desperation, faced with the end of war work, the company sought more war work. In desperation, faced with the end of war employment, the union sought more war employment. In desperation, faced with the breakdown of the war economy, the White House sought more war economy. And in desperation, faced with the implications of peace, the spokesman of the Hill turned back in nervous haste to the familiar mechanisms of war. It was an ominous portent for the future.

Despite 12 years of unhampered experimentation, despite government planning, the primed pump, and all the dreams and visions of a long decade, when you take away the artificial stimulus of the greatest war in history you find us right where we started. We still don't know how to handle the industrial system.

MAY 31, 1944. A Judiciary subcommittee composed of Hatch, O'Mahoney, Happy Chandler, Ferguson and Alexander Wiley voted today to report out a resolution extending the statute of limitations governing the time when trials must be held in the Kimmel–Short Pearl Harbor court-martials until Dec. 7 this year. That was as amended: the original resolution, by Ferguson, extended it only to Sept. 7. The present resolution governing the case expires next week, on June 7. Naturally a lot of people are doing some fast scrambling to get it delayed. Over in the House the Rules Committee has given the go-ahead to a resolution extending it to June 7, 1945, an even more desirable suggestion from some points of view. Meanwhile, in a pathetic, plaintive letter to Ferguson, Kimmel has renewed his plea that he be tried immediately. The Roberts report, he says, is not the whole story of Pearl Harbor. What that story is the country will apparently not be allowed to find out so long as the Administration can prolong the case. Meanwhile witnesses, scattered either deliberately or by the fortunes of war, are dying off in some cases, gradually forgetting in others. Time is being used to achieve a purpose that a forthright investigation would apparently defeat.

The debt-limit bill passed today, boosting to $260,000,000,000 the artificial figure on one side of which we feel safe and on the other uncertain. It is a worthless piece of paper, yet if someone were to propose a resolution reading "Whereas, the United States will obviously spend as much money as it needs to win the war, therefore it is the sense of the Congress that all debt limitations be removed for the duration of hostilities," the country in all probability would feel financially lost to the point of panic. Words are strange fetishes, sometimes.

With the debt-limit bill out of the way, Overton asked unanimous consent to take up the Rivers and Harbors bill, a glorious catch-all that includes everything in the way of pet projects but the kitchen sink, but White and Robertson blocked him. "Is the Senate supposed to sit still," Overton demanded, "simply because the OPA bill is not ready to be brought up until Monday?" White argued in his quavery voice and earnest manner that he would rather see the Senate maintain the "understanding and agreement" that OPA was to come up first, even if it meant sitting still. After a long wrangle, the Senate went over to tomorrow, when it will do nothing except recess until Monday, meaning that it will do nothing on Friday or Saturday either. Meanwhile the conventions come closer and closer, and a grand fooforaw in which complicated legislation is jammed through with sloppy haste becomes virtually inevitable. There is no excuse for it, despite White's reiteration of "an understanding among Senators."

JUNE 1, 1944. The Senate met today for 12 minutes and went over to Monday. The understanding has been maintained.

In Judiciary this morning the full committee voted to report out Ferguson's resolution on Pearl Harbor, but extended the time to June 7, 1945. The resolution does take the positive step of directing the services to begin an investigation and gather the facts; this they must do within the year. The Navy began such a proceeding in March. Significantly, Hatch told us the Army "only agreed to do so this morning." Ferguson, who was arguing with Abe Murdock with some heat as the executive session broke up, told us he was satisfied, so long as the facts could be gathered "before they are all forgotten." Happy Chandler was voluble and upset and maintained consistently that the resolution says "in their discretion" the services will press charges after the investigation. " 'In their discretion' means after the war," he pointed out with some emphasis. It was not entirely clear where Hap stood in all this, but he was certainly fed up with the whole situation. He was very good-natured but talked a flood while Carl Hatch laughed and soothed him like one talking to a volatile child, which Happy, the complete extrovert, sometimes resembles. Anyway, Ferguson seemed satisfied, and the committee voted unanimously—with the exception of Connally, who claimed the resolution cast doubt on the integrity of the services and he wouldn't be a party to it.

The fantastic idea I first heard more than five months ago—that some of the Southern states might name electors who would vote against Roosevelt in the Electoral College—is bearing fruit in surprising fashion. The Texas Democratic convention demanded certain things in the national platform and announced that if they were not granted, Texas' electors would be instructed to vote, not for the nominee, but for some other Democrat of their choice. South Carolina's recent convention recessed without instructing its electors, to meet again in August after the national convention; and the rumor that Mississippi will "hit the front pages soon" is afloat on the Hill.

JUNE 3, 1944. Today the President made a slip in his endless little game with the rest of the country. Greeting a Congressional delegation he spotted bald Bill Lemke of North Dakota who ran against him in 1936. "Well, Bill," he asked with a laugh, "are you going to run against me this year?" There was a moment's silence, broken by muffled amusement. The President blushed and added hastily, "That is, if I run." People who get all excited about such things thought that was awfully cute and revealing, but most of the press gallery dismissed it with a shrug. The whole topic is becoming just a mite, just a trifle boring.

13

PRECONVENTION

JUNE 5, 1944. Theodore Bilbo, whose dangerousness is compounded by the fact that he is by no means unintelligent or stupid, but on the contrary shrewd and ruthless, got up today to attack the Court. The motive obviously was the recent Texas case decision giving Negroes the right to vote in primaries, but the approach was a trifle oblique. "Split-hair definitions" drew his ire at some length. Frankfurter, although unnamed, came in for an acid paragraph. The Court, said Theodore, is engaged upon a systematic attempt to invade the prerogatives of the legislative and executive branches. There are times in Washington when one gets the impression, to hear the talk, that three independent authorities are engaged in constant raiding parties against one another. Bilbo did what he could to strengthen the impression today. Senators who agree with him were undoubtedly encouraged in their belief when word drifted over from across Capitol Plaza that a decision holding insurance to be commerce within the meaning of the interstate commerce clause [and therefore subject to the controls O'Mahoney has been advocating] had been handed down.

O'Mahoney, of course, was jubilant. Six months' work has not been in vain, the Senator indicated in his happy statement to the press. "I had no doubt as to the outcome," he remarked. His one-man filibuster in committee has borne the fruit he hoped it would, and his ambition has been achieved.

The OPA fight began today, starting a debate which promises to turn into a wrangle much longer than Wagner had fondly hoped. Taft's amendment providing that after July 1, 1945, no subsidies shall be paid without specific Congressional appropriation sailed through 50–22. The anti-subsidy sentiment in the Senate has apparently not diminished. Taft, who once during the hearings remarked with a rather rueful laugh "Maybe this time we had better add a clause saying, 'This time we mean it!'" seems to be succeeding in his attempts to do just that.

Bankhead has come out with an angry statement attacking "OPA propaganda" against his cotton amendments.

Out of order in the midst of the debate Carl Hatch called up the Pearl Harbor resolution and got it passed in a couple of minutes.

JUNE 6, 1944. D-Day came today, for me at 6:30 in the morning when the office called. "Al," said someone on the desk laconically, "the show is on." Color at the Capitol might be needed, he said; I departed for the Hill forthwith. Subsequently it was decided that I would write none, for indeed there was none to write. Just a beautiful cool morning, the flag rippling in the wind, the sun slanting across the front of the huge old building, a few cars passing early from Union Station, green grass glistening, an air of quiet peace. Elsewhere time hung suspended and young men who would never see another day plunged forward into hell. On Capitol Hill at that early hour it was just another June morning, nature as always impervious to man.

On the floor at noon both houses stopped for prayer. In the House this solemn period lasted for half an hour, in the Senate somewhat less. The business of the day was then resumed with customary vigor. Already this evening some commentators are making stern remarks about the way in which Congress "stopped to pray and then went right back to arguing." What else the Congress might do it is hard to see. It is unlikely that any purpose could be served if everybody dropped everything and sat around thinking about the invasion. Aside from the deep underlying prayer everyone will carry with him from now until it is over, nothing could be gained by such oversentimentalizing. The job of the troops in England was to cross the Channel. The job of the Congress is to legislate. It was perfectly fitting that both should attend to their duties.

Wherry beat Abe Murdock in a fair fight on Wherry's OPA amendment today after a really good debate in which both gentlemen argued with convincing earnestness. Wherry was the more convincing, all the logic in fact being on his side, but Murdock put up a good battle. Wherry finally beat him down to one last, weak argument—that Wherry's proposed amendment would "overburden" the price administrator ("We've heard a lot here today about doing justice to the poor, overworked price administrator," Walter George thundered later. "I'm interested in doing a little justice to the poor American citizen"), and then proceeded to demolish that. The committee had approved an amendment giving convicted defendants in OPA criminal suits the right to file within 5 days after judgment a protest against the regulation under which they were tried. If the regulation should be found invalid, the case would be closed and the charges dismissed. Wherry wanted to know why this shouldn't be extended to civil suits. Despite the fact that Murdock argued with him for nearly an hour, there just wasn't any answer. When a vote was finally taken all but the most dutiful OPA-lovers laid aside partisanship and paid tribute to the Nebraskan's logic with an approving vote of 48 to 26.

After that Walter George got up, r'ared back, and passed his usual miracle. The only man who tackles Walter is Bob La Follette, and today he agreed with him so there wasn't any argument. The George amendment would require OPA to bring suit in the area where the defendant resides, and is of course only sensible.

In the evening I went to a dinner at the Mayflower given by the National Cotton Council. Bankhead, who never makes the slightest bones about the lobbyists who infest his office, hang on his arm, write his bills for him and tell him how to vote—"They're my boys," he says complacently, "they're my boys"—was toastmaster. Surrounding him were Ed O'Neal, Albert Goss, the Cotton Council and all the other farm representatives who camp on Congress' doorstep. A lot of Congressmen were there, not very impressed. McFarland was on hand, rather uncomfortable and disconsolate, and Harry Truman and Dick Russell also came along. It was one of those lobbying dinners one reads about in dark stories about pressure groups in Washington: from the conversation around me it didn't change a single vote. These affairs are apparently so routine that nobody pays much attention to them: it's free drinks and free food, and if the poor suckers think that's the way to get votes, well, hell, why turn it down? Congressmen, despite the popular impression, are not easily flattered by such innocuous social gatherings. The Cotton Council president's statement that he had umpty-ump thousand members in 14 states was far more to the point.

Paul McNutt played liaison man for the White House at this particular affair, and after the main address spoke briefly in rotund generalizations. He is the sort of speaker who swoops down on his sentences, lowering his head on the first half and then giving 'em the old chin on the last half. "Isn't he a hell of an attractive-looking man?" murmured Harry Truman, sitting nearby. "I think he's a *hell* of an attractive man." The fabulous Paul, with his dark skin, white hair, dark eyes and handsome features, deserves the comment. The thoughts expressed, however, would never set the world on fire.

JUNE 7, 1944. After a long, acrimonious argument between those two old buddies from Kentucky who would gladly drop one another in the Potomac if they could, the good Alben and the exuberant Happy, the Senate added today an amendment to OPA that would make ignorance of the law—providing the defendant could prove it—an adequate defense against an OPA suit. The curtailment of treble damages and the added provision that the Emergency Court of Appeals might impose only one and one-half times that amount were also included in the same amendment. This provoked Taft's opposition. One's surprise at Taft's liberal stands evaporates before the knowledge that he has an honest mind and considerable integrity. To adopt the amendment, he said rather scornfully,

would be to make the whole bill useless. "I don't like price control," he said flatly, "but it is a necessity for the war effort, and so long as we have it it must be enforced. The essence of price control is regulation. It cannot be maintained without it." Despite the fact that Barkley also jumped in and got quite openly annoyed at Chandler—their relations, always wary, are apt to break through the standard veneer of Senatorial chumminess on rather slight provocation at times—the Senate decided to approve the amendment and did so 47–27.

A Senate–House conference committee met hastily this morning on the Pearl Harbor resolution after the House Republicans yesterday steamrollered through an extension of only three months. The conferees split the difference with the Senate's one year and sent to the White House late in the day a bill providing that the Kimmel–Short court-martials will begin not later than December 7 of this year.

June 8, 1944. The Senate spent 5 hours and 25 minutes today arguing over the Bankhead amendments protecting cotton from OPA. Bankhead himself had the floor when the session began and held it until 3 o'clock. Then Eastland took over. In and around and between, people like Radcliffe and Murdock and the vociferous Charles Tobey attempted to debate them down, to no avail. No vote was reached, and the hopes for disposing of the bill this week became increasingly slim. Around 6 Chester Bowles took it upon himself to issue a statement advising the Senate that it had better watch what it was doing and not get too uppity—a bad move from a strategy standpoint, and one which will probably be waved like a red flag by the cotton boys tomorrow.

June 9, 1944. The Senate ran till nearly 7 tonight, in a long, drawn-out session that finally passed Bankhead's escalator amendment, 39–35. Late in the session Chester Bowles was subjected to a scathing attack by Ed Moore in his flat, dry voice. The wizened little Oklahoman made his usual brief for unrestricted enterprise. The OPA should never have been created at all, it ought to be abolished at once, price control is counter to everything American. Ed and his colleague Elmer Thomas wanted to add an amendment raising the price of oil $1.65 per barrel. "Why," cried Taft scornfully, "it is utterly ridiculous to expect us to pass a law that oil should receive a certain number of cents above a given price." The same sentiments came from Vandenberg with equal force and better grace, since he had voted against the Bankhead amendment. The oil amendment lost by a resounding margin, as though a lot of people were easing their consciences. It was a tattered and lopsided piece of legislation that finally emerged from the Senate, even though its procedural amendments, such as those by Wherry and George, are probably all to the good and much less damaging than the agency tries to make out.

JUNE 10, 1944. A Special Post Offices and Post Roads subcommittee was named to investigate the Office of Censorship after Representative Coffee of Washington broke a story about Vivien Kellems, Connecticut industrialist, and her correspondence with a Count von Zedlitz.* The subcommittee met this morning and had itself quite a session. So far the committee has done pretty well, gradually narrowing the trail down to the State Department. It has been an interesting thing to follow, developing a picture of a censorship organization that makes "intercepts" of some 12,000 letters a week, passes out the intercepts to some 8 or 10 government departments and agencies, which in turn distribute them to a good many thousands of people, some of whom turn up at cocktail parties later with what are laughingly termed "pocket editions." The grossest possible violations of personal privacy have occurred and are occurring every day under this bland system. Old Mack, Clyde Reed, Ferguson, reasonable John McClellan, and Jim Eastland are gradually getting together quite a record on it. In the main their investigation has been singularly free from side issues.

Today they had before them George P. Shaw, head of State's foreign-activities correlation division, an honest man trying to cooperate. He divulged the rather astonishing information that probably upwards of 500 people in the department get intercepts every day, that no record is kept of them once they are sent out from his office, which receives them first from Censorship, and that so far as he knows they are never destroyed or otherwise disposed of. The Senators seem to have some hope of threading their way through this labyrinth to the real culprit, but it sometimes

---

* Coffee charged that the correspondence revealed a "love affair" between Miss Kellems and Von Zedlitz, a resident of Argentina who was on the State Department's blacklist as a representative of Hermann Goering's metals syndicate. Miss Kellems denied the charge.

seems a wan one. When they asked Shaw to put his copies of the Kellems–von Zedlitz intercepts in the record for the committee, he refused on the ground that he was under written instructions from his superiors, who were themselves under written instructions from Censorship Director Byron Price, not to divulge them to anyone outside the department.

Reed promptly had a clerk call Price, and in about 15 minutes, his round pink face worried and his eyes beneath their heavy lids looking from side to side rather desperately, he arrived and was put on the griddle. Very shortly thereafter the issue reverted to the familiar Executive versus Legislature. Would Price permit Shaw to place the copies in the record? No, he would not; he would be violating his trust and revealing "secrets of the war." "It's my job to protect the integrity of this correspondence," he said doggedly. "You think you've done that a hundred per cent?" asked Clyde Reed. "No, sir," said Price. "That's why we're here," Reed told him. McClellan then pointed out (he's a great clarifier, McClellan, and really a very able man) that after all, if they wanted to make an issue of it they might as well not make it on Mr. Shaw, but on Mr. Price himself, the man who gave the orders. Very well, agreed Clyde Reed: would Price put his originals in the record for the committee? No, he would not. It wound up with Ferguson asking: "Your position is, then, that you yourself will be glad to come back Monday to testify but you won't bring the intercepts unless we subpoena them?" "I won't bring them without one," said Price crisply. Later on in the day Mack played very cagy when I called him up, but I gathered that a subpoena will probably be forthcoming, and Ferguson said he didn't see how they could avoid it. "After all," he said, "the issue is fundamental. If we haven't got the right to get the facts, we might as well call it quits and go home." Once again we are up against the Constitution, a document whose vigor and vitality I never really appreciated until I came to Capitol Hill.

JUNE 12, 1944. Jimmy Byrnes, ex-Congressman, ex-Senator, ex-Justice, present War Mobilizer, came up today to testify on the George–Murray reconversion bill. An amiable man with a face that narrows down sharply to a small amiable mouth, he has watery bluish eyes, a clear, barely accented voice, and a reasonable manner. As long as he was reading from his prepared statement he made a great deal of sense and his stirring picture of reconversion plans being carried into effect with meticulous care was forthright and impressive. Done with his statement and forced to answer the pointed questions of his erstwhile colleagues, the Honorable Jimmy floundered rather sadly in a sea of his own tortuous sentences. Vandenberg, looking heavy, pontifical, soured and monumentally disapproving, pinned him down several times. Murray's questions were more respectful and not so deep. Walter George looked omniscient but said little, Warren Austin typically wanted a question of legal phraseology straightened out, Scott Lucas looked tanned, handsome, and disagreeable, Chapman Revercomb impeccably polite but speechless, and Bushfield glowered thoughtfully at the former Justice. There was not, in truth, much to be said. The problem of reconversion and demobilization is not being handled the way it should be, and everyone knows it. The war-contracts termination bill which passed the Senate nearly a month ago is lying dormant in the House, with scant chance of passage before the conventions recess. The George–Murray bill has even less chance of emerging from committee before conventions, let alone passing either house. The Brewster factory expedient is the prime example of how far the nation's plans have gone. The Honorable Jimmy's ideas sound mighty fine on paper, but put to the test they have yet to prove their value.

The fascinating tale of the Purloined Letters, or Alice in the State Department, continued before the Post Office Committee this afternoon. Byron Price got the subpoena he wanted, and in return submitted his originals of the Kellems–von Zedlitz correspondence. George Shaw returned to remark with a rather helpless air of amusement that "everyone but the office boys and the charwomen" in the State Department has a chance to see the intercepts Censorship sends over. Intercepts which are not filed, he added, are burned by "a responsible officer." And who is the responsible officer? Well, Raymond Geist, chief of the communications and records division, knows. Raymond was accordingly yanked out of his placid office and rushed to the Hill posthaste. Half an hour later he arrived, composed if a trifle winded. Who burns the papers, Ray? Why, Jackson burns them. And what is Jackson's first name? "I don't really know—we just call him Jackson." Just-Called-Jackson, it turned out, is a $1620-a-year colored man who burns the intercepts. Geist hastened to add that he does it "under supervision of an armed guard." And who is the armed guard? Why, one of the department's regular police. And when did he assume this interesting protective duty? Why, "three or four months ago." And how are the intercepts protected? Why, Just-Called-Jackson opens them "hastily" in a room on the fourth floor to make sure no important papers are included among them. He then places them in a trunk, "throws a canvas over it," and he and the guard then hop cozily into an elevator and plummet to the basement. There, amid the subterranean pillars of the State Department, Just-Called-Jackson burns the intercepts. "You see," said Geist seriously, "we take every precaution to protect the integrity of these letters." "And you mean to say that these confidential papers are disposed of by a $1620-a-year nigger—" snorted John McClellan in disgust. "That's ridiculous!" But whether it was the method, the nigger, or the $1620 that shocked John most, we never learned.

Bob Reynolds is starting to do just what people have expected he would do when he left the Senate. In a scathing statement issued today he announced formation of nationwide clubs to stop "America's drift toward internationalism." Apparently he is making his plans to reap the whirlwind of the reaction which he has assured us so often from the Senate floor will come when the war is over. Bob is a shrewd, sardonic, clever man, who accepts the appellation of fop and the derogatory title "Buncombe Bob" with impassive suavity, secure in the knowledge that they will induce in the public mind just the attitude of amused contempt he needs to foster his purposes.

JUNE 13, 1944. The man who worries the House terrifically these days and has Rufus Holman walking around talking to himself—Sidney Hillman of the CIO Political Action Committee—came to the Hill today to tell the Senate Campaign Expenditures Committee all about it. A short, trim, stocky man with a square, good-looking face and keenly intelligent eyes, he speaks in a heavy accent that betrays his Russian birth, smiles often and shrugs most amiably when hard-pressed. Green, looking glummer and glummer, presided over a session devoted almost exclusively to Republican questioning. Tunnell, rather displeased but philosophic, as though he knew that the Democrats' day would come, interjected a biting comment from time to time; otherwise the field was left open to Joe Ball and Ferguson. The former made his point effectively: the Political Action Committee is certainly indulging in political action. Hillman's counsel maintained, however, that endorsements of Roosevelt were entirely legal, since no campaign has begun. It's all just an attempt to beseech the convention to name him, "just an attempt to urge him to make himself available for the nomination." This task, presumably very difficult, has resulted in a number of posters and publications which Ball spread about the committee table with diligent drama. When all was said and done he had proved very little. He told me later with drowsy disgust that "it wouldn't do any good to ask the present Department of Justice to prosecute, because the CIO Political Action Committee is on their team."

On the floor this afternoon Carl Hatch, who is industriously embarrassing the Republicans by putting Willkie's articles in the Record every day, attacked the GOP's foreign policy and aroused the ire of Vandenberg. The Michigander rose in high dudgeon to put him in his place. Before the argument ceased Tom Connally was in the thick of it, bandying the Administration's program back and forth with Styles Bridges. Bridges made the undeniable statement that no one knows what America's peace aims are because the President refuses to state them. Marse Tom came forth with the old standby about "we can't reach those agreements while the war is under way. We've got to wait until the war is over." Remembering the results of that policy in the industrial field, it was hard not to wonder what would happen if we suddenly found ourselves faced with a Brewster case in international affairs. Supposing the Germans collapsed tomorrow, an event not entirely beyond the realm of possibility? What would become of the Do-Nothings then?

JUNE 14, 1944. The Senate was in recess today, having been driven into another little vacation in the midst of a pressing legislative schedule by a Southern threat to filibuster. The War Agencies Appropriations bill has come out of committee after a hot fight in which a six-man Southern subcommittee tried to kill the Fair Employment Practices Committee. The rest of the committee wouldn't stand for it, and on a 14–6 vote the agency was placed back in the bill from which the subcommittee had neatly removed it. Dick Russell promised us "There'll be a fight on the floor," and at once rumors of filibuster began to fly. A meeting was held—one of those meetings which are always used for their propaganda value by the Southerners—and apparently Barkley and White began to get scared. An "agreement" was reached, and despite the desperate need for a little work to be done if any sort of convention recess is to be possible, the Senate decided to skip a day and go over to Thursday. Today was to be taken up with a lot of peacemaking and compromising. All it produced, however, was another meeting and another announcement by Russell that the Southerners had decided to make the FEPC the issue to prove whether "we are going to have a government by constitutional means or by Presidential directive." Tomorrow promises to be a heated day in the Senate, with a good prospect that a filibuster may develop.

Over in the House they finally passed their version of OPA and appointed conferees, after turning down their counterpart of the Bankhead cotton amendment nearly two to one. They spoiled the moral effect of this, however, by adding a boost in the price of oil and a few other such elements. The Senate will probably name its conferees tomorrow and the conferences will then begin. If they produce anything but a patchwork bill before conventions it will only be by dint of day-and-night sessions.

JUNE 15, 1944. The FEPC fight failed to develop today. La Follette passed an amendment to the War Agencies bill instead. As the bill came out of committee it carried $25,000,000 for unemployment compensation through the Social Security Board. This agitated Wiley, who asserted that it should be $31,000,000 in order to maintain the program. He became excited about this after the third reading of the bill had been ordered prior to passage. Unanimous consent was required to amend at that time, and McKellar wouldn't grant it. The House had approved $25,000,000, he said, the Senate committee had approved it, and he just wasn't going to open it to amendment now. Sometime during this exchange Bob La Follette wandered onto the floor, found out what was going on, and decided to come to the aid of his jovial but ineffective colleague. Within five minutes the McKellar who wouldn't give unanimous consent to Wiley had given it to La Follette.

"Now, Mr. President," Bob began, "I want to make just a few brief remarks——" With him this always means at least an hour's speech, so everyone settled back to await the long debate. Alexander Wiley, shrewd enough to realize that the ball was now in the hands of the star player on the Wisconsin team, shut up like a clam and said no more. After about two hours in which Vandenberg and Burton came to La Follette's aid, the amendment went through 45–19. Once again La Follette, simply by making a cogent speech in his effective manner, had secured passage of a liberal proposal.

JUNE 16, 1944. Dick Russell, who like John McClellan is one of the ablest men in the Senate, and like McClellan has his blind spot—the Negro—took the floor against FEPC today and talked until 4:30 without permitting a vote. The Senate bowed to the inevitable and went over to Monday. A week from tomorrow is supposed to be the official preconvention deadline.

A number of Negroes were in the audience today. We seldom seem to have these visitors except when the poll tax or the FEPC is under discussion. It is as though somebody had the idea that their presence might be a silent reproach. It is utterly wasted on the Southerners, although it may needle some Republican consciences.

The OPA conference began today, and already it promises to turn into a marathon similar to that conducted on the soldier vote. Only two amendments out of the hodgepodge of legislation were winnowed out this afternoon. Wagner hinted that a Sunday session may be necessary, and predicted a bill "by Sunday night." Taft grinned and shook his head. "Maybe we can get through soon," he said with a laugh, "but, gee, there's a lot of things to be done."

JUNE 17, 1944. The OPA conferees met from 10:30 until 2 today. From time to time Maloney would wander out and back in again, or Taft would hurry forth to ask for Richard Field, the OPA general counsel; or bumbling old Brent Spence, chairman of House Banking and Currency, would bumble out, bumble "Well, we're makin' progress, we're makin' progress," and bumble back in again. As usual the press hung around outside and swapped shop talk, gossip and acid comments on the amount of time wasted on executive meetings which don't produce much news.

At 2 the meeting broke up until Monday, and once more we surrounded Wagner. Today, however, it was without success. With an amiable smile and a number of wisecracks he faded away to the elevator and disappeared into the depths below with a wave of the hand and a wistful "Sorry." We were sorry too, a condition we expressed in varying degrees of profanity. The next best bet—or really the best bet, all things considered—was Taft,

Sen. Taft at Dinner

and scouting parties at once set out after him. We eventually ran him
to ground in the Senators' restaurant, launched upon a roll which he had
broken in half and was briskly buttering. Watching him enviously, for
by that time we were rather hungry too, we enveloped the table all
around and proceeded to ask him questions. "Senator Wagner wouldn't
give us any news, Senator Taft," said AP. "We've turned to you for help,
Senator," said UP. "Senator, was anything decided today?" asked INS.
"How about the Bankhead amendment?" suggested the Washington *Star*.
"Were any votes taken?" urged Transradio Press. The Senator shook his
head with an amused smile. "I can't tell you anything," he said. "We're
making progress, some tentative agreements have been reached, nothing
binding. We haven't got to the Bankhead amendment yet." "Was anything
done on court review, Senator?" someone asked. "I can't tell you anything,"
he repeated, biting into the roll with gusto. A little silence fell. "I don't
suppose you could even give us a general idea, Senator—" began somebody else rather forlornly. "Nope" (another hearty bite of roll) "Nope, I
can't tell you anything." Another little silence, while the Senator, undisturbed, continued eating. AP picked up the menu and looked it over
thoughtfully; for a moment we all considered ordering and a polite form
of the third degree. Knowing our man, however, we realized this would
be useless. A bowl of bean soup arrived, we all got hungrier; the soup
began to disappear. "Over in the House restaurant," said AP brightly,
"they've been stopping us at the door in the last couple of days and making
us show our press passes." "Have they?" said Taft. "I guess they're trying to
keep people like us from annoying the members," added AP. "Oh, that's
all right," said our prey with a quick little laugh, "you aren't bothering me
in the least." Obviously we weren't. Along about the tenth spoonful of
soup we left, having been beaten very politely and amicably at our own
game.

The Senate's second casualty, D. Worth Clark of Idaho, has gone down
to defeat in the primary to a singing cowboy, Glen Taylor.

JUNE 18, 1944. There's some talk that Jesse is behind the revolt of the
Texas electors. Pappy O'Daniel, though, thinks it's "strong, silent folk of
Texas with blood in their eyes . . . big, tall, sun-tanned men from Texas."
The COMMON PEOPLE, Pappy says, are really behind it all. Pappy is doing
a lot of evangelizing with the COMMON PEOPLE right now, making speeches
over the radio that sound just like Huey in the old days. Pappy's sober
presence on the Senate floor still does not jibe with this other Pappy, who

is perhaps rather more of a danger, in his busy industrious fashion, than most people realize.

JUNE 19, 1944. The FEPC debate dragged on and on this afternoon, without ever reaching a vote, although the Senate met until 6 P.M. Jim Mead made a rather weak defense of the agency. Dennis Chavez, after quietly demolishing several of Eastland's arguments with a few well-placed and deadly questions, did a much better job of it. The Senator has a very real interest in anything that helps minorities, and as a defender of the group he always scrupulously refers to as the "so-called" Mexican people, he made an able and moving appeal. Either we are all free, he said, or we fail: democracy must belong to all of us. There was no very good rebuttal for that.

The OPA conferees met at 10:30 A.M. in Barkley's office diagonally opposite the old Supreme Court room in the Senate wing of the Capitol. At 12:30, still "makin' progress, makin' progress," they emerged and went to lunch. At 1:30 they came back, as amiable and noncommittal as ever, to continue until 7. At 8 they resumed their deliberations, while five or six faithfuls of the press read magazines, gossiped and pitched pennies in the hallowed corridor where Webster and Clay once walked burdened with affairs of state. At 10:30 Taft emerged and went off to a radio station to make a speech. "I've offered to come back at 11:30 if they're still in," he told us. We groaned: we had been afraid of that. Time passed. OPA's counsels, Richard Field and Henry Hart, sat out the watch with us. "It's like waiting in a hospital for an operation to end," remarked Field. "You don't know what condition the patient will be in, but you know he'll be on a stretcher." We began to refer to our vigil as "the salt mines." More time passed. At midnight roly-poly little Jesse Wolcott of Michigan came out, predicted a bill "in an hour," got a drink of water and went back in. At 12:30 A.M. the Senate conferees kicked out the House members and went into a huddle. At 12:45 they ended the huddle and called the House members in again. At 1 A.M. the conference ended in a sort of quasi-final decision in which a number of procedural amendments were adopted but the Bankhead cotton clause still remained undecided. Another meeting tomorrow at 11, Wagner said, and then if no agreement can be reached, back to the Senate for a vote and instructions tomorrow afternoon. Field refused to comment until he had read the bill, but one provision in particular, providing that protests may be filed at any time against any OPA order, seemed to guarantee a great complication of administrative detail. Most of the inflationary amendments, however, were stricken.

JUNE 20, 1944. The FEPC appropriation was sustained today, after a vicious, dirty speech by Bilbo, who was hissed from the galleries and deserved it. Walter George also spoke, thundering for a while against agencies created by executive fiat.

After Bilbo had his say, attacking the Negroes, Eleanor Roosevelt, the residents of the District of Columbia and everyone else who came to his venomous mind, and after other representatives of the South had contributed their bit, the Senate voted. Several amendments were adopted after the appropriation was approved, one of them—that the FEPC shall make no rule or regulation "which repeals a law of Congress"—being so basic that nobody could honestly oppose it. The Senate then moved on to other things, having cleared its biggest hurdle on the way to adjournment.

In the afternoon, after several more hours of heated discussion the OPA conferees emerged with a compromise on Bankhead's amendment—it would apply only to "major" cotton textiles, and the President might require producers to pay parity prices to cotton farmers. This concession, which satisfied Bankhead and therefore could not have been such a very severe defeat, was promptly hailed by Administration spokesmen as "non-inflationary," "a reasonable amendment," etc., etc., etc. Whatever it was, it cleared the way for final approval of the conference report, expected tomorrow.

Hiram Johnson of California came back to the Senate today after six months in Florida. Clad in a cream-colored suit, with a heavy dark tan setting off his snow-white hair and distinguished face, the old man looked fit and well. Across to his desk from all parts of the chamber came other Senators to shake his hand and welcome him back. The man who lives on in the heart of California as "the greatest governor the state ever had," possesses still at 77 a great prestige among his colleagues. He carries virtually no weight any more when it comes to voting, he influences no decisions, he takes very little part in debate or committees, he contributes nothing but his presence, but in that an undeniable force still remains. This is Hiram Johnson, it seems to say: he has been a power in his time. To that past and that power the Senate still pays affectionate and respectful tribute.

JUNE 21, 1944. The Senate went abruptly into high gear today, putting on a final burst of speed and effort in the drive toward adjournment. Everybody involved worked hard, the Senators, the clerks, the press, and the pages. Not till 7:30 did the session end.

In that time the Senate passed the OPA conference report and sent it to the House; received from the House the contract-termination conference report, passed it and sent it to the White House; received from the

House the conference report on the War Department Civil Functions appropriations bill, passed it and sent it to the White House; passed the District of Columbia appropriations bill and sent it to conference with the House; received from the House, passed and sent to the White House the Interior and Agriculture appropriations bills; received from the House the Labor-Federal Security appropriations conference report, refused to accept it, added an amendment, and sent it back to the House for further conference. The Congress may not always earn its recesses by the work it does during the average run of time, but it certainly earns them in the last week or so before they begin.

Late in the session Barkley announced that he intended to move a call of the calendar tomorrow to dispose of routine bills, and later still Pepper arose and attempted to call up a calendar bill out of order. There ensued a discussion which was characteristic and enlightening. White of course objected, in the interests of the minority; Senators like to plan to be on hand when the calendar is called, because sometimes there are bills they want to oppose. Pepper said he wished White would withdraw his objection. White was pleasant but adamant. Walter George arose majestically. If the Senator from Maine, he said, would agree to dispose of amendments to the bill, so that the Senator from Florida could be absent from the Senate tomorrow as he wished to be, then, said Walter George, "I will see that it pass at the proper time." In that serene and truthful statement—"I will see that it pass"—much was explained about Walter George and his position in the Senate. White agreed promptly.

JUNE 22, 1944. The reading of the calendar passed without notable incident today, as usual, although at one point Aiken got very upset with Tydings. Early in the session the Senate came to a bill to promote Emory Land of the War Shipping Administration from rear admiral to vice-admiral on the retired list. The admiral, a wispy, perky gentleman who is in solid on the Hill, does not elicit the admiration of Aiken in quite the same degree he does that of other Senators. Aiken, in fact, considers him generally incompetent, wasteful and inefficient. Accordingly, he had planned to make a fight on the bill, and in his absence Wherry dutifully asked that it go over, to be taken up later. Some time after this Millard Tydings wandered onto the floor for the first time, saw that the bill had gone over, got up and moved that it be reconsidered and passed. Wherry made a halfhearted protest and whoever was in the chair asked the usual, "Is there objection? The Chair hears none, and the bill is passed." Shortly after that George Aiken came in, and with him the wrath of a Vermonter betrayed. "I don't like that kind of dealin's, Mr. President," he said angrily, his voice choked with emotion. "I don't like those kind of sharp practices!

That isn't the way I'm used to doin' business." His obvious anger produced an instantaneous reaction from Tydings, apparently innocent, and four or five others. The next half-hour was taken up with explaining to the Senator from Vermont, who was so upset that he was unable to get the drift for a while, just what had happened. Some deep, innate suspicion which Aiken has way down underneath, some faint lingering suspicion of the country feller for the city feller, seemed to complicate and confuse his understanding. Somebody was trying to pull a fast one, and he just wasn't havin' any, Mr. President, he just wasn't. Tydings, long and lean and right out of the bandbox, wearing a dark blue coat and vest and light trousers, smiling amiably with perfect self-possession, only seemed to infuriate Aiken more. Not until Henrik Shipstead gave Aiken an exhaustive recapitulation of just what had happened was the Vermonter mollified. The vote of passage was rescinded, and the bill was put over to tomorrow, when Aiken plans to speak.

With the calendar finished, the Senate proceeded to clear up some more major bills. It received, passed and sent to the White House the conference reports on Lend-Lease and UNRRA; received, passed and sent to the White House the War Agencies conference report; received, rejected and sent back to conference the War Department appropriations bill; passed (after the Appropriations Committee, working only from typewritten notes, so great was its haste, reported it out) and sent to conference the Second Deficiency appropriations bill; received, passed and sent to the White House the State, Justice and Commerce appropriations bill.

On several of these the situation was such that the Senate passed its version of the bill, sent it to immediate conference, and then stayed in session to receive the conference report and dispose of it before closing the session. To do this, several "temporary recesses at the call of the Chair" were taken as the hour moved on past 6, 6:30, 7 and on to 7:30. At the end things got very informal and there occurred an enjoyable scene that more people should have seen, for it would have done much to increase their understanding of their Senate. A handful of Senators, perhaps 11, remained on the floor; Lister Hill, Barkley, White, frail old Capper, Jim Davis of Pennsylvania, jovial young Arthur Walsh of New Jersey, Tom Connally, a few others. Greetings, comments, requests for speed and wisecracks began to be exchanged between the floor and the Press Gallery; the tourists had gone long since and we were among friends. Walsh began squeezing his hands together to produce a slightly vulgar sound. This trick soon communicated itself to the Press Gallery, and to other Senators: Jim Davis and White listened attentively, Lister Hill tried it once or twice. Suddenly Jim Davis decided to sing, and placing his hands over his heart and broadly burlesquing an operatic baritone, he launched into, "Come,

come, I love you only—" "Mr. President!" cried Barkley, jumping to his feet hastily from his seat beside Connally, "Mr. President, I move for cloture!" Jim Davis' singing ended in a burst of laughter. Walsh went back to making funny noises, and in a moment or two had all the pages, fascinated, gathered around his desk. In no time, 10 or 12 of them were making noises too. More wisecracks passed between floor and gallery; suddenly a clerk appeared at the door and McKellar rose hurriedly. "All right!" he called out. "All right!" Lister Hill jumped up and sprinted onto the dais. "The Senate will be in order," he cried hastily. "Mr. President," said McKellar formally, "I lay before the Senate a conference report and ask for its immediate consideration." "Without objection," Lister Hill replied smartly, "the report is passed and the Senate stands in recess until noon tomorrow." It was 7:47 and all concerned were tired, as they say, but happy.

JUNE 23, 1944. Today, the last of the preconvention session, the Democrats decided to have a family squabble. With their convention scarcely three weeks away, with party harmony at a premium, they certainly did little to increase it this afternoon. It centered, as do most of these intramural fights, around Joe Guffey.

The Pennsylvanian began it by arising to attack Josiah Bailey for his statements last week attacking Sidney Hillman. Bailey was not in the Senate: Byrd remarked later when he got up to denounce Guffey that the Senator has a habit of waiting until other Senators are absent before assailing them. The Guffey speech was short, sarcastic, blunt. At its conclusion Aiken made a brief statement on Admiral Land, Radcliffe replied with many laudatory defenses, and the promotion bill was passed. All during Radcliffe's speech Byrd stood patiently by his desk waiting for him to finish. When he did, Byrd got the floor. Guffey by that time had left the chamber. In about five minutes Byrd did the neatest job of personal denunciation the Senate has heard in quite some time. In all his 12 years in the Senate, he said, he had never heard an attack so vindictive and so cowardly as that the Senator from Pennsylvania had just made upon the Senator from North Carolina. The Senator from North Carolina, he said, was absent because of an illness necessitating an operation. The Senator from Pennsylvania knew this, and he deliberately waited to make his attack until the Senator from North Carolina could not be present. Nothing the Senator from Pennsylvania might say could detract from the reputation of the Senator from North Carolina. "It has often been said that the Senator from Pennsylvania has the political hide of a rhinoceros. When the Senator from North Carolina gets through with him, that hide will be nailed on the floor of the Senate."

At this point Guffey returned. Byrd said he wanted to tell him to his face that he had made the most cowardly attack upon another Senator he, Byrd, had ever heard. Guffey protested that he had based his remarks upon a letter from North Carolina charging that Senator Bailey—"If the Senator wants to start reading charges on the floor of the Senate against other Senators," Byrd shouted angrily, "I have plenty of charges which have come to me, true charges, against the Senator from Pennsylvania. I have a stack of charges that high (he gestured with both hands), and the Senator will find that others can play that game." Guffey said he would be glad to be present "next week, next month, or next year," to hear about them. He then sat down, disgruntled, while the more-than-usually pink-faced Byrd, who, aside from these occasional exchanges with Guffey confines his activities to filing economy reports, retired to his chair beside his inseparable crony, the gray-faced Peter Gerry of Rhode Island. Presently his high laughter was heard in the chamber, and the incident was apparently over. Guffey glowered alone.

Later in the day, however, bitterness flared again. The resentment Byrd expressed when he told Guffey that "the South knows how to handle its own problems. Stop trying to run us!" revived when Guffey once more obtained the floor to introduce a resolution abolishing the Electoral College. "I know there is little hope that it will be passed before recess," said Joe Guffey, knowing perfectly well it will never pass. But, he said, the recent disturbances in Texas and elsewhere had prompted him reluctantly to take this action. Carl Hatch arose to spread oil on troubled waters in his slow, courtly manner. The people of the South, he said, were honorable people; he didn't worry about them. If the "revolt" went through, however, "the Constitution will be changed faster than it has ever been changed before." Claude Pepper followed, charging darkly that "the roots of this thing go perhaps into the opposition party itself, or into the great financial citadels of this country." Walter George told him bluntly that he was interfering in the affairs of the states, and that the South could tend to its own difficulties without outside advice. This hit home hard with Pepper. "Mr. President," he cried bitterly, "it is sometimes forgotten, but I am no stranger to this South! I am a Southerner too!" Tom Connally, remarking to someone who asked him to yield that—gesturing to Guffey —"I want to answer this fellow," read Section 2 of Article I "of the Constitution, which is the ruling document around here, although the Senator from Pennsylvania doesn't seem to know it." He then put an end to the argument by remarking acidly that "we wish these political doctors with their pill-bags would stay in their own states and not try to come out and doctor the rest of us."

At 5 P.M., having cleared the decks of the War Department conference report and the Second Deficiency bill, the Senate adjourned until noon, August 1. Five Republicans and 11 Democrats were on the floor as the session ended. Barkley stepped across the aisle to shake hands with White, other Senators started quickly for the doors. A definite feeling of "School's out!" was in the air.

Reporters waiting in Senate

14

CONVENTION RECESS

JUNE 24, 1944. Ball, Burton, Hatch and Hill have issued another manifesto on internationalism, a rather cautious document that assails the balance-of-power theory and takes some issue, quite mild, with the Administration's general partiality for spheres of influence. The genesis of the thing is rather interesting. The four Senators were closeted with Hull for two hours Thursday. He told them that he wanted a strong international organization but felt himself to be "ahead of the people." This apparently disturbed him, and he asked the Senators to be the advance guard. Of the Hull thesis the Senators were rather skeptical, but they were glad to issue another statement.

The American people, who for a time in this war were willing and eager to go far out in front for international cooperation, have already begun to recede from that position; and by the time the President and the Secretary of State, cautious and calculating every step of the way, have advanced a little distance on the road to peace, they will meet the American people coming back and there will then ensue that perfect marriage of true minds the Administration is apparently hoping for. We shall then accept not what we must have to save civilization but what our leaders have been able to persuade us we can have. It does not look now as though it would be enough.

JUNE 25, 1944. Among odds and ends left over from the last day of the session is the information that Harry Byrd for the Rules Committee reported out Maloney's resolution setting up a joint Congressional committee to study the streamlining of Congress—the first time such a measure has ever got beyond committee. Apparently members have decided at last that it is time to begin to give serious consideration to the problem of bringing the Legislature up to date. It fits logically into the picture of a Congress determined to re-establish itself as the dominant branch. [*This aim, like so many absolutist goals in the American system, is never achieved for long, and never abandoned. Congress did, at any rate, get itself re-organized, in due course, in the La Follette–Monroney Act of 1947.*]

JUNE 26, 1944. An indignant editorial this morning comments on the recess and points out acidly that the outstanding piece of unfinished business—the reconversion bill—is still unfinished. There is no excuse for this, the editorial says, and true enough, there isn't. Just the fact that Walter George and Jim Murray put in one bill, and Harley Kilgore put in another, and mutual jealousy has resulted in duplicated hearings and an inability to report out either. These personal difficulties are hard for the general public to understand, but they play a considerable role in much of the legislation developed here.

The Republicans opened their convention in Chicago today, with Dewey a certainty and Warren of California almost as certain for second place.

JUNE 27, 1944. Convention doldrums have settled on the Hill. Only a few Senators remain in the Office Building, their number decreasing daily as more and more depart for home. Democrats all, they are ready and able to make incisive comments on the doings at Chicago, but other than that they have little to say. Their own day is coming, and of the battles ahead they refuse to speak. All is not well with the Democracy, even though it has its candidate. The pressures of time, the inevitable deteriorations of the men-who-stayed-too-long, are sapping the strength of the party. The fight in the Senate Friday was only an opener for the conflicts to come.

JUNE 28, 1944. A Republican convention listless in the Chicago heat today nominated the clever little man from Albany for President and gave him for running mate the handsome if vacuous John Bricker of Ohio. Warren, making a decision that might have been inspired by a number of considerations but in any case was politically right, refused to accept second place and returned to California to complete his governorship and await the blessings of the future.

Of the Senators commenting several, like Jim Murray, were very kind to Dewey, asserting their respect for his abilities as a lawyer but doubting his broader qualifications for the job to which he aspires. Carl Hatch chose to be quizzical and humorous. A contract with the people of California prevented Warren from taking second place, he pointed out dreamily, but apparently a contract with the people of New York was no bar to Dewey taking first. "Not critical," he emphasized gently several times throughout his statement, "Not critical. Just curious." Lister Hill, old-boying and old-manning and old-fellowing with every other breath, as is his genial custom, was much less restrained than his colleagues. The wraps came off, with Lister, and the knife came out. "A nomination of a little man who satisfies the reactionary interests which dominate the Republican Party," he said crisply. "How's that, old boy? Is that enough, old fellow? I guess it ought to be, old man, oughtn't it? How about that, old boy? How about that? That'll take care of it, won't it, old man?" I said I thought it would.

One Democrat, not at the moment too popular with his elder brethren, was already looking forward rather wistfully to his own party conclave. Claude Pepper, wearing the air of earnest self-righteousness which so infuriates his colleagues, commented some more this afternoon about the Southern revolt. The thing that worried him most, he said practically, is the fact that in the Electoral College lies the only strength of the South. "If this revolt succeeds and it results in the abolition of the Electoral College and the direct election of Presidents," he pointed out, "that will mean the end of any influence the South might have. Our whole voting strength lies in the Electoral College, because many of our people don't vote. Our vote would be negligible in a popular election." Florida's gift to liberalism is rather closer to Walter George's philosophy, perhaps, than Walter George dreams. The ultimate purpose, to preserve the influence of the South, is evidently the same.

JUNE 29, 1944. Elbert Thomas, back from his tour of duty as American representative to the International Labor Organization convention in Philadelphia, remarked today with his quiet little laugh, "My party in Utah has decided to nominate me for Vice-President if there's a contest. A man will make a speech and so on. I don't suppose that's news, but"—he chuckled—"you can run me for Vice-President if you want to." I went back to the gallery, wrote my story, and did so.

Out in North Dakota Gerald Nye, first behind and then ahead in the primary race, is battling desperately for his political life.

JUNE 30, 1944. The President signed the OPA bill today, his pen dripping honey as he dwelt on the "statesmanship and courage" of Congress in "resisting group pressure and in protecting the public interest." All is sweetness and light now. "Relief for the greedy instead of the needy" is no more to be found on Capitol Hill. They are statesmen all, perfect in every way, and the greatest politician of them all is hard at work removing a basic issue in his coming campaign.

JULY 1, 1944. A few Republicans are beginning to wander back from Mecca, among them Harold Burton, disgruntled to a certain extent about the foreign-policy plank but doing what he can to maintain a good front about it. He emphasizes, however, that as it stands it is weak, and that it will be up to the candidate to strengthen it by interpretation. Clyde Reed says Dewey is "the first formidable opposition, the first real opposition," Roosevelt has ever had. If he's elected, Clyde Reed says, "and if I come back to the Senate next year, which I am planning to do, I may get along with him and I may not. He knows what he's doing, all right." Chapman Revercomb, his blue eyes bland, at his most courtly and gracious, is convinced of the candidate's "sincerity." "He's so sincere, so very sincere," Chapman Revercomb says. Chapman Revercomb is optimistic, too, very much so, although Clyde Reed says "a fifty-fifty chance" and doesn't go out on any limbs. Joe Ball, slow and uncommunicative, has little to say: the foreign-policy plank is weaker than the Republicans' Mackinac Island Declaration and it needs strengthening—he doesn't know yet whether he will take part in the campaign to any extent—he yawns and you leave.

JULY 2, 1944. The Democrats have chosen Sam Jackson of Indiana as their convention chairman. A bald, square-faced, dark-visaged man of 49 with a little streak of black hair running to the center of his forehead, he goes about his business in the Senate, where he has sat five months, with an air of brisk, pragmatic efficiency. Possessed of a businesslike presence and a good speaking voice, he has so far voted quite consistently with the Administration—when he has been here. Out in Indiana they criticize him for "missing more roll calls in a shorter time than any other man in the history of the Congress." He replies that he occupies Fred Van Nuy's seat only "to keep it warm for Governor Shricker" and refuses to change his ways. With the press he is generally popular. After making his maiden speech a couple of weeks ago—discussing hogs—he sent copies of it, with a bottle of Seagram's, to the Press Gallery. Hogs could not compete with the war or the appropriations bill, and I doubt if any of us carried it, but the whiskey made a hit. He seems to be a sound, fair-minded man, the sort who ought to stay in the Senate. The party has other plans, however, and he is running for governor instead. His first statements as chairman were reasonable and restrained. Aside from the comments of a few eager beavers like Lister Hill and Claude Pepper, the campaign so far is extremely polite. The slugging will begin a little later.

JULY 3, 1944. In the cooperative endeavor that so frequently distinguishes the press on the Hill, a couple of us decided to pool our resources today and go out beating the bushes for news. Our search through the Office Building was not very rewarding; one office after another was either closed or devoid of its Senator. Tom Connally was in, however, and with him we had a pleasant if not very productive talk. He has a sudden kind smile about his eyes that is rather unexpected in view of his usual dry sarcasm. He likes to talk to people, he likes to be talked to. Sitting high in his chair, with the gold studs gleaming down the front of his shirt, his flowing black coat open and casual, the gray hair swirling down over the back of his collar, the Senate is fully as picturesque as his reputation. He is also a thoroughly shrewd politician, walking with all the delicacy of one walking on eggs across the dangerous ground of the Texas revolt. Marse Tom is no rebel this time; Marse Tom is too closely tied up with the Administration through the Foreign Relations chairmanship. At the same time, there's no use rilin' up the boys back home. The way out of this particular problem, he has evidently decided, is silence. He isn't talking, at least for publication. As for the convention, "I'm not even a delegate. Might go as a bystander, as an observer." About the Republicans, that's another matter, although even there the famous Connally acid is being sprinkled lightly. "I want to keep this foreign-policy business as nonpartisan as possible. I've got to get all this peace machinery through up here, and I don't want to rile them up." However, "peace forces," the delicate phrase adopted by the GOP resolutions committee under Taft, hardly suits Tall Tom. "We've had too many 'peace forces,' that's what's the matter now." The wording will have to be stronger than that, he thinks, and he thinks the Democrats will supply it in their platform. As for the Republicans, "maybe they've got an outfit that will win, I don't know. But I just don't see how it can." There is "something behind" Warren's withdrawal, Tom thinks, more than money and "promises to the people of California." As for the Democratic Vice-Presidency, he too had heard the rumor which is flooding the Capitol today: that "the White House" has decided on Barkley. This report, which is very logical if looked at from the standpoint of a candidate who wants to prove his oneness with Congress, interested Tom a good deal, but he hadn't heard anything definite about it. "I'm tryin' to get my news from the source," he said. "You tell me. You're the molders of public opinion, or the poisoners of the public mind, which is it? You tell me." But we couldn't tell him, except to repeat the rumors.

These he discussed with interest, but without any more positive facts than we possessed. On Henry Wallace he had an opinion: the opinion that Henry won't make it. "Not that I have anything against Wallace," he said, "but you know, it's amazing to me the depth of the bitterness against Henry Wallace throughout the country." Who might step forward to receive the blessing, however, Marse Tom would not predict.

JULY 4, 1944. Walter George was returned to office today by an apparently overwhelming majority, and in Mississippi John Rankin, the strange demagogue who sometimes acts like a statesman, was re-elected four to one. In Georgia the Negroes were refused the right to vote, a denial of civil liberties so forthright, yet withal so polite and cordial, that it is almost hard to realize it happened. The complacent words of the young Southern Senator came again to mind. "Niggers don't vote in my state, and niggers aren't going to vote in my state." Constitutional amendments, laws, Supreme Court decisions, what have you—nothing matters. That's the way things are.

JULY 5, 1944. By what quirk of fate it is that one man of 51 is interested and progressive and liberal, with a head bubbling with ideas, and some other is set and conservative and stodgy, with blinders on both eyes, probably no one will ever be able to say exactly. The forces shaping one may be much the same as the forces shaping the other, and both, as I have seen it happen, may wind up in the United States Senate. Yet there is something, some individual way of looking at things, some saving or destroying grace, which is the making of one and the end of the other. Harley Kilgore of West Virginia belongs in the first category. His mind is alive and alert and on the go and, while it sometimes goes too far, it has a commendable vigor.

Today I caught him in the midst of lunch, his round amiable face with its wide amiable mouth buried up to the eyes in a lettuce sandwich. Between bites the conversation began, and was continued thereafter to an accompaniment of more sandwiches and a glass of iced tea. After this was out of the way, it still went on. All told, it must have run close to an hour. In that time we went pretty thoroughly over the ground charted by a man who wants to encourage enterprise and democracy in many direct and rather unorthodox ways.

There is, for instance, the national office of scientific research and investigation, which he wants to set up on a permanent basis. ("That's one of those bills I introduced back three years ago. It's going to pass itself, one of these days.") Its purpose would be to sponsor and underwrite experiment as does any private foundation, such as the Guggenheim for instance. The only thing wrong with it, from the standpoint of popular (in the sense of organized) appeal, is the fact that no one would be allowed to profit from the patents developed. They would be national property, and aside from a reasonable reward to the men who did the inventing, would be distributed for the widest possible use by all. It is at this point, as the Senator admitted with a rueful chuckle, that the whole project runs afoul of a lot of powerful interests who definitely do not approve. But in the long run, he thinks it will prevail, because the trend is in the times and eventually public opinion will override the interests, no matter how powerful.

There is also his reconversion bill, running its neck-and-neck competition with the George–Murray bill and probably destined to go in the ash-can when all is said and done. "The human side of demobilization," that is; the bill to "tide us over," to "reconvert," to "put things back on a stable level." But it is too liberal—the Federal government is given too much—the purpose, admirable, can be attacked too easily on the ground of centralization. The Senator is not abandoning it until he sees the whites of their eyes, however, and action in August, he predicts, is inevitable. "In some form or other, we're going to pass something, because the pressure is getting so terrific that we can't afford not to." (Over in the House Majority Whip Robert Ramspeck of Georgia says "another recess until Labor Day," because "there just isn't anything to be done.")

And finally there is the Senator's plan for postwar military training. First comes two years of it, for high school juniors and seniors—everybody, with an integrated program during the year and a summer camp devoted exclusively to training during the vacation months. Then comes a plan for the Regular Army: enlistment for 16 years, 4 active, 12 reserve; the three summer months of each active year to be devoted to rigorous maneuvers in the field; the nine months of each active year to be given on detached service at a university, getting an education and a diploma. At the end of four years, graduation from college, thoroughly trained in both civilian and military pursuits, and into the reserve. "Within 15 years," says Harley Kilgore, "this would give us 300,000 highly educated, highly trained reserve officers. If we ever needed them, we could call them up, give them a refresher, and there would be the most competent officer group you could ask for to run your army." And after that four years? Well, there's another idea, "but this is so way out of bounds that I don't bother to mention it." Why not make West Point and Annapolis places where the most brilliant of your four-year student soldiers could go to take the degree of Master of Military Science. "Why not say, 'To hell with you, Congressman or Senator, forget your appointments.' And, 'To hell with you, West Point and Annapolis, give everybody a chance, democratically and fairly on the basis of merit.' Why not make the academies the place where you develop your staff men, and your great military leaders. Why not open them to all? Why, it would give you the best-trained, the most democratic—especially the most democratic—bunch of officers you've ever seen."

"But the ideas I have like that," says Kilgore of West Virginia, "I don't talk about, because people might think I'm crazy."

Outside Senate Chamber

15

V.P. FEVER

JULY 6, 1944. Brisk Sam Jackson started to hurry by our table in the Office Building cafeteria this noon. We hailed him and he stopped to talk for a moment, his dark chubby face beaming as he prepared to say *no.* "Senator," we said, "we think you ought to tell us something that would make news." "Look," he said, "crowbars and wild horses couldn't drag anything out of me. I just don't know anything." "But surely——" "Nope," he repeated, "I don't know a *thing.*" Everybody laughed, skeptically. "Well, Senator, what do you think of Joe O'Mahoney as a Vice-Presidential candidate?" "Joe's a wonderful fellow," said Sam Jackson promptly. "He'd do a fine job wherever you put him." He beamed, and so did we. Somebody made one last attempt. "What do you think of a Westerner for Vice-President?" "Anybody west of the Mississippi would be fine," said Sam Jackson thoughtfully. "Anybody west of the Mississippi——" "Yes?" we said. "Or anybody east of it," added Sam Jackson with a laugh. We had to laugh too. The Democrats have picked a convention chairman who has mastered one of the toughest of all political skills—to tell the press absolutely nothing and still hold its friendship.

The Vice-Presidential bug, as a matter of fact, is running rampant at the moment in the Office Building. The only person who isn't in the race, as somebody remarked yesterday, is Carter Glass—and even he may be mentioned. Fond hopes are blossoming in a dozen Senatorial breasts. The thing to do, as the latest gag has it, is to make a list of those who are *not* candidates, and save yourself a lot of time. Barkley and Truman seem to have a fairly good chance, with Thomas of Utah and O'Mahoney being "considered." Reports that the convention may be "thrown open" in the secondary contest are countered by reports that the White House, fearful that rambunctious Southern strength would swing to billion-pinching Harry Byrd, will permit no such thing to happen. Henry Wallace, unhappy and unloved, still looks to have the inside track, principally because he is in and may prove in the last analysis to be the only solvent for many antagonistic mixtures.

JULY 7, 1944. The latest V.P. rumor going around is that the President wants Wallace but also wants three or four "acceptable" people built up in case the convention won't swallow Henry and he has to back down and let the delegates make a "free" choice. Of these, the word has it, Barkley is the leading contender. An intensive four-day campaign, "with a lot of money spent," will be launched for him at Chicago.

Down in Louisiana, Overton, bowing to the inevitable, has made the decision everyone expected and will run again.

JULY 8, 1944. Three of America's best public servants—Donald Nelson, Harry Truman and Jim Murray—have suddenly become involved in the reconversion controversy that has gradually been developing within WPB and the military. Both Senators and their committees have recommended for months that small business be permitted to reconvert as materials and men become available. Recently Nelson promised Truman that the orders would go out on July 1. Meanwhile he fell ill of pneumonia, and in his absence his big-business subalterns have blandly refused to do anything. Today Truman issued an admonitory statement, and from his sickbed Donald Nelson promised action. Later in the day Murray came to his support. The reaction in WPB was presumably violent, though not vocal, but from the armed services came a formal blast against Nelson. His plans would "prolong the war," and so on—the same familiar nonsense. How much of this is due to natural military caution and how much to the civilian backgrounds of the service liaison men in WPB is one of those interesting things Truman ought to go into. This whole fight within WPB is at any rate beginning to come into the open. Significantly, Truman is fighting the services—which, candidly, hate his guts—on the eve of the convention at which, presumably, he might be offered second place. The effect of this controversy might be to kill his chances. This does not stop Harry Truman.

JULY 9, 1944. Harry Byrd's machine, which holds Virginia in a sure and viselike grip, rolled along smoothly at the state Democratic convention yesterday. When all was said and done, despite some unruly demonstrations for the President, the Senator had everything pretty well under control. The delegation to Chicago was specifically uninstructed on the Presidency. It was also specifically instructed to oppose Henry Wallace for second place.

With this Welcome Home ringing in his ears, the V.P. arrived in Seattle

Senator Byrd

from China today and went on the air with one of the earnest, eager, sincere speeches which mean so much to his partisans and prove so galling to his enemies. Very close to the start of it he went out of his way to emphasize that he is an American. The more he sees of other countries, Henry said, the more he likes America. This statement may have been too little and too late, but he made it just the same.

The latest rumor now has it that Roosevelt has decided to dump him completely. Obviously, however, all these rumors are rumors and nothing more.

JULY 10, 1944. The V.P. got back to town today and promptly issued a statement to the press. He said he was glad to be back.

JULY 11, 1944. From one of our "informed sources"—this one within a couple of So-and-So-told-me's from the White House, and so perhaps a little bit more authentic than most—we received today the flat prediction that "by Thursday" the President will have issued a statement endorsing Wallace for Vice-President. The President's own candidacy is no longer in question. In a letter to Bob Hannigan he has agreed with a fine reluctance to be the standard-bearer once again. (I shall never forget the expressions on the faces of three Democratic Senators in committee this morning when they heard the news. It was as though the sun had burst from the clouds and glory surrounded the world. Relief, and I mean relief, was written on every face. The meal ticket was still the meal ticket and all was well with the party. They almost sang out loud.) This removes one pawn from the board but leaves the other still in doubt. Despite some other contenders—among them Justice Douglas, who, our source says, has the backing of Harold Ickes, Joseph Kennedy and Tommy Corcoran —our friend insists that Henry has it in the bag. Not only the endorsement, in fact, but the nomination as well. "By Thursday," he says, offering to bet $5 on it. He had no takers.

Late in the afternoon the office sent me around to the Wardman Park to the Wallace apartment. Mrs. Wallace came to the door, a most sweet and gracious and charming woman, and relayed my questions to the man of the house. But the V.P. wouldn't talk, despite an afternoon spent at the White House. "He can't, really," his wife explained; and of course he couldn't.

JULY 12, 1944. The Senate's incumbents did rather well today in three of their races. Out in Utah, Elbert Thomas won renomination on the Democratic ticket without opposition, although he will face what may be a close fight in the runoff. In Oklahoma Elmer Thomas captured his party's endorsement over two opponents, and in New Hampshire the lively Charles Tobey, master of the most unintelligible high-speed delivery and florid oratory in the Senate, subdued an ambitious Representative by a comfortable margin.

No word from the White House on the V.P. today, but another meeting with party leaders and a hectic atmosphere of corridor gossip and rumors, counter-rumors, reports and counter-reports.

JULY 13, 1944. The Vice-Presidential situation began to emerge a little more clearly today. One of the "informed sources" who is really informed went to the White House yesterday afternoon and when he got back told us the general outlook. Probably on Friday, in any case not later than Saturday—because on Saturday the President is "going away," a long, long way—a statement will be issued: a very typical statement. "If I were a delegate, I would vote for Henry A. Wallace"—that kind of a statement. This technique, the most obvious and the most standard in the Roosevelt repertoire, is expected to dump poor Henry.

Donald Nelson has apparently won his fight with the big-business boys. Jimmy Byrnes has come to his assistance with a sort of pseudo "compromise" that still retains Nelson's basic plans for reconversion. The issue, however, is by no means dead.

JULY 14, 1944. This is the Thursday on which the President was supposed to issue his milk-and-water "endorsement" of Henry Wallace for Vice-President, but it hasn't come yet. Nonetheless the atmosphere around the V.P.'s office is much more relaxed and optimistic than it was yesterday, when people went around under an obvious strain and dealt rather abruptly with the subject. Meanwhile, other reports are current. Happy, one report says, is behind the drive for Barkley for reasons connected with the Kentucky situation. Pappy O'Daniel, another report has it, is going to accept the nomination of the American National Democratic Party, the divide-and-let-the-Republicans-rule organization which was dreamed up somewhere out on the fringe as a means of splitting the vote and doing Roosevelt in. Pappy denies it. His job, he says, is to do the best he can at the job he holds.

Out in Missouri, Harry Truman has bowed out, reiterating a statement he has made many times on the Hill, that he does not want the Vice-Presidency. Tom Connally says the same thing. O'Mahoney chuckled when asked if he would accept the job and remarked, "I think my answer to you is: it hasn't been offered to me." The Vice-Presidency, he added candidly, isn't something you run for, anyway. "You get it given to you." Elmer Thomas, out in Oklahoma, has issued a statement echoing Mc-Kellar's a week or so ago, that it would not be in the best interests of the Democratic Party to renominate Henry Wallace.

Meanwhile on the movie screens downtown, the pictures of the V.P. in China are receiving enthusiastic applause. The old American love of the underdog is beginning to work. At the moment his fate is hanging entirely in the balance, Henry Wallace for the first time has become popular with his countrymen.

JULY 15, 1944. "Everything that comes in on peace is referred to us," remarked the secretary in Foreign Relations this morning. "We just acknowledge it with a card and file it away." Less innocently and with less intention to go through the files at a later date, others around the world are doing the same.

JULY 16, 1944. The President, who left town Friday, is presumed to have left his letter of "endorsement" for Wallace with Bob Hannegan, but in Chicago the Democratic chairman won't talk. The center of interest, in any case, has now moved west, and no longer are we bothered with the problem along the quiet corridors of the Hill.

Apparently determined to make Taft and the Congress look ridiculous, a task at which it has admirably succeeded, the War Department has chosen to interpret most literally the ban on political literature in the soldier-vote law. Charles Beard's *Republic*, Catherine Drinker Bowen's *Yankee from Olympus*, various tracts of a mild and innocuous nature, have been put on the official index. This is a lot of fun and gives everybody a good laugh, but the chances are excellent that the Congress will have the last word.

JULY 17, 1944. Out in Chicago Guffey has reiterated his support for Wallace. It seems to indicate one thing definitely, which is that the President would not be averse to having the good Henry renominated. Guffey wouldn't be for him otherwise. "Who will you vote for for Vice-President?" someone asked him the other day. "Whoever Frank Roosevelt tells me to," was his instant reply.

JULY 18, 1944. The President's letter, perhaps the coolest and cruelest brush-off in all the long Roosevelt career, has been released by Sam Jackson. If he were a delegate, he would vote for Henry, all right, but as

President he can't say much for him. Here he is, it says in effect. If you want him, well, OK. If you don't, well, OK. Suit yourself. And so long, Henry.

The V.P.'s official reticence these last few days has proved a considerable problem for the press. Aside from a Saturday incident when he momentarily lost control of himself and tossed a photographer headlong, his relations with us have been on a polite but distant plane. He hasn't talked in his office, he hasn't talked at home, he won't talk coming or going. This has necessitated a lot of special-detail work. In an attempt to catch him on his way to Chicago tonight, we had a man stationed at the Wardman Park, a man stationed at his office, and seven more men stationed at Union Station, one of them with reservations on both the Pennsylvania and the B & O, to be used as necessary. Even so the difficult gentleman eluded us, whisking on at Silver Springs, Maryland, up the line, with a cheery "Good-by—no comment," and a wave of the hand. They will nab him in Chicago, however.

JULY 19, 1944. The President has now revealed to his undictated-to convention that Harry Truman or Justice Douglas would be "acceptable" provided Wallace gets the boot this new letter so thoughtfully invites for him. Sidney Hillman has put the kibosh on Jimmy Byrnes, thereby displaying the power of the CIO in the convention and ending that candidacy in a hurry. "In deference to the wishes of the President," the wispy little Justice said, he would withdraw. The good Henry arrived, got a good hand, and was apparently much encouraged. Joe Guffey, crying "Politics!" with complete consistency, has assailed Bob Hannegan for his active sponsorship of Truman. Few people can hate one another with more cordial enthusiasm than a bunch of Democrats.

JULY 20, 1944. Barkley, after coming within an ace of staging another revolt because of the President's opposition to his own hopes for second place, made the nominating speech today. It was accepted by the President, traveling on the West Coast, "in pursuit of my duties under the Constitution. . . ." Harry Byrd got a handful of protest votes and half the Texas delegation walked out. Near midnight a Wallace demonstration, carefully staged by the CIO and quickly crushed by Hannegan and Sam Jackson, threatened for a moment to upset all the carefully laid plans. It was probably Henry's only chance. The boys in the back room killed it.

JULY 21, 1944. Henry Wallace went down to defeat on the second ballot tonight and Harry Truman became the Democratic Vice-Presidential

nominee. There are both good and bad features about this Roosevelt-dominated "free choice." On the credit side, the Senator is a fine man: no one would do a better job of it in the White House if he had to. On the other hand, the Pendergast background makes him entirely too vulnerable to Republican attack, and no one who knows him likes to see him subjected to that kind of smearing in view of the forthright job he does in the Senate. Also, he has announced that he intends to resign the chairmanship of the Committee immediately, which is a considerable loss to the country.

In adversity and defeat Henry Wallace for the first time has emerged in something of his true stature before the country. Everything which has been said about his unfitness for administrative office, his ineptitude, his impracticality, still finds adherents; but his moral character, his integrity and his good will, if they were ever in serious doubt, are no longer so. His has been a regrettable personal tragedy: like so many others, he knows now what it means to be a politically dispensable friend of Franklin Roosevelt.

JULY 22, 1944. The convention which might go down in history as "The Battle of the Bosses"—Hague, Kelly, Hannegan and Flynn versus Hillman, Murray, bland-eyed, heavy-set young Dick Frankensteen of the UAW—has ended with a legacy of hatreds from which the party may not soon recover. The South's feelings are perhaps best epitomized by one item which has already drifted back to the Hill from Chicago: the Mississippi delegation in caucus came within a couple of votes of supporting

Henry Wallace for Vice-President on the deliberate assumption that he would be the best choice to weaken the ticket.

JULY 23, 1944. It has remained for Bob Reynolds, who when he likes a man goes all-out for him, and when he doesn't like him, goes all-out against him, to sum up what everyone on the Hill feels about Truman.

"I am very pleased with the nomination of Senator Truman," Bob Reynolds says. "He will make a fine candidate, for he bears no enmity, is extremely popular in the Senate, and with the rest of the folks who work up here at the Capitol with the Senators. As a member of my committee he has been relied upon for his sound judgment and good attendance. His work on his own special committee has been excellent. I think Senator Truman is one of the finest men I know."

To that the rest of us say *Amen.*

16

BACK TO WORK

JULY 24, 1944. The Senators are beginning to return to the Hill, amid rumors of going over to Labor Day and from then until after the elections. The imperative logic of the German situation, however, is expected to change all that when Congress reconvenes.

Tydings, looking lean and well-satisfied—as well he might, considering the fact that all he has to do in Maryland in November is walk into office again—was back today. Chavez, subtle and at times sardonic, also turned up. In the cafeteria in the Office Building at noon McKellar could be observed surrounded by his secretaries. Tall, old, perennially ill Charles Andrews of Florida, who with Bob Reynolds is one of the only two members who have stayed straight through, was also on hand. Joe Guffey is back, too, disgruntled and soured about Wallace, but for once holding his tongue. Apparently Frank Roosevelt told him.

Tydings' purpose in town was the first meeting of the Filipino Rehabilitation Commission, established several months ago by Congressional action. The Senator had on his left the bland, soft-voiced, aging Oriental who is Vice-President of the Philippines, Sergio Osmena; Joaquin Elizalde, the Resident Commissioner, a dark, birdlike man with sharp features and an impatient, nervous manner; and the round-faced, youthful-looking Pulitzer Prize winner, Colonel Carlos P. Romulo. Other assorted members of both nationalities completed the group, which met for perhaps 20 minutes, named a subcommittee on progam and adjourned at the call of the chair until September. There may not be jockeying for power against a background of the tragic Commonwealth, but it is not too hard to sense friction in the air which surrounds the exile government. So long as Quezon lives, you feel, will the uneasy truce prevail— just so long. Probably no longer.

Chavez, knowing his Latin Americans, wanted to reassure them about Wallace and did so in a soothing statement. The political fortunes of "one or two individuals," he said, had little to do with the Good Neighbor policy, which after all is based upon the whole spirit of the government and the attitude of the whole American people. "They're all for one man or another down there," he said with his slight lisp and a rather fatherly air. "They can't understand that with us it's a matter of principle and attitudes. We have our great swings of sentiment and our leaders become the people who best interpret and express them. Down there it's the individual man who matters, and whatever he does is all right with them providing they like him." His small eyes twinkled thoughtfully as he interspersed this analysis with his favorite expression, "You get me?" Although disappointed in the Wallace defeat, he shares the general feeling about Truman. The racial plank, he said, is "very weak—much weaker than the Republicans'," but "the candidates and the Congress" will take care of that. As his own contribution he intends to push his bill for a permanent FEPC.

Down in Mississippi Eastland has pledged his full support to the party ticket. Apparently the Mississippi revolt is over, otherwise the Senator, who is a most politically circumspect young man, would have been less hearty in his endorsement.

JULY 25, 1944. Old Mack, sleepy-eyed and drowsy-voiced and in a mood to ramble on at length, was at his most amiable this morning. Did he like the convention? Oh, *yes*, oh, *yes*. Fine convention, fine convention. And what did he think of the Vice-Presidency? Well suh, Mistuh Wallace is a ve'y good man; Ah don't criticize him puhsonally. His ideas (this with his characteristic dryness) in no way coincide with mine. No suh. In no way coincide with mine. Ah've been heah now with five—no, six—Vice-Presidents, and of them all Mistuh Wallace is the only one—well, Senutuh Truman will make a good candidate. Strengthen the ticket. Yes, suh. Of six Vice-Presidents; yes suh, six. What did he think of the platform? Well, suh, the Tennessee delegation withheld endorsement of the platfo'm; as you know it included se'v'al things which Ah have consistently voted against in the Senate. Ve'y pooah platfo'm. But aftuh all—who cayehs about the platfo'm? Doesn't mean anythin' anyway. Seems to me the votuhs won't change ho'ses in the middle of the stream. Yes, suh; yes, suh. Not in the middle of the stream. What did he think about the monetary agreement at Bretton Woods? Well, suh, Ah don't rightly know yet; Ah haven't had time to read it ovuh yet; Ah ruthuh suspect Ah'm not goin' to like it much. Ah keep readin' in all these columnists—youah not a columnist, are you?—in all these columnists wheah weah goin' to put up the money to reconstruct France and all these othuh countries. Wonduh wheah the money's comin' from? You know? Ah haven't been able to find out wheah the money's comin' from. Ah just caint find out wheah. Seem's to me like weah assumin' an awful lot 'thout knowin' wheah the money's comin' from. Doesn't it seem that way to you?

From the acting chairman of Appropriations that seemed like a question which he himself might ultimately answer. The money might not come from anywheah, if Mack has the say of it. And Mack has.

JULY 26, 1944. Cotton Ed and Hattie have been defeated for renomination and already the industrious are beginning to read all sorts of Roosevelt significance into it. No one who knows the two Senators, however, can be misled into such exaggerations, for both were ripe for defeat and now it has come to them. That's about all there is to it.

Cotton Ed, reactionary, unyielding, violent, unrestrained, the whispery shadow of a once-powerful indignation, was just too old; and Hattie, the quiet little grandmother who never won anything, lost anything, said anything or did anything, was just too colorless and inactive. Cotton Ed through the chairmanship of Agriculture and Forestry was a power, more often for ill than good. Hattie held no such position of influence and carried no weight one way or the other.

Of their opponents, Governor Olin Johnston of South Carolina has a reputation which suggests that it will be the same record with a new needle. In Hattie's case the situation is far different. Representative Fulbright, who stands the best chance of winning in the runoff, is 39 years old, a former Rhodes scholar, former president of the University of Arkansas, author of the "permanent peace" resolution in the House—in him the Senate has something. A lot will be expected of him when he gets here in January.

While Cotton Ed's defeat was long overdue and nothing much to be regetted, in Hattie's case it will always seem too bad that she made so

little of her Senatorship. The only woman ever elected—and twice elected, at that—to the office, she had a great opportunity to make a record for herself and for her sex. She did nothing with it. It was her misfortune to be a nice little old lady, very unassuming and quiet, thrust by the whim of the electorate into a job far beyond her capacities. The result was a rather pathetic comedy of errors. The record she might have made awaits some younger and more vigorous woman. [*In time, most ably and actively, came Margaret Chase Smith of Maine and Maurine Neuberger of Oregon to make the most of the opportunity Hattie let slip.*]

JULY 27, 1944. Jimmy Byrnes has wired Barkley and John McCormack over in the House urging that Congress stay in session until the reconversion legislation is completed, and from Michigan the great Van has addressed a telegram to his Republican colleagues calling them to conference next Tuesday with the same end in view. Bob Reynolds, anxious to oblige, has also taken to the telegraph, dispatching wires to the members of Military Affairs asking them to return to the Hill for a special meeting Tuesday, at which time he hopes to report out a bill. With all these hopeful gestures being made, the number of Senators who are planning to be on hand August 1 still does not add up to very much on the basis of an informal poll.

At any rate, the pressure is on and may be expected to increase in the next few days. The Congress is being placed on the spot, something it does not enjoy. Indignation may be expected to follow, and presently action. August may prove to be a rather warm month inside the Capitol as well as out.

JULY 28, 1944. A few Senators will be on hand Tuesday, probably enough for a quorum—although it may be what the press gallery refers to as a "fast count," when the V.P. briskly announces, "Forty-nine Senators having answered to their names, a quorum is present!" when there are about 20 people on the floor. Possibly Lister Hill can be prevailed upon to shirk his principal duty, which is to suggest the absence of a quorum. Possibly no quorum will be necessary at all, in view of an immediate adjournment. Chances of that, however, are becoming increasingly slim.

Jimmy Byrnes has now issued another demand for action on reconversion. Vandenberg's telegram is getting a good play everywhere in the country. From Elmira, N.Y., where he is on a Truman Committee trip with Ferguson, Kilgore has added his bit, thanking Van for his support and getting in a few licks for his own bill. More and more it begins to look as though the Congress is going to stay on the job next month.

Over several offices these days hangs a visible aura of disintegration, as though they had been hit by a cyclone whose material debris has been cleared away but whose psychological shock still remains. Hattie Caraway's secretaries "don't know when she'll be back. We don't know anything. We don't know how long we'll be here." Cotton Ed's folks are similarly upset. Rufus Holman has gone home to Oregon, marrying the widow of the late Senator Lundeen on the way, and will not be back until November; packing has begun. In D. Worth Clark's office, boxes of papers, books and documents stand about, pictures have already come down off some of the walls, the wreckage of a public career that began at 32 with two terms in the House and is ending at 42 after one term in the Senate speaks in eloquent terms through the packaged bric-a-brac of an office. And there will be others.

Bob Wagner, lovable and philosophic as always, refuses to worry about his own chances. "After all, why worry?" he says. "The people will decide. They always do. You can't tell. I ran the first time in 1904, that's 40 years ago. Somebody was telling me the other day that I've been at it long enough, maybe I'd better retire. Well, maybe he's right. I'm not worrying about it." Things like the Bretton Woods monetary agreement interest him more. "If nations can agree on economic matters, which after all form the basic causes of wars, then it seems a hopeful sign that they might be able to agree on other matters." At times "the going got rather rough" at the international conference in New Hampshire, he remarked dreamily: Russia proved difficult in spots. "But we worked it out all right. That's the value some of us old fellows were able to contribute—we know how to compromise. These experts, you know"—jamming his hands together tightly—" 'Kill him'—that's what they want to do when they run into trouble. But we worked it out." There was "a very good spirit of co-operation there—very good. It's a real hope for the future." How did I think the end of the war would affect the President's chances? I did? "Well, you know, it's funny. I had a young man—well, he's not such a young man either, he's 42, but he's a lot younger than I am—and a young woman in here the other day. The young man felt just the way you do, but the young woman took exactly the opposite view. Well, I don't know. You can't tell. The people will decide."

JULY 29, 1944. White and Burton came back today, both anxious to get going on reconversion legislation. The Minority Leader held a press conference for us, and talked along for a while about the legislative situation, Tom Dewey, and the world in general. Reconversion ought to be tended to, he said; after that, nothing much is hanging fire. He would favor a session straight through August and as far into September as necessary, with a recess in October just before election—"that's near the

time when the firin' squads get to work, and no one
will want to stay here then, anyway." With Dewey
he was "very favorably impressed—very favorably
impressed. He's a man who takes a lot of advice
and studies things very hard and then makes up
his mind. Of course he treated the Maine delegation very ably when we went to see him—asked us
what the situation was in the state of Maine, then
asked our views on the national situation and the
campaign—very deferential. My gosh, really made
us feel as though we might be important, after all!
But he makes up his own mind, there's no doubt
of that." The main problem, White thinks, is one
of timing: "if he can start his campaign before people have made up their minds but not so long be-

fore election that th·y'll be all talked out when election rolls around."
Dewey, he predicted, will make a "very intelligent campaign, a very able
campaign, and I think a very appealing campaign." The word "winning,"
however, did not enter the Minority Leader's conversation. He said they
were able to tell Dewey what Maine would do, but "after all, I'm not
qualified to speak on the rest of the country."

Burton, the compact, the capable, was eager to get to work too. Speaking in his clipped, hurried fashion he said much the same as White:
finish reconversion and then go home. On politics he brushed aside the
foreign-policy issue rather impatiently. "There can't be any controversy
on foreign policy," he said. "After all, we're all agreed on the need for a
strong one." A stable foreign policy, he added aptly, is after all a domestic necessity. The thing paramount over all others, he maintained, is the
need for a domestic policy that can handle reconversion and reconstruction after the war, a "sympathetic attitude" toward the problems of recovery. He thinks the Republicans may take the House. "We won't carry
the Senate, but we'll come so close to a majority that it will be practically
certain. And with the Southern opposition—they'll follow us."

JULY 30, 1944. The atmosphere on the Hill is beginning to get that little
extra bustle in it that always precedes the opening of a session. The
cafeteria in the Office Building, always full during recess when everything else is closed, is even fuller now. More and more Senators are
beginning to appear, secretaries are coming back from vacations. Over in
the Capitol the pageboys are busily at work distributing copies of bills
to all the desks in the chamber. The empty room which for five weeks
has been just an empty room is being prepared for the rituals that will

once again turn it into the Senate of the United States. The press is back in force and impatient to get to work. With the exception of the members, everyone is eager to begin.

As things stand now, it appears that the first week or so is going to be a mere formality anyway. Jim Murray is on the Coast holding hearings which will run through August 5. Nothing can be done to bring his reconversion bill out of his Military Affairs subcommittee until he returns. His feud with Kilgore has now reached epic proportions. Walter George has withdrawn from the battle and left Murray to fight on alone, and Kilgore claims he has enough proxies in his pocket to pass his own bill through the whole committee. Murray is not going to be pleased about this. The deadlock that has existed for nearly a year is about to be broken now, however. The public has at last become interested, and the Congress can't duck the genuine sort of pressure that drifts in day by day through the mails.

JULY 31, 1944. Barkley held a press conference today, looking soured and somewhat sobered by the death of his hopes at Chicago. His words were conventional and circumspect, a certain remoteness characterized his tone. As for the session, he and White have agreed that it should begin tomorow as scheduled. Three-day recesses until Military Affairs can report out the reconversion bill seem to be indicated, he said. It is going to be a rather half-hearted affair, this session that very few of the Senators want. They feel they have been bludgeoned into it by Vandenberg and the public, and they don't like it. If anything has bludgeoned them into it, however, it is the dilly-dallying procrastination which has permitted this legislation to drag on and on and on up to the last possible deadline.

Not more than 25 Senators are expected on the floor tomorrow. Not before mid-August will a majority be back. It will be legislation in a vacuum while the Senate waits for Military Affairs. Bob Reynolds, joined by Barkley, has dispatched another telegram to his recalcitrant members urging their immediate return.

Taft, disapproving the Bretton Woods agreement, agreed today with Wagner's suggestion that the debate go over until after election. This made a good story, and he presently came forth with another, his amendment to the soldier-vote law. He is submitting it to the Council on Books in Wartime today, and expects to introduce it sometime this week. It will place upon the Secretaries of War and Navy the burden of deciding what is and isn't political propaganda. "That ought to permit these officers down the line to relax a little and not lean over backward." He agreed that "in a way" it looked as though the Army might be trying to ridicule Congress with its strict interpretation of the law, but on the other hand he was more inclined to think that maybe it was "just that old Army fear of taking responsibility." The Army, he added, wanted to take the words "and calculated" out of the phrase "political propaganda designed and calculated to influence the outcome of any election." This, he said, he refuses to do. Did he regard the Dewey campaign as sound so far? "Yes (rather coldly).... Yes. He seems to be doing a good job of it. I was up there about 10 days ago.... He seems to be doing a good job." From there the talk drifted to his own campaign. Would he have much trouble? "Well" (with his sudden smile) "I think I'll win, but—I'm not going to be sure until I have. You never know." He seemed neither optimistic nor pessimistic nor particularly interested; just a practical politician, aware of the risks and prepared for anything.

17

GEORGE HAS THE VOTES

AUGUST 1, 1944. Thirty-four Senators met for 50 minutes today to open the summer session. Vandenberg urged Action with much emphasis, Barkley did the same. Tom Connally drily cautioned against giving the country the idea that the war is about over, and Van countered with equal dryness that "the Senate doesn't have to loiter to prove to people that there's still a war on." The first committee meeting has been postponed to Tuesday and Ed Johnson, Hill, Chan Gurney and Kilgore have promised to be back. The committee quorum is six, so there will be enough on hand to do business.

Meanwhile, the desperate intrigue as Senators maneuver to gain for themselves the credit of the reconversion bill has been stepped up to dizzying speeds. Walter George with impeccable blandness has now put in an entirely new bill which carefully appropriates to his own Finance Committee the unemployment-compensation features of the original Murray bill. He may succeed in taking the unemployment side of the problem right away from his ambitious competitors. A majority of the Finance Committee is in town and George has called a meeting for tomorrow morning. If he can possibly swing it, and he probably can, a bill ought to be on the calendar ready for action within a week.

Simultaneously, Murray and Kilgore have once more joined battle. Murray has abruptly canceled his West Coast hearings and is flying back to Washington. "Because of an emergency," he told them out there. "What emergency?" queried the San Francisco News. We couldn't tell them: because it looks as though Kilgore might get his bill through committee and, by George, that's emergency enough for Murray. In the middle of the afternoon Murray's committee suddenly released a new bill— sponsored by himself and by Harry Truman, who with obliging impartiality also has his name on Kilgore's bill as cosponsor. The new Murray–Truman bill is a neat little number that simply engulfs Kilgore's bill and serves it up under new management. All the Federal-centraliza-

tion features have been appropriated; unemployment compensation is
served up with a lavish hand. The states'-rights emphasis has utterly
vanished. Murray, after months of work, has revised an old political saw
and is trying to lick 'em by swallowing 'em. The addition of Truman,
with its appeal to Democrats who want to help the ticket, may give him
the extra strength he needs to emerge victorious.

Kilgore's reaction, somewhat resembling the agony of a wounded bull,
has taken the form of an acid statement damning Murray's measure with
faint praise. The Senator is apparently determined to fight it out on this
line if it takes all summer, and the mere fact that Murray has appropriated
his bill and Harry Truman along with it is evidently not going to stop him.
There may not have been a quorum on the floor today, lots of Senators
may be still away, the tempo—so far as the public knows—may be slow,
but the Senate is back in session, all right.

In another sector, political strategists were also busy outmaneuvering
one another today. Theodore Francis Green and Scott Lucas, moving
briskly to steal the spotlight from their most relentless critic, have beaten
Taft to the punch with an amendment to relax the censorship restrictions
in the soldier-vote law. Queried on this by telephone Taft told me thoughtfully that he "probably would" introduce his own amendment for the sake
of the record, "but I won't push it if the Green–Lucas amendment is
satisfactory." He wanted to study it, and he refused to say what his final
course would be. However: "I don't want to start the old argument all
over again. I don't want to get into a lot of controversy. I just want us to
take care of the specific issue."

AUGUST 2, 1944. Walter George swung his Finance Committee into line
behind him today, as he usually manages to do, and reported out his
version of the reconversion bill. This beats everybody to the tape, and the
Senator says it will be taken up on the floor on Tuesday. There is a
reasonably good chance that it may be out of the way by the end of next
week.

The well-worn path which leads about the Office Building from door
to door yielded three good interviews today, with Guy Gillette, Robertson
of Wyoming, and Chapman Revercomb. The genial Guy, just back from
a month in Iowa, was glad to analyze the Midwest political situation at
some length. "They hate Roosevelt," he said, "but they just can't see
Dewey. There is an accumulated bitterness—a host of irritants—against
the President which in any normal year would sweep the Democratic
Administration and everyone connected with it out of office. But this isn't
a normal year. They wonder about Dewey's ability, about his interest and
understanding in the field of foreign affairs. They wonder what he stands

for—they wonder if he stands for anything. They don't know, they can't find out. They'll vote for Roosevelt because they just can't find what they want in Dewey. In a region which is normally two- to three-to-one Republican, the Dewey candidacy simply has not clicked. And now you want to know my own situation?" (this with the characteristic sober beginning which always ends in a twinkle) "well, I'm not having any trouble at all. All I have to do is hold all the Democratic registration and pick up about 40 per cent of the Republican and I'm in. That's all there is to it. Very simple." It can hardly be said that the Senator is desperately concerned about his probable defeat. Few men on the Hill are more detached or more likable than Guy Gillette.

Joe O'Mahoney's portly, shrewd little Scottish colleague, E. V. Robertson, with his level, liquid, clipped accent, his keen dark eyes, and his shrewd and practical approach to the problems of politics, turned out to be a gold mine of news today. As a member of the Republican Senatorial campaign committee with jurisdiction over the Western states, he was in receipt of a number of reports from the field, and these he was willing to divulge for the press—in our working parlance he would "stand still for it," meaning that we could quote him direct rather than having to resort to some indirect attribution such as "it is understood," or, "it is reported." His comments were in the main quite optimistic. Like many of the minority he has visions of picking up five or six seats. Wayne Morse, he says, has Oregon "sewed up." "I do hope," he said, "that Rufus Holman's new wife is taking his mind off his troubles. I watched him in the Senate after he got beaten—he couldn't concentrate on anything, all he could do was think about it. Rufus is a lovable old fellow, but after all—any man who

Senator Guy Gillette

goes into public life has got to expect that eventually the voters are going to retire him. It's all part of the game. You can't take it to heart too much."

Bennett Champ Clark had need of that philosophy today, as he went down to a resounding 17,000-vote defeat. Harry Truman's support did not carry Republican-bound Missouri for him.

Chapman Revercomb was cordial as always and as always not too productive of news. But what he did say—that the Republicans would carry the border states "and that would include the Senate seats"—tied in well enough with Robertson's statements and gave me what I wanted. The interview could not end without some comment on the reconversion issue. The new Murray–Truman bill is "a typical Hillman idea—it reads like something born on the steppes of Russia." The figures the Senator quotes are admittedly impressive—something like $1200 unemployment compensation for $900 annual work, and so on. "If we've got to legislate to maintain employment, let's do it—if we've got to subsidize, and that's what it would be, all right—but let's don't penalize the people who do work to support the people who don't. No, sir. I just couldn't go along with the boys on that one. I just couldn't go along." Very obviously one of two things is going to happen on this bill: either the Senate is going to rush through a Santa Claus grab-basket beyond anyone's wildest dreams or it is going to spend considerable time hammering out a calmer and more sensible measure. With Republican opposition virtually certain, and with conservative Democrats falling into line, the chances seem to be weighted on the side of the latter possibility.

AUGUST 3, 1944. Military Affairs met for two hours this morning and then came back at 2 P.M. to go on to 6:15. As always in the Senate, when they really want to work, they can, and they are at it now. Ed Johnson has put in a bill to handle surplus-property distribution (it padlocks durable goods for five years so as not to interfere with resuming civilian production) and Kilgore and Murray after a heated tussle have agreed to separate surplus property from the other features of their bills. This simplifies matters somewhat. The hope now is to have a bill ready for the Senate by Tuesday. In the meantime, as Kilgore promised with humorous grimness this afternoon, "some heads are going to be knocked together." A battle royal is under way in the committee room.

Harry Truman resigned this morning, both as chairman and as a member of his committee. He came out of the executive session in his usual brisk fashion, distributing copies of the letter he had just sent to Wallace as President of the Senate. His decision was universally regretted, but as he said he had "considered all the angles and my mind is made up." The Truman mind, once made up, generally stays that way.

Some strange characters infest his office these days. Of course the normal stream of visitors has greatly increased, and among them are some prize numbers. While waiting for his resignation statement today a couple of us got to talking to one of them, a florid-faced gentleman with a shifty eye and an easy shrug and a pragmatic manner, a doctor from Kansas City, well-to-do and voluble. In about five minutes he gave us the best thumbnail portrait of the corrupt political mind it would be possible to get anywhere. "They say Harry was sent here by the Pendergast machine," he said indignantly, "but what the hell. He's always been an honest man. And anyway, I've never been able to see all this fuss about machines, have you? Why, there's always graft. Somebody's got to get it. You might as well have a machine you know and can trust to do you some favors. Isn't that right? They say it's all wrong, but it's only human nature. You find it in all cities, mayor or council or what have you—there's always a strong man, there's always somebody who's boss. Of course sometimes they do things that may be wrong; I don't know. (He shrugged and winked.) Now, you take Kansas City; when I was on the payroll there, why, one time they needed some money to balance the city budget. So what did they do? They threw everything wide open—gambling and everything. The town was roaring for about a month, then they closed it down again. Well, maybe it was wrong. But they got the money. See what I mean? It's all a matter of give and take anyway. Now you take another friend of mine, Frank Hague over in Jersey City. All Frank wants is the judgeships, it's just a matter of trading the governorship for the judgeships. That's all it is every time, Republican or Democratic, it doesn't matter which. Frank is behind them all. He gives them the governorships and they give him the judgeships. That's what I mean—it happens everywhere, it's just human nature. There's always a boss. Maybe it's wrong, but I don't know. Do you?"

To this interesting dissertation we agreed with the amiable and meaningless acquiescence of politicians and newspapermen who depend on banana oil to grease the wheels of society, but as my friend remarked later in a shocked tone of voice, "What a hell of a thing for Truman to have a man like that in his office! With us, we don't think anything about it, we're used to that type; but suppose some constituent had heard all that—why, it would be a hell of a thing. He's so vulnerable anyway." We decided it must be one of those old friends ("I've known him ever since he was a kid, I grew up with Harry") to whom Truman is so admirably loyal, but even so, we agreed that he was not safe company for a Vice-Presidential nominee.

With this in mind we were even more impressed with Truman's letter to Wallace in his capacity as President of the Senate.

Dear Mr. President (wrote the man who has come out of this background to be one of the honest miracles of America), I herewith submit my resignation as chairman and as a member of the Special Committee of the United States Senate Investigating the National Defense Program.

It is one of the regrets of my lifetime that this had to be done. But frankly, under the present circumstances, I am of the opinion that any statement, hearing, or report for which I would be responsible would be considered by many to have been motivated by political considerations.

The accomplishments of the Committee in the past largely have been due to the fact that all its members, Democratic and Republican alike, were able to work together in harmony without partisanship. I know they would all sincerely try to continue this, and I appreciate the very great compliment which the Republican members have paid me by requesting me to continue and pledging me their support.

However, I have been nominated for the office of Vice President of the United States by the Democratic Party, and as candidate for that office it is my obligation to present to the people the accomplishments of the Democratic Party and the reasons why it should continue to be entrusted with the administration of the government in this great national emergency.

I do not want even the shadow of suspicion that the Committee's activities in any way are determined or influenced by political considerations.

Sincerely yours,
Harry S. Truman, Chairman
Special Committee Investigating
the National Defense Program

AUGUST 4, 1944. A Frankenstein monster in the guise of Santa Claus came to the Hill today. His uneasy spirit presided over Military Affairs along with Bob Reynolds, and when it was all over a bill which one Press Gallery cynic termed "the most desperate SOS for votes in history" had been reported out. The fantastic measure, on which Murray and Kilgore reached sufficient agreement to accept coauthorship (Harry Truman prudently withdrawing) holds out a bonanza to the unions with one hand and beats them over the head with a club with the other. Their fervid endorsement, given so often in advance, may be somewhat modified when they have had a chance to study the bill.

Approved on a strict 10–7 party vote by 8 committee members and their proxies—only Reynolds, Ed Johnson, Hill, Murray, Kilgore, Austin, Revercomb and Gurney were actually present—the bill creates a Work Administrator who may withhold unemployment benefits from any jobless worker who refuses to accept a job ordered by the government, and gives the Work Administrator "if he deems it necessary" the right to set aside state standards and rulings on employment benefits ranging as high as $35 a week. As Chapman Revercomb pointed out with some asperity, it would make the Work Administrator "a dictator over all employment in the country," and it would place the jobless in the iron grip of the government, to be herded into unions or out of them according to whichever philosophy prevailed at 1600 Pennsylvania. Warren Austin's national service, so innocent of authorship and so dangerous of administration, can't compare with this bland device. All the Work Administrator could do to a man if he wouldn't take the job the government wanted him to is let him starve. Kind-hearted Warren Austin never thought of that one.

The Republicans are united solidly against this strange proposal, and so are the conservative Democrats led by Walter George. The chances are good that it will not pass without drastic revision. The Senate's innate caution is of some purpose here. Never has there been a more peculiar hodgepodge of good intentions and bad lawmaking than this weird, inexcusable measure which Kilgore's proxies, all of whom are absent and none of whom as of today probably has the slightest idea what his name has been put to, have recommended to the Senate. By a combination of political fright, vaulting ambition, liberalism amok and sloppy drafting, a peculiar deed has been done. Some days will be consumed by the Senate, doggedly and with intense internecine bitterness, undoing it.

AUGUST 7, 1944. The Murray–Kilgore brainchild continues to agitate the Senate. The genesis of the Work Administrator's dictatorial powers now becomes a little clearer. It is a CIO-sponsored bill, we are given to understand; Kilgore accepted their version without much change. Viewed in that light, the compulsive features by which a jobless worker might be forced into a union make a little more sense. Obviously, however, it has never occurred to the CIO that the bill might someday be administered by an Administrator who wanted to break the CIO instead of strengthen it.

With the authorship in mind, the Republicans are even more determined to throw it out, and the conservative Democrats—and not all of them are from the South, either—are equally antagonistic. The Democratic Steering Committee held one of its rare meetings this afternoon, but if Murray and Kilgore thought they were going to get anything like a solid front to meet the Republicans, they were sadly mistaken. Walter

George, whose personal influence would outweigh 10 of Murray and Kilgore, won the first round: an agreement to take up his bill first tomorrow. Barkley held a press conference after the meeting and told us about it, but the things he had to say about the internal fight in the majority were noncommittal in the extreme. A harmonious conference, concerned with "procedure." "We tried to keep it out of politics," and he had "made no canvass of other Senators" and could not predict the sentiment or the vote. Asked about his own position, he remarked with a chuckle that he expected to explain at the proper time his reasons for voting as he will, "but I don't want to tell you now—I don't want to scoop myself." And his face fell into its familiar easygoing joviality. In the same fashion he said he had "made no plans for the campaign." "Is that for the national ticket or the Barkley ticket?" he was asked. "In Kentucky," he said quickly, and laughed heartily with us, "the national ticket *is* the Barkley ticket." His personal charm and his political instinct remain unchanged despite his unhappy days in Chicago.

As for the reconversion fight itself, although Barkley predicted "passage of a bill by the end of this week," few others are so optimistic. The Senate has an invariable habit of overestimating its own ability to make time, and this occasion will probably be no different from the rest. Republicans are rather grim about it, and so are Walter George and his crowd. Kilgore and Murray talk a good fight, but already they are beginning to act a little guilty and not quite sure of themselves.

AUGUST 8, 1944. Amid fireworks the fight began today on the floor. George called up his bill with a brief speech. Murray promptly countered by offering his bill as an amendment to George's bill, striking out everything after the enacting clause and substituting the first three sections of his own measure. As a second amendment Murray proposed to pick up the George bill *in toto*, and after it add the rest of his bill—a neat sort of whale-swallowing-Jonah business that would simply engulf George's bill in the verbiage of the Murray–Kilgore bill and let it go at that. The majestic Walter, not to be outdone, countered presently in his turn with a left hook to the jaw in the form of an amendment to Murray's amendment (after the session we spent 15 minutes with Charlie Watkins, the parliamentarian, getting this all straight) which would strike out most of Murray's bill, substitute a new George bill which includes all the old unemployment-compensation features and a much-watered version of the Work Administrator, and then pick up the last two innocuous sections of the Murray–Kilgore bill on public works and housing.

George's amendment to Murray's amendment takes precedence and is now the pending business for tomorrow, which means that the first vote will come, in practical effect, on the George bill. If it is agreed to, as everyone is certain it will be, that will be the end of the Murray–Kilgore bill. Any compromise that might save some of it will not come from them, because, as one of their youthful assistants told us, "They aren't authorized to accept any compromise." When we asked, "Authorized by Military Affairs Committee or the CIO?" he shrugged and grinned and told us to draw our own conclusions. We did.

Barkley still has "taken no canvass," he told us after the session, but it is obvious that he has no more illusions about the Murray–Kilgore bill's chances than anyone else. In common with us all, he "likes some features of both bills and dislikes other features of both bills." Although he refused to predict which would win out, the outcome is not hard to see. Walter George's bill goes just far enough to the left to pull in the practical liberals who know the Senate won't take anything more, and stays just close enough to dead center to satisfy Taft and the Republicans. It is a shrewd compromise, as befits a shrewd man.

AUGUST 9, 1944. Denouncing the Philadelphia transit strike, Dick Russell served one more of the South's increasingly regular warnings on the FEPC. The strike, he charged, was deliberately instigated by the FEPC, with a ruling against racial discrimination in hiring, in order to make the Army come in and break it, thereby giving an "object lesson" to any other workers who might wish to disregard FEPC rulings. If the FEPC, he said soberly, attempts to repeat "the Philadelphia story" in the South, then it will set in motion a train of events that will be of the gravest consequence to America.

AUGUST 10, 1944. "George has the votes," Kilgore admitted glumly today, "but he won't talk to me." In desperation the West Virginian and his Montana sidekick are beginning to talk compromise, but the stately Georgian refuses to have anything to do with them. "George has the votes," the slogan which has so often tipped us in advance to the outcome of a legislative battle, is once more the watchword of the Senate. And George is sitting tight.

He did so all day long today, and at 4:30, when the Murray–Kilgore group wanted to recess until tomorrow in order to give the unions, and possibly the President, time to bring more pressure to bear on the George supporters, he rose in wrath and denounced the proposition. The Senate returned to work, he said, and there was no reason why it should not do so. Wallace White took the cue and jumped up to second the statement. The afternoon, he said, was "hardly half over." "We have been here almost a week," the Minority Leader said, "and we have done almost nothing."

Sheridan Downey, who had made a point of no quorum knowing perfectly well that the necessary 49 Senators could not be found that late in the afternoon, which would mean an automatic recess, remarked with some asperity that "if this bill is so important, and if we must work so hard, then it seems to me that we should at least have a quorum instead of 25 or 30 Senators on the floor. Speaking to empty seats can hardly contribute to our knowledge of the problem." However, he said, he would leave it up to Kilgore, who was about to speak; if he wanted the point of no quorum withdrawn, it would be. Kilgore decided to withdraw it, and launched into his speech. At 5 Barkley prevailed on George to relent, and a recess was ordered. The Senate meets again at 11 tomorrow. The afternoon did not produce much of note aside from a speech by Taft, making one of his able analytical dissections of a bill he doesn't like.

Bob Reynolds spoke for an hour and a half, his face redder than ever, his sharp nose and flowing hair swinging from side to side in emphasis, starting out on the merits of the Murray–Kilgore bill and ending up with his favorite topic—the "beellions and beellions of dollars which we ah spending on ouah Allies ovahseas. Beellions and beellions, Mr. President; *beellions* and *beellions!*" On the whole, not much progress was made today. "George has the votes." It's just a matter now of letting everybody get talked out so that he can produce them.

AUGUST 11, 1944. George delivered his votes today, 49 to 25 on the question of his amendment to the Murray–Kilgore amendment, and a smashing 55 to 19 on the final passage of his own bill. The Senate met for eight solid hours, convening at 11 and adjourning until Tuesday at 7 P.M. It was a long, dramatic day, filled with hurried conferences on the floor, caucuses called in cloakrooms, sudden switches, deals, attempts at compromise, last-minute amendments in a desperate effort to get votes, and several valiant attempts to recommit the bills to committee—one of those days when little signals flicker over the surface of the Senate—a Senator crossing to another, a third carefully tallying up his votes on a roll-call sheet, more and more outspoken denunciations of "politics" as losers begin to feel themselves irrevocably slipping, and a number of heated exchanges. Murray remained glumly in his seat, conferring intently all day long with an ever-changing stream of his bright young men, while Kilgore, holding voluminous papers embodying his last desperate amendments, wandered back and forth around the floor looking more and more tired and confused and despondent. Walter George sat placidly in his seat, his only sign of life coming in a powerful thunderous denunciation when Maloney, asserting that nobody knew what it was all about, moved to recommit. Other than that, the Georgian sat tight.

Taft, who loves politicking, conferred busily with Byrd and other Senators, counting up votes in plain sight of everyone. Once Pepper came over to his desk, looking abashed and disconsolate, and argued with him briefly. Taft kept shaking his head, unsmiling. His right hand rose and fell forcefully. The words "cost billions and billions and billions of dollars!" came clearly to the gallery. Bennett Champ Clark came back in defeat from Missouri nursing his grudge against the CIO and eager for the chance to chop it down with his vote. Many Senators went across and shook his hand and offered their commiserations. The portly, red-faced Bennett took off his glasses and wiped his eyes repeatedly, growing sadder and sadder; not until Hattie came over and shook his hand heartily did his face break into laughter and relax. Both of them seemed to feel better about it, and Hattie, too, for the first time since she has been back, seemed more philosophic. When Vandenberg got up to shout in his heavy gravel voice that all bills had received earnest consideration of the committees, that the Murray–Kilgore bill "is the result of six months' work by the War Mobilization subcommittee and the Military Affairs Committee," Bennett Champ shot out, "and the CIO!" in a loud voice which broke the tension and made everybody laugh. Barkley made a roaring speech, growing even redder in the face than usual, when Maloney moved to recommit.

Sheridan Downey in his high, indignant voice made an able address urging positive legislation to promote production rather than defeatist legislation accepting the certainty of millions of unemployed. Tydings, lean and reasonable, chopped Kilgore into little pieces with a calm and logical statement of a basic fact: that someday, sometime, somehow, somebody in Washington is going to have to start thinking about where the money is to come from. Warren Austin was upset for a number of reasons about the Murray–Kilgore version of his own national service law ("Now you simply cut off a man's relief, you permit him to starve, you do away with all appeals and all pretenses at justice!") and Aiken, honestly angry still about the way in which agriculture was ignored, rose to second in a choked voice Maloney's motion to recommit. After the vote O'Mahoney took the floor to point out calmly that the reconversion process is continuing, and that "this is not the last hour, or the last day, or the last month or the last year" in which Congress will be considering the problem. Hatch interjected bitterly that "for all the Senator's fine words, the philosophy [of liberalism] is being killed right now and he knows it." Pepper, characteristically singing the swan song after everything was over, made an unfortunate oratorical assertion to the fact that asking the states to increase their compensation was a pious hope like the Lord's Prayer, and when a man is out of work, what use is the Lord's Prayer? Happy Chandler protested, the debate ended on a note of general ill-temper. Walter George walked off the floor, his expression still dignified, calm, impassive, and entirely unemotional. He knew he would win, and he did.

Thus the reconversion fight moves across the Capitol to the House, to return in conference within a week or two to be thrashed out in final form. Many in the Senate were of a mood expressed perfectly by Maloney when he said that "one bill goes so far as to be almost an absurdity. The other does not go far enough. With great reluctance I shall vote for the George bill. With no compunction whatsoever I shall vote against the Murray–Kilgore bill." The George bill is not satisfactory, it does not do what must inevitably some day be done—establish a minimum standard for state unemployment compensation—but it is so much better than the Murray–Kilgore bill, with its fantastic Work Administrator with his enormous powers to force a man into a union, which might so easily be used to force a man out of a union; with its gaping holes as wide as a barn door, its innumerable legislative jokers, its sloppy drafting—in short, its complete ineptness—that there was no choice in the final showdown.

"The people behind this bill," one correspondent summed it up succinctly afterwards, "were a bunch of hams and they were up against a man like Walter George and they were licked from the start. Kilgore and his amendments and Murray and his compromises! Why didn't they get together and work something out at the very beginning, instead of hanging on to the end and then going around trying to promise everybody everything? All it got them was contempt. If their bill wasn't dead already, that killed it."

Once again the all-or-nothing-at-all theory has proved its weakness for democracy. It shows so little understanding of the legislative process, so little appreciation for the hard fact that everything enacted on the Hill is the child of compromise to some degree. That's the way Congress functions—it's the way democracy functions. Three times now—the soldier-vote bill, the anti-poll-tax bill, and the Murray–Kilgore bill—the bludgeon method has been tried, and three times it has failed. It will always fail as long as this is a free Congress and a free country. And right now, Congress is very free.

AUGUST 12, 1944. "For the past two years," said Carl Hatch bitterly, "the Republican minority, aided by certain elements among the Democrats, has controlled the United States Senate." Through the exercise of this control, he told Tony Vaccaro of AP and me, the Republicans prevented George from compromising. "From what I know of Senator George," Hatch said, "I know he favors a broader and more comprehensive coverage of the problem than the bill passed by the Senate affords. If the Republicans had let him, Senator George would have compromised. They would not do so." Consequently, he said, features of the Murray–Kilgore bill that might have been salvaged were lost.

This statement, regretted sharply by O'Mahoney when we told him about it, provoked from the slow-spoken Georgian himself only the calm comment that he "didn't care to become involved in controversy based upon the philosophy projected in the Murray-Kilgore bill." He did not admit the Hatch analysis, and he was not perturbed about it. Doubtless the Republicans will be, but it didn't worry Walter. His whole attitude implied that it was a rather wild exaggeration, and so it seems to be. George didn't compromise because George didn't want to compromise and George didn't have to compromise. The Republicans couldn't force him not to, because there wasn't anywhere else for them to go if he had. It was his own decision, and Hatch seems to have let his disappointment run away with him.

Senator Walter George

To Vandenberg, who as usual would not talk and said so with a smug bluntness verging characteristically on the downright rude, it was a matter that should not be boasted about. "I never believe in boasting," he said in his pompous voice, as though he had done it all single-handed, an impression he may quite possibly be victim of. "No, no comment." We did manage to stay with him at least 10 minutes, however, which was some sort of a record. Usually it takes about 10 seconds for him to say *no* and you to decide you have much better ways to use your energies than in attempting to drag a florid statement out of the florid statesman from Michigan.

To Albert Hawkes of New Jersey, his eyes narrowing sharply from time to time, the inevitable cigar in his hand, his coat off, his suspenders showing, his rich, well-fed hearty voice bearing down hard on the emphatic points customary to an ex-president of Congoleum-Nairn and the U.S. Chamber of Commerce, the Murray–Kilgore debacle was "brought about because the Senate knew the people all over the country wanted to stop further centralization of power in a centralized government." The bill was "a false promise. . . . Now there is no greater friend to labor in the United States than I am"—the tone, the appearance, the aura of wealth and power which surround him have to be experienced to make this oft-reiterated statement of the Senator as effective as it always is—"but the CIO (C–I–O) simply went off half-cocked on this thing. You've got to compromise; compromise is the law of life. That's one thing I've studied and learned since I came down here—that you've got to compromise. When you come here from business, you know, where all you have to do is push a button and tell them what the policy is going to be—well, I've learned a lot down here. I pray all the time that I can be fair and never lose my temper in the United States Senate. I want to be fair. The hard thing, wanting to do everything you can for labor as I do, is to bear down on the false leaders of labor and still be fair to the laboring people themselves. That's the problem on everything here, balance and fairness. Everybody has some ax to grind. Why, these *businessmen*" (and his tone became sarcastic and he hunched forward acidly over his desk) "coming to me on this subsidy fight. 'Of course we're against subsidies, but now if you'll just leave us alone for a year or two on our part of it—' Hmph! Everybody has an ax to grind. Same way on this poll-tax fight a while back. Now, there isn't a *better*, a more *sincere*, a more earnest *friend of the Negro* than I am in the United States. But you have to be fair. That's the thing I've studied and worked on down here—you've got to be fair. Everybody's got an ax to grind."

18

SURPLUS

August 13, 1944. Surplus property is next on the docket. Murray, with an amiable tolerance that probably baffles the CIO but is certainly no surprise to anyone familiar with the Congress, has decided to line up with the same Bob Taft who only a day or so ago was among the leaders of his bitter opposition. Together with Tom Stewart they have drawn up a surplus-property bill and introduced it, and obviously, although there are seven other bills pending on the same subject, it is the Murray–Stewart–Taft bill which is going to get the go-ahead from Military Affairs. A liberal measure, sound in principle and practical of execution, it may be modified but its essential structure will probably emerge undamaged. This time Murray has joined hands with the one man he needs on his side to win. Had there been the same foresight shown a couple of weeks ago, the Murray–Kilgore debacle might have taken a different course.

August 14, 1944. Dr. Richard Lamb, Phil Murray's legislative representative, came up today to testify on the surplus-property bills. A young, neat-featured man with a worried forehead, a clipped professional voice, and a pleasant smile, he betrayed a little of the CIO's inner bafflement at the strange business of legislating. "We have been interested to note," he told the committee earnestly, "that a number of bills on this subject have been presented, and that there seems to be a tendency to borrow from other bills, to exchange sections, and modify them, and to adopt other ideas. This would seem to be a healthy sign, and perhaps provides an indication of the way good legislation should be drawn." "I guess," he added, rather plaintively; so plaintively, in fact, that Ed Johnson could not suppress a slight twinkle despite his attempts to do so.

On this proposition, which is a business matter, the union's emphasis is of course directly contrary to its attitude last week. The idea of setting up a Surplus Property Administrator who might flood the market with surpluses that could cripple new production upsets them. "This is too big a problem for a government administrator to handle alone," said Lamb seriously. "We must make very sure that his authority is hedged about with all possible restrictions. You don't want to confer such broad powers; you don't know what a man might do with them." The CIO on this bill stands just where the coalition stood last week on the Work Administrator, while Taft has now moved over to the opposite side. Only Jim Murray is the constant factor in this process, the undeviating link between the two bills. He is right where he was before, willing to confer any powers to do anything so long as an "advisory board" can be set up and the mere vestige of Congressional control can be maintained.

From one who knows has come another post mortem on the Murray–Kilgore bill. "We finally told Kilgore to get as many proxies as he could and dynamite that bill out of committee," he said. "It was the only way to get something done. It meant a sloppy bill, but otherwise we never would have had anything at all to work on."

And Bob Reynolds, asked about his determined support for the bill, says in his florid voice and humorously overdone manner: "Why, Ah knew it would get beaten. Ah sat there in committee and didn't say a wuhd. Ah let 'em put in eve'y crazy thing they could think of and didn't raise a finger. Ah knew they'd beat it on the floah. And the unions wanted it. What could you lose?"

AUGUST 15, 1944. The Green–Lucas–Taft amendment to the soldier-vote law, relaxing censorship restrictions on reading matter sent overseas, went through this afternoon, and for a little while it seemed that we had suddenly been transported back six months. Across the way in the diplomatic gallery sat Colonel Cutler, brooding thoughtfully on an unruly Senate; at their desks in unchanged asperity Taft and Pepper and Green and Hatch contended. Not a shade of the bitterness has gone. The same ugly dislikes that characterized the original debate are still there, just under the surface, and ready to come out at the drop of a hat. It is one of the issues since I have been in the Senate on which real bitterness has been aroused; the feeling is undiminished to this day. Taft has the same suspicions of the Army, the same grim determination to block its "undue anxiety to get out the vote in November." Green has the same sarcastic contempt for "the Congress which would pass such a ridiculous law." Pepper and Hatch still condemned with the same violence "those who are so afraid of the servicemen that they refuse to permit them the franchise." Only the absence of a large attendance prevented the resumption of a full-scale fight.

Later McKellar, growing increasingly isolationist—or at any rate increasingly acquisitive for the United States—put in a rather surprising resolution this afternoon binding the government to enter into no treaty or agreement which does not provide for U.S. control of all Japanese-owned and Japanese-mandated islands, including Formosa and the Ryukyus. In addition, he would have the U.S. acquire Bermuda and all islands in the West Indies owned by European powers, and would request the President to begin immediate negotiations with Ecuador looking toward the acquisition of the Gallapagos Islands.

Truman, as friendly and forthright and eager-to-be-liked as a cocker spaniel, was in his usual amiable mood after the session today when I dropped in to see him. The man who may quite possibly be the next Vice-President, and perhaps the President, of the United States, is, as he likes to say, "as plain as an old shoe." No pomp and no circumstance for Harry Truman, and no hesitation about telling you what he thinks. He is so frank, in fact, that unfortunately nine-tenths of it must remain off the record, but it certainly makes him an enjoyable person to talk to. He is planning to meet the President on Thursday or Friday to map the campaign, and he wants to make as few speeches as possible. "A short campaign is better than a long one," he says briskly, a philosophy quite possibly dictated by his distaste for public speaking. His voice is good but his delivery, at least in the Senate, gallops. It sounds like "Oh-God-when-will-I-be-finished" while he's talking and "Thank-God-I-am-finished" when he hits the last sentence. He had a good deal to say on the Murray–Kilgore fight and gave the shrewdest and most accurate analysis, man by man, of his colleagues on the Truman Committee that anyone could possibly give. "My committee," he calls it still, and obviously will never be entirely reconciled to the fact that he had to leave it. He talks rapidly, laughs often, is entirely natural and completely likable. And the press, without exception, eats out of his hand, principally because his best stories are usually on himself. As for instance the story about the testimonial dinner they gave him after he resigned from the committee. The historian Douglas Freeman spoke, and: "Why, good Lord," Truman said, "to hear the way he laid it on you'd have thought I really *was* somebody. After we got through with the meeting Art Walsh of New Jersey said to me, 'You know what I'm going to do, Harry? I'm going to set up seats around the Reflecting Pool in front of the Lincoln Memorial and raise money for the Democratic campaign by charging people to see you walk on the water. After that build-up I'm convinced you must be Christ's half-brother.'" Truman laughed delightedly. "After I made arrangements to split the profits," he added briskly, "I said I'd do it."

AUGUST 16, 1944. The surplus-property bills moved into full committee today and three gentlemen from downtown turned up to testify, the

pugnacious Mr. Ickes, the blunt Mr. Maverick, and the smooth Mr. Clayton. Each was plugging his particular interest, and the old, old story of
interdepartmental jockeying for power was told all over again. Honest
Harold, possessed of a bulldog face and a gentle voice which only occasionally strays to acerbity—he is beginning to age, and acerbity is only
used when it is really worth it—wants surplus lands in the General Land
Office, where O'Mahoney want them. The details of the Senator's amendment did not quite suit Harold in some respects, and there were some
politely acid interchanges. "After all," O'Mahoney said blandly once,
"when I put in that provision I knew what I was doing. It was not an
inadvertent error." "Oh, I'm sure of it," said Ickes, "I'm sure of it. The
Senator always knows what he is doing." On the whole, however, he
endorsed the amendment.

The bull-necked, outspoken and bluntly honest Maury, fighting his
battle for little business like a Texas Tantalus who can never quite slake
his all-consuming thirst, praised the Murray–Taft bill but demanded more
consideration for the Smaller War Plants Corporation. The Colmer bill
which the House is now debating ignores little business, but the Senate
is very little-business-conscious, and Maury will probably be taken care of
in the final draft of the bill.

Will Clayton is a big, tall, well-built Texan in his 60s, with gray hair, a
handsome, rather rugged face, and the smoothest manner imaginable
when it comes to handling recalcitrant committees. The Colmer bill, he
said frankly, was written by his assistants in the present temporary Surplus
Property Administration set-up, and "it is a fine bill." If all restrictions
could just be taken off the Administrator in the Murray–Taft bill, it too
would be a very fine bill. O'Mahoney doesn't stand for that kind of talk,
and neither do Ed Johnson and Happy Chandler, and Clayton had a
rather warm time of it for a while. He defended himself ably and very
suavely, never lost his temper and never really conceded an error.

Out in Wisconsin Alexander Wiley has won renomination by a thundering majority, while in Kansas Clyde Reed's Democratic opponent has
withdrawn, ending his worries. The outcome in Wisconsin has been very
surprising to the press.

AUGUST 17, 1944. Will Clayton came back today, and for a while the
Military Affairs Committee was in executive session. Then, apparently
deciding that the gentleman should be put on the record, and also that
the press should have a chance to see that on this bill (in contrast to the
Murray–Kilgore) the committee is really using a fine-tooth comb, they
decided to open it up. The result was not much news but an interesting
insight into the way Senators function when engaged in the word-by-

word dissection that is the first preliminary to reporting out a bill.

Although Chan Gurney usually sits in amiable, round-faced silence, and Warren Austin only occasionally gives an opinion when someone asks for it, the others were in a mood to put Clayton over the ropes. Bob Reynolds, leaning back in his chair as always, with an intent, thoughtful frown on his face as he listened, presided in his heavy, ornate voice whenever the need arose. "Now, ge'mun," he would say occasionally, "what's youah pleasuah?" And whenever the discussion lagged he would go down the line calling the roll for more questions: "Sen'tuh Austin? Sen'tuh Chandluh? Sen'tuh O'Mahoney?" Will Clayton he bowed in and bowed out, as he does all witnesses, shaking hands with a single thorough grip, telling him "how much we 'preciate havin' you with us, havin' you take youah valu'ble time to come up heah and give us the ben'fit of youah 'sperience." O'Mahoney, unimpressed, challenged the administrator frequently in his light, husky, Massachusetts–Wyoming voice, putting his pince-nez on his nose and popping them off again to express varying degrees of surprise, interest and/or skepticism. His questions, as always, were filled with an amiable acid, and in his polite way he managed to imply that he thought rather little of Clayton's general philosophy. "As I see it, Mr. Clayton," he said, "there are two attitudes here. You take the attitude that this surplus property should be disposed of as fast as possible for as big a financial return as possible, whereas the committee believes that it should be used to encourage employment, promote education and farming, and in general strengthen the national economy." "There isn't any difference, Senator," Clayton protested. "If I thought I could strengthen the national economy by doing as this bill suggests, I wouldn't hesitate one moment." O'Mahoney nodded politely. "Well," he said, "of course it may be that the philosophy is the same on both our parts, and that it is only my poor understanding that prevents us from finding complete accord." Clayton, perhaps understandably, looked a trifle frustrated.

Happy also does a pretty good job of asking questions. He doesn't always know what it's all about, but he never hesitates to ask and find out. "Warren," he demanded of Austin at one point, "what do you mean here when you say 'or otherwise' in this section? What does that mean?" "Well," said Austin rather drily, bestirring himself, "of course I didn't write the bill——" "No, I know," said Happy, "but you're the legal expert around here. What would you say that means?" His questions to Clayton, amiable but frequently quite pointed, were answered by the administrator with a little more ease than O'Mahoney's, but even so Happy got the clarification he wanted.

Ed Johnson, having conceded that his 5-year padlock idea is lost, was particularly anxious to set Clayton on the right track concerning surplus lands. As with all Westerners, Ed wants to encourage small farms and he doesn't want to play into the hands of the land companies. Clayton, who proposed nothing more drastic than a series of 8 or 10 amendments that would remove all restrictions from the administrator and give him a free hand to sell as much of anything to anybody as he chooses, does not see this. Ed kept asking slow, friendly, common-sense questions in a manner which implied that he wouldn't take any nonsense for an answer. Clayton, whatever his views may be, never hesitates to state them with complete frankness, and his replies seemed to suit Johnson even if the sentiments did not.

Lister Hill can always be counted on to sum everything up in a rather nervous rush of words about every five minutes. When he is not engaged in this, he occasionally asks some quite shrewd questions. In between times, he betrays a jocose and frequently rather disconcerting humor which is usually directed against his colleagues, or former Congressmen such as Maverick. "Of course you know some of the names they call us downtown," Maverick said yesterday. "Lame ducks?" suggested Lister Hill promptly; Maverick ignored the interruption. Again Maverick paid Sheridan Downey a rather heavy-handed compliment about "always agreeing with the speeches he makes out in California." "Ham and eggs?" suggested Lister Hill promptly; Downey ignored the interruption.

AUGUST 18, 1944. Military Affairs met most of the day today, winding up with a vote of 7 to 4 which abolished Will Clayton's office and approved instead a seven-man board to run surplus-property disposal. So much for the handsome Texan's hold on the Senate. Over in the House, of course, they are eating out of his hand, dutifully passing his bill just as fast as they can.

The Senate met in lackadaisical fashion today, marking time until the committee brings out a bill. McKellar took the occasion to defend his island-grabbing resolution, which has been greeted with virtually unanimous silence by his colleagues. Bob Reynolds praised Mack's objectives, making the speech a day with which he is favoring us as his days in the Senate draw to a close. Bill Langer, speaking in his furious whistling voice which no one can understand for long, brought to the Senate's attention the plight of North Dakota farmers who cannot get equipment because it is going across the border to Canada under Lend-Lease.

AUGUST 19, 1944. Although he refused to be associated with McKellar's resolution today, Hatch too would like to see the United States acquire island bases "with as much ownership as possible" in both the Pacific and Atlantic approaches. The Senator's internationalism, like that of the bulk of the Senate's constructive thinkers, is tinged with a strong practicality. It extends as well to the Republicans. The selection of John Foster Dulles as Dewey's representative to confer with Hull is a good thing, Hatch thinks—anything that will commit the Republicans "irrevocably" to a strong peace is a good thing. "I want to do everything I can to get them on the record once and for all so that they can't back down, ever." This for several reasons, but the principal one is "because there is a possibility that the man may be the next President of the United States." Hatch, who has always been fair in his comments on Dewey, advocates an internationalism which, while based upon an idealism as great as any, is also filled with considerable common sense. It is men like that who will lead the Senate as far toward international cooperation as it is prepared to go in this second war.

Tom Connally, in contrast, is beginning to get more and more soured on the world in general. "I'm getting sick of sugaring the world with money," he told us when asked about Lend-Lease, "bribing people to do what they ought to do." And he too wants islands, all we need, particularly in the Pacific north of the equator. Reminded that the British have already run up their flag over islands scarcely cleared of American dead, he exploded into anger. "God damn their black souls in hell," he said bitterly. "I can't turn my back on them for a moment." But he will go along, because that is his responsibility—go along for a while, at least. A day may finally come when he is not so compliant.

Taft, refusing to comment on islands ("Bob Reynolds"—with a grin—"took care of that"), approved the Dulles choice. "Foster," he said—"we've known each other since we were boys—is an excellent selection, as good as Dewey could find, very intelligent and possessed of very sound judgement. He represents the Wilsonian view of the League of Nations and expresses the attitude of the Republican Party." The Senator, whose reputation for rampant isolationism always carefully ignores his constantly reiterated support of a league organization ("I think we'll be surprised how far Taft will go," Hatch said), shook off questions about his own views. "After all, it's what the Republican Party thinks and the people think and not what thirty-nine Senators think." When we begged leave to disagree, he grinned again. "I think they'll go along on a vote," he said, "almost all of them. Certainly they will if this Hull plan is set up, where one nation can veto the use of force. Certainly nobody would object to that." He himself, he added truthfully, would like to go much farther in the direction of real cooperation than that.

AUGUST 20, 1944. The Berrymans have done another good job in the *Evening Star* today. Their cartoon shows Henry Wallace talking to Donald

Nelson, about to leave on a special Far East mission for the President. "So you're going to China, Mr. Nelson?" the V.P. is saying. "What will you do when you get back?"

"Why don't you take a trip to China?" is the latest gag in this wonderful city.

AUGUST 21, 1944. The House is entering the second week of debate on its surplus-property bill and there is increasing talk of shelving the George reconversion bill until after elections. The surplus-property debate is dragging on and on, not at all according to plan. About 130 members were on the floor when I was over there today, and there was a rather desultory interest in what was going on. The boyish-looking, perennially worried Jerry Voorhis of California spoke for five minutes vehemently on an amendment to require the widest possible advertising of surplus sales. The able and contentious Jessie Sumners of Illinois challenged him a couple of times, gesturing vigorously with one hand, the other on her hip, asserting her views with the unhesitating forcefulness which makes her one of the best rough-and-tumble arguers in the House. Clare Luce, wearing a new hairdo and looking slim and other-worldly as usual, sat in her seat and chatted calmly with various colleagues as they wandered by. John Rankin, the man who runs the House when he wants to, moved around restlessly at the back of the room. Voices droned on over the microphones. The circus atmosphere was still there, but only one ring was in operation. After a while I left.

On the Senate side Military Affairs moved closer to reporting out a surplus property bill—close enough, in fact, so that only a brief routine session will be necessary tomorrow before the bill can be sent to the floor, where debate will begin Wednesday. O'Mahoney and Happy formed a working alliance to secure passage of O'Mahoney's surplus-lands amendment, and got it through during the afternoon. ("See?" Happy told us delightedly after the meeting. "Just like we told you it was goin' to be, this morning. Just like we told you. See there? Just like we told you!") The bill as it now stands provides for an eight-man board, puts surplus agricultural land under the Agriculture Department and other lands under Interior's General Land Office, provides for strict anti-monopoly controls, emphasizes the role of small business, aids local political units, and in general is a very excellent measure. How much of it will be retained in conference is another matter. Clayton's friends in the House are awfully loyal.

AUGUST 22, 1944. All the Democrats have been playing it very close to the belt, but Wherry and Ferguson have led off the pack in the outcry over

Nelson's trip to China. At the other end of the Avenue this has been taken into account in a sharp defensive statement. The mission is not a "kick in the teeth," it has been shortened to three or four weeks, and all is well. Nelson and his principal aides have reconsidered their plans to resign and a temporary armistice has been patched up. It begins to seem, however, that the day cannot be far distant when WPB is going to blow up like Vesuvius.

In the Senate, marking time until tomorrow when debate can begin on surplus property, the discussion this afternoon turned to the Dumbarton Oaks conference. No one knows what will come out of the Georgetown estate with its line of MPs around the grounds and its hush-hush aloofness from the press. Tom Connally, however, did his duty and expressed the hopes everyone has. In an earnest demonstration of unity Hatch and Pepper and Vandenberg and White joined in to pledge their own good wishes to the cause. All the speeches were able and sincere, Vandenberg's almost desperately so. If the same unity prevails when the time comes to make the generalities specific it will be a wonderful thing.

AUGUST 23, 1944. The debate on surplus property began today, and immediately a flood of amendments started. Apparently it doesn't matter, much, whether a committee spends a lot of time writing a good bill or gives a lick and a promise to a bad one: once it enters the lions' den it has to fight for its life regardless. Vandenberg is eyeing the bill warily, Wherry is upset, Aiken wants some changes made, and Walter George is mulling it over with a warning gleam in his eye. Already Senators are beginning to make cracks privately about "socialistic nonsense," and "plans to change the economy through surpluses." The painstaking work of the Military Affairs Committee, characterized by agreement between such diverse viewpoints as those of Warren Austin and Joe O'Mahoney, has apparently been in vain. Not only will the bill be under fire from the House, it may not even get through the Senate without drastic revisions.

Simultaneously on the House side the Ways and Means Committee has taken out its little hatchet and gone after the George bill. Not content with the measure as it passed the Senate, the House had decided to water it down still further. Chairman Bob Doughton of North Carolina, not nicknamed "Muley" for nothing, doesn't want to go along with Walter George, even to the limited extent the Senator's bill would provide. His committee feels the same. Two principal emotions dictate this attitude. The first is resentment, very lively, against Senate initiation of a bill which will require taxation, the House's constitutional prerogative. The second is resentment against the CIO, regarded as the principal force demanding the legislation.

On this latter point, in fact, House resentment approaches near-violence. The bludgeon methods of the Political Action Committee are bearing their unhappy fruit; understandably enough, the House is determined not to give Sidney Hillman what he wants. He is out to get them, they feel, and they are out to get him, and if the civilian economy suffers in the process, that's too bad. If suitable reconversion legislation fails in this session, the blame in the last analysis can be laid at the door of the PAC—not because it is such a very bad outfit, but just because it was foolish enough and unwise enough to mistake force for persuasion in its dealings with free men.

AUGUST 24, 1944. McKellar, Eastland, and McFarland collaborated today on an amendment to the surplus bill that kept the Senate busy for five hours. Thoroughly sound in principle—to stop speculation—it is completely impractical of administration. Where Mack got the idea, nobody knows, but once committed to a thing he never backs down unless a way can be found to save his face. Consequently considerable argument has developed.

The amendment provides that in all subsequent resales of surplus property after it leaves the government's hands—even if it is the tenth resale and occurs 20 years from now—the Surplus Property Board shall have the right to examine the records of the transaction. If it finds that "excessive profits" have occurred, it may institute court proceedings to recover twice the amount of the sum deemed to be excessive, turning it over to the Treasury as miscellaneous receipts. All of the millions upon millions of items included in an estimated $100,000,000 worth of surplus property, and all the millions and millions of sales and resales of such items, would come within the scope of this proposition. Naturally the Senate is against it, Taft terming it "an administrative impossibility," and O'Mahoney remarking scornfully that "no one would buy if he knew his records were going to be subject to examination forever after." After four hours of testy argument, Ed Johnson suggested that McKellar draw up a compromise and submit it to the Senate tomorrow; and Lister Hill, laying on the compliments with a trowel as he invariably does, commended Mack highly on his idea but hinted delicately that it might be a good idea to draw up something else. Nobody really wants to make the old man angry, so everybody scurries around trying to find an out for him. With a good 40 votes on the floor against him, he was deferentially asked if he would "consider a compromise." Such is the power of McKellar.

The War Production Board blew up this afternoon, as everyone had expected it would. Big Charlie Wilson of General Electric, his square face red with anger, resigned in a scathing letter to the President, who promptly tried to make out that all was rosy with Donald Nelson despite Wilson's

direct and vitriolic criticism. Wilson then came to the Hill for a previously
scheduled meeting with the Truman Committee and after that was over
the committee too tried to make out that all was rosy with Nelson. Wilson
then returned to his office, held a one-hour press conference, and blasted
all this hypocrisy sky-high by saying exactly what he thought of Nelson
—which wasn't much. The delay in reconversion was all Don's fault,
Charlie said, and the charge that the chairman was opposed by the vice-
chairman in his plans for little business was all a deliberate smear. The
truth in this tangled mess probably lies somewhere between, but at any
rate one thing is certain. Another of the President's hydra-headed administrative monsters has bitten itself in the neck.

AUGUST 25, 1944. The surplus-property bill passed on a voice vote today
substantially unchanged after McKellar's amendment went down to a
resounding 31–18 defeat and a number of other amendments were speedily
disposed of. Taft, attempting to the last to centralize authority on the
theory that a board is "long, wooden and narrow," put in an amendment
that would have given the President the right to select one member of the
eight-man board as administrator, exercising the board's authority. "This
seems to me to be the best possible compromise," he said firmly, provoking
the Press Gallery to muffled laughter. In the first place there wasn't any
need for compromise, at least within the Senate, and in the second place
the remark and the determination were both so typical of the Senator. If
there is a compromise to be found ("That A in his name stands for Amendment," a reporter remarked), Taft will find it—a valuable trait, but one
which can be overdone. He got swamped in a roar of nos, and that was
that.

Walter George, unyielding, says he regards the bill as an "unworkable,
ill-advised measure." The chances for an acrimonious conference are unfortunately good.

19

"THAT'S HOW YOUR GOVERNMENT WORKS"

AUGUST 26, 1944. Harold Burton, he of the hurried speech, the quick manner, the tumbling little laugh, and the idealistic approach, came forth with a novel idea this morning. There will be no need for Congress to retain control of the warmaking power if a postwar organization clearly establishing the conditions of peace is created in the treaties. The President would then be free to employ force without Congressional approval, as he saw fit, as long as it was in pursuit of America's obligations. Warmaking would become "a purely administrative job." Therefore no question of Congressional jurisdiction would ever arise, because naturally the country would be committed to certain things and the President would have every right to do them. The same "purely administrative" aspects would do away with the threat to world peace implicit in the Roosevelt concept of the major-power veto. Doubts as to the stubbornness and jealousy of major powers and the United States Congress he brushed away with an impatient smile. He just didn't see how any problem could arise, he said, so long as the treaties were clear.

Later Walter George, closing his eyes for long periods of time as he talked, as is his usual custom, and rolling forth an impromptu flood of impressive language which fell instinctively into Senatorial patterns, was willing to be quoted on what the House has done to his reconversion bill. Acknowledging the fact that it is not wise to criticize the proud gentlemen of the other branch, and being careful to pay tribute to the hard work of the Ways and Means Committee, he nonetheless was annoyed with its wholesale slaughter of his legislative child. He is going into conference with a powerful determination to restore it to a shape at least resembling the original. By a combination of personal prestige, stately logic and practical horsetrading he will probably manage pretty well—as well as Muley Doughton will let him.

255

AUGUST 27, 1944. Carter Manasco of Alabama, the shrewd little gentleman who will head the House conferees on surplus property, remarked today that "it looks like a long conference." Going through the two bills and digesting their provisions in the margins for easy reference, I find that I have written "Disagrees with House" in no less than 34 places in the Senate bill. It looks like a long conference indeed.

AUGUST 28, 1944. J. A. Krug, the heavy-set, earnestly belligerent 36-year-old who has succeeded to the town's biggest hot seat appeared before the Truman Committee today at its invitation, to get acquainted. The newly appointed acting chairman of WPB looks honest and speaks determinedly. His words did not indicate the supposedly temporary nature of his assignment, nor did the attitude of the committee and the press. By tacit agreement Donald Nelson, just a week ago the all-powerful czar of the American industrial machine, is kaput following Charles Wilson's angry resignation. That, as they say with an ironic shrug, is Washington.

As for "the Nelson crowd and the Wilson crowd," Krug promised the committee firmly, "they will work together in one group or they won't work there. That's a harsh policy, but if it's needed I'll do it." Impressed by his determination, everyone forgot for the moment that this stout do-or-die assertion has prefaced more than one pyrotechnic failure. The committee pledged its support, however, and the press gave him a good writeup, and everybody went away feeling thankful that the job was his worry and not theirs.

AUGUST 29, 1944. Attorney General Francis Biddle, possessed of a square, staring face with huge eyes, a tired expression, prominent cheekbones, a downturning mouth and a mustache to match it, came before Kilgore's War Mobilization subcommittee today to speak in his petulant Main Line voice about cartels. The things he said were very important, robbed somewhat of their effectiveness by his poor presentation; the atmosphere in which he spoke, however, could not have been more ideal. No disturbing questions were asked and all was harmony. Kilgore presided, and the A.G. was definitely among friends.

Lister Hill told us today that the Senate will do "absolutely nothing of importance" until the surplus-property conference concludes.

AUGUST 30, 1944. Although Elbert Thomas told us after the meeting today with his gently philosophic smile "We haven't reached the toughness stage yet," the surplus-property conference has already deadlocked on the fundamental issue of the single administrator versus the eight-man board. The first vote has been taken—7 Senators voting solidly for the board, 5 Representatives for the administration. "I'd call them stubborn," confided one Senator with a grin, "except that they might call us that. . . . Those House guys," he added, "are tougher'n hell—like a rock." The Senators show a tendency to "wander off in all directions." When it came to a vote, however, "everyone stood firm. Nobody is going to break yet." Happy Chandler remarked with a laugh, "We haven't got past Page 1." The process of squaring off and sizing each other up is still going on, apparently. The horsetrading will come next week.

Dennis Chavez has started hearings on his permanent FEPC bill—a noble gesture that is good for the Democratic Party and doesn't worry the Southerners because they know they've got it stopped cold when it gets to the floor. Essentially it's just good politics—a gesture which can fool some of the people enough of the time to get them to vote the right way and then can be abandoned if necessary. Chavez and the majority of the Education and Labor Committee are of course sincerely behind it, but they aren't kidding themselves that they're going to get anywhere.

The committee room is packed with hopeful Negroes who applaud the witnesses eagerly and from time to time stand in silent prayer that the bill will pass.

AUGUST 31, 1944. "Let's light our pipes and sit back and talk this thing over," said Warren Austin comfortably, settling back in his chair and suiting the action to the words. Time was hanging heavy on his hands prior to a 4 P.M. broadcast and he seemed to welcome the chance to talk. The topic was the surplus-property conference, still deadlocked, but from there the conversation went to Dumbarton Oaks and the likelihood that an international organization may be set up before the peace treaties are written.

Austin thinks it must be, in order to get the "atmosphere of peace" necessary for really sound treaty-writing, and he also thinks that the draft of the proposed organization may come to the Senate at a time which "may not be so far off" as next spring. The Dumbarton Oaks conference, he says, will of course have to be followed by a conference "on a higher level," after which he expects the government to submit the proposal to the Senate. Sometime after election, apparently, or early next year, the test will come and the great debate will begin. In it Warren Austin may be expected to maintain the same constructive international leadership he has always shown. "Some people," he said with sarcastic indignation, "want to hold back the international organization from the people for political reasons," but he is confident the Administration will not do it that way. The "some people" he did not identify, but clearly enough they are in his own party and among his own colleagues. They had their reason for deciding that good-hearted Warren Austin, who used to be McNary's right-hand man and confidently expected to become Minority Leader when he died, should be carefully excluded from any post of responsibility in the Republican organization. Every once in a while, in a sudden sarcastic barb which comes rather unexpectedly from one so kind and fatherly, he reminds you that it still rankles, as well it might.

The House, with a disturbing conservatism far beyond the Senate's, has emasculated the George reconversion bill to an empty shell and passed it by an overwhelming voice vote.

SEPTEMBER 1, 1944. Austin and Chandler proposed a surplus-property compromise today in committee but it didn't get very far—to set up a four-man board with a veto over a single executive administrator. It was discussed "very tentatively" and no decision was reached. Earlier Happy offered a compromise retaining the board's authority but reducing it to six in number. The House proved cool, although George Bender of Ohio and Charles Gifford of Massachusetts, the two Republicans, voted with the Senate when it came to an issue. The rest of the time was spent in argument and dickering, in the immemorial fashion of free men around a table. Bender and Gifford are apparently the weak links in the House armor, and perky little Carter Manasco confines himself to talking about "three sure votes" when he discusses the line-up.

George, Walsh of Massachusetts, Barkley, Vandenberg and Taft, a powerful battery, have been appointed Senate conferees on the reconversion bill. Downtown Barney Baruch has issued a blast against it, increasing talk that if the conferees cannot strengthen it, it is going to run head-on into a veto.

SEPTEMBER 2, 1944. Happy took time out from the surplus-property conference to light a bomb under the State Department and the British today, releasing a cable which "fell into his hands." It was from an official in New Delhi to his superiors in London, declaring former Ambassador William Phillips *persona non grata*. Pearson began all this a week or so ago with one of his undeniable scoops, printing excerpts from a letter Phillips wrote the President in May 1943 concerning the Indian situation. A typically American communication, it settled the Indian problem in a few concise sentences and arrogated to the United States the right to demand from the British that they do this, that and the other to straighten the situation out. Naturally the British were annoyed with the publication of the letter and a day or two later Phillips resigned as Eisenhower's political adviser in London and came home. Happy thereupon made a speech assailing "British interference" with American diplomacy, and Halifax * promptly countered by denying everything. When the cable from India "fell into his hands," Happy promptly told the press. Later in the day he confided with a pleased chuckle that the State Department had called him on the phone and demanded to know where he had got it, but "I didn't tell 'em. They sure asked me, but I didn't tell 'em."

As for the conference itself, the four-man policy-making board with a single executive administrator was formally adopted today—the complete and perfect compromise, going right down the line between the two houses. Next thing on the schedule is surplus lands, discussed but not agreed upon this afternoon. Happy tried to tell us that the Senate bill's provision had been approved "without substantial disagreement," but Carter wouldn't let him get away with it. "I'm not going to have the Interior Department coming into my state," he said. "They'll be in there," Happy assured him. "We won't accept the bill without it." "We won't accept the bill with it," Manasco replied. The meeting ended with Happy dashing off to catch a train. It seems he's going home until after election. He has left his proxy on all important issues, he told us, and "everything is under control." "Goin' to see my family," he assured us happily. "Goin' to do some visitin' around." So far none of the other conferees has decided to leave Washington, otherwise it might turn into an interesting affair, conducted from a dozen different states.

SEPTEMBER 4, 1944. Joe Ball, back from a month's rest in Minnesota and looking more animated and alive than he has for a long time, today set mid-January as his prediction for the date when the world organization treaty will come up. That there will be a fight over it he has no doubt. "There'd be a fight," he remarked acidly, "if you tried to ratify the Lord's Prayer." He apparently expects to play an active part, "especially if they try any of their reservations. Then there really will be a fight." He is not, however, "worried so much" about the outcome. He thinks the so-called American Plan [to establish a world organization in one treaty, an international police force in a subsequent treaty] is too weak—"I'd like to go much farther. I'd like to see an international police force, and I think we could get it. I think Britain would support it, I think Russia would support it, I think the Senate would support it"—but he will go along with the plan

* Lord Halifax, British Foreign Secretary.

as "the best they seem to be able to give us." The idea of picking up islands he dismissed with a snort. First of all they would have to be defended, even if 7000 miles away; secondly, their acquisition would destroy all moral right America might have to challenge others who want to seize "defense areas." "The only sensible thing to do is internationalize them, let all the United Nations use them. We'll be the principal users for the next 20 years anyway—and that's as long as you can plan for." With his gray hair at 40, his massive size, his rugged face and his Gary Cooper bashfulness, the Senator is an effective-looking character. Now that he seems to have licked the illness which has kept him worn down for so long, the effectiveness appears to extend to his actions as well. It is a good thing, for he is going to be needed.

It is interesting to note, these days, the way in which, all over the Hill, thoughts are beginning to turn to the Senate and the coming peace debate. From the House side comes word that responsible members are not too enthused about a recent idea in the press that they share the ratifying responsibility. They are afraid of the House, of its sudden emotionalism, its tendency to be stampeded by men like John Rankin and Ham Fish; they are not so sure they want the responsibility. Strangely enough, in view of the lively jealousy between the two houses, they trust the Senate more than they do themselves.

On the Senate side, deep down underneath, all of us are afraid of what the Senate will do. The press is afraid, the Senate itself is afraid. The responsibility is so great, and no one can be sure that the strength will be found to meet it. It is no wonder, perhaps, that everyone in and around the Senate feels a little uneasiness, a growing concern. We can hope—we can hope desperately—but we cannot be sure. Not until the votes are counted can anyone be sure. It is in a troubled and uncertain mood that the Senate side moves inexorably closer to the hour of its great decision. A restless pessimism, hoping against hope, in some measure grips us all.

SEPTEMBER 5, 1944. We got the preview today. Bushfield touched it off, showing himself as always no mean spokesman for the far-right point of view. The Senator who looks like Andy Jackson speaks with a drily acid humor, a considerable logic, and an undeflectable persistence in hammering his questions despite attempts to evade them. Under the American Plan, he charged, the President would become "a real dictator, the absolute despot of the American people" through his power to commit American troops to prevent aggression without the consent of Congress. Connally rose to answer, doing his duty like a good soldier. He had tried consistently, he said, to keep foreign policy out of politics; his tone sounded rather tired and lifeless. Then he began to warm up, the old Connally fire began to flare, the famous hunchings and pokings and gesturings and pacings began to come into play. Sarcasm began to drip from his tongue and his responses became more amusing as they became less pertinent. Bushfield kept his temper and baited him politely, returning to the point at issue with the dogged determination that is one of his commendable qualities. In no time at all Connally was telling us all about the American Plan, heretofore a subject of rumors and speculations and carefully managed State Department leaks. The four major powers, he said, will compose the council. An undetermined number of smaller powers will be added through election by the assembly. The use of force may be vetoed by any one of the four major powers. A second master agreement setting forth the number of troops to be contributed by each country and the conditions of their employment will have to be drawn. "Does the Senator consider France a major power?" Bushfield asked. "France has played the part of a little nation in this war," said Connally promptly, bringing into the open a disparagement he expressed to the press privately a couple of weeks ago. "France has played a very sorry spectacle in this war." Nobody had consulted him, he said, but if it were left to him he would make France undergo a period of probation before admitting her to the council.

During this Vandenberg and White, amused and shocked, looked at one another warily from time to time. Bushfield, persisting, wanted to know if Connally favored giving the Executive the right to use troops without Congressional approval. Connally responded by citing a long list of precedents. "I want to thank the Senator for the position in which he has placed himself in these last few minutes," Bushfield said. "You have now put yourself in a position of upholding the Executive's action in making war without a declaration by Congress." "This isn't a declaration of war!" Connally shouted. "It's a declaration of peace!" The squabble went along for a few more minutes until Vandenberg, unable to contain himself longer, came to Connally's assistance. Bushfield was quibbling, he implied, and if Senators wanted to quibble, nothing would ever be done to enforce the peace. The thing to do, he said, was set up the international rules in such a way as to make an aggressor "exhaust the rule of reason" first—then there would never be any moral question as to his guilt. As for the delegate, "we shall govern our delegate," and the result will be never to put the United States into war without a declaration by Congress.

It was an interesting debate, and the participants were significant of what is to come: the anti-cooperationist, logical and shrewd, the official defender, vitriolic and exclamatory, and the confused but desperately earnest cooperationist, vacillating between, one foot on this side, one on that. All the explosive potentialities of the argument to come were here presented. In a chair toward the back sat Gerald Nye, grave and judicious and faintly amused.

SEPTEMBER 6, 1944. The surplus-property conference is moving very slowly; this is the third day on the land provisions. Manasco, amiable little soul with a big cigar, told us that they "spent all day today on three or four paragraphs," and that is just the way it has been going. Asked if he thought they would conclude before the end of the war, Thomas with his gentle and very quiet humor said, "I'm hopeful we can conclude before the final stages of the war. After all, some of us have to get home to run for re-election, or we may be defeated, and that would be bad, wouldn't it?" Then he chuckled gravely. "I find, though," he added, "that the less I see of people the more votes I get." Beneath his philosophic and mellow exterior he is really quite worried about his campaign and would like very much to get away. If he does lose, he can truly say that he sacrificed his public career for the good of the country, for he has not hesitated to stay on the job. He has placed the writing of a good bill above his personal interests, and that deserves considerable commendation.

Over on the other side, the George reconversion-bill conferees have bogged down already in almost complete disagreement. Dave Walsh, acting chairman in the absence of George, who slipped and fell and fractured his collarbone the other evening, says the Senate will insist upon a full House vote before receding. There now arises the question of finding a quorum in the House in order to get a vote, something that seems improbable at the moment. Consequently there is already talk that the whole thing may go over until after election.

Waiting for the surplus-property conference to break up this morning we were joined by Maverick, looking rather disconsolate and weighed down with the cares of the world and small business. "How does it look, Congressman?" I asked him. "Are they going to take care of you in there?" "They are if Ah have anything to say about it," he said promptly. "The Senate bill is better than the House on small business, isn't it?" I said. "Everything the Senate does right now is better than the House," he said glumly. "Ah don't know what's got into 'em, but they're sure mad about something." "You don't suppose they feel somebody or something is trying to push them around, do you?" He shrugged. "Ah don' know," he said disconsolately, "but they're certainly in a bad mood."

SEPTEMBER 7, 1944. We have fallen into the habit of meeting with Thomas after the conference sessions in the President's Room, an ornate gilt-and-gold affair just off the floor on the Senate side. This is a stock tourist attraction ("Decorated by Lincoln," the guides say, "and used by every President from Lincoln to Woodrow Wilson to sign bills on the last day of the session; now used as the room where the incoming and outgoing Presidents meet on Inauguration Day. This hasn't happened for some time now. [Laughter]") and while we were interviewing the Senator today a group came through. "Tell them to go right ahead," Thomas said to the guide, waving amiably. "This is a press conference. Let them see what it's like." They watched and we worked. Presently Thomas halted the flow of questions and raising his voice, explained in his fatherly fashion: "This is a press conference. We have been meeting this morning on the surplus-property bill, one of the two major reconversion bills before Congress. The House passed a bill and the Senate passed a bill. Now representatives of both houses are meeting to work out a compromise. We have been meeting all morning. People want to know what we have done, so we are meeting with the press to tell them about it. That's how your government works.... That," he added with a chuckle, "is Political Science Lecture No. 1." It was a very effective little speech. It's too bad such things aren't on tap all the time for tourists to see, because that *is* how their government works, and it is good for them to know it.

SEPTEMBER 8, 1944. Mr. Big looked like the devil this morning, but seemed otherwise in an amiable mood. More than either of the other two times when I have been at the White House, the charm was present today. And well it might be, after all, for everything is rolling smoothly, the trip to Quebec is just a couple of days away, the master strategist has everything in hand, both the Commander-in-Chief and the Democratic Candidate are doing nicely, thank you. The snappishness which has subdued the correspondents so much at recent conferences—they do not, of course, enjoy being sneered at by a man whose office protects him from retaliation in kind—seemed to have vanished as if by magic. Physically he looks desperately tired, his face is very deeply lined and drawn, he rubbed his eyes several times with a hand which very visibly trembled. It is no wonder people go away from each conference wondering if it has been the last.

He began in a very low tone of voice, as he always does. He told us about Jimmy Byrnes' new reconversion plan, which will be made part of the new law when Congress gets through with it. He told us about UNRRA in Italy and about a letter to Hull advising him to keep an eye on international cartels. He wanted us to be sure to note that reconstruction loans to Italy are to be charged to Italy. "In other words, don't get the idea that they're gifts." He concluded and looked up for questions.

"Mr. President," somebody said, "have you received any peace overtures from inside Germany?"

"No," he said promptly, an answer which few people bothered to believe, since his categorical *Nos* do not always mean what they say.

"Is there anything new you can tell us about the progress of the Dumbarton Oaks conference, Mr. President?" somebody else wanted to know.

"No, nothing new. They're nearly through. They're making excellent progress."

"Mr. President"—and here came the question everyone had been wait-

ing for—"you said in your acceptance speech that you would correct any misrepresentations of fact—"

"Oh, wait a minute," he said quickly. "I said I would *feel free* to correct any misrepresentations of fact. I didn't say I would. Let's keep the record straight."

Everybody laughed.

"Well, did you hear Mr. Dewey's speech last night?"

Mr. Big considered Mr. Little for a moment.

"I didn't listen to it myself," he said thoughtfully. "One member of my family did and told me about it. I've read about half of it."

"He quoted General Hershey as saying that men would be kept in the Army because that was cheaper than taking care of them when they couldn't find work outside. Do you agree with that?"

"Is General Hershey's job to keep men in the Army?" he asked. "Isn't his job to put men into the Army?"

"That wasn't my question," the questioner said, frustrated, and everybody laughed again.

"No," he said, "but it's a pretty good answer."

"Do you agree that the Administration is afraid to demobilize?" someone else pursued the point.

"You can say the President smiled broadly," Mr. Big replied, and laughter again rewarded him.

"Do you consider your Administration a tired, defeatist, quarrelsome Administration, Mr. President?"

He thought for a moment and spoke slowly.

"Well," he said, "all I can say is to repeat what I have said many times before, that I would like to go home to Hyde Park.... But," he added with a toss of the head, "I'm not tired and I'm not defeated."

Again we laughed, and—maneuvered to a standstill—fell silent. The moment lengthened and lengthened. Nobody could think of anything to ask. Suddenly somebody blurted, "Thank you, Mr. President," and we all echoed it and trailed out laughing again. Mr. Big laughed too, and so did Steve Early and so did Admiral Leahy and so did everybody.

Mr. Big had got by very nicely, this day.

SEPTEMBER 9, 1944. Gerald Nye sat for a while and talked with us in the Office Building cafeteria this morning, critical of Dewey's Louisville endorsement of an international organization to keep the peace. On the record, the Senator was able to go along. His agreement was not overwhelming, and there were significant reservations, but he is still "absolutely" able to support the candidate. A likable man in many respects, the Senator was more interested in trying to sell us a story about the way in which Langer tried to rob him of the Senate nomination this year. He has been peddling this talk for months, but it is too libelous to handle just on his say-so. Consequently nobody has. Now he has decided to make a speech in the Senate, on Tuesday, which will make it privileged and permit us to use it. What happens when one United States Senator accuses another of bribery is at the moment obscure—probably nothing. At any rate, it will be an interesting squabble between two men who hate one another as violently as any two on the Hill. Aside from his comments on Langer, which were vitriolic, Nye's conversation ranged from Mc-Kellar ("He's still the cleverest operator in the Senate") to the possibility of adjournment ("Some of us are afraid to go home because of the war, but some of us" [with a grin] "are afraid not to because of the elections"). Intelligent, shrewd, forceful and attractive, Gerald Nye has much to commend him. It is one of the tragedies of Washington, perhaps, that over the course of the years the liberal Young Lochinvar who came out of the West should have dedicated his abilities to purposes which are too easily suspect.

Harry Truman, back from the hustings, commented briefly on Dewey. "I've made it a point," he said, "never to say anything to the personal detriment of my opponents, but I sincerely hope Mr. Dewey keeps on campaigning."

The Truman office is turning out photographs and processing visitors like a factory these days; we were just able to squeeze in between one eager guest and an appointment with "the Boss." This we learned through a telephone conversation. "I'd like to," Truman told the party on the other end, "but I can't. I've got to see the Boss in just a few minutes." "Who's the Boss?" we asked promptly, although that is what the Senator always calls him, and we knew. "You know," Truman said, "sometimes I wish I was able to lie, but I just can't. I guess I'm just not made that way. I'm meeting the President, but it's entirely off the record, and you'll forget you ever heard about it, won't you?" We said we would. "I don't want to do things that way myself," he added, "but that's the way he wants it, so——" He shrugged.

Surplus-property conference has agreed on nearly everything and has finally come smack up against the metal-stockpiling provision. Johnson and Thomas want to keep it in the bill in order to prevent release of surplus metals to compete with their mining industries, but the House is against it. It will probably take most of next week to reach an agreement.

SEPTEMBER 10, 1944. Ferguson and a number of Republicans in the House are beginning to get worried again about Pearl Harbor. This perennial "King Charles' head" of the Roosevelt Administration refuses to be consigned to the limbo where the Democrats would prefer to have it, and particularly now that an election approaches it is of even more interest to the Republicans. Ferguson says he intends to introduce a resolution calling for a special Congressional investigating committee, sometime between now and Dec. 7, when the most recent extension of the statute of limitations expires.

SEPTEMBER 11, 1944. Connally's enthusiastic endorsement of Dewey's foreign-policy speech, he told us with a humorous little smile today, "prob'ly didn't suit some of 'em downtown," but he was glad to make it anyway. He wants to get him committed, he said, "get him tied down." Old Tom isn't so dumb. His own nonpartisanship on this issue is sincere and despite "some of 'em downtown" he is going his best to head off any purely political attack on the peace. The structure of the peace, of course, is another matter, and as he proved in the debate last week he may not hesitate to express his own views on it when the time comes.

The surplus-property conferees are still temporarily deadlocked over the metal-stockpiling issue. The suggestion that all surplus metals and minerals be stockpiled under the Treasury Procurement Division sounds fine to Elbert Thomas from Utah and Ed Johnson from Colorado, but to House members who have few mines in their states it does not appeal so much. There is a disposition to compromise, however, and chances that the bill will be finished by the end of the week look increasingly good.

SEPTEMBER 12, 1944. North Dakota politics, which Nye's secretary says are "conducted with blackjacks and brass knuckles," boiled over today. The Senate's bitterest feudists, clawing one another politically like wild animals, brought their hatred into the open with a bang. The general reaction to this pretty display was summed up later, privately, by another Senator from out their way. "Personally," he said candidly, "I think if we could take both of North Dakota's Senators and drop them in the river the Senate and the country would be a lot better off."

Nye began it, making the speech he promised us several days ago. Characteristically he refrained from mentioning Langer by name; it was just "a Senator" from North Dakota. This Senator on Sept. 14, 1943, brought together a "Mr. McSheehan"—identified by Nye as Joseph B. Keenan, former assistant attorney general in the Roosevelt Administration —and six disabled First World War veterans from North Dakota. An offer of money was made by Keenan, Nye said—$110,000 if one of them would run against Nye for the Republican nomination. The offer was rejected. The veterans were told that whether one of them took it or not, there would be a veteran in the race against Nye. Having thus told off

Langer, praised his self-denying constituents, and done a neat job of attacking by indirection Lynn Stambaugh, the veteran who is running
against him as an independent, Nye sat down. Langer, taken by surprise,
sat furiously silent through this recital. Then he rose in a rage and roared
his protest. Joseph B. Keenan never gave anyone one dollar to be a candidate for anything, he shouted. "I state upon my honor as a gentleman,
upon my honor as a United States Senator, and upon my honor as a citizen of the state of North Dakota in which I was born, that Mr. Keenan
never offered anybody one single penny." He would, he said, reply "item
by item, paragraph by paragraph" to his colleague in the near future.
There the incident ended for the time being. An hour later when I went
around to Nye's office he had left for North Dakota. The timing, his secretary said, was something they had worked over for months. Langer, the
secretary said, had been riding high in North Dakota for 12 years—
"through his Non-Partisan League he *is* North Dakota, just as Roosevelt
is the Democratic Party." The only time Langer ever got beaten, he said,
was when he ran against Nye in 1938. Now Nye is trying to capture the
state machine as well as win re-election to the Senate. "In North Dakota
we play politics with blackjacks and brass knuckles," the secretary said,
"but we keep our noses clean." He seemed very happy about the whole
thing.

SEPTEMBER 13, 1944. The surplus-property conferees, after adopting a compromise that in effect freezes surplus metals for 15 months after the end of the war, announced complete agreement on all points and recessed to Friday, when they will read the committee print of the bill and prepare to report it out. Probably it will be approved by both houses and will soon be on its way to the White House.

The postwar highways bill, authorizing a Federal expenditure of $1,650,000,000 over three consecutive postwar years, to be matched on a 60–40 basis by the states, was called up today and a typical Senate reaction ensued. This was a bill over which there was going to be no controversy: all was harmony, everybody was for it (except Taft, who never hesitates to say what he thinks, letting the political chips fall where they may) and it was set to go through in an hour. The moment the matter came up, however, the whole picture changed. Amendments began to land on the Clerk's desk like bombs on Berlin, and in no time at all 8 or 10 Senators were engaged in a lively argument. All estimates of time were immediately revised, and Carl Hayden, in charge of the bill, finally asked that he be permitted to take bill and amendments back to committee. This was granted, and the argument went over to Friday.

SEPTEMBER 14, 1944. Wallace White is so tickled about the Maine primary elections he can't get over it. "Of course the thing that worries me," he says with a chuckle, "is that the Republicans rolled up such a whoppin' vote when I was down heah instead of bein' up theah campaignin'. Kind of a reflection on me, in a way—they seem to do bettuh when I'm not around." His own home town, he said, went Democratic. "But that's nothin' new. It always has. I ran for mayuh three times and got licked every time. That was before I decided to enlarge my constituency and run for the House." Since then, he added, he hasn't had any trouble.

The Post Office and Post Roads Committee decided to lop approximately $500,000,000 off the highways bill and make the Federal-state ratio 50–50 instead of 60–40. Hopes for passage tomorrow are brighter, and a recess by the end of next week now seems almost certain.

SEPTEMBER 15, 1944. In the fashion of conferences, the surplus-property conferees' "final agreement" has proved to be no more final than any of the endless finalities of the soldier-vote conference. Helped along by Will Clayton, who wrote a letter to Jimmy Byrnes attacking the four-man board, one-man administrator idea—administratively unworkable, he said, and he could not accept appointment as administrator under such a bill (a righteous renunciation of something the Senate would never give him anyway)—the House suddenly kicked over the traces and renewed its demand for a single administrator with supreme authority. The jovial atmosphere which has usually surrounded the meetings was not present today: this was a little too abrupt an about-face for the Senate to forgive or forget. The issue was forced to a vote and both sides refused to yield. The House conferees then suggested one more compromise, which was more or less finally adopted. Disposal powers are now to be vested in a three-man board which will be both policy-making and administrative. Thomas and Manasco both declared that the issue's reopening had nothing to do with Clayton's letter. It was one of those denials that events so often force people on the Hill to say with a straight face, and which the press is adept at accepting with a similar blandness.

SEPTEMBER 16, 1944. The surplus-property conferees, in a bad humor with each other and life in general, signed the report at 9 o'clock last night and called it quits. Carter Manasco, still muttering darkly about the Senate's "hydra-headed monster," was not pleased with the outcome. Nobody was, in fact. After all those meetings and endless discussions and constant attempts to be charitable, sheer annoyance with each other suddenly got the best of everyone. That and Clayton's letter, which didn't help much.

Anyway, it is now out of the way, and so is the highways bill, which went through late yesterday without much trouble. The Senate's docket is now clear; it is waiting to approve the two conference reports and then it is ready to go home. In the meantime, it will probably pass the Connally–Taft resolution to guarantee "the world right of all men" to write, send and publish news without interference by government or private monopoly—"a gesture," as Barkley remarked today, but one worth making.

The Judiciary subcommittee handling the insurance bill has decided to report it out to the full committee. O'Mahoney says he is of course going to oppose it, and will make a speech on the floor. The principal thing he has left to do now, he said, is "begin counting noses." Also, he adds, there are witnesses who might be heard. "In other words," the press suggested, "your best bet now lies in dilatory tactics." "I don't know what you mean," the Senator said with a grin. "I don't know what dilatory tactics are." Whatever the outcome, he has done a brilliant job of maneuvering the bill to a standstill this past year. It is the single most brilliant piece of parliamentary work by a Senator, in fact, since I have been on the Hill.

SEPTEMBER 17, 1944. Opposition to the surplus conference report seems to be developing in the House over the week end. Simultaneously, the big test for the George reconversion bill looms tomorrow. A quorum of the House is in town, and a vote is scheduled for tomorrow afternoon.

There is absolutely no justification whatsoever for not giving Federal employees the right to unemployment compensation if they need it. Many of them came to Washington with the patriotic urge to help the war, and many of them have just managed to squeak by in this absurdly overpriced city on their meager Civil Service salaries. But the House is on the rampage, and the odds against this very meek liberalization of the George bill are overwhelming.

SEPTEMBER 18, 1944. I was over in the House today, a rather frightening assemblage when its erratic moods stampede it down the blind alleys of absolute conservatism. Travel pay home for war workers? No! said the House. Unemployment compensation for Federal employees? No! said the House. A surplus-property bill? Well, said the House grudgingly, with a handful of votes for margin, perhaps.

On the Senate side, O'Mahoney finally went down bloody but unbowed before the onslaught of Pat McCarran and a majority of the Judiciary Committee. The insurance bill was reported out on a vote of 11 to 6. As always, the Senator from Wyoming had the attention of the press. We wrote our stories and gave him the play he wanted, just as we have done throughout this whole fight. His battle has been the news, and that is the way we have written it. He has complained consistently to us, every time we have been in to see him, that his actions and sentiments have been strangely absent from the printed page. But we have been able to reply with a clear conscience. We have done our duty, by him and by the news. What has happened to it in editorial offices has not been our responsibility.

The Connally–Taft free-press resolution has suddenly been transferred to a subcommittee of Foreign Relations. Objections, many of them quibbling, have developed. There is a tendency to scoff at it as "just a gesture, absolutely impractical of operation." This is sufficient for some. Others, more specific, have united on one main thesis: the attempt, in both Taft's resolution and Connally's, to direct the Dumbarton Oaks conference and the peace-framers to write the free-press clause into the peace treaties. The matter should be handled separately, some say, and there may be some logic in their position. At any rate, it has been consigned to a subcommittee. Some say it will pass before recess, some say it won't.

About recess itself, there is general agreement that it will begin by the end of the week. A few odds and ends remain to be disposed of—Langer has to have his say about Nye, and so on. Aside from these minor matters, the decks are clear and a lot of relieved people can go home and start campaigning.

20

"IT IS ON THE MAIN ISSUE"

SEPTEMBER 19, 1944. "The great question at issue is whether the United States shall reverse the decision it made in 1919 and this time join a world organization having the authority and the force necessary to outlaw aggressive war. Let us not permit some fancied encroachment on the prerogatives of Congress to distract our attention from that major question: should the United States help preserve peace.

"It is on the main issue, and not the secondary questions, that we must answer to our consciences and to posterity. The peace of the world and of these United States, for generations to come, may depend upon our answer."

So spoke Joe Ball, at the end of a long and most able and most idealistic defense of Dumbarton Oaks today; and quite to the opposite spoke his fellow Minnesotan, Henrik Shipstead, preceding him on the floor. The tall old man, with his dry, clipped, sardonic, humorless peasant's humor, attacked the conference as "a step by President Roosevelt to dominate the world with three or four other men representing the great powers." Harold Burton spoke too, later, defending the deliberations with much the same ability and idealism as Ball, although directing his argument along slightly different lines. Carl Hatch joined in, rising to request the floor of Ball for a few moments to read article by Mark Sullivan concerning the shifting moods of the American people. Burton Wheeler, back after three months in Montana and the West, attempted to talk on Ball's time also. The young Senator pointed out that he had been waiting for nearly 15 minutes while Shipstead and Hatch argued bitterly. Wheeler disregarded him and began talking. "Mr. President!" said Ball angrily. "Have I the floor or haven't I?" Wheeler went on impatiently, only to be drowned out by Ball, beginning his address. "Will the Senator yield?" Wheeler demanded. "I decline to yield," Ball snapped. "The Senator declines to yield to me for just a minute?" Wheeler persisted. "For how long?" Ball wanted to know. "For two minutes," said Wheeler. "I yield," said Ball shortly, pulling back his coat sleeve and looking at his watch with utter contempt and the barest of civility.

There is no love lost there; nor, indeed, was there any love lost anywhere in today's debate. We have been given another preview; once again the Senate's great responsibility has been revealed, once again the outlines of the coming battle have been clarified. This is the first issue since the soldier-vote fight in which real hostility of Senator against Senator has been aroused, and there is a great deal of it. It will be a bitter fight in the next few months, as the forces of idealism led by Ball and Burton and Hatch go forth to battle with those of unrepentant isolation lead by Wheeler. The brilliant Montanan is not worried yet, that is obvious. He has been here a long time and he knows how to fight in the way that will do the most good.

SEPTEMBER 20, 1944. Burt Wheeler, the Massachusetts Yankee who went West but never got over a certain Calvinistic indignation where his own beliefs are concerned, was in an amiable mood when I corralled him for an interview this afternoon. One of the most likable men alive, in his bright, blunt, sarcastic fashion, he turns to the press these days with even more than his usual cooperation. He needs publicity and he needs public support, and he is ready and willing to talk to get them.

His comment on the coming debate was terse and concise. "There'll be a hell of a fight," he promised promptly. "This idea of creating a peace organization before you know what the peace treaties are going to be is absolutely absurd. The reason they're trying to do it that way is because they're scared of what the peace treaties are going to be. They know the American people wouldn't accept the peace organization if they could know the kind of treaties it is going to have to enforce."

Would it pass the Senate? "I couldn't say until we have a chance to see what's in it. The other side may have strength enough to put it over. We'll have to wait and see. But I can promise you there'll be a hell of a fight."

The Russo-Finnish armistice he pointed to as an example of what the peace may be. "It doesn't bode very well for the kind of peace that's going to come out of this war. There's a better feeling in the United States for Russia than there has been at any time in history. That sentiment, however, can change very rapidly if Russia seems to be grabbing up all the Baltics and all the Balkans, part of Poland and whatever she desires in Asia. This is one reason why I have suggested that we should go slow about setting up machinery for some world organization until we know definitely what the imperialistic desires of Great Britain and Russia may be."

Here he paused in his endless pacing—around his desk to the window, back again, around his desk to the window, back again—and thought for a moment. Then he resumed:

"The American people subscribe to the idealistic purposes of the Atlantic Charter. We have built up the greatest army in the world, a greater navy than all the navies of the world combined, a greater air force than all the air forces in the world combined. We're in a position now to demand the kind of a peace that we want, if our leaders will insist upon it. We can demand a United States of Europe" (one of his pet projects) "and the kind of peace that the boys who fought and died would be proud of, the kind of a peace our grandchildren will be proud of. But we can't do it—we can't do it if we're going to let any of our allies grab for the territory of other countries as we did after the last war." He paused abruptly and grinned. "There. That's enough of a speech for you."

I thanked him and left, impressed as always by his very real sincerity, his very real ability, his unyielding isolationism, and the fact that he is a most shrewd and dangerous opponent of the things many people believe must be done if the world is to live.

The Senate, having disposed late yesterday of both the George reconversion bill and the surplus-property bill, spent the afternoon today indulging in personalities, North Dakota politics, and the Pearl Harbor case. Langer lavished some 41 pages and a good hour and a half on his colleague, and was rewarded with a rather larger attendance than usual.

Other members have been interested in this intramural fight, and a good many of them stayed on the floor to hear about it.

Langer was at his loudest and most indignant. "Oh, Mr. Prezshident!" he cried in his curious whistling voice. "Politicsh, politicsh, politicsh!" The incident described by Nye he admitted, but placed upon it an entirely different interpretation: he himself had suggested that someone run against Nye, he himself had proposed raising not $110,000 but $10,000 to finance the campaign. He himself, he said, had secured Nye's first endorsement for Congress, he himself had bought him clothes and paid the unpaid debts he left behind him. Little did he know, he said, that Nye, instead of working for North Dakota, would spend his time in social circles where "blondes and cocktail bars" are more important than legislating. "Politicsh, politicsh, politicsh!" He ended by challenging Nye to waive immunity and appear under oath with him before the Campaign Expenditures Committee. "Dare he accshept that challenge?" Langer demanded. The question, rhetorical, died out sternly upon the tortured air of the Senate chamber.

On Pearl Harbor, Alexander Wiley began it by remarking that his constituents were writing him demanding to know why Congress was delaying the court-martials of Admiral Kimmel and General Short. Alexander was in a rather more earnest mood than usual; his easily evoked indignation had a ring of unusual anger today. Carl Hatch arose to defend the action of the Judiciary Committee in approving the resolution to extend the statute of limitations. Somewhere along the way he also defended the President. Homer Ferguson charged that responsibility for the delay "ought to be placed squarely on the doorstep of the Commander-in-Chief." O'Mahoney rose to make a brief but very forceful speech, pointing out that, "It is not without significance that no clamor, either in the press or on the floor of either house of Congress, broke out for these court-martials until a political campaign began." On the whole, there was considerable bad temper today, and everyone seemed agreed afterwards that it is just as well that a recess is going to occur. There is enough bad feeling in the Senate anyway without increasing it by the enforced strain of having to remain together during the campaign. This way there will be a month and a half of peace and then controversy—for a long time to come.

SEPTEMBER 21, 1944. The Truman Committee—even Jim Mead, now chairman, still calls it that, partly from habit and partly from deference to its former chairman—has a habit, sometimes, of making up its mind about something ahead of time and then looking for the facts to bolster

the conviction. Today it met its match, however, in Irvin Wexler, alias
Waxey Gordon. Mr. Wexler is a heavy-set, aging, phlegmatic and completely self-possessed individual who has been breaking the law ever
since he became old enough to find out there was a law to break. His
manner implied that he had come up against prosecutors a lot tougher
than these, and by a judicious combination of contempt, good nature,
belligerence and sarcasm he successfully fought them to a standstill for
more than two hours.

Mr. Wexler did so, in fact, despite the assistance given the committee
by the Fiorello La Guardias. All the La Guardias were on hand in force,
at their most charming and most indignant and most laughable. The
La Guardias threatened to steal the show, for a while, until Mr. Wexler
took over. The La Guardias did make certain charges—that Mr. Wexler
was behind two firms in New York which are dealing in surplus property
at exorbitant prices. The La Guardias also hinted at a tie-up with
officials in the Treasury Procurement Division. The La Guardias said
the whole thing began when New York wanted to buy some tires and
got rooked by Mr. Wexler's companies. "Of course," the La Guardias
said with a cherubic smile, "if I had wanted what goes inside the tires
I could have produced it myself." Everybody roared when the La
Guardias said that.

The La Guardias were convinced that Mr. Wexler was involved in
these two firms, and the La Guardias' conviction had been imparted to
the committee. Hatch repeatedly told Mr. Wexler that the committee
didn't believe him when he said he had nothing to do with the businesses.
Neither did anybody else believe Mr. Wexler. The only weak point in
the committee's case was that it never once offered specific proof of its
charges. Mr. Wexler said he wasn't involved, and nobody ever got Mr.
Wexler to admit he was. Consequently it was a very enjoyable performance, but it certainly didn't prove anything.

Mr. Wexler disclosed himself to be a most competent witness. Did so
and so happen? "It's possible," said Mr. Wexler calmly. "It's possible."
When a committee aide lost his temper and began to rail at Mr. Wexler
indignantly, Mr. Wexler said bluntly, "You're asking me to tell you about
conversations which took place months ago. What did you have for
dinner Tuesday night? Tell me that! What did you have for dinner
Tuesday night? And don't give me no deviated answers!" When Hatch,
switching his approach from forceful anger to smooth friendliness, attempted to elicit some damaging answer, Mr. Wexler said, "You know,
when you get so proper and smile sweet I know I got to watch you.
When you give me that sweet smile, Senator, as much as to say, 'Who
you kiddin',' I know I got to watch you close." To the news photographers,

straining for a colorful angle, Mr. Wexler said, "Don't be always shootin' me. Don't be always shootin' me. I know what yuh want, I'll give it yuh. Yuh want something like this, see—something vigorous with the arms." Occasionally, bored by it all, Mr. Wexler would give a shrug and an amused smile. "Surplus, surplus!" Mr. Wexler would say. "Who wants to talk about surplus? I'd rather talk about the fights, baseball, something. . . ."

Mr. Wexler handled his investigation of the Truman Committee, in fact, very, very well.*

On the floor, the Senate met until nearly 6 o'clock and then adjourned until Nov. 14. All the speeches that hadn't been made before were delivered, the calendar was called and a number of routine bills were disposed of. Shortly before adjournment the Congress of the United States and a small group of hard-lobbying reporters passed the free-press resolution. Everything ended on a note of harmony and gratification on the part of all concerned.

SEPTEMBER 22, 1944. The recess slump is beginning to settle on the Hill again. A good many Senators have already left and those who remain are as eager for news as we are. Neither of us has any.

Theodore Francis Green, busy and professorial, has decided to investigate Pappy's activities in Texas. The *W. Lee O'Daniel News*, the letters, the speeches, the broadcasts—the Senator thinks they ought to be looked into, particularly since Campaign Expenditures Committee has sent two different requests for information, both ignored, to O'Daniel. The committee is also going to send an investigator into Arkansas, where terrific amounts of money were spent to beat poor Hattie.

SEPTEMBER 23, 1944. In a certain Senatorial office, which is known to many as "The Whispering Gallery," we were treated today to one of its occupant's most subtle performances. There was, as always, the air of intimacy, the sly wink, the confidential, forward-hunching over the desk, the same delicate smearing of the people he doesn't like. Did we notice where the PAC had indorsed George Aiken? "That explains why he's voted the way he has on everything lately; that explains it. Right down the line, he's been for everything labor wants and everything that will spend money. I guess it's clear now why he's done so." (Aiken, eating lunch with me earlier, explained with a chuckle, "I'm the Republican Sidney can point to for the PAC now. As a matter of fact, a joint meeting of the A.F. of L., the Railway Brotherhoods and the Vermont CIO was held about six months ago. The A.F. of L. moved to endorse me and the others made it unanimous. Now the PAC is tryin' to jump on

* Better than did his colleagues in the rackets, who ultimately gunned him down.

the bandwagon, just as they've done with Saltonstall in Massachusetts. I get along fine with the Vermont CIO, I never had any trouble with labor when I was governor, but there are lots of times when I don't see eye to eye with the national CIO.")

"I see where Roosevelt's speaking tonight," the whisperer went on. "You know, I've heard an interesting thing from a source I know is close to the White House. A lot of them there didn't want him to run, simply on the grounds of health—afraid he might break down while making one of his speeches. Rosenman's scared to death. Admiral McIntire didn't want him to run, General Watson didn't want him to run. The family wanted him to, and Roosevelt himself wanted to, but a lot of his intimates didn't—just on the ground of health...." The talk passed to other things, but presently the tie-in came. "I heard an interesting thing about Truman," the whisperer said. "It seems FDR called him to the White House for a secret conference and told him not to ride on any more commercial planes during the campaign. I don't know why, unless it's just that equipment's getting so old. But that's what he told him—don't ride on any more commercial planes."

The talk turned to North Dakota, and the whisperer seemed shocked.

"Did you hear Langer's speech?" he asked. "Wasn't that a honey? That's about the most vicious personal attack I've ever heard in the Senate. The thing about Langer," said the whisperer, who isn't such a bad fellow except that for him politics is just a little too much of a game, "is that he hasn't got any scruples. He just doesn't have any scruples."

SEPTEMBER 24, 1944. Styles Bridges, clever and able, speaking shortly before the Senate adjourned Thursday, gave an excellent exposition of the middle ground in the coming debate—the middle ground where those Senators who want to add Versailles Treaty-type reservations may find their adherents and their necessary strength. Stressing the Atlantic Charter and its original purposes, he demanded of the President where those purposes have gone to and what has become of that Charter. He pointed to all the aggravating, explosive things the Russians have done and the British have done, and he asked what the U.S. was doing. Although the Atlantic Charter has gradually become the favorite symbol for those who don't really believe in it but recognize its value as a divisive argument, the Senator's speech nonetheless set forth a very sound proposition: that if all the idealism and all the good will are reserved to the United States alone, and if the United States stands by without protest while other nations indulge their tendencies toward devious self-interest, then the peace is going to be a shaky thing indeed.

SEPTEMBER 26, 1944. Someone who has known Clyde Reed for 25 years gave a good analysis of the cantankerous Kansan today. The 72-year-old hell-raiser, he said, "is the best watchdog you could want. He'll drive away the wolves and the tramps, and if there aren't any wolves and tramps he'll go into the kitchen and bite the cook. He loves to stir up trouble, he loves to make people mad. He's the best-hated, least-liked and most capable governmental brain in the prairie states. He's very efficient and he knows more about freight rates and railroad problems than the railroads do themselves. He hits everybody but the way to get along with him is to hit right back. He'll respect you for it. Clyde carried his own precinct in the primary this time—hadn't been back there for six years. People in Kansas hate his guts, but they're going to give him a whopping good majority this fall." The analysis rang true to anyone familiar with the Senate, where the Senator may be disliked but where he is never overlooked or minimized. He can't be overlooked or minimized, in fact; he just raises too much rumpus.

"There'll be a fight all right," commented Tom Connally sarcastically today, discussing the coming treaty debate. "There'll be a fight. Some of 'em are already beginning to maneuver around here. They say they're for it, you know, but they always leave a little hole for ingress and egress to help them get around it when the pinch comes."

Joe Ball has urged the electorate to purge the isolationist Senators in November, remarking truthfully that the treaty fight will be decided by the men in the Senate and not by any letters and telegrams to Senators after election.

SEPTEMBER 27, 1944. Confronted with two choices—whether to let Joe Ball's call for a purge die down and be forgotten, thereby helping to strengthen vitally necessary harmony in the Senate, or whether to try to embarrass the Republicans, Claude Pepper never hesitated today. "Senator," we said as we entered his office, "what's on your mind?" Before we were really seated he had launched into one of his flowing and erudite speeches. Thirty minutes later we broke away with a story to the effect that:

"Senator Ball would win the acclaim of the nation if he would rise above party lines and lend his character not only to defeating isolationist Senators and keeping isolationists out of the Senate, but to keeping Roosevelt and Hull in charge of negotiating our foreign policy in the

four dangerous years ahead.... Ball can't be consistent and urge us to
experiment with a Dewey and a Dulles and turn out true and tried
friends of world peace like Roosevelt and Hull.... I agree with every
word that Senator Ball said, but I go one step further. Let's not only keep
isolationists out of the Senate—let's keep out of the White House those
who were isolationists until they become candidates, and let's keep out of
the State Department those who did nothing for international collaboration until they became prospective Secretaries of State...."

(Told about this later, Joe gave one of his Gary Cooperish, aw-shucks
laughs. "You guys," he said, "are just hard up for a story." Pepper had
every right to say it, he intimated, "just as I have every right to refuse
to take the bait.")

Furthermore, Pepper went on (he had apparently
been waiting for the press—either that, or his passionate love of language enticed him onward), "It is
clearly apparent that the cabal between the Republicans and the Democratic isolationists is coming out
of hiding.... The same crowd that defeated the
League and obstructed preparation for war is getting
ready to defeat the peace.... The signs are too ominous to be ignored that the die-hard Old Guard, aided
by derelict Democrats, is trying to do to Roosevelt
what they did to Wilson. If they succeed, they will
condemn the nation again to depression and their own
sons to another war.... I think the present Senate" (and here he departed from text with sudden emphasis) "in fact, I *know* the present
Senate won't accept an organization sufficiently strong to prevent another
war. They won't do it. They just won't do it."

SEPTEMBER 28, 1944. Two shrewd, irascible, political-minded oldsters,
Clyde Reed and Harold Ickes, took one another's measure today over
the gasoline situation. Apprised from somewhere downtown that Honest
Harold was planning to increase civilian rations in October, the Kansas
Senator decided that two could play that game. Accordingly a Reed
press conference was held. He assailed Mr. Ickes and quoted figures,
evidently secured from someone in Mr. Ickes' own office, concerning the
amount of surplus gas on hand. That was yesterday. Today another Reed
conference was held. This time it was a telegram to Bennett Champ
Clark demanding hearings by the special committee on Midwestern fuel
resources. "Mischievous" and "irresponsible" were the words which
hurtled out of the Interior Department on that one. Honest Harold,

caught temporarily off base on his plans for a preelection bonanza, resorted as usual to invective. "It seems to be impossible for Harold Ickes to act like a gentleman," said Clyde Reed with pained indignation. Off the record he said other things. To date the honors have gone to the Senator. Whether the hearings are held or not, he can point to his personal campaign for increased rations on the day when Harold decides to bless the populace. If Harold had gotten away with doing it his way, it would of course have had nothing to do with the election; and with Clyde trying to do it his way, it of course hasn't anything to do with it either.

SEPTEMBER 29, 1944. The last feeble embers of the Great Southern Revolt flicker and die on the Hill these days. Josiah Bailey, last to capitulate, has issued an apologia in the form of a purported "interview." Senator Bailey said a number of stern things in this particular interview, dismissing with pointed scorn one anti-Roosevelt question after another. Others have been equally circumspect. The dinner bell is ringing and the wayward youths are turning home. All the furious indignations, the violent damnations, the dark, desperate threats—all, all are forgotten, swallowed with an obvious effort and a great, convulsive gulp. Only Pappy the Indomitable remains upright and firm in the midst of this darkling scene. Good old Pappy, staunch and stalwart: NEW DEAL SKULDUGGERY agitates him still. It is his redeeming feature. Unlike these others, when Pappy said it Pappy meant it. If only by contrast, the integrity of his disaffection is notable.

SEPTEMBER 30, 1944. To the St. Paul paper Joe Ball has issued a forthright and courageous statement expressing his doubt that Dewey will fight for a strong international organization and announcing that he consequently cannot campaign for him "at this time." Naturally it has been something of a sensation. The Senator's integrity and honest conviction cannot be minimized; his practical political wisdom is still in serious doubt. Young men who call for a purge of their own party and denounce their own candidate do not gather the votes with which to pass treaties. It has delighted the Democrats and disturbed the Republicans. No one questions his motives even though many deplore his methods. Ken Wherry, much concerned, says it is "unfortunate. Ball's a damned good man. We need him," and Harold Burton, without commenting directly, says firmly that he has "no hesitation" in endorsing Dewey and will speak for him whenever requested. An honest gesture, appreciated by many at the moment it was made, it will not be forgotten

later on. In a sense Joe Ball has left the party, and in a sense it will
never take him back. Certainly it will not take him back during the angry
months ahead. He has been true to his own convictions, but a good
fighter for the good cause has been seriously weakened by his own
deliberate decision. Without demeaning that decision, it is still just to
point out that it has done much to turn a potential leader into a
glamorous but powerless lone wolf.

21

SOME THOUGHTS ON PUFFY THE PIG

OCTOBER 2, 1944. Taft, back in town for a couple of days between speeches to catch up on correspondence and attend to the myriad demands of the constituency, was in his usual friendly mood today. Ohio, he says philosophically, "looks pretty good," both for him and for Dewey. "I'm surprised," he said in a sincerely shocked tone, "at the depth of the hatred for Roosevelt I find in rural Ohio. They *hate* him." He expected to find active dislike, apparently, but the intensity of it he was not quite prepared for. The CIO, he said, "is saying I did things I never did, but I don't think it's hurting me much."

OCTOBER 4, 1944. Harry Truman gave us his itinerary today, a rather modest trip that will cover 7500 miles but will only include four major speeches. ("The trouble with me," he remarked candidly, "is that I'm not photogenic and I'm a hell of a public speaker.") His comments on Dewey were colorful and unprintable and amiably good-natured. He does not seem disturbed by the fact that he has furnished the Republican candidate with many of his most effective texts. He himself, he says, "will answer arguments with undeniable facts, something our opponents have not done." His press conference as usual produced little news but sent us away thinking what a nice fellow he is. In the midst of it he called in his secretary to tell her to "Get my mama on the phone—no, my mama," he said, when she started to dial his home phone. "Oh," she said, surprised; "I thought you meant—" "It goes through the St. Louis exchange," he told her firmly. "Hello, Mama," he said warmly when the call came through, "how are you? . . . Are you? That's fine. I'll be seeing you soon—I'll be in St. Louis tomorrow and I'll call you. . . . That's right. I'll call you when I get to St. Louis. . . . You have? . . . He did? Well, what do you know. You've done a good job all right, if you've got him lined up. . . . Well, we'll hope so. I'm not admitting it can be any other way.... That's right. Well, I'll call you. Good-by, Mama." He hung up and turned back to us. "Ninety-two years old and the grandest old lady in the world," he told us. "Tells me she's got the Republican preacher to vote for me. I told her that was a good job, because he's a mighty hard man to convince." As we left he said, as he so often has, "You boys have been mighty nice to me, I'll tell you that. You really have." That is one of his great talents, of course: it's impossible not to be.

OCTOBER 5, 1944. Homer Bone, his acid and rhetorical humor tinged with a certain amount of quizzical bitterness, was in his office for a little while today, supervising packing, arranging records, getting ready finally to pull out and leave for the Coast to take his seat on the Ninth Circuit Court. His hip, after five years of agony, is at last beginning to mend enough so that he feels he can start the new job without having to return immediately to the hospital. "Sometime before Congress returns" on November 14 he will resign, and one of its most colorful liberals will be gone from the Senate.

"I am glad to go from public life," he told us, talking in his rapid sardonic fashion, "in these days when the comic strips have more influence with the American people than all their leaders combined, and when Puffy the Pig means more than a United States Senator. There's a change coming, and it will be here very soon. There are waves of opinion in America, you know, up and down, up and down; when you've been in public office as long as I have, you know. We've been up for a while and now we're about to go down. They've had too much reform, they're sick of it; they want to sink back into the restful arms of conservative Morpheus for a while, until something happens to make them wake up again. Jesus Christ! Liberalism! Look at Norris—40 years of a man's life, and what did it all add up to? Oh, I know he accomplished some things—some things. But from a long life as a representative of the law I know that a man never does accomplish half the things he wants to accomplish. Puffy the Pig and Little Orphan Annie! In them is found all knowledge.... I am glad to leave. I've fought hard for the things I believe in, but it isn't worth it. They don't want it. All they want is Little Orphan Annie and Puffy the Pig." His eyes narrowed and a glint of battle came into them. His wisp of a frame hunched about swiftly in his chair. "When I sit on that bench," he said flatly, "I'm at least going to have my say, even if I'm a perpetual minority of one. There'll be some dissents, written in my glittering and no doubt deathless prose, which will make even Puffy the Pig sit up and take notice. I've been fighting for these laws all my life; now I'll get a chance to see that they're enforced as they ought to be. Maybe then I'll feel that I've accomplished something before I totter off into limbo with this God-damned creaking frame of mine. Puffy the Pig! Jesus!"

OCTOBER 6, 1944. The V.P., bashful as ever but finally at peace with himself and his surroundings, held a press conference today to announce his campaign plans. Strictly on his own, without help from the Democratic National Committee at present dominated by the friends of his successor, Henry is going to stump the hustings for the fourth-term ticket. A lonely voice of disembodied liberalism, he is off to the wars, an uneasy wind troubling the surface of the waters. There is such selflessness and purity of purpose, for Henry Wallace has it, along with a lot of other qualities more open to ridicule. Within his gallantry lies the burning seed of a great ambition. That it is his own, no one can say for sure, but that it agitates his office no one who has been in there can deny. "Wallace in '48!"—the cry has rung through a hundred halls, and it has been heard with an attentive ear by his secretary, Harold Young. The huge, roly-poly Texan is thinking ahead, thinking ahead. Somebody had the idea, and Henry is doing it: forget the bright lights and the big stages, go out and talk to the grass-roots boys, the small fry who keep the big fry swimming. Shake hands, duck the head, laugh the whu-whu laugh, show them what a good soul you are. Henry is not yet buried, though he may be politically dead.

OCTOBER 7, 1944. Shockingly sudden—the life of Wendell Willkie came to an end today. The Great Crusader died at 52, his heart figuratively and perhaps literally broken by the terrific beating he took for four straight years. The Wisconsin defeat, topped by the treatment he received at the hands of the GOP convention managers—not even being named as a delegate, not even being asked to speak, being in fact totally shut out in one of the cruelest brush-offs in the cruel history of American politics—apparently proved just too much when added to the poor physical care he took of himself. "He came on the American scene like a meteor," someone said, "and like a meteor he burned himself out." He goes at a time when the things for which he stood and his monumental courage were never more needed.

What it will all add up to when the histories are finally written, time alone can tell. Out of all those four, hectic, furious, excited years, what will remain, what permanent impress will be left upon America? One wonders, a little, whether there will be any—but there may be a lot. It is hard to tell now. Inept in many ways, unable to perceive that there is nothing inherently vicious in compromise but only in the uses the self-interested put it to, he was still a challenging figure possessed of an integrity, honesty and courage far beyond the average measure. He went into politics and politics killed him, but that need not discourage the idealistic. Where he failed others can win. And others will.

OCTOBER 8, 1944. Joe Guffey, sounding a popular keynote for Democratic commentators, has seized upon the occasion of Willkie's death to assail the Republican Party and shed deep moving tears over the man whom only yesterday he was attacking with all the venom at his command. Others are joining in the chorus, others from his own party as well as others from the opposition. Roosevelt, Dewey, Ickes, Taft—an interesting array to mourn for the fallen, some few sincere, the rest relieved. One would never have imagined that a man could so soon achieve greatness by the simple act of dying.

Out of the big old house in Georgetown has finally come the Dumbarton Oaks Agreement, the "suggestions" for a "United Nations Security Organization." Such timid minds, these were, so petty and so small. Apparently afraid to formulate a really strong world body, they have been content to propose instead a method for organizing international chaos in the most thoroughly respectable manner. It probably deserves to pass the Senate, for it is apparently the best the frightened little men who run the world can manage, but no one need be under any illusions that it will prevent a third world war.

OCTOBER 11, 1944. Joe Ball drew the biggest crowd in months today when he held a press conference to lay the groundwork for his probable apostasy. He posed three questions to the two candidates: did they favor immediate formation of a world peace organization, did they favor its formation before the peace treaties were signed, and did they favor empowering the American delegate to commit an "agreed-upon quota" of American troops to keep the peace without prior approval of Congress. On these three questions, said the Senator from Minnesota, he would base his decision in the election. He doubted that Dewey could satisfy him, but refused to say so on the record. The indications are excellent that he will support Roosevelt. This made a good story—Ajax defying the lightning—and wonderful headlines: "Willkie's mantle" was the phrase in one enthusiastic story. The Senator as always looked, talked and acted like a very sincere individual.

OCTOBER 30, 1944. Back from vacation, the Hill seems even deader than before. Joe Ball, running true to form, has endorsed Roosevelt. Looking haggard and rather as though he hadn't quite known what he was getting into, he reports his mail running 50–50. Ed Johnson, veteran of the political wars of 30 years, comments with an undisturbed smile that "Senator Ball is taking himself too seriously." One Republican office, adept at giving the knife to colleagues it doesn't like, terms it "juvenile delinquency." The rest are furious.

Using the phrase which infuriates the Hill perhaps more than any other, Ball has asserted that the President if re-elected will have received "a clear mandate" for the unrestricted use of force by the American delegate. While the election will of course be no such thing, the argument will be used. Looked at in the sober light of day, the Minnesotan's action seems odder and odder, particularly in view of the fact that the two candidates, far from being miles apart on foreign policy, are on the contrary virtually rubbing elbows. He does not seem altogether at ease about it. Hailed noisily by Lister Hill in the cafeteria the other day he seemed rather more embarrassed than pleased. Joe Guffey and others are of course going out of their way to make the most of it.

OCTOBER 31, 1944. The new isolationist strategy—or at any rate one of the new isolationist strategies—was outlined calmly today by one of the young bloods who will be in there helping the old warriors when the chips are down. The obvious and sensible thing to do, he said reasonably, is to put it in the form of a constitutional amendment and submit it to the American people. Shall we join the world organization or shan't we? What better way to find out than to let the people themselves decide? The states would have seven years to make up their minds, and certainly that would give plenty of time for the issues to be thoroughly thrashed out. This proposal, which may or may not be used but at any rate is being seriously considered right now, is the shrewdest one yet. It has all the appealing elements—the Constitution, the people, full and free discussion. There are some clever minds at work on this thing, and if it isn't killed off it won't be because they didn't try.

22

SOMEBODY MUST BE WRONG

NOVEMBER 1, 1944. "Washington's wonderful!" Ferguson exclaimed today with a delighted chuckle. "You can always get in a fight about something down here. You're right in the thick of it!" His newest fight is simply a continuation of the old one—Pearl Harbor. The Army and Navy boards have made their reports to Stimson and Forrestal, marked them *Secret* and *Top secret* and refused to give them to the press or to the Congress which ordered the investigations. This has of course aroused a good many people on the Hill. Obviously, Ferguson declared, the Roberts report must now be considered totally inadequate and incomplete, since it was never marked *Secret* or *Top secret;* obviously, we are right back where we were on Dec. 8, 1941. Asked if he had talked to Justice Roberts about it, he looked startled and said, "Say, that's a good idea!" Within five minutes he had called the Justice, made an appointment, clapped on his hat, and high-tailed it over to the Court. Upon his return he was evasive and bland. Again he repeated his charge against the Justice's report. "Did Justice Roberts agree with that analysis?" we asked. "Don't you think it's a fair one?" the Senator replied with a smile. Whatever went on at the conference, however, the impression had been established: Ferguson attacks Roberts Report, confers with Roberts, announces determination to continue probe of Pearl Harbor secrecy. It may have been only Hello and Good-by, but the public has the picture and can draw its own conclusions. A great many things in Washington go just about that deep.

NOVEMBER 2, 1944. The Young Lincoln, as he is called by some of his more acid critics, was in his office today surrounded by stacks of approving and disapproving mail when some of us went in to see him. We asked him some rather pointed questions, the same ones raised in a number of places by a number of people. We wanted to know what he had to say about them. Had he been sold a bill of goods at the conference with Roosevelt? Was he simply trying to kill off Dewey to better Stassen's chances? Did he hope to switch to the Democratic Party in '48 and reap the reward for it? The answer was *No*, delivered in the same amiable spirit in which the questions were asked. Nobody dislikes Joe Ball, except maybe his Republican colleagues; we were willing to give him the benefit of the doubt. "Lord," he remarked with a laugh, "this is a hell of a place. Whenever you do something people always have to look for a motive and imply you've got some secret deal on. It never occurs to them that you might just feel that way and sit down at your typewriter and do it." He had been interested to note, he said with another laugh, that nothing could have been better timed than his revolt from Republicanism. "Betty and I got to looking back over it," he said, "and Lord, it couldn't have been any better if we'd sat down and calculated it out to the last minute. As a matter of fact, of course, I wasn't going to say anything if I couldn't go along with Dewey. Then I went out home and the papers got after me, and I issued my first statement. Then I got back here and you were all wanting something, so I drew up my three questions. Then I heard the two foreign-policy speeches and that decided me. But, Lord! It was perfect. It couldn't have been better if you'd planned it." We asked him how he liked politics. "Sometimes I get damned sick and tired of them," he replied promptly. "Sometimes you can see why 89 per cent of the American people don't want their children to go into them." We suggested that he ought to stay in them, because if the good people get out and leave them to the bad people, then government really will go to pot and 99.9 per cent of the American people won't want their children involved. "That's why I took this job in the first place," he admitted. What lies ahead for him, we wanted to know. He shrugged. "I'm damned if I know," he said.

NOVEMBER 3-10, 1944. In New York to handle the election story, some of us went to Madison Square Garden on the evening of Saturday, November 4, to hear "the next President of the United States!" It took three hours of patient sitting in an overflowing, hysterically excited Garden to produce this pleasure, and when all was said and done it remained a little doubtful whether it was worth it. It is true we had movie stars, Adolphe Menjou desperately in earnest—"Sidney Hillman is playing for keeps!"—Eddie Bracken mimicking the President; Gloria Swanson; even Babe Ruth, terribly happy. All about us the enormous crowd applauded and roared in the mammoth building. Back of the platform, high up, large banners proclaimed three CIO locals "against the PAC!" Elsewhere Republican groups hung out their banners. Huge American flags were all down the length of the hall, photographs of the

candidate were conspicuous in many places. A fife-and-drum corps
paraded through, hundreds of policemen stood about warily. The tension mounted and mounted, and the air hummed constantly with the
familiar, half-heard sibilance of a great excited crowd.

Promptly at 10:30 the Republican candidate for Senator stepped to
the microphone and announced the Republican candidate for President.
A trim little man with a shiny forehead and a large black mustache
trotted onto the platform with his wife. Pandemonium began and lasted
for five minutes. Promptly at 10:35 pandemonium got a competitor as
the little man began to speak; pandemonium subsided, to reburst every
two or three minutes. Over and over again, in that hearty, well-modulated
tone (This man, if elected, could be imagined saying, "Bully!" too), came
the familiar chant, "And *that's* why it's time for a change!" Once a
reference to his opponent seemed to arouse a hitherto-suppressed emotion. The speaker jabbed viciously at his mustache with his right hand.
At 11 P.M. he concluded. The crowd roared. Off the air, and with an informality just a little too polite to be quite informal enough, he returned
to thank us, to inspire us, to call us once again to a crusade to "save the
best country in all the world!" Then he paused for a few more pictures,
shook a few more hands, waved and waved, and left. The great moment
was over and the crowd pushed out to rejoin the city's Saturday-night
millions.

Touched to a degree by the processes of American democracy, which
are naïve and wonderful and stirring and laughable and thrilling all in
one, I could not help but think back to another crusade which now seems
long ago. There had been the huge crowd then, a San Francisco crowd
that time, but the same crowd really, the same thing, America. Instead of
the little man there had been a big man, and instead of the intellectual
rhetoric there had been an overwhelming emotional appeal. It was not
his fault, perhaps, that the little man suffered by the comparison, for human warmth is something you either have or haven't, and there is no adequate substitute; but suffer he did. Across four hectic years and out of a
grave the big man still spoke, and his personality burned as brightly as a
flame. It took no effort to conjure him up, to see him again, to hear the big,
powerful, touseled figure crying hoarsely, "Join me, join me! Help me,
help me!"—until at last, if you were at all of the persuasion, you came to
feel that you had joined him, that you did want to help him, that he was
in a sense your creation in which you had a personal interest and in which
you could believe. Not so this other. Excellent though his abilities may
be, admirable though his character, he does not inspire. He interests, he
perhaps persuades, but he does not inspire. You may have believed with
him intellectually that in a confused and deteriorating Administration it

is indeed time for a change; but for the man himself you could feel only an analytical interest. Would he make it or would he not? And if he did not, what would become of him? And would it matter? There was nowhere the feeling, as there had been with the big man, that he *must* make it, that he *must* try it again, that if he should be lost something vague but irreparable would have been done to America.

On Election Night, when the returns came in, there was little jubilation, little regret. It was over and it was a good thing to have it out of the way. Relief was the predominant emotion; relief and the special wonder which is always preserved for the realization that all over a great land free men and women actually rule themselves. Placed against the dark background of Europe and the endless centuries of oppression, that miracle which is the essence of America seems at election-time to be the most miraculous in all of human history. "We, the People"—the proudest words which were ever said.

Also on that day the membership of the United States Senate changed to some degree. Brilliant John Danaher, his enormous industry and statesmanlike mind unable to salvage a voting record which laid itself open too fatally to the smear of "isolationist," went down to defeat. In Iowa Guy Gillette, making an excellent showing considering the circumstances, rolled up a big vote but fell behind. In Indiana the Democratic seat fell to Republican Homer Capehart. Leverett Saltonstall, the lean Yankee, rolled up an overwhelming tally in otherwise Democratic Massachusetts. Fulbright succeeded to Hattie Caraway's seat in Arkansas. H. Alexander Smith, reportedly internationalist, won in New Jersey. Out in North Dakota the end came for Gerald Nye. Jim Davis, his fate not to be known until Pennsylvania counts her soldier vote on Nov. 22, trailed the Guffey-sponsored Myers by 11,000 votes. No other incumbents lost out, although out in Ohio Bob Taft, like Danaher too easily tarred with the brush of isolation, ran a bare 17,000 ahead in a total vote of more than 3,000,000. Basically the make-up of the Senate has been changed very little. One or two of the most astute contrivers have been removed, one or two of the more obvious drawbacks. Otherwise the situation is much the same. The balance toward internationalism has been tipped a little more, but the Republican–Southern Democrat coalition, which may ultimately decide the peace as it has decided so much else, remains a lively and a going concern.

NOVEMBER 12, 1944. Four major projects are apparently on the docket when the Congress reconvenes on Tuesday: Second War Powers extension, Flood Control, Rivers and Harbors, and another Pearl Harbor resolution. Also around are the insurance bill, providing O'Mahoney can't delay it until the new Congress; Gillette's equal rights amendment which he says he will push even though chances for passage seem remote; and the highways bill, still awaiting action by the House. Not much else is expected to develop. Major fights are in prospect on Flood Control and Rivers and Harbors, with possibly a bitter battle on Pearl Harbor. Second War Powers [*a hodgepodge measure correlating many of the President's emergency authorities*] will probably be extended without much trouble.

NOVEMBER 13, 1944. "You know, you can only carry so much," Gillette said philosophically today. "And that was just too much—just too much. I did my duty, as they wanted me to. They said I owed it to the party to run, and I did. I did. So I agreed to do it. I discharged my obligation. When you don't want to run, and you know you're going to get licked, your heart isn't entirely in it, but I did what I could. I paid my debt. I was glad to do it for them. But you can only carry so much—and this was too much."

Elsewhere on the first floor of the Office Building Ken Wherry also discussed the ABC's of practical politics. The best organization man on the Republican side made a typical comment on his next-door neighbor. "Joe Ball," he said bluntly, "made the greatest speech on international policy that's been given in the United States Senate since I've been in it. Hell, I'm not mad at Joe Ball. Joe Ball's a damned fine man. He has a right to his opinions, and as far as I'm concerned he can express them. Any man who stands up on his own two feet and says what he thinks, honestly and sincerely, I've got a place in my heart for him. I don't agree with Ball on lots of things, but he's a damned fine man. Of course I don't know what Taft and Vandenberg and those boys want to do about it, but the way I look at it is that you need everybody you can get. You've got to have organization and you've got to have everybody in it. I want to take all of 'em into it, I want Joe Ball along with everybody else. We're all Republicans, we've all got to stand together, we all need each other. Take 'em all in, see what I mean, have lots of meetings, talk everything over, exchange your ideas. Maybe you can even convince me sometimes, see what I mean? That's the only way to do it! That's the only way to have a real organization! I haven't heard anything about reading Joe Ball out of the party—how the hell can you do it, he's in it, isn't he?—but if I do I shall most certainly be opposed to it.

"You've got to have organization. That's what's been the trouble with this whole damned campaign. We're never going to get anywhere until we have a real practical politician as national chairman—somebody who knows what it means to ring doorbells. Why, hell! These boys were young this time, they were nice fellows, but hell! They didn't have any more idea of what it means to organize a precinct than the man in the moon. Dewey did a fine job of mending fences—on the upper level. But we're not going to get anywhere until we've got somebody who knows every precinct worker in the United States by his first name. You've got to do it that way, you've got to deliver it right where it counts, and that's in the ballot box. Roosevelt plays along with some peculiar people, maybe, but they get the votes. They know what they can count on, and on election day they produce it. I'm not saying that's the sort of tie-up we ought to have, but we ought to get it right down to the real grass roots. Hell, the way things are going now it'll take a national catastrophe, a revolution or a great depression or something before we get Roosevelt out, if he lives. Organization, that's the only way to do it. Yes, sir!"

NOVEMBER 14, 1944. The largest turnout for an opening in some months —50—showed up today to start the short session. Joe Ball, prepared to get the cold shoulder, seemed slightly abashed by his elders as they went out of their way to shake his hand. Whatever the knifing to be done, apparently, it will not be done in public. The Democrats surrounded Harry Truman and Barkley, both looking very pleased. A hum of talk and chatter filled the chamber; Wallace beat futilely for order from time to time. Guy Gillette was on hand, taking it like the trooper he is. Hattie came in in her customary fashion, sat down calmly, opened her newspaper and began to read. Bennett Clark was there. Gerald Nye, not too happy, received the condolences of his colleagues. Jim Davis, trailing 11,000 votes, took his seat with undisturbed aplomb. Danaher had not returned.

Later in Gerald Nye's office the North Dakotan gave the standard Republican analysis of the elections: isolationism was a minor issue. The PAC, the "silent vote," other things (in his case a three-way race) were to blame; there was no "mandate." Regarding the North Dakota situation he was probably right. The vote of the independent, Stambaugh, added to his own, would have been enough to beat John Moses. "You'll be missed around here, Senator." He chuckled. "Well, you know," he said, in his grave, effective voice, "you're going to be surprised at how well things keep going right along without me." There is bound to be, he said, "a certain hurt remaining, when you feel that you have done a good job for your state over many years and then are rejected." The campaign, he said, had been "vicious—oh, my, it was vicious." He showed me some of the literature, and it was vicious; what the output had been from his own camp he did not reveal. And "enormous sums" had been spent to beat him. What were his plans? "I think I shall go back and try to get re-established in the economic life of the state which has done so much for me." Nothing political, nothing anti-Langer? "That suggestion has been made to me from many quarters, but I don't think so. I shall just try to get re-established in the economic and political life of the state." Not as a candidate for office, he thought—"after you have been here for a long time and have worked up to a position (ranking Republican on Appropriations) where you could really wield some influence when your party gains control—then there is some point to running. But to lose all your seniority, to start over again. . . ." He shrugged. "But I expected it. When we lost our fight and war came, I said to myself then, 'Well, brother, you can forget all about coming back here. You're through.' But it was worth it. I'd do it again. I don't regret any of it—any of it. There is a great reaction coming—call it 'isolationism' if you will—after this war; such a reaction as you never saw." And would he speak again, in this reaction? "The time is not right for it now," said Gerald Nye, defeated, "the time is not right."

NOVEMBER 15, 1944. McKellar, like the imperial prima donna he is, has decided to be president pro tempore of the Senate. His method of getting the job is very simple: short notes to all of his Democratic colleagues requesting them to vote for him. This royal command will undoubtedly be treated with the deference it deserves when the 79th Congress reconvenes in January.

John Overton, who ran on a platform of killing the St. Lawrence Seaway in order to end any real or supposed threat to the seaborne commerce of the Mississippi Delta states, has finally aroused George Aiken by his dilatory tactics. Aiken's bill to authorize completion of the project, stymied in Overton's commerce subcommittee since March 1943, will be offered as an amendment to either the Rivers and Harbors or the Flood Control bill, the Vermonter says. His dander is up and he is through being patient with the portly Louisianan. The situation promises to offer the hottest fight of the lame-duck session.

NOVEMBER 16, 1944. From Joe Ball, Warren Austin and George Aiken come earnest demands that the Republican Party overhaul itself and move left with the times. "Unless the party becomes more liberal in domestic policies and also in foreign policies, there's going to be a hell of a blow-up and probably a new party," the Minnesotan says. "We must lead in foreign policy," says his friend Austin. "We mustn't always be followers." From other Republican offices comes another tune. "With twenty-two million votes? Why should we liberalize? What do you mean, *liberalize?* We're doing all right."

Somebody must be wrong.

23

POWER

NOVEMBER 17, 1944. The Connally strategy on foreign policy, removed from the partisan encumbrances of the campaign which led him into several attacks on Dewey, has reverted to type. Old Tom is out once more to entrap the opposition with a judicious combination of honey and vinegar. Endorsing an earnest plea by Warren Austin that the minority take a constructive stand, Connally rose today to pay tribute to the Republican candidate and the Republican platform. To his Republican colleagues, also, he extended a fulsome pat on the back. Later on he chuckled about it, pleased with his apparent success. "I wanted to brag on 'em a little," he told us, "make 'em feel good, get 'em committed. I wanted to coax 'em along a little, get 'em lined up on the right side." The election, he thought, would be salutary. "Some of these Republicans that are right on the line, you know, waverin' back and forth, maybe it'll make 'em stop and think a little." Vandenberg, he said, worries him most because "he's the key man."

NOVEMBER 18, 1944. Claude Pepper, who has more faith than most in the efficacy of passing a resolution to solve the world's ills, held hearings today on his proposal to authorize wage increases to 65 cents an hour without War Labor Board approval. The A.F. of L. was on the stand today; the CIO, as befits its new status, headlined the proceedings yesterday. Lewis Hines, A.F. of L. legislative representative, termed the resolution a "tottering, childlike step." He added, however, that he was for it. William Davis came up in the afternoon, as unimpressed by Senators as ever, his dogged face and slow, almost quavering voice expressing at every point his unshaken determination to hold the line. The War Labor Board chairman has weathered many storms, and a slight buffeting from Claude Pepper was nothing to him. The big drive to break the Little Steel formula, which Pepper, Tunnell and Aiken would like to do, may have excited some people but it has not bothered Bill Davis. He would regard the resolution as a guide rather than a mandate if it should be passed, he said. "After all, just passing a resolution doesn't solve everything. You've got to make your wage adjustments in such a way that industry can absorb them and still make a profit." Pepper, unprepared for such orthodox testimony from a supposedly compliant witness, looked a trifle annoyed. "Well, wouldn't 65 cents an hour be a fair standard?" he demanded. "It seems to me," Davis replied mildly, "that one of the best of all fair standards would be the old American one of trying to find out how much people can afford to pay." WLB, he added, would under no circumstances consider itself freed from its obligation to help stabilize the economy. Having thus expressed himself in his slow, unperturbed fashion, he departed from the annoyed committee.

NOVEMBER 19, 1944. Cotton Ed was buried in South Carolina today, having passed away Friday in Lynchburg, in the year of his age the eightieth, of his Senatorship the thirty-sixth. The longest Senatorial term in the history of the nation came to an end in defeat and amid the unrelenting attacks of the old man's enemies. Not content with his death, editorialists and commentators threw a few last stones at his coffin before it was lowered away. What purpose was served by all this it was hard to say. The man was dead and could do no more damage. But Cotton Ed was a symbol, and a symbol had to be suitably disposed of. Catcalls such as he himself might have hooted after an enemy followed him to his grave.

The naïve, however, were those who read into his passing "the end of an era in the South"; "a symbol of the change which is coming upon the states below the Mason-Dixon line"; "the new spirit"; "the new age." Cotton Ed's going marks indeed the end of an era, but it is an era of bombast which is passing, not an era of substance. The old things will be there still, coming out of the South, only now they will be streamlined a little, perhaps a little more modern, done with a somewhat suaver manner. Cotton Ed is dead, but the things for which he stood are living still.

NOVEMBER 20, 1944. The developing fight on the flood-control bill has grown by giant strides over the week end. Some optimist has mentioned December 10 as the date of the Christmas recess, but he is behind the times already. At the rate the Senate is moving now it will be later than that before everything is done.

The essential fight centers around the Missouri Valley. The upper valley states want water for irrigation, the lower for navigation. Overton, professing to stand in the middle, maintains that the bill as now written can satisfy both; multiple-purpose dams can be built, he says, storing up water for irrigation, releasing it when needed for navigation. Basic to the whole debate is the need for a new clarification of the Federal power policy.

Cheap-power advocates like Lister Hill ("The TVA is the greatest thing which ever happened to the South") and utility-company defenders like Josiah Bailey ("Destroy these companies and you destroy free enterprise in the power industry and presently in many other things") are about to fight it out. It promises to be a long process.

NOVEMBER 21, 1944. Homer Ferguson has put in two resolutions, one passed immediately and the other referred to Military Affairs, to extend the statute of limitations on the Kimmell–Short court-martials, and to set up a 10-man Senate committee to investigate Pearl Harbor. The extension went through virtually without debate, but the other of course ran into trouble from the Democrats. Carl Hatch, who told us yesterday that he would support it with a single qualification—that it not interfere with the war effort—began to hedge today, apparently regretting his haste. Barkley, deploring this tendency to look backward instead of forward, expressed the customary Administration willingness to forget the whole thing. As the event recedes farther and farther into the past and the Roosevelt Administration continues to combat successfully all attempts to disclose the truth, it begins to seem more and more likely that neither the American people nor history will ever know what really happened on the morning of Dec. 7, 1941—or why.

NOVEMBER 22, 1944. The Commerce subcommittee met today to hear testimony on the question of whether or not the St. Lawrence agreement with Canada is an executive agreement or a treaty. The State Department's chief legal adviser, a harrassed little man named Green H. Hackworth, found himself backed into a corner repeatedly by indignant Senators after he made the initial and inept mistake of declaring it to be the President's right to decide "by its wording and the manner in which it is presented to Congress" whether a document should be ratified by two-thirds of the Senate as a treaty or by a majority of both houses as an executive agreement. This is a point of Senatorial touchiness so elemental that it seemed astonishing that a man holding so responsible a position with State would blunder against it; but he did, apparently all-unsuspecting, whereupon the wrath of the gods descended.

It was a fascinating and in many ways a very significant performance; one of those times when Senators are more than just Senators, human and likable; one of those times when they become, not Senators, but The Senate, a branch of the American government under the Constitution of the United States. This is an impressive, albeit a rather frightening, process. It flustered Mr. Hackworth, but his desperate attempts to get out of it did no good. The Senate was aroused and the issue was decided. Whatever the St. Lawrence seaway compact may have been before, the moment the assertion was made that the President had sole authority to decide its nature, it became a treaty.

Vandenberg, sitting silent throughout, summed up the general reaction at the end. "I came down here," he said bluntly, "inclined to believe this thing could be done by agreement. But if this is to be a symbol of the philosophy of government set forth by Mr. Hackworth, that the treaty-ratification processes directed by the Constitution are a matter of choice by the President, then I am certainly opposed to that symbolism."

NOVEMBER 24, 1944. Bad tempers boiled over in the Senate today. Bennett Champ Clark, apparently determined to pay off some old scores and annoy everybody before bidding the upper house farewell, served as middleman for Overton as he beat off concentrated attacks by both Murray and Aiken. Both are in the same boat: Murray put in his Missouri Valley Authority bill and Overton sat on it; Aiken put in the St. Lawrence seaway and Overton sat on it. In phrases strongly reminiscent of each other, the junior Senators from Montana and Vermont took the senior Senator from Louisiana over the bumps. The portly, aggressive B. C. did what he could to needle both of them and encourage Overton.

At times this process degenerated into farce. Murray had the floor and yielded to Aiken for 15 minutes. Clark asserted that Murray had given it up altogether. Murray said he was leaning against his desk and hadn't sat down. Later Clark got the floor and yielded to Overton for 15 minutes. Murray challenged him. "I was leaning against my desk," B. C. responded.

Later Clark reminded Overton that technically he had yielded to him for a question; would he, in conformity with the rules of the Senate, care to state it? "How is the Senator's health?" asked Overton. "Very fine," said Bennett Champ Clark. There were moments, however, when this mood of kindergarten levity departed. Aiken quoted Overton's campaign literature and his promises to block the St. Lawrence proposal. Overton defended himself with righteous anger, a choked voice, and the suspicion of a tear. Clark demanded of Murray what right he had to "lock himself in his office, perhaps with a representative of the CIO," and determine what the course of legislation ought to be. Murray, his usually inaudible voice for once carrying clearly to the galleries, replied sharply that he had never been locked in his office with a representative of the CIO, was not a CIO stooge, had never introduced or sponsored a piece of legislation offered by the CIO. Bennett Champ, confronted with this flat assertion, had no choice but to apologize. A man who wears skepticism like a mantle, his real opinion of Murray's denial was not hard to perceive.

All in all, it was a bitter, rather childish wrangle, of the sort the Senate gets into occasionally when somebody breaks through the veil of necessary courtesy and really reveals what he thinks of somebody else. The future course of the legislation is even more uncertain. Clark served notice that he would filibuster if Aiken proposes the St. Lawrence seaway, and made virtually the same promise with regard to the MVA. Murray announced that he would call up the MVA amendment regardless. The real basic issue, of course, is Federal power development. One of the great controversies of the Roosevelt years, never settled but only suppressed, has emerged again.

NOVEMBER 25, 1944. "Flood control is only incidental," Aiken said quietly today. "What we're really fightin' about in the Senate right now is whether we're goin' to conserve the remainin' natural resources of the United States for the 12,000,000 in service and their descendants or whether we're goin' to turn them over to a small group of private utilities." Asked about Clark's threat to filibuster, he shrugged. "If they want to sacrifice everything in the bill by talkin' it to death, that's their lookout," he said. He isn't sure yet, he added, when he will offer his amendment. If the flood-control bill is in sufficiently good shape when the Senate gets through with it so that the President can sign it, he will offer the St. Lawrence proposal. If it is so bad that the President will have to veto it, then St. Lawrence will go over to the new Congress. "I wouldn't want to put him in a spot where he had to veto the St. Lawrence. I certainly wouldn't put him on a spot like that."

NOVEMBER 26, 1944. Over in the House, Chairman Sol Bloom of the Foreign Relations Committee has suddenly started talking about a constitutional amendment to take away the Senate's treaty-ratifying power and place the responsibility in a simple majority of both houses. Obediently a House Judiciary subcommittee has decided to report out a resolution to that effect. The sponsors hope to have it through by the end of the session, they say, naïvely certain that the Senate will go along because of the "pressure of public opinion." The idea is finding enormous support on the editorial pages, not much in the House, and virtually none in the Senate. One thing all these hopeful people who talk about abolishing the two-thirds rule can put down in their little black books, and that is this: the Senate will never give it up. Therefore, unless the never-used process of Constitutional amendment on the initiative of two-thirds of the states is finally resorted to, treaties will continue in perpetuity to be ratified by two-thirds of the Senate and nobody else. Carter Manasco, chipper and amiable, summed it up for us at the press table in the House restaurant yesterday. "What they're tryin' to do," he said, "is take away one of the basic powers. It would be just like the Senate offering a bill to cut itself in on our power to make appropriations. We'd just never stand for it, and neither will they."

NOVEMBER 27, 1944. Hull's resignation, rumored for many weeks, was accepted at the White House today. Four hours later Edward Stettinius was nominated for the post. Time and ill health have worked a change where the Republicans could not.

None of the attitude with which the Secretary is regarded on the Hill —that peculiar mixture of respect and skepticism—seeped through the official statements this afternoon. Connally, Chandler, Vandenberg, Burton, McKellar, the procession of eulogists was impressive, and the words they used were fulsome. "Great" was the mildest. They ranged up the scale from there.

As for his successor, the appointment was hardly as effective as the appointment of Jimmy Byrnes would have been. The wispy little Justice, for all that many Senators dislike him, still knows how to handle them; that is the most important qualification in a Secretary of State today. Money may be appropriated, armies and armadas may be built, men may die: the ultimate decision lies in the United States Senate. If it refuses to go along, the whole thing will be as nothing. If a clever Secretary can persuade it to his point of view, the battle that wins the war will have been successfully consummated. Stettinius will have a hard row to hoe, and not the least of his difficulties will be the fact that he does not know the Hill, is not acquainted there, and has nothing of the instinctive political familiarity with Congress which saved Hull in so many situations and made his over-all record a worthy one.

After all the glowing words and wonderful tributes were said, after he had been hailed as the greatest of the great, men in cloakrooms later spoke with a certain wry humor on the circumstance that took a minor Tennessee politician and lifted him into a place in history where he could not escape greatness, or at least the reputation for greatness.

NOVEMBER 29, 1944. The flood-control bill moved forward toward final passage on the floor today. At the last moment, when all else was decided,

Murray got up and offered an amendment that would transfer water-conservation reservoirs in 17 Western states from the Army Engineers to the Bureau of Reclamation. It hasn't a ghost of a chance, but is part of his whole general strategy of delaying the bill as long as he can, possibly until next session.

NOVEMBER 30, 1944. Murray's amendment was beaten today, and toward the end of the session he was also persuaded to drop the MVA for the remainder of the year. Lister Hill, Wherry and White mollified and cajoled and promised full debate next year. Murray, assessing this familiar technique for what it was worth, nonetheless agreed finally to abandon the fight. He had made his record, which was what he wanted, and the MVA is by that much advanced. [*Though not, as it turned out, very far. It has not passed yet.*]

Prior to this decision, Langer held the floor for two and a half hours. His subject was the Stettinius appointment and he roared on about it in his usual unintelligible way. "Wall Shtreet influensh" drew his ire; his shouting voice echoed about the Senate side like the wail of some aggravated banshee. "Wall Shtreet, Mr. Preszhident," he cried, "Wall Shtreet!" Connally, moved to protest at one point, was submerged in a roar of sound, and decided to let him go on and talk himself out. When he had done so the Texan moved that the nomination be approved. A roll call was taken and the vote stood 68–1. Langer's baby filibuster had gained him great publicity, strengthened his hold on the Dakota farms where attacks on Wall Street are great stuff, and annoyed everybody. Listening to him shout, his whole body hunching forward and shaking with rage, it was easy to see where he could have been a danger if once, long ago, he had learned self-control. His flow of facts and his obvious intelligence cannot be denied any more than can the questionable nature of the uses he puts them to.

DECEMBER 1, 1944. In another of those actions which are causing his most vociferous supporters to express pained and rather pathetic surprise, the President has nominated two controversial people to the Surplus Property Board. Former Governor Robert Hurley of Connecticut, twice rejected at the polls, and Lieutenant Colonel Edmund Heller, husband of the Democratic National Committeewoman from California, have received the nod. Guy Gillette is to be the third member, although that will have to wait until he leaves the Senate.

Cognizant of this, Gillette and Danaher, meeting in the corridor, exchanged amiable remarks. "Well, John," said Guy, "it won't be long before we lame ducks will be migrating." Danaher chuckled. "I think this year we've been declared surplus property, haven't we?" Good losers both, they laughed heartily together and walked off.

DECEMBER 2, 1944. With flood control out of the way, Rivers and Harbors is next on the schedule. To it Aiken will offer his St. Lawrence seaway amendment. "What will you do?" we asked today. "What can we do?" he demanded in reply. "Just start fightin' and keep on fightin' if it takes 10 years, for this project to benefit 135,000,000 people." He is a slow man to anger, the Vermonter, but he is angry now, and he will beat Overton and the Southern crowd if he can. He thinks he has the votes and is preparing to talk the bill to death in this session if necessary, if its managers won't permit a decision. Asked about this, Overton spread his hands and shrugged. "No comment," he said, and shrugged again. "No comment." Then he relaxed and gave us one. "By murdering the Rivers and Harbors bill he will not put life into his St. Lawrence seaway." That was all he would say. The South will filibuster too, fearful of competition from Great Lakes commerce and, aided by the private utilities, fearful of competition from Federal power. It is a formidable combination Aiken is contending with. But he thinks he has the votes.

DECEMBER 3, 1944. Tom Connally has killed the Anglo-American oil treaty [*which his constituents were afraid would liberalize the flow of oil from British-held areas into this country*] in one brief paragraph. Almost as if it were an afterthought he issued it yesterday through his secretary and then went off to the Army–Navy game with Jimmy Byrnes. The months and months of delicate negotiation, the exasperating labors which have gone on at all levels from the top on down, the desperate necessity for convincing the world that the Senate is not unreasonably uncooperative —all these were nothing to Tall Tom. The treaty, he said, would not be practical and is not in the public interest. Accordingly it will never be ratified by the Foreign Relations Committee or the Senate. Might as well bury it now and stop folks fussin'. So bury it he did.

The summary fashion in which this was done—without hearings, without warning—must have sent a cold wind blowing through the State Department and the chancelleries of the democratic world. It was a lesson and it will not be easily forgotten in a world still remembering the last lesson it got from the United States Senate. Let the mighty strive as they may, it will avail them nothing if the fancy strikes. A shrewd old man from Texas is mightier than them all.

DECEMBER 4, 1944. Brehon Somervell came up today to testify on the manpower shortage before the Mead Committee, which its chairman still refers to as the Truman Committee. Offered a straw by Ferguson—a "war

workers' bonus" suggested this morning by Julius Krug of the WPB—
the general grasped at it eagerly; the thing began to assume major proportions by the afternoon editions. Neither Krug nor the general had
worked it out: some sort of extra inducement, given at the end of the war
to those who stay on the job. It seemed like a good idea and turned into
a one-day wonder. Something may come of it, but perhaps no more than
will come of Somervell's warning that unless manpower shortages
(311,000, he says, for Army Service Forces programs), are met within 30
days, "we shall have to ask for national service legislation." This produced
a smile among the press and a certain mild skepticism among Senators, for
it is as dead as it ever was and not even Somervell can revive it. He did
say that ample supplies are reaching the unloading areas, which cast some
question upon his testimony. Before the hearing began the general went
up to the committee counsel. "Look," he said confidentially, "try not to
interrupt me, will you? I mean, if it's possible not to, I'd appreciate it. I'm
going to make one of the most important speeches of my life in a couple
of days, and I'd certainly appreciate it if you'd kind of go easy on me today," "Well," said the counsel doubtfully. "Of course we'll have to reserve
the right to get the facts. But we'll see. Just be sure you don't put yourself
in the position of not giving the full picture." "Oh, no," said Brehon Somervell hastily. "Certainly not."

DECEMBER 5, 1944. Rivers and Harbors is moving along slowly on the
floor, but is nearing completion. Aiken will call up the St. Lawrence
amendment tomorrow and from then on it will be anybody's guess what
will ultimately happen. Adjournment by December 15, one optimistic
prediction, seems remote.

Ferguson's Pearl Harbor resolution is having tough sledding in view
of the unexpected Army and Navy statements clearing Admiral Kimmel
and General Short and expressing the official determination to keep the
lid on the entire matter until the end of the war. Ed Johnson says the conflict between their statements and the Roberts Report makes a Congressional investigation "absolutely necessary," but it will apparently not be
until the next Congress, and probably not then.

DECEMBER 6, 1944. Aiken began the St. Lawrence fight today with a long
discussion of the project's history—something which is boring but has to
be placed in the Record. The strategy of his group, he says, is to argue
the merits of the case first and then call up the amendment at the end—
to avoid a "parliamentary tangle," the nature of which he does not specify.
Overton has acquired a habit of coming over to the Republican side and
sitting a few seats away from his bitterest enemy, listening intently without a trace of expression on his round, bland face. The two are barely on

speaking terms, even on the floor. Off it, their comments on one another are dignified but frigid. The latest rumor is that the Southern group is going to bring pressure to bear on Aiken to drop St. Lawrence in return for their agreement to leave the "Connecticut compromise"—an amendment giving Vermont considerable say in the building of eight dams in the upper Connecticut Valley—in the flood-control bill when it goes to conference. If he won't give in, so the story runs, then conferees led by Bailey, Overton, Bennett Clark, Hattie and Bilbo will abandon the compromise. This is a rather neat scheme in a ruthless sort of way. Questioned about it, Overton won't confirm or deny but grins and shrugs and chuckles that he has "heard something about it." Aiken also chuckles. "I don't respond very good to pressure," is the way he puts it.

Conference on the Tomorrowville Trolley

24

SIX FOR STATE

DECEMBER 7, 1944. The first major break with the White House since the tax veto came in the Senate today, causing some gallery wit to remark, "Well, I guess the fourth-term honeymoon is over." It was indeed, and with a vengeance.

Once again the cause was appointments, this time to the State Department. Will Clayton, Archibald MacLeish, Nelson Rockefeller, James Dunn, General Julius Holmes, assistants; Joseph Grew, undersecretary. Nothing excessively wrong with any, perhaps, although all were vulnerable to some sections of the populace; but it was just the old, old story of somebody down the Avenue getting the idea that it is slick and smart and "efficient" to steamroller things through without giving the Senate sufficient time to look them over. Tom Connally, just a few days ago acting as hatchetman on the oil treaty, turned around and did the Administration's work on the nominations. An executive session of Foreign Relations was held yesterday, the nominations were approved and placed on the calendar, and Tom was set to pass them in about two minutes. Unfortunately for the White House, and for him, the course of history did not run quite as expected. The Senate made some changes.

Joe Guffey led off, and when Joe Guffey goes against the White House it is a sign that the skies have fallen and the earth caved in. He read an editorial from the Philadelphia *Record* attacking the appointments and concluded by stating in a spiteful tone of voice, "I thought on the morning after the election that the liberals had won a great victory. Now I'm not so sure." He even said he was disappointed in President Roosevelt, a Guffey heresy of the first water. This attracted Bennett Clark, determined these days to settle a lot of old scores before bidding the Senate farewell, and although opposing the nominations himself he proceeded to tangle with Guffey on the loyalties of the publisher of the *Record*, "who has profited almost more than any other man under the New Deal Administration." This, an example of pure needling, provoked Guffey into an answer and several minutes of quarreling. Following that Happy Chandler and Joe O'Mahoney arose and the debate began to move onto a really moving and historic plane from which Connally's attempts at sarcasm did not succeed in dislodging it.

Happy, his voice beginning to rise shrilly with excitement and his words beginning to tumble out of him, demanded to know what the war was being fought for, and who won the election. We were told, Happy said, that the little folks won it, but it looked to him like Wall Street did. Our Republican friends told us during the campaign about "Clear everything with Sidney." Now Sidney was over in London telling them how American politics operated, and it was beginning to look like "Clear everything with Harry Hopkins." What did these State Department nominations mean? What was the policy that would come out of them? All over the world people were asking what had become of the Atlantic Charter; all over the world people were looking to America for the answer to the future, little folks, wondering. Senator Russell would tell them, he knew from their recent trip abroad together how all over the world people would say they wanted to be freed from the control of one or another of our allies. It was things like that which made it important to hold full and free hearings on these nominations "where Senators and citizens of the republic can come and learn what the views of these men are." That was why he would support a motion to recommit the names. That was why it was so desperately important that the Senate examine these men so closely. That was why the record must be made.

Joe O'Mahoney, using the beautiful English which is his in moments of stress, followed with the motion to recommit and the oration that guaranteed its passage. Must the Senate be expected to vote in ignorance? Were Senators to be asked to cast their votes for men about whom they knew nothing? We hear much, he cried in anger, about the Executive taking powers away from the Legislature. Was not this an example of that very thing? Was not this a case in which the Senate, given no information, asked to vote in blindness, was bowing supinely to the President? No, Mr. President; as for him he would not be satisfied until a full, fair hearing had been held. There were many questions to ask Mr. Clayton, for instance, concerning his attitude on postwar economic adjustments, many questions. The public interest would not be served by these nominations until they had been asked. Accordingly he would move that the names be recommitted, and did so move. The motion carried, 37–27.

In this tense moment, in which the Senate sat gravely quiet and concerned as it always does in its times of drama, Connally made a rather poor showing. By flippancy and sarcasm and the assertion that the President ran the State Department anyway, he attempted to justify the high-handed fashion in which his committee sought to steamroller the names of men who would inevitably make each day a thousand decisions of their own that would subtly affect the drift of events. It was the familiar Connally technique, good for a poll-tax fight, perhaps, or a soldier-vote debate, or some other issue of perhaps not completely major importance. The technique when applied to Happy seemed like kid stuff, for Happy, although he allowed himself to be dragged into the same sort of thing momentarily, was in desperate earnest. Applied to Joe O'Mahoney it seemed in bad taste, for the Senator from Wyoming was speaking with the wrath of a righteous man. Connally's final attempt to make it a personal issue—"I never voted to send anything back to your committee!" he cried bitterly at Bob Wagner, striding down the aisle and gesturing wildly as the New Yorker voted—failed, as it should have. Republicans and New Dealers found themselves side by side as one White House man after another—Wagner, Mead, Murray, Guffey, Tunnell—swung over. Perhaps it was suspicion of Clayton, perhaps it was Burton Wheeler, lecturing like a Dutch uncle—"Listen to me, you Democrats! I've been here 20 years and I know how these things operate. If Herbert Hoover sent up the names of a Rockefeller and a Clayton and someone connected with the house of Morgan, there would be all sorts of opposition on this side of the aisle"—which decided them; at any rate, their votes were against the Administration they admire. The beginnings of a new split in a Senate already split four ways from Sunday were perhaps given birth on the day it was decided to rubber-stamp the State Department nominations. One thing it guaranteed, in any case: if there has ever been the slightest chance that there would not be a continuing conflict between the White House and the Hill, that chance has vanished now.

DECEMBER 8, 1944. Foreign Relations met and voted unanimously to hold public hearings, starting next Tuesday. Connally, spiteful, predicted a "circus," but there is no need for it, providing he does his duty by the public, the Senate, and the press.

   Through with sufficient votes to override a veto should one be forthcoming went the social security tax freeze, opposed by the President. Coming on the heels of a House vote similarly overwhelming, this marked the second Administration defeat of the new era.

DECEMBER 10, 1944. Indications seem to be that Aiken is losing ground very definitely in the St. Lawrence fight. Two main issues seem to be strengthening his opponents—sincere doubts about the constitutional propriety of offering the project as an executive agreement instead of a treaty, and the possibility, transformed in some quarters into an open threat, that the Southerners will filibuster the Rivers and Harbors bill to death if the amendment is adopted. Faced with the prospect of losing all those surveys and authorizations and profitable projects for the post-war, many members are beginning to think very seriously whether they want to run the risk of seeing the bill die this session. The sincere Constitutionalists like Austin and Danaher, always alive to the very real importance of precedent, are beginning to look askance from that angle. It is too bad, because Aiken has put his heart into it in a way few men here are capable of, and he is about to undergo an experience rather rare on the Hill. He is not only going to get defeated, he is going to get hurt. Few of the experienced men here throw themselves deeply enough into a cause for that.

DECEMBER 11, 1944. The Military Affairs Committee resumed hearings today on Lieutenant Colonel Heller and former Governor Hurley, the Surplus Property Board nominees. Warren Austin, dignified, solemn, with a very gentle, sometimes regretful, sometimes sarcastic note in his voice, carried on such cross-examination as there was. Bob Reynolds, in his element in these last few days of his tenure, was at his usual fulsome best. Spying Vandenberg at one point in the proceedings, he made a typical remark. Most chairmen would say, "Senator Vandenberg is with us today. Senator, would you care to ask any questions?" But not Bob. "Ge'mum, weah ve'y hono'hed to have with us today the distinguished Senutuh from Mich'gan, the *senyuh* Senutuh from Mich'gan, the Hono'hble Ahthuh H. Vandenberg. Senutuh Vandenberg, weah ve'y highly hono-hed to have you with us, sir, and we'd sho'ly 'preciate anythin' you might cayuh to contribute to these procedin's. We know you have doubtless some ve'y searchin' questions you-all want to ask the witness. Ge'mum, Senutuh Vandenberg. Senutuh?" Vandenberg's chuckled "No, thanks. I'm just an innocent bystander" came as rather an anticlimax.

At the close of the session today Aiken and Overton reached an agreement to vote on the St. Lawrence proposal not later than 3 P.M. tomorrow, the time from noon to 3 to be controlled equally by the two opponents. Each will parcel out the time to his supporters. Thus it will be one of those rare occasions when the phrase heard so often in the House— "The time of the gentleman ('Senator' in this case) from So-and-So has expired!"—will be heard in the Senate.

The agreement is something of an endorsement of the wisdom of Lister Hill, acting Majority Leader, in Barkley's absence, who told us last Thursday after the session that he wouldn't try to get a Saturday session to complete work on the bill. The situation would work itself out, he said, as soon as everybody had delivered himself of whatever he had to say, and it wouldn't do any good to force the issue. "This old Senate, you know," he said affectionately, "is a hundred and sixty years old—you can lead it sometimes, jest a *leetle*. But you sure can't drive it!"

DECEMBER 12, 1944. The Foreign Relations Committee met this morning in a blaze of lights and glory. Nearly 25 Senators were on hand, plus the 6 State Department nominees, plus enough of the general public to pack the Caucus Room to the doors and beyond. Flashbulbs flashed and the bright glare of movie spots beat down upon the committee and its witnesses. Tom Connally, taking pains to display his skeptical impatience with the whole thing, ran the hearing with an iron hand. Everything that threatened to become embarrassing or even instructive was immediately classified as "something for an executive meeting." When the nominees seemed about to undergo questioning that might produce something of some value, the questioner was summarily choked off. As a matter of fact, the nominees did not need this diligent protection from the chairman. From bland Joseph Grew, with his unperturbed good humor, his hearing aid, and his convenient ability to miss things that might be hard to answer, through ingenuous young Nelson Rockefeller to the handsome, competent, and unimpressed Will Clayton, they were fully able to handle themselves.

Stettinius himself led off, filled with the glow of good health and moral purpose, and living up to the reputation for good looks that once caused a member of the House to remark admiringly to a colleague, "There! You see what God can do when He really tries." Grew referred to the "liberal spirit" that now infuses the State Department. "I would like your interpretation of that phrase," Tunnell told him amiably. "The word 'liberal' does not seem to coincide very well with the newspaper advertising which this new team of appointments has received." Grew made some diplomatic rejoinder and the moment passed. Archibald MacLeish, slight and dapper, asserted his faith in democracy and his detestation of communism and successfully survived a few half-hearted jabs from Bennett Champ Clark. The hearing concluded after Clayton read his prepared statement and challenged his critics. They will cross-examine him tomorrow.

On the floor this afternoon Aiken went down to defeat with a crushing 56–25 vote against his St. Lawrence amendment to the Rivers and Harbors conference report. The Southern threat to filibuster did the trick. In a last impassioned plea the Vermonter urged the Senate to "vote for America!" The nature of the bill and the nature of the opposition proved too much for him, and many good friends who would have voted for the St. Lawrence had it been brought before the Senate as a separate measure crossed over to vote it down. Later in the day, disappointed and sick at heart, he made a futile fight against the conference report on the flood-control bill on the ground that the Connecticut dam compromise endangered the West River Valley in Vermont. Austin, astounded, arose to argue with his colleague at some length, first patiently and then with some anger. "We talked this all over before the compromise was adopted," he said, "and I can't see why we are wasting all this time. I can't see the purpose of it." "I am trying to protect the state of Vermont," said Aiken. "And the inference is that I am not?" demanded Austin angrily. "No," said Aiken lamely, "but I want the Senate to know what it is doing." The West River Valley, he said, "means more to me than any other valley in America. The Senate doesn't know what it means to me." Finally Connally broke in sarcastically. "Does the Senator think he can kill the conference report?" he asked. "What does he want to do about it?" "I know I can't kill it," Aiken said, his voice trembling a little by then. "I just want the Senate to know what it is doing." He sat down, a New Englander beaten, and the conference report went through.

DECEMBER 13, 1944. Will Clayton returned today to face a barrage of questions from critical Senators which somehow did not add up to the searching examination that had been forecast. Bob La Follette attempted unsuccessfully to prove that the cotton firm of Anderson and Clayton traded with Germany and Japan after war broke out in Europe. By coming to the witness stand loaded down with secret documents the press was not permitted to see and showing them confidentially to Clayton, he did manage to elicit the admission that some subsidiaries might have had such dealings. But he never succeeded in tying Clayton to it. Claude Pepper's questions concerning Clayton's membership in the anti-Roosevelt Liberty League in 1936, somewhat irrelevant to the main issue, were summarily dismissed by the witness. He had joined at the request of a friend; subsequently he had allowed his membership to lapse. His tone indicated that he considered the whole matter rather unimportant in view of his four years of service in the Roosevelt Administration. John Bankhead, so blind to everything but cotton that he can only be termed a fanatic on the subject, took over the questioning for a time; a hot argument developed. Clayton reiterated his frequently stated view that there are two alternatives: either the South can go on producing a failing crop which the taxpayers of the nation must support with a government dole, or the government can encourage diversified farming in the South and gradually do away with subsidies and support prices. This enraged Bankhead, who made wild charges about "dumping in the foreign market," "throwing millions of people out of work," and so on. The attitude of mind so typical of the planters of the South, who love the millstone around their necks so much that they will drown rather than throw it off, was amply displayed by the senior Senator from Alabama. Confronted with it in its most indignant form, Clayton sounded patient and rather hopeless. This may affect a few votes, but the chances of his confirmation seem very good.

In the afternoon Archibald MacLeish came back, to be subjected to more needling by Bennett Champ Clark. The irascible Missourian, who spent the morning passing books of MacLeish's poetry among his colleagues with raucous snorts and chortles, challenged him with direct quotes in the afternoon session. MacLeish, a little better prepared for the sort of no-holds-barred rough-and-tumble at which B. C. excels than he was yesterday, squirmed occasionally but on the whole handled himself fairly well. "That's the trouble with being a poet," he said. "It lets you in for things like this." Citing Robert Browning's remark that when he was young only he and God knew what his poetry meant, while now only God knew, the dapper little man received the laughter of the audience, and with it was able to parry Bennett Champ with reasonable success. He too will probably be confirmed, although with the smallest vote of any.

On the floor the crop-insurance bill [*a hedge against agricultural disaster which, combined with wartime subsidies, led on ultimately to today's unmanageable farm program*], which was going to sail through without any trouble, ran into the usual Senatorial difficulties. Maybank tried to amend it with a rider to the effect that banks might absorb credit charges for purposes of exchange, and immediately a fight began that dragged on well into the afternoon. Elmer Thomas of Oklahoma, in charge of the bill, expressed the hope that a vote might be obtained before the end of the session, but Taft, confronted, as he remarked later, with the fact that "there weren't many Democrats around and I wasn't sure of those who were there. Harry Byrd wasn't on hand, and it just didn't seem safe," jumped up and informed the Senate that he intended to speak against the Maybank amendment and would like to have it go over to tomorrow. This was finally agreed to, but not before an exchange between Thomas and White. Thomas bemoaned the fact that "if this amendment goes over to tomorrow, Senators know what will happen. We will be swamped with telegrams demanding that we vote one way or another on it." "In view of our rather long experience in politics and political life," White said gently, "does the Senator think such telegrams will have very much influence on any of us?" Thomas smiled and admitted that they wouldn't.

DECEMBER 14, 1944. With Maybank's amendment beaten, the crop-insurance bill was passed today and the Senate began consideration of the Hurley–Heller nominations to the Surplus Property Board. As with the State Department nominees, these men have rather vague and fuzzy outlines. Hurley, a tall, hawk-faced, droop-eyed individual with a nervous manner, and Heller, a slight, dark man with a black mustache and a pleasant manner, are relatively unknown to the Senate. Consequently the debate proceeded along strictly political lines, a forecast of the way the vote is going to go when all is said and done. Austin led the fight against them, aided from time to time by Danaher and others on the Republican side. Sheridan Downey defended Heller with effective indignation, using more emphasis and vigor than he usually does.

DECEMBER 15, 1944. Foreign Relations, tying itself into knots over the nominations, met repeatedly today to cast its votes. All the nominees save MacLeish's to be an Assistant Secretary got safely by with a favorable recommendation. In the poet's case the vote stood 10–10, the recommendation unfavorable after the morning's meeting. [*The unsubstantiated off-the-record comment that he was "fuzzy-minded" seemed to sum up most of the opposition.*] Guffey voted against him, but later changed his mind and demanded another meeting to change his vote. Clark insisted that the committee must approve such an action. Another meeting was held, a vote taken: Guffey was denied the privilege. Late in the day Wagner, out of town, telephoned his vote and MacLeish was approved. Pepper is hinting about a resolution to send the names back to the President, and a Guffey–Pepper–Murray–La Follette filibuster seems to be in the making. The word "filibuster" is abhorrent to the gentlemen, but the fact is undeniable. Some of the most peculiar political line-ups ever are being organized to fight the "team" of jolly Big Ed Stettinius.

DECEMBER 16, 1944. Right down the party line the Democrats today confirmed Hurley and Heller. Only Ed Johnson, whose guts and integrity are never in question, voted his convictions on Hurley. It was the lone Democratic *no*. Hiram Johnson voted for both men, as did Langer, ever the maverick. Albert Hawkes crossed over to vote for Heller, although against Hurley; all the rest were strictly party. Just before the vote the brilliant Connecticut team put on its last performance. Maloney defending Hurley, Danaher denouncing him. Danaher, taking cognizance of his own position, began by remarking that "Since Nov. 7 I have deliberately refrained from making any statements on general government policy." It was the final appearance together of the two men who have for 6 years formed one of the best delegations any state has ever had in the Senate.

DECEMBER 17, 1944. Into the midst of the State Department fight has come the harsh reward for four years of sloppy diplomacy, personal intrigue and tin-horn politicking on a world-wide scale. The boys who are playing for keeps informed the United States, which apparently isn't, about the facts of life in Europe. To Stettinius' naïve condemnation of the British [*support of neo-fascist elements*] in Italy, Churchill and Bevan have given blunt reply: the policy was initialed by the President at Quebec. To the Polish government-in-exile, clinging desperately to its last shred of hope, Churchill and the Russians have given blunt rejection: it must be sacrificed, along with half of Poland and nearly all the honor of the Allies. It has been a rude awakening for the dreamy squires of Washington, who lived in a Never-Never Land of Let's Pretend for just a little too long.

The reaction has of course been just what might be expected: violent denunciations from New Deal Senators, I-told-you-sos from Wheeler and Reynolds and Nye, bewildered dismay from Austin and Ball and Burton. Of these three groups the most inconsistent and the most pathetically laughable, perhaps, are the people who have been arguing for months about "Russia's right to security and self-defense." Somehow they can't seem to take it when this is translated into cold power and all the fine rationalizations are stripped away—it seems too cruel a blow. With one  accord they have taken the out afforded them and have turned in savage rage upon the British, whose only crime has been to give Russia exactly what her apologists have been saying all along she should have. This tortuous reasoning, filled with a hysterical hatred and a desperate fear, might be rather amusing were it not so sad. How did they ever get so far away from moral principle? And will they ever get back? It seems unlikely.

Off in rainy Georgia the President sits relaxing from his cares. Soon he will return to us, and once again all will be well.

DECEMBER 18, 1944. The formal debate on confirmation of the State Department appointments began today amid threats from Pepper, Guffey, Murray and La Follette to launch their filibuster. Burt Wheeler, sitting in his chair and chuckling happily at the whole situation, arose from time to time to needle the Senator from Florida with an expert hand. He had differed often in the past with the Senator from Florida, Wheeler said, but one thing he would hand him: no man in the Senate knows sooner or more accurately what the policy of this Administration is to be in the field of foreign affairs. He would like to point out to the Senator from Florida that the Stettinius "team," selected by the President and dominated by him, would undoubtedly give the Senator from Florida exactly the foreign policy he wants. So why all the fuss? Furthermore, the President has a right to his own advisers, and if he wants advisers as incompetent as these, then he ought to be given them. He would not even vote, said Wheeler, momentarily forgetting the name, to reject MacNitch if the President wanted him. If the President thought MacNitch would be a suitable man, as well as all these others, then he, Wheeler, was prepared to vote for them. Even MacNitch had a right to be confirmed under these circumstances.

Pepper, on the spot and knowing it, indulged in the strange left-field reasoning people of his political persuasion go in for when the cold facts stare them in the face. He would be against these nominations, he declared stoutly, "if the President himself told me he was for them." Anyway, he knew the President could not be for them because they were "out of character with the President's appointments." (Out of character with which of the President's appointments, Wheeler demanded. Knudsen? Don Nelson? Charlie Wilson? Frank Knox? Henry Stimson? Stettinius?) Somebody—that black conservative leprechaun the liberals always credit with somehow speaking Roosevelt's words and doing Roosevelt's deeds—must have sent up the nominations, according to Claude, because it certainly wasn't the President. It just wasn't in character. He just knew it wasn't, and the skeptical and obvious smiles of his colleagues on both sides of the aisle did not deter him from saying so.

Hiram Johnson arose midway in the debate for one of his rare speeches. His voice is almost gone, and only stray fragments of a former thunder came to the galleries. It was a rambling little speech, very brief, about Greece and the fact that "weapons we furnished are being used to shoot men and women down like dogs." His colleagues sat in a circle around him and a straining silence settled on the Senate. He wished he still had strength, the Senator said, to talk with them about these problems; but he had not, and so would not be long. At the end of five minutes he sat down after a moving and rather pathetic little performance.

DECEMBER 19, 1944. The great revolt of Pepper, Guffey, Murray and La Follette collapsed with a gentle whoosh of wind today after a telephone conversation between the Senator from Florida and the Boss. Bob La Follette unapprised, started off the session by asking that the reading of yesterday's journal, usually dispensed with by unanimous consent, be reserved until later in the day "for other purposes." This favorite filibuster technique was overruled by Henry Wallace, who pointed out that the Senate was in executive session, not legislative, and consequently the journal need not be read at all. Before La Follette could do much about it Pepper got the floor and read the Senate his apologia: the President had assured him that even if the nominations should be sent back to him, he would resubmit the same names late in January, and he had promised to remove immediately any man on the team who did not carry out his policies explicitly. (Audible laughter, led by Wheeler and Vandenberg, rippled around the chamber on that one.) Consequently, Claude said, the Four Horsemen would abandon their intention to speak against the nominees but would reserve the right to vote against them. Bennett Champ Clark, who announced yesterday that he would support all the nominees in view of the people who were against them, couldn't let this awkward situation pass without applying the knife a little. In an acid exchange with Joe Guffey he said the whole thing reminded him of a famous King of France who "had an army of ten thousand men, marched them up the hill and marched them down again." Furthermore, said B. C., after the votes were counted, when the army was seen in its proper size there were only 7 men in it anyway. Guffey sputtered, but Clark, enjoying himself on his last day in the Senate, emerged victorious in the encounter. Tom Connally made a number of enemies during the day, challenging McKellar, attempting to interrupt Langer (who simply buried him under a roaring torrent of sound), fussing at Chandler, and generally acting prickly and undiplomatic. Perhaps disgusted, like so many others, with the trend of events abroad, the man who will need all the friends he can get to push the Dumbarton Oaks agreement through successfully did very little to win friends today. His whole strategy during the fight, in fact, has been such as to place him in the position of battling with the Senate instead of leading it along. He has emerged from the contest definitely weakened, and by that much has the treaty itself been weakened.

When the roll call came all the nominees were confirmed by safe, and in some cases handsome, majorities. Guffey, Pepper and Murray voted against everyone but MacLeish; Bob La Follette voted against them all. Bennett Champ Clark, perverse to the end, cast his vote for Archibald MacLeish and all the others. The State Department fight, leaving many scars that will become apparent later in the peace debates, was over.

The session then dragged on until 8:22 P.M. as Jim Mead attempted to secure passage of a bill to raise the basic salary scale of postal employees $400. The raise is logical—they haven't had a basic increase since 1925—but Josiah Bailey, piqued and disappointed because the Senate would not yield on the Rivers and Harbors bill, proceeded to talk it to death. The House insisted in conference upon an amendment to Rivers and Harbors that would suspend Bureau of Reclamation laws limiting to 160 acres the amount of land which could be irrigated with water from California's Central Valley Project; the Senate wanted to strike it out. Bailey asked the Senate to yield, the Senate refused; the $500,000,000 bill died with the 78th Congress, much to Bailey's disgust. All the long battle, the hearings, the St. Lawrence controversy went for nothing. It will all have to be done over again next year. The good Josiah could be seen almost visibly determining to raise hell in reprisal. He launched into his indignant oratory and in no time was threatening the nation with inflation and loss of the war if the postal employees were granted the extra $400. Jim Mead, arguing with some skill and his rather dry humor, deprecated these terrible consequences and expressed his great concern for the postal clerks. Other Senators hopped up from time to time to state their profound approval of the measure; Josiah Bailey argued on. Somewhere during the course of it Barkley got through the customary formal joint resolution adjourning the 78th Congress *sine die* and sent it to the House, which promptly passed it and departed. Stocky little white-haired Jim Davis made the final swan-song speech of the day, following Gerald Nye and Bob Reynolds. John Danaher began moving about the floor on one of the hardest missions a defeated man can have, saying good-by to those who will go on without him. Time passed, the attendance, over 60 during the State Department voting, began to dwindle into the 40s. Josiah talked on. Finally he made the parliamentary point of order that the postal bill was brought in on the legislative day of December 14. The Senate was still in the legislative day of December 14, Bailey said, since the legislative day does not change unless the Senate adjourns between sessions. It had not adjourned since December 14, only recessed. Under the rules a bill must lie over one legislative day before it can be acted upon: consequently the bill could not be acted upon. A parliamentary argument at once developed. Finally Connally in the chair ruled that Josiah Bailey was probably right. Jim Mead began an appeal to the Senate to override the ruling. Further controversy loomed. Determined to have the last word, Clark jumped up. "Mr. President," he said, "I suggest the absence of a quorum." The Clerk called the roll. Thirty-eight Senators answered to their names; a quorum was not present. Barkley moved that the Senate adjourn *sine die*.

In an entirely typical fashion, after a parliamentary wrangle, in a bad humor, and on a point of no quorum raised by Bennett Champ Clark, the 78th Congress of the United States of America passed into history.

25

"THEY'RE SICK AT HEART, THAT'S WHAT THEY ARE"

DECEMBER 20, 1944. Today Joe Ball and Burt Wheeler agreed. The agreement made a good story and served to bring to light a situation of desperate seriousness which is developing in the Senate.

Wheeler told us: "It would be pointless for the President to send the Dumbarton Oaks proposals to the Senate unless Britain and Russia changed their present policies in Europe."

And Joe Ball, murmuring, "For once I agree with Mr. Wheeler," remarked: "If the present trend of unilateral decisions by the Allied nations in the liberated areas of Europe continues, it may do irreparable damage to the principles of international collaboration set forth in the Dumbarton Oaks proposals."

"You know what the matter is, don't you?" Wheeler said. "These internationalists who brought in this damned thing, and have been pushing it all the time, they're sick at heart, that's what they are, they're sick at heart. Why, damn it, they're stuck and they know it."

"I don't want to blame anybody," said Joe Ball cautiously, "but things can't go on like this and get anywhere."

The tragedy of it is not that the consistency of men like Wheeler is being justified by events, but that the earnest idealism of men like Joe Ball, who had such hope and wanted to do so much, is being mocked so cruelly by the very policies they have done so much to support. They deserve so much better than that, and so did the world. They are beginning to realize that it is not to be.

DECEMBER 21, 1944. Pepper is expressing some wistful ambitions these days. It seems that the liberal bloc which opposed the State Department nominations is going to remain organized and consult with the President regularly on policy. This will prevent such sad incidents as the conserva-

tive Stettinius "team," they hope, and the President's conservative leprechaun will not be able to take the functions of his office right away from
him in that embarrassing fashion. Included in this plan are Pepper,
Guffey, Murray and Kilgore; there may be others, they hope. Meanwhile,
the man they are going to advise and consult has put them neatly in their
places with nasty finality. What did he say to Claude Pepper that made
him drop his filibuster? he asked his press conference. For the life of
him, he couldn't remember. He didn't know what he said that caused
Claude to react that way. It was a puzzle to him. Undaunted, the Four
Horsemen are out to get that leprechaun.

Three and one-half Horsemen, it might perhaps be more accurately
stated. "Of course you know," says Joe Guffey with his sardonic and
ironic humor, "that I'm not really a liberal. I didn't really become a liberal
until I joined in the State Department fight. Before that they thought I
was a boss from Pennsylvania. But I'm really holy now."

DECEMBER 22, 1944. White, Vandenberg, Taft and Wherry, and four
GOP leaders from the House conferred yesterday with Dewey in New
York. The meeting was general, explosive, and not very satisfactory to the
Senator from Nebraska. "The only way we can hope to win is to get a
full-time chairman and a full-time organization and work like hell from
the top level to the grass roots, starting right now," he told us, striding
up and down behind his desk and banging out his words as he always
does. "I really told 'em, boy, I laid it into 'em." It had not, however, done
much good. "I tell you, I was sick. Brownell's going to stay on as chairman
and Dewey's going to be the candidate in 1948. The whole psychology of
defeat is going to keep right on with that set-up, and it's going to be a part-
time proposition. We've got to get the organization working, it's the only
way we can do it. You should have heard 'em talk. Oh, they thought I
had a fine idea; oh, sure. And then they're going right along the way
they've always gone. And we just can't win that way."

To Wallace White, however, it was "a satisfactory discussion"; to Taft,
"a stimulating exchange of ideas, showing a cooperative spirit on the
part of Mr. Dewey." Vandenberg's sentiments, undivulged, were presumably much the same. "We've got to get rid of the Old Guard!" cried Ken
Wherry hopelessly, knowing it can't be done.

DECEMBER 23, 1944. Carl Hatch and Joe Ball made the trek to Mecca
today, at their own request. After an hour-long conference with the
President they returned to the Hill to face the press. Their words were
circumspect, their attitude amiable, but beneath the surface could be
sensed a glum discontent. They had gone down the Avenue hoping for

enlightenment and encouragement. The enlightenment they got was very evidently not encouraging.

What did they talk about? "The whole international picture." Were they satisfied with what they got? What *did* they get? "We got information—period," said Joe Ball. Information about what? "Information about the President's views on foreign policy." Did the views coincide with theirs? "No comment," said Joe Ball. Couldn't they tell us anything? There followed a hurried, whispered conclave on the other side of the desk, while we strained our ears in attentive silence trying to overhear it. A formal statement was drawn up, edited, and given us. After conferring with the President they were "more convinced than ever" of the need for the immediate formation of an international organization. The United States "must make immediate efforts" to solve the problems facing it in the foreign field. Did the imperative not indicate dissatisfaction, and who "must" take the necessary steps? "Obviously, of course," said Carl Hatch, "the President has the chief responsibility. But the Senate," he added hastily, "must ratify it when completed." Did Joe Ball care to add anything to his warning about the fate of Dumbarton Oaks? "I have nothing to add to my statement on Dumbarton Oaks." "They're heart-sick," said Burt Wheeler, "that's what they are, they're heart-sick." It was the consensus of the press that the description, or something very near to it, fitted very adequately the senior Senator from New Mexico and the junior Senator from Minnesota after their conference with the President of the United States.

DECEMBER 24, 1944. In these hard days, when the Germans are on the offensive in Belgium and America's foreign policy is going to hell in a fast freight, it is reassuring to turn to the press releases of the Honorable Alexander Wiley, a Senator from the state of Wisconsin. There is to be found in these a quality like nothing else on heaven or earth. The latest, delivered to the Press Gallery yesterday (there will be another today) is a case in point. It is headlined WILEY QUESTIONS 'ERSATZ NEW DEAL' ON PLANS FOR ERSATZ CHRISTMAS DIETS IN FUTURE, and it runs in part:

> Senator Alexander Wiley (R., Wisc.), today publicly addressed a question to all New Dealers whether they are deliberately planning for ersatz Christmas diets and all-year diets in the future such as we are having in 1944.
>
> The newly re-elected Senator from the Badger State called attention to the absence, particularly evident at Christmas, of many traditional and natural American delicacies, such as butter, from the kitchen table. He asked "in the name of Christmas honesty" that the

New Deal, "which is nothing but an ersatz imitation of European socialism," "come clean" on plans to maintain a perpetual scarcity in natural foods and accustom American palates to synthetics such as oleomargerine.

Senator Wiley voiced the fear of the American farmer that the home market is being "progressively destroyed for vital and pure items of nourishment by their officially-fostered replacement with artificial and cheap imitations."

"Is the New Deal, with Nazi-like stealth, planning to complete such destruction of the home market, by employing high-sounding but wretched excuses now and after the war?" the Senator asked. . . .

[Senator Wiley] served warning that he will be on the lookout for underhanded schemes to drive from the American table, now or at any time in the future, the natural dairy and other foods beloved by all generations.

This is the unique spirit just re-elected by an overwhelming majority by the state which rejected Willkie and has for 20 years maintained the excellent La Follette in the Senate. Evidently Alec, with his war on oleo and his appeal for butter, has found the key to all these puzzling contradictions.

DECEMBER 25, 1944. Not since Bataan and Corregidor has there been such cold comfort for a cold Christmas. Americans are retreating again, this time in the "Bulge" in Europe, and the future is dark and overshadowed. The President has gone to Hyde Park to read *A Christmas Carol*, while most of the House and some of the Senate has departed for home. The Atlantic Charter, an airy myth dismissed at last by its light-hearted creator, no longer clutters the pathways of realistic diplomacy, and the peace of swords is casting its intimations on the earth. Everywhere is good will toward men who are undismayed by conscience or principle, and in the holy temples of government the deaths of unimportant millions are being assessed for purposes they never knew.

DECEMBER 26, 1944. From three fine men on this day after Christmas come three significant statements.

"We must have a determination to create conditions which will postpone as far as possible another war," says Warren Austin, his eyes dark with worry, his mind far away, unable to concentrate for long as he thinks of his son fighting in the black night of Belgium.

"I'm not ready to lie down and quit yet," says Carl Hatch, with a defiance that sounds hopeless already.

"If I can't accomplish anything else," says Joe Ball grimly, "at least I can get up on my hind legs and say what I think."

The Warren Austin who six months ago would have called for the determination to make another war impossible, now hopes only to postpone it. The Carl Hatch who would not before have admitted the possibility of lying down and quitting admits it now. The Joe Ball who once hoped to do so much more will be happy now to do "the least" he can, since it seems that perhaps he "can't accomplish anything else."

All through the Senate doubt and disillusion are beginning to come to the surface. It is saddest and most disturbing among the men who have done their best to persuade the Senate to take a strong and constructive stand, for there are no finer men than these, and none have worked harder or more earnestly at the task. Even before the issue is joined, however, they have begun to lose the battle. Events and men have conspired against them, and against the great majority of their colleagues who were really convinced, for a while, that maybe this time they should give it a try. Faced with the revival of power politics in Europe, faced with a vacillating acquiescence in the White House, the Senate has begun to go back home to the suspicious isolation it has known so long. Only a miracle can save Dumbarton Oaks now. And no miracle is in sight in any sector.

DECEMBER 27, 1944. Wayne Morse of Oregon arrived today, a spare, trim man with heavy black eyebrows, a black mustache, a keen expression and a tendency to twinkle as he talks. He went over big with the press, which has high hopes for him in the Senate. On the basis of first acquaintance, at least, it does not seem likely that he will disappoint them.

The new Senator, former dean of the University of Oregon law school and former public member of the War Labor Board, talked of his campaign and of labor and of his views on foreign policy with a forthright and humorous frankness. Midway in the campaign, he admitted, he was sure he was licked; he still seemed surprised that he led the ticket. As for labor, "it seems to me vital to the Republican Party that it adopt a progressive labor policy. And I do sincerely believe that collective bargaining can operate better under our party than it can under the sort of thing I've seen here in Washington under this administration." He is proud of the fact that all labor groups in Oregon supported him, "but I made it clear in the campaign that I did not solicit their support, and that I would not consider myself bound to do more than give labor a fair deal according to my conception of the best interests of the country." On foreign policy, "No one has the blueprint yet, but the objectives of the Dumbarton Oaks agreement come closest to it. We mustn't let our tendency to exaggerate details aid the development of doubts and cynicisms because of the revival of power politics in Europe." As for committee assignments, "I applied for Foreign Relations, which I know I haven't a hope of getting, for Education and Labor and for Agriculture. I don't much care where they put me, though. There's a job to be done wherever it is." What he wants to do, he said, is maintain a "flexible" attitude toward social change. "Americans are so used to thinking of things in terms of static situations. But social relationships aren't static; they're flexible. That's the way we've got to meet them here." There is a sense of fairness, intelligence and liberal moderation about the new man from Oregon which promises very well for his state, the Senate and the nation. Barring some unforeseen mistake in policy, he should become established as a national leader in a very short time. And he seems far too steady to make any such mistake.

Wallace White today joined the men who warn the President. "If this diplomatic discord isn't cleared up right away," he said, "it seems to me there may be a considerable delay in considering the Dumbarton Oaks proposal." And the delay, he indicated, may well mean complete defeat.

DECEMBER 28, 1944. Committee assignments, the principal plums of a new Congress, are being much sought after these days. Five vacancies are open on Foreign Relations, three for the Democrats, two for the Republicans. Styles Bridges, ill and absent in recent months, has first priority on one Republican seat. Taft, logical choice for the other, has turned it down, preferring to remain on Finance and Banking and Currency where his statistical mind can be employed to best advantage. That leaves a field of equal-ranking members that seems to be narrowing down to stocky, silent little Chan Gurney and the exuberant Wiley. There seems a fair chance that Wiley may get it. Among the Democrats

McKellar would like one seat, and Wheeler thinks he would like to have one of the others. Hatch and Hill, far down the list in seniority, and Fulbright, knowing he hasn't a chance, have made the gesture of applying.

In all these selections, of course, seniority prevails. The institution comes in for much bitter criticism by people outside the Senate, but a moment's thought reveals the reason for it. It is all very well to say, Elect your chairman, elect your committee members: that sounds easy. Apply it to 96 men, however, who have to live and work together on the nation's business day after day, month after month, year after year, and it is not so simple. The vote-trading, the intense bitterness and jealousy, the harmful effect on future legislation of the animosities and the deals of selection-time—they would prove a very real detriment to sound democracy. The same thing, to a lesser but nonetheless imperative degree, applies to the House. The institutions just aren't large enough to do it successfully any other way. These aren't machines, they're men; and the method of seniority, accepted and acknowledged and deferred to in the automatic tradition of 160 years, is one of the necessary mechanisms of their getting along together. Its results are not always what people outside the Congress would wish (or people inside either), but as long as they are accepted peaceably by the members, seniority has served a worthy purpose.

DECEMBER 30, 1944. One of the supreme strategists of the Senate—the Honorable B. K. Wheeler of Montana—has stepped in neatly and cut the ground out from under nearly everybody. A shrewder piece of timing has not recently been recorded.

It comes in the form of a resolution he will introduce next Wednesday. It reaffirms the Atlantic Charter, which of course embarrasses the President. It demands the immediate creation of a United Nations council, which of course steals the thunder of the Ball–Hatch crowd. It proposes the adoption of a universal bill of rights, which of course entraps the liberals. And it calls for the creation of a general federation of European nations, which of course emphasizes once more the Senator's own pet solution for the ills of mankind.

The internationalist group, caught flat-footed, have refused to comment —as well they might. The shrewd old fighter has them exactly where he wants them. Of course they don't dare attack the Atlantic Charter, because the American people wouldn't stand for that. Of course they can't challenge the immediate creation of a United Nations council, for it is exactly what they have been calling for. Of course they can't condemn the universal bill of rights, or the United States of Europe, for both are reasonable aspirations of the world. All they can do, in fact, is gulp and gag and swallow it down.

The Senator's motives in this seem to be compounded in about equal parts of strategy and sincerity. He does believe in a United States of Europe, and the other things would be nice if they could be attained. To demand them at the moment, however, is simply to embarrass the President and throw a bombshell into the enemy camp. Idealism coincides neatly with political warfare, and Burton K., the old campaigner, has once more proved that he can give lessons any day to the idealistic Ball, the hopeful Hatch, the earnest and kindly Austin.

DECEMBER 31, 1944. Ed Johnson, staring thoughtfully into space and contemplating the future, added his warning to the rest this afternoon. "The present political maneuvering of the Big Three is casting a shadow on Dumbarton Oaks," he said. "I am convinced that there is a strong sentiment in the Senate for some kind of a world security plan and organization. However, any selfish finagling by any of the Big Three can spoil everything. Sentiment in the Senate can change overnight." He stated the picture as he saw it, and it was as black as all the rest of us see it. Then he sighed. "You know," he said with thoughtful grimness, "we're in for one hell of a damned bad time."

26

NEWCOMERS

JANUARY 1, 1945. Jimmy Byrnes, reacting in the only way Washington knows to disaster, has come forth with stern threats to the home front. Harsh measures are under way to atone for the high command's failure in the Bulge. Race horses won't be allowed to run, and a few other drastic things will be done. Warren Austin, questioned, says with exasperation that he will reintroduce national service legislation if there is a real need for it, but adds with asperity that "I'm not introducing legislation just for the sake of introducing legislation." Over in the House shaggy Joe Martin says the Republicans will view with some alarm any Administration attempt to rush through compulsory military training. The Roosevelt Administration's apparent answer to the problems of peace—the military state—is being received rather roughly in its first, tentative stages.

JANUARY 2, 1945. A newcomer from the House, Warren Magnuson of Washington, 39, short, stocky and blond, thinks the United States ought to acquire naval bases in the Pacific. He's going to get up and speak his mind in the Senate if he doesn't see a peace parley shaping up that will permit it, he says. We have the paramount responsibility in the Pacific, and we've got to maintain peace there. Also, upon our trade with the Pacific will depend those 60,000,000 jobs. Also, if we don't get there first Russia will. Dumbarton Oaks is a good blueprint, but it had better give us those bases in the Pacific or the Senator will be heard from. On domestic issues he will vote "liberal," but "not automatically. There, too, local conditions must be taken into account, the broad general picture." Bachelor veteran of four years in the House, he has a sensible approach and a manner that goes with his inevitable cigar.

Clyde Hoey of North Carolina, successor to the one and only Reynolds, is 67, tall, bent, with a crumpled face like a kindly rag doll and the same cutaway coat, bow tie and flowing hair affected by Tom Connally. A sensible man of quiet and obvious ability, he intends to follow a moderate middle line on domestic policy, work for world cooperation in the international field. Modest in attitude and businesslike in manner, he comes like a breath of cool air after the effulgent blast of his dapper predecessor.

Barkley is back, his infected eye still troubling him a good deal but otherwise ready to tackle the headaches of a highly controversial session. The legislative conference with the President this morning produced little of note, he said. The President did not tip them off on what he wants done, or when he plans to get together with Churchill and Stalin. "It was just a friendly talk," the Majority Leader said, like so many others. The annual message will come up Saturday, to be read by the Clerk of the House at the joint session which will count the electoral vote. This week will be given over to organization in both houses, and the trend of legislative development will probably not become clear until some time after inauguration.

Harry Truman, homespun as ever, chuckled about the conference. "I can't tell you much about it," he said. "After all, I was just there as an onlooker. The Vice-President was there, and Barkley and the House leaders. There wasn't much for a junior Senator to do." "This is the meeting where we haze Harry," the President had said; and, well, when the President wants to haze somebody there isn't much you can do. "Anyway," he remarked with a laugh, "you know how it is when you go to see the President. He does all the talking, and he talks about what he wants to talk about, and he never talks about anything you want to talk about, so there isn't much you can do." As for what will be in the annual message, "I don't know, and that's the truth. I didn't ask him because I knew you'd ask me, and if I didn't know I could tell you I didn't know and I wouldn't be lying." The new V.P., unchanged by fame and glory and the Damocles sword above his head, remains the same shrewd judge of people he has always been.

JANUARY 3, 1945. The 79th Congress began today at 12 noon. In the Senate the galleries were full and most of the members were on the floor. The hum and chatter and buzz of a full house echoed through the chamber. Newcomers, shepherded by their colleagues, moved about shaking hands and getting acquainted. Glen Taylor, the singing cowboy from Idaho, appeared in a dark business suit, looking youthful and Western with a long, broad, big-boned face. Several Senators who have been absent for months, among them the ebullient Tobey, returned amid lusty handshakings and backslappings. Men who parted two weeks ago with an expression that indicated poison at the least greeted one another like long-lost brothers. Such hearty conviviality has not been seen on the Senate floor for some time. It won't be seen again for some time, either.

Presently Henry Wallace rapped for order and called for the new Senators. Four by four, each on the arm of his colleague, they came to the desk and were sworn in. The tall, white-haired John Moses, victor over Gerald Nye, was there; stocky, dark-haired Brien McMahon of Connecticut, on the arm of Theodore Francis Green, who rose later to explain that Maloney was ill in Connecticut and could not be present to do the honors; chubby Homer Capehart of Indiana; the keen and capable Oregon team, Wayne Morse and Guy Cordon; Olin Johnston of South Carolina, a big, lumpy man with a young-looking face. Along with the newcomers came the re-elected veterans, Barkley and George and Claude Pepper, Elmer and Elbert Thomas, the carefree Wiley, making some hearty wisecrack to Vandenberg as he came down the aisle on Bob La Follette's arm. Off on the edge of the floor, bowing and exclaiming and effusive, Bob Reynolds exercised his prerogative as an ex-Senator to lend to the proceedings the note which only he can give.

With the swearing-in completed, Barkley moved the traditional quorum call. A quorum was found to be present, and he introduced the traditional resolution calling for the appointment of two Senators to join with two House members to wait upon the President of the United States and inform him that the Congress is in session and ready to receive any messages he may wish to transmit. While Barkley and White were absent on this errand, Lister Hill arose to introduce the traditional resolution informing the House that the Senate is in session and ready to do business. Barkley and White returned after five minutes on the telephone in the Democratic cloakroom to inform the Senate that they had waited upon the President "with dispatch." "He told us he was glad Congress was back in session," Barkley said, a statement greeted with a flicker of amusement throughout the chamber. Theodore Francis Green arose and introduced the traditional resolution providing for a joint meeting of the House and Senate to count the electoral vote and certify to the election of a President and a Vice-President. Barkley moved recess until Saturday, and at 12:45 the first meeting of the 79th Senate came to an end after proving once again that perhaps the greatest thrill and the greatest strength of democracy is simply the matter-of-fact habit of it.

Over in the House things were not so nice and decorous. The atmosphere of sweet harmony induced by the speeches of Martin and Sam Rayburn was rudely shattered by the most powerful man in the other branch. John Rankin, the master demagogue, the master parliamentarian, the man no wise observer ever underestimates, wrote the House Un-American Activities Committee into law as a permanent standing committee of the House. He did it by proposing an amendment to the rules of the House, a tactic Majority Leader McCormack cried out against as

The beginning of
The 79th Congress

"breaking the precedent of 150 years." On a division, or standing vote, a fast count showed Rankin beaten. He demanded the Yeas and Nays. The Clerk called the roll. 207–186, with nearly the full membership of that brave new liberal Congress of the Democrats' voting, the committee was confirmed and the Administration had received its first defeat at the hands of the 79th Congress.

JANUARY 4, 1945. John Moses of North Dakota, a man with a personality which hits one with an almost physical impact, is 6 feet 4 inches tall, medium thin, with a keen, sharp-featured face that begins with a small chin and a small, rather severe mouth and then flares out broadly at the top to include large eyes made even larger by very thick glasses, white, thinning hair, and the most fabulous eyebrows since John L. Lewis, a good inch in width and shaggy in proportion. The Senator speaks with just enough Scandinavian accent to betray his Norwegian birth, has a habit of turning his head up and away from you as he speaks and then turning suddenly and peering down sharply at you from among the eyebrows by way of emphasis. It is no wonder that North Dakota has elected him governor three times and it is only surprising that he has not entered the national picture sooner.

"You ask me what I think of a Missouri Valley Authority?" he said bluntly. "Well, I'm for it. But it seems to me that for Congress to attempt to pass an MVA bill at the present time is premature. What we should have is a complete survey of the Valley's needs by a board of experts supported by a Congressional appropriation. It shouldn't be a study to support one particular point of view; it should be a study to get the facts. The problem isn't a simple one of just transplanting TVA to the Missouri Valley, good as TVA is. The Missouri Valley's problems are too vast and complex for that. We have plenty of time, anyway. There won't be a shovel turn on it until after the war, and that's a good three years away. We can afford to find out what we're doing." Would he introduce the legislation for the survey himself? "No. No. Say I'm working on it—say I'm working on it. I've seen too many of these stories about new Senators and new Representatives coming down here and telling the world what they're going to do. Frankly I'm damned sick and tired of it. Just say I'm working on it." Something new in the Senate has definitely been added by North Dakota.

JANUARY 5, 1945. Glen Taylor, more than a little awed by his newfound eminence, yet determined to conceal it with the facility acquired from years in what he terms "the theatrical profession," remarked today with a pleasant but rather worried smile that he was "afraid maybe some of the others might be a little offended by my publicity." He didn't mind wisecracks, he said, he more or less had to expect them, but "Senate Sinatra" seemed a little strong. (The title was acquired rather inadvertently when he and his family appeared on the Capitol steps to sing, "Oh, give us a home near the Capitol dome," in the hope of breaking down some Washington landlord's resistance. The photographers made the most of it.) If we wanted to make wisecracks, well, he supposed that was our privilege, but if we could go a little easy just at first, he'd appreciate it. We said we would. "I'm not going to stick my neck out for a while," he assured us. "I'm down here to learn and find out what this is all about.... You boys keep an eye on me," he added earnestly. "You'll see me listening to everything that goes on. I'm not going to read newspapers and carry on private conversations on the floor. I'm going to listen to everything." We murmured tactfully that this was a fine ambition, but that he would soon find himself acquiring the knack of listening to routine matters with half an ear while tending to the daily social and political business of the floor. "Well, I don't know," he said. "I'm going to try it and see. I suppose a lot of it is just for the *Record* anyway." "Not so much as it is in the House," we assured him. "Well, you drop in and see me anytime," he told us. "When nobody else'll talk to you, I will. We're just common folks here, and we're glad to see you."

JANUARY 6, 1945. The Senate assembled and marched in a body to the House today for the joint session to count the electoral ballots and hear the President's message. The hosts dutifully vacated the first two rows of seats and turned them over to the Senators for the occasion. Henry Wallace and Sam Rayburn sat side by side on the Speaker's platform. Theodore Francis Green and Warren Austin served as tellers for the Senate, Gene Worley and shrewd little Ralph Gamble of New York as tellers for the House. "The duly elected electors of the state of So-and-So having cast their votes," one of the tellers would intone, "it appears that Franklin Delano Roosevelt (or Thomas E. Dewey) has received so many votes for President, and Harry S. Truman (or John W. Bricker) so many votes for Vice-President." After the roll of the states had been called, Wallace read the formal phraseology which declares that opening of the ballots in the presence of a joint session of Congress shall be deemed a sufficient certification of election, and the triumph of Franklin Roosevelt was official. Scattered applause greeted the votes of the individual states.

Following that the 8000-word message was read by the Clerk. A rather lifeless affair, somehow, and one that bored rather than inspired the Congress to which it was addressed. The one thing that could have salvaged it—the presence of the star performer—was lacking. Consequently members listened with wandering attention as the Clerk read on, unable to escape the feeling that if the Boss didn't feel it was sufficiently worthwhile to warrant his coming up, then they couldn't really regard it as so very important either. This was an unfortunate but inevitable effect of the rather remote and offhand manner in which the statement on the State of the Union was passed off on the Reading Clerk of the House.

JANUARY 7, 1945. Congressional reaction to the President's speech is not too good. Warren Austin, who has learned his lesson, remarks testily that he will certainly not reintroduce his national service bill unless there is "a real effort" on the part of the White House to back him up. Over in the House Jim Wadsworth of New York says the same, having grown tired of running the ball without the help of the rest of the team. Bailey and Brewster have put in their "4-F work-or-fight" bill again, a measure which is given slightly more chance of passage than it had in the last Congress. Editorialists are already expressing dismay at these evidences that the President's call for universal service is falling on deaf ears. The explanations are of course simple: hardly anyone in Congress trusts Franklin Roosevelt with the enormous power envisaged in national service. Furthermore, hardly anyone in Congress, confronted with the welter of inefficient administration downtown, can quite believe that to subject the whole nation instead of just a part of it to that sort of thing would in any way contribute to the winning of the war. And, finally, there is little enough evidence to show that the armed services, which have made such inefficient use of untold thousands of men and women already subject to their disciplines, would do any better if confronted with the task of assigning civilians as well. The whole thing, in short, just doesn't ring true.

On the score of foreign policy the message has fallen equally flat. The President's call for compromise and his attack on "perfectionism"—an apparent step to prepare the country for the compromises he is going to have to accept at the next Big Three meeting—soured the idealists, confirmed the isolationists, and disturbed the middle-of-the-roaders. The official outlook was optimistic, all right, but there was nothing specific to back it up. Certainly the White House is doing nothing to counteract the growing disillusionment and uncertainty on the Hill.

JANUARY 8, 1945. J. William Fulbright of Arkansas, 39, is a trim little fellow with an amiable face, little eyes and a little mouth that crinkles up when he smiles, and a great deal of charm of which he is not, perhaps understandably, entirely unaware. A former Rhodes scholar and president of the University of Arkansas, he has every claim to the brains he exhibits, and the impression he makes on the press is uniformly good.

He talked with us for a long time this morning, about foreign policy and politics and the ticklish technique of a new man's baptism in the Senate. As a veteran of the House, however, he showed the same disregard as Magnuson for the tradition that new Senators should be seen and not heard: he was willing to be quoted. The President said, he pointed out, that United States foreign policy is being carried forward in a manner which is "vigorous and forthright." "It doesn't seem that way to me," he told us. "It was 16 months ago that the House passed the (Fulbright) peace resolution, and nothing has been done. That hardly seems vigorous and forthright to me." Blunders of inaction, rather than blunders of action, are at the root of the trouble, he said. "We just aren't doing anything. Delay and delay and more delay. No wonder disillusionment is beginning to crop up in the Senate." Burt Wheeler, who carried his crusade once again to the American people in a shrewd radio address Friday night, is "a very clever man; very clever, very shrewd. He knows how to appeal to people. He may be able to get some support here." The need for a world organization now is imperative: "Details don't matter so much once we get it set up and operating. The important thing is to get us into it, to let the world know that we will stay in it, to get it functioning. Of course we may have to accept compromises, but that's inevitable. Providing they are compromises we all understand, it will be all right. The main thing is to get everybody around a table working it out. Then if we have to take compromise, well, it will be just like it is in Congress. If something comes up you don't like, you vote against it, but if you're beaten on the vote, well, you accept it as the best available compromise, knowing that it's been reached democratically and in an orderly fashion. That same principle could be applied in international affairs, and will be if we get the organization set up. But there's too much delay. It's got to move faster than this."

Tom Connally, in a bad humor and looking forward without eagerness to the foreign-policy debate which is expected to break on Wednesday, seemed glum and rather petulant when we saw him later. No, he wouldn't comment; he had his hands full and he wasn't talkin'. The present mood of the Foreign Relations chairman seems to vacillate between angry disgust and moody pessimism. Officially, of course, everything's "goin' along all right."

At 3 P.M. Leverett Saltonstall arrived, a fellow so nice and instantly likable that everybody succumbs to his charm immediately. It is a quiet charm, rather elusive, compounded of friendliness and unobtrusive humor and quality, which no substitute can quite approximate, and he has it in overwhelming measure. Tall as they have described him, pink-cheeked, lantern-jawed, buck-toothed, droop-eyed, one of the plainest men imaginable, he walked into his office rather shyly, shook hands with his secretaries and the press, and the place was his. He has that effect.

He said he wasn't sayin' much—just goin' to listen and learn for a while. He opened the windows and let in a big draft of cold air, which made him feel at home; he poked a few buzzers experimentally and found out how to call his staff; he chatted about his family and his housing problems. He said he had been concerned mainly with local problems, didn't want to say anything on the national picture yet. He was glad to be coming down at the start of such an interesting session. "Some very difficult things to vote on. I hope I have a friend left in the Senate at the end of two years." We talked along for a little longer, not a very consequential conversation, not any real news. Just Leverett Saltonstall. For the present, at least, it seemed enough.

JANUARY 9, 1945. The Democratic Steering Committee, in a deliberate slap at the Republicans, who asked for it and deserved it, has named three strong internationalists to the vacancies on Foreign Relations. Carl Hatch, Lister Hill and Scott Lucas were elected on open votes which tossed seniority out the window. The Republicans had laid themselves wide open by naming Wiley, with his reputation for conservative isolationism, and the chance was too good to miss. Add to that the ability and general liberalism of at least two of the selections, and the decision was inevitable. The defiant gesture of the Republicans seems increasingly short-sighted and stupid as time goes by.

JANUARY 10, 1945. The foreign-policy discussion did not turn into much of a debate today, but it did serve as the framework for a very fine and statesmanlike speech by Vandenberg. The former isolationist, who has made a completely sincere and earnest—and successful—attempt to see the other side of the question, spoke on a high level of nonpartisanship and constructive suggestion. He expressed the fears and the doubts of the Senate and the American people concerning power politics in Europe; he expressed the shocked surprise of the nation at the President's blithe dismissal of the Atlantic Charter. Then he became more specific. Three things should be done, he said: an immediate permanent military alliance of the Allies should be formed against Germany and Japan—Dumbarton Oaks should be completed and ratified at the earliest possible moment— the President should be given the right, within the framework of the military alliance against Germany and Japan, to use American troops to prevent aggression without referring the matter back to Congress. This placed the Republicans' most powerful spokesman on foreign affairs far out in front of both his own party and the leader of the opposition. It augured well for the future of the peace treaty providing it can be sent up soon, providing present developments in Europe take a turn for the better, and providing the President accepts the invitation for a little constructive leadership. All three factors seem at the moment remote.

Following Vandenberg's address, Ferguson rose to make a briefer, almost equally able statement along the same lines, and propose a resolution for the immediate formation of a United Nations political council. He did not formally introduce it, preferring, he said, to consult with other Senators before doing so, but he is working on it, apparently as a countermove to Burt Wheeler. From the Democratic side, significantly, has come no such concerted attempt to maintain American principles and ideals in the past few days. It is the Republicans who are making the suggestions and fighting the fight at the moment. Or perhaps more correctly, it is the Republicans from Michigan.

Up to the Hill from the White House came a placating little message today. There seemed to be some concern over the proposed oil treaty, the President said. Some people were afraid it would prove to be detrimental to the petroleum industry. In order to correct such unfortunate impressions, would the Senate return the treaty to him so that the matter might be ironed out with the British and a new draft prepared? The Senate would.

JANUARY 11, 1945. Asked about his plans for his United Nations resolution today, Ferguson smiled. "I'm working on it," he said. "I've been talking to other Senators about it. The newcomers had a meeting today and I even went down and talked to them and gave them copies of it. It's the first time I've really campaigned for anything in the Senate. But I want above all to get this thing settled in the right way. The thing I don't want to see is for a treaty to be all drawn up and completed and come up here, and then have somebody say 'I won't vote for this because I don't like the position of this period, this semicolon ought to be somewhere else, why isn't this comma changed?' That's what we got into in 1919 and I don't want to see it happen again. If there's anything I can do to prevent it, I want to do it. Too much is at stake." The President can still salvage the peace if he will come to the aid of the men on the Hill who want to help him. But he is going to have to act fast and with more comprehension of what it is all about than he has shown so far.

Down in Glen Taylor's office on the second floor the junior Senator from Idaho was concerned about the performance of the Congress for the folks who foot the bill. "When you're experienced in that sort of thing," he assured us, "you can sense the audience reaction. The reaction we get isn't so hot." Two things are wrong, he thinks. In the first place, tourists just can't understand why all the members aren't on the floor all the time, and in the second place—at least in the Senate—they can't hear very well. "Anybody who knows about stage business knows that marble doesn't reflect your voice very well," he said. "Maybe we ought to re-model the chamber, let some good acoustics engineer take it over and do a job on it. Maybe we ought to get rid of a little of that marbelized beauty. It's pretty, but after all we're there to work, and if it would make the acoustics better I'd be all for it." As for the lack of members on the floor, and the inability of tourists to realize that they are either in com-mittee, attending to constituents' mail, or downtown running some thank-less errand for the folks back home, he thought maybe visitors should be given a printed slip explaining the situation. "But we ought to do some-thing, because it's bad. There must be thousands of people here every year, and unless they happen to hit it on a real lively day when something big is on they go home and spread propaganda against Congress. Some-thing ought to be done about it." As for himself, he said, he wouldn't attend half the time if it wasn't for the looks of the thing. "I do it for appearances," he explained candidly. Viewed from the gallery, where he can be seen leaning forward intently with an expression of earnest strain on his face, he always appears to be giving a good performance.

JANUARY 12, 1945. With the best of intentions, Tom Connally has put his foot in it again. Not content with having followed Vandenberg's splendid speech with a semisarcastic appeal to the personal ("I hope when the Senator comes to vote on it," he said piously after Vandenberg had fin-ished giving the Administration the biggest boost it has received in a long, long time, "I hope he will cast his vote along the same lines as he has been speaking"), he has now come forth with the statement that there should be no resolutions and no debate on foreign policy at the present time. This attitude, so counter to the entire spirit of Vandenberg's address and so dangerous to real public understanding of the issues, has provoked an immediate hornet's nest. Vandenberg himself remarks rather scornfully that all he can do is repeat what he said in his speech, that he fails to see why America should be the silent partner. Carl Hatch, perturbed, asserts that a gag on debate will simply encourage the isolationists to give the world the impression that they speak for America. And swarthy little Allen Ellender urges the Administration to make use of "the most power-ful weapon America has"—free public discussion. The gap between the Foreign Relations chairman and the Senate which he must persuade is becoming steadily wider due to a series of little annoyances and missteps and irritations, none very important in itself but all adding up to a feeling of ominous significance to the treaty.

JANUARY 13, 1945. The wonder which is Washington was pictured for us today by one of our best news sources. "I've got a letter here which you might be interested in," he said, mentioning the name of one of the most influential men in America. "Now the story behind it is this. The other day he called me up and asked me if I would write him a letter asking him some questions. He gave me all the questions he wanted me to ask, and I wrote them all down. Here's a copy of my letter. All those questions are the ones he wanted me to ask him. I've dressed it up with a little malarkey, asking his advice, and so on, but they're all his questions. Here's a copy of his answer to my request for information. Now, he didn't say so over the telephone, and he doesn't say so in this letter, but I assume he wants it in the papers. I'm damned if I know what he's getting at, but he's an awfully shrewd old boy, so it must be something. Anyway, here it is. That's what's behind it, for your information. Maybe he'll be surprised as hell when he sees it in the press, but somehow I rather doubt it." We observed the bargain and handled it straight. The public was interested to learn that Senator So-and-So had requested information on such-and-such from Mr. Baruch. Probably they thought Senator So-and-So was pretty smart to have asked all those questions, and we were sure that the logic of Mr. Baruch would suitably impress them. Anyway, that's Washington.

27

THE KEY IS ELBERT

JANUARY 14, 1945. "The key to this manpower situation," said Ed Johnson, the shrewdest judge of men and events in the Senate, "is Elbert Thomas. You watch the way Elbert jumps and you'll know whether the President really wants national service or not." As far as he could see to date, Ed said, Elbert isn't going to jump very far. In the first place, he doesn't like the bill himself, and in the second place he apparently hasn't received even a telephone call from the President. This is the acid test of Roosevelt sincerity, of course: if he really wants it, he will contact the chairman of the Military Affairs Committee. (Elbert moved up when Bob Reynolds moved out.) So far he has made no move to do so, and the suspicion is growing on the Hill that his speech, hailed so fervently by the press, was simply for the purposes of making a record. "If the Old Man really wanted it," Ed said, "he could probably get it. But has he put on any pressure? I haven't heard of any." The interpretation gaining ground rapidly in Congress is the same interpretation that was placed on the same situation a year ago. Some vocal groups want national service, so the Boss will make a speech calling for it—but some other vocal groups, particularly labor, don't want it, so the Boss won't press the matter with Congress. The Boss can thus eat his cake and have it too, with another black eye for Congress thrown in for good measure. It's the same old act, of course, but it still seems to fool the customers. Here on the Hill, where words mean little and headlines less, the master politician is being assessed for what he is by others of his kind.

JANUARY 15, 1945. The Administration policy of confusion, contradiction, uncertainty and delay today produced its inevitable result. After urging all Senators to refrain from proposals and discussions on foreign policy, Connally suddenly came forth over the week end with a plea for an interim United Nations council—a move to take credit and publicity

338

away from Vandenberg so obvious that it simply gave further credence
to the growing belief that the Administration will accept nothing which
does not originate in the White House. It was also an attempt to shut
out Burt Wheeler, already annoyed by Connally's attempt to impose gag
rule on the Senate. The Montanan arose and addressed his colleagues for
three irascible hours this afternoon, precipitating a bitter debate filled
with intimations of the fight to come.

Dumbarton Oaks, Wheeler said, is simply "a plan to underwrite tyranny." He will vote against any plan that gives an American delegate
the right to send American boys to war without reference to Congress. He
will oppose "any unnecessary involvement in the quarrels of Europe."

Furthermore, he said, and he cited chapter and verse, an increasing
number of spokesmen are admitting that the world situation is steadily
deteriorating. Quoting exhaustively from Roosevelt, Churchill, Stalin and
many publications, the Senator built up a damning picture of the collapse
of Allied morality and the betrayal of Allied purpose. Time and again
he returned to his attack on Russia, an obvious but nonetheless effective
attempt to embarrass the President at the coming Big Three conference.
Time and again he assailed unconditional surrender and the Morgenthau
plan for a deindustrialized Germany. Time and again he taunted "the
internationalist crowd" with the few small crumbs that remain of the
bread they cast forth upon the waters. Time and again he proved that
Burt Wheeler, isolationist, is a powerful debater, a shrewd opponent, and
a man who will devote the utmost diligence to the destruction of a cause
or a leader with whom he does not agree.

Confronted with this, Connally sat silent, the wisest thing he could do
under the circumstances. Barkley moved about the Democratic side
dutifully trying to persuade others to do the same. A number of quiet
conferences were held at different desks. All but Claude Pepper yielded
to the Majority Leader's persuasion: the galleries were interested, the
President was being attacked, the dragon confronted St. George. Claude
sprang eagerly to battle.

His first tactic proved hardly as effective as he obviously had thought
it would be. It consisted of asking questions in a shocked tone of voice
which indicated that he certainly didn't believe *anybody* could answer in
the affirmative. Did the Senator mean that he was against Dumbarton
Oaks? He did, said Wheeler bluntly. Did he mean that he was against
the use of armed force to repel aggression? If it meant American boys
policing the world, yes, said Wheeler. Did he mean he was against con-
tributing American forces to a world security organization? Yes, said
Wheeler, unimpressed and speaking with the blunt impatience of a dedicated Yankee. Pepper sounded as though he could hardly believe it, but

Wheeler eventually convinced him. The Floridian set out on another angle: help for Hitler.

That's what Wheeler was doing, he charged: helping Hitler. Giving Goebbels weapons. Saying things which would give great comfort to the enemy. Maybe the disclosure of Morgenthau's plan [*for reducing Germany to an agrarian economy—which revived the flagging German will to fight on*] did cost thousands of American lives, but Wheeler's speeches would cost more. For anyone with the able Senator's national reputation ("Perhaps no Senator's sentiments in this matter are more important than those of the able Senator," he said truthfully) to get up on the floor and say things like that—well, the able Senator had no conception of the damage he was doing.

Then he turned to the Senate itself. "Within these four walls the peace of this nation and of the future will be decided!" Yes, Mr. President, within these four walls. There should be a new dedication and patriotism here, a new spirit of consecration. Why, Mr. President, the world could be made over in one short week if there could be a new spirit in the United States Senate—the Senate which lost the last peace and did so much to bring on this new war.

At that bald, deep-voiced Gene Millikin of Colorado jumped into the debate with a deliberately thunderous indignation. "I resent that implication!" he cried. "That is a terrible thing to say about this nation and this Senate! I challenge the Senator to demonstrate that statement! I challenge him to show how the blood of this war can be placed upon Senators of the United States, either now or those who came before us!" Millikin, who does not usually raise his voice above a grave, impressive murmur, grew red in the face and strode dramatically across the aisle. Pepper's voice rose too and he launched into the old, bitter story of Versailles and the elder Henry Cabot Lodge. Millikin, spitting out his words, pointed out angrily that the war began when German troops crossed the frontier into Poland; it spread when they crossed the frontier into France. "Show me where we are responsible for not stopping that aggression, and what we could have done!" Pepper retreated further into words about Versailles. "I will not argue history with the able Senator," he finally remarked. "The Senator quarrels with history." "I do not quarrel with history, sir," Millikin snapped. "I cooperate with the inevitable. When the Senator attempts to place a gag on any Senator and tries to say when a speech is divisive and when it is not, I say to him that he is simply scratching an unwholesome itch." "It is not the unwholesome itches in the Senate which concern me," Pepper shot back. "It is the unwholesome cancers in the Senate!"

He sat down, heated and not too sure that he had won the argument, and Wheeler rose for his brief rebuttal. He was not surprised, he said, to find himself charged with helping Hitler and Goebbels. That sort of argument didn't surprise him when it came from the Senator from Florida. "But I can take it, Mr. President. There isn't anybody going to stop me from saying what I think." The Senator from Florida, he said, of course knew more than anybody else about the war, he recognized that. However, for any Senator to imply that any other Senator was helping Germany and Japan hardly represented fair play in the United States Senate or anywhere else. He himself, he said, had never implied that any Senator was doing anything to help the enemy in any way. And he sat down, his voice cracked and hoarse and almost gone from three hours of debate and an incipient cold.

"Mr. President," said Barkley into the calm that followed, "I move that the Senate adjourn until noon on Thursday next."

JANUARY 16, 1945. The Boss apparently intends to do a little more than usual about national service this time. He called in the Hill's representatives this morning and had a heart-to-heart talk. Elbert Thomas emerged from it to announce that a new message on national service would be forthcoming "in the next couple of days." As for the Senate, he said with gentle dryness, "No, no. We don't want speed. We want to be very judicious and careful and make sure we are getting the best possible bill. We look to the House to work out a good compromise. Then it will come over to us and we'll hold hearings. We won't speed it." Perhaps this time there is really a conflict between the White House and the Hill on this ill-fated and dangerous legislation.

The brilliant Connecticut team had put on its last performance indeed on December 16, although no one could know then how tragically final it was. Dead at 50 is Francis Maloney, shrewd, practical, perceptive, one of the finest of men and most capable of Senators. Influenza, turning to pneumonia, complicated by recurrent heart attacks, proved too much for the stocky little Irishman from Meriden; a worthy career of public service has been cut short far too soon. In the short space of one month, the Democrat by death and the Republican by defeat, Connecticut has lost two of the best men who ever sat in the United States Senate.

As is inevitable in this political atmosphere, a man is not cold before speculation begins on his successor. Discussion on the Hill centers on two names. Will Clare Luce try it? Or will Danaher come back? The decision rests with a Republican governor, who must make his peace some way with a Democratic legislature.

JANUARY 17, 1945. As the hour of the falling of the ax draws near for the retiring V.P., the tide of rumor swirls higher around his tousled head. He seems to be wrapped in an aura of self-content and confidence these days, which encourages people to believe that something definite is in the offing. On the other hand, he has been confident before and come out on the short end of it, so no one can be sure. This uncertainty extends even to his secretary, Harold Young. Harold asks the reporters as many questions as they ask him, and is always taking them off to the Office Building cafeteria for coffee and long philosophic dissertations on the future of Aygard [*the Southernism for Agard, the V.P.'s middle name*] as he is referred to in some circles. Today Aygard gave a luncheon for all the new Senators, both Republican and Democratic. "He's giving his in here," said Harold, standing about the Capitol halls to direct the guests to their destination, "and Ellender's giving another in there. Ellender's got duck, we've got fricaseed chicken. I tried to get Ellender to give me a couple of ducks, and he said he'd be glad to give them to me, but he wouldn't give any to Wallace." The attitude, joking on the part of Ellender, who likes Wallace, is expressed more seriously by other Senate veterans. Aygard may have to be confirmed, if he gets that Cabinet nomination, and the chances are good that he will need all the votes he can get.

Meanwhile down at the White House Tom Connally and Josiah Bailey conferred with the President on the possibility of giving Aygard Commerce and easing Jesse Jones out of it into a sort of superduper financing post in which he would retain control of RFC and all the government lending agencies. This would give Henry a job, save Jesse's face, and placate Senators who would never vote for Wallace for anything which involved the distribution of funds. People still expect a terrific yelp from Jesse, who will not permit Henry to get his revenge for the Board of Economic Warfare fight in the early days of the war without a protest.

JANUARY 18, 1945. The Senate confirmed a number of nominations today, among them Guy Gillette for the Surplus Property Board, and then paid brief tribute to Maloney and recessed until Monday. The legislative program is still not under way in the upper house, where members are

waiting on the House to finish up the work-or-fight bill and send it along
to them for consideration. As time goes by and the first flush of enthusiasm
wears off, the inevitable reaction is beginning to set in against the measure. It will probably be some time before it is finally passed—if it is finally
passed. Prospects do not seem good at the moment.

Encouraged by the Administration's coolness toward Vandenberg's proposals, the usual petty sniping has begun in journals which range as
widely apart as the *Daily Worker* and the Washington *Post*. Maybe he
was sincere, the careful articles point out, but just the same, similar tactics
were used by Lodge and others 25 years ago. Maybe he has had a change
of heart, but just the same, who can be sure? Such carping does not seem
to have impressed the self-congratulatory Michigander. "Wallace," he
challenged White before the session the other day, "I've just been going
back over the World Court fight. I find that you voted against it and I
voted for it. How did that happen? You're the internationalist and I'm
the isolationist. How did you happen to do that?" White protested feebly
that he "really couldn't say what got into me." "What made you do it—
you, the internationalist—" Vandenberg pressed him, "when I, the isolationist, voted for it? I just couldn't figure that one." "Really, Arthur," said
White, "I don't remember now." "Well, that was really something," said
Vandenberg, looking satisfied, "that was really something." There is nothing phony about the great Van's conversion. He is tickled pink with it.

JANUARY 19, 1945. Fulbright and Austin appeared together in New York
the other night, their speeches an illustration of the confusion of tongues
on the internationalist side. Austin, clinging with the desperation of a
man who sees no other to a hope he knows is inferior, stoutly maintained
that Dumbarton Oaks represents a great advance over the League and
stoutly upheld the unilateral actions already taken in Europe. Everything
is moving forward, the Vermonter maintained: all that happens is for the
best. The corroding doubts which beset him in private he does not yet
place on the public record. His son is somewhere near Strasbourg, the
world is in darkness, and Austin fights gallantly on in a cause which he
hopes will yet be made valid. Not so Fulbright, the young and the clever.
In slashing irony he assailed "inspirational conferences . . . the sin of doing
nothing . . . sixteen months which have passed without anything more
than an incomplete blueprint. . . ." Peace, he said with some justice, is a
continuing process, "something more than a big red seal on a charter."
Dumbarton Oaks, incomplete though it is, must be organized immediately,
he cried. If not, then an interim council of foreign ministers. But action,
action! The hour is late and the opportunity must not be lost.

Last night in New York Ken Wherry offered his contribution: the

Reciprocal Trade Agreements Act, Dumbarton Oaks and the Bretton Woods proposals mean "the end of self-government in the United States." And on the Town Meeting of the Air, Pepper urged immediate formation of an international organization, Ellender and Tobey gave it qualified approval and called for complete disarmament of Germany and Japan, and practical Dennis Chavez advised the State Department to get the advice of the Senate if it plans to "render effective any international commitment for American participation in a world organization."

The one dominant note in all these increasingly numerous statements is concern. It is a concern the President may yet direct to the saving of the world if he will but show the leadership to do so. But the hour is indeed very late.

JANUARY 20, 1945. A little group of people stood about in the snow at the White House, a President was sworn in. He looked grimmer, Senators said, than they had ever seen him. "There wasn't any smiling," said Ed Johnson, "there wasn't any smiling at all. It was all solemnity this time. Very solemn." Dick Russell and others confirmed the fact. Some praise was given the speech, very brief and suitably innocuous, attempting to appeal to a moral righteousness events long since turned into a wan mockery. Then it was over, and life went on. There were balls and dinners, and some social fluster, but life went on. The fourth began in a drab mood which augured ill.

Concerning Henry, the rumors continue to fly unfounded. "Going to vote to confirm Henry for Secretary of Commerce, Senator?" we asked Ed. "I will if it's just for Commerce," he replied. "If it's to head up all the loaning agencies too, I won't. I doubt if the Senate will either. There'll be a hell of a fight." He agreed, however, that Connally's compromise would probably be accepted. The same indications came from Tall Tom. "You can speculate, of course," he said. "What I hear, it's going to be that way." He seemed pleased and happy and in a better mood than he has been in recent weeks.

28

SOMETHING FOR HENRY

JANUARY 21, 1945. The President has found something for Henry and all hell has broken loose. That it was planned this way seems highly unlikely in view of the crude frankness of his letter firing Jesse Jones. Apparently it was all to remain a state secret, a private exchange of letters, unknown to the simple public. Mr. Big figured without his man. In Texas they fight different.

Written shortly after inauguration yesterday and released by Jesse at 8:30 this evening, the Jones–Roosevelt correspondence will undoubtedly go down in history as one of the more noteworthy events of a crowded era. There has probably never been an exchange of sentiments between Chief Executive and Cabinet officer quite like it. Jesse has done a marvelous job, the President said, only he's got to get out because Henry wants his job. Henry's stalwart service "for the ticket" gives him the right to "anything he wants." What Henry wants, with an apparent ambition for power and desire for revenge that seem strange in his generally idealistic character, is Commerce. So Jesse can just pack his bags and git—with one afterthought. If he really wants something, he might "see Ed Stettinius." An ambassadorship or two is available. Just drop the word to the Secretary of State and everything will be taken care of, just like Henry. With warmest regards and the family stiletto, he is, as always, Franklin D. Roosevelt.

To this Jesse replied with a masterpiece of sarcasm. Unfortunately, he said, he could agree with neither the President nor Henry concerning Henry's qualifications for the vast financial responsibility of the RFC and the other lending agencies under the department. In view of the President's encomiums—and he threw them back in his teeth virtually word for word—it seemed to him strange that he must be removed. He had no desire to go into the State Department, Jesse said. He believed his work should lie along the same lines of business and finance he had followed all his life. "But I seek no job."

From the spokesmen of the Hill have come startled statements of antagonized concern. Connally, furious, has issued a diplomatic statement regretting the passing of Jesse Jones; it sounds as though the man were dead. The general tide of comment is much the same. There is little mention of Wallace, and only Lister Hill and the inevitable Langer have come forth to endorse him. What is referred to privately as "one hell of a fight" is getting under way, and the chances for bashful Henry do not seem good.

As for the act itself, the principle reaction underlying all others is complete bafflement. On the eve of his departure for overseas, at a time when his relations with the Senate are of the utmost importance to the cause of world peace, the President has chosen deliberately to do the one thing that would antagonize them more than anything else. The Henry who was such excess baggage that he could be shelved without remorse at Chicago has suddenly acquired a stranglehold on the loyalty and conscience of the man who has never shown loyalty or conscience where he was concerned before. The compromise giving Henry Commerce and leaving Jesse in charge of the lending agencies could have been worked out—Jesse was agreeable, and Henry could have been forced to take it. Instead, this. It just doesn't make sense—unless, as some are already saying, the President simply wished to pass the buck to the Senate and let them kill off Henry because he didn't have the guts to do it himself. That might be a valid explanation, were it not for the wider implications and the wider effect on his relations with the treaty-ratifying branch. Possibly it is still valid. At any rate, it is the only one that even remotely makes sense of any kind. All the others wind up in baffled and profane bewilderment.

JANUARY 22, 1945. The Senate met today, but its mind wasn't on its work. Its mind was on battle lines, which were rapidly being drawn. Off in the wilderness somewhere Claude Pepper and friends were setting up one headquarters. On the right the Friends of Jesse, Inc., were organizing. Somewhere in the middle, uncertain which way to jump, a number of stray Republicans looked nervously for shelter. The utmost anybody will concede Henry at the moment is 35 votes. The tally against him mounts into the 50s.

Into this situation Walter George introduced the best possible compromise: a bill to remove all the loan agencies from Commerce and return them to an independent Federal Loan Administrator. Aware of the Senate's deep-seated distaste for denying a President the Cabinet he wants, the powerful Georgian says sincerely that he has no wish to criticize Mr. Wallace. He just wants to neutralize him, removing all his fangs and making him harmless so that the Senate can confirm him with a clear conscience. This is the best way out, and indeed the only one if a head-on clash with the White House is to be avoided. The attitude of Henry, who can have what he wants, remains to be seen. Maybe Henry won't want Commerce without those nice billion-dollar corporations. Then what?

On another topic, momentarily obscured but nonetheless important, Mead and Ferguson gave the best possible answer to the hysterical cry for labor-draft legislation. They dropped down to the Norfolk Navy Yard the other day, and the conditions they found were appalling. Hundreds of men stood about idle, encouraged in their idleness by their superiors. Labor hoarding was glaringly apparent. "The armed services are always telling us about their desperate need for manpower," said Jim Mead bitterly. This was how they made use of what they had. Ferguson backed him up, waving a mahogany checkerboard made at the Yard for some officer on government time—on war time. Later in the day there came from the Navy, prim and self-righteous, the standard denials. Nonetheless, the facts were there on the record. They will probably defeat the work-or-fight bill, and they should. The Mead Committee's call for War Manpower Commission authority to force management to utilize labor to the full was much more to the point.

JANUARY 23, 1945. Josiah Bailey, slow-spoken and pedantic and enjoying the nervous agonies of the press, droned along through a press conference after the Commerce Committee meeting this morning telling us about the Rivers and Harbors bill. It has been approved and goes back on the calendar for another battle at some later date.

Eventually Josiah, having had his little joke, came to the crux of the matter. The Committee voted to take up the George bill first, turning down a motion by Brewster to take up the Wallace nomination first. The compromise is apparently going to be attempted, with a delay in the nomination sufficient to ascertain whether or not the President will veto the bill. A public hearing will be held tomorrow afternoon. Jesse will be invited to testify—"on the merits of the bill." Thursday morning Henry will be given the same privilege. After that the committee will decide what to do.

Meanwhile, the President has departed Washington for parts unknown. Henry and the little band of regulars have been left to fight on alone.

JANUARY 24, 1945. Jesse was among friends today, and Jesse put on a good show. Chewing gum and looking about sharply among the audience with his shrewd old eyes, he came into the overflowing Caucus Room in the midst of Walter George's testimony. Immediately things ground to a halt.

Photographers and newsreel cameramen swarmed toward the witness stand to take his picture. Obligingly he waved his hand. For a good 10 minutes this went on. Finally the room quieted down, the photographers withdrew, George continued. Jesse moved about in his chair restlessly, looking, looking. Along the committee table his friends and supporters beamed placidly upon him, Claude Pepper alone showing open disapproval.

When George concluded—after being questioned so closely by Pepper on the timing of his bill that he finally retreated into an indignant "I am not answerable to this committee or any other committee for my motives" —Jesse took over. Before he began his page-and-a-half statement attacking "amateur experimentation," "visionary planning," and "idealistic dreamers," he asked to be allowed to make a statement off the record. "I suppose you may," said Bailey rather doubtfully. "I'm just wondering who gets the gate receipts," said Jesse. Everybody laughed and Jesse was off to a flying start.

After his opening statement Jesse submitted to questioning and gradually a rather appalling picture emerged. Total Reconstruction Finance Corporation war authorizations, $32,000,000,000; disbursements, $18,000,

000,000; returns, $9,000,000,000; still in the fund, roughly, $8,000,000,000. "How do you make loans," he was asked; "by what system? How do you determine the amount and the length of time?" "We loan what we think we should," he said, "on the terms we think we should." It's a telephone business, he explained. "People call up, want $100,000,000 here, $60,000,-000 there; we talk it over and OK it. Telephone business, mostly." Were there any restrictions under law? "We use our own judgment." It is this power the President proposes to turn over to Henry. More basic than that, it is this power a foolish Congress has permitted to become concentrated in the hands of one man. Never has the fallacy of tailoring government to individuals been more forcefully proven. In a way, this whole situation serves the Congress right.

The whole realm of Jesse's power seemed to possess a beautiful vagueness. Did Jesse know the length of term for which he was appointed head of the RFC? "No, I don't know. I'm not sure." He swung around in his chair and asked the crowd: "Does anybody know?" Again everybody laughed.

Toward the end Claude Pepper attempted to pin him down as he had Walter George. Apparently, he said, Jesse believed that the combined jobs of Secretary of Commerce and Federal Loan Administrator could be held by one man, but they could not be held by Henry Wallace, only by a man who had "grown up with the RFC." That could only mean that Jesse considered himself the only man capable of holding both jobs. Was that right?

"I want to tell the witness," Bailey interrupted in his slow, deliberate voice, "that he doesn't need to answer that. He wasn't brought here for the purpose of answering questions like that."

"I decline to answer," said Jesse finally, after Claude had tried unsuccessfully again. Bailey seemed pleased.

At least five times during the hearing Jesse made some amusing sally and the crowd broke into heavy applause. Finally Pepper made a telling point, and a light scattering of approval could be heard. Bailey leaned forward instantly and held up his hand. "Please," he said. "Please let's don't have these demonstrations. Let's keep order in the committee room."

"I hope," said Pepper bitterly to the press afterward, "that the chairman will be fair enough to give the former Vice-President of the United States the same consideration tomorrow that he has accorded the former Secretary of Commerce of the United States today.... I think he will," he added for the sake of harmony, but without much conviction.

JANUARY 25, 1945. For five hours today Henry Wallace of Iowa faced men who don't like him and argued for his principles with the really rather magnificent candor and courage which are his two best qualities. He spoke of a dreamer's America, but it was the same kind of dreaming that America was originally and that America someday yet may be—an America of peace and prosperity and good will and humanity, with jobs for all and food for all and business for all and bountiful plenty for all, and evil banished forever from a fair and pleasant land. Watching him testify, tense and nervous and yet handling himself fairly well, it was hard not to feel a little ashamed of the fact that he should be called upon to recount, painfully, to skeptical men, the story of how he grew corn and supervised the Agriculture Department and gained his "experience" in business. All these issues seemed crass and presumptuous in the face of one of the very few sincerely moral characters of the present Washington generation. There was something almost obscene about the fact that a man as essentially good as he is had to be subjected to such an ordeal.

Yet it has to be done, just as his nomination, when it finally comes before the Senate, will have to be rejected unless the George bill has passed. For Henry has aspired to monumental power and would, if given it, proceed in his headlong fashion to impose upon the country a blueprint for which it is not yet ready. It is one thing to have the dream and it is another to attempt to drive the country into it. Henry's world is one of plans and programs, imposed with an eager compulsion upon folks who may not always agree. The happy way of the reformer might too easily lead to destruction. Possibly without the RFC, in an honorary secretaryship where he could devote his time and talents to preaching the new world, Henry might do great good in gradually moulding public opinion. Given the club of untold billions and the unrestrained impulses of a desperately sincere Messiah, there is no telling where he might end up. And always, of course, he would mean well, and his heart, full of love for the common man, would be in the right place. It is that basic goodness that makes his erratic course through American life such a personal and political tragedy. A little more maturity, a little more stability, a little better timing and a little more common sense, and Henry might be an effective great man. As it is he is probably a great one, but he is certainly not effective.

One concession he did make to his critics. He will take Commerce without RFC, he said, but only for the duration. He would prefer to have both jobs, and if he does get them will use RFC "for the benefit of all the American people." Politely and firmly he described exactly the program he would follow: the President's "economic bill of rights." He did not bow to his conservative opponents, nor did he pull his punches in any respect. He got a three-minute ovation when he came in and a one-minute ovation when he finished his statement. Jesse's crowd had given way to a more progressive breed.

As for the votes, he apparently changed none of them. Leaders of the fight against him estimate the Yeas in the 20s, the Nays in the 50s, with RFC. Without it, one estimate rises, the other goes down, but the predictions of his defeat still hold good. "A lot of us," said Harry Byrd, "are just simply against everything he represents. We just don't agree with the things he proposes. We might as well meet the issue head-on and make it clear where we stand once and for all."

On the floor a compromise insurance bill, suspending the anti-trust laws for the industry until 1948, went through after an exhaustive discussion. Although authored by Pat McCarran and Ferguson its real father, O'Mahoney, says, "the end of a long fight." It has been a long one, and it has all been his. By using every trick in the book, by delay and compromise and the shrewdest of strategy, he has finally won; a brilliant performance that should not go entirely unsung.

The freshman Senators have sent the President a round-robin pledging their support in foreign policy, a good move and inevitably helpful.

JANUARY 26, 1945. The Commerce Committee voted today, 14–5, against the nomination of Henry A. Wallace of Iowa to be Secretary of Commerce. At the same meeting it voted 15–4 for the George bill to remove all lending agencies from the Department of Commerce. As an added indication of its faith and trust in the President of the United States, it added an amendment forbidding him to transfer the agencies back to the department. The fight goes to the floor on Monday, where the probable course of events is at the moment obscure. The nomination goes on the executive calendar and comes up automatically at the end of the day's session. The bill goes on the legislative calendar and may not come up for some time. Pepper and his group may attempt to delay the nomination and force consideration of the bill, knowing that if the nomination comes up first Henry will almost certainly be beaten; but there are ways of dealing with that strategy, and doubtless Henry's opponents know them. So important is the issue that Senators are beginning to give out formal statements making their positions clear. Ed Johnson cannot vote for Wallace with the RFC. Neither can the two Marylanders, Tydings and Radcliffe. Joe Ball, on the other hand, can. So can Aiken and Langer. Harry Byrd has already expressed himself as being against Wallace in any form. Others are going on the record daily. The comparison with the Supreme Court fight of 1937 (of which some scars still remain) is not inappropriate. This is a major battle here, and men, rightly or wrongly, feel that issues of the deepest import to the nation are involved in the fate of this earnest, ill-starred man.

JANUARY 27, 1945. McKellar has called for the defeat of Henry Wallace in a scathing letter sent yesterday to the CIO council in Memphis. Shrewd, blunt, merciless, it lacerates the unfortunate nominee with all the acid at the Senator's command. He would not vote for Mr. Wallace, Mack says, under any circumstances, with the George bill or without it. Mr. Wallace is one of those fortunate men whose father left him a fortune. "He dissipated it in short order." During his eight years as Secretary of Agriculture "one of his fads" was killing pigs. He was generally incompetent. His four years as Vice-President were equally hopeless. "He never knew anything about the rules and he never learned anything about the rules." When he left the Senate the other day "not one Senator" said anything about it, and no Senator could say anything about it because of the poor job he had done. "He is a failure in politics." He has never been able to carry his own state even with the President to help him. It may be that he helped the ticket by speaking for it, but in Mack's opinion Mr. Roosevelt would have received more votes if Mr. Wallace had never said anything for him at all. He has never done anything for labor except make speeches when he wants labor to give him something. "The people of Tennessee," as the CIO council informs him, may be demanding Mr. Wallace's confirmation, but somehow Mack cannot accept that analysis of their attitude. No, suh.

Led by Tom Connally, other Southerners are attempting desperately to get Wallace either to withdraw or request the Senate to pass the George bill before considering his nomination. They don't want the "embarrassment," Tom says, of having to vote against him. If Henry will not accede, he indicates, they are ready to endure the embarrassment.

JANUARY 28, 1945. On the basis of an informal poll taken over the week end, the vote against Henry now stands 39–21. Estimates by Harry Byrd and others raise the total against to 51. Josiah Bailey, key to the whole situation, has not yet indicated which report he will file first, the nomination or the bill. Meanwhile Henry has gone off to New York for a triumphal visit among his friends. The mantle of martyrdom, never far from his shoulders, is being tried on for size as the Senate moves toward its decision on his fate.

JANUARY 29, 1945. In a long, dragging session overshadowed by the death of Colonel Edwin Halsey, Secretary of the Senate, Josiah Bailey procured permission to file his reports on the Wallace matter during the recess of the Senate. The administration strategy of delay, strengthened now that

Barkley has returned to the hospital for treatment of his eye and left Lister Hill in charge, has guaranteed a two-day interval before the Senate meets again on Thursday. It is apparently the hope that pressure can be brought to bear, that thousands and thousands of those telegrams which White once referred to so truthfully as "not having any great influence on any of us," can be delivered at the Office Building—that obdurate men can somehow be persuaded by hysterical propaganda. The hope seems forlorn at the moment. It seemed even more remote late in the day when from New York came word that Henry, encouraged by his friends, now says that he would prefer not to have the secretaryship without the RFC.

During the session Langer joined the prophets of doom for Dumbarton Oaks. The thing is dead, he said, and the only hope for the world lies in the abolition of small states and the regrouping of civilization into five regional units. The tactic of killing a thing by absurdity is one the wily North Dakotan knows with a sure and practiced knowledge.

As simply as though it were a minor resolution, the Rivers and Harbors bill, that minor storm center of the last session, passed without trouble this afternoon. Stripped to its essentials and with all controversial amendments left out, it seemed almost an afterthought after the battles of December.

JANUARY 30, 1945. Claude Pepper, perturbed by Henry's surprising shift toward firmness in New York, called a hasty press conference today to assure us that it was all a mistake. Henry still wants the job, Claude said. "He will be a good soldier." Whatever his latest statement may have been, he will really take it without the RFC. The Senator's candidate had gotten out of hand, and the Senator was working hard to put him back in line. It was an attempt not entirely successful.

Half an hour after Pepper's press conference began, Josiah Bailey held one. The press rather unceremoniously abandoned Claude and hastened to Josiah. Josiah's comments were a stall for time, a slow-moving discussion of his plans that added up to virtually nothing. His real plan, which came from other sources, is to move for an executive session at the earliest opportunity tomorrow. If the motion carries, Henry's name will automatically come up ahead of the George bill and that will be the end of Henry.

That Josiah's motion will be approved seems uncertain now. He doesn't have the votes he had a couple of days ago. A number of Republicans, persuaded by the valid argument that a President should have the men he wants in the Cabinet, have begun to swing over. Estimates of the defection run as high as 14 votes.

Meanwhile, Barkley is going ahead with plans to move consideration of the George bill as soon as Truman will recognize him for the purpose. A party caucus has been called for day after tomorrow.

JANUARY 31, 1945. "Looks like maybe Jesse is being made the scapegoat, doesn't it?" somebody asked Harold Young today. "Jesse!" said the hefty Texan disconsolately. "What about Aygard? You remember the Ed Flynn nomination." That famed occasion, when the President got rid of his national chairman by tossing him to the Senate with a diplomatic nomination, has been mentioned frequently of late. More and more people on the Hill are coming to feel that the President's action, jeopardizing the peace treaty and possibly the fate of the world, was done simply to rid himself of two embarrassing domestic liabilities. [*Jesse's power, according to this theory, having grown so great and drawn so much criticism as to make his presence as awkward as Henry's.*] No other valid explanation has been offered, at any rate.

FEBRUARY 1, 1945. The Democrats met in caucus this morning, but a two-hour session produced little harmony. Everybody made speeches, Barkley said he would move to take up the George bill, Bailey said he would move an executive session. Nothing was decided, some additional tempers were inflamed, and at 12 noon the issue went to the floor.

There Bailey made his motion within a half hour of the opening gavel. A dramatic roll call followed, the votes pacing each other down the tally sheet until they hit liberal Democratic territory, when the Nos began to creep ahead. Farther down, the solid Republican bloc of Wherry, White, Wiley, Willis and Wilson that concludes the list swung the balance back again. The vote stood 42–42 and the motion was lost. Taft jumped up immediately and asked to be allowed to change his vote to Nay, a necessary parliamentary preliminary which would place him on the winning side and permit him to move that the vote be reconsidered. Barkley, who had the floor, changed his mind in a split second and after saying he would yield for that purpose, refused to do so. Taft objected strenuously and Truman ruled that he might make the motion to reconsider "at any later time." Barkley proceeded to call up the George bill and the moment had passed. The high tide against Wallace had been reached and had receded—on a tie.

The consideration of the George bill moved on slowly for another two hours. Finally everything there was to be said had been said. The Yeas and Nays were asked for. The Senate certified its faith in Henry Wallace by voting 74–12 to strip him of the RFC and its lending authorities.

Legislative business concluded, Barkley moved an executive session. It was agreed to. Barkley moved that the nomination of Henry Wallace be delayed until March 1. The delay, he said, was due to the fact that he had been notified by the House that it would speed action on the bill; the delay would also give the President time to sign it. He was confident the President would do so, Barkley said, because he had a letter from him saying so. He read the letter. The President would sign. Still and all, the motion had better read March 1 so people could be sure. The Senate certified its faith in the word of Franklin Roosevelt by giving unanimous approval to the Barkley motion.

Later, Taft and Wherry signified their intention to continue the fight against Wallace. Josiah Bailey, talking around the point but remarking "A lot can happen in 30 days," did the same. McKellar declared that he was "going shopping for votes." Henry's chances look better but they are still not absolute.

House Office Building

29

THE DRIVE BEGINS

FEBRUARY 2, 1945. The House has finished with the May bill to force workers into war plants and make the sort of situation the Mead Committee found at Norfolk the national policy to win the war. This fanciful measure, conceived in ambition and delivered in hysteria, has now come to the Senate. Its fate in the upper chamber is momentarily obscure.

To begin with, there is a considerable feeling in Military Affairs that the whole business has been a sort of trumped-up shenanigan by administrative officials who are demonstrably incapable of doing a good job with the manpower controls they now have. Elbert Thomas is against it on principle, and others are equally wary. Ed Johnson has come around and will go along, simply because the services have bellyached for so long that he has come to the conclusion that the only way to shut them up is to give them their lollypop. O'Mahoney is suspicious and prepared to urge delay. It is perhaps just as well, for one strange inconsistency has emerged from the committee's meetings: they want to give Jimmy Byrnes as War Mobilizer "vast and unprecedented powers" over the nation's manpower. They want to center the whole thing in him, make Jimmy the czar. They know Jimmy, you see, and that makes it all right. Having just been presented, in the Jones–Wallace situation, with the most glaring example of the fatal stupidity of concentrating "vast and unprecedented powers" in the hands of favorite pets who are neither immortal nor certain of tenure, they are now willing to turn right around and do it all over again. Apparently nothing has been learned. It is still to be tailor-made government, at least for boys like Jimmy. This state of mind is really very seriously dangerous to democracy, easy though it may be to shrug it off in the pragmatic atmosphere of the Hill.

FEBRUARY 3, 1945. The hearings on the Mexican water treaty drag on and on before Foreign Relations. The pattern has by now become well established. There is the ritual of the box of cigars, passed around to all Senators at the start of the meeting by the clerk. There is the bullying of witnesses by Tom Connally. There is the hearty, vacuous joking of Alexander Wiley, and his rambling clarifying questions. There is the slow, humorous, persistent questioning of McFarland, the shrewd probing of Murdock, Milikin's brilliant legal mind in operation, and Joe O'Mahoney jousting like a lancer with recalcitrant spokesmen for the cause of California. There is California itself, appearing in great numbers headed by its attorney general, the chubby, smooth, ambitious Bob Kenny; there is the obvious jealousy and animosity of the other Western states toward the favored sister on the Pacific. There is the endless repetition of the facts of the argument: the 1,500,000 acre feet of Colorado River water guaranteed annually to Mexico, through whose territory the river flows finally to the sea; the 350,000 acre feet of Rio Grande River water guaranteed annually to the United States; the more than 5,000,000 acre feet of Colorado River water annually obligated by contract to California users; the fear of California that Mexico's treaty guarantee will breach her contracts; the fear of the upper basin that if California kills the treaty Mexico will insist upon international arbitration and may get much more than the treaty gives her, which in turn will jeopardize the development of the upper basin. Over and over, running through like a constant thread, is the waspish dislike for California evidenced by the representatives of Wyoming and Utah and Colorado, New Mexico, Arizona and Nevada.

And each day also there is the little vignette of the Hiram Johnsons, repeated in unvarying routine. Promptly at 10:30 in the morning Mrs. Johnson, a tiny old lady, lively and spry, brings in the Senator. He walks very slowly, shuffling along the corridor with a cane. She sees that he is seated comfortably and then retires to a chair in the back of the room, where she listens intently, occasionally whispering to her neighbors, more often silently keeping an eye on her husband. Infrequently during the hearing he will address a question to the witness, speaking in a barely audible, painfully difficult voice which everyone strains to hear, spacing out his words: "Is—it—not—true—that——" Once in a while he gets into a laborious spat with Connally, who treats him with affectionate disrespect. Around 1 he gets restless; Connally usually recesses until 2:30 at his request. Mrs. Johnson comes forward, takes his hand, asks him about his hat, he gets it and slowly, slowly they depart. At 2:30 they return again, again she gets him settled, once more she retires. At 4:30, like a vague ghost-voice somewhere in the room, he can be heard urging Connally to recess. Usually it is done. Mrs. Johnson comes forward and helps him out, and slowly, slowly they depart. He plans, his secretary says, to run again in 1946.

FEBRUARY 4, 1945. Ed Johnson, his good-natured soul incensed to its depths, has come out with a violent blast against the War Department. Ed's heart is set on Jimmy Byrnes to administer the May manpower bill. On the record he says the War Department has favored the same thing. Behind the backs of the press and most of the committee, however, he says, "top officials" have been calling Senators and urging that the power be placed in Selective Service. "This is a good example of the dirty double-crossing which goes on in the executive departments of this Administration," he says bitterly. The Senator from Colorado, who takes a long time to come to a boil, has apparently reached boiling point now.

Highlighted by his explosion, the predicament of the legislation appears to be growing more intense. The happy rush and enthusiastic hurry with which it was whooped through the House are apparently giving way to a much more sober view. It is just as well. There are some peculiar motives and some strange jockeyings for power in this bill. The arguments of its proponents are beginning to wear a little thin as the Senate's instinctive suspicion of the Executive (which always exists to some degree, no matter who the Executive is) results in a lengthening delay.

FEBRUARY 5, 1945. California's candidate for President, Governor Earl Warren, appeared before Foreign Relations today, a massive, impressive, good-looking man who spoke ably and well along familiar lines. There was little new that he had to add to the Mexican treaty discussion, but it was an intelligent and logical presentation by the intelligent and logical man who is the Pacific Coast's most popular and most skillful leader. After he had finished, the photographers moved up toward the witness table. "Wait for the pictures!" cried Alec Wiley jovially. "He will," said Connally spitefully. "He's willin'." The governor laughed pleasantly in his face, which was just about what he deserved.

Military Affairs, beginning to go through the same agonies and labor pains that struck it last summer during surplus-property days, seems to be in the process of tying itself into knots over manpower. O'Mahoney and Chandler, once again an effective team, insisted upon hearings. Happy wanted them open, but Elbert Thomas was able to hold 8 members in line. The Nay vote stood 9-7. O'Mahoney then moved that the hearings be executive. The motion was agreed to 14-3. They will be limited, Elbert says, and a specific list of witnesses will be called to testify. They will consume, he estimates, at least a week. Chapman Revercomb, Taft and Edward Robertson have introduced a substitute designed to give the War Manpower Commission more authority to control manpower, a logical move which lost by only 10 votes in the House.

As an outgrowth of the Wallace situation, Byrd and Butler have joined forces to introduce a bill requiring all government corporations to make an annual estimate of expenditures, placing them all under annual audit, and requiring them to lend only for projects specified in the annual estimate. Meanwhile in the House the Republicans are planning to amend the George bill if they can, to place a permanent ban on the President's right to transfer agencies. John Rankin, who has his own ideas and his own methods for achieving them, wants to pigeonhole the George bill altogether and force the Senate to reject Wallace for the full secretaryship on March 1. Henry is far from out of the woods.

FEBRUARY 6, 1945. Military Affairs held its first executive hearing on the manpower bill this morning, and later released the statements of its witnesses about 5 o'clock after the best news-hour had passed and the wires were beginning to close down. This annoyed the press, but perhaps in the long run it didn't matter much. The statements on this topic are familiar in every detail. They go over and over and over the same ground, whether they come from Stimson or Forrestal or Patterson or Krug, and they contain the same basic contradiction: of course the war is going well and of course we can win it without this bill and of course the bill won't be used—but we want the bill. This makes a lot of sense, about as much as the newest argument, the one about its "being necessary to the morale of the boys at the front." In the first place the boys at the front aren't concerned with much of anything except getting through and getting home, and in the second place, if the morale of the boys at the front is so shaky that the only way to strengthen it is to impose military dictatorship on the country, then we had all better get through and go home because there won't be much point in what any of us are doing. The war is heading toward its final stages, public worry over the Bulge is beginning to diminish, the last chance to clamp a vise on the nation is beginning to slip away. No wonder there is a desperate scramble of errand-boys to the Hill. And no wonder the Senate receives them with the skepticism they deserve.

FEBRUARY 7, 1945. Over in the House the Banking and Currency Committee has reported out the George bill to strip Commerce of the lending agencies, beating down Republican attempts to amend it. It now goes to the Rules Committee, where Southern Democrats link hands familiarly with the minority, and where it seems possible that the bill may be bottled up just as John Rankin wants it to be, thereby sharply decreasing Wallace's chances in the Senate. Meanwhile a lot of Democratic opponents of the unfortunate ex-V.P. are beginning to get cold feet, on the theory that to defeat him altogether would be to "make a martyr out of him and build him up for 1948." Such an argument seems shaky. Four years is a long time to keep a martyrdom alive. Not even Wendell Wilkie with all his great ability and dynamic appeal could manage it, and it seems unlikely that Henry could either.

FEBRUARY 9, 1945. The mechanics of the way you create pressure for a manpower bill "necessary to the morale of the boys at the front" were revealed today by the alertness of the American press. First Bob Patterson issues a statement demanding it. Then the War Department sends an urgent query to *Stars and Stripes* asking whether it intends to run an editorial on it. Then the editors of *Stars and Stripes*, understandably eager to comply, write the editorial. Then the wire services pick up the editorial and give it widespread play back home. Then Bob Patterson comes up to the Hill and talks about "the morale of the boys at the front" and the circle is complete. It is all very neat if it doesn't leak to the press. This time it did.

It is no wonder that the gap between civilian and soldier widens daily, when the troops are played upon deliberately with self-serving propaganda of this type by officers of the executive branch.

FEBRUARY 10, 1945. Henry, still in hot water, has run into a new snag in the House. The Banking and Currency Committee went along all right, reporting out the bill without amendment, but then it had to run the gantlet of the Rules Committee. The balance of power there is a coalition balance, faithfully reflecting the picture in the whole Congress, and it is against poor Henry. The Rules Committee, in fact, has refused to grant the bill a rule that would bring it to the floor. Consequently Banking and Currency now expects to wait until next Wednesday, calendar day, and attempt to call it up then independently of Rules. When this technique is followed a bill is wide open to every sort of amendment from the floor. This may mean a night session. In any case it will probably mean one of those tense House affairs when changes of opinion rush across the surface of the multitude like a physical wave and men like John Rankin are in their howling glory.

FEBRUARY 11, 1945. Kilgore and Murray, those two industrious gentlemen, are beginning to talk about their own substitute for what is now becoming known more and more widely in the press as the work-or-jail (manpower) bill—a measure which would appropriate the Voorhis idea to give the WMC more authority and at the same time require an investigation of the utilization of manpower by the Army and Navy. This latter provision of course is the last thing that services want, and their pressure on the Hill will undoubtedly increase in desperation. To have somebody really look into the situation and really discover all those thousands and thousands of men and women who through no fault of their own are wasting out the war at petty, trivial and unnecessary tasks in order to preserve the station complement of ambitious commanders—that would never do. That would have the most terrible effect upon the morale of our boys at the front of the Pentagon and the Navy Building. Nothing could be more deadly to the war effort. To horse, therefore, and into battle in the glorious cause of entrenched stupidity. Kilgore and Murray have proposed the single most constructive step in the whole manpower mess. Let them look into the services. The answer is there.

FEBRUARY 12, 1945. The three men by whom the world is temporarily run have issued their latest pronouncement, and the effect on the Congress has been on the whole good. Meeting for eight days at Yalta in the Crimea, they have made a few positive and constructive forward steps— at least on paper. There may come the tacit wearing away of belief, the easy dismissal, but as of this moment, it looks on the surface as though they have actually agreed on something. America's basic interest lies in the provisions that require free elections in liberated areas and joint provisional administrations by the three great powers. It lies also in the apparent ability to meet, to discuss, to compromise and to agree. True, the ultimate victor has been Russia, and the so-called "solution" of the Polish problem is only half a solution, but at least an accord has been reached, something definite has been done, and in one respect—the calling of a United Nations conference in San Francisco on April 25—a warrant of great hope has been issued. Six months or a year from now it will become clear whether or not it is to be redeemed.

On the Hill, and particularly in the Senate, reaction is generally approving. Carl Hatch is much relieved, Joe Ball is pleased but still shrewd enough to be cautious, Barkley has gone overboard and Wallace White has tagged along, Vandenberg has given his blessing. Some doubts are expressed over Poland, but Poland is becoming an accomplished fact, and gradually the moral issue is yielding to the finished deed. All in all, the signs are good. Dumbarton Oaks' chances, which fluctuate with the headlines, are momentarily on the upgrade. Everything now begins to depend upon San Francisco.

FEBRUARY 13, 1945. The President has selected Hull, Stettinius, Vandenberg, Dean Virginia Gildersleeve of Barnard College, Stassen, Connally and Representatives Sol Bloom and Charles Eaton as the American delegates to San Francisco. The President, who knows the right men to get

committed in order to embarrass the Republicans and also strengthen
the peace, has done a good job of picking with Vandenberg. Although
faced with an election in '46 and a ticklish problem in reconciling his
Polish constituents and the Yalta declaration, Arthur is expected to accept.
He is temporarily stalling off the press by saying that he "hasn't received
the President's invitation yet," but as one of his colleagues remarked,
"You don't turn down an invitation to a peace conference."

FEBRUARY 14, 1945. Over in the House, the Rules Committee has relented
somewhat and now agrees to send the George bill to the floor with a rule
on the amendment by industrious Jesse Wolcott of Michigan which would
also strip Henry of membership on the Export-Import Bank. Other
amendments are likely to be lost without Rules Committee endorsement,
but at least the bill now has a fair chance of getting through.

FEBRUARY 15, 1945. Hiram Johnson may be aged and ailing, but there are
still flashes of the grand old warrior left. The constant bickering and
bitterness of the water-treaty hearings came to a head today in a head-on
clash between the senior Senators from Texas and California. The senior
Senator from California won and the senior Senator from Texas slammed
out of the room.

As usual, Sheridan Downey, doing an able job of presenting California's
case under great provocation from the chairman, was the cause of the
squabble. A witness was testifying and Downey wanted to question him.
"Let him finish!" said Connally peremptorily. Hiram Johnson's eyes
snapped and he turned toward him in his chair. "The chairman of this
committee," he said, his echo of a voice becoming firm with indignation,
"is attempting to arrogate to himself all direction of the testimony before
this committee." "That's all very well," snapped Connally, "but I'm not
going to turn the whole thing over to Mr. Downey of California. By all
the rules of the Senate, Senators who are not members of committees
have no right to question witnesses. I have permitted Senator Downey
to ask questions, I have extended him that courtesy, and I shall continue
to do so. But he has no right to do so." "When a witness, or a member of
the committee, or a member of the Senate," said Johnson, slowly but
firmly, "wants to ask a decent question he should be permitted to do it
without your placing your construction of his remarks in the record."
"Senator," said Connally reasonably, "I have given you every courtesy
as a member of this committee, I have permitted you to ask any question
you wanted, I have given you everything you desired, because you are
a member of this committee, and because"—and he sounded, and was,
sincere—"like every other member of the Senate I regard the senior

Senator from California with great respect and affection." "Oh," said
Johnson slowly. "Oh. Thank you. I appreciate that a great deal, and I
accept it—I accept it in the spirit in which it ought to be meant." "Well,"
said Connally, understandably angry again, "if you are going to place that
insinuation on it, I withdraw the statement. I was only trying to be helpful to the Senator from California." "The Senator from California can take
care of himself!" said Johnson angrily. "Make no mistake about that.
The Senator from California can take care of himself. I am getting rather
tired of seeing the chairman of this committee designedly directing the
testimony in this matter." The witness on the stand, slightly overcome by
the crosswinds of Senatorial anger, began to read his statement again
hesitantly; Connally and Jim Tunnell began to whisper together. "Well,
now," interrupted Johnson. "You're reading and they're talking and I
can't hear you." Connally rose huffily and followed by Tunnell, started
to leave the room. Johnson swung about in his chair. "Hey!" he cried.
"Don't go away!" Connally slammed the door behind him. Later in the
day, of course, the two were bickering together amiably like the cronies
they are; but Hiram Johnson at 78 had put Tom Connally in his place,
something younger men are rarely able to do.

FEBRUARY 16, 1945. The George bill passed the House today by a vote of
204–196 after surviving a move to recommit—one more significant indication of the regard in which the Congress holds Henry Wallace. It was a
lively session, with rotund Jesse Wolcott persistently trying to amend
the bill and bumbling Brent Spence, chairman of Banking and Currency,
persistently making points of order against him. These were uniformly
sustained by the Chair. Finally Spence moved an end of debate and a vote
on the bill. Wilson of Indiana moved to recommit. Joe Martin hopped
up and demanded the Yeas and Nays. Many others seconded, and the
long laborious process began. At the end of the roll call an 8-vote gap
separated the two sides. The Clerk called the roll of the absentees, a fair
number answered, the vote continued parallel. The 8-vote margin spelled
Henry's victory when it was over. Spence moved passage of the bill, again
the Yeas and Nays were ordered, 399–2 the bill went through. In exactly
the same spirit as the Senate, the House had come within a hair's-breadth
of rejecting Henry altogether, and then had voted virtually unanimously
to give him his job but strip it of everything he wants.

FEBRUARY 17, 1945. Wagner and Tobey have put in a bill to take the
United States into the Bretton Woods monetary agreement to establish an
International Monetary Fund and an International Bank for Reconstruc-
tion and Development. Although Tobey is sanguine enough to predict

"two weeks" to get action, two months would be more like it for Bretton Woods, a topic so complicated that the burden of starting work on it is generally regarded with great reluctance on the Hill.

Across the river in Virginia a little wind has been stirring around the ivory tower of Carter Glass. The suggestion, made with a suitable hesitation and an almost frightened daring, has been bruited about here and there: Carter is useless and Carter should resign. Carter is 87, Carter has not been in the Senate since 1942, Virginia in actual fact has only one Senator: Carter should resign. From the guarded suite at the Mayflower, through whose doors no outsider has passed in many months to see what lies within, has come the usual answer. Mrs. Glass has replied for the Senator. The suggestion will not be considered. The incident is closed. The winds have shaken a little the heavy curtain over the door of the tower, but with a firm hand its diligent keeper has drawn it taut again. Within, the Senator sleeps on.

30

THE PRESSURE GROWS

FEBRUARY 18, 1945. Henry Stimson has made a strange speech, playing with emotions so violent that he probably has no conception at all of what he is doing. In a deliberately divisive address, which could have been no better designed to turn the country against Congress had Goebbels himself contrived it, he has come forth with a desperate wail for the manpower bill. The Stimson speech sounded hysterical, and it may have been. At any rate it attempted to stir up the most bitter passions among the families of the men in the services, and among the men themselves. Oversimplified, glaring, dangerous and false, the arguments it used were familiar. They were given an ugly shrillness that seems ominous indeed.

To the nation that has produced for all the world, War's aging servant cried bitterly to see the example of others. Others have compulsory labor, he cried: does not this nation, which has produced and produced and produced to become the miracle of the centuries, feel a sense of shame that it has managed to do it without the whip? Is it not terrible that America, the free, should have accomplished what America, the slave, could never do? Should not this America that has won the war in many ways without which it could never have been won at all, should not this America castigate itself because it did it with liberty? Is not America ashamed to be successful and free at one and the same time? How dare America have the unforgivable arrogance to be both successful and free? Can America ever be at ease with her own conscience again if she does not welcome slavery? Can she face the verdict of history if she triumphed without compulsion?

Not in the mind of Henry Stimson, apparently, for so in substance he said tonight in an inflammatory speech whose exaggerations were not salvaged but made more grim by the fading old voice in which it was delivered. The Administration wants this compulsive bill and it wants it with a determination that is strange and dismaying, for its officers will tell you, when you question them privately, that there is no need for it and they know it.

FEBRUARY 19, 1945. The Stimson speech has probably killed the punitive May manpower bill, and for that thanks can be given. O'Mahoney, aroused and at his most acid, has assailed the Secretary for attempting to use misleading and false propaganda to inflame the passions of the country. The Senator is deeply disturbed by it, as are most of the members. Ed Johnson says tersely that he is "not impressed by the Secretary's attempt to dictate legislation." Sentiment in the Military Affairs Committee has veered even further away from compulsion than it was on Saturday. The Kilgore substitute now looks to be the thing. There will be a debate, consuming some time, and then the conference with the House, consuming some more. Then possibly Germany will be fallen and the bill will die. If not, the measure that emerges will probably be a fairly good one, designed to go to the heart of the problem and do the job. Certainly the Senate is in no mood any more to grant the power the House would so blithely have given.

FEBRUARY 20, 1945. Military Affairs * voted today 12–6 to drop the May bill and take up its own substitute version. The work of the Secretary of War and his colleagues in the Cabinet has produced its just result. They wanted too much and they tried too hard to get it. Reasonably sound legislation should emerge from the committee's deliberations.

In midmorning Barkley released a rather peculiar statement to the press. It was dated Feb. 11 and entitled, "Memorandum for Senator Barkley from the President." It consisted of two sentences, which were immediately analyzed for doubletalk. He favored the *principle* of the May bill, the President said. It would provide ammunition and strengthen our arms. The initials *F.D.R.* appeared at the bottom. It furnished a new mystery. If the President really wanted the bill, why didn't he address the chairman of the committee? Why wasn't it a formal request? Why was it released on Feb. 20, nine days after it was received? It was a curiosity, but it influenced no one.

FEBRUARY 21, 1945. Military Affairs, which has a greater capacity for doing things it can't explain later than any other committee in the Senate, suddenly reinjected some teeth into its substitute "voluntary" manpower

* The Military and Naval Affairs committees of both houses were combined into a single Armed Services Committee of each in the La Follette–Monroney Legislative Reorganization Act of 1946.

bill. Nobody seems to know quite why Austin's amendment was adopted; nobody, not even Austin, seems to know whether it applies to the employer, the employee, or both. The $10,000 fine and year's imprisonment which it provides for infractions "changes the whole philosophy of the bill," as Elbert Thomas pointed out later to the press. The adoption of a Tydings amendment, which in effect freezes farm labor on the farm while leaving urban labor free to move about at will, also "changes the philosophy." Somehow Military Affairs never fails. It starts out with a clear-cut prejudice and a good idea of what it wants and then at the last moment a sort of hasty indecision grips it and it suddenly goes crazy. "Changes in philosophy" then become the order of the day. It will vote on reporting out the substitute tomorrow, Thomas said, after a preliminary vote of 9–7 to do so. All members, he said, have reserved the right to oppose the bill when it gets to the floor.

FEBRUARY 22, 1945. The substitute manpower bill came out of committee today on a vote of 11–4. Both the Austin and Tydings amendments were retained. So were "vast, unprecedented powers" for Jimmy Byrnes. For no apparent reason except that Jimmy keeps his fences mended, the Senators have made the War Manpower Commission's authority subject to the direction and control of the Director of War Mobilization and Reconversion. This represents virtually full circle, since the military does everything in that office but sign the checks. The proviso for a survey of manpower in the services has been retained. The bill heads now for a stiff fight on the floor, where the May bill will probably be offered as an amendment. Chances seem good, however, that the substitute will pass.

Vandenberg says he is delaying his acceptance of the invitation to San Francisco until the President returns. He wants a specific statement from him, the Senator says, that he goes as a free agent, free to oppose the treaty when it reaches the Senate if he deems it advisable, and in no way committing the Republican Party. The Republican Party is reported to be equally anxious to get a guarantee from Arthur on this last point.

FEBRUARY 23, 1945. The President, still abroad, hasn't signed the George bill yet, causing thereby a certain uneasiness among some people. The opposition to Wallace seems to be dwindling into a party affair, with the burden of opposition resting on the Republicans and a few dissident Democrats going along with them. There seems to be no doubt whatever that Henry will be confirmed.

Barkley, always optimistic about the Senate's speed, talks about reaching a vote on the manpower bill by Tuesday. Others, not so hopeful, are beginning to talk about at least a week's debate and possibly much more. There is a sizable sentiment for filibustering the bill until some decisive development has occurred in the Allied favor on the Western front.

FEBRUARY 24, 1945. "That guy is a brilliant man. He's really a shrewd operator." The words, rueful, were Wayne Morse's, and they concerned Bob Taft. The Senator from Oregon, representing the progressive left of the Republican Party, is engaging in his first contest with the Senator from Ohio, representing the right center of the Republican Party. The experience has amused and enlightened him. He does not show much dismay, however.

The issue is the Federal aid-to-education bill, which Taft killed more than a year ago, and which he will kill again if he can. As now presented it provides $100,000,000 to be distributed equally among the states, and an additional $200,000,000 to give a blanket $200 war emergency raise to the nation's 1,000,000 teachers. This latter provision is frankly admitted by everybody to be simply a means of getting votes for the bill, and is dismissed as such with a grin and a shrug. On the other point, however, controversy has arisen. Taft has adopted the line of argument that the grant should be based upon a sliding scale. As it stands, he argues, states that don't need it, such as Ohio, get Federal funds in the same amount as states which do need it, such as Georgia. It is not a bill to equalize, he argues, it is a bill to maintain inequality. This argument, very clever, is hard to answer. Morse, who regards the measure as "a well-drawn and desirable bill," is fighting back with a skillful catholicity of weapons that is rather surprising in a newcomer. He has obtained some facts on Ohio's underpaid teachers and presented them to the committee. He notified Taft of this, he said, and sent him a copy, and the Ohioan hasn't shown up at committee since. This is probably not due to Morse's tactics, or to any embarrassing plight of the teachers in rural Ohio. Nonetheless, tentatively and in a first-skirmish fashion, the issue has been joined in the Education and Labor Committee between the two clashing elements of the Republican Party. It may be the first sign of a contest that will ultimately engulf the national organization.

As for Taft himself, he remarked with a shrug and a grin, "The main argument seems to be that teachers aren't paid enough. Well, lots of people aren't paid enough. The theory is that there's an emergency, but if they get on the national payroll they'll never get off. The only real difficulty is that they've lost a lot of teachers, but $200 extra isn't going to stop turnover when war jobs are as attractive as they are." He is working, he said, on a substitute proposal that will give aid to the states on a sliding-scale basis: states will be required to contribute a certain per-

centage of their own income to education; if the percentage doesn't meet
the Federal standard, the Federal government will make up the difference.
"That way it will really be equalized, instead of being designed to maintain inequality, as the present bill does." The whole problem, he said, "is
to keep the primary responsibility a local responsibility. That's what my
own aim always is. I'm working on a housing bill, a health bill, and an
education bill. The basic emphasis in all of them is to start in on a small
scale and try it out. I don't believe in this wholesale-donation type of
legislation. It seems to me that the Federal responsibility—if there is one
—is simply to make up the difference, to come to the aid of the states only
when absolutely necessary. It isn't to assume an over-all responsibility to
give everybody a full education, or full housing, or full health security.
It's to act as the balance when it's needed."

Joe Ball, swinging about in the GOP like an erratic pendulum according to his own convictions, agreed with this. Aiken sided with Morse,
"providing we can keep the Federal government from controlling the
courses." All four Senators admitted candidly that this last admirable aim
could not be entirely achieved. "It seems to me inevitable in the nature
of human nature," Taft said, "that where you spend a lot of Federal
money you will have a certain amount of Federal influence. We'll do
everything we can to legislate against it, but a certain amount of it will
come regardless of everything we do."

On the manpower bill he was similarly explicit. The grant of power to
the Director of War Mobilization and the War Manpower Commissioner
"seems an extraordinary and absurd thing to do. They can practically
write their own manpower bill under this authority." Reminded of the
analogy between this and the Jesse Jones debacle, he smiled. "The trouble
is," he said candidly, "that everybody talks about restricting the powers,
and then when you come right down to it nobody knows how to write the
exact language which will do it. Congress does it every time. We all know
it, but we don't seem to be able to do anything about it."

FEBRUARY 25, 1945. Debate began today on the manpower bill. Elbert
Thomas led off, remarking sadly that "there comes a time when you have
to go along in spite of your own convictions"—as frank an admission of
surrender to browbeating by the services as could possibly be uttered.
The bill, he said, is not perfect, but it will do the job. It is the best compromise between the compulsion demanded by the Administration and
the liberty desired by the Senators. Pass it, Elbert urged, and solve the
problem.

To this Happy Chandler and Joe O'Mahoney replied with scathing and
violent sarcasm. Happy, his face growing red with anger, cried out against

the opportunism of the military. The German breakthrough gave them their chance, he cried, "and they used it to try to horsewhip the American people into regimentation." Did the Secretary of War say this legislation was necessary for the morale of the boys at the front? "Mr. President, I must disagree with the Secretary of War. It seems to me if the word goes out to the boys at the front that the democratic system has failed and the government has had to apply Fascist methods to the folks back home, then nothing could be worse for morale." O'Mahoney referred with acid sarcasm to the plea that every country but the United States works under forced labor. "We have equipped the greatest military machine in history, and we have furnished arms for the army of Britain, which has forced labor, and the army of Russia, which has forced labor. Who is it who will say that America must have forced labor?" Kilgore and Tydings, arguing on a less violent plane, Tydings for, Kilgore against, also contributed to the debate. Elbert Thomas looked harassed and sounded philosophical even when he was most upset. Obviously he had a great distaste for the task he was performing.

The Judiciary Committee, hot on the heels of some eager editorials about the House committee's action in reporting out the constitutional amendment to ratify treaties by majority vote of both houses, met this morning and voted to ban consideration of all constitutional amendments until the end of the war. This kills off the treaty amendment, the Presidential-tenure amendment, the poll-tax amendment, and any others that may be in the wind. "The issue is squarely up to the Senate," the editorials cried fervently. "The hell you say," said the Senate.

FEBRUARY 26, 1945. The manpower debate began to settle into the familiar pattern today: all predictions of speed began to seem overly optimistic as more and more people jumped into the argument. Bushfield and Kilgore have both put in amendments to strike out all penalty clauses; Revercomb has put in a complete substitute. Sentiment at the moment is so divided that there is a good chance that no bill at all will emerge. Only the realization that the men in the services have been propagandized by their leaders to the point where they could never understand a complete rejection of any legislation at all remains to salvage some sort of half-hearted legislation.

Late in the day the conference report on the insurance bill came up and Pepper immediately jumped up to challenge it on the ground that it sets aside the Supreme Court decision. O'Mahoney, feeling frustrated by this sudden threat to upset the apple cart after his more than a year of work on the bill, attempted to point out in carefully veiled language that it was the best compromise anybody could get and Pepper had better shut up and be thankful. Claude was not convinced, however, and insisted that the matter go over to tomorrow. Manpower will be further delayed.

FEBRUARY 27, 1945. Pepper argued for three hours today, after which the insurance report was approved. The Senate then returned to manpower and Josiah Bailey made a long, sarcastic and amusing speech attacking the substitute and demanding revival of the May bill. "This isn't a work-or-fight bill," he cried. "There isn't any work in it. There isn't any fight in it. It's a 'wait-and-see' bill." Bobbing up and down like a circling game cock and chuckling openly at some of his own sallies, Josiah had a good time. "I see where it says," he said, thumbing slowly through the substitute, "the War Manpower Commissioner shall coordinate—the War Manpower Commissioner shall investigate—the War Manpower Commissioner shall survey and regulate. Activate, coordinate, cooperate, survey and regulate! What an army we are bringing up! That's throwing in the reserves! That will put the fear of God into Hitler's heart—regulate and coordinate!" He spoke for an hour, calling upon the conscience of his colleagues and making frequent appeals in the name of "the boys at the front." It changed no votes and leaned far more heavily on rhetoric than it did on logic, but it was an amusing performance by one of the Senate's best performers.

FEBRUARY 28, 1945. Revercomb and Burton spoke for some time today on the manpower bill. A long session dragged on to its close. Progress was perfunctory and nothing much was accomplished. In Europe the new Allied offensive pushed on, lessening with each mile chances for the bill.

MARCH 1, 1945. The President, looking tired and drawn, spoke from the well of the House today on the Yalta conference. He sat at a desk facing the Congress and the packed galleries, with a cluster of microphones before him, a glass of water at his elbow, and floodlights trained upon him from every angle of the chamber. Throughout, his talk was punctured by the sudden glare of flashbulbs as the still cameramen took his picture; the newsreels ground steadily on. Above in the galleries sat his wife, his daughter, and his son-in-law; Crown Princess Martha of Norway; Barney Baruch; Lord Halifax; others of importance. In a row of single chairs immediately in front of him sat his Cabinet, Ickes and Frances Perkins watching him soberly, Henry Morgenthau with an almost continuous smile on his face, Francis Biddle leaning forward bolt upright like a little boy watching teacher. Just beyond in the first three rows sat the men in whose hands his ultimate place in history may lie, the Senate of the United States; beyond them, the House. One hundred and sixty years ago clever

Joint session
packs House to
hear F.D.R. report
on Yalta.

men said it should be so, and 160 years later it still was. The majesty of America, made up of so many commonplaces, seemed suddenly quite majestic indeed.

As for the speech, it was a long, rambling, rather lifeless affair, delivered in a rambling and rather lifeless fashion. He just talked along, a very good approach at first, but soon wearing upon the listener. He said nothing new except for a few departures from the script, only one of them being of much significance. "Of course there were a few other little matters," he remarked, "but I won't go into them here." Out of the few other little matters in the next few months all the world's troubles will probably come. For the most part it was a review of the newspaper reports of the conference, with nothing added and nothing taken away. When it was over the Congress stood and applauded, he smiled and waved, and then looked around with a sudden impatient annoyance for someone to wheel him away. Aides hurried forward and he was taken out. Behind him the Congress, which had heard him in the attentive and rather wondering silence with which it always hears him—"The Congress knows," he said, looking them straight in the eye, "no one believes more in constitutional processes than I"—continued to applaud for a moment more. Then the Senate rose and departed for its chamber and the House adjourned.

Comment was respectful but one theme ran throughout: "There wasn't anything new in it." Everybody said so: a note of real disappointment ran through every statement. Many people were disposed to make humorously sarcastic comments. "What did you think of the speech, Senator?" we asked Truman as he hurried past us in the hall. "One of the greatest ever given," he replied promptly and burst into hearty laughter in which we all joined. "Privately, my statement will be as informative as the speech," said Wallace White and proceeded to live up to his promise. "I'm so thrilled by all this I can't read it straight," he apologized, fumbling for his notes. That was the general tone. Once again the man who makes foreign policy had a chance to convince the men who can break it, and once again he had lost it.

Back in the chamber, the Senate debated Henry Wallace for two hours. Lister Hill and Aiken spoke for, Hawkes and Burton and Wiley against. Brewster spoke briefly in Henry's favor, Taft rebutted, also briefly. Byrd, O'Daniel, McKellar, Stewart and McCarran voted with the Republicans against. Aiken, Ball, Burton, Saltonstall, Morse, Shipstead and several others crossed the line to vote with the Democrats for. 52 to 32 Henry A. Wallace of Iowa became Secretary of Commerce and the fight that began so violently fizzled out gently in the benign atmosphere created by the President's hasty signature of the George bill upon his return to the White House yesterday.

MARCH 2, 1945. Aubrey Williams, the second left-of-center appointment of the new term, has received an unfavorable recommendation from the Agriculture Committee after three weeks of controversial, persecution-filled hearings. McKellar has succeeded in lining up a number of votes against the nominee for Rural Electrification Administrator. In committee the tally stood 12 to 8 against, and on the floor the proportion may be even higher.

Williams, a slow-spoken idealist who overdoes it a trifle, would seem, on the basis of the hearings, to be earnest, ill-advised, and reasonably competent. McKellar has attacked him on several side issues, such as his religion, but the real motive behind his rejection lies in the fact that he wrote several articles for the National Farmers Union assailing "Southern tories in Congress." That killed Aubrey. Mack has concentrated his wrath on him, and many other Southerners, who have had a hard time struggling with their consciences since they voted for Wallace, are inclined to balance that vote with a vote against Williams. The President's right to name his own Cabinet, a very real issue with many Senators, does not apply to this sub-Cabinet job.

MARCH 3, 1945. John Moses, the man from Norway, has died in the Mayo Clinic just two months after he was sworn in as junior Senator from North Dakota. A man of powerful personality and great potential, he would have been an able Senator. There is immediate talk that Gerald Nye will come back, either through appointment or by running in the next election to succeed some temporary nominee. Langer has rushed home to do what he can to stop it, but the governor is not a Langer man, and smooth-spoken Gerald may yet return from oblivion.

Following a talk with Truman, Aubrey Williams has announced flatly that he will not withdraw as a candidate for the REA post. Truman, denying modestly that he has any influence in the matter—"After all, I'm just a—what do they call it?—political eunuch"—is nonetheless beginning to emerge as a V.P. who may presently become a very powerful man. He loves politics and he is well loved by the Senate, and he is doing a great deal of stirring around these days, visiting and talking and conferring and discussing and running errands and getting them run. His power to refer bills to committees—which has become quite an issue since he turned Murray's MVA bill over to the openly inimical Commerce Committee—gives him a lever if he wants to use it. He apparently does. He is no man's stooge, and he goes about the business of politics with a youthful enthusiasm and a mature skill. The man who selected him for running mate because Harry was a good, average man who wouldn't make any trouble may wake up one of these days and find Harry, with the Senate behind him, doing the dictating on a number of things.

MARCH 4, 1945. Fred Vinson, one of Congress' darlings and an able man in his own right, has been nominated Federal Loan Administrator to succeed Jesse. This is greeted with great approval in the Senate, where Fred is a deservedly popular man. All talk of separating the vast, fantastic and inexcusable powers of the agency has of course automatically stopped with the appointment of a fellow everybody likes.

MARCH 5, 1945. The Senate met briefly and recessed out of respect for Moses. In the Banking and Currency Committee Vinson's nomination was unanimously approved and sent to the floor.

MARCH 6, 1945. "The Senate has spent enough time fooling around and messing around on this subject," its Majority Leader told it indignantly today after extraneous speeches not dealing with the manpower bill had consumed the first three hours of the session. "I do hope Senators will give some consideration to restraining themselves in the delivery of addresses which have nothing to do with it," he added. Alben was obviously fed up, and perhaps with some justification.

Earlier Bushfield, sounding the note he echoes with increasing persistence these days, had attacked Dumbarton Oaks at some length as "a new League of Nations." Voicing the growing uneasiness in the Senate concerning the Yalta settlements—now that the first hearty flush of desperate enthusiasm has died away and the cold gray light of afterthought has begun to shine—he attacked the Polish partition and turned the knife in all the open wounds there are among the Allies. The basic picture he drew was too close to reality for comfort. The isolationists have right along been handed their ammunition on a silver platter as step by step there comes into being the shabby peace of a shabby war.

Bushfield concluded, the Senate turned to the manpower bill, and once again the issue was drawn. Tom Stewart summed up best the one basic argument of those who want compulsion. "General Marshall wants it," he cried, "Admiral King wants it, the Commander-in-Chief wants it, the Secretary of War wants it, the Secretary of the Navy wants it!" Albert Hawkes nailed that argument, if such it could be called, subsequently. "Simply because these gentlemen know what should be done in the military sphere," he said, "does that mean that they know everything about civilian production? And supposing they do tell us they should have compulsion. Is there no obligation on us to make up our own minds? Have we no responsibility in this Senate of the United States to exercise our own judgment?"

MARCH 7, 1945. The Senate just doesn't like dictatorship. It made that abundantly clear today in three overwhelming votes. The first came on taking the penalty clause out of the manpower bill. This clause, inserted by Austin, was so vague that no one could be sure who it applied to, employers or employees. The Senate knocked it down 44 to 35. The next vote came on Bailey's attempt to amend Revercomb's "draft loafers" substitute so that it would hit every male between the ages of 18 and 45 not employed in some industry essential to the war effort. The Senate knocked it down 60 to 23. The third vote came on Revercomb's substitute for the whole bill, unamended but partially compulsive. The Senate knocked it down 54 to 27.

MARCH 8, 1945. 63–16 the manpower bill passed the Senate today, late in a long, irascible session. Prior to the final vote the penalty clause was put back in—in a new form, submitted by Joe Ball, which clearly defined the employer's liability and provided for conviction through the courts. In that form it was acceptable on a vote of 40–36.

Joe Guffey

As the session opened, in one of those extraneous speeches Senators cannot be prevented from giving, Joe Guffey sounded the tocsin of alarm against the Republicans in Pennsylvania in 1946. Apparently feeling the hot winds of an off-year campaign blowing on his neck, Joe sailed into "the Pews and other oily fat cats" who are "trying to steal the election of 1946." He also attacked Bushfield and the Republican National Committee. Brewster, rising to ask a question at one point, remarked delicately, "In Maine we are innocent of such sums. But I of course recognize the Senator from Pennsylvania as an authority on political corruption." Old Joe, with a hide like a rhinoceros, grinned and cracked back, "I ought to be, I grew up in that atmosphere—although not in my own party." Brewster grinned too and sat down. Others laughed.

Bailey, also extraneous, went into a long philosophic discussion of Henry Wallace and Jesse Jones and the theory of 60,000,000 jobs. Presently Dick Russell arose and with his characteristic able use of sarcasm, asked Barkley if it would be against the rules of the Senate if he spoke on the pending bill. Barkley said drily that it would be, but he thought

Russell might get unanimous consent if he wanted to do it. Russell went on into an indignant, entertaining plea for the more compulsive May bill, but despite his amusing sallies ("General Guffey, General Taft and General Pepper wheeling up their battalions to defeat this measure," etc.) he did not answer a single one of the specific facts on national production offered by the bill's opponents. Later Pepper got the floor and in an urbane and witty speech accepted the promotion to general and repeated the arguments on his side of the issue.

On the final vote Happy, and one or two others against all legislation of any sort on this problem, joined Harry Byrd and a handful of Southerners eager to get absolute compulsion to make the 16 votes against the modified and watered-down Senate bill. All others fell into line behind it, and it went to the House with a very definite expression of opinion to support it.

Senate Barbershop

31

"WE'D BETTER COUNT TEN"

MARCH 9, 1945. The State Department, still at this late date playing the dangerous game of trying to bypass the Senate, has run head-on into the Foreign Relations Committee. An understanding was reached, some time back, that the international aviation agreements made at Chicago should not be formally concluded until it could be determined whether they were executive agreements or treaties. It now appears that the department has been proceeding as though they were executive agreements and Foreign Relations is understandably upset. A resolution was introduced (and came within an ace of passing) to censure the department and declare the agreements treaties. Barkley, still the peacemaker after all these storms and stresses, interposed and hastily promised to take the matter up directly with the President. Somewhat mollified, the committee agreed to wait and see. A little more suspicion, a little more dislike and mistrust, have been added to the heavy burden Dumbarton Oaks must carry when it comes to the Hill.

MARCH 10, 1945. Old Mack from Tennessee, the feudin' boy, is still after TVA. His Appropriations Committee reported out the Independent Offices Appropriations bill this morning with an amendment canceling the agency's revolving fund. As a corollary to this McKellar has an amendment he will offer from the floor, requiring TVA to turn all receipts in to the Treasury and get its operating expenses direct from Congress. This is the same amendment he offered last year. Despite his persistent attacks on Lilienthal during the hearings, the Senator insists that this is just a matter of principle with him. No matter who was chairman, he would feel the same.

MARCH 11, 1945. Another first-class fight seems to be brewing in the House on the manpower bill. The Senate's version was not received on Friday, when it might have been put directly to a vote before anybody had time to get organized. The official story is that the Senate's messenger went over and tried to deliver it, was not recognized immediately, and left in disgust when a roll call began. This was the first time anyone could remember when the messenger's feelings have been so easily hurt, and the popular interpretation is that he was instructed not to linger because if he did the House might approve the Senate version and the House conferees then would not be able to take their own May bill into conference. Chairman Andy May of the House Military Affairs Committee insists that his bill will prevail, but Ed Johnson remarks bluntly that in view of the war news he'd better take the Senate bill and be thankful, or there won't be any bill at all.

MARCH 12, 1945. "I have a sense of dedication to this cause," said Warren Austin recently, "which overshadows everything I have ever undertaken either in public or private life." Back from Mexico City, where they helped draft the temporary wartime Act of Chapultepec providing that aggression by one American state upon another would be regarded as aggression against all, he and Tom Connally reported to the Senate. There was everywhere, they said, a spirit of friendliness and hope, a sense of co-operation and unity [*fortified at the Rio Conference of 1947 which made the arrangement permanent*]. Connally spoke at some length and at one time was confronted by a group of Senators waiting to be recognized which included Bridges, Ed Johnson, Butler, and Taft and Wiley. He settled on Johnson, who caught him short in the statement that the American republics accepted the Monroe Doctrine. Did they? Ed wondered. Did the Senator mean that? Well, the spirit of it, Tom said. Later, speaking in his ringing tones, Alexander Wiley made his inevitable address for the day, pointing out as surely as Fate that "some months ago I introduced a resolution——" The resolution urged the Executive to take the Senate into his confidence on foreign policy. The Austin–Connally report cast some light, Alec felt. He praised it, expressed regret that there was no greater frankness from the President himself, and sat down to look about him with his bright vague grin.

McKellar came armed with piles and piles of papers, reports and books, but the opportunity did not arrive: committee amendments to the Independent Offices bill took up the day and TVA was not reached. Mack is ready, however, and the ammunition is waiting at his desk.

MARCH 13, 1945. War Manpower Commissioner Paul McNutt, testifying before cherubic Harry Byrd, impatient old Muley Doughton and quizzical, blunt-spoken Harold Knutson of Minnesota, took nearly two hours this morning to tell the Joint Committee on the Reduction of Nonessential Expenditures that he has no real authority to enforce the orders of the War Manpower Commission. This admission, damning enough and disturbing enough to the manpower program, was not to be drawn with ease from the handsome, rather impatient commissioner. In fact, he never did come out with it in so many words. "I can't understand why you won't tell us just what your authority is," said Harold Knutson, knowing perfectly well. "You seem to be just a sort of benign persuader." McNutt, exactly that, did his best to avoid saying so, and was finally dismissed with the quiet, fatherly advice from Byrd that he present the committee with an exact statement of his powers and authorities. He said he would.

Over in the crowded little Commerce room in the Capitol the newly confirmed Secretary appeared before a crowded audience to testify on the international air agreements. To help him understand these problems, Henry Wallace said, he was going to learn to fly.

On the floor, the Senate spent a long time deciding to uphold the Appropriations Committee in its grant of $35,000,000 to states and municipalities for postwar planning. Bob La Follette wanted to raise it to $75,000,000, on the ground that plans had better be complete and adequate or trouble will ensue. Bob Taft, acrid in his contempt for "the popular idea that the government will always finance public works to stop unemployment"—which the government of course will do—argued against it. So did Dick Russell, citing the $75,000,000 sarcastically as "an example of our economy." The bill, reduced $5,000,000,000 under the 1945 figure, could probably have stood the $75,000,000 but it was voted down overwhelmingly, as was a later attempt to make the figure $50,000,000.

That done, McKellar tried to get through an amendment requiring the states to contribute on a 50–50 matching basis. This drew scathing denunciation from such diverse people as Wayne Morse and Walter George, the latter pointing out that "this perfectly ridiculous proposal" would make the states contribute 50 per cent to something which is, under the terms of the Reconversion Act, only a loan in the first place. It too was beaten.

Then the executive session began, and Tom Connally immediately tried to call up the Mexican water treaty. McKellar interrupted and asked for an immediate consideration of Aubrey Williams. Connally said the treaty was too important to be laid aside "for one little bitty 2-by-4 job," and refused to permit it. The treaty, he said, had precedence, and he intended to go ahead with it. Sheridan Downey ventured the prediction that between "30 and 35 Senators" wished to speak on the treaty. McKellar asked with a grin if Downey could say what year they would conclude. He added piously that he *did* hope they could vote promptly on Mr. Williams. The most Connally would do, grudgingly, was say that if Senators anxious to vote on Williams could work out an agreement and set a definite time, then the treaty might be laid aside. But he wasn't promising anything. There the matter rested as the session ended.

MARCH 14, 1945. McKellar, recognizing the impossibility of getting a two-thirds vote to permit him to suspend the rules and add his legislative amendment against TVA to the Independent Offices bill, dropped the project today after a long, violent denunciation of people who say he is against the Authority. "Every one of those dams with one exception I got," he told the Senate. "All I did was get every dollar for those dams." Though the great Nebraskan has been dead now for nearly a year, Mack continued his feud with George Norris. What really happened to bring about TVA, he said, was that the President, visiting the Tennessee with a Congressional junket, turned to Norris and asked him to introduce the TVA bill already introduced by Lister Hill, then a Representative, in the House. So all along it was Lister Hill's doing, and not George Norris'. And people who say McKellar wants the patronage in TVA? Why, Mr. President, there isn't a word of truth in it. The truth of the matter is that patronage is a detriment to a Senator and he is better off without it.

That task completed, Mack left the floor and fainted in the washroom. Immediately the ghost of Death, never far from the mind of the Senate, began to walk. Les Biffle hurried about, getting and giving information, Barkley and White conferred worriedly, other Senators gathered in little groups. Outside in the reading room George Carver, the Capitol physician, diagnosed the ailment as a too-hasty meal before coming to the floor. Barkley and White agreed to recess the Senate. Old Mack arose under his own steam, badly shaken but as grimly tenacious of life as he is of everything else. The Senate relaxed.

Elsewhere today, in the little old Education and Labor Committee room tucked away in the Capitol, the Joint Committee on the Reorganization of Congress got under way. Bob La Follette, succeeding Maloney as chairman, presided with the very able Mike Monroney of Oklahoma from the House. Under an amendment introduced by John Bankhead, fearful of an attempt to do away with the filibuster, the committee has no authority to make any recommendation to change the rules. The task before it is of the utmost importance, and the forces arrayed against its ever achieving anything are enormous. They include Congressional inertia, vested interest in outmoded traditions, and perhaps above all the unthinking tendency of too large a part of the public to greet with scorn the very modernizations and increased staffs and emoluments that are imperative if their Congress is to do the job that lies ahead of it.

MARCH 15, 1945. The Russians, ever-sensitive to people who don't agree with them in every particular, have come out with an attack on Vandenberg for his attack on them for their Polish policy. The sage of Grand Rapids, armed with an exchange of letters from the President which specifically guarantees his independence of action at San Francisco, arose the other day to condemn the repressions of the Lublin government. He was much disturbed, Van said, and he expressed his disturbance in no uncertain terms. What he said was of course entirely reasonable but naturally somewhat critical of the Russians. The Russians yelped, as usual. More and more it seems likely that San Francisco will be the all-important place, and that in that all-important place the all-important man will be the Senator from Michigan.

Finance Committee took approximately one minute this morning to approve the bill raising the debt limit to $300,000,000,000. The executive session in which this was done followed an open hearing during which dark, trim little Undersecretary Daniel Bell of the Treasury submitted to questioning. On hand in unexpended balances at this moment, he said, is $151,000,000,000, but "We know full well we will be back before the end of fiscal 1946 asking you for another increase." The incongruity between these two statements was never explained. It never is. During the morning the all-around ability a Senator develops was once again amply demonstrated. Thick and fast and technical, with facts and figures and financial terms most people outside Treasury never even hear of, the questions were tossed at Daniel Bell. In Finance Committee a Senator knows finance, but from Finance he may go to Agriculture, and in Agriculture he knows agriculture—and so on. It is worthy of considerable respect, the vast fund of knowledge on government and the nation's affairs members of this much-maligned institution have. They know what they're talking about, most of them, and it is no small amount.

MARCH 16, 1945. Josiah Bailey, battling on all fronts these days, engaged in a long jurisdictional spat with Wheeler today. Harry Truman as usual was in the middle: he had referred the aviation bills to Josiah's Commerce Committee instead of to Burt's Interstate Commerce Committee. "The Chair will say," he remarked plaintively the other day, "that he certainly hopes the committee on the reorganization of Congress will be able to recommend some rule which will clearly define where bills are to go. The

Chair has been accused of all sorts of ulterior motives in his referral of bills, and he would certainly appreciate a guide."

The opponents of Aubrey Williams, as anxious to get a prompt vote as his friends are to delay one, attempted again today to break into the water-treaty debate. Connally, making the opening statement for the treaty, repulsed them indignantly. Although against Williams himself, he said, he didn't want to "send the Senate off on a rabbit-hunt." Barkley, delighted to have his help in stalling off a vote, waxed equally sarcastic and finally got quite angry, to the point of snapping at Wallace White, something he rarely does. White, expressing his earnest desire to get the matter settled, suggested, "What I want—" "It doesn't matter what you want," said Barkley bluntly. "There won't be any vote today." Bankhead finally got the floor and introduced a resolution to lay aside the treaty and take up Aubrey. It was made the pending business and the Senate went over to Monday.

MARCH 17, 1945. "No, I'm not going to support Bankhead's resolution," Connally said irritably today. "I'm going to speak against it. 'Course I know what they want. They're afraid if they can't get a vote right away, the other side will persuade enough doubters to get him confirmed. I'm against him myself, but I'm not going to lay aside the treaty if I can help it. I'm gettin' fed up with all this fuss over these damned confirmations. They aren't important, and all they do is divide us and make everybody mad and leave scars and wounds. I'm gettin' fed up."

John Bankhead said prospects for his resolution look good. "I think we'll pass it," he said. "I'm sure we will. Obviously the people who are for Williams know we will, you could see that from the way Barkley acted yesterday. We'll pass it all right."

Later in the day another Williams opponent was equally jubilant. Calling Bilbo on another matter I began, "Senator, this is Allen Drury of United Press—" "He-llo there, Alfonso-Renaldo!" he yelled in his characteristic way. "How you-all?" "I'm fine, Senator," I said, "and how are you?" "Oh, I'm fine," said Bilbo, "I'm fine. Rarin' to go and no one to go with. What can I do for you?" I told him. "I'm sorry," he said elaborately, "but that's a mattuh of military secrecy and I don't care to comment." "Well, what about Aubrey Williams?" I said. "The ban of secrecy on Mistuh Williams has been removed," said the Senator from Mississippi. "He's on his way out. Yes, sir, he's on his way out. Call again, friend scribe and reporter!" And he banged down the receiver with a jubiliant cackle dying away on the wire.

On the manpower front, Warren Austin, the inevitable compromiser, is already busy with a new plan for the conferees to consider when they meet Monday. It will "localize the obligation," he said, "and show up these spurious claims of coercion and slavery for what they are."

MARCH 18, 1945. Various facts come gradually to light concerning the desperate behind-the-scenes struggle waged by the services for the House's May manpower bill. There was the War Manpower Commission, browbeaten and threatened into withholding its January report showing "the best manpower situation since the war began," a report that would of course have greatly weakened arguments of the bill's proponents. There were the Secretary of War and the Secretary of the Navy, cajoling, threatening, propagandizing, twisting the facts to suit the fable. There was the Congress, placed under the whip and told that if it didn't pass the bill the services wanted, retribution would be forthcoming. One member of Naval Affairs Committee in the Senate—and he is typical of many—was told that if he didn't go along, important contracts in his state would be canceled. (This for the bill which was to "help us win the war"—"increase production"—"get the necessary weapons for victory.") Many others were subjected to a pressure as ruthless, as vicious and as dangerous to democracy. And all the time, sowing the seeds of a tragic misunderstanding no amount of explanation can ever quite kill off, the propaganda went out through all the services' broadcasts and newspapers and official journals to the troops that the Congress was letting them down, that the folks back home were betraying them, that the civilians—those despicable people— weren't fighting the war. Downtown in the Pentagon and the Navy Building smooth-talking incompetents schemed and schemed and schemed for power.

Ultimately Jimmy Byrnes became disturbed: this was carrying a good thing too far. The word went out—officially. In the office of the Secretary of War and the Secretary of the Navy, the tactics were suddenly changed. The watchword became "Hands off" and sweet reason. Pressure was suddenly relaxed, but not before the May bill was dead in the Senate. Ambition had over-reached itself, and the country may always be grateful for that. For these men knew they needed no bill. These men knew what the truth of the situation was, and they knew what they were doing. And they did it just the same.

Nor is the battle yet over. The conference begins tomorrow, and 10 men are easier to handle than 531. Maybe there will be a new offensive up the Avenue. Maybe the reserves will come up once more. Maybe the Battle of Capitol Hill will enter a new phase. We shall see.

MARCH 19, 1945. 52 to 33 the Senate voted today to lay aside the Mexican water treaty and take up immediately the nomination of Aubrey Williams. His supporters, stunned and disappointed by the size of the vote—they had expected a trouncing, but nothing like that—rallied gamely and began to make their case. Scott Lucas took the floor for the first time since the soldier-vote fight, his handsome face deeply tanned from a vacation in Florida, his mouth bitter as he assailed McKellar and his friends. Carl Hatch, determined to embarrass Williams' opponents, made a point of no quorum six times during the afternoon, each time over McKellar's protest. Lucas assailed McKellar's charges of Communism against the nominee. There had been an editorial in one of the papers of his state, said Lucas scathingly, entitled "Comrade Lucas." "Mr. President," he said, "if I'm a Communist, so is every other member of the United States Senate. And that includes you," he said to McKellar. "You too, Mr. Bushfield," he said, looking across the aisle. Bushfield grinned. The charges against Williams, admittedly shaky and unsubstantiated, were sarcastically denounced. Once Taft precipitated a flurry by charging that "Mr. Williams and his friends have called on every Senator asking him to make up his mind yes or no." Tunnell and Hatch sprang up indignantly and denied it. There was much real personal bitterness today.

The strategy of the opponents is simply to sit still and let the proponents talk themselves out. They have the votes, and there's no point in overexertion under that circumstance.

James Forrestal, rapid of speech and brisk of manner, trim and self-possessed, appeared before an Interstate Commerce subcommittee today to testify on a Navy proposition for a monopolistic cartel over all postwar overseas communications. "I have reached this conclusion reluctantly," he said, and so he should have, for the plan was obviously thought up by some of his ambitious underlings in uniform. The corporation would be "privately owned but government supervised." Independence of action would be retained for it by having a 20-man board of directors. Of these only five would represent the government (State, War, Navy, Commerce and Post Office), and all they would do would be to exercise a veto over routes, managerial policies, personnel, technical developments, and plans for expansion. Otherwise, the civilians on the board would be quite free to do as they pleased. The essential principle of consolidation may be inevitable, but the Navy's plan is a plan to keep the Navy and Army in control of a very important facility when the war ends. It served as a reminder that the day when the services are cut right back down to size cannot come too soon. It is imperative that it be done at the earliest possible moment.

The manpower conference began this afternoon, a three-hour session that produced little news. Nobody budged. It was that first preliminary circling-around and sounding-out that always starts a Congressional conference. Neither house is in any mood to yield, although Warren Austin is hard at work on his compromise if anybody wants to.

MARCH 20, 1945. John Moses' successor was sworn in today, Milton Young, a tall, shy, scholarly-looking farmer. Langer escorted him down the aisle for the ceremony. Elsewhere on the floor, exercising his prerogative as an ex-Senator, Gerald Nye looked on with an impassive, expressionless face. Bennett Champ Clark was back too, shaking hands and conferring and listening to the debate, seeming to restrain himself with difficulty from springing up instinctively to raise a point of parliamentary order and tangle everybody up.

In the manpower conference, the Austin compromise was outlined to the conferees. The reactions were varied, but the general tenor was unfavorable. It is apparently much stronger than either the House or the Senate bill. The conference is recessing until Thursday to give members a chance to study it.

The Williams debate settled into the marathon stage this afternoon, with Lucas and Ellender taking McKellar to task for his testimony before the Agriculture Committee. It was chiefly of interest as a demonstration in McKellar techniques. The two proponents attacked Mack's lack of evidence for the charge that Williams was a Communist. Mack jumped up. "Mistuh President," he cried indignantly, "I do hope the Senutuhs will quote me correctly. I nevuh—I *nevuh*—attacked Mr. Williams' intelligence in my life. This is what I said about Mistuh Williams' intelligence—" and he proceeded to read from the record of the hearings, where he had referred to Williams as "a most delightful, most intelligent man." Lucas and Ellender attempted to point out that they were discussing the charge of communism, but—"I nevuh attacked his intelligence in my life, Mr. President!" He was quite indignant about it.

MARCH 21, 1945. The Austin manpower-bill compromise, in the words of one Senate conferee, is "a holy terror. It doesn't leave anything to the imagination. It has more teeth than a shark. It's worse than anything either the Senate or the House ever dreamed up." Another called it "a monstrosity," another "fantastic." House members were cautious, but Ewing Thomason of Texas considered it "a pretty good omelette, especially since it includes many features of the House bill." What it does is apply the voluntary methods of the Senate bill, with their compulsions on employers, and then—when the War Mobilization Director, at the behest of his service-dominated Manpower Priorities Committee, finds that voluntary methods have failed—it applies the outright labor-draft of the House bill. In addition it clamps a job freeze on all workers now in war industry. "A holy terror" is not too strong. "In my opinion," said O'Mahoney candidly, "It doesn't have a chance." Its author is not under many illusions either. "It gives us something to talk about," he said. "That's the funniest bunch of men I ever saw. We got together and we didn't have a thing we could agree on. This at least gives us a starting point."

A few Republicans, Willis and Shipstead among them, spoke against Aubrey Williams today. Joe Guffey arose to reply to a Bushfield speech which in turn was a reply to his speech attacking Bushfield last week. Ellender attempted to tackle McKellar again and was badly beaten for his pains. Yesterday Ellender said McKellar said that the head of REA should be a businessman and an engineer and a farmer. McKellar challenged him to produce the evidence that he had ever said any such thing. Elender read the hearings before the committee: Mack had said just that. "Does the Senator deny that what I said yesterday was true?" Ellender demanded, gesturing violently and bobbing up and down. "Ah suhtinly do," said McKellar slowly. "Yes, suh, Ah suhtinly do. What you read from the committee record, now, Ah stand behind that 100 per cent. But what you said yesterday—no, suh. Mistuh President!" he cried indignantly, raising his right hand above his head and bringing it down violently in his characteristic way, "Ah have been surprised and shocked at the attacks made against me by the Senatuh from Louisiana and the Senatuh from Illinois. You would think Ah was the candidate for this job. But Mistah Williams is. These two gentlemen have devoted theah time to attackin' me, Mistuh President. Now, Mistuh President, why do they make these attacks on me? Ah'm not the candidate. There aren't two more lovable or more able membuhs of this Senate, Mistuh President, but" (he turned to them in a fatherly way and his voice dropped to its most gently dulcet and confidential) "Ah do think you would get more votes if you would tell us about the good points of Mistuh Williams and not spend your time attacking me."

Late in the afternoon McKellar attempted to get an agreement that a vote be held not later than 2 P.M. tomorrow. Ellender objected. Then Barkley attempted to get an agreement limiting each Senator to 20 minutes; Ellender objected. Barkley raised it to 30 minutes; Ellender was satisfied but Happy objected. As he remarked later, he had "sat there every day and suffered, and if Ah want to speak tomorrow Ah don't intend to be closed off. It's just the foot under the door if we get into the habit of these agreements limiting debate; it's just the foot under the door and you don't know where it might lead to. Ah'm not havin' any of that."

Earlier in the day La Follette in a slow-paced, very effective if somewhat flamboyant speech ("Mr. President," he began soberly, "already I hear the rumble of the tumbrils") conceded that "the rejection of this nomination is a foregone conclusion." And John McClellan estimated in an interview "from 8 to 10 votes margin against him." Burt Wheeler spoke bitterly on intolerance ("Already you see creeping in this country the intolerance which you saw creeping in Europe after the last war, and which is already following this. You can see it will ultimately result in an upheaval") and Glen Taylor, speaking in an effective, slightly over-heavy voice, remarked that "there is a tide in history, and the people know it. After we have produced all this for destruction, they are not going to accept any more the idea that there is not enough for everyone." This theme, basic to the age, is beginning to crop up in Senate debate more and more frequently as the war nears its end and the artificial stimulus of organized chaos begins to give way to the blank, staring fact that we know no more now than we ever did about how to control and operate the machine we have created.

MARCH 22, 1945. Gathering in the beautiful Presidential Room of the Statler for the annual dinner of the White House Correspondents Association, we stood about talking at the tables, slow to sit down, knowing that the moment would come when we would have to rise. At 7:30 it came. Over to the side, at the end of the long head table, they drew the curtains apart; the director of the Navy Band raised his baton. There came a blare of trumpets and "Hail to the Chief." Surrounded by his guards and his cops and the Secret Service, leaning forward in his wheel chair, looking old and thin and scrawny-necked, they brought in the Prisoner of the Presidency.

Curiously, he paid no attention to us at all as we stood and applauded. Not even when he had reached his place at the center and shifted into his seat and was staring straight out at us did he acknowledge the reception in any way. We might not have been there at all, and for a moment it gave one the uneasy feeling that, perhaps preoccupied beyond all such social graces, he didn't know we were. After a minute or two more we sat down. Presently, when the Association president, Merriman Smith of United Press, introduced him formally, we arose and applauded again. This time he noticed, snapped out of it, waved and laughed a little

in a deprecating way as though, really, this wasn't necessary. Whatever
had been on his mind, that banished it. From then on he came to life and
began to enjoy himself.

All down the head table and scattered at the tables about the gleaming
room, the powers of the Roosevelt Administration were on hand—more
of them in one room and one place, probably, than at any time or place
since the fourth inauguration. To the President's right, separated from
him by Joe Fox of the *Star*, Harry Truman looked spick and span in a
dark suit with a handkerchief, carefully folded so that exactly four corners
showed, stuck in his breast pocket; beginning to seem, already, like a man
who is getting a great deal of experience in the social life. Merriman sat
on the President's left, and beyond him the Earl of Athlone, Governor
General of Canada, a very tall old Englishman with a rosy-domed head,
a huge walrus mustache, and amiable, obligingly interested eyes. On
down the table on either side of the President were Leahy and Marshall
and King, and Ickes and Biddle and Morgenthau, Wickard and Jimmy
Byrnes. Six seats to the left of the President the Secretary of Commerce
sat in bashful soberness, drawn out occasionally by John Crider of *The
New York Times*, sitting on his left, but more often silent and earnestly intent, even in the midst of the most uproarious laughter. Mr. Justices Jackson, Douglas and Rutledge represented the Court. Out among the tables
sat some of the men so important to the man at the head of the table: the
amiable Alben, slow, enormous Joe Ball, Dick Russell, Warren Austin,
Scott Lucas, quizzically able Wayne Morse.

Danny Kaye, a magnificent entertainer, a player in the old, traditional
sense, headlined the entertainment, getting his gilt-edged audience to
furnish unintelligible gibberish as a background for his rendition of Min-
nie the Moocher. With him were Jimmy Durante, a bundle of energy with
a sloppy brown hat and a cigar ("What a stinker that General Marshall
gave me," he said indignantly, "what a stinker!") keeping up a running
patter against the background of his trademark tune, "You gotta start the
day with a song"; Fanny Brice, passing from Baby Snooks on into Fanny
Brice singing "I'm a second-hand Rose, with second-hand clothes . . ."
and the humor furnished by the correspondents themselves. "We knew it
was time for a change," said Joe Fox, assuming the presidency of the Association, "and *we* made it."

But in all the entertainment, there was one principal performer, and
to him after every sally on the stage hundreds of eyes turned and among
the tables the little remarks passed back and forth: "He's really enjoying
it, isn't he? . . . He likes that. . . . The Old Man is getting a kick out of it,
all right. . . . He takes everything in stride, doesn't he?" And more soberly,

the other questions, the questions he faces in increasing number everywhere he goes: "How does he look?...Well, what do you think of him? ...Looks pretty thin, doesn't he? Looking pretty old...."

Impervious to our interest, as one who has faced thousands upon thousands of audiences must eventually become impervious, the President did enjoy himself, smoking steadily and steadily drinking wine, leaning forward often with his hand cupped behind his ear to have Merriman tell him the joke as the laughter welled up in the room, sometimes joining in it wholeheartedly, sometimes just sitting there listening with an intent, vague expression on his face, letting his jaw drop and his mouth fall open so that he looked at moments almost too intent, almost too vague.

Watching him closely, as we all did throughout the evening, there came again the strange wonderment, the puzzled question implicit in the attitude of every audience he meets here in the city that knows him better than any other—for it knows him not at all. "What manner of man is this?" men seem to ask; and they never find the answer. You think of all the things he has done, all the good things and all the bad things, the glowing idealisms, the shabby, inexcusable expediencies, the great gestures and the devious ambitions, and you wonder in bafflement, for there is no answer, what goes on inside. What is he really like, the aging politico, the four-times President, the curious symbol of a desperate hope? Will anyone ever know? It does not seem likely.

At the end, suffering from a cold and speaking with a convivial glibness, he said he was going to give us a story. "But first I want to give you a word, the word *Humanity*. We all love Humanity, you love Humanity, I love Humanity. Humanity's with me all the time. I go to bed and I dream of Humanity, I get up and I eat breakfast and there's Humanity, Humanity follows me around all day. So with that in mind, with that word, Humanity, here's your headline and here's your story—I am calling off the press conference for tomorrow morning." We laughed and applauded and again we stood, for he was shifting back into his wheel chair, and in a moment they were wheeling him out. The applause rose and increased, and just before he went out the door he acknowledged it with the old, familiar gesture, so that the last we saw of Franklin Roosevelt was the head going up with a toss, the smile breaking out, the hand uplifted and waving in the old, familiar way.*

MARCH 23, 1945. By a 16-vote margin, 52–36, the Senate today rejected

---

* These words, written the next morning, were significant enough of the growing premonitions in Washington concerning the President's health—as they were a tribute, also, to the amazing powers of recuperation which, even then, enabled him to begin an evening in virtual stupor and conclude it with a fair semblance of his earlier self.

Aubrey Williams. The decision, a certainty almost from the beginning, was made in a flurry of bitter charge and countercharge. Inflammatory statements that confused the issue on both sides were uttered by indignant men, some of whom saw in the issue the basic problem of the times, some of whom—on both sides of the aisle—saw a chance for political advantage. Whether it is true or not that the fate of nations depends upon these nominations, a hysterical propaganda from the left has insisted so in three fights now—the State Department fight, the Wallace fight, and the Williams fight. "This is the first battle in a total war," said James Patton of the Farmers Union later with a flamboyance understood on the Hill but perhaps misunderstood in the country: "We will meet these Senators where they live." And he announced a "victory" dinner next Wednesday at which the President's wife will speak for Aubrey Williams. Statements equally inflammatory were made throughout the debate on both sides. Some people meant them, others did not; but the country, having no standards by which to judge, has doubtless taken them all at face value.

That is the basic danger: that whether there is an economic and social conflict or not, we may never be able to solve our problems by peaceable democratic means because the country has been propagandized into believing that they cannot be solved by those means.

MARCH 24, 1945. George Aiken, the Republican's left-of-center maverick, discussed the Williams rejection today in his quiet, sober, sound, Vermont way. "I think we'd better count 10," he said concerning the Farmers Union statement, but, he said, "regardless of the sincerity of much of the opposition to Aubrey Williams—and I know most of the opposition to him was sincere—the outcome will inevitably be regarded as a victory for the enemies of REA. I hope the President will insist that whoever is administrator of the REA will be friendly to the objectives of this great organization. ... As far as the political effect is concerned, only time can tell. There is unquestionably an increasing cleavage in this country between those who believe in full employment and plenty and those who believe in monopoly and scarcity and control of our economic system by a few. We'd be blind not to recognize that. I think we're about in the middle of a fight which will continue for the next few years and will end with victory for those who believe in plenty. It will be felt in '46 and will probably be decisive in the election of 1948.... ("You mean social and political conflict, I judge," I said. "You don't think there's a chance for physical conflict." "I think there's a hell of a good chance," said George Aiken.) If both Democrats and Republicans put up reactionary candidates in 1948, there will be a third ticket—not a third party—in the field. There will be a struggle within the parties themselves. The main body of voters who voted the Republican ticket last fall are out of sympathy with the policies advocated by some of the Republicans' most vocal national spokesmen.... The Republicans *must* stop their backward-looking attitude before they can hope to win national elections. They've got to about-face—they've got to about-face like hell."

To Leverett Saltonstall, pink-cheeked, toothy and amiable, I put the following question: "Senator," I said, "I've been talking to Senator Aiken and he thinks there is a basic social conflict in the country which will be felt in '46 and may be decisive in the 1948 election. He thinks the Republican party must liberalize if it expects to win in '48. Do you have any thoughts along that line you might care to express?"

That was what I asked him and this is what he told me: "I have always had faith in the reactions of our people when they understand the facts and the facts are brought home to them. Their emotions are generally right. I believe in telling them the truth as circumstances arise in each case. How their reactions will be to conditions in 1946 and 1948 it is impossible to determine. Everyone is interested in cleaning up the war as quickly as possible and making as lasting a peace as possible. When our boys and girls come out of the armed forces they will be the biggest single minority group in the country. They can make or break this country. It is for this reason that I am very anxious to see they have the opportunity for education, for with education comes understanding of their responsibility toward themselves and toward the country. I believe that the average boy and girl wants what I have wanted and what every American citizen wants—a good home, a job that will give a feeling of security, and an opportunity to educate children a little better than they were educated, in a decent community."

He gave me this statement in the presence of his secretary and when he had concluded he made me read it back. "Do you want to qualify 'lasting peace?'" suggested his secretary. "Make it just 'lasting peace,'" said Leverett Saltonstall. "Take out the 'as possible.'" I read it again. "That's my story," he said. "Thank you, Senator," I said, "it will help me with mine." I left, after an experience a Capitol Hill reporter has rather often. There are two explanations for the secretary-in-the-room, read-it-back-to-me technique. It is a sign of a very cautious man—or a Candidate. Unfortunately the two are far too often synonymous.

Surprising everyone, on a motion by shrewd Ed Johnson, who knows his Senate, the manpower conferees suddenly agreed upon a bill today. It does away with the labor draft but it imposes a "labor freeze," and places penalties on both employers and employees. "Taken in conjunction with Selective Service," said Andy May, "this amounts to a labor draft." Then he got cautious and took that off the record, afraid that such an admission from the House would further antagonize the Senate. The House is expected to accept the bill dutifully. The outcome in the Senate is in doubt. Not even shrewd Ed Johnson, who knows his Senate, would predict the decision there.

32

"A GREAT DEAL DEPENDS"

MARCH 25, 1945. The manpower conference report upon examination turns out to be even more of a holy terror than the Austin compromise, even though the motion to get it to the floor was made by Ed Johnson, who applied that term to Austin's bill. The new blockbuster makes Jimmy Byrnes literally a dictator, backed with statutory authority running to June 30, 1946. Under the bill, relying entirely on his own whims and judgments, for there are absolutely no guiding standards set up, the Director of War Mobilization may, as he "deems" necessary: (1) establish labor ceilings in any area, activity, or industry he pleases; (2) impose a labor freeze upon any individual, any industry, any area, any farm he pleases; (3) regulate by such policies as he pleases the hiring and rehiring of workers in any area, industry or activity he pleases; (4) prohibit the acceptance of employment by any worker he pleases in any area, industry or activity he pleases. Imprisonment for a year or $10,000 fine, or both, is imposed upon anyone violating the unknown regulations which he may at any future time, with complete freedom of choice (for there are no standards in the bill), impose upon the country.

"A great deal depends upon the way this bill is administered," Elbert Thomas told us yesterday in his gentle voice. "It won't be abused," he added with calm confidence. "No, it won't be abused. It will be spotty, always remember that. It will be spotty." Out of the minds of 8 men—O'Mahoney and Dewey Short of Missouri from the House would have none of it—has come the most fantastic, fascistic bill ever proposed in America. It is a strange commentary on the times that it is expected to have no trouble in the House, and perhaps not too much in the Senate. By so tenuous and fragile a thread does our democracy hang, and here in the Congress, by gentle Elbert and shrewd Ed and idealistic Harold Burton and good-hearted Warren Austin, by pragmatic Andy May and matter-of-fact Ewing Thomason and amiable Walter Andrews and agreeable Overton Brooks, the thread is about to be cut. Only the full

Senate stands between the country and such a consummation. What the full Senate will do is today anyone's guess.

MARCH 26, 1945. O'Mahoney made one last attempt in the final manpower conference today to take the labor freeze out of the bill, and then he took his battle to the floor. In an impassioned speech which he obviously meant, he cried out bitterly against the conferees and their monstrous measure, which he said is "one of the things pushing this country, almost powerless to resist, toward I don't know what final determination.... We are in the grip of forces beyond our comprehension, yet we seem powerless to resist the stream which carries us on." The conference report, he said, "is the repudiation of democracy. It is the sacrifice of freedom. It is the adoption of the principle by which Hitler regimented the people of Germany and by which Joseph Stalin and his predecessor, Lenin, regimented the people of Russia." At the very hour, he said, "when the patriotic men and women of America are proving their ability to triumph over the forces of tyranny, we are asked on the floor of the House and the Senate to forge chains for them." Its defenders, he said, "will tell you, 'Oh, Justice Byrnes will not abuse the powers.' If Justice Byrnes had the time to write the regulations, that might be true. But regulations are written in secret, in private rooms, in places where the people they are to affect can never see them. When Congress legislates, it is in the open; when Congress has a bill before it, the bill is printed and lies on the desk of every member. It is not so with directives and regulations." Bitterly he remarked that he had told the conferees that "No man who votes for this bill should ever again raise his voice in this Congress against delegation of powers and administrative regulations." It would, he said, give one man supreme control over the lives of 50,000,000 Americans.

The Senate, last court of appeals, listened with an impassive air that could not be analyzed. It was one of those times when one observes them fearfully and wonders, "What will they do?" There was no indication from Fulbright, listening without expression; Barkley and Hill, joking together at the back; Walter George, reading the papers on his desk unmoved, or the rest. Free America might very well be in her last days, but you would never know it from looking at the Senate. You could only hope that when the time came they would vote as they almost always do in the last analysis, to preserve the freedom and the democracy of their land.

The House acts tomorrow, and having a different view than some of freedom and democracy, will pass the bill.

"Where in the bill do you exercise control over the Director?" I asked

Elbert Thomas after the session. "Supposing he doesn't administer it
the way you want, what then?" He looked at me sharply, a rare antagonistic expression on his face, as though I were trying to pin him down.
I was. "Oh, there are always the courts," he said softly. "Where in the
bill does it provide for appeal to the courts, Senator?" asked another
reporter. "It doesn't provide it," he said, sounding a little annoyed. "But
there are still the rights of American citizens."

But he could not find them for us in the bill.

MARCH 27, 1945. There were many sober men on both sides of the aisle
today, yet it was in a somehow almost-picnic atmosphere that a majority
of the House of Representatives voted to throw democracy away. Watching, one was struck with the strangeness of it, as though no mood, no
atmosphere could match what was going on here. Perhaps, one had
thought, it would come, if it ever came, to the crash of physical violence,
with great pain and bloodshed, a horrible thing, recognized and fought
against to the last desperation. One realized today that it could come
thus quietly, on a beautiful day on Capitol Hill, in the House chamber
familiar as an old shoe, in a kind of daze, without a real understanding
at all of what was actually happening.

The vote came after an hour and a half of debate, concluded by
Majority Leader McCormack, waving the told totemistic symbol. The
name of it this time was Marshall, but it might as well have been King
or Leahy or Stimson or Forrestal or some other name representing not
democracy but the military oligarchy that now stands on the threshold
of ruling the land. The roll call began, careful and slow and deliberate,
as it always is in the House. The Yeas went into the lead in the 60s, fell
equal and then behind over the hump into the hundreds, then surged
ahead again as the vote crossed the 200 mark. Forty-eight Democrats
jumped the line to vote against the bill, some of them as powerful and
respected as Judge Hatton Sumners of Texas, Carter Manasco of Alabama, but others stayed loyal. In some peculiar fashion Andy May had
been able to convince them; and they stayed loyal. There came the
Great Liberals, Marcantonio and Celler of New York, Helen Gahagan
Douglas and Jerry Voorhis of California, voting for the bill. There came
the lesser fry, many from the South. Presently it was over. 167 to 160
the House had adopted the conference report.

Across on the other side lay the last hope of turning back the tide.

There Wallace White remarked amiably that he thought it'd pass
"because you know the Senate has a habit of adoptin' conference reports."
"On something so basic, Senator, do you think the habit would hold?"
we asked. "I don't know," he said with a smile. "I'm not predictin', except

to say that the Senate has that habit." Others were not so sure, although Barkley loyally went along, praised the bill and said it would pass. O'Mahoney and Kilgore, in an act reminiscent of the crusading zeal of the days when the Senate fought Roosevelt's plan to pack the Supreme Court, sent out telegrams to each of the 61 Senators who joined them in voting for the original Senate bill, urging them to join in the fight against the report. Kenneth McKellar said he would vote against it "because to change our system at the last moment and adopt the system we are fighting against in this war seems totally inadvisable." Murdock, representing the New Dealers, indicated that their opposition has not changed at all. "It is extremely untimely," he put it. Taft said he would "probably be against it." Most of the Republicans, he ventured, will "line up about the way they did before"—against the bill. Significantly, John McClellan, hell-and-brimstone for work-or-jail a month ago, said now that "the picture has changed so much abroad that there's a real question in my mind whether we need it." Ken Wherry said it would be "very close . . . might pass . . . a real fight." "If it does pass the Senate," he said, "it will be because of the great confidence the Congress has in Jimmy Byrnes." "Would you vote for it if it were going to be administered by Henry Wallace?" someone asked. He laughed. "That would be a different proposition. Say!" he demanded, "Are you lobbying me?"

So it has come about, just as the dark Cassandras said it would—the last great battle for democracy has not come on a foreign field. It has come here, at home, on the Hill. Almost unnoticed out in the country save in the intemperate editorials that have consistently misrepresented the case and begged with masochistic eagerness for the very dictatorship the press is theoretically so dead-set against, it has gathered in the House and in the Senate over the past two months. And now it has been lost in the House and only the Senate remains. It may be the hysteria of the moment, and perhaps time will prove it to have all been a harmless thing—yet it seems no exaggeration at this moment, here where the thing is taking place, to say that the vote the Senate will cast sometime in the next few days is the most important it has cast. Everything which is America is at stake; and the frightful knowledge about it is that men on the other side of the Capitol, men just as patriotic and just as sincere and just as freedom-loving, have just voted calmly and matter-of-factly, and as though this were no less routine than an appropriations bill, to throw it away.

MARCH 28, 1945. The manpower conference report was called up by Elbert Thomas today in a long, weak, contradictory speech in which he admitted that "we have here a bill so strong that if it is recklessly or foolishly administered it would create chaos such as we have never known in this country ... if recklessly administered it would do not good but infinite harm to war production." It is a matter, he added lamely, of "trust in the Director." Burt Wheeler, joining the increasing number who are avowedly against it, snapped back that it isn't a matter of trust in the Director at all: it's a matter of who's going to write the regulations and who's going to administer it, and what check is there in it upon the terrible powers which are conferred. The issue of whether or not it is an anti-strike bill was raised: Taft maintained that it could be so used by interpretation. Not so, cried Warren Austin and Ed Johnson, "because the conferees were unanimously agreed in their discussions that it could not be so interpreted." What effect that would have on the Director once he had the unchecked power, Austin and Ed were unable to point out. Thomas began to look glummer and glummer, although he continued to argue without much conviction and without much skill for a measure which, in his heart, he does not like and does not want.

Midway in the afternoon O'Mahoney sent word up to the Press Gallery that he wanted to hold a press conference. We all trooped down to the President's Room, and presently he joined us. There was about the Senator from Wyoming, whom somebody once referred to with great truth as "an operator," an air of unmistakable confidence. Never a man to go out on limbs unless he is absolutely sure of himself, he told us flatly: "I am very much of the opinion, on the basis of numerous conferences this morning, that the conference report is beaten. When it is, I shall make a motion to recommit it to conference, so that it can be redrawn, now that its weaknesses have been pointed out." And he added to his statement a reference to the fact that the Navy last night canceled 72 of 84 ships scheduled to be built on March 6. Thus in one short month, he said, and while the bill was under discussion, the Navy has abandoned 75 per cent of its recently announced program—the program being one of the excuses it has given for wanting a manpower bill.

Up from the White House to "Dear Elbert" came a letter from a man who has apparently decided, now that the conferees have produced something beyond anyone's wildest dreams, to really get in and fight for it. He urged the passage of the conference report "because the manpower situation is still critical." Once Congress has passed it, he said smoothly, the full obligation would then rest on the Executive, and there would be no doubt where the responsibility should be placed. There would also be no doubt, although he did not say so, that Congress, having "discharged its obligation," would be left with absolutely no control whatsoever over the absolutely dictatorial powers conferred upon the Director of War Mobilization, and through him upon the military.

Late in the day when we went down on the floor to see Barkley after the session, he sidestepped, very much aware of how things are shaping up. "It looks pretty good," was the most he would say, and that was grudgingly. "It looks pretty good.... Of course Joe here," he said, poking O'Mahoney in the arm, "thinks it looks pretty good for him, too, so I don't know." He left us laughing, as he always does.

MARCH 29, 1945. With the House now in an informal Easter recess, meeting only every three days, and then without a quorum call, some Senators too have gone home—"between 30 and 35," according to Barkley's estimate yesterday. The strategy of the manpower bill's opponents, who think they have enough votes but want to be good and sure, is delay. Where as many voluble men as there are in this body feel as deeply as they do about this bill, delay is easily come by. The debate is lengthening.

Meanwhile the American armies are plunging forward into Ger-

many, and the psychology of victory is becoming steadily stronger. Downtown Paul McNutt, whom the services and their aiders and abettors would get rid of if they could, has told an embarrassing truth—that the manpower situation right now is "in excellent shape." Taken in conjunction with the WPB's latest report that February production was the highest ever, it all adds up to the most irrefutable answer to the proponents of the bill. They are left, in essence, only with the fake argument that "it is necessary for the morale of the boys at the front." Not bothering to point out the obvious, that the boys at the front are creating their own morale with each new mile they conquer, Taft the logical pointed to the very real danger to morale which the bill contains. Under it, he noted, the Director could channel any discharged serviceman into any job he pleased and freeze him in it. Tell that to the servicemen, Taft said, that they could only expect to come out of the Army and go right back into compulsion, and imagine the effect on morale. Harley Kilgore, following the same tack and making a scathing reference to the services' "verbal hiding in the foxholes" whenever they are attacked, also summed it up. "What every man in the Army wants," he said, "is one of two things. He wants to complete his education, or he wants to work. And he doesn't want to work under some sort of Army military discipline system. He's had enough of that."

Few people spoke for the bill today. Elbert Thomas, returning from a hasty conference at the White House attended also by Barkley, attempted to answer Kilgore a little but then gave it up. Warren Austin, the only man in the Senate who is really deeply, passionately, devotedly in favor of the bill, replied indignantly to McKellar's charge that it is "involuntary servitude" by arguing that the same "involuntary servitude" applies to drafting a man into the armed forces. McKellar responded that working for the government and working for private employers making private profit are two different things. The vote originally hoped for by Friday is now being hoped for by Monday, and there is talk that it may be delayed even longer. The bill is beaten and everyone knows it, but its foes are taking no chances. They want all the Senators on hand they can get, and they want it killed good and dead. Said Barkley after the session: "Informal polls show a very close vote—but I still think there's a chance to win." And Elbert Thomas, with a weary candor: "A very close vote, with a tendency to beat the bill."

MARCH 30, 1945. There is an amiable little Navy lieutenant who runs around this place, checking on people and taking polls. He works out of the Navy Liaison Office in the Senate Office Building, and today he seemed quite worried. Somehow—he did not reveal how—he had seen

Taft's poll on the bill. It showed 36 for, 39 against. Worse than that, however—far, far worse—he had made one of his own. And shocking and sad to relate, it showed 36 for and 52 against. "The situation," he confided earnestly, "is desperate." Sympathetically the reporter he was talking to agreed. Obviously another Pearl Harbor, of a sort, was about to overtake a proud service.

From other sources came much the same story. All figures except the Navy's seem to stay within the 30–40 bracket; between 32 and 36 for and 39 against. As of today, close but beaten.

The debate did not do much to change the situation one way or the other, except insofar as it delayed a vote. Langer, a past master at this, challenged McKellar on the Treasury Department Appropriations bill which he called up during the afternoon, and a good hour and a half was consumed by an item giving Treasury $15,000,000 for the disposal of surplus property. Langer pointed out, and Aiken joined him most reasonably—and it was a real issue quite aside from its bearing on the manpower vote—that the Surplus Property Board had been established to dispose of surplus property. What was the Treasury doing, anyway? Furthermore, what was the RFC doing, and the Army doing and the Navy doing? The good Gillette, harrassed and worried by this lack of cooperation, has come to the place where he can always find friends, the Senate, and his story has received a sympathetic hearing. George Aiken placed it in its proper perspective when he summarized the characteristic formula succinctly. "There is apparently," he said with quiet bitterness, "a definite effort to see that this board does not function in the manner in which Congress intended it should function. Unless something is done, in a few months' time someone will come before Congress and say, 'Now, see what you have done. The board you set up has been a miserable failure. You have got to have this matter of disposing surplus war property handled by one strong man, and we know just the man.'" Eventually the appropriation was amended to permit Treasury to use it "unless and until" the Surplus Property Board assumes jurisdiction. But George Aiken had called the turn. That is how it is done, this clever, backhanded destruction of the ways of democracy. You don't pervert the intent of Congress, you just ignore it. You just harass and hamstring its boards and its agencies, and then presently you come before it and you ask for "one strong man." And then maybe someday, not too far off, all your efforts culminate and you get One Strong Man who *is* a strong man; and then you have done it.

On the international front hell also popped this afternoon. Forced out of the White House after 47 days of discreet silence, one of those "other little things" the President told us about at the joint session on

Yalta has finally come into the open. It seems Britain has been promised 6 votes in the General Assembly, and Russia and the United States are going to get 3 each because of it. The reaction has been profound on the Hill, and must be equally profound among the smaller nations abroad. Criticism is sharp and follows two lines. There are those who demand that the United States have a vote equal to Britain's. And there are those, more perceptive of the ultimate issue, who demand that the nonsense be stopped and each nation be given one and one only. Essentially, however, the basic criticism common to all is the manner in which the news was divulged: by a carefully planted leak to the New York *Herald-Tribune* which finally forced the White House to come clean. Joe Ball, clutching his ideals desperately in a howling gale, is at least consistent with them. Sharply he calls it "a gratuitous slap at the smaller nations." Vandenberg is equally sharp, although more circumspect. Connally says the President told the San Francisco delegation about it last Friday, and indicates that he thinks one of them let it leak to the *Herald-Tribune* in order to smoke out the White House. Barkley and Lister Hill, good, obedient, loyal servants, rationalize and excuse and speak smoothly about "little details" which "must not be allowed to endanger the larger objectives"—not realizing, apparently, that the larger objectives may eventually be completely destroyed by the little details.

But whatever the stupidity, and whatever the justification, one thing is certain today. More bitterness, more mistrust, more suspicion have been created between the White House and the Hill. Giving all the breaks one can, and being as fair as it is possible to be, it is nonetheless true that this is one more clear-cut time when the blame for it is in no way the responsibility of the Congress.

MARCH 31, 1945. Tonight Jimmy Byrnes will issue his second report as Director of War Mobilization and Reconversion. Asked to comment for an advance story, Ed Johnson gave us a rather historic piece of paper. On it he had written:

"Justice Byrnes has effectively destroyed all chances for Senate adoption of the Manpower Conference Report by his grotesque statement that 'the need for manpower legislation continues . . . not only for war production but also for the production of essential civilian goods; and later to facilitate reconversion.'

"It has been understood all along that this was very definitely war legislation and not as its opponents contended, 'for the permanent regimentation of American manpower.' The conference report is dead."

This he gave to us rather grimly, and when we asked him "Will you yourself vote for it, Senator?" the author of the motion that sent the conference bill to the floor replied bluntly, "Hell, no. I wouldn't vote to give Jimmy Byrnes or anybody else that much control over manpower in peacetime. He said it was necessary for the war. Now he wants it for civilian goods and reconversion. That does it." In the game of mate and checkmate that goes on here on so many issues, the Senator from Colorado, as he often does, has ended up with checkmate. The ex-Senator from South Carolina gave him his chance and he took it. With his statement, if there had been any doubt, the life of the conference report did come to an end. All that remains now is the formal burial. It will be interesting to see if other proponents are as shrewd at finding an out for themselves as Big Ed Johnson has been.

Elbert Thomas, game to the end, refused to comment on Johnson's statement. However, he said that "Senator Byrnes is ill-advised and ill-informed. The bill is not a peacetime measure, it is a wartime measure. It expressly provides for termination. No, he's mistaken on that." And he added, "I don't think it will affect the chances of the bill."

O'Mahoney, told of Ed's decision, gave a brief, sardonic chortle and refused to comment.

APRIL 1, 1945. From one who knows comes an interesting picture of the discussions that produced the manpower conference report. Nobody, he maintains stoutly, wanted a bill that could, even inadvertently, be used to shackle the American nation on into peacetime. To that effect, he said, Joe O'Mahoney made "an impassioned speech." "Senator," said Andy May, "I agree with you 100 per cent. But this is war." Apparently nobody had any idea, or at any rate would admit it, that the bill would be used as a weapon of reconversion. "That's terrific power," our informant said thoughtfully. "My, that's terrific." "Well, Senator," we said, "that's what's puzzled all of us reporters about this. If you felt that way about it, how did you ever produce such a thing?" "Well, they told us they had to have it," he said. He gave a wondering little laugh. "Hasn't this been the damnedest thing?" he said. "Have you ever seen anything like it?" "No, Senator," we said, "we never have."

APRIL 2, 1945. Wayne Morse, acting with an assurance and an obvious ability which annoyed some Senators who opposed him and consequently chose to regard him as an upstart (Senators on his side were very approving) made his maiden speech today against the manpower bill. With a disconcerting bluntness he went straight to the heart of it. The Administration, he charged, demands the bill because it is afraid of unemployment, has no cure for it, and hopes to stave it off by forcing people to move about from job to job at the whim of the government. To

this Elbert Thomas replied gently from time to time. At one point when
Morse pointed out that the Director of War Mobilization might turn over
the writing of regulations to persons who would misuse the power for
"a program which I believe to be not in the best interests of representative democratic government," Thomas got up and answered with his
patient, rather embarrassed, kindly smile. "The American government
just doesn't function that way," he said quietly. "The Senator is mistaken.
This bill is a people's bill, and it will be administered in the spirit of
a free people." Morse, confronted by an idealism and faith almost beyond
belief, looked momentarily frustrated but returned to the attack. The
remark, however, was typical of the many Thomas has made throughout
the debate. Disliking the bill himself, he dislikes it on other grounds.
It is never the dangers to freedom in it which concern him, for this is
America and in America such things could never happen.

Killing the bill even further, Jimmy Byrnes resigned today and Fred
Vinson was immediately nominated to succeed him. The move has cost
possibly two or three votes, although the bill is dead already. Most
Senators have reasons much deeper than Jimmy Byrnes to be for or
against it, but in a very few wavering cases, Jimmy Byrnes has helped.
Now even this is gone. We asked Barkley after the session how he was
getting along. "Well," he said, with his easy chuckle rippling through
him, "it reminds me of trying to drive chickens through a picket fence.
You think you've got 'em all coraled and then some old hen runs back
through and they all follow her." He too has perhaps some doubts about
the wisdom of the bill, but he is going along like the good soldier he is.
That phrase, in fact, would make a good epitaph for some of the good-
and-faithfuls on the Hill: Here lies So-and-So. He went along.

APRIL 3, 1945. Forty-six Senators decided today that the country should
not go under dictatorship. The House of Representatives was against
them, 29 of their colleagues were against them, all the agencies of the
executive branch of the government were against them, the President
was against them, the Army and Navy were against them, a sizable,
unthinking portion of the press was against them. They stood firm. They
knew where the ultimate necessity lay, and they voted accordingly.
Their responsibility was for the preservation of the freedom of America,
whatever the passing storm, and they maintained it. But there were only
46. Out of all the people of power in America, there were only 46. It
was not a large margin to save the work of 160 years. Yet it sufficed.

Of course there were some few who had other reasons. "You don't
know my state," said one New Dealer drily when he was challenged later

on his vote. A handful more were subject to similar pressures. In the main, however, a majority of the 46 Senators who voted against the manpower bill were sincerely convinced that its adoption could only mean the loss of the American heritage. Confronted by the alliance between the big industrialists and the military, a pattern which if carried just a little farther—as far as the conference bill would permit—would be the perfect pattern of the fascist state, they rebelled and voted it down. Had they not done so, the chances of their being able to end the threat of tyranny in the future by an act so simple as the one word "no" might almost certainly have been placed in jeopardy beyond recall.

Afterwards some of us talked to Elbert Thomas. He was, we told him, the happiest unhappy man we had seen in some time. "Oh, the Senate bill was better," he said softly. "The Senate bill was infinitely better. But we were confronted with the situation. The conference report was the bill before us. We didn't really have a choice." And what of the future? What of the proposed nurses' draft? "Well, we'll report it out. But it hardly seems fair to draft one segment of the population when you refuse to draft all." "Senator," someone said with a laugh, "you really would have been much happier if you'd  stayed on as chairman of Education and Labor, wouldn't you?" He gave a quizzical little smile, and when he spoke it was with the very soft but very definite irony he sometimes uses. "Oh," he said, "I've been a great success in Military Affairs. We've made nine generals and investigated a dog. Elliott Roosevelt's a brigadier general. We've accomplished a great deal. Yes. We've accomplished a great deal."

*Heart of the Manpower Conference Report,
passed by the House 167–160, March 27, 1945;
killed by the Senate 46–29, April 3, 1945*

Sec. 5(a) To the extent deemed by the Director [of War Mobilization] to be necessary and appropriate to carry out the purposes and means declared in section 2 of this act and also for the purpose of keeping activities and places of employment essential to the war effort in productive operation, the Director is authorized, by regulation—

(1) to prescribe employment ceilings in designated areas, activities, or places of employment, fixing the maximum number of workers by age, sex, or occupational qualifications, who may be there employed, and prohibiting the employment of workers beyond such maximum numbers;

(2) to prohibit or regulate the hiring, rehiring, solicitation or recruitment of new workers by employers and the acceptance of employment by workers; and

(3) to prohibit the individuals employed in designated areas, activities, plants, facilities and farms, which the Director deems are essential to the war effort, from voluntarily discontinuing such employment unless, in the case of any individual so employed, the Director determines that it is no longer necessary to the interest of the war effort for him to remain in such employment or that he has a justifiable reason for leaving such employment.

(b) Whoever wilfully violates the provisions of any regulation made under subsection (a) shall be guilty of a misdemeanor and, upon conviction thereof, shall be punished by imprisonment for not more than twelve months or by a fine not to exceed $10,000, or both.

33

IF NEWSPAPERMEN EVER PRAY

APRIL 4, 1945. Two new items to increase mistrust. The State Department announced that it has concluded an agreement with Chile at Mexico City to retire American nitrate plants so as not to compete with Chile's. A week ago Tom Connally and Warren Austin assured Taft in entire good faith that no such agreements were made at Mexico City. That was where they reckoned without the State Department. Out of that smart gesture have come some really good, some really get-in-the-international-groove-and-let's-have-unity dividends. Taft is made more suspicious, Connally and Austin, confronted with the knowledge that they have unwittingly told a lie, more troubled. "Damn it," said Connally bitterly, "they didn't have any authority to do that." With just such bricks as these do the architects of tomorrow busily build their house of peace. If it does not topple on their heads it will be through no fault of theirs.

The second item is the President's decision to ask for only one vote at San Francisco. Some praised it—or dismissed it with a rather tired disgust that passed for praise when you saw it in print—but Bob La Follette said bluntly what they all knew, that "it makes a confused situation more confounded." All the rosy haze of Yalta has vanished, rather more quickly than has been usual on such occasions. The attitude on the Hill now is, Well, what next?

APRIL 5, 1945. The Navy, now that it has lost the manpower bill, announces blandly that its draft quotas for the coming month will be cut one-half. Strangely, the manpower crisis seems to be all gone from the minds of our mimeograph admirals.

APRIL 6, 1945. The Mexican water-treaty debate is dragging along on the floor with Downey and Millikin carrying the ball. Connally and the Administration are attempting to make great capital out of the thesis that it is necessary as "proof of our willingness to cooperate with the rest of the world." All we have done, of course, is send our armies to the ends

407

of the earth and donate $40,000,000,000, but we must still give "proof of our willingness to cooperate with the rest of the world." This is an interesting theory that is nonetheless effective despite its palpable absurdity: there is a certain pride of reputation in the Senate and it still smarts under the lacerating charges of the post-Versailles era. A good many Senators incline to be influenced by the idea of redeeming their international prestige.

Sheridan Downey, able and never at a loss for words, carries the fight for the opponents of the treaty. Hiram Johnson sits beside him with his cane and jabs him in the leg whenever he thinks an opposition argument needs answering. Downey jumps up obediently.

APRIL 7, 1945. Connally, forced into it by his scene-stealing fellow delegate, Arthur Vandenberg, says that of course "some minor amendments" may be made to the Dumbarton Oaks proposals at San Francisco. He doesn't sound as though he will be disposed to accept very many of them, however. Van, making speeches right and left and issuing suggestions in the same fashion, has effectively taken the play away from Connally, who doesn't like it one little bit.

APRIL 8, 1945. The President plans to go to San Francisco to address the delegates in person and open the conference. Apparently husbanding his strength for the journey, he has gone to Warm Springs. His fortunes have rarely been at so low an ebb in the Senate which must ratify the treaty he will send to it. The bitter aftermath of Yalta, the destruction of one more hope, the knowledge that Stalin has refused to dignify his delegation by sending Foreign Minister V. M. Molotov to the conference, the knowledge that Roosevelt is apparently helpless to do anything about it, the whole general atmosphere in the Senate toward the White House— all bode ill for Dumbarton Oaks. The old touch is gone and only a memory remains. It is a moot question at this point whether it will be enough to swing the victory.

APRIL 9, 1945. Barkley, his likable soul enraged by Senatorial absenteeism, arose in indignation today to give his colleagues the severest dressing-down they have had in some time. The least they could do, he informed them scathingly, was remain at their desks and try to give the impression that they were doing their duty whether they were or not. His outburst brought applause from the galleries and will doubtless be followed by many approving editorials. A few members attempted to point out that they sometimes do have committee meetings in the afternoon, that constituents do call on them, that there are errands to be run in the departments. Barkley was unyielding. Later Bob La Follette endorsed his remarks and added a few of his own. It made quite a story—and provoked a lot of disgusted comment from other Senators later.

Vandenberg made an able speech for extension of the Lend-Lease act today, but warned bluntly that it must not be used for postwar relief, rehabilitation or reconstruction. Taft put in an amendment which he said would make that desire absolutely ironclad. His amendment would strengthen a House amendment that leaves the way open for readjustments of Lend-Lease contracts. Considerable sentiment seems to be developing for the Taft proposal, and one more slap in the face may be on its way to the White House.

APRIL 10, 1945. Harry Truman, with all the brisk eagerness of someone who is bored to death, seized his first chance to vote in the Senate today and made the most of it. The vote wasn't necessary, for under the rules a tie kills a proposal, but he cast it anyway, with obvious satisfaction. Taft's Lend-Lease amendment, significant straw in the wind, rolled up a vote of 39 to 39. The Clerk reported this to the V.P., and the V.P. settled the issue once and for all. "On this amendment," Harry Truman called out rapidly, "the Yeas are 39 and the Nays are 39. The Chair votes No. The amendment is not agreed to."

With elaborate carefulness several Senators got up today and asked unanimous consent to be absent from the Senate. It was granted amid chuckles.

The other service has revealed its cupidity. The War Department, announcing the cancellation of 12 tank plants and a 10-per-cent reduction in artillery, says blandly:

"American production is now at a level which assures fighting men of a sufficient production rate to complete the war against Germany and provide the output necessary to supply forces to be used against Japan."

Three and four weeks ago, lying in their teeth about the sad state of production, and knowing it, the top men of the War Department misused the truth ruthlessly in their desperate attempt to get a dictatorial manpower bill through Congress.

APRIL 11, 1945. We had an amiable talk with Harry Truman today down on the floor after the session. The V.P., restless, and not afraid to say so, under the restraints of his office ("Mr. Vice-President—" someone addressed him the other day. "Smile when you say that," said the heir-apparent), was in a mood to relax. He got as big a kick as anybody out of the absenteeism squabble. "I take care of that," he told us with a grin. "When they hold up two fingers and say they want to go to Appropriations Committee, I tell them they can go to Appropriations Committee. When they hold up one finger, I tell them they can sit there and suffer."

He laughed and gave a reminiscent sigh. "It's wonderful, this Senate," he said. "It's the greatest place on earth. That takes in a lot of territory, but I say it and I mean it. The grandest bunch of fellows you could ever find anywhere. And there isn't one of 'em who couldn't do better in private business. I was sitting there today looking them over, and you know, there isn't a one but what could make three times what he does here if he worked for some private corporation. And there isn't one of us who would be anywhere else if he could. We wouldn't be anywhere else." "It's a good place for public service, isn't it, Senator?" somebody asked. "It's the best place there is," he said soberly. "If you really want to do public service, this is the place for it." "You did what you could, didn't you, Senator?" "Well—" he grinned. "I did what I could. I did my best. I was getting along fine until I stuck my neck out too far and got too famous—and then they made me V.P. and now I can't do anything. No, sir," said Harry Truman, smiling but more than a little serious, "I can't do anything."

APRIL 12, 1945. Around 3 P.M. this afternoon, looking down from the gallery, we saw Harry Truman come in, cross to the Republican side and go into an obviously friendly huddle with Alexander Wiley and Ken Wherry. We watched him for a moment, enjoying as always his enjoyment of other people and theirs of him. "You know," I said, "Roosevelt has an awfully good man in that Truman when it comes to dealing with the Senate if he'll only make use of him." Tony Vaccaro of the AP, one of Truman's best friends and close enough to know, shook his head and frowned. "He doesn't make use of him, though," he said. "Truman doesn't know what's going on. Roosevelt won't tell him anything."

Such was the legacy and such the condition which at 4:35 this afternoon fell into the hands of one of the squarest shooters who ever lived. Far off in springtime Georgia the Champ met the Contender he couldn't lick, and suddenly in three swift hours the magic voice, the magic presence, were gone forever. All the great triumphs, the millions of hopeful hearts, the eager upturned faces seen from the back platforms, the cheering crowds, the great applaudings, the ambitions and ideals and expediencies and betrayals, the commitments and understandings and projects and agreements, all the flashing caravan of 12 fantastic years, ground abruptly to a halt in the face of the one fact from which there is no retreat and no appeal, that all men are mortal and all men must die. At 1 P.M. he said, "I have a terrific headache." At 1:15 he fainted. At 4:57, President but unaware of it, Harry Truman adjourned the Senate after finishing a letter to his mother, written at his desk. At 5:20, President and terribly aware of it, Harry Truman reached the White House. "The President has passed away," said the gallant woman he met there. "What can I do?" he asked her. "Tell us what we can do to help you," she said gravely. At 7:09 he

Truman sworn in as
President of U.S.

took the oath of office, farm boy, soldier, failure, child of Pendergast, Senator, Vice-President, one of the most honest people in creation. So ended an era and so began another.

On the Hill, getting ready to go downtown to our offices, we got the flash just before 6. For a long moment people ran back and forth through the gallery saying the same things being said everywhere: "Roosevelt's dead. What? Roosevelt's *dead?* My God, Roosevelt's dead!" For about 30 seconds this condition continued; then the press was galvanized into action. People leaped into telephone booths and began calling Senators for comment. Others dashed over to the Office Building to Truman's office. Others rushed out, hopped into cabs and tore down to the White House. In the sort of supreme community skill that characterizes the press in moments of crises, everybody had a job to do and everybody did it with an efficiency and a speed rarely matched, in its complexity and its completeness, by craftsmen in any other trade.

Later in the evening as we came out of the Press Building, away from the clattering teletypes, the typewriters and the telephones, the copy paper strewn all over the desks and the floor, the atmosphere of tension slowly relaxing after a job superbly done, we bought the papers. PRES. ROOSEVELT DEAD, they said. ROOSEVELT DEAD. We read them; and we could not believe it. We read them again; and we could not believe it. We had helped write the great story; still we could not believe it.

APRIL 13, 1945. Harry Truman came back to us on the Hill for a little while today, in the shrewd first step of a shrewd Administration. Aware as only one from Congress can be aware of the vital importance of the relationship between the Executive and the Legislature, he wanted to meet with the leaders of the House and of the Senate. Characteristically he came to them. He did not, this first time, ask them to come to him. It was his instinct to come home for reassurance in his terrifying hour, and he came.

With him came the entourage, for now he was the Prisoner. The cops were there, the Secret Service; he walked in an open square of armed men through the halls where literally only yesterday he passed briskly and alone. In the office of the Secretary of the Senate he met his colleagues for a while before the luncheon began: Democrat and Republican, in ones and twos, the Senate went in to shake his hand and wish him luck. Outside stood the press, and presently we too grew anxious to see him again. Our emissary went in and came out with the warning, "Just hello. No interviews. Just hello." We promised just hello, and in a moment were taken into the inner reception room where we formed a circle. The door opened and our friend walked in. He looked gray-cheeked and tense, but when he saw us his face lighted up. He smiled and tears came into his eyes.

"Well, isn't this nice," he said, coming forward and shaking hands with us two by two, using both hands. "This is really nice." "Good luck, Mr. President," said somebody. "I wish you didn't have to call me that," he said. We laughed, the tension broke a little: George Aiken came through. "Hello, Harry," he said, "can I say hello to you?" "George, go right along in," Truman said. "I'll be along in a minute." He turned back to us. "If you fellows know what it's like to have a bull or a load of hay fall on you," he said, "you know how I felt last night. I felt as though the moon and a couple of planets had fallen on me. I have the most terrible responsibility any man ever faced." He paused a moment and then went on gravely. "If newspapermen ever pray," he said quietly, "pray for me." Then he was gone, leaving us very moved. For just a moment he had taken us into his confidence and shown us frankly the frightening thing that had happened to him—shown us, who represented something, a free and easy cameraderie and naturalness to which he knew he could never, for the rest of his life, quite return.

Later he came out of the office, the luncheon completed. We trailed him out and saw him off. Passing through the galleryway back of the Senate chamber he turned suddenly and walked over to the doors. Throwing them wide he stood for a long moment looking out at the Senate: a ham actor's gesture with anybody else, but not with Harry Truman. Then he let them swing to and started on. By the Vice-President's office he paused and stepped in quickly to shake the hand of a secretary and wish him luck. "Come and see us often, Mr. President," somebody called. "I'd like to," he said with a trace of annoyance in his voice, "but you see how many people it takes to get me up here and back now." Then down the stairs and out, and into the gleaming sedan, and down the Hill in the screaming cavalcade like others before him. If affection from the Senate side can help him meet his destiny, he need have no fears.

APRIL 14, 1945. Once again through Washington the Old Man came home, passing from Union Station, past the Senate Office Building, down Constitution Avenue to the slow cadence of muffled drums, the dirge of mourning music, the crack of hands on rifle stocks, the clop of horses' hoofs. Thousands upon thousands lined the way to see the coffin pass upon its caisson under the muggy April sky; some cried, most were silent. So much had this man dominated their lives, so inextricably had he entwined himself with their destinies, that they could hardly grasp the reality of his last parade. In him an age had died, and whether for better or for worse no one in that hour could rightly say. For him or against him, the sure knowledge came that with that somber procession as it moved down Constitution Avenue a door was being shut, irrevocably, and forever.

That afternoon at the White House there was a 25-minute service. Harry Truman, so they said, sat unmoving with his eyes upon the coffin. But if there was confusion and uncertainty in his mind, he did not show it this day to the world. Already he has decided that the San Francisco conference will go on. Already he has asked the Cabinet, for the time being at least, to remain. Already he has plunged into a whirlwind schedule of conferences with everyone, anyone, who can unravel the tangled skein his predecessor bequeathed him. Already he has achieved something Roosevelt couldn't do—secured from Joseph Stalin, by the simple expedient of asking for it bluntly and directly and with neither equivocation nor appeasement, the assignment of V. M. Molotov as head of the Russian delegation to San Francisco.

APRIL 15, 1945. Here in Washington, where he long ago ceased to inspire men and where they had come to look upon him with grudging admiration as a great politician, a master of expedient, a devotee of success at any price who nine times out of ten did succeed, the death of the man who was buried today at Hyde Park is assessed as one more example of his fantastic fortune: he died at exactly the right time. His luck held to the end. The war is coming to successful conclusion, the bitter fruits of Yalta and the rest have yet to be harvested in full, the promise has been made without the necessity for redemption. Upon Harry Truman falls the burden of unemployment and the peace. Destiny timed it perfectly, and the legend has been made secure.

That it will mean a drastic change, no one doubts. That it will mean the reaction joyous conservatives predict, many doubt. That it will be like a breath of fresh air blowing through the government, all agree.

The page has turned, the slate is clean. As someone remarked on the Hill yesterday, "Already you can see it even in little things. Already the single word *Administration* means something else. It doesn't mean Roosevelt and Blaze and Elliott and all the rest of it any more. It means something new." Gone as if by magic are the accumulated bitternesses and hatreds and mistrusts and antagonisms of 12 embattled years. Gone are all the angry emotions the name and the presence of the departed so quickly evoked in so many hearts. Gone are the lacerating memories in Congress of the tax fight and the State Department fight and the Wallace fight and the Williams fight and the manpower fight. Gone, all gone. By so much, harsh though it may be to say it in this hour of universal memorial, has the nation gained.

By so much also has the chance for peace been bettered. Roosevelt's prestige and influence in the Senate, steadily declining for many months, were never lower than they were on the day of his death. ("Mr. Roosevelt's last months," the columnists wrote, "were devoted to strengthening his relations with the Senate, for he was well aware of its vital role in ratifying the peace. To that he subordinated every other consideration." Was that why he made the State Department nominations? Was that why he nominated Henry Wallace? Was that why he tossed in Aubrey Williams, like a slap in the face? Was that why, in the last six months, he deliberately did one thing after another that he knew would antagonize and infuriate the Senate?) Dumbarton Oaks, handicapped by his sponsorship, would have had heavy going; too many past antagonisms would have been riding with it. It is no untruth to say, and everyone who knows the Senate knows it, that the chances for American participation in the world organization are considerably better under Harry Truman than they could ever have been under Franklin Roosevelt.

Furthermore, there is the domestic side of it. A mercurial presence is gone, true, and all there is to take its place is a blunt honesty which says what it means and means what it says and stands by it. This will be dull, perhaps—or will it?—but at any rate it will be enduring. Administration will be straightforward and candid and practical. The social reforms will be maintained and strengthened, and they will be administered with a moral integrity and a democratic conviction that will lift their foundations from the shifting quicksand of one elusive personality and place them solidly upon the rock of established processes.

Much that was remarkable, and possibly much that was great, died with Franklin Roosevelt. But here in the Washington which knew him day by day, there are no illusions though there are all the formal rituals. As he declined, so his Administration declined. Everything was on a toboggan, going steadily downhill. Just before the toboggan picked up speed, Death intervened. By history, which does not rationalize, sentimentalize, or excuse, the toboggan will not be overlooked.

34

"I MEAN TO BE THE PRESIDENT"

APRIL 16, 1945. The trim gray Senator came back to the Hill again today, President of the United States and Commander-in-Chief, to address the Congress and the world. To "you, my friends and colleagues of the Congress," he spoke for some 15 minutes, slowly and carefully and sincerely and well. Almost unnoticed an implied criticism of his predecessor crept into his speech. It is the duty of the great powers, he said, "to serve not dominate the world." And in his prepared text where the favorite words of yesterday, "the peace-loving nations of the world," were waiting to be said, he dropped the "peace-loving" as he spoke and urged instead an organization for all the nations of the world. And on a note long absent in Presidential speeches he ended earnestly: "I ask only that I may be a good and faithful servant to my Lord and my people." When he had done and was standing, irresolute and anxious to be gone, on the rostrum, all the crowded chamber, packed with humanity from top to bottom, burst into prolonged applause that continued as the diplomatic corps, led by Anthony Eden, walked up the aisle and out, followed by the Cabinet; continued until the President left, and then continued after for a little in personal tribute to a modest man obviously determined—and capable of making that determination come true—to make good at his new job.

Looking over the Cabinet as the President spoke, it was easy to see that most were sobered and saddened. Only Henry Wallace, however, looked really tragic, unhappy and alone. When Truman concluded he applauded, but it was perfunctory applause. The thoughts of Henry Wallace, The Man Who Might Have Been, must have been interesting too.

APRIL 17, 1945. What a President does, in the last analysis, more than any one physical thing, is furnish the mental and moral climate in which the country lives. If he is one sort of man, certain things can be done in his Presidency which, if he were another sort of man, could not be done. Harry Truman is providing already a very different climate from that of Franklin Roosevelt.

This was most notable in the rather awestruck reports that followed his first press conference today. Here was a man who spoke right out without reservations and without equivocation. Some article referred to the absence of "the subtle interplay, the intellectual game, which Mr. Roosevelt loved to indulge in." Someone else put it more bluntly: "There wasn't any doubletalk." It was Harry Truman's purpose to tell the truth, to answer all the questions he could and say frankly when he couldn't. He handled himself admirably, perfectly poised, good-natured and natural. "I mean to be the President," he told someone yesterday, and already he has become so. It caused a sensation among the correspondents who had not known him on the Hill. Remembering the old days, the devious statements, the winding answers, frequently the downright untruths, the atmosphere of hostility and discomfort, it was a major change. Without doubt the President has captured the imaginations and the loyalty of such of the press as did not know him already. It is a most auspicious start.

From the Hill come words of fulsome, and—at least for the present—entirely genuine support. The reputation for integrity, loyalty and cooperative friendship is paying dividends. There will be some issues to come, as Ken Wherry puts it candidly, when "we'll meet this man head-on," but for the moment, all is serene. The same is true throughout the country. Few Presidents in history have started off on such a wave of universal good will and good hope as has come to Harry Truman.

APRIL 18, 1945. The Republican Steering Committee followed the well-worn path to the White House door today, carrying good will and good wishes. Bob Taft said whimsically that it was the first time he'd been in the executive offices since the Hoover Administration. The visit lasted perhaps 10 minutes. Taken in conjunction with the formal telegram of support from the Senate Republican Conference last Friday, it was a significant thing. Certainly it could never have happened to the man before him.

In the Senate, after long debate, many delays and much heated argument, the Mexican water treaty was ratified 76 to 10. In the international arena, Moscow has once more demanded San Francisco representation for the Lublin Polish Provisional Government, and the United States has once again refused. The President's first big issue is shaping up. Meanwhile he is following a backbreaking schedule of work and appointments which starts promptly at 8 and ends at 4:30 or 5 after a stream of eager visitors has departed.

APRIL 19, 1945. Taft went back to the White House again today for another conference with the President. "There were a lot of other people there yesterday," he explained. "I couldn't really talk to him. I just had some general suggestions to make, things I thought ought to be done." It was typical. These days everybody has advice for Harry.

Back on the Hill George Aiken said calmly, "Oh, it won't last. He'll make enemies sooner or later. If he doesn't make enemies he just won't be a very good President, that's all."

Truman's endorsement of Bretton Woods and the Reciprocal Trade Agreements Act may be the tipoff that he will make some enemies soon. Both are issues on which, as Ken Wherry put it, he will run "head-on" into the GOP.

APRIL 20, 1945. Connally and Vandenberg, backed up by the President from his desk "right where I belong" (again that implied criticism), arose in the Senate today to make their farewells before leaving for San Francisco. Connally promised there would be "no slavish devotion to every clause and every line" of Dumbarton Oaks; Vandenberg spoke of opening the Golden Gate to a better tomorrow. Both were good speeches, topped off by expressions of confidence and trust by Barkley and White. After it was all over, Barkley proposed a recess as a sign of respect to the delegates, because legislative business (extension of the draft act) "seems out of place in view of the noble sentiments expressed here this afternoon." Before the session began he expressed some doubt that he would be able to hold a quorum because of the opening of the baseball season. Apparently he wasn't able to.

Down on the floor after recess he had a short talk with tall Tom, shaking his hand long and earnestly. "If there's anything I can do, now," he said, "if there's anything you want me to canvass for you, or anything like that, don't hesitate to call on me. I mean it." Tom thanked him, gave his hand a last shake, shook hands with us and prepared to depart. "Did you see 'em get up and applaud me after I spoke?" he said with satisfaction. "Broke a tradition of the Senate," we assured him. "Did you put that in your stories?" he wanted to know. "We certainly did, Senator," we said. "Well, all right," he said with an amiable grin. "All right." He waved a little and walked out of the Senate, a knight of peace off on his perilous mission.

APRIL 21, 1945. Carl Hatch went down to see the President today. Truman called him down "just to talk over things in general and have a friendly talk." The two have always been very close, but Hatch remarked with a smile that he "just wasn't interested" in any Cabinet position, hadn't been offered any, and would turn it down if it were offered. "I regard the office of Senator as next to the Presidency," he said. "This is the place for real public service." He mentioned his friend thoughtfully. "I think people will like him a lot," he said. Then surprisingly and significantly for a man who supported Roosevelt so strongly, a note almost of annoyance came into his voice. "The American people like his simplicity and his honesty," he said forcibly. "The American people don't need brilliance. They don't need a Hitler to dominate them. They greatly appreciate a man who is simply—himself." He said this with positive conviction and an air close to defiance. We didn't argue.

APRIL 23, 1945. Barkley, George, Elbert Thomas, Curley Brooks, Ken Wherry, Leverett Saltonstall and 6 Representatives have been invited by General Eisenhower to inspect the German atrocity camps. The manner in which the selections were made—behind closed doors in the office of Secretary of the Senate, Les Biffle, without consultation with the full Senate and without its authority—stirred up a tempest in a teapot today. Many Senators were annoyed by it and said so. Lister Hill, acting Majority Leader in Barkley's absence, attempted to back out of a tight spot by saying with inadvertent truthfulness that "the War Department designated the members of the committee." Later he amended this to "the War Department in consultation with the Majority and Minority Leaders," but the damage was done. George Aiken and Wayne Morse remarked acidly that it didn't matter to them what the War Department liked, it was a fine situation when any Executive department presumed to tell the Senate who could and could not inspect the public business. Millard Tydings, deploring "these self-appointed committees, these committees appointed by little cliques and little groups," waxed equally sarcastic. Finally Wallace White, indignant and deploring, arose to accept the responsibility for naming the Republican members. Barkley was assigned the responsibility on the other side. The "great reluctance," undoubtedly sincere, of the committee members was stressed. Lister Hill put in a resolution to constitute them a formal committee of the Senate and then withdrew it on White's objection that he was sure the Senators, now in Europe, "would feel that they had been subjected to a vote of censure if the resolution passed." The whole business was a rather sorry, slipshod affair ("vicious government," Wayne Morse called it later), and the soundness of the Aiken, Morse and Tydings objections was amply proved by the bitter wrangle inspired by the methods which were used.

Eating dinner at the Press Club tonight, I was joined for a while by Theodore Francis Green. The visit of 40 Democratic Senators to the White House this morning entered the conversation; he laughed jovially. "O'Daniel got off an awfully good one," he said. "When we were all lined up there, just before the President spoke, O'Daniel called out, 'Mr. Presi-

dent, I suggest the presence of a quorum.' Wasn't that good?" We laughed
about it. "How was the President?" I asked. "Oh, he was fine," the Senator
said. "He made an awfully nice little speech. Everything he said was just
right, it came from the heart, it was sincere, it made you feel good." "He
has that talent," I said. "Yes," he said. Then, like Hatch, he made a
revealing little comment. "He isn't glamorous and he isn't brilliant," he
said, "but he's honest and he's sincere and he's efficient. He's made a
tremendous impression already, hasn't he? He's plunged right into it. He
hasn't said he wanted time to get used to his job, or anything like that.
He's stepped right in and taken over. You know, it's a remarkable thing,
isn't it? In spite of the great shock which it was to the country, America
has gone right along just as though nothing had happened. What other
country could do that? It's really a remarkable thing."

Also at the White House, Molotov called today; and the President
conferred with his military and diplomatic leaders; and Molotov called
again; and Anthony Eden and Stettinius, looking upset, conferred together; and the rumors grew. No one at the moment knows just what
is in the wind, but to many who know Harry Truman it looks very much
as though a poker-player from Missouri is about to call the bluff of one
from Moscow. At any rate, Molotov complained to Stettinius that "no
man" had ever given him such a dressing-down as he received from
Harry Truman.

APRIL 24, 1945. The Senate passed the draft-extension act today after
a long, acrimonious afternoon. Since the manpower fight members have
become very restive under the continued ubiquitous presence of the
military. There is a very strong tendency, prompted by the devious bad
faith of the two service departments in that unlovely battle, to kick them
in the teeth whenever possible. The handwriting is on the wall for the
roll-top regulars of the Pentagon and the Navy Building, and much as
they hate it their little fling at ruling America is entering its final stages
with the war.

Before it approved the bill the Senate wrote in one restrictive amendment—a requirement that 18-year-olds must be given 6 months' pre-
combat training. This was by a vote of 50 to 25, and despite impassioned
appeals by Lister Hill and such other Army's Men as Warren Austin,
Harold Burton, Chan Gurney and Josiah Bailey. Once again there was
trotted out on parade the string of glittering names and epaulets. "General Marshall is against it, Secretary Forrestal is against it," and so on;
the same blind abdication of responsibility. "Who are we to set ourselves
up over General Marshall and tell him what he should do?" cried Lister
Hill wildly: he was only addressing the Senate of the United States.

Brewster, aware that he got taken into camp on the manpower bill and prepared to retaliate, remarked bitterly that "George Marshall like the President has become an institution, and like the President he must rely upon advisers. I have come more and more to the conclusion in these last few days that he is receiving very poor advice on the situation in this Congress and this country."

APRIL 25, 1945. Off in San Francisco in a mingled atmosphere of skepticism and hope, the United Nations conference opened today. Harry Truman spoke briefly from the White House, stressing the moral basis which for him is paramount in the construction of the peace. Others, equally idealistic—for they were all Americans—mentioned it earnestly too. The name of Roosevelt was dutifully invoked. Meanwhile the problem Roosevelt bequeathed continues to trouble the waters. Russia still insists on the admission of the Lublin Polish government; Harry Truman says flatly, *No*. Stalin and Molotov, who like so many others before them seem to have read too much into the easy acquiescence of their late friend, are apparently at a loss to understand the new President's firmness. Russo-American relations have entered a touch-and-go stage in which everyone concerned is playing with dynamite. Harry Truman in his practical fashion does not seem in the least perturbed by this.

APRIL 26, 1945. The House surprisingly enough is getting ready to accept the Senate's 18-year-old amendment to the draft act. Andy May says the House will be allowed to vote on it without conference. Apparently even there the stock of the military is at last returning to proper value on the political exchange.

APRIL 28, 1945. Clyde Reed remarked today that the world security charter ought to be delayed until fall. The country and the Senate, he said, ought to have time to talk it over. The idea is just beginning to gain ground in the Senate, and not from isolationists alone. There seems to be a growing disposition to go slow and look it over. Truman's leadership probably guarantees almost anything within reason, but something of the urgency associated with it seems to have been buried with his predecessor.

APRIL 29, 1945. Far from the Hill, yet adding immeasurably to the burden the men upon it must bear, the Thousand-Year Reich is coming to an end in blood and shame and agony. The lost mad minds who wanted to conquer the world and almost succeeded are reaping their savage reward.

The brilliant twisted spirit who was in himself the perfect synthesis of all the evils of a black, sick century is either dying, vanished or dead. At any rate, the dream is over—the temporal dream, the dream of evil translated into empire. The evil lives on, and the strains and stresses of these bitter years of which Adolf Hitler was the supreme embodiment have not fallen to the guns and planes and tanks and splendid youth of the Allied nations. They are with us still. We know who has won the last great battle, but who has won the war? It will be a confident and knowing man who dares point to the democracies and call them Victor. That is not decided yet.

APRIL 30, 1945. A Republican liberal in the Senate has a novel but possibly sound theory about Truman's ascension. Unlike so many others, striking a strange note in the paean of praise, he was disconsolate and moody when I went in to see him today. "Look," he said crisply, "you mark my words. Liberal Republicans in the Senate aren't going to get along half so well under Truman as we did under Roosevelt. We're going to get pushed into the background. We're going to be ignored and our influence is going to be reduced to the point where we'll have hardly any voice left at all. This will be done for two reasons: first, because it is his political training and instinct to work through party organizations; and second, because that way he can build up the conservative side of the party and encourage the nomination of a reactionary Republican to run against him in '48. You see who he's talking to already: Taft and that crowd. Has he called any of us in? No. Why should he? He knows who holds the power, and he isn't going to start any fights trying to transfer it to somebody else. Even if his instincts are liberal, as I'm willing to grant they are, he won't encourage Republican liberals because he knows they can't deliver and he isn't interested enough to help them reach a point where they can. Also, what's his best bet for '48? It's to deliberately foster the nomination of a reactionary Republican. he can knock over easily. You wait and see. Roosevelt was more interested in the idea, and would work with anyone who wanted the same idea, but not Truman—it isn't his instinct and it isn't to his advantage. The Republican liberals in the Senate are going to be the orphans of the Truman Administration. You wait and see."

MAY 1, 1945. The first faint doubts of the honeymoon, the first faint questionings and uncertainties, began to appear today as Truman bluntly lashed out at "irresponsible critics" of OPA. Over in the Senate, where Elmer Thomas of Oklahoma, white-haired, thin-lipped, dry-humored, heads a food investigation that has become increasingly critical of the agency, this was received with a rather startled silence broken by a few acrid Republican comments. Bob Taft responded, a note of disappointment in his tone; a few others spoke up. Most chose to regard it as an unfortunate break that might be better ignored, but a lot of people began to wonder. Harry is supposed to behave. He isn't supposed to say things like that. "He'll make enemies," predicted George Aiken comfortably; and George may have been right.

In the House today, nobody could have said anything bad about Harry Truman. Because he had already visited the Senate and wished to be fair to the House, and also because he likes people and wants to meet them, and also because he is no man's fool, he dropped in for a visit. The House recessed in his honor, and in Sam Rayburn's office, taking off his ring, he shook 400 hands and more as delighted members walked through. The visit represented an investment of approximately two hours. It will pay dividends for a good six months on the Hill. By means so simple does the new President operate, and while he may make enemies, they will be reluctant and it will be a while before they organize to oppose him actively.

MAY 2, 1945. Congress went around in a warm glow today as Harry Truman slashed the budget by $7,000,000,000. The crack going the rounds—"Harry Truman is the white man's Lincoln"—seemed borne out. Certainly many seemed to think so, and his stock on Capitol Hill was at its peak.

Possibly with that in mind, and aware that he has buttered McKellar up beyond the old man's fondest dreams by inviting him to sit in at Cabinet meetings, he announced briskly to his press conference that he would reappoint Dave Lilienthal chairman of TVA. He also announced he would name Bob Hannegan of Missouri to succeed Frank Walker as Postmaster General. Hannegan, continuing an old tradition, will retain the chairmanship of the Democratic National Committee. "By 1948," predicted my liberal Republican friend glumly, "they'll have built up a political machine such as you never saw the like of." But the Democrats still have the majority, and the privilege of a President to select his Cabinet still holds good. Hannegan will be confirmed, and so will Lilienthal.

MAY 3, 1945. Borrowing on his credit, the President vetoed a bill to reaffirm and enlarge the Tydings amendment to the draft bill deferring farm workers. The bill would have given all agricultural workers a blanket deferment regardless of any standards of need, either on the farm or in the service. It was special privilege for one group, Truman

said, "and consequently I am returning it without my approval." In his
first clash with the Congress he won handily. A majority of the House
voted to override the veto, but it was a very slim majority and came
nowhere near the necessary two-thirds. The Senate, relieved, watched
the performance without comment. "The House took care of that," Ed
Johnson said with his slow grin, "so I guess I won't bother to comment."
There is no desire to rush the day when the upper house must turn
against its former member.

With Elbert Thomas absent in Europe, Lister Hill has been casting
about for a way to duck the nurses' draft bill. Finally on Monday he
suddenly suggested that McCarran's $1,000,000,000 postwar airport bill
be made the unfinished business for Thursday. By the time the Senate
had registered some objection and Pat had withdrawn it, the crisis had
been passed: The nurses' draft was relegated to the background where
it will presently die. It is just as well for the Army's sake that this should
be so. Ed Johnson, who has carefully collected the most damning set of
figures concerning the nurse-recruitment program, the misuse and mis-
assignment of nurses in service, and the general incompetence of the
Army's handling of the program, was prepared to make a speech on
the subject. He told Hill bluntly that he would blast the Army from
hell to breakfast, and Hill, who knew he could do it, decided the matter
had better be dropped. In the general routine of the Senate the bill
is gradually being forgotten by unanimous consent.

MAY 5, 1945. Wayne Morse, expressing an idea heard with increasing
frequency these days, has joined Clyde Reed in the suggestion that the
peace treaty be delayed until fall. He says that unless it is understood
and supported by the American people it will fail. Joe Ball says it may
well be delayed until fall by the necessity for some sort of summer
recess to give members a chance to rest—everyone on the Hill has been
working hard and steadily since January and a recess will be welcomed
by all of us—but he does not favor delay as a deliberate policy. McKellar,
veteran of the last treaty fight, remarks with drowsy irony that "delay
didn't do the treaty in the last war any good." It should be sent up
immediately, he said. Asked if that was the Administration's plan he
remarked hastily, "Ah don't know, Ah'm suah. No, suh, Ah don't know
at all." Out in San Francisco, where everything that happens has its
bearing on what the Senate will do to the treaty, Molotov has announced casually that 16 Polish democratic leaders have been arrested
for "diversionary activities against the Red Army." Eden and Stettinius,
confronted suddenly with the ghastly resurrected face of the Thing
which has just been put down at such terrible cost, have demanded an

explanation and suspended all negotiations on the Polish question. On the Hill suspicion of Russia has flared violently anew. It is under such handicaps that Dumbarton Oaks must deliver itself.

MAY 6, 1945. At Rheims the Germans have surrendered, and already American newsreels recapitulate the past like some horrible shadow-show: the fanatic genius, his gang, his people. He screams in angry frenzy above the animal mobs of Nürnberg, and Americans in victory laugh. The lesson so plainly seen seems already forgotten: that nation went mad. It could go mad again. The thought is fantastic in our comfortable theaters, in the hour of victory.

Out in San Francisco, where they are supposed to be preventing such things, a kind of paralysis of moral purpose seems to lie heavy on the delegates. There are conferences and there are compromises, but a shabby proposal is emerging shabbier still. Over and over again in the reports and the columns recurs the phrase, "one of the things bequeathed to us from Yalta." Three men, filled with the arrogance to defy history, met and thought they could decide the world. But only one was in a position to do so, for only one was absolute in his own great land. The other two, although they seemed to forget it, were responsible to democracy. It is not surprising now that it should be the one all-powerful who temporarily dominates, free from the psychological pressures of public opinion, free from the necessity for considering the welfare of his people, free from deferring to their wishes. And it is not surprising that the heirs and assigns of the other two, scurrying about in confusion, should be sinking deeper and deeper in a morass of self-interest and compromise and power-politics diplomacy. Such is the cold, hard penalty, proved over and over again quite beyond the hysterical charges of campaign orators, for one-man rule. Unless government, both foreign and domestic, is of public record and public approval, unless it is grounded firmly on the understanding of all the nation, it is as though it were written in sand which the vagrant winds dissipate and none can restore.

MAY 7, 1945. The nomination of Bob Hannegan to be Postmaster General came before the Senate today. Forrest Donnell, Bennett Champ Clark's successor, his tousled hair askew and a pout on his face like a hurt little boy, argued ably and well for two hours about the genial nominee's political past, taking the Senate on a personally conducted tour of the cesspool of Missouri politics through which Harry Truman passed to glory. Wayne Morse, arguing once again on principle, attacked McKellar for the way in which the nomination was circulated about the Senate floor—members of the Post Office Committee were contacted by the clerk and asked to sign their names as a token of approval, the whole thing was done in one brief afternoon. Donnell refused to sign, asked for time to consider; Morse was never contacted at all. The nomination was reported out favorably regardless. Old Mack waxed sarcastic, amusing and indignant all at one and the same time. There are times, when he knows he has the votes and isn't worried by his opposition, he can really put on a delightful performance, witty and shrewd and excellently entertaining. He did so today while Donnell, absolutely serious and humorless, argued back, and Morse, speaking with a dispassionate and lacerating acid, stripped all McKellar's righteous pretenses bare. Donnell finally moved to recommit the nomination. The Republicans stood by him, the Democrats remained Democrats, the motion was beaten. Hannegan was then confirmed 60 to 2, Donnell and Taft holding out to the end. Morse wasn't hurt a bit by his fight. "The Republican steering committee wanted to let it go through without opposition," he said later. "They said we were licked anyway. I told them I certainly intended to have my say on it, as a matter of principle. It always strengthens both the man and the party to make a fight on principle. It doesn't matter if you get licked."

MAY 9, 1945. "The answer," said Bob Wagner, giving us the greeting he always gives reporters, "is No." We laughed and he laughed and the interview was off to its customary amiable start.

What we wanted to find out about was OPA, but before we were through we were reminiscing about public life and Roosevelt and politics. OPA, which is in the Hill's doghouse this year as it has never been before, has been given a couple of weeks' of grace to put its house in order before Banking and Currency reports out the extension bill. If no improvement is visible then, there will be some drastic amendments. Chester Bowles, complete with charts and charm, has not been able to beguile his critics so well this year as last; there is even some talk that he ought to resign. Wagner is doing what he can for him, but even he, most mellow and philosophic of men, is beginning to get a trifle fed up.

OPA disposed of, we turned to other things. What did he regard as the most important matters facing Congress now that the war was over in Europe? Well, the international organization treaty, of course, and Bretton Woods. Suddenly he fell silent for a moment, his eyes saddened. "Isn't it too bad Roosevelt couldn't be here to see this!" he said. "Isn't it really a damned shame?" "Senator," we said, "you ought to write a book sometime about your friendship with Mr. Roosevelt. There must be a great many things which would be of interest in the historical record." He smiled and shrugged. "Well, I don't know. . . . I don't know. He helped elect me leader of the New York state senate, you know—that was back in 1911, we served together. There was quite a bunch, the young bloods, you know, the young radicals—Frank Roosevelt and Wagner and the rest. They had a conference in New York City with the leader of Tammany Hall. 'We want a new leader,' 'Well,' he said, 'I suppose you want somebody from upstate.' 'No, we'll take one of your own men—we'll take Bob Wagner.' So that's how it was done. That was 1911." He paused and thought back over the years. "I started in 1905," he said with a smile. "Assemblyman, state senator, lieutenant governor, state supreme court justice, appellate court judge, United States Senator . . . 40 years. Well"—he grinned—"that's boasting, and I wouldn't want to boast. I guess I'd better stop it right now. You don't want to hear all about me, anyway." We said we did. "You know," he said, "I don't want to be like a young friend of mine—swell fellow, you know, swell fellow. Used to be a lawyer. Then he got an appointment to a city court job, you know—just a little job, really, but important to him then. The next time I saw him after his appointment"—Wagner hopped out of his chair, puffed out his chest, set his face solemnly and stomped forward—"I said, 'Hello, Bill.' 'Howdye-do, Senator,' he said" (Wagner's tone became heavily pompous) " 'Howdye-do.' " He suddenly reverted from his self-important friend to Bob Wagner and returned to his chair. "So, that's how it goes," he said. "That's how it goes. Come in and see me again. I never have any news, but I like to talk to you. Come in again."

MAY 11, 1945. Henrik Shipstead, grim and shrewd and sardonically humorous, admitted today that there might be some chance that the world-security treaty will get through the Senate. If it does, he said, it may keep the peace for "25 or 30 years." "Until the big powers decide to fight each other," he added in his dry, clipped accent. He spoke on for a while of hated Britain and dangerous Russia and the stupid naïveté of the United States, waxing violently indignant from time to time. The charges he repeated were standard and many of them were true—the fatally confusing factor in this great debate. He spoke with a sincere and bitter conviction. Like all the isolationists in the Senate, the patriotism of the towering old Viking from Minnesota cannot be impeached. This is his country, and this is how to save it. On every side of this unhappy argument the same conviction prevails. It is an apparently insoluble conflict that can only be ended by the final vote in the Senate. There seems little ground for compromise, and little inclination for it.

MAY 12, 1945. Speaking from London, sounding tired and old, Winston Churchill today served notice on transgressors he did not identify that the democracies did not fight the war to permit the deliberate perversion, for political purposes, of the words "democracy," "freedom," and "liberation." "On the continent of Europe," he said, "we have yet to make sure that the simple and honorable purposes for which we entered the war are not brushed aside—and that the words 'freedom,' 'democracy,' and 'liberation' are not distorted from their true meaning as we have understood them."

Across the water in Washington the government announced that Lend-Lease shipments to Russia will be drastically curtailed now the fighting in Europe is over. Under the vast powers granted in the Lend-Lease act, this decision is the responsibility of one man only. Without fuss and without fanfare, walking very softly and carrying a very big stick, he is continuing the revolution that began on April 12.

MAY 13, 1945. Tom Stewart of Tennessee and his colleague Kenneth McKellar bowed to the inevitable today—not an easy thing for Mack to do, but he knows when he is licked. Dave Lilienthal, they said in their joint statement which Stewart read to the Senate late in the afternoon, is "personally and politically obnoxious, offensive and displeasing to each of us." However, they admitted glumly, the President, "whom we like," has been adamant about reappointing him. Accordingly they would make this statement, vote against confirmation, "and leave the matter there."

There have been indignant editorials in some places about the unworthy impropriety of the President's inviting "such a political spoilsman as McKellar" to sit with the Cabinet. It was, however, a practical political situation, solved practically by a practical politician. There is nothing like obligating the most powerful man in the Senate. Harry Truman knew what he was doing, and the people who disapproved obviously didn't know what he was doing. It has been no secret on the Hill, however.

Speaking before the Washington Building Contractors meeting at the Mayflower, Joe Ball has raised one more storm warning to indicate the Senate's temper. "Russia's attitude," he said, "is the big question mark as to whether this world organization will work or not. We've got to make it clear to Russia that you can't eat your cake and have it too. She can't go ahead on a strictly unilateral basis and on an international-security basis at the same time."

Everywhere the signs are showing. If the Russians, who are not fools and who have their own means of gauging American opinion, ignore them, it will be because the Russians are determined to ignore them.

MAY 15, 1945. Ken Wherry remarked today with grudging admiration and the energetic vigor which is his outstanding characteristic that Harry Truman is just doing too good a job to suit the Republicans. "Why," he said with a reluctant grin, "we aren't going to have any issue in 1946 if this keeps up. He's sticking too close to the middle of the road. He's done some conservative things that I think have been pretty good, and at the same time he says he's going to support Roosevelt's program, and he's endorsed Bretton Woods and the Reciprocal Trade Agreements act. I tell you, we're going to have to step some. Now, if Henry Wallace were in there, we'd have something. But what are you going to tie into with Truman? Also, Hannegan's doing just what I thought he would—they're getting to work already on the '46 elections. They'll be in every county, you wait and see. And what are we doing? Well, damn it, I've criticized the national committee too much already, but I keep telling them you've *got* to have an organization, you've *got* to get to work early, you can't win by just sitting around drawing up programs. They're nice fellows down at headquarters, I guess, but they certainly aren't getting to work. We're going to have a terrific fight and we can't win it if people are too proud to work."

35

PROBABLY A VERY UNWISE BILL

MAY 16, 1945. In the Banking and Currency Committee this morning they voted unanimous approval of Bob Wagner's bill to absorb five more government corporations into the RFC. Thus does Jesse's empire grow and proliferate, even without him. Taft remarked rather wistfully that he did hope they would be able to get some sort of survey of the actual powers and expenditures of the agency. Truman's appointee, the unemotional, businesslike banker John Snyder, said that would be all right with him. Nobody at all any more talks about breaking RFC up into components which can be controlled. The only impulse to kill the octopus came with Henry's nomination. After that was taken care of, the impulse faded away.

MAY 17, 1945. The basic truism about the South—that you cannot legislate emotion, you can only educate it—was proved again today when five Southerners, several of them liberal, kicked over the traces in the Education and Labor Committee and refused to go along with Chavez' bill for a permanent compulsory FEPC. Lister Hill, Fulbright, big good-natured Olin Johnston of South Carolina, Allen Ellender and Claude Pepper emerged in revolt from the executive committee meeting. Ellender and Johnston promptly threatened a filibuster if the bill ever comes up on the floor. Hill assailed it as "regimentation," and Pepper, although casting about for a compromise, seemed equally against it. Ordinarily no one is more willing to force people into line on social issues than those two gentlemen, but now the practice has been brought too close to home for comfort. They know what the result would be, and they are taking the only stand consistent with the realities of the South. Taft's compromise, an educative, persuasive commission rather than a compulsive, mandatory agency, has been bitterly attacked in the New York press. Consequently those committee members who take their cue from the New York press made no attempt to offer it to the Southerners first. There was some chance they might have accepted it. Now that too is out the window. Once again the all-or-nothing-at-all philosophy has produced its inevitable result.

MAY 18, 1945. Happy Chandler, although elected baseball commissioner, has decided to stay in the Senate for a while, much to the annoyance of the GOP. Hap kind of figures maybe he ought to stick around "for security reasons," as his secretary puts it with a grin—security against Republicans, who would certainly gain another seat if he left. This has caused consternation in the ranks of the minority, who find themselves confronted with something of the same situation they faced with Homer Bone. This disconcerting habit Democrats have of getting other jobs and then staying on in the Senate to block Republican successors is getting to be too much! There is some disposition to forgive Happy, however, who is very popular personally. The votes he casts are not too far from the minority line, in any case.

MAY 20, 1945. In New York, speaking before the American-Polish Associations, Taft came out today in qualified support of the San Francisco Charter. Russia's insistence on a veto, he said, makes it impossible to achieve international law, and there is no use fooling ourselves that the thing is perfect. However, he said, the men at San Francisco "have done a great job," and he for one intends to support the result. Burt Wheeler, off in Europe at the head of a touring Interstate Commerce subcommittee, is becoming more and more isolated in his isolation.

MAY 21, 1945. Over in the House today, before a joint session, the President personally presented the hundredth Congressional Medal of Honor to be awarded an infantryman in this war. It went to T/Sgt. Jake M. Lindsey of Luceville, Mississippi, a slight, shy young soldier who seemed as awed as any soldier might be to be escorted in by the Chief of Staff ("Give him a bow," Marshall murmured out of the side of his mouth just before he sent his young charge forward to get the medal) to be honored by the President and the Congress of the United States. His folks sat down front, along with the Cabinet and other guests of honor and distinction. Marshall read the citation, Truman hung the medal around the sergeant's neck, the galleries applauded long and loud. There was the sort of comfortable, touching, family feeling about it that America's moments of symbolism and state so often have.

After he finished reading his brief speech—each single sentence typed neatly in the center of an individual sheet of paper in his notebook— Truman acknowledged the applause for a moment and then turned to shake hands with Rayburn and McKellar above him at the Speaker's desk in back. They exchanged some humorous comment; he started away, then thought of something else and turned back quickly. As the applause went on he ignored the Congress, grasped the rail of the Speaker's desk with both hands, stood on tiptoe and shouted something additional to McKellar. Then he turned back and left the dais and started out, waving to the Senate, shaking hands hastily with Carl Hatch, saying, "Hello, Bob," to Bob La Follette on the aisle, and smiling his pleased, broad grin. Marshall and Sergeant Lindsey left last, receiving a special ovation of their own as they went out the door.

Back in the Senate, Lilienthal's nomination was confirmed by voice vote after McKellar read again the same statement Stewart read last Thursday. Barkley, attempting to spread a little oil on the waters, inadvertently trod on Mack's sensitive toes. McKellar charged him violently with "doing everything he can" to bring Lilienthal into the Senate in McKellar's place. "I don't want to see anyone else in the Senator's place," said Barkley patiently. After the old man calmed down, and after Stewart took a few more cracks at Lilienthal, the nomination was put to a vote. "Aye," said everyone else. "No!" shouted Mack and Stewart. "The nomination is confirmed and the President will be notified," said the Chair calmly.

MAY 22, 1945. Pepper has definitely decided to drop his plans for a compromise on the permanent FEPC and will oppose the bill—"sitting there at his desk with his Abe Lincoln bookends!" as one of my indignant colleagues told me later. The good Claude, however, who is a sincere liberal and a real one, knows his South too well to do anything else.

Appropriations decided this morning to follow the lead of the House and approve a $2500 tax-exempt expense account for the Senate. The money is entirely justifiable on the basis of need, and is indeed far too miserly to be an adequate solution. The way in which it is being done, however, adding it to other legislation instead of letting it stand on its own merits, can only lay the Congress open to new and deserved criticisms.

MAY 23, 1945. The Education and Labor Committee voted 12 to 6 today to report out the permanent FEPC bill. Taft joined the Southerners to oppose it. Thus have some political debts been paid off, some others deferred. Chavez hailed the "bipartisan action" by which Democrats joined Republicans to send the bill to the floor: a couple of rather embarrassing platform promises have been taken care of. One of the nicest and truest liberals on the committee summed up the situation succinctly later. "I think it's probably a very unwise bill," he said with a candid grin. "I'd never vote for it if I thought it would pass."

MAY 24, 1945. Up from 1600 Pennsylvania Avenue today came a reasonable and logical message requesting legislation as soon as possible to permit the President to reorganize the Executive branch. It proposed the safeguard of a Congressional veto within 60 days of any given reorganization proposal, and was received with considerable approval on the Hill. Some Republicans, realizing like Ken Wherry that they are being gradually stripped of all their issues, let out indignant squawks, but there wasn't much they could do about it. To be consistent with their campaign speeches in three elections, they will have to vote for whatever proposal is finally put before them—or else they will have to face the charge that they have simply been playing politics all these years.

Also from the White House came announcement of the resignations of Francis Biddle, to be succeeded by Tom Clark of Texas in the Attorney Generalship; Frances Perkins, giving way to Judge Lewis Schwellenbach, former Senator from Washington; and Claude Wickard, to be replaced at Agriculture by Representative Clinton P. Anderson of New Mexico.

The President, Barkley + McKellar

Wickard will move to the Rural Electrification Administration if the Senate confirms him; it probably will. Francis Biddle leaves unwept and unregretted. Frances Perkins, good woman and thoroughly competent Secretary of Labor within the limits set for her by the late President, takes with her a very real respect and appreciation from the Congress which once criticized her so much.

In the Senate this afternoon Bob Wagner, still carrying the banner of liberalism undaunted, introduced the latest version of the Wagner–Murray–Dingell social security bill. Perhaps the most significant and important piece of social legislation to come before Congress in a decade, it will probably be another decade before it is passed. That it or something like it someday will be, however, there can be no doubt, for its vision of expanded social security, public health insurance, old-age pensions and better living is one that cannot be denied the nation much longer. Many things in the bill as it now stands need amendment and revision and much discussion, but the essential purposes are sound and they are good, and it is only a matter of time before they prevail.

MAY 25, 1945. Opposition to the Senate's expense account is growing apace. Ed Johnson announced yesterday after a rather acrimonious debate that he will make a point of order Monday to the effect that the proposal is legislation in an appropriations bill, something forbidden by the rules. Overton is hurrying around trying to work out a compromise with the House—the House is getting huffy—and it begins to seem doubtful whether the Senate will vote itself the increase. A question that was rather academic to the Senate's many wealthy men is beginning to become more important as it becomes more controversial. To the Senate's poorer men, a windfall that might have helped them considerably is beginning to be a matter of principle they must seriously consider before voting. "I am interested in maintaining the integrity of the Congress," Ed Johnson said. "That's the most important thing there is in this country today, the integrity of the Congress." And though his statement aroused a momentary amusement, second thought indicated that he was probably right.

MAY 26, 1945. Elbert Thomas has released a letter from Undersecretary of War Robert Patterson. In view of the changed circumstances of the past six weeks, says the efficient gentleman with the tired face and the stern, impatient mind, the War Department no longer feels it necessary to have a nurses' draft bill. The voluntary program has worked wonders, he says, the Cadet Nurse Corps has come through with flying colors, the Germans have surrendered completely instead of undertaking guerrilla warfare. Accordingly the War Department is taking the extraordinary step of urging the Senate to drop the bill. Thus suavely the department is bowing to the inevitable and attempting to save such meager face as it still has in the Senate, which by now has come to know it too bitterly and too well. Elbert Thomas hails the decision, much relieved. Others smile sardonically and make, but not for publication, the obvious comment.

Over in the House this afternoon Harry Truman survived his first real test handsomely. The Reciprocal Trade Agreements Act was extended by a vote of 239–153. Now it comes to the Senate, where its prospects are not so clear. It will probably pass all right, but whether it will carry the increased authority to reduce tariffs the House granted remains to be seen.

Continuing his fascinating act of carrying Democrats on one shoulder and Republicans on the other, the President has invited the GOP's only living former Executive to confer with him Monday on the European food situation. Herbert Hoover, pleased, has accepted the bid.

MAY 27, 1945. Out in San Francisco the work is nearly done. All the compromises with principle and history have been worked out, the uncomfortable liveliness of the smaller nations in demanding greater power in the organization has been firmly suppressed,* the basic charter for power-politics-made-respectable has been worked out, every attempt to change it being greeted with the cry, "This was decided at Yalta!" Decided at Yalta it was indeed, and a worse decision history does not record. "Let us make this a lasting memorial to Franklin Roosevelt!" cry the delegates lustily, struggling frantically in the morass of half-kept promises, unfinished commitments and tentative "understandings" he left them. Memorial it may be, but if so it will be grim.

In the Senate an inertia lies upon the men who must make the final decision. Aware that Connally and Vandenberg are twice as timorous as they might otherwise be because of their fear of "what the Senate will accept," its internationalists do not speak out in constructive debate to help them in their work. Twenty-five members are overseas, among them such as Joe Ball and Homer Ferguson; the voice of the Senate is silent. "I'd rather wait until I see what comes out of San Francisco," men say, permitting the desperately wrong results to develop without raising their voices to indicate where the Senate stands and just exactly what it *will* accept. It is much more, in all probability, than it is going to get.

MAY 28, 1945. The Senate decided today that Representatives are worth $2500 more than Senators. It was an unhesitating decision, endorsed by

* Or so its architects thought then, 15 years before the retreat of colonialism brought more than 50 new nations surging into the UN to demand their say in things.

an overwhelming vote. It kept the Senate from breaking the Little Steel formula and it left the House out on a limb. Each house got something. The Senate got the glory and the House got the cash. It was quite a lively afternoon.

It began with Lucas attacking the expense-account amendment for the Senate and Overton defending it. Later Hatch got the floor and spoke in favor. Wayne Morse spoke with great conviction and moral purity of purpose to the effect that the Senate mustn't break the Little Steel formula and "start an inflationary spiral." "What of the 435 members of the House who will get this increase whether the Senate does or not?" Carl Hatch wanted to know; Wayne Morse expressed the pious hope that the House, abashed, would repeal the provision. Others pointed out that it couldn't be done unless the House provision was amended so that it could go to conference. Hatch offered a substitute amendment. Barkley tried to amend it to bring the figure down to $1500; Barkley was beaten. Struggling desperately to bring the action of the two houses into line, Barkley pleaded earnestly with his colleagues to amend the House provision with the same $1500 figure; the idea got lost in the shuffle. Styles Bridges, frank to say the Senate should have the increase, fought in vain to secure it. The vote came: down went the Senate amendment 43 to 9. Promptly Bridges offered another, a straight pay raise of $1500, the magical 15 per cent of the Little Steel formula. Down it went, 38–12. Ed Johnson, defeated earlier on a point of order against the Senate amendment, offered an amendment to strike out the House provision—an attempt to overturn a precedent of 160 years that one house does not interfere with the other on its own appropriations. For a little while it looked as though the precedent would be overturned; at the end of the first roll call, with Barkley voting Aye in an attempt to throw the whole thing into conference and align the houses, the vote stood 22–22. Six Senators entered late: they were all against it. 28–22 Ed Johnson's motion lost. Styles Bridges exploded angrily at his colleagues' apparent determination "to go on record as making this a millionaire's club and forcing out the poorer men, so that only men of great wealth, men who have inherited it or have married wealthy wives, can serve in the Senate." Barkley looked glum and unhappy. When the angry debate was over, the Senate had decided that it would not accept the increase for itself; it would not refuse it to the House; it would not even make a *pro forma* amendment to the House provision so that the whole thing could be worked out equitably in conference. So the record stands: Congressmen $12,500—Senators $10,000. It will take a devil of a lot of squabbling to get them back together again in the future.

MAY 29, 1945. The House put on a defiant show today about being pleased with its expense account and to hell with the Senate, but members are beginning to feel very much out on a limb and lonesome in the national spotlight. The mail is beginning to run very heavily, and it is not approving. The Representatives have worked themselves into a nice spot, and for once the Senate has decided to give rein to its occasional annoyance with them and let them sit and stew on it.

In San Francisco, cozy and encouraging, Edward Stettinius spoke last night and warmly hailed the "strong and democratic" Charter that is emerging. It is not strong and it is not democratic. What kind of fools do they think we are?

36

RECIPROCAL TRADE

MAY 30, 1945. The Administration opened its case for the Reciprocal Trade Agreements Act in the Senate today. Will Clayton, patient, reasonable, smooth as butter, put on his usual beautiful performance of testifying earnestly and intelligently before a generally hostile committee. Bushfield, who may be as conservative as his critics say but is certainly no slouch when it comes to cross-examination, came the closest of anyone to ruffling the apparently unruffleable Texan. Butler heckled him occasionally also, Dave Walsh was critical, Ed Johnson asked some pointed questions, Josiah Bailey, slow and ministerial, sounded quite inimical to the whole program, O'Mahoney tossed a few darts and received them back again, sharp end first. Even Peter Gerry of Rhode Island came to life. When Clayton argued that tariffs could be reduced more efficiently and more profitably by the Executive than by Congress, Gerry leaned forward sharply. "Are you familiar with what Senator Underwood said in 1922 on the fallacy of that argument?" he asked severely. "No sir, I'm not," Clayton said. "I didn't think you were," said Peter Gerry sternly. Then he sank back in his chair and was thereafter silent. It was the first thing he had said in months.

All in all, Walter George has his hands full with the Finance Committee. Most of them concede that the act will be renewed, but there is a strong tendency to knock out the authority to reduce tariffs by an additional 50 per cent. The House, always generous, gave this without a qualm. The Senate, always cautious—frequently with good reason—is not so sure. There will be a stiff fight.

Banking and Currency has finally reported out the OPA extension act. There will be a fight on that too. All amendments were beaten in committee, but some will be offered again on the floor.

MAY 31, 1945. Bob La Follette today made the second major speech of the peace debate, the first being Vandenberg's on January 10. The stocky little liberal from Wisconsin ("Every time I come away after talking to that guy," said one of the reporters later, "I feel that I've been talking to one of the most honest men in the Senate") had had the speech "stewing around inside" him for a long time, he said. It was obvious before he started that he knew it was an important thing. He was nervous, something he very rarely is, and after he obtained the floor and was yielding to other Senators for insertions in the *Record*, he bobbed around tensely at his desk, impatient to begin. It became apparent why this was when he finally began to speak.

His speech was a damning, specific indictment, which lasted three hours, of Russia, Britain and the United States and all their mistakes of omission and commission. He started with Versailles, quoting chapter and verse from those who were there, and he drew all the deadly parallels with the present situation. He cited the broken pledges of Yalta, attacked the haste with which the big powers are attempting to rush the San Francisco conference to a close, scathingly denounced Russia's ruthless imperialism and Britain's both-ends-against-the-middle diplomacy, concluded with a demand for a broader and more democratic organization, and put his finger bluntly on the hypocrisy that surrounds the veto. He pointed to the French attack on Syria, at its peak today, and he noted that when the organization is established France will be able to veto even the discussion of any such event in the future. He said over and over again that he wanted to "get it on the record"—the tragic stupidity with which the great powers are walking once again down the blind alley they first stumbled into at Versailles. Fulbright attempted to interrupt from time to time, rather confused interruptions that La Follette batted down angrily. Fulbright wasn't making too much of an argument, anyway—his remarks more often paralleled La Follette's than diverged from them. He was strongly skeptical of the Senate's ratification of the treaty without the veto in it and he did express strong disappointment that the Senate is not engaging in more policy debates to help guide the delegates at San Francisco. He praised La Follette's contribution to this, and La Follette thanked him. He didn't expect his remarks to carry any weight or influence, he said, but he wanted to get it on the record. Barkley said he thought La Follette underestimated his own influence. "I'll withdraw the remark if it offends the Senator," said Bob La Follette with an acid promptness and a rather tense laugh. He was very definitely on edge throughout his speech, and there was no denying the enormous impact of his sincerity. He was just fed up, and he let fly with everything he had. "It wasn't as bad as we expected," Barkley told us afterwards. "It was really a pretty good speech." He seemed impressed by it, and so were we all. La Follette doesn't go in for needling, and when he makes a major speech people listen.

JUNE 1, 1945. In an exhaustive 9000-word message, the President today painted the picture of the Japanese war the military contemplate: the Army sent against Europe to be doubled for Japan, the full might of the Navy to be used. Partly, no doubt, it was propaganda for the Japanese; partly it was fact.

To his press conference, also, the President said that he was attempting to bring his ideas on postwar military training and those of the Army and Navy, and of Congress, into some sort of over-all agreement. He does not agree, he said, with the Army and Navy. The House starts hearings on the subject next week, and all the big guns of an intensive propaganda are once more being brought to bear. From Taft and Ed Johnson comes confirmation of reports that the Army and Navy have been holding secret meetings in the Pentagon with leaders of women's groups, professional veterans organizations, and others, lining them up behind this proposition. It is a strange, suspect procedure for the military of a free republic to follow. Once again it raises squarely the issue of the manpower bill in this new bill. Placed against the background of this maneuvering by the services, it becomes a thing of desperate concern. What do they want? What are they after, that they must go skulking and sneaking behind the public's back? What is the reason for this sneak-thief approach to Congress? Are they afraid of a fair fight on a fair issue, or are they after something a fair fight wouldn't give them?

JUNE 2, 1945. Ed Johnson confessed today to great concern about the compulsory military training idea. "You look at the tie-up between the brass hats and big business," he said, "and you'll be worried too. This is all part of it, this military training bill. What do you suppose they've been holding all these secret meetings for? Can you figure it out? I can't. Oh, I don't like it, I don't like it at all. They're sure trying to run things, and if you give them this control it's going to mean that we never will get rid of them. I'm sure as hell going to fight it with everything I've got." Usually an excellent judge of sentiment in the Senate, he confessed to uncertainty. The House, he thought, would probably go along as usual.

So it is beginning to shape up, the next great fight with the military. Over in the House (where the Senate, because of the expense account, is now referred to informally as "Those bastards"), there is some doubt that members will be quite as pliant as the Senator thinks. They have gone a long way in this war and have been far more generous with the people's liberties than the Senate, but there are signs of a change, even there. The testimony, the letters, the telegrams, the importuning of the ladies and gentlemen who went to school at the Pentagon, may not be quite so effective in the long run as the old, saving instinct of what is best for a free country. There are still some who believe in that, and perceive also that liberty is indivisible and that you either have it or you do not have it, without any quibble in between.

JUNE 3, 1945. Down in the District of Columbia Building where the Surplus Property Board has its rather harried offices, Guy Gillette yesterday met the press, looking his usual good-natured self. His resignation on Thursday has caused much comment. Rumors and rumors of rumors circulate about his head. We were in a mood to ask questions, and after an exhaustive discussion of a new regulation on veterans' preference, somebody began it. "Senator, I can't go back to my office without asking this: why did you resign?" The military officers who sat at his elbow tensed, the Senator looked embarrassed, but being an honest man, he smiled and answered. He took the job, he said, on a temporary basis. He never wanted it. The basic program of directives was under way. He felt he could resign without being accused of running out on the job. So he was. Colonel Heller, his fellow Board member, broke in to remark that the reports of dissension in the Board were entirely untrue. He and Governor Hurley, he said, were "most unhappy" to see the Senator leave. The basic issue, the basic conflict—Gillette's contention that war plants should not be sold to the big monopolies until small operators were given first chance to bid, Heller's and Hurley's determination to permit the owning agencies to sell them without restriction to whomever they please —was ignored smoothly. All was harmony, Colonel Heller said; Guy Gillette, on a spot where he had no choice, echoed the sentiments suavely. ("I'm going to issue a statement which will bring this whole mess into the open," he told one of his former colleagues the other day. He did not do so.) The meeting broke up on a note of amiability, the Army's watchdogs relaxed and departed. One of my colleagues, an old Senate hand, and I went up to say hello to Gillette. "Well," he said with a pleased smile as he shook hands, "here's a couple of old warhorses. Nice to see you, nice to see you." We returned the sentiment. "What's next, Senator?" we asked. "I don't know," he said frankly. "The President offered me a seat on the Federal bench, but I turned it down. I'm not qualified for a judgeship. I told him I hadn't practiced law for 25 years. They told me at the White House I could 'brush up.' Well, you can't very well 'brush up' for a Federal judgeship and do a good job of it. The President told me he wanted me to stay on in official life, but whether anything will come of it, I don't know." So spoke Guy Gillette, in all probability one of the few men in history who has turned down a lifetime Federal judgeship because he didn't consider himself qualified. It may be, as some say, that part of the trouble on the Board has been his own hesitancy about coming to decisions on matters of major policy. It may be that along with all his many fine qualities there is also the one a former colleague summed up the other day when he told us: "Guy has a hard time making up his mind. He used to tell me that he went to the Lord for advice on how he should vote here. Frequently I thought the Lord was giving him very poor advice." Whether that is true or not, the fact remains that he is an excellent public servant.

JUNE 4, 1945. The Finance Committee, on a speed-up schedule in an attempt to get the Reciprocal Trade Agreements extension to the floor in time to meet the June 12 expiration date, is whipping through witnesses like a house afire these days. Most of them have already testified endlessly in the House (a constantly recurring argument for joint committee sessions) and both George and Dave Walsh, second in command, show a strong tendency to cut them off swiftly at the conclusion of their prepared statements and hurry on to the next man. Not so Taft, whose constant clashes with them furnish virtually the only news out of the committee. From time to time Scott Lucas, speaking in a slow tone of heavy sarcasm, interrupts to throw the knife into the Senator from Ohio. Taft ignores it or snaps back an answer. Now and then portly, able young Brien McMahon, the man who beat Danaher, attempts to follow Lucas' example in a portly, husky voice. Taft handles him too, sometimes ably, sometimes not so well. Over and over again the Republicans (Butler and Bushfield help out, occasionally clipped-voiced Robertson of Wyoming joins in) attack the theory that the trade agreements have anything to do with the Bretton Woods agreement, the San Francisco Charter, or the international Food and Agriculture Organization. Each, they argue, should stand on its own merits. They are gaining ground day by day. Sentiment also is growing for O'Mahoney's amendment to provide Congressional review. A poll of the committee shows that the bill will come out stripped of the House's grant of an extra 50-per-cent tariff-reducing power.

JUNE 5, 1945. The President, who is rapidly becoming the most industrious writer of messages to Congress in history, today walked deliberately into a hornet's nest by addressing a letter to Chairman Adolph Sabath of the House Rules Committee. The FEPC, he pointed out, is about to die without a fair vote of the House because of the Appropriations Committee's decision to cut off its funds and the Rules Committee's decision to prevent the permanent FEPC bill from reaching the floor. Accordingly he requested the committee to give the bill a rule—a rare intervention by a President in the workings of Congress, and probably excusable on the Hill only by virtue of his past employment as a member —so that the House could vote on its merits. There is some doubt that the committee will comply, but it is an interesting event. It is interesting to note, also, the mildly expressed but increasing sense of annoyance many people are beginning to feel at the unending stream of requests, suggestions, admonitions and advice that is ascending from the White House. It's nice to be loved, after so much hatred, but it is beginning to make Congress feel a trifle uneasy, deep down inside.

At the trade-agreements hearing this afternoon we were afforded an interesting study in family resemblances when Charles Taft, foreign economic adviser to the State Department, turned up to testify for the bill. His brother Bob, with whom he disagrees violently on this issue, tactfully stayed away, perhaps by arrangement. The younger Taft is a rather handsome gentleman with large dark eyes, the determined family mouth, and an impatient, rather peremptory manner which is also characteristic. His voice is pitched higher than his brother's, but there is the same banging emphasis on individual words, delivered with the same forceful movements of shoulders and arms and head. Whatever the geniality of the late President may have been, he certainly bequeathed his sons very positive and decided personalities. Charles Taft ignored the Republican side of the committee, shook hands cordially with Barkley and McMahon and Lucas ("Look at that!" Bushfield murmured indignantly to Butler), and replied to GOP questioning with a prickly arrogance that indicated it would brook no argument and consequently got little. Like his brother when annoyed, he bites; and Bushfield and Butler, after testing him out a little, decided to leave him alone. It was a sensible decision of the Senator not to come around. He and Charlie would have had a spat if he had, there's no doubt about it.

JUNE 6, 1945. The debate on OPA extension began today, with Wagner once again doing the honors for the Administration. The bill has come out of committee, where it was delayed for two months while conferences were held to try to persuade the agency to be more cooperative, with a solid lineup of Democrats versus Republicans. The greatest bitterness against the agency this year seems to stem from the fact that it is imposing 1942 prices on reconversion production, thereby, as Taft argues, discouraging new business, driving marginal operators out of business, and helping to create an unemployment which the sponsors of 60,000,000 jobs elsewhere in the Administration do not contemplate in their blueprints. Apparently frightened at last, Chester Bowles is issuing statements right and left to the effect that he will interpret this section of the law and that section of the law "just as Congress wants it." Why this obliging willingness to obey the law has had to wait until so late in the day to appear he does not reveal.

JUNE 7, 1945. The House, grimly determined to stand by its guns, took up the expense account today and upheld it handsomely on a roll-call vote. At the other end of the Avenue Harry Truman remarked with brisk candor that he knew what it was to be a member of an underpaid Congress, and added that a bill ought to be put in to raise salaries to some point between $15,000 and $25,000. He would, he added, sign such a bill. Wayne Morse in the Senate issued an indignant statement that the President was threatening to break the Little Steel formula by condoning the "wage grab of the House," but most Senators felt a little sheepish about it all.

JUNE 8, 1945. Overton and Bridges, gratefully accepting the lead proffered by the White House, today introduced a bill to raise all Congressional salaries to $20,000, boost the V.P. and the Speaker to $25,000, and raise Cabinet officers to $20,000. Again Wayne Morse lectured his colleagues severely, but the general attitude was favorable.

The OPA debate dragged on at some length. The usual predictions about finishing the debate "in two or three days" are turning out to be quite as optimistic as always.

The Finance Committee reported out the Reciprocal Trade Agreements bill after stripping it of the extra tariff-reducing authority by a vote of 10–9. A determined attempt will be made to write it back in on the floor.

JUNE 9, 1945. "I don't know how it happens," said Ed Johnson with a grin, "but somehow it always seems that a day or two before you come to voting on reciprocal trade you always have enough votes to beat it, but then when you vote somehow all your votes disappear and it passes." One of the Democrats who joined the Republicans in committee to strike out the 50-per-cent clause, he seemed inclined to think it will be put back in on the floor. O'Mahoney's Congressional-review amendment will be brought up on the floor, as will Taft's attempt to shorten the extension period. Both went down by narrow votes in committee.

On another international front, Bob Wagner announces that Banking and Currency will start hearings Tuesday on the Bretton Woods monetary agreement.

JUNE 10, 1945. Finance Committee, after two hearings, is getting ready to act on a bill by Fulbright to repeal the (Hiram) Johnson Act prohibiting private loans to countries in default on their First World War debts. The central picture is dramatic—Fulbright, the young internationalist confronting Johnson, the Ancient Warrior of isolationism. The youthful Senator has been quite abashed and embarrassed at having to oppose the old, and has refrained from looking at him while he has made a feeble, pathetic attempt to stall off the repeal of his law. First he demanded a week's delay to permit him "to get my evidence together—I have been occupied with other things in these recent months ... other things. ..." (His voice has trailed away and there have been long, painful silences while he gathered his thoughts.) The delay was granted. Then the old man attempted to delay some more, standing before the committee with his cane, turning occasionally to the audience, whispering on hesitantly in his fading voice which now and then rises to a strident echo of its former vigor. Walter George, Barkley, Dave Walsh have talked to him patiently, going over and over the situation. He has charged them with "trying this like a court. ... I want time to gather my evidence. ... Why do you rush me along? Why do you hasten so to do this thing? ... Why will you not ... allow me. ..." Finally the committee has been forced to go ahead; Johnson has subsided into a chair. Once in a while he has risen on his cane. A word, a sentence, a phrase—they have started and trailed away. It has been unpleasant for everyone. "If I only had the strength I once had," he has sometimes said in whispering protest. But he has not.

JUNE 11, 1945. The Senate passed the OPA extension today after a cantankerous debate and a parliamentary muddle that wound things up in a tangle of frayed tempers. After the bill was passed by unanimous voice vote, Walter George got permission to make reciprocal trade the pending business, and tomorrow the fight begins on that.

JUNE 12, 1945. The trade-agreements debate began today as George arose majestic and thunderous to denounce his erring committee members for their deletion of the extra tariff-reducing powers. He developed an interesting argument—that the act must be extended with the added power "to aid the President in his great fight for a free economy" against the collectivist economy of Soviet Russia. Everywhere the trend to collectivism continues, the Georgian said; everywhere the comparison is being drawn between the free economy of the United States and the collectivist economy of Russia—"and the influence of Russia will extend as far as it can go. ... It devolves upon the United States to bear the burden of proving the strength of a free economy."

When he finished, O'Mahoney obtained the floor, and the outlines of this interesting debate became clear—two of the Senate's most powerful and most skillful fighters, squaring away to oppose one another with all the tricks they know. There is no more able or persuasive man in the

Senate, O'Mahoney began, than the Senator from Georgia. How, then, could he contemplate without concern in an age of creeping totalitarianism the abject surrender of Congressional control over tariffs? Everywhere, everywhere, Mr. President, the most wondrous wonder of wonderful Wyoming cried in impressive anguish, the governments of free men are at bay. A great step will be taken toward totalitarianism if Congressional review of tariff reduction is not restored. Basic to our time is the issue of free government versus executive control. It was much the same argument he gave on the manpower bill, the same he has applied to so many other things.

It was a rare entertainment, as well as a discussion of issues that are indeed basic to this land as to so many others. George replied softly and sarcastically from time to time, reserving his thunder in the colloquies, implying gently only that O'Mahoney was exaggerating, that he was being absurd, that there was nothing to it. The Senate sat in rapt silence as two of its giants tangled head-on. It will be very interesting to watch the debate develop. Somebody is going to lose, but neither George nor O'Mahoney has the habit.

Down the Avenue for the first time Truman backed water. He sent a letter to Speaker Sam Rayburn and Mc-Kellar: apparently Wayne Morse's lecture and the pressure of his own stabilization officials was too much. He urged the Congress to stay within the Little Steel formula and raise its wages $1500 only; later on salaries might go to $15,000. His remarks to his press conference were "misinterpreted." For once there was a momentary echo of the past.

In the House they went through their annual futility by passing the anti-poll-tax bill again. Once again it is on its way over here, where it will eventually be buried once again with suitable honors. And the Rules Committee, 6–6, refused to give the go-ahead to the permanent FEPC bill.

JUNE 13, 1945. After a conference at the White House, Barkley returned today to announce that the President will send up the San Francisco

Charter immediately upon its completion, probably by June 25. There will then be a speed-up campaign to get the Senate to rush it through, presumably so that Truman can take it with him to the next Big Three conference, now scheduled for the middle of July. Despite confident opening statements, however, everybody hedged on it before they finished their comments. Barkley said he saw no reason why they shouldn't be able to pass it in two or three weeks, including hearings—but there should be time for reasonable discussion. Walter George presumed that there would have to be quite extensive hearings, "perhaps two or three weeks—at least two or three weeks." Wallace White said much the same, so did Styles Bridges, so did the rest. For a little while the unfortunate impression went around that the White House was trying to jam it through and not give time for ample discussion. This impression is always fatal to the best-laid plans, in the Senate. Later Charlie Ross, the press secretary, issued a statement that Truman certainly wasn't demanding such speed. He would like to have the United States among the first to ratify, but he would be content to go along with whatever the Senate decided. Things settled back down to normal again after a moment's uneasiness. There definitely will be an attempt to expedite it, however, and if conducted reasonably it should meet with success. Much will depend on the way Connally handles the hearings before Foreign Relations.

In the trade-agreements debate Tobey furnished us the best story of the day by suddenly jumping up in vociferous anger to lash out at "five fat sleek lobbyists, sitting out there just outside the Senate, calling us out and putting screws on Senators to get them to vote against this bill!" (On the opposite side of the chamber, outside the other door, several sleek, slim lobbyists from the State Department, among them Assistant Secretary Dean Acheson, were calling Senators aside and putting the screws on them to get them to vote for the bill. So it goes.) "I say they can go straight to—" cried Tobey, New Hampshire's liberal tornado, banging on his desk, "—you know where they can go to!" We interviewed him immediately afterwards, and talking in his extremely rapid fashion, with his pleasant toothy smile coming and going on his professorial face, he gave us some more good quotes. "There they are," he said forcefully, "five fat lobbyists. They're fat and they're sleek and they've got round bottoms and round heads. They can't wait to get back to the good old Smoot–Hawley days [*of high protectionist tariffs established in the Smoot–Hawley Tariff Act of 1931.*] They're panting for it, their tongues are hanging out for it." A Republican leader, he added, was out there helping them, calling Senators aside and counting noses. Then, in an outburst reminiscent of George Aiken and Wayne Morse and Austin

and Joe Ball and a few others—a very few others—he said angrily, "The
Republican Party just hasn't learned anything! Damn it, we never are
going to get back into power unless we stop opposing things just for the
sake of opposing and once in a while vote for something for the good of
all the people of the country. It takes heart, that's what it takes, you've
got to have love in your heart, you've got to understand people, all the
people, not just this group or that group. Damn it, what did Jesus say?
Love the Lord they God, and love thy neighbor as thyself. And who is
thy neighbor? It's everyone, all the people of this country and of all
countries. We're all in this together, see what I mean, and we all rise and
fall together. You've got to have heart—" he concluded earnestly. "You
can't just look at this narrowly, for this little group or that one."

JUNE 14, 1945. Walter George, confident he has the votes, predicted today that the extra tariff-reducing authority will be put back in the reciprocal trade bill when the Senate votes. This event is now delayed until Monday by the return of a number of travelers, some of whom want
to speak on the subject. Burt Wheeler, George said with a chuckle, "is
coming in here loaded for bear." Then too, he added drily, "Senator
Langer says he is going to speak, and he is sometimes apt to be a little
lengthy." But he has the votes, George thinks. He is not making predictions yet on O'Mahoney's amendment to require Congressional review.

JUNE 15, 1945. Wheeler, annoyed with the Russians and full of dark tales
he will undoubtedly make use of when the time comes, met the press
today upon his return from Europe. Pacing up and down, he gave his
opinion on the treaty schedule: he objects to it. It seems to him, he said,
that the Charter might very well wait until the peace settlements have
been made and the country knows what its sacrifices have been used to
underwrite. This argument will probably be one of the main weapons in
his arsenal when the fight begins, and like most of the others he will use,
it is perfectly sound and perfectly rational and thereby doubly destructive to the opposition.

Homer Capehart of Indiana, who made the grand tour with the
shrewd Montanan, echoed his sentiments faithfully. Let's wait until the
peace treaties have been signed, Capehart urged: let's find out what
we're getting. That always seemed like good business to him, said the
man who made those handsome radios. Let's don't take a pig in a poke.

Elsewhere in the Senate, in a reaction from the burst of optimism
several days ago, members are beginning to sober down and realize that
after all it just isn't possible to get the Charter through in anything like

the three weeks originally proposed. It will be a longer fight, and a tougher one, than that.

JUNE 16, 1945. Homer Ferguson, back from Europe, was reasonably optimistic about the chances for cooperation with Russia when we went in to see him today. He emphasized, however, that it was a hard task to create democracy in Europe. It takes education, he said, it takes time, "and above all it takes the courts, you know? The courts are the heart of it, really—the assurance that every man will have a fair trial under a law which is universal and recognized by all. That's what we have—oh" (quickly), "I know there are many exceptions, but on the whole that's how it is with us right down to the traffic courts. It's the indispensable basis.... There are many difficulties with Russia, and I heard a lot about how impossible it will be for us to get along with her—mostly from our military men over there. But I think we can do it. I think these things will straighten themselves out." On another topic, the charges of graft and incompetence leveled at the Army Engineers by quiet Roberston of Wyoming for their activities along the Alcan Highway and the Pan-American Highway, he said the Mead Committee is making a preliminary investigation. He showed his customary undaunted willingness to go after the services again, in the old, old battle the committee has had to fight for so long.

JUNE 18, 1945. Coming down the aisle of the House flanked by a joint Senate-House committee and welcomed by a roaring Congress, General Dwight D. Eisenhower, Supreme Commander of the Allied forces in Europe, looked nervous and embarrassed and rather like the high school valedictorian just prior to his speech today. Everyone but the President was on hand to greet him (tactfully he stayed away, this being Eisenhower's day): the Congress, the Cabinet (four of its Roosevelt-appointed members appearing for the last time), Marshall, King, Leahy, and the rest. He gave his amiable, friendly grin, put on his glasses, gripped the lectern firmly and began to speak in the voice of Kansas, flat, honest, forthright. His words were conventional and stereotyped, an inevitable consequence of the situation and his position; he delivered them rapidly. Something about the event bore a strong resemblance to the last joint session, when another honest and likable man spoke to the Congress and the country. With both, the fact that the words are conventional does not seem nearly so important as the fact that the words are sincere and earnest and full of common sense. "The American people don't need brilliance," said Carl Hatch once. It is brilliance they have in Truman and

Eisenhower, but it is the brilliance of the common denominator, candidly expressed.

Over across the Plaza the Court wound up its season with a flurry of decisions, entailing the hardworking activity of a good portion of the press. Associated Press, they ruled, is a monopoly; Harry Bridges, they ruled, is not a Communist and may remain in the country. (His lawyers, a tall girl in green and three or four husky young gentlemen, put through a call to him in the phone booths just off the press alcove. "He says he's breaking out the champagne," the girl reported, and everybody laughed, jubilant.) Having thus cleared the docket and called each other a few more names—the reasoning in the AP case, Roberts remarked acidly, was "nothing added to nothing," Stone, Roberts and Frankfurter were terse and sharp in their dissent on Bridges—the gentlemen of the Law bade one another farewell and scattered till October, Douglas to his beloved Oregon mountains, Bob Jackson to Europe for the war-criminal trials, the others to their various relaxing-places.

JUNE 19, 1945. Up from the White House today came a candid message on a subject a lot of people have been worrying back and forth in private —the succession to the Presidency. In the event of "my death or inability to act," he said, the Secretary of State would succeed under present law; the President, be he former Vice-President elevated by death, virtually has the right to name his own successor. In a democracy, this is a power the Chief Executive should not have. ("As a matter of fact," remarked one Democratic Senator later in the wave of annoyance that greeted the message, "the President always selects the Vice-President and we all know it.") Accordingly, he would suggest that Congress immediately enact legislation to provide that the succession go to the Speaker of the House and then to the President *pro tem* of the Senate, and thereafter to the Cabinet as under present law. He then departed by plane for the West Coast, emphasizing his remarks. In a couple of weeks both he and Stettinius will be gone overseas to Potsdam, emphasizing them further. The reaction on the Hill was interesting to watch.

Over in the House Joe Martin, heir-apparent to the Speakership if the Republicans gain control, was all for it. In the Senate, Styles Bridges promptly introduced a bill. During the reading of the message the House broke into applause. The Senate listened with a skeptical air. On the record comments were cautiously polite, off the record Democrats were acrid. In the first place, this was all the President's idea, he didn't consult with anybody before he sent it. In the second place, it was all so unnecessary. Presidents name their own Vice-Presidents, anyway—the country has managed nicely so far with the Secretary of State next in line after the V.P.—and besides the House might go Republican next year, and if that happened there could be a Republican President. The House was generally pleased, but not the Senate. Some very important Democrats were quite put out. "Why in hell did he have to go and stir this up?" one of them demanded. The succession message marked the first real trace of annoyance with Truman on the Democratic side of the aisle.

By the comfortable margin of 14 votes, 47–33, the Senate today put back in the reciprocal-trade bill the 50-per-cent tariff-reducing authority requested by the President. George had the votes once more, beyond even his most optimistic hopes. He seems to be in very good shape on the O'Mahoney amendment, too, which comes up tomorrow.

Once more Tobey furnished a laugh. Taft, arguing forcefully in a lost cause, maintained flatly that while there had been talk of lobbying, "I really think there's been less lobbying on this bill than on any other I can remember." "Will the Senator yield?" Tobey cried, jumping up and coming toward him eagerly. "Will the Senator yield right there?" "I can't yield," said Taft shortly. "My time is limited." "You're going to miss something good," Tobey assured him. "I prefer to miss it!" snapped Taft.

JUNE 20, 1945. After a powerful argument in which his angry voice thundered all through the hallways and echoed back and forth majestically in the chamber, Walter George marshaled his votes and swamped the O'Mahoney amendment today 49–27. The Wyoming Senator argued powerfully himself, but it wasn't good enough. Again George had the votes. O'Mahoney's argument, he declared, was "supremely fantastic." Down to defeat went able Joe's contention that the Congress was taking steps toward executive government in its surrender of the tariff-making power. ("If you say we have not time, and are incapable of doing it," he cried bitterly the other day, "then have the courage to vote the appropriations to see to it that we are adequately and efficiently staffed and can do it!") Whatever the merit of his argument, it was lost in George's show of overwhelming moral indignation. On quick roll calls thereafter the Senate beat down a series of minor amendments and late in the afternoon passed the bill 54–21.

Ball, Burton and Hatch today introduced a bill that will probably become one of the most controversial before the Senate—a comprehensive overhaul of the labor-relations laws to set up a five-man board to handle conciliation and mediation and a three-man board to handle complaints of unfair labor practices. It also makes arbitration compulsory in public-utility strikes and requires unions holding closed-shop contracts to maintain certain democratic methods. The three Senators told us that the bill represents 18 months of study by "labor relations experts" headed by

Donald Richberg, former head of the National Recovery Administration. His co-workers, drawn heavily from industry, prompted Wayne Morse to attack the bill as "industry-slanted." He praised it as a starting point for discussion, however, and that may ultimately be its principal value. As for Lister Hill, the missing member of the Ball–Burton–Hatch–Hill ("B²H²") idealists who stormed the citadel of isolation a year and a half ago with their peace resolution, he is playing it very close to the belt. "We've kept him fully informed of what we're doing," Hatch told us. "We're counting very heavily on his help as a member of the Education and Labor Committee. We're counting on him very heavily." Lister Hill, when we talked to him later, did not seem to be one too willing to bear the burden of this heavy dependence. "I didn't join in the sponsorship of it," he said, with a blank look and momentarily at a loss for further comment. Then his face brightened. "You can say that as a member of the Education and Labor Committee I will give it my every consideration. Yes, sir, old boy, my every consideration, that's what I'll do. As a member of the Education and Labor Committee, old man, I'll give it my every consideration, my every consideration."

Appropriations Committee, preparing a couple of good fights that will consume a little time between now and June 30, the end of the fiscal year, reported out the War Agencies bill with a boost for the Office of War Information that brings it pretty close to the budget estimate trimmed so drastically by the House. It also authorized Dennis Chavez to introduce an amendment from the floor giving the FEPC upwards of half a million. This last was somewhat in the nature of doubletalk, since under the rules his amendment will take a two-thirds vote even to bring it up, and the Southerners are already wheeling up their big guns and preparing for battle. Unless he gets his two-thirds or works out a compromise, the agency will be terminated.

Senate Appropriations
Committee

J&R Senators Joseph C. Mahoney, Carl Hayden,
Theodore F. Green, Elmer Thomas, Kenneth McKellar,
Styles Bridges, Clyde M. Reed, and Homer Ferguson

37

SO FAR AS I AM CONCERNED

June 22, 1945. The Presidential succession bill was taken up by the Privileges and Elections Committee today. Afterward Theodore Francis Green told the press that "certain constitutional questions" had come up. He did not enlighten us on what they were, nor did he indicate any great urge for speed on the part of the majority. The Truman suggestions, based as they are upon what he conceives to be best for the country, are apparently going to be sacrificed to what his colleagues conceive to be best for the party. This can hardly surprise him, the practical politician, so very much.*

June 23, 1945. Out in San Francisco, Vandenberg has thrown a certain amount of cold water on plans to hurry the Charter through. He doubts if hearings can begin for at least two weeks after the conference ends, he says, because Foreign Relations will want to wait until it has the full print of the deliberations before it. He predicts a good eight weeks of consideration, and inclines to the view that an opportunity for full discussion should be accorded every Senator. This last goes without saying in the nature of the Senate, but it is just as well to have it on the record. Meanwhile, first polls show a sizable majority for it, and Connally's confident prediction that it will be overwhelmingly ratified may be amply justified by events. Burt Wheeler, "loaded for bear," has not been heard from, however, and until he is predictions are idle. A master of in-fighting and delay, his strategy has yet to be divulged. The picture will shape up a little better after it is.

June 24, 1945. Bilbo and his cohorts are talking filibuster on the FEPC appropriation. "I'll fight it from now till Christmas," Mississippi's mighty mite assured us yesterday. "Will there be a filibuster, Senator?" we asked. "We don't have filibusters," he explained elaborately, "just extended ex-

* This judgment was unfair, for in 1947 Congress passed the act as he proposed it.

454

planations." "Will you engage in an extended explanation?" "Well"—with a cackle—"I'm full of my subject."

As a matter of fact, the Senate as usual is getting right up against the June 30 deadline on the appropriations bills, and the Southerners may be able to get what they want with a minimum expenditure of breath. War Agencies, which carries the Office of War Information fight in addition to the Fair Employment Practices Commission, is pending. The War Department appropriation hasn't even passed the House yet. The Labor–Federal Security appropriation is just out of committee. With five days to June 30, "extended explanations" could kill FEPC completely. The temporary agency, Bilbo said, "is just as bad as the permanent measure. It's just throwing away the people's money on a damnfool project."

James Scrugham of Nevada has died in San Diego after a long illness. A short man with a bald head and an impassive expression, he has only been in the Senate once since 1943. That occasion was the State Department fight. They helped him in and they helped him out, and when it came time to vote he got unanimous consent to remain seated. The balance will be unchanged politically; a Democrat will succeed.

JUNE 25, 1945. John McClellan, discussing the Charter thoughtfully, said optimistically this morning (as so many do) that it will "sail through without any trouble." He said it should be discussed and considered, but anticipates little opposition. On the FEPC appropriation he said he knows of "no organized effort" to oppose it. His eyes darkened, he looked off into space thoughtfully for a moment, and when he spoke it was with an air of uneasy restlessness. "I *wish* they'd leave us alone," he said.

Banking and Currency, heading into the home stretch on the Bretton Woods hearings, entertained one of its most industrious and familiar witnesses today, W. Randolph Burgess, president of the American Bankers Association. A tall man with an open, ingenuous face, an honest expression, and an eager, placating smile, he does a very smooth job of testifying in a hesitant, earnest, thoughtful way. This does not impress the committee, which knows him of old. Some members, in fact, regard him as though they were regarding a very capable puff-adder, responding only grudgingly to his diligent charm. Murdock in particular looks severe, and other Democrats are almost as cool. Taft, bitterly opposed to Bretton Woods and always cordial to the ABA, seemed nonplused this morning to find Burgess reversing his position before the House committee to endorse the international monetary fund. Over there he opposed it, but, he admitted candidly today, "It is no longer a question of 'yes' or 'no.' These hearings and the trend of public opinion indicate that people are in favor of international monetary cooperation. It is a matter

of amendment now, to make the fund work more efficiently." He remarked gently that there did seem to be "an almost pathological urge"
toward world cooperation (something on which Sheridan Downey challenged him sharply. He laughed amiably, qualified somewhat, admitted
the word might have been ill-chosen, but conveyed the impression that
he still thought it was the right one). People, he said, seemed to be "sold
on hopeful preambles." However, he would not stand in the way. "You
no longer recommend elimination of the fund?" Barkley asked. He
laughed. "We wouldn't like to make up your minds for you—" he began.
"I want you to make up your minds for yourselves," Alben assured him.
He laughed again. Taft jumped in. "What you mean," he told Burgess
bluntly, "is that you think the operation of the fund should be postponed,
but you're bowing to the pressure of the inevitable." Burgess laughed
again. "Well, not exactly," he said. "We think the fund should be safe-
guarded." He laughed again, very amiably. Murdock looked stern.

JUNE 26, 1945. After 26 years of popular worry over "what the Senate
will do" to another world-cooperation treaty, the whole thing fizzled out
today as Burton K. Wheeler told me:
"So far as I am concerned, there is going to be no organized fight
against the treaty."
This was bulletin-matter. SEN. WHEELER GIVES GREEN LIGHT TO TREATY,
said the Washington *Daily News*, and so, in effect, he did. He did it without much fanfare, to the accompaniment of a black, bleak, off-the-record
picture of what is going on in Europe. He did it reserving his right to
speak against it if he chose, and with some acid comments on the Administration's strategy. But he did it. That was the news.
Rounding out the picture later, Hatch said:
"As a matter of fact, Senator Wheeler told me today that he might vote
for ratification. Senator Wheeler is a man of absolute integrity. When he
says that he may vote for ratification, I take it for full face value because
Burt Wheeler does not make idle statements to his colleagues."
"I'm tremendously gratified," said Lister Hill. Joe Ball's face broke into
a sudden smile. "His statement is an indication of the overwhelming public support for our joining the organization," he said accurately. "It is in
line with my expectations," said Harold Burton. "I don't know how I'll
vote yet," said Bill Langer, chewing his customary soggy, gooey, cello-
phane-covered cigar. "I want to read the damned thing first. I want to
find out something about it." Henrik Shipstead was out of town, Hiram
Johnson is in Bethesda Naval Hospital. "I would like very much to see
the San Francisco Charter agreed to unanimously," Hatch remarked. It
won't be quite that, but it is going to come pretty close.

Suddenly all the clouds are lifting for the New World blueprint. So easily are they rolling away that one can only wonder what might not have been accomplished in the way of really constructive and courageous achievement at San Francisco, had there been the will and the vision to attain it. If all the men who have been bound for so long to the terrifying legend of "what the Senate will do" had only been a little braver, what might they not have done?

JUNE 27, 1945. Connally and Vandenburg reappeared on the floor today, interrupting Langer in midvoice. It was the first time anyone had ever seen the vociferous North Dakotan silenced. He stopped what he was saying gracefully, however, and joined in the general applause that broke out as Senators crowded down toward the well of the chamber to shake hands with the tall Texan and his natty, smiling colleague. Both looked supremely pleased. Both intend to speak before the week is up, and Connally says Foreign Relations will meet Saturday to decide upon a schedule for hearings. Speed is the word.

Unlimited debate, the Senate's great weapon with which it has so often in these war years blocked or modified unwise and dangerous legislation sent over from the House, showed its reverse side today as Theodore Bilbo began his filibuster against FEPC. He did so in the midst of much hurrying and scurrying as Barkley and Biffle attempted to work out a compromise. He refused to yield to Chavez on several occasions, finally permitting him to ask a few acid questions. These Bilbo parried with the sort of crude, cruel humor so characteristic of him. He then launched into an attack on "niggers and Jews," giving to both words an ugly, vicious intonation that made of his hatred an almost palpable entity. Elsewhere on the floor other Southerners waited patiently for their squad leader to falter. He did not do so, however. The session ended late with Bilbo still going strong. With elaborate exaggeration he denied several times that this was a filibuster. This was meant for humor. A few snickered.

JUNE 28, 1945. There came today an immediate, though temporary, end to the easy harmony which had heretofore prevailed on the Charter. John Overton got Connally's OK on a resolution that would have done away with all hearings on the document. Overton meant well and so, presumably, did Tom. The Senate, however, blew up. In the 20 minutes of irascible debate that followed, more bad feeling was set afloat in the Senate than it has known in months.

Wallace White, white-faced and trembling, condemned the proposal violently. Barkley, confronted once more by one of his ever-recurring problems, attempted to pour oil on the waters. Bob La Follette, saying he would support the Charter, condemned the speed-up proposition. Walter George thundered that everyone should have an opportunity to be heard. Curley Brooks, violently indignant, threatened to filibuster the Charter if such tactics were adopted. Everybody got upset. Overton, arguing angrily that Connally had encouraged him to do it, was argued down. The resolution was referred to Foreign Relations with the strong indication that it had better be pigeonholed. But the damage had been done and a totally unnecessary wave of ill-feeling had been aroused. Connally was absent during all this.

The Senate ran on and on as Bilbo's filibuster began to develop in earnest. Tempers were frayed on a number of counts. Wherry and Chan Gurney attempted to modify the OPA conference report, which dropped a pet Wherry amendment, but they got swamped. The report passed and went to the House. A few other matters were disposed of. Bilbo talked on, to 6 and beyond. The session lengthened. Barkley offered a compromise to cut the FEPC appropriation in half; Chavez was agreeable but Bilbo turned it down. Wallace White and Taft went around getting signatures on a cloture petition; Barkley refused to yield to permit them to introduce it. Instead he moved to recess until tomorrow. Taft demanded the Yeas and Nays. At 10:10 P.M. the Senate voted 28–19 to stay in session. Endless quorum calls were held, the last, near midnight, precipitated by Walter George, who suddenly got very annoyed with Barkley, made the point of no quorum and then stalked off the floor. Wall Doxey, ex-Senator from Mississippi and Sergeant-at-Arms, went about cautiously hauling Republicans up from downtown, well aware of what happened to his predecessor when he made the mistake of arresting Democrats to compel attendance and found Kenneth McKellar in the lot. That was the end of *him*. Doxey was taking no chances. Thin, ascetic, professorial Alexander Smith of New Jersey wandered in. Brewster and Wherry rushed up to greet him, hands outstretched, and escorted him elaborately down the aisle to record his name. Barkley and several others crossed the aisle to congratulate him, amid appropriate horseplay. Homer Capehart came in; later Alec Wiley, chortling, snorting, bouncing, poking, slapping, giggling hysterically at his own jokes; O'Mahoney arrived, after midnight. A quorum was found to be present, Taft introduced the cloture petition, which must lie over a day before it can come to a vote; the Senate recessed. The great light that hangs in the Capitol dome during night sessions, like a bright star above the town, went out.

JUNE 29, 1945. Vandenberg made a powerful and excellent speech on the Charter today, receiving for it the same accolade of applause and approval which yesterday greeted Connally's similar effort. The able Michigander's address, filled with rhetoric and his love for empurpled passages, nonetheless answered a number of specific objections to the Charter and answered them very well. Both he and Connally were careful to say that none of the document's authors considers it perfect; but as a half a loaf—or possibly a quarter, or maybe even an eighth—they consider it better than nothing. So it obviously is, however tragically short it may fall of the terrible sacrifices of the 40,000,000 who died to give it birth— or of those others who must die if it should fail.

Eastland carried on the filibuster today, saying things about the racial situation that sounded frightening in the United States Senate. They had to be heard to be believed. Fortunately not many heard them.

Francis Biddle and Frances Perkins came on the floor today to say good-by to their friends. Francis didn't look too happy, but Frances seemed quite relieved.

38

SENTIMENTAL JOURNEY

June 29–July 16, 1945. Traveling west to California for vacation, we swept along the Potomac and into lush Pennsylvania. Somewhere along the way a deer came down to the water's edge to drink; the pastoral scene flashed into the window and was gone. Here and there a house lay back among the trees. The evening came on apace. Already Washington was slipping away, beginning to seem remote. The inevitable process of revaluation, the restoration of the fabulous city to its proper place in the whole, was under way. The world, discovered anew, was not ending at the District Line.

Next morning we passed the great steel mills at Gary, glimpsed the lake, plunged on to Chicago fronting majestically on the water. Rich farms followed, rich land, rich harvest. Delegates to San Francisco, so they say, watched the spectacle in awe. Americans do too. Washington sank to a dateline in the papers.

Onto the high plateau and the vast grazing-lands, we came near noon to pleasant Cheyenne, capital of the pyrotechnic O'Mahoney, the shrewd and able Robertson. But the end of the land was not yet. Jimmy Byrnes for State, the papers said. It stirred mild interest on the train: people approved. Washington momentarily loomed larger, then sank away again.

In the evening at Salt Lake City the man Franklin Roosevelt ran against in four elections left the train from the car behind us. He was wearing his characteristic high collar, a hat too small on his round chubby head. A little crowd gathered, curious, appraising, silent, still at this late date half-inimical. There was no applause, no demonstration; there was nothing. His skin was puffy and yellowing with age, he looked old and tired and not too happy. A photographer came and he posed patiently for three or four pictures; his sons appeared and he greeted them with a kiss on the cheek, relaxing and smiling for a moment. A local reporter not long out of college haunted his elbow with nervous questions and he answered them patiently. His whole manner seemed to say: "Why do you bother me? What have I left to give you? What do you want of me?" "*Booooaard!*" called the porters along the train; the little crowd dwindled away. Dusk was closing in on Deseret. Almost unnoticed, almost alone, Herbert Hoover, 31st President of the United States, trudged with an old man's heavy slowness down the empty platform as the train pulled out.

The train shot along the plains by the Great Salt Lake and the purple afterglow lay on the vast shimmering mountains rising from them sharply, as the businessman and I settled the affairs of the world.

"I'm just telling you what I find in my travels," he said. "I travel a lot and I talk to lots of businessmen. What we want is America for the Americans, know what I mean? I find a lot of people want that. They don't want all this nonsense."

Somewhat surprised, for I had supposed that the reaction to "all this nonsense" had abated somewhat in the wait-and-see political honeymoon, I suggested that Truman probably intended to do something about it as soon as he could get around to it. The businessman looked unconvinced.

"Well, maybe," he said doubtfully, "I certainly hope so. Because a lot of us feel that way, but we don't know where to take hold, we don't know where to begin. We're waiting for leadership, something that will give us America for the Americans."

"I'd say the best thing to do is get organized for 1948 and get behind the man who best represents what you want," I said. He snorted.

"1948's too far away!" he said. "We want something done about it sooner than 1948."

"Then I would suggest that you organize for the Congressional elections next year and try to change the House."

"Well, maybe, yes," he agreed. "Yes, that might be it. That might be the way to do it."

But I had the impression that he didn't really think so.

Through the great Mojave, the endless desert ending, the names becoming familiar with a quickening excitement, Barstow, Riverside, San Berdoo, the level productive fields beginning to stretch away on every side, the groves appearing. Into Union Station two hours later, into Los Angeles, brawling, sprawling, vulgar, vigorous, alive, into wonderful, pleasant, wonderfully balmly Southern California, into the atmosphere like nothing else on earth.

Then the bus station and the bus, and up over the Ridge and down again, and still the familiar names, always the familiar names, San Fernando, Junction, Castaic, Lebec, Summit; and then Grapevine and the jumping-off place and stretching out ahead 200 miles and more, flat and shimmering in the 105-degree heat, the great brown San Joaquin, the ever-same, the ever-changing, and the towns of pleasant memory, Bakersfield, Corcoran, Hanford, Tulare, Lindsay, Strathmore, and so to Porterville and home and the family waiting.

The ex-Senator brought the Charter to the Senate, his ex-colleagues applauded. In mind's eye the scene stood out, then Washington faded again. In the Sierra pines, on the green lawn beside the swimming pool, along the rushing river, for five days it seemed far away.

"This is our Munich," said some. "Unless we stand up to Russia now we're going under. . . ."

"We'd better pull out of there and pull out fast," said the close friend, a veteran of the Elbe, home on his way to the Pacific. "We're in something we don't know anything about and the sooner we get out the better." What of the rest, when a veteran of his intelligence feels thus?

Riding down to Los Angeles again in the starbright California night, we heard the voice of Harlan Bushfield coming drily over the radio. He was convinced, he said, that the Charter was unconstitutional, but he intended to support it nonetheless. The public is for it. And truly it is, for everywhere is the easy, unthinking acceptance, the fatal American belief that all you need is a gadget and your worries are over. Nobody knows quite what we are getting into, nobody realizes quite what a revolutionary step it is. But the public is for it, and probably rightly. Congress, faithfully reflecting, is for it too. For a moment Washington came alive again, and with it a historic doubt. If it is thus easy for public pressure to get international cooperation from the Senate, was public opinion so truly for the League in 1920? Was Henry Cabot Lodge quite such an unrelieved villain? Or were Woodrow Wilson's partisans excusing his own ineptitude? It seems a fair question when the thing is done so easily now.

Wonderful Southern California—wonderful, wonderful. JESUS SAVES . . . and the great lazy beach at Santa Monica in the sun . . . and the opulence of Wilshire Boulevard, Miracle Mile and Sunset Strip . . . and the lush night clubs and the theaters and Hollywood... and the beautiful homes in the beautiful hills ... and the bright cars on the bright highways running through the bright land ... and the easy doing, the easy living, the easy laughter, the easy life of the suntanned golden children of the Golden State.... "The weather is so monotonous," my eastern friends tell me. Monotony, I'm your man.

And again the primeval wastes of desert, the fascinating, suffocating expanses. Up through New Mexico, the green hills of lower Colorado, flat Kansas. Again the rich farms, the rich lands, the rich harvest. Again Chicago, again Gary, again the Potomac and lush Pennsylvania. Again America, so vast, so magnificent, so strong, holding so much of hope and promise still.

"Washington!" the porter said. Vinson to Treasury, FEPC approved, the Charter out of Foreign Relations 21–1, the Bretton Woods debate about to begin.

39

"BOB CAN HAVE THE BRAINS"

JULY 17, 1945. Tobey took the floor today to respond to Taft's attack on Bretton Woods yesterday, and Murdock and Barkley helped him out. The day was still the vigorous Ohioan's. Arguing passionately and sincerely and with a fair amount of sound argument on his side, he attacked the bank and the fund in a losing battle. Reciprocal trade, Bretton Woods, the Charter—for better or for worse, the trend is all the other way. "You know," remarked one reporter during the debate today, "a bill like this wouldn't have a prayer under normal conditions." It is with this abnormal impetus that we rush forward into arrangements into which normal conditions must ultimately be fitted. The attitude in the Senate—and once again it is faithfully reflecting the country—is a shrug and a quizzical smile and the wry admission: after all, we've tried everything else. Might as well try this. Nothing to lose. Disillusion is an erratic tide—one generation it sweeps out of world affairs and the next it sweeps in. Thus the strange Americans, a very decent people, who do almost everything with their hearts and almost nothing with their heads. May God protect them, for they mean so well.

In Mead Committee this morning members found themselves up against their oldest and most incorrigible opponent, the Army. The item at issue was a 900-mile section of the Pan-American Highway, supposed to cost $14,714,000 but costing $42,715,000, supposed to be completed in one year but not completed in two, supposed to be contingent upon its not interfering with the war effort but continued long after it was declared so—a typical situation. Somewhere in the background, concerned in the strange delays, the off-the-cuff decisions, the blunders that led to so much waste and confusion, was a familiar figure—Brehon B. Somervell. Strange it is, but sooner or later most of the committee's investigation lead back to this dynamic, forceful figure. It is difficult to imagine why this should be so, but definitely it is.

JULY 18, 1945. Taft, showing a comprehensive grasp of Bretton Woods unmatched anywhere else in the Senate, continued to make his record today against the agreement, going into his third day of argument. His main points he repeated, but he buttressed them with a continuing flow of new facts and figures which he produced out of his head and made use of where they would do the most good. It was a brilliant *tour de force* in economics by a brilliant man whose ability is thoroughly respected even by those of his colleagues who disagree with him most. Despite the fact that he and Assistant Secretary of the Treasury Harry Dexter White told each other acridly during the hearings that neither was competent to understand what Bretton Woods is all about, it seems very likely that they are the two men in the country with the soundest knowledge of its details. Everyone else is being swept along on the tide. The country has only the foggiest notion of what it is all about, and the same applies to the Senate. Barkley attempted to argue with Ohio's voluble son, and Abe Murdock tilted with him a few times. Bob Wagner, ostensibly in charge of the bill, gave up after being demolished decisively a few times. One of the reporters met Wagner in the hall today. "Well, Senator," he said, "I'll bet you'll be glad when Bretton Woods is out of the way." "Oh, *God*," said the chairman of Banking and Currency.

Taft, however, doesn't have the votes, something he has known from the beginning. He is simply making the record, pointing out all the pitfalls and the weaknesses and the possibilities for failure in the Bretton Woods agreement. If it succeeds, then he will still have made a sound, if pessimistic, contribution. If it fails, he will be a prophet confirmed. On several tests today he got beaten thoroughly, once on a motion to postpone the bill until November, again on a motion to recommit. Joe Ball surprisingly came to his support on the motion to postpone. Taft, he said, had proved conclusively that the United States, by rushing into everything so fast, is losing all her bargaining power abroad. "Let's let someone else get committed to something," urged the earnest idealist whose wildest hopes for U.S. cooperation have come rather embarrassingly true. It was to no avail. The Congress and the country are in one of those psychological states when neither is capable of changing direction in the slightest degree. We may not know exactly where we're going, but we're certainly hell-bent on the way. The mood has swung completely to cooperation and, typically, the mood allows for no hesitations. This curious psychosis extended even to amendments, several of which were proposed. Some were rather reasonable, but the Senate like an automaton refused even to consider them. "This amendment would kill the bill," Barkley would assert about some innocuous provision. "Oh, the Senator knows this would kill the bill," Wagner would echo.

This produced one rather curious result. Bill Langer offered an amendment to prohibit any member nation from using funds from the international organization to purchase armaments and matériel of war. "All in favor of the amendment," said McKellar. "Aye," said a few scattered voices. "All opposed." "*NO!*" roared the Senate.

JULY 19, 1945. "I'll bet Senator Taft knows more about Bretton Woods than any other two men on the floor," one of my colleagues said to Barkley today. The Majority Leader, who is really very fond of Taft, gave one of the progressive chuckles that start at the top of his head and shake down gradually and engagingly to his feet until his whole body is involved. "Bob can have the brains," he said. "I've got the votes."

This he proved late in the afternoon when the final vote came. 61–19 the Senate followed the House into the Bretton Woods agreement. Shortly before the end Barkley, Ball, the vociferous and idealistic Tobey and several others paid tribute to Taft's bitter-end fight. But Barkley had the votes, and that was that.

Thereafter the session dragged on until after 9 o'clock as Walter George tried to get through the corporation tax-relief bill. Bob La Follette, stocky and earnest and determined as always, stood squarely in the way as he has so often before in financial matters the powerful Georgian has wanted to expedite. And, as so often before, Bob La Follette won. He is the only man in the Senate who can beat Walter George, and he nearly always does it because he argues with an intensity and a sincerity that give him a terrific moral force. Here is a really honest man, one thinks, and opposition fades before his reasonable insistence. George wanted the bill to go through with an amendment which would give unusually generous tax relief to several merging railroads. The bill went through, all right, but when Bob La Follette got through with it the amendment was out. There are some fine and brilliant men in the Senate, but Bob La Follette comes as near as any to being the ideal public servant—a man who works tirelessly and consistently and honestly, through many defeats, toward the goal of a better society for his fellow men. They say on the Hill that he is "going to be in trouble" when he runs for re-election next year. If Wisconsin, the state which has just sent Alec Wiley whooping and hollering back into office, turns out Bob La Follette, it will deserve to be sent to the bottom of the class, there to remain. A state doesn't get such representation very often. If it is wise, it hangs onto it. [*But it did not, and Joseph R. McCarthy came to Washington. Six years later Bob La Follette lay dead by his own hand. Nobody ever knew why for sure, but the concensus among those who*

*knew him on the Hill was that he had finally broken under the crushing
feeling that he had let his family and his father down by losing to such a
successor the seat they had held between them for 40 years.*]

JULY 20, 1945. By unanimous voice vote the Senate today approved a bill
to increase the capital stock of the Export-Import Bank to $1,000,000,000
and increase its lending power to $3,500,000,000. Taft joined the pro-
ponents, making one of his I'm-going-to-vote-for-this-but-I-want-you-to-
know-what-you're-doing speeches in the process. What the Senate was
doing, in effect, he said, was approve a supplement to Lend-Lease and
a weapon to be used in bargaining with Europe. Tobey, who used to be
an isolationist but has sincerely found the true faith now, quoted Max-
well Anderson and implied that Taft was quibbling too much. However, they were on the same side today. Without trouble the bill sailed
through.

With that out of the way, the calendar was called. That completed,
Barkley moved to call up the resolution authorizing United States membership in the United Nations Food and Agriculture Organization. Chapman Revercomb objected and argued for two hours with Warren Austin
while the Democrats sat back and enjoyed it. Finally unanimous agreement was secured to vote on the bill not later than 2 P.M. tomorrow.
Again Barkley has the votes—the motion to take it up was passed by
a wide margin.

Late in the afternoon Wayne Morse (referred to in the press gallery
as "the Five O'Clock Shadow" because of his habit of choosing that in-
convenient hour to make speeches against the OPA) once more damned
Chester Bowles up and down for his handling of the Oregon lamb situation. This sort of thing has been going on for a week—a daily speech
from the Senator, always neatly timed so that it will annoy Barkley
as much as possible. Today this strategy seemed to have produced results,
for Guy Gordon said he had been informed by the Secretary of Agriculture that he was recommending a suspension of ration points on Oregon
lamb. "I shall continue to speak until the Democrats across the aisle
exercise the responsibility of a majority and see that something is done,"
Morse said crisply the other day. His campaign has been annoying but
it has been effective. He makes a lot of enemies, but he gets results.

Midway in the day the chamber stirred with excitement. In the diplomatic gallery a committee composed of McKellar, George and Fulbright
escorted in one of the great romantic symbols of the between-wars era
—a slight little man with a pink face, puffy eyes and blond hair, who
once upon a time was King of England and before that Prince of Wales.

He looked very trim and slight and youthful in his neat blue suit, trotting down the steps and later trotting up. One uniformed aide was all that remained of the pomp and circumstance of yesterday. He showed a lively interest, but inasmuch as he stayed about as long as the average tourist he probably got about the same grasp of what was going on. The Senate paid no attention but went on arguing the Export-Import Bank.

JULY 21, 1945. Early in the session today the Senate boiled over with the transportation problem. The Army, as usual trying to shift the blame for its own inefficiency onto the backs of the civilian population and profit therefrom as much as possible with the servicemen, has been doing its best to make everyone believe that the lack of sufficient Pullmans for redeployment of troops is not its fault. This little game, which has gone on so often on so many things, was shown up yesterday for what it is by the Mead Committee. In a sharply worded statement by Jim Mead the responsibility for the lack of coordination was placed right back where it belongs, in the Pentagon. Today Scott Lucas arose in horrified concern to protest this criticism. The committee was criticizing the Army, cried Illinois' statesman, because it hadn't set its schedules right, because it was bringing back too many men on a certain day, because it didn't follow a reasonable system and permit the Office of Defense Transportation and the railroads to know about it in advance. Why, he wished the Army could bring back a million men right away! He wanted as many to get back right away as the Army could bring! He welcomed them back! This argument, which ignored the very justifiable bases for the committee's complaint, brought both Mead and Ferguson to their feet with an angry roar. Why didn't they work out a program, Ferguson demanded, why didn't they coordinate their redeployment? Why didn't they let ODT know what the score was so that it could have the Pullmans available, instead of bungling the job and then trying to blame somebody else? Both the excellent Michigander and the chairman of the committee shouted in righteous anger at Lucas' unwarranted attack. Lucas, never · to be outdone in such exchanges, shouted right back. It was a bitter debate, made more so by the committee's prompt assumption that the Army had planted the protest with Lucas. However that may have been, it filled them with an added determination to work the Army over when the committee starts its investigation Monday.

Later the Senate added one more chapter to the history of how America went into world cooperation like a house afire by passing the resolution authorizing participation in the United Nations Food and Agriculture Organization. This concomitant of Bretton Woods passed easily over the protests of Chapman Revercomb and a handful of farm-staters, arguing darkly against an institution which will do little more than study, correlate and distribute vital information on the world agricultural picture.

Everything is now clear for the Charter debate, which is not expected to run much more than one week.

40

THE GREAT DEBATE

JULY 23, 1945. This was the Great Debate. It began in an atmosphere of anticlimax, in the shadow of a certainty, and with a lackadaisical disinterest rather embarrassing in view of all the tourists who turned out, apparently expecting to witness some great forensic tussle. All they saw was a dispirited parade of orators, some good, some not so good, relating their plans to vote for ratification. Once they even saw the Charter laid aside while Kilgore, Ed Johnson and Pepper spoke at some length on a bill they were introducing to establish a national research foundation. Three times they saw the Senate forced into quorum calls because of lack of attendance and a lack of speakers that had to be filled in somehow, and so was filled in with the standard time-killer, a quorum call. It was not much of a show after 25 years of worried anticipation. Everybody wants cooperation these days. Hell, yes. Who's going to be so stupid as to vote against that?

It was this "docility," indeed, which prompted Bill Fulbright to express some concern when he got up to speak. Everything was too easy, the able Arkansan implied. "I wish there had been a little more opposition.... Perhaps the Charter has been oversold, both to the Senate and the public...." But that's the way it is, and Bill Fulbright, the only voice raised today in constructive criticism ("Only totalitarian or Fascist states are 'sovereign'... the Charter attempts to revive and revitalize an outmoded concept...") knew like everyone else that nothing can stop the early, the easy, the offhand, casual, afterthought vote.

Tom Connally began the parade, echoing the speech he made several weeks ago. Now and then he waxed dramatic; the arms shot out, the gestures gestured, the dry sarcastic voice belabored opposition—only there was no opposition. Vandenberg, thundering and indignant, found criticism, an anonymous editorial, and against it he fulminated violently till his face grew red and his hair fell down over his eye—but there was no opposition. Dennis Chavez spoke, Pappy O'Daniel read a statement he had issued three weeks ago endorsing the Charter. There was no opposition. By 2 P.M. attendance had dwindled until there were 10 Senators on the floor. Pappy concluded, an embarrassing silence fell. Nobody was ready to speak. Kilgore asked for a quorum, the chamber slowly filled again, he and Johnson and Pepper had their say. Tom Connally pleaded with Senators to be ready to speak and to make it as brief as possible; Joe Guffey complied sardonically in less than one minute, announcing his support. Elbert Thomas spoke, idealistic, philosophic, historical and earnest. Sixteen Senators were on the floor. Another quorum call. Fulbright spoke, ably and well. Alexander Wiley spoke. There was no opposition. After the session Barkley thought a vote might be reached Wednesday, perhaps no later than Thursday. Burt Wheeler plans to speak—that may be opposition. But the juggernaut is rolling, rolling, and a very boring debate, reported in exhaustive detail by the press, is moving inexorably toward its predetermined conclusion.

JULY 24, 1945. The debate picked up today, thanks largely to Wheeler, who furnished the opportunity for conflict. The opportunity was seized by Carl Hatch and Scott Lucas. Wheeler, arguing with the passionately bitter honesty that has characterized him on this issue since the war began, said he would "reluctantly—very reluctantly" vote for the Charter. "What I am doing by supporting this measure," he said, "is to give the framers of this document an opportunity to prove their good faith and their good intentions. But I want to serve notice, here and now, that when the peace treaties are made, when any question of further appeasement arises, and when any threat to the continued democratic representation of the people of America comes before this Senate body I shall be in the vanguard of those citizens and those members of this body who will feel it to be their duty exhaustively to scrutinize, analyze, and prove the wisdom of the creators of this Charter, to the end that the sovereignty of this people's government and its Constitution may be preserved."

Before he reached that peroration, however, he spent nearly three hours, in a speech heavy with the world's unhappiness, painting with acrid honesty the picture of things as they are. It is not a pretty picture, but it exists. There are some—indeed, there are many—both in the Senate and in the country, who do their best to gloss it over. They are those who have faith, who have hope, who believe that just possibly, by some strange, remote, fantastic miracle, this thing will work and the world will be saved. Knowing themselves to be on the defensive, however, their tempers are apt to be short, their nerves touchy. They do not like a too-steady dose of the truth, which is what Wheeler gave them for three hours. It is not surprising, perhaps, that Claude Pepper should have charged him with changing his vote because he wants to be re-elected next year, that Alben Barkley should have shouted that he would "take him on anytime" on the powers of the American delegate, that Carl Hatch should have demanded indignantly, "Let's fight it out now!" that Scott Lucas should have announced bitterly that he will speak tomorrow on the issues raised. Burt Wheeler is constitutionally incapable of wearing rose-colored glasses. It is no wonder if those who do resent it when he knocks them off.

Above the tumult and the shouting the State Department, represented by the tall, mustachioed Dean Acheson and four or five of his cohorts, sat in a nervous little huddle in the first row of the gallery across the way, plotting high strategy and from time to time sending out runners to the men in the field. Of these the most cooperative was Scott Lucas. He received the nod when it came time to challenge Wheeler's assumption that all agreements reached under the Charter will be brought back to the Senate to be ratified as treaties. The State Department, as usual, wants them to be executive agreements ratified by joint resolution. The injection of this idea provoked Wheeler to increased bitterness, and prompted both Connally and Vandenberg to make it very clear that the intent of the American delegation was that the agreements should be approved by Congress—they didn't care much whether by the Senate alone or with the House, but *by Congress,* and with no possibility that the President alone could initiate action entirely on his own responsibility.

Earlier Barkley made a standard speech in support, Lister Hill did the same, Homer Ferguson, Ed Johnson, Ernest McFarland, the same. Out of the day's debate there emerged the figure of Montana's angry man, looking out upon a world black, black, black, unable by reason of his own rigid and unsparing honesty to see it any other way, pacing back and forth along the desks, wheeling like some cornered tiger at the pin-prick barbs of Claude Pepper attacking his motives, and the rest. Whatever one thinks of Wheeler's conclusions, it is impossible not to respect his integrity and his character. And it is also impossible to believe that his opponents, with their idealistic purposes but their empty phrases and their empty platitudes about the certainties of a just and stable peace, are debating on the same plane at all. It is as though Wheeler went beyond and through their pretenses and had his eyes on a darker reality far deeper than they perceive. This is not the case, for they perceive it too. It is just that they will not admit it, needing so desperately to hope, while he, who has virtually abandoned hope, admits it with the frightening coldness of despair.

JULY 25, 1945. John Foster Dulles, a man whose importance to the world organization is perhaps not quite so great as the Senate has assumed for two days, dominated debate until nearly 3 o'clock this afternoon. Mr. Dulles, present not in flesh but in spirit, testified during the committee hearings that he assumed the military agreement for the use of troops under the Charter would be submitted for ratification as a treaty. His testimony was quoted at great length, and repeatedly, by Wheeler and others, Wheeler having promised yesterday that "a real fight" will come when the military phases come up for action. Opponents of the Dulles interpretation argued back. It was, after all, only the opinion of one man, and of little material weight in the final balance. Yet supporters clung to it like a rock in the sea and opponents belabored it like the world's best whipping boy. Finally Vandenberg, remarking drily that he had taken the unusual course of asking Mr. Dulles by telephone just what he did mean, announced that Mr. Dulles meant that he merely assumed that it would be a treaty because the Charter said it should be ratified by member states according to their "constitutional practices." This precipitated another long argument over what "ratification" meant and what "constitutional practices" meant. In between and around this Scott Lucas made his speech, provoking Tom Connally to the statement that the argument on interpretation was like "going after the fox and then jumping a rabbit or two," which in turn provoked Lucas to the indignant statement that Tom wasn't going to cut off debate so he might as well not try. Connally denied that he was trying to cut off debate. He was always, he said, "entertained and amused" by the remarks of the Senator from Illinois. Lucas accepted that one acidly, and Tom remarked with hurt good nature that he just couldn't understand the Senator, he was always taking offense. He tried to pay him a compliment, Tom said, but it was always misunderstood. Lucas looked skeptical and concluded.

Millikin spoke briefly, Taft elucidated a few points, Smith of New Jersey, confessing frankly, "I am by nature conservative," told in rather embarrassing detail how he had found the internationalist faith. Albert Hawkes announced his support, and Tommy Hart of Connecticut did likewise, combining it with a surprising attack on the British, on America's inept use of bargaining power, and on the dangers of promising too much help to the world in the reconstruction period. Connecticut's Admiral-Senator, appointed to succeed Maloney, is a slight, quiet, inconspicuous man who during his professional days in the Navy commanded the Asiatic Fleet in the opening months of the Japanese war. He speaks with a slow, dispassionate, careful delivery, shot through occasionally with a gleam of wry and acid humor. His opinions on the

British, perhaps harking back to his days aboard ship, are not compli-
mentary.

The galleries continued full today, the State Department was in its
accustomed place. Over to our left in the Family Gallery Ed Stettinius,
startlingly tanned and startlingly white-haired, maintained his faithful
daily attendance.

JULY 26, 1945. "What are you going to do about Oregon lambs, Senator?"
somebody asked Barkley after the session today. "I'm going to take one
Oregon lamb out and roast him," replied the Majority Leader with a
rather grim chuckle.

Wayne Morse, continuing his violent campaign against the OPA regulation on marketing lambs from his state is battling against the odds
while his elders, increasingly annoyed, cast about desperately for ways
to silence him and evade the issue he poses. His attack is direct—he not
only flays the OPA but the Democratic majority as well—and this hurts.
Today Tom Connally tried to prevent Morse from having his say by
moving that no one be allowed to speak on any subject other than the
Charter for more than five minutes. Morse objected to this. Connally
promptly moved that the Senate recess. On a standing vote the Senate
refused to support the motion. It furnished a lively few moments in an
otherwise dull debate which simply added more names to the lengthening list of people who will vote for the Charter. By the end of the session
today, upwards of 26 members had expressed their approval. Warren
Austin spoke at length on the legal aspects, Claude Pepper warned darkly
of later attacks upon the organization and Jim Tunnell cried "Treason!"
against various unnamed people who are flooding his office with anti-
Charter propaganda. Once again, the sum total of debate added up to a
pious hope and a determined whistling past the graveyard of the world's
lost chances.

A little over a month ago Barkley brought onto the floor a little, clerkish man with a long, narrow, bald head, a clipped little black mustache,
a manner most polite and 'umble. As Senators passed his desk, Barkley
introduced the visitor to them. Finally he asked the Senate to suspend
for five minutes so that all members might meet the deputy prime
minister of Great Britain, the Right Honorable Clement R. Attlee. This
they did. Today the little clerkish man became Prime Minister in a smashing Labor sweep that sent the second of the original Triumvirate into
limbo after five terrible, triumphant years. Comment on the Hill took
three lines. Some emphasized that it would make no difference in our
relations with Britain—some saw it as "the era of the common man"

(whoever he is)—some feared the movement left. Uneasily those who calculate began to calculate. No one knows yet just what the portent means, but all are aware that portent it is.

JULY 27, 1945. For the first time something of the world's agony and its terrible tragedy were brought into the debate today as Walter George, overcome with emotion and the memory of his lost son, spoke for the Charter. It was not one of his best speeches, it didn't hang together very well, it wasn't very well-connected or rounded, but it came from the heart, and was profoundly moving. There were moments when he was unable to speak at all, when he stood fighting for control at his desk, one hand gripping it tightly, the other tracing nervous patterns over the surface. There were times when he would begin to speak and then have to stop, too choked to go on. There were times when, almost dazed, he repeated himself and wandered in his words. But from Walter George, more than from any other who has spoken to date, there came the reason why it is such a desperate need and such a desperate hope that something, anything, prevent another war. When he had finished Tobey proposed that the Senate rise in silent respect and sympathy. It did so solemnly. Saltonstall and Hart, both of whom have also lost sons, passed by George's desk to shake his hand.

It was, on the whole, a day of able speeches. Joe Ball, like Fulbright true to his original idealism, criticized the Charter severely for its weaknesses but accepted it with the hope that time and gradually growing prestige may give it the strength it needs. Henrik Shipstead urged the tightest possible control of the American delegate in a bitter speech reminiscent of Wheeler's, and never did indicate exactly whether or not he would vote for it. Later in the day we heard that Hiram Johnson, ill at Bethesda Naval Hospital, will probably be unable to attend for the vote. Forty members have now spoken and a decision is hoped for before recess tomorrow. Connally put in the resolution for ratification after an hour-long argument about the way Wayne Morse was treated yesterday. Morse, indignant, announced that "no method of disciplining freshman Senators" would make him stop talking about Oregon lambs. The moment he left the floor Connally rushed forward and poked Barkley. Barkley jumped up and asked unanimous consent for Connally to file the ratification resolution. "Mr. President," said Wallace White obediently, "I have no objection." The motion was approved and Connally introduced the resolution. It was all rather like little boys in grammar school sneaking something over when teacher was out of the room. When teacher returned he announced with some annoyance that he had never had any intention of blocking a vote on the Charter, but would protest any attempt to limit debate. Barkley, who wants to vote not later than 5 tomorrow, may find some way to get around that one, too.

The Pentagon mind, that strange amalgam, was displayed to the Mead Committee today at its hearing on the redeployment muddle. The committee has seen it all before, and so has the press, but it was such a perfect example that it should be preserved, pickled in formaldehyde, perhaps, as a warning and a sign. Previously the committee had heard retired Colonel J. Monroe Johnson, head of the Civilian Office of Defense Transportation, a violent, cantankerously able old man whose face looks as though it had been hewn out of a piece of granite that couldn't be used for anything else, testify that the Army has consistently refused to cooperate in informing him how many troops would be returning each day. Obviously under that circumstance ODT has been unable to furnish adequate Pullman accommodations. This has been the Army's fault almost entirely. Bob Patterson, of course, held a press conference and blamed ODT and other civilian agencies for the Army's mistake. Dutifully a certain sycophantic portion of the press parroted the terrible things the civilians were doing to our returning soldiers. This infuriated Johnson, disturbed the committee, and disturbed everyone else who is at all concerned about the Army's habit of shifting the blame for its own mistakes. Johnson told the weary, familiar tale of how the Army issued a schedule of arrivals, happily found it could return more men than it had estimated, unhappily failed to inform ODT, thoroughly gummed everything up, and then went tattling to the press with its little bucket of tar.

Today the Army Transportation Corps came up to testify. It developed that: (1) The Army "doesn't see" how daily knowledge of troop arrivals could help ODT arrange adequate Pullman transportation for them. (2) The Army did not begin to furnish such reports to ODT until after the whole story broke and Fred Vinson as War Mobilizer wrote the War Department and demanded that it be done. (3) The Army is refusing to speed discharge of skilled railroad workers eligible under the point system "because it would destroy the troops' respect for the point system and endanger the war with Japan." ("Isn't the breakdown of rail transportation something of concern to the war with Japan?" demanded Jim Mead in weary disgust. Well, it might be, the Army grudgingly agreed.) (4) The Army has consistently refused to permit Railroad Retirement Board officials to interview dischargees at separation centers and encourage them to take railroad jobs.

"Don't you think," demanded Homer Ferguson of a snip little colonel with a chip in his voice, "that redeployment of troops within this country might be a civilian problem as well as an Army problem?" "It might be a matter of comfort," the colonel said. "If it interfered with the strategic picture in the Pacific, it might be a civilian problem too." "But don't you see that it would help the ODT to arrange better transportation for these men if it knew from day to day how many were arriving?" Ferguson persisted. "I can't see that it would help the ODT any," said the colonel. Redeployment, he advised the committee tolerantly, "is something for the general staff corps. I don't see that we are under any obligation to let civilian agencies know about it."

Having created an inexcusable muddle, the Army has tried, with a cynicism that cannot be excused or forgiven, to make the troops think it was the civilians' fault. What will come riding, riding, out of this cleavage so carefully nurtured over the years, no one now can say. If we are lucky, nothing; if we are not so lucky, much more than nothing.

JULY 28, 1945. "So ends the Great Debate in the Great Anti-Climax!" cried one cynical reporter as he rushed for the telephone to transmit the result shortly after 5 P.M. this afternoon. It may have been a sound judg-

rush for the phone

ment, it may not. Sound or not, it summed up rather neatly the mood of six ritualistic days.

Even so, however, there was drama, and perhaps, for a moment or two, some real realization of the enormous step here taken so easily, so casually, so expediently. ("Hell, I'm the biggest isolationist that ever lived," one Middle-Westerner remarked the other day with an ironic chuckle, "but I'm sure as hell not going to vote against the Charter.") Some voted prayerfully, some voted skeptically, some voted because it was their political scalps if they didn't. Two remained true to bitter conviction and a third, Hiram Johnson, was announced as siding with them even though he could not be present to repeat the negative vote he cast against the Charter in committee. Very nearly a full Senate voted. Only the sick Glass, Thomas of Idaho, Johnson, Clyde Reed and Josiah Bailey were absent. 89 to 2 the Charter was ratified.

The session that did it began at 10 A.M. The galleries were jammed full to overflowing and along the hallway to the House tourists waited four abreast in the futile hope of getting in. A constant hum and rustle filled the chamber as the speeches dragged along. Taft spoke ably, reviewing a personal record that has been basically internationalist despite the easy smearings of his opponents. Glen Taylor made a brief and popular statement, exhibiting his easy use of the human touch. He hadn't planned on saying anything, he said, but a lot of Senators had been coming to him and urging him to speak so that history would know what his feelings were on this great occasion. That didn't carry much weight, he said, but when they asked if he didn't want to have something to tell his grandchildren, well, that was different. Of course, he added, mindful of little A-rod, 10, and P.J., 3½, he didn't expect to meet his grandchildren for some time yet. He expressed himself with his usual natural felicity and then sat down. Jim Mead read a long letter he said he had written to a serviceman to tell him "what the Charter really means." Forrest Donnell of Missouri, always the meticulous legalist, shouted for half an hour that the President's assurance, received yesterday from the Potsdam Conference by McKellar, that agreements under the Charter will be approved by Congress, might be interpreted in three different ways. After he had stated and restated them at exhaustive length, Barkley asked if he didn't agree that in any case the President had promised that nothing would be done by Executive order alone. Donnell rather grudgingly admitted it. Raymond Willis spoke, Sheridan Downey, very briefly, Joe O'Mahoney, inserting an earlier radio address on the Charter as his sensibly time-saving contribution. Wayne Morse, needling Connally and paying a nice tribute to George Wilson of Iowa, asked insertion in the Record of "the first attempt by anyone to get an international conference," Wilson's 1943 resolution urging the President to call the nations together. Barkley hopped up and went back to Connally's desk, poked his arm. If he didn't say, "I guess that shows you," it looked like something very close to it; both chuckled. Finally Bill Langer obtained the floor, inserting letter after letter in the *Record* on the lack of farm machinery in the Northwest, concluding with a statement that brought a startled silence from the galleries and caused some excitement among the press.

When he came down here, said Wild William of the Prairies, he took his oath to defend the Constitution. He could not violate that oath now by voting for the Charter. Some professed to see hope for peace in it; he could not perceive it. To him it seemed a guarantee of the enslavement of millions of people and a state of perpetual war. Accordingly, he must vote against it. Henrik Shipstead arose immediately and walked up to Wheeler's desk. The Montanan got up and they walked together up the aisle, pausing in front of the door for a hasty conference, the tall old man from Minnesota in blue, the tall old man from Montana in brown. After a moment Wheeler shook his head and they returned to their seats. Apparently Shipstead's last-minute plea had failed. Langer concluded amid cries of "Vote! Vote! Vote!" His tall, embarrassed colleague, Milton Young, said very briefly that he regretted the split in the North Dakota delegation but he intended to vote for ratification. "Vote! Vote!" came the cry again. Barkley asked for a quorum call. The Clerk completed it hastily. "The vote is on the resolution of ratification," McKellar announced. The Clerk began to call the roll. The galleries fell silent as "Aye" after "Aye" came up from the floor. Langer's "No" was so quiet that few could hear it, but when Shipstead voted "No" a little audible gasp and stir ran through the crowd. Burt Wheeler, true to his word, cast his vote for the Charter. The excuses of the absentees ("Absent on official business," "because of illness," "necessarily absent") were given by Wherry and Hill. The Clerk recapitulated the roll swiftly, turned to McKellar. "On this vote," said the president *pro tempore*, "the vote is 89 Yeas and 2 Nays, and the resolution of ratification is approved by the necessary two-thirds majority."

Somewhere in the gallery somebody started to clap hesitantly. When Barkley jumped up to ask that the President be immediately notified, the moment passed, the impulse died. In silence the galleries accepted the vote and in comparative silence they filed out. Vandenberg crossed to Connally and they shook hands happily. The Senate went on to other business amid the after-vote hubbub that follows every crucial ballot.

So it has come to pass after 26 years, and so, for good or ill, it has been done. All that remains now is to infuse the Charter with decency and justice, tolerance and good will, trust and honor and integrity. All that remains now is to give it heart and give it life.

In the effort so to do the Senators of the United States, so human, so likable, so certain and so confused, so noble and so petty, so statesmanlike and so expedient, so wonderfully representative of their own human, likable, certain, confused, noble, petty, statesmanlike, expedient country, will of necessity play a great and vital part. That they and their colleagues in the House will play it as the country would is certain, for here on the Hill, in a way that is the wonder and the strength of America, they *are* the country.

AFTERWORD

In the Senate then, as in the Senate now and always, certain men predominated, as some do in this Journal. If the names of Connally and Vandenberg, Taft and La Follette, Ball and Barkley, Ed Johnson and Elbert Thomas stand out in this narrative, it is because they stood out in the flow of days of the 78th and 79th Congresses. If the names of Mansfield and Dirksen, Humphrey and Javits, Douglas and Russell and Byrd stand out today, it is because they are the prime generators of news now. The makers and movers of the Senate have always formed the nucleus of "the club within the club," the inner command post of that "Citadel" so lovingly described by William S. White. Yet there are many others of diligent service and honorable record, too, and so to round out this report of a tense and dramatic era, to honor those now at rest and those still here, and to pay tribute to all who served in those days, this brief "where are they now."

You will note two things: first, the basic similarity of pattern in many of these lives, by which a man moves (usually through the law) into state and then national legislative pursuits; and second, the enormous turnover in the Senate.

Of the 96 men serving in 1943–1945, only 15 remain among the 100 who now, with the accession to statehood of Alaska and Hawaii, compose the Senate. Another, Claude Pepper of Florida, was elected in 1962 to the House, after many years' retirement and so has come back to Capitol Hill. Of the rest, 34 are still living at date of writing, either in some other government service, in business, or retired.

Those still serving (listed alphabetically by their states):

LISTER HILL, Democrat, of Alabama: born in Alabama 1894, educated at the University of Alabama; lawyer; served in the House of Representatives 1923–1938, in the Senate since 1938; the South's outstanding and most tenacious liberal, still fighting the good fight in his old boy, old man, jovial way.

CARL HAYDEN, Democrat, of Arizona: born in Arizona Territory 1877, attended Stanford University, treasurer and sheriff of Maricopa County; elected to the House on Arizona's admission to statehood and served 1912–1926; elected to the Senate in 1926 and has served continuously since; chairman of Appropriations, President *pro tempore*, of the Senate, still a shrewd and canny operator who remains silent in the press and powerful in the cloakrooms.

JOHN L. MCCLELLAN, Democrat, of Arkansas: born in Arkansas 1896, educated in public schools, admitted to the bar in 1913, practiced law; served in the House 1935–1939; ran for Senator, lost, resumed his law practice; tried again in 1942, won, and has served continuously since; a man of moral purpose and mighty indignations who has given invaluable service to the country in his investigations of labor-management corruption and racketeering.

J. WILLIAM FULBRIGHT, Democrat, of Arkansas: born in Missouri 1905, resident of Arkansas since 1906; University of Arkansas graduate, Rhodes scholar at Oxford, law degree at George Washington University in Washington, 1934; attorney in the anti-trust division of the Department of Justice; taught law at the University of Arkansas, was elected its president in 1939, served until 1941; elected to the House in 1943; succeeded Hattie Caraway in the Senate in 1945 and now is chairman of Foreign Relations Committee, where his excellent mind has full play over the subjects which interest him.

RICHARD B. RUSSELL, Democrat, of Georgia: born Georgia 1897; graduate of the law school of the University of Georgia; practicing lawyer for two years; member, state house of representatives 1921–1931; Governor of Georgia 1931–1933; in the Senate since 1933; chairman of Armed Services Committee; powerful, astute and dignified leader of the Southern bloc.

BOURKE B. HICKENLOOPER, Republican, of Iowa: born Iowa 1896; law graduate, University of Iowa; practicing lawyer; state house of representatives 1934–1937; lieutenant-governor of Iowa 1939–1942; Governor of Iowa 1943–1944; elected to the Senate 1944; ranking Republican on Foreign Relations, where a certain practical shrewdness sometimes offsets the occasionally more casual approach of his chairman.

ALLEN J. ELLENDER, Democrat, of Louisiana: born Louisiana 1891; law graduate, Tulane University; Louisiana house of representatives 1924–1936, floor leader 1928–1932, speaker 1932–1936, in the days of Huey Long; elected to the Senate 1936; chairman of Agriculture and Forestry, diligent worker, earnest and unsuccessful foe of many of the sloppier aspects of the foreign aid program.

LEVERETT SALTONSTALL, Republican, of Massachusetts: born Massachusetts 1892; Harvard University; state house of representatives 1923–1936; Governor of Massachusetts 1939–1944; elected to the Senate in 1944 to succeed Cabot Lodge; ranking Republican on Appropriations; still charming, still careful, still cautious.

JAMES O. EASTLAND, Democrat, of Mississippi: born Mississippi 1904; lawyer, farmer, landowner; state house of representatives 1928–1932; in the Senate since 1941; chairman of Judiciary, where he does his skillful best to keep civil-rights legislation from becoming the law of the land.

MILTON R. YOUNG, Republican, of North Dakota: born North Dakota 1897; graduate of North Dakota State Agricultural College at Fargo; farmer; state house of representatives 1932–1934, state senate 1934–1945; in the Senate since 1945; second-ranking Republican on Appropriations and Agriculture; quiet, decent, diligent.

WAYNE MORSE, Democrat, of Oregon: born Wisconsin 1900; educated University of Wisconsin, law schools of Minnesota and Columbia Universities; moved to Oregon to teach law at the University of Oregon; dean of law 1931–1944; elected to the Senate in 1944 as a Republican; became an Independent; became a Democrat; survived it all to continue to win reelection, most recently in 1962; intelligent, embittered, alone.

OLIN D. JOHNSTON, Democrat, of South Carolina: born South Carolina 1896; law graduate, University of South Carolina; member of the state house of representatives 1923–1924, 1927–1930; Governor of South Carolina 1935–1939; again Governor 1943–1944; elected to the Senate 1944; chairman of Post Office, and Civil Service Committees, ranking Democrat on Agriculture; known along the corridors of the Senate as "Olin the Solon."

GEORGE D. AIKEN, Republican, of Vermont: born in Vermont 1892; fruit farmer, nurseryman; member of the state house of representatives 1931–1934; lieutenant governor 1935–1937; Governor of Vermont 1937–1940; in the Senate since 1940; ranking Republican on Agriculture, second-ranking on Foreign Relations; shrewd, kindly, unimpressed, an undismayed Yankee liberal still.

HARRY F. BYRD, Democrat, of Virginia: born West Virginia 1887, family moved to Virginia the same year; educated Shenandoah Valley Academy, Winchester; publisher and apple grower; state senate 1915–1925; Governor of Virginia 1926–1930; in Senate since 1933; chairman of Finance, ranking Democrat on Armed Services; delightful gentleman, dedicated conservative, grim opponent of waste in government.

WARREN MAGNUSON, Democrat, of Washington: born Minnesota 1905; law graduate, University of Washington; member of the state house of representatives 1933–1934; member of U.S. House, 1937–1944; in the Senate since 1944; chairman of Commerce; a blunt, pragmatic, easygoing, take-it-as-it-comes legislator, universally liked.

CLAUDE PEPPER, Democrat, of Florida: born Alabama 1900; graduate of University of Alabama 1921, Harvard Law School 1924; taught law at the University of Arkansas; moved to Florida, practiced law; member of state house of representatives 1929–1930; in the Senate 1936–1950; defeated for renomination 1950, returned to law; elected to the House 1962.

THOSE IN OTHER PURSUITS

ERNEST W. McFARLAND, Democrat, of Arizona: born Oklahoma 1894; University of Oklahoma, Stanford University Law School; moved to Arizona; lawyer, judge; elected to the Senate 1940, defeated 1952; Majority Leader succeeding Scott Lucas; Governor of Arizona 1954–56, 1956–1958; ran unsuccessfully for the Senate against Barry Goldwater 1958; now practices law in Phoenix.

EDWIN C. JOHNSON, Democrat, of Colorado: born Kansas 1884; moved to Nebraska with parents, attended Lincoln High School; railroad laborer, telegrapher, train dispatcher, Colorado; Colorado state house of representatives 1923–1931; lieutenant governor 1931–1933; Governor of Colorado 1933–1937; elected to the Senate 1942, retired in 1954; Governor again 1954–1956; retired, in Denver.

JOHN A. DANAHER, Republican, of Connecticut: born Connecticut 1899; Yale Law School; assistant U.S. district attorney in Connecticut, secretary of state of Connecticut; elected to Senate in 1938, defeated in 1944; appointed judge of the U.S. Circuit Court of Appeals for the District of Columbia Circuit by President Eisenhower, and has served since 1953.

THOMAS C. HART, Republican, of Connecticut: born Michigan 1887, graduate of Annapolis; served in the Navy in the Spanish-American War and both World Wars, with rank of Admiral in the South Pacific in World War II; appointed to the Senate Feb. 15, 1945, served to Nov. 5, 1946; retired, in Connecticut.

C. DOUGLASS BUCK, Republican, of Delaware: born Delaware 1890; University of Pennsylvania Engineering School; Delaware state engineer; banker; Governor of Delaware 1929–1937; elected to the Senate 1942, defeated 1948; in banking in Delaware.

GLEN H. TAYLOR, Democrat, of Idaho: born Oregon 1904; public schools of Idaho; owned and managed a dramatic stock company; elected to the Senate 1944; ran as Vice Presidential candidate with Henry Wallace on the Progressives ticket 1948, was defeated; defeated for renomination

1950; president of successful wig business, Taylor Topper, since 1957; resides in Idaho.

SCOTT W. LUCAS, Democrat, of Illinois: born Illinois 1892; Illinois Wesleyan Law School; practiced law, served as chairman of state tax commission; in the House 1935–1939; elected to the Senate 1938, defeated in 1950; Majority Leader succeeding Barkley; practices law in Illinois and Washington.

HOMER E. CAPEHART, Republican, of Indiana: born Indiana 1897; farmer, radio-phono-TV manufacturer; elected to the Senate 1944, defeated 1962; returned to business and farming.

GUY M. GILLETTE, Democrat, of Iowa: born Iowa 1879; Drake University law graduate; lawyer, farmer; member state senate 1912–1916; served in the House of Representatives 1933–1936; in the Senate 1936–1944; defeated 1944; surplus property board; re-elected to Senate 1948, defeated 1954; retired, in Iowa.

ALBERT B. CHANDLER, Democrat, of Kentucky: born Kentucky 1898; Harvard; University of Kentucky Law School; state senate 1930–31; lieutenant-governor 1931–35; Governor of Kentucky 1935–39; in the Senate 1939–1945, when he resigned to become baseball commissioner; resigned as commissioner 1950; Governor of Kentucky 1955–59; publisher, other business interests, in Kentucky.

ELMER THOMAS, Democrat, of Oklahoma: born Oklahoma 1876; De Pauw University; lawyer; state senate 1907–1920; House of Representatives 1923–1927; elected to the Senate 1926, defeated for renomination 1950; retired, in Oklahoma.

GEORGE L. RADCLIFFE, Democrat, of Maryland: born Maryland 1877; Johns Hopkins University, University of Maryland Law School; engaged in law, banking, farming; elected to the Senate 1934, defeated 1946; resumed business interests; resides in Maryland.

HENRY CABOT LODGE, Republican, of Massachusetts: born Massachusetts 1902; Harvard; newspaperman; elected to the Senate 1936, resigned 1944 to enter Army; re-elected to Senate 1946, defeated by John F. Kennedy 1952; U.S. Ambassador to the United Nations 1953–60; unsuccessful Republican candidate for Vice President 1960; now in private business in Washington.

HOMER FERGUSON, Republican, of Michigan: born Pennsylvania 1898; lawyer; elected to the Senate 1942, defeated 1954; judge of the Military Court of Appeals in Washington.

JOSEPH H. BALL, Republican, of Minnesota: born Minnesota 1905; University of Minnesota; reporter and political writer; appointed to the Senate 1940, defeated 1948; active in the shipping industry in New York City.

HARRY S. TRUMAN, Democrat, of Missouri: born Missouri 1884; farmer, haberdasher, county court judge; in the Senate 1940–1944; Vice-President January–April 1945; President of the United States April 1945—January 1953; active in politics.

BURTON K. WHEELER, Democrat, of Montana: born Massachusetts 1882; law graduate, University of Michigan; moved to Montana, practiced law; member state house of representatives 1910–1912; U.S. district attorney for Montana 1913–1918; elected to the Senate 1922 (Vice-Presidential candidate with Robert M. La Follette, Sr., on the Progressive ticket, 1924); served in the Senate until his defeat in 1946; practices law in Washington.

FORREST C. DONNELL, Republican, of Missouri: born Missouri 1884; law graduate, University of Missouri; Governor of Missouri 1941–1945; elected to the Senate 1944, defeated 1950; practices law in Missouri.

ALBERT HAWKES, Republican, of New Jersey: born Illinois 1878; engaged in law, chemical industries; elected to the Senate 1942, defeated 1948; returned to business; retired, in California.

H. ALEXANDER SMITH, Republican, of New Jersey: born New York 1880; Princeton, Columbia Law School; executive secretary of Princeton 1919–27; lawyer; elected to the Senate 1944, served until his retirement in January 1953; retired, in New Jersey.

CARL A. HATCH, Democrat, of New Mexico: born Kansas 1889; law graduate, Cumberland University, Tennessee; moved to New Mexico, practiced law; district judge; in the Senate 1933 until his retirement in 1948; appointed U.S. District Judge for the District of New Mexico by Harry Truman and has served since 1949.

JAMES M. MEAD, Democrat, of New York: born New York 1885; state assembly 1915–1918; House of Representatives 1919–1938; elected to the Senate 1938, retired in 1946; Federal Trade Commission; represented N.Y. Department of Commerce in Washington briefly; retired, in Florida.

GERALD NYE, Republican, of North Dakota: born Wisconsin 1892; editor and publisher; in the Senate 1925 until his defeat in 1944; in business in Washington.

HAROLD H. BURTON, Republican, of Ohio: born Massachusetts 1888; Bowdoin, Harvard Law School; moved to Ohio, practiced law; state house of representatives 1929; mayor of Cleveland 1935–1940; elected to the Senate in 1940 and served until appointed an Associate Justice of the United States Supreme Court by Harry Truman in 1945; retired in 1958; resides in Washington.

GUY CORDON, Republican, of Oregon: born Oregon 1874; Stanford University; lawyer; appointed to the Senate to succeed Charles McNary in 1944 and served until his defeat in 1954; practices law in Washington.

THEODORE FRANCIS GREEN, Democrat, of Rhode Island: born Rhode Island 1867; Brown, Harvard Law School; active in many business enterprises; state house of representatives 1907; Governor of Rhode Island 1933–1936; elected to the Senate 1936 and served until his retirement in 1960; retired, in Rhode Island.

CHAN GURNEY, Republican, of South Dakota: born South Dakota 1896; high school graduate; gasoline, seed, and nursery business; elected to the Senate 1938 and served until defeated in 1950; member of the Civil Aeronautics Board, Washington.

TOM STEWART, Democrat, of Tennessee: born Tennessee 1892; Cumberland University; lawyer; appointed to the Senate 1938 and served until his defeat for renomination 1948; resides in Nashville.

TOM CONNALLY, Democrat, of Texas: born Texas 1877; Baylor University; law graduate, University of Texas; served in the House 1917–1929; elected to the Senate in 1928 and served until his retirement in 1952; resides in Washington.

W. LEE O'DANIEL, Democrat, of Texas: born Ohio 1890; business school; moved to Texas to engage in grain and milling business; Governor of Texas 1938–1941 when he resigned to fill a Senate vacancy; served in the Senate until his retirement in 1948; active in life insurance and business activities in Texas.

ABE MURDOCK, Democrat, of Utah: born Nevada 1893; moved to Utah 1898; lawyer; served in House 1933–1940; elected to the Senate 1940, defeated 1946; resumed law and farming; member of the National Labor Relations Board 1947–1957; retired, in Washington.

HOMER T. BONE, Democrat, of Washington: born Indiana 1883; graduate Tacoma Law School 1911; state house of representatives 1923–1924; elected to the Senate 1932 and served until he resigned 1944 to become judge of the U.S. Circuit Court of Appeals for the Ninth Judicial Circuit; retired 1956; resides in Washington.

CHAPMAN REVERCOMB, Republican, of West Virginia: born Virginia 1895; law graduate, University of Virginia; moved to West Virginia 1922; practiced law; elected to the Senate 1942, defeated 1948, re-elected 1956 to fill unexpired term of Harley Kilgore, defeated for re-election 1958; practices law in West Virginia.

ALEXANDER WILEY, Republican, of Wisconsin: born Wisconsin 1884; University of Michigan; University of Wisconsin law school; district attorney of Chippewa County; elected to the Senate 1938, served until his defeat in 1962.

DECEASED

JOHN BANKHEAD, Democrat, Alabama, Senator 1930–1946
HATTIE W. CARAWAY, Democrat, Arkansas, Senator 1932–1944
HIRAM W. JOHNSON, Republican, California, Senator 1916–1945

SHERIDAN DOWNEY, Democrat, California, Senator 1938–1950

EUGENE D. MILLIKIN, Republican, Colorado, Senator 1943–1956

FRANCIS MALONEY, Democrat, Connecticut, Senator 1934–1945

BRIEN MCMAHON, Democrat, Connecticut, Senator 1944–1952

JAMES M. TUNNELL, Democrat, Delaware, Senator 1940–1946

CHARLES O. ANDREWS, Democrat, Florida, Senator 1936–1946

D. WORTH CLARK, Democrat, Idaho, Senator 1938–1944

JOHN THOMAS, Republican, Idaho, Senator 1928–1932, 1940–1945

C. WAYLAND BROOKS, Republican, Illinois, Senator 1940–1948

RAYMOND E. WILLIS, Republican, Indiana, Senator 1940–1946

FRED VAN NUYS, Democrat, Indiana, Senator 1932–1944

SAMUEL D. JACKSON, Democrat, Indiana, Senator 1944

GEORGE A. WILSON, Republican, Iowa, Senator 1942–1948

ARTHUR CAPPER, Republican, Kansas, Senator 1918–1948

CLYDE M. REED, Republican, Kansas, Senator 1938–1949

ALBEN W. BARKLEY, Democrat, Kentucky, Senator 1926–1949; Vice-President of the United States, 1949–1952; Senator 1952–1956

JOHN H. OVERTON, Democrat, Louisiana, Senator 1932–1948

WALLACE H. WHITE, Republican, Maine, Senator 1930–1948

OWEN BREWSTER, Republican, Maine, Senator 1940–1952

MILLARD E. TYDINGS, Democrat, Maryland, Senator 1926–1950

DAVID I. WALSH, Democrat, Massachusetts, Senator 1918–1924, 1926–1946

ARTHUR H. VANDENBERG, Republican, Michigan, Senator 1928–1951

HENRIK SHIPSTEAD, Republican, Minnesota, Senator 1922–1946

THEODORE G. BILBO, Democrat, Mississippi, Senator 1934–1947

BENNETT CHAMP CLARK, Democrat, Missouri, Senator 1932–1944

JAMES E. MURRAY, Democrat, Montana, Senator 1934–1960

HUGH BUTLER, Republican, Nebraska, Senator 1940–1954

KENNETH S. WHERRY, Republican, Nebraska, Senator 1942–1951

PAT MCCARRAN, Democrat, Nevada, Senator 1932–1954

JAMES G. SCRUGHAM, Democrat, Nevada, Senator 1942–1945

STYLES BRIDGES, Republican, New Hampshire, Senator 1936–1961

CHARLES W. TOBEY, Republican, New Hampshire, Senator 1938–1953

ARTHUR WALSH, Democrat, New Jersey, Senator 1944

DENNIS CHAVEZ, Democrat, New Mexico, Senator 1935–1962

ROBERT F. WAGNER, Democrat, New York, Senator 1926–1949

JOSIAH W. BAILEY, Democrat, North Carolina, Senator 1930–1946

ROBERT R. REYNOLDS, Democrat, North Carolina, Senator 1932–1944

CLYDE R. HOEY, Democrat, North Carolina, Senator 1944–1954

WILLIAM LANGER, Republican, North Dakota, Senator 1940–1959

JOHN MOSES, Democrat, North Dakota, Senator 1945

ROBERT A. TAFT, Republican, Ohio, Senator 1938–1953
ELMER THOMAS, Democrat, Oklahoma, Senator 1926–1950
EDWARD H. MOORE, Republican, Oklahoma, Senator 1942–1948
RUFUS C. HOLMAN, Republican, Oregon, Senator 1938–1944
CHARLES McNARY, Republican, Oregon, Senator 1917–1944
JAMES J. DAVIS, Republican, Pennsylvania, Senator 1930–1947
JOSEPH F. GUFFEY, Democrat, Pennsylvania, Senator 1934–1946
PETER GERRY, Democrat, Rhode Island, Senator 1916–1928, 1934–1946
ELLISON D. SMITH, Democrat, South Carolina, Senator 1908–1944
BURNET R. MAYBANK, Democrat, South Carolina, Senator 1941–1958
HARLAN J. BUSHFIELD, Republican, South Dakota, Senator 1942–1948
KENNETH McKELLAR, Democrat, Tennessee, Senator 1916–1952
ELBERT D. THOMAS, Democrat, Utah, Senator 1932–1950
WARREN R. AUSTIN, Republican, Vermont, Senator 1931–1946
CARTER GLASS, Democrat, Virginia, Senator 1919–1946
MON C. WALLGREN, Democrat, Washington, Senator 1940–1945
HARLEY M. KILGORE, Democrat, Washington, Senator 1940–1956
ROBERT M. LA FOLLETTE, JR., Republican, Wisconsin, Senator 1925–
    1946
JOSEPH C. O'MAHONEY, Democrat, Wyoming, Senator 1933–1952, 1954–
    1960
EDWARD V. ROBERTSON, Republican, Wyoming, Senator 1942–1948

Of the others prominently mentioned here, John Elliott Rankin, a Representative from the state of Mississippi, is dead; Andrew May, a Representative from the state of Kentucky, is dead; Fiorello La Guardia, a Representative from the state of New York and later Mayor of New York City, is dead. Of the two contestants in the Battle of the Commerce Department, Jesse Jones is dead. Henry Wallace, fired by Harry Truman from the Secretaryship, unsuccessful Presidential candidate in 1948 with Senator Glen Taylor of Idaho on the Progressive ticket, lives quietly in retirement in New York, running a farm and conducting more of the experiments that have contributed so much to the development of American agriculture.

INDEX

Allen Drury was born in Houston, Texas, on September 2, 1918, and graduated with a B.A. degree from Stanford University in 1939. A year later he became the editor of the *Tulare* (California) *Bee*—a position he held until 1942, when a call to serve in the United States Army took precedence over journalistic pursuits. In 1943, following a medical discharge, he traveled East to Washington, D.C., where he joined the staff of United Press as a Senate reporter, covering that "beat" until 1945. Following a year of free-lance work in Washington as a correspondent he became the Nation Editor for *Pathfinder Magazine,* joined the National Staff of the *Washington Evening Star* in 1953, and from 1954 to 1959 was a member of the Senate staff of *The New York Times.*

What he saw and heard during those years of covering politics and affairs of state was later to provide the background for his first novel, *Advise and Consent,* one of the great best-sellers of our time which won the Pulitzer Prize for Fiction in 1960, and its worthy successor, *A Shade of Difference,* the novel of the United Nations which was published in 1962. His third book, A *Senate Journal: 1943–1945,* is his first work of nonfiction—a personal diary of the great issues and people in the United States Senate during two of its most trying and interesting years.